Pitt

The Story
of the
University of
Pittsburgh
1787–1987

Pitt

The Story
of the
University of
Pittsburgh
1787 – 1987

Robert C. Alberts

48 0520

University of Pittsburgh Press

378.748
Al 14

Published by the

University of Pittsburgh Press,

Pittsburgh, Pa., 15260

Copyright © 1986, University of Pittsburgh Press

Feffer and Simons, Inc., London

Manufactured in the United States of America

Library of Congress Cataloging-in-Publication Data

Alberts, Robert C.
  Pitt: the story of the University of Pittsburgh, 1787–1987.

  Bibliography: p. 511
  Includes index.
  1. University of Pittsburgh—History.   I. Title.
LD6013.A43   1986   378.748′86   86-5461
ISBN 0-8229-1150-7

Contents

Foreword

John Funari

This history of the University of Pittsburgh is told in the lives of its chancellors, its faculty, and its students. It is a story of trustees bent on proper stewardship, of University administrators stubbornly dreaming visions grander even than the institution itself and, surprising even themselves, bringing a new reality and vitality to the intellectual life of the city and region. The texture of this history of the University reflects the texture of the culture of the city and region itself: gritty, taciturn, stubbornly persistent, doggedly hard-working, wary of the new and disdainful of the ostentatious, and above all, deeply loyal to church, political party, union, class, neighborhood, and friends. This bicentennial commemoration of the people who brought the University from its early and lowly beginnings through uncertain times to its current prominence is a testament to their quiet devotion, at times unarticulated, to higher education, to the life of the mind, and to the search for meaning.

There were times when the faculty, the students, and the University leaders seemed embarrassed and even reluctant to assert the primacy of the intellect. In the context of the sometimes turbulent and always kinetic society of nineteenth- and twentieth-century Western Pennsylvania, contemplation and introspection were not prime values—neither for persons of social standing and wealth, nor for those who aspired to them. The direct, vital, and causal linkages between learning and a prosperous economy and between scientific research and material advancement were not always evident nor generally accepted. This history tells of these times. More important, it tells of the times when the people of the University of Pittsburgh, eloquent in their restraint, courageous in their persistence, and visionary in their leadership, not only defended learning and education, but wove it into the tapestry of the society of Western Pennsylvania.

The prevailing, organizing themes of this history of the University are recurring ones. The reader will be struck, for example, by the continuation of the debate in 1985 about the "mission" of the University: should it serve the immediate needs of the Pittsburgh and Western Pennsylvania region or should it seek to become an international university? The latter choice conjures up images and forebodings in the minds of its opponents that the University would answer to a different, remote, and elitist constituency or master. Stating the possibilities in an either/or fashion, of course, assumes, almost certainly wrongly, that the two goals are mutually exclusive or contradictory or inherently in conflict. Leave aside for the moment the merits of the issue or how it is phrased. The reassuring aspect is that in this history one sees the same dichotomy arising in the 1840s, in 1900 when the University moved to Oakland, during the Bowman chancellorship, and with starkly exhilarating and personally tragic results during the Litchfield period, 1955–1965. The debate continues to the present day. One need only read the *Report to the Trustees on the University Plan, 1985,* by President Posvar, to see how persistently recurring this theme is in the history of the University.

It is a theme that goes to the heart of the culture and the society from which the University sprung two hundred years ago. The Scots-Irish who first crossed the Alleghenies from New York and Philadelphia, and in almost equal numbers came north and west through the valleys from Virginia, were characterized by their independence of mind, dedication to hard work, and stolidity of spirit. By the very act of emigrating they were spurning the social structure of the eastern seaboard of the United States as they had spurned the established church and the ruling class of Britain and Europe. By the early and middle 1700s, the eastern seaboard was becoming a sophisticated society with urban centers, but with insufficient economic or educational opportunities for the steady influx of new immigrants. The very act of creating a new society west of the Alleghenies signified a strongly held bias against the world and the culture that had been left behind. Thus, significantly, one of the first and most violent challenges to the new American Republic was the Whiskey Rebellion in 1794; Western Pennsylvanians simply would not accept without a fight the attempt by the "ruling interests" of the East to exploit them by a tax on the manufacture of distilled liquors, their principal method of disposing of surplus grain. Not even the august and revered General-President Washington at the head of federal troops

prevented the populist Jeffersonian farmers and traders from asserting their defiance of the suspect and "exploitative" Hamiltonian easterners.

The successive waves of immigration, pushed by political, social, and economic conditions in Europe and pulled by the opportunities of land and new industry in Pittsburgh, only served to confirm that cast of mind that the original Scots-Irish pioneers and settlers brought with them: scornful of old ways, convinced that they were little understood by the powers back East, suspicious that they had been exploited and, even worse, patronized by the bankers and government leaders of Philadelphia, New York, Boston and, later, Washington.

By the early decades of the nineteenth century, Western Pennsylvanians were looking westward to the expanses of the Ohio and Mississippi valleys. The emerging demand for new products and services provided by and through the port of Pittsburgh created attractive opportunities for the enterprising second generation. Local ventures into coal, iron, timber, transportation, and banking made Pittsburgh a competitor with the eastern cities and reinforced the sense of insularity of the area's inhabitants, who used their new wealth and power to counter the dominance of the eastern seaboard.

The German, Swiss, Dutch, and French religious and political dissenters and reformers migrating to the area in 1790 to 1850 differed from the earlier Scots-Irish principally in their language, not in their values. Their defiance of oppression, economic, political, or religious, real or only perceived, echoed that of their predecessors a generation or two before. In many cases even the symbols of their rebellion were the same. The Scots-Irish Covenanter Presbyterian thistle was also the "flower" of Alsace-Lorraine brought to the counties north of Pittsburgh in the 1820s and 1850s by immigrants from that embattled area between Germany and France. The motto around the thistle of Alsace-Lorraine was perfect for Western Pennsylvania: "Touch me not, I scratch."

When the eastern and southern Europeans began to arrive in 1870–1880 to work the mines, mills, railroads, and factories of Western Pennsylvania, eastern Ohio, and northern West Virginia, the University of Pittsburgh was already nearing its centennial. The new arrivals found a landscape and society that were different in almost every respect from the ones they had left. But the new immigrants brought with them the same populist egalitarianism and contempt for the effete, established order they had experienced in rural Poland, mountainous Italy, the remote villages and hills of the Austro-Hungarian Empire. In their adopted country, they faced a newly formed class of bankers and industrialists and managers who were the descendants of the immigrants who had cut their way across the Alleghenies a scant one hundred years before. This new "ruling class" was not at all like the hereditary, quasifeudal system that the immigrants had known in the "Old Country." This new class had only recently earned their money and position. Thus, however sharp the differences between those who had arrived earlier and were now the "new rich" and each successive wave of new immigrants coming across the mountains from the ports of Baltimore, Philadelphia, and New York, they shared at least two things: geographical space and a heritage of hard work and self-reliance.

African-Americans had, of course, been among the very first settlers to come to Western Pennsylvania and the Upper Ohio Valley. The historian Walter Worthington reports that Black Americans assisted Braddock and Forbes in their negotiations with Indian tribal leaders. At the time of the founding of the University, there was already in Pittsburgh a Black community active in trade, services, and the professions. The migration in later years from the South, largely Virginia, brought Blacks, both manumitted slaves and those escaping slavery, into an already existing Black community. The Underground Railroad that led to Canada passed through Western Pennsylvania and eastern Ohio, where jobs in the iron, steel, coal, and railroad industries were as attractive to Blacks from the American South as they were to other ethnic groups from the European South. The massive migration of American Blacks to northern and western cities shortly after World War II tended to bypass Pittsburgh because the decline of heavy industry relative to other cities was already beginning in the 1950s.

Because the migration had been earlier and more gradual than in other areas, the Western Pennsylvania Black community was more rooted and therefore less confrontational in matters of social justice and civil rights. This is not to say that Blacks received any better treatment or were any less segregated or discriminated against in Pittsburgh or Western Pennsylvania. It is only to say that both white and black Pittsburghers share the same characteristics of loyal attachment to work, family, church, class, and neighborhood, and a resentment against the haughty attitudes of the societies they had rejected in Europe, the eastern American seaboard, and, in the case of Blacks, slave-owning gentry in Virginia.

The effect of these migrations on the University of Pittsburgh was profound. As early as 1835, the University was pressed, albeit with mixed results, to provide a "practical" education for the young people of the immediate region as well as education for the professions. That controversy continued for some years but the underlying, uniquely American contribution to higher education and scholarship was evolving: education should be open to all with an ability to learn, and the curricula should be relevant, concrete, and pragmatic. John Dewey and William James were the most eloquent proponents of the American view of education in a democratic society committed to pragmatism as a philosophy and to progress as the overarching ethos.

At the same time, the process of American higher education has led to connections, relationships, and dialogues with the encompassing network of international scholarship, in recognition of the fundamental truth that science, art, technology, and understanding are human, not national or ethnic, phenomena. Even Emerson's declaration of independence for the "American Scholar," in 1837, fifty years after the founding of the University of Pittsburgh, intensifies the persistent duality in American higher education. The practical and the populist ideals of higher education, epitomized by the land-grant university, are pitted against the concept of the university as part of the older tradition and the larger community of scholars free of the obligations to taxpayer, state, contributor, and parent. This dynamic tension, as energizing as it may be, has hidden the synthesis of these models or concepts. Even universities that are now thought of as national or international in standing and scope—Harvard, Stanford, Princeton, Virginia—originated as community colleges or regional universities. They were created to serve the needs and transmit the values of the societies that surrounded them. The courses of study, the schools and departments established, and the faculty hired were all, in the beginning and for a considerable time thereafter, designed to train the student for working life as well as to break new intellectual ground. These universities were founded to meet society's need for graduates with the skills, credentials, and training for participation in the economy and the polity. Contemplation of a larger, external world and more abstract concepts were to come later.

The quintessential American institutions of higher education, and one of the most valuable contributions of American life and culture to the world, are the land-grant university, the state college, the urban university. Those who contrast the University of Pittsburgh with, for example, Harvard, and point out with a sigh that the latter is not a parochial institution, should read more closely the history of Harvard, which was and is both a regional institution serving local needs as well as a world-renowned center of scholarship and learning. One must quietly point out: so is Pitt.

Throughout this history of Pitt, one sees again and again the dynamic tension of this conflict. It is inherent in American higher education, even after two or three centuries; it is even more pronounced at Pittsburgh because of our historical rejection of the world on the other side of the Alleghenies and across the ocean. The history of our University is a constant juggling of the legitimate demands that it serve the interests and needs of its client students and employers and also fulfill its historical function as a bridge of understanding to our past and to our future. It is no accident that the architectural style of the most distinctive educational building in the world, the Cathedral of Learning, combines the modern skyscraper with the medieval Gothic cathedral. The symbol of industrial and commercial America is thus united with the symbol of a more spiritual and contemplative, but feudal and stifling, time and place—our distant ancestry.

To understand fully the social and cultural history of the United States is to understand that absolutely fundamental to that history is the concept that education—particularly higher education—is an instrument for social, political, and individual change. It has become a cliché in American theater, in American sociology, and in American literature to depict immigrant parents struggling against great odds and postponing pleasures to send their children to college. One immigrant grandmother put it succinctly, "They can take away everything else, but they cannot take away what you learn; and what you learn can make you both free and rich."

The University of Pittsburgh is, of course, not unique. For example, Columbia, New York University, and the City College of New York in the 1920s and 1930s were urban centers of creativity in American social sciences, arts, literature, and natural sciences. Most of all they were the means by which the sons and daughters of immigrants moved to positions of prominence and power. Nor were the urban universities, whether in New York, Chicago, Philadelphia, or Pittsburgh, the only American institutions of *public* higher education. Thomas Jefferson so prized his founding of the University of Virginia, in 1817, thirty years after Pittsburgh, that he included it, along with his authorship of the Declaration of Independence and the Virginia Bill of Rights, as his epitaph. All the rest of his accomplishments and attainments and honors he considered secondary. Whether funded directly by the state, or by church, or by private contributions, the American university was to serve as the instrument for social change and individual fulfillment. Indeed, education became the secular religion of America.

It is striking that architectural and building concepts of successive chancellors and boards of trustees at the University of Pittsburgh were similar to the ones used by Jefferson and others at an earlier time. The Greek city-state was the theme of the grandiose building plan for the University of Pittsburgh when it moved to Oakland at the turn of the century. The hill was to be the acropolis, and descending the hillside was to be a cascade of Greek revival buildings housing the University. (Pennsylvania Hall and the Mineral Industries building are survivors of that plan which, most fortunately, was never funded.) Bowman's theme a generation or so later was the medieval village with the "cathedral" at its center, a reprise of the "academical village" of Jefferson in Virginia. This was one of the boldest architectural statements of America's secular religion. The "cathedral" was completed, but as this history of the University recounts in detail, the concept of the closed-in medieval village was never built. That, too, was a blessing, despite the aesthetic appeal of the drawings submitted which proposed the area, around the Cathedral, now open, to be enclosed by Gothic buildings. However appealing the drawings made the buildings seem, the image of a "closed" university was simply contrary to the grand vision of the role of the university in American life.

While the University of Pittsburgh has been in the mainstream of higher education in the United States during its entire history, it is important to read this history in the context of the University's function within this region. An outside observer would be struck by one statistic in particular that Pitt always cites in its information handouts; few if any other universities or colleges in America even keep the data, much less call attention to it. That statistic, among the usual ones, is the number of students who are the first in their family to go to college or university. For as long as most of us can remember, that percentage is always given each year, so that now we hardly even think it unusual; we are almost casual in quoting it. To the external observer—say an anthropologist or a sociologist or a social psychologist—the citing of such a statistic is a trace of a deeper meaning. It is a manifestation of the truculent pride that characterizes the subculture of Western Pennsylvania and of the trans-Appalachian people from Pennsylvania to Kentucky. It is as if Pitt were saying, "See, however humble the origins and proletarian the roots, our students are fulfilling the dream that brought their ancestors here in the first place." It is also the manifestation of the second theme that runs through this history of the University of Pittsburgh: that of the University as a vehicle for the advancement of the individuals of that subculture. Without the University of Pittsburgh, it would have been more difficult if not impossible for many to fulfill their aspirations.

In 1986 the University is sometimes criticized for not performing enough "public service," which often, if somewhat cynically, can be translated as not performing the particular "public service" that the critic wants at the expense of the sacrifice of the University's other purposes. What the critics overlook is that the public service the University has provided is the most revolutionary and radical of all: the broadening of the minds and the sharpening of the skills of more than a quarter-million students who have made the intellectual and social migration that parallels in importance the geographical migration of their parents and grandparents.

In the 1970s it was sometimes remarked snidely that Pitt was becoming a "Black" institution. This racist comment implied that the University had lowered its standards of admission and graduation in an effort to lower the temperature of Black rage and frustration. This comment was not only snide and corrosive; it was erroneous and showed an ignorance of the traditional role of the University. Blacks, like every other immigrant group in Western Pennsylvania, saw education as the route to a better life. By making the University more accessible to them in 1965–1975 Pitt was only fulfilling its traditional and historical function—in the case of its Black citizens delayed by over a century—as it had done in the past for other groups.

Some of those who offered this criticism of Pitt were members of ethnic, nationality, or religious groups whose young people had been educated at the University in earlier decades. For example, high school students who were considering attending Pitt in the 1930s or 1940s were almost routinely informed, subtly or directly, that Pitt had become "a largely Jewish institution," with whatever unsettling consequences that was supposed to have for a student going here. Elsewhere, expressions of ugly anti-Semitism would have been viewed with distaste or revulsion. In Pittsburgh, a person's religious affiliation or ethnic origin is often a subject of teasing or jovial banter. What this hides is the dark and dangerous side of the ethnicity in which great pride is taken as evidence of the colorful variety of the people and the culture. Identification by ancestry or cultural heritage—by "blood"—can be a positive source of pride, to be sure. At the same time, this persistent sense of being classified and assigned forever to a closed ethnic group, with loyalty divorced from rationality, can be a negative force that divides, separates, and demeans. The Nationality Rooms of the University are glorious and beautiful examples of the very best that the ethnic groups and cultures of Pittsburgh and Western Pennsylvania have produced. Nonetheless, the University, no less than its social environment, has paid a price for accepting too easily the beauties of the ethnic mosaic without recognizing or acknowledging the racism, ethnic slurs, and religious bigotry that too often are the dark costs of that mosaic.

What is heartening about this aspect of the University's history is that if Pitt was Black in the 1970s and Jewish in the 1930s and 1940s, it was Slavic and Italian in the 1920s and 1930s and Scots-Irish and Anglo-Saxon in the 1820s and 1830s, and German, French, Scandanavian, and Eastern and Southern European in the years between, before, and after. It should be remembered that the "first-family-member-in-college" students included, in his time, Thomas Mellon. The point is that the 200-year history of this University could as well have been written by a sociologist or a demographer as by a historian, because it is a history that has been marked by successive waves of students who were loosely or strongly bound to their ethnic origins and who proceeded through the University to a full and integrated life.

Thus, not only is this history of the University a story of an institution conditioned by the dichotomy of an insular-regional versus a national-international perspective, it is a history of social mobility and an instrumentality for individual students to understand both their own ancestry and the larger meaning of the American experience. The University opened larger personal perspectives and prepared its graduates for material advancement. That the University also provided industry, commerce, business, the health and social professions with trained personnel was a laudable and not altogether secondary consequence.

Whatever one's opinion, adoring or sarcastic, of the Cathedral of Learning as a work of architecture, no one can deny its value as an inspiration for this upward mobility and attainment. The recollection of a Pitt alumnus, B.A. and Ph.D., a former faculty member and now a prominent executive in the city, illustrates this poignantly.

Each morning when I was roused by my parents to get ready for school, one of the first things I saw out my window was the upper floors of the Cathedral of Learning. Our house in the Hill District actually looked down on Oakland and the University, but I always thought of it as my "looking up" to the Cathedral. My one hope, almost consuming, was that I might somehow, some way, some day be able to go there to college. And each day, while I grew up with all my brothers and sisters, and worried with my parents about how the family could make a living, I would see the Cathedral through the window last thing at night, first thing in the morning. I knew that was my way up and where I wanted to be.

A third theme that runs through this bicentennial history of the University of Pittsburgh is how often the events at the University mirrored what was happening in the larger nation and wider world. This history describes the attacks on academic freedom and the student dissent in the 1930s, the fever of the McCarthy period, and the convulsions of the Vietnam War. The sometimes discreetly hidden conflicts between trustees and chancellors in the 1850s and in 1939 and 1965 were also expressions of larger battles and conflicts taking place in the mainstream of American life. We are reminded by this history that a university with pretensions to greatness must be a setting in which its faculty and students can be both reflective observers and active participants in the gripping issues of the time. One should read this history, therefore, with an awareness of the larger significance that the events in these pages take on when placed in the wider context of world events. It is a source of satisfaction to see the University become mature enough, self-confident enough, to be a vigorous and lively marketplace of ideas, even for the outrageous.

Throughout this history the evidence accumulates, like paint on a large mural, that here is an institution that is larger than the people who have built it, haltingly but lovingly, over the years. The history of any university is more than a march at measured pace. The history told in these pages is therefore not a tale of steady, straight-line progress and growth. It is a tale of major attainments and missed opportunities; of dreams realized and dreams shattered; of intellectual, scientific, and artistic distinction amidst the pedestrian and prosaic; of periods of dash and dormancy; and often of plodding persistence succeeding where facile eloquence failed. Through this tale the institution emerges, takes on form, color, perspective, and purpose; the picture has depth and light and shadow, and most of all, promise.

Celebrating lifts the spirit; celebrating a bicentennial could make us giddy. It is at once both sobering and profoundly reassuring to remember that when the University of Pittsburgh was holding its first class in 1789 in a North American wilderness, the University of Mexico in Mexico City and the University of San Marcos in Lima had already celebrated *their* bicentennials as leading universities in the Americas. So let us not lose a sense of perspective in our own high spirits as we read this history and celebrate our accomplishments.

If stopping to look back is a refreshing pause, turning to face a distant and murky future should sober the soul even while it steels the will. Justice Holmes observed that the inevitable comes about through sweat and hard work. There was nothing inevitable about the development of the University of Pittsburgh, and it is not inevitable that it will continue as a "great research university" of international renown. This history tells us clearly that the University is a product of its economy and its society as well as a driving force behind that economy's and society's evolution and development. It tells us that while the University's existence may be secure, its excellence has to be won again and again with unceasing, Sisyphean efforts. One reads of the controversies in the early life of Pitt and of the later battles that surrounded the proposals to build the Cathedral, to create the Health Center, to build the high

technology complex in Panther Hollow, and that surrounded as well the gift from Miss Frick, the Salk vaccine research, and the personally tragic end of the Litchfield chancellorship. Reading about them in this recounting makes us realize that the past of the University of Pittsburgh is not the homogenous, monolithic life that the past so often seems. The fire and acrimony of those controversies, advances, and setbacks of the past sharpens our capacity to assess and our ability to endure the controversies of the present and future. Thus, this history serves a larger purpose than celebrating the bicentennial of Pitt, as important as that purpose is; it serves to prepare us for the future that will bring its share of intractable problems. This history forces us to conclude that the University will attain future prominence and excellence only through a firm, even stubborn, leadership and wearying hard work. One is reminded that "mankind makes progress only with great friction and clamor, sparks flying heavenward." It could be a description of the old blast furnaces along the Monongahela; it certainly describes the history of the University of Pittsburgh.

We need not, as faculty, administration, students, or alumni, shrink from that history of controversy. Rather, we should accept it as the necessary condition for the evolution of a university struggling to live up to its reputation of greatness. Controversy is in the nature of an institution, and arguments will be intense and passionate where daily concerns are truth, beauty, the newest technology of the human mind, the health of the human body, the maintenance of life, even the meaning of life itself, the redefinition of old questions and the search for new answers, ancient values, and new discoveries that challenge these values and startle the soul. What is unacceptable is a placid acceptance of the mediocre and the otiose, of weak programs and curricula, inadequate research facilities. Academic institutions require constant attention and care, building and rebuilding, pruning, cutting, and fertilization, patience and sometimes a touch of the chiliastic. This history shows that inaction, nostalgia, and stasis are the real enemies; the really killing regrets are for the things that were not attempted.

Finally, it should not escape mention that the

bicentennials of the University of Pittsburgh and of the American Constitution occur in the same year. It would stretch credulity to say that the two events were causal rather than casual. Still, it is an intriguing parallel: the U.S. Constitution—"the greatest written plan for human government struck by the hand of man," as Walter Bagehot described it—and the University of Pittsburgh—"a candle lit in the forested wilderness"—illuminating the mind of man. Both are being celebrated in 1987 with the hope rather than the certainty that their respective founders in 1787 created institutions that will last beyond our measured time.

In 1787 American society, in an act of monumental faith, made a commitment to the notion that the education of the public was the single most sure guarantee of the continuance of our liberty, and to improve our health, our lives, and our ability to pursue the significance and meaning of the human experience. The University of Pittsburgh, estab-

lished the same year, is an expression of that act of faith, repeated by successive generations since those who came west of the Alleghenies from Africa, the British Isles, Central, Southern and Eastern Europe, Asia and Latin America. They came in tumbling waves through this University from spirit-killing societies that had neither faith in freedom nor opportunities for learning. We can be happy but not satisfied with the results.

It is the function of universities, and the destiny of Pitt, to make change happen, to challenge assumptions, to disturb complacency, to engineer innovation, to look with a fresh eye, to devise new social structures, to create new sciences, to energize our natural instincts. This history is a recital of the chronology of our past. Like the University itself, it should animate our assault on the challenges of our future. That is the prime reason for the existence of a university. That is the real point of Pittsburgh.

Preface

Robert C. Alberts

My purpose in writing this book is to tell the story of an American urban university from its birth on the western frontier in the eighteenth century down to the year in which it celebrates its two-hundredth anniversary. As a professional historian and biographer working outside academic circles, I was asked by the University in 1980 to write a history that would be at once scholarly, readable, and useful to a wide audience.

The president of the university issued a public commitment laced with a liberal measure of hope: "The book will not be a dry school-by-school repetition of tired data but an attempt to tell the story as it is, to flesh out the characters, and to face up to the controversies and the politics inevitable in an institution this size and this old. We think that in telling our story we will be adding historical perspective to the entire mosaic of higher education in this country."

I closed out all other endeavors and began my research in February 1981. I stopped work on the book in March 1986, when the printer pulled down and locked the window. I found the intervening five years—through thirty-five formal interviews, thirty-six chapters, some 2,700 handwritten manuscript pages, 300,000 words—a surprising and edifying experience.

In several respects I was fortunate. The research papers were concentrated in one city and largely in one library. That was not true of most of my earlier books, where the documents were scattered over two continents. The librarians and custodians were friendly. I was overjoyed to find in the University archives some thousands of pages of an academic diary kept over a seventeen-year period (1938–1955) by the provost-become-chancellor. In it he made notes on conversations, reported every crisis, and recorded his daily thoughts, decisions, and actions.

The story, moreover, was much better than any author undertaking such a project has any right or reason to expect. There was drama; there was tragedy; there were indeed controversy and politics. There were, unexpectedly, rich veins of humor, occasionally of comedy. There were at least five academic experiences in the history of the University that attracted prolonged national attention.

There was also, not least, a wealth of history,—of fresh episodes of everyday life, of academic life in other times—to report and describe. I think of certain incidents and experiences, major and minor.

For example:

In September 1891 there occurred a casual matter that somehow better than any other depicts the wide gap between university life in the 1890s and in the 1980s. This was an incident in which Dr. William J. Holland, a naturalist and chancellor, established a natural history society among his students. "We went out," he wrote to his parents, "and shot a few birds, and I gave them a lesson in the art of stuffing them, and besides gave them a lesson in practical botany. We had a very pleasant forenoon together."

In the 1920s the University undertook a monumental effort to raise $10 million with which to build a 52-story skyscraper in an open field on the Pitt campus. The campaign, never fully reported, was the first milestone in a new profession, that of fund raising.

In 1934–1936 there was a historic conflict of wills between a stubborn history professor of liberal inclinations and an equally stubborn conservative chancellor. They had at each other while the American Association of University Professors, a state legislative investigating committee, the popular press and the nation looked on.

In 1939 there was an investigation of the same chancellor's illiberal academic policies, conducted by a special committee of seven trustees. The trustees were conservatives, but they rendered an unexpected judgment.

In 1959, while the world watched and the University braced itself, a potentate from the east descended on the campus, accompanied by his wife, children, four ambassadors, and 325 American and foreign news correspondents. This was Nikita Khrushchev, and now we discover that he was also accompanied by a KGB agent who in 1978 became the highest ranking Soviet official ever to defect to the West.

And in the decade 1956–1965 occurred the tragic story of a chancellor who took the University on a great educational leap forward; who gambled that the millions of dollars he spent to pay for it would be forthcoming from somewhere or someone; but who, as it turned out, was mistaken.

In writing the history of a university, an author faces a problem and must make a decision. How, in Thomas Macaulay's phrase, are the parts to be ordered? Is the history to be organized chronologically in the conventional manner, according to the narrative succession of presidential administrations? Or should it be structured and written by topics, by subjects, by schools and departments, in a manner sometimes considered more progressive?

I studied a number of published university histories. I found that writing the history of an institution by topics does indeed make it possible to include many details, such as the founding and growth of every department, major appointments and promotions, awards and accomplishments—some of which details, however important and deserving, cannot always be worked or wedged into copy that is subject to the discipline of chronology and a narrative line.

Topicality, however, can lead to a grievous mistake: that of attempting to do too much, of trying to cover everything, and in so doing, of beclouding major themes and reducing interest in the book as a whole. Topicality, moreover, may confuse the reader as he is taken back and forth in time from past to present and back again to past as each subject is introduced and developed. (A Boston editor once instructed me, "Never write flashbacks unless you are Joseph Conrad.") And such a structure sacrifices the unifying, clarifying effect of chronology and the heightened interest that even a little suspense may generate in straightforward narrative.*

I elected in 1981 to organize this history around the presidents and chancellors as they came on the

---

*The Modern Researcher by Jacques Barzun and Henry F. Graff analyzes the conflict between topical order and chronological order. An amusing passage applies topical treatment to a biography and by this device reduces it to the ridiculous. The subject's character is taken through boyhood, youth, maturity, and old age, and then his hobbies are taken through boyhood, youth, maturity, and old age, and then his health, his income, and finally his friends.

scene beginning in 1787, attempting as I did so to develop as strong a chronological narrative thrust as I could. Fortunately, the principals are through twenty decades, each in a different way, interesting, distinctive, and three-dimensional. Each had a strong supporting cast. Each made his contribution to the University—generally the one that seemed to be most needed at that time.

I regret the events that were precluded by this auctorial decision—the names that were not recognized, triumphs not recorded, honors not acknowledged, the schools and programs not exhaustively described or even mentioned. I grieve that, even in 446 pages, not everything and everybody could be covered.

Notes and sources appear on pages 459–509, keyed to the text by page number and an identifying phrase and to the bibliography by a short title. This allows uninterupted reading of the main text and in some degree makes the back notes readable and understandable in themselves. Acknowledgments to the good people to whom I owe an immeasurable debt of gratitude for help and counsel in writing this history appear on pages 451–52.

Book I
1787-1921

Pittsburgh is in plain sight, at half a mile distance. It is an irregular, poorly built place. The number of houses, mostly built of logs, about one hundred and fifty. The inhabitants (perhaps because they lead too easy a life) incline to be extravagant and lazy. They are subject, however, to frequent alarms from the savages of the wilderness. The situation is agreeable, and the soil good.

Journal of John May
May 7, 1788

In the roaring decades following the Civil War, when Pittsburgh was supplying the iron and steel for building the North and opening the West, the growth of this area was one of the raw wonders of the nineteenth-century world. Great mills proliferated up and down the narrow riverbanks, the building city staggered helter-skelter up precipitous hills and valleys, and some of the greatest U.S. fortunes were laid. By 1900 more wealth had probably been beaten and torn from the 750 square miles of Allegheny County, whose capital is Pittsburgh, than from any like plot on earth.

Fortune
February 1947

1

The Articulate Audible Voice of the Past

Whereas the education of youth ought to be a primary object with every government: And whereas any School or College yet established is greatly distant from the country west of the Allegheny mountain: And whereas the town of Pittsburgh is most central to that settlement, and accommodation for students can be most conveniently obtained in that town . . .

Preamble to AN ACT for the establishment of an Academy or public School in the Town of Pittsburgh, February 28, 1787

Pittsburgh from the south, as depicted in a painting by Louis Brantz, 1790.

Hugh Henry Brackenridge was admitted to the Philadelphia bar in December 1780 at the age of thirty-two. He was one of the dozen remarkable men in Pennsylvania who, it has been said, could have served with distinction in 1787–1788 if the original framers of the Constitution had been dead, dying, abroad, or otherwise occupied. Nevertheless, he left Philadelphia four months later. "I saw no chance," he said, "for being anything in that city, there were such great men before me."

He chose to travel 320 miles to the west, across seven ridges of mountains, to take up residence in Pittsburgh. The War for Independence was still being fought on the western frontier, and communities there were being brutally assaulted by Indian raiding parties led by British officers. He found a trading post and garrison town surrounded by wild country. It had fewer than 400 inhabitants, most of them Scots (like himself), Scots-Irish, and German, living in a town, he said, not "distinguishable by house or street." There were perhaps 1,500 inhabitants in the area about Pittsburgh, most of them to the south in busy communities in Washington and Fayette counties.

Why Pittsburgh?

Though a poor boy brought from Scotland to Pennsylvania at the age of five, Brackenridge had learned Latin and studied the classics as a child. At fifteen he was in charge of a free school in Maryland, and at nineteen he entered the College of New Jersey at Princeton. James Madison was a classmate there; Aaron Burr was one year behind him; with Philip Freneau, another classmate, he wrote *Father Bombo's Pilgrimage,* perhaps the first prose fiction written in America, and at commencement exercises he recited to much applause a patriotic poem he and Freneau had composed together, "The Rising Glory of America." In the succession of occupations that followed he studied divinity while heading an academy in Maryland; returned to Princeton for a master's degree; served as a chaplain in the field with Washington's army; founded and edited a monthly publication in Philadelphia called the *United States Magazine;* and studied law under the great Samuel Chase in Annapolis. Indeed, why Pittsburgh?

He chose Pittsburgh because he saw more there than most of his compatriots. He recognized its role as a port of supply and transit that was sending a stream of traffic down the Ohio River to Kentucky—in one six-month period in the winter of 1786–1787, 177 boats carrying 2,689 people, 1,333 horses, 766 cattle, 102 wagons, and one phaeton, a count that did not include those vessels that passed in the night. "The bulk of the inhabitants," Brackenridge wrote with an eye on an eastern audience, "are traders, mechanics, and laborers. Of mechanics and laborers there is still a great want; indeed from this circumstance, the improvement of the town in buildings is greatly retarded. This town must in future time be a place of great manufactory. Indeed the greatest on the continent, or perhaps in the world." He had, he said, "a strong interest to prompt me to offer myself to that place. My object was to advance the country and thereby myself."

He was admitted to the practice of law in Washington County and at Hanna's Town, the seat of Westmoreland County (which, until September 1787, encompassed Pittsburgh). He soon became a leading member of the bar, acquired property, and took a wife, a Miss Montgomery, of whom nothing is known except that she died two years later, leaving him with an infant son. Two years after her death he was on his way home from a Washington County court session when he stopped at the farmhouse of a German farmer named Wolfe to seek shelter from a rainstorm and have his horse fed. A contemporary relates that Mr. Wolfe had a beautiful black-eyed daughter named Sabina, who was directed by her father to bring the gentleman's horse to the door when he departed.

Brackenridge traveled a few miles toward Pittsburgh, stopped, turned his horse around, and returned to the farmhouse. There he asked Mr. Wolfe for his daughter's hand in marriage. When he was persuaded that Brackenridge was serious, Mr. Wolfe protested that Miss Sabina was employed in shrubbing a meadow, which saved him an annual expense of ten dollars. Brackenridge gave him a sum of money, obtained Miss Sabina's consent, and took her to Pittsburgh. Almost immediately after the wedding he sent her to Philadelphia "under the

Hugh Henry Brackenridge. Portrait by Gilbert Stuart.

Sabina Wolfe Brackenridge. Portrait by Rembrandt Peale.

Governance of a reputable female Character, whose business will be to polish the Manners, and wipe off the Rusticities which Mrs. Brackenridge has acquired whilst a Wolfe."

Brackenridge's attitude toward the town of his choice was very similar to his attitude toward Mrs. Brackenridge. He intended, in the words of his biographer, to plant the values of Enlightenment in the life of the frontier town. He would adapt the place to his own personality—that is, he would civilize and educate it, improve its cultural life, and correct the morals of its people.

In a town that had virtually nothing, he began by establishing the institution he needed most: a newspaper. He persuaded John Scull, a young Philadelphian of good family, to transport a printing press over the mountains and to start the weekly *Pittsburgh Gazette.* Scull also printed books and pamphlets, and he was able to establish a weekly mail delivery to and from Philadelphia. From New Jersey Brackenridge then brought Zadok Cramer, a bookbinder who started a bookstore and a circulating library on Market Street.

To accomplish his larger goals, Brackenridge needed front-stage political power. To get it he used the *Pittsburgh Gazette* almost as though it were a personal vehicle, and on October 10, 1786, he was elected to the state assembly.

The first session of Pennsylvania's eleventh general assembly opened in the State House in Philadelphia on October 25, 1786, but Brackenridge did not present himself until November 13. Such tardiness was common at the time, especially of those traveling long distances from the west. Brackenridge was able nevertheless to begin work at once on the legislative program he carried with him. On November 17 he was put on the committee appointed to draw up a plan for the sale of lands lying north of Pittsburgh, 10,000 acres of which he hoped to obtain for financing one of the undertakings on his program. On November 30 he was assigned to the committee that brought in a bill that established Allegheny, a new western county, made Pittsburgh a borough within it, and placed there the county seat and the court of justice. He successfully

entered a bill that resulted in an improved road from Carlisle to Bedford, and another bill that incorporated a nonsectarian Christian church in Pittsburgh. In December he read aloud and entered a petition, written by himself, to charter an academy of learning in Pittsburgh.

He had prepared the way by publishing in the *Gazette* on September 2, 1786, a long article giving the reasons why the state should grant the charter and give financial aid to the academy.

The situation of the town of Pittsburgh is greatly to be chosen for a seat of learning; the fine air, the excellent water, the plenty and cheapness of provisions, render it highly favorable. . . . I do not know that the legislature could do a more acceptable service to the commonwealth than by endowing a school at this place. It will introduce money to Pennsylvania . . . from the whole western country. It will institute knowledge and ability in this extreme of government. We well know the strength of a state greatly consists in the superior mental powers of the inhabitants. . . .

I should rejoice to see Pennsylvania at all times able to produce mathematicians, philosophers, historians, and statesmen, equal to any in the confederacy. . . .

The country west of the mountain certainly deserves a particular attention from the commonwealth. It has been a barrier of the war against the savages, and has greatly suffered from the depredations. To the inhabitants the whole war has been a tour of duty.

Brackenridge had used Benjamin Franklin's Philadelphia Academy, founded in 1749, as a model for his western academy, in that it was to receive some support from the state government but would be governed by an independent board of trustees. His petition was signed by twenty-one incorporators who would serve as trustees: eight lawyers or jurists, six clergymen (five of them graduates of Princeton), four army officers who had served in the Revolution, two physicians, and one merchant. The bill that founded an academy of learning in Pittsburgh was passed by the assembly on February 28, 1787—just ten weeks before the opening of the convention that was to write a new federal constitution. Thus the Pittsburgh Academy, grandfather of the University of Pittsburgh, became the first institution of learning west of the Allegheny Mountains to be established by a charter of the Pennsylvania legislature.*

Brackenridge returned to his home county with an impressive record of legislative accomplishment, which was enhanced by a gift he had obtained from the Penn family: one square of land in Pittsburgh in what was known as Ewalt's Field, bounded by Second (Boulevard of the Allies) and Third streets to the south and north, Smithfield Street to the west, and Cherry Way to the east. Two of his other undertakings, however, were less successful. He had asked that the assembly give as an endowment for the Academy the proceeds from the sale of 10,000 acres of public western lands, but in September 1787 this area was reduced in debate to 5,000 acres, and the state sold these at so low a price that the money gave very little help. And he found on his return from Philadelphia that the church he had chartered—the nonsectarian church open to all Christian denominations—had been taken over and was controlled by a Presbyterian congregation.

Although the Academy's charter was granted on February 28, 1787, and land was obtained, formal instruction did not begin for two years. The schoolhouse stood somewhere on the Academy lot. The story that the first school building was a log house has persisted, and it may be true—in Pittsburgh at the time there were more log houses than other kinds of structures—but there is no direct evidence to support this agreeable version of the Cathedral of Learning's ancestor. On March 12, 1789, the trustees elected George Welch as principal and gave notice that the curriculum would include "the Learned Languages, English, and the Mathematicks." In 1795 a new master, Reverend Mr. Arthur, a Virginian who specialized in rhetoric and belles-lettres, taught "the reading of English according to the most improved method."

The Reverend Mr. Robert Andrews, who became principal in 1796, was introduced by the trustees as one who "finished his education in two of the most celebrated seminaries in Europe, and has been in the habit of teaching for several years, especially in the Royal Military and Marine Academy in Dublin, and has also spent three years in the same habit in America in two respectable places of literature, with general approbation." The first complete catalogue of courses followed:

The principles of English Grammar and Geography will make a particular part of the academic course, with their application to parsing and explaining the English language, a knowledge of Globes, Maps &c. The lower classes will be taught Orthography agreeable to standards of the first taste. . . . Reading and a just pronunciation will be a peculiar object of Mr. Andrews personal attention. Writing, Mercantile Arithmetic, Navigation, Surveying, and Book keeping will be taught by the most respectable masters that can be procured; and the usual branches of classical education, with a succinct view of the histories of Ancient Greece and Rome . . . paying particular attention to the Antiquities and Mythology of the same people . . . together with a stated course of examination on the Belles Letters.

A French and dancing master would also attend "for those who may wish their children instructed in those graceful parts of a polite education." The cost of tuition, payable quarterly in advance, varied from three pounds per annum for instruction in reading to six pounds for the teaching of another language.

The Reverend Mr. Robert Steele, pastor of the First Presbyterian Church, was made principal in 1800. An Irishman who wore satin breeches, silk stockings, knee buckles, and pumps, he gave frequent public examinations to his pupils, "considering examinations best calculated to bring into operation two powerful incentives to application: the love of praise, and the dread of disgrace." The notice of his appointment in the *Gazette* also contained some helpful advice:

The present establishment, and future prospects of more extensive usefulness of the Pittsburgh Academy, so well situated for the general benefit of the Western Country, must be highly pleasing to all who value the education of youth. . . . It is proper to remark for the information of those who live at a distance . . . that from the present moderate prices in the Pittsburgh market, boarding is considerably reduced below the high rates which the former market prices rendered necessary. There are now in

*This claim is conservative. See Appendix A.

this borough, more and better chances for good and for cheap boarding, than can be found elsewhere.

The Reverend Mr. John Taylor, a large, handsome man of more than six feet, weighing two hundred pounds, and a talented singer and violinist, arrived at the Academy in 1801 with a set of globes and apparatus for making astronomical calculations. He notified the readers of the *Gazette* "that he intends to open a NIGHT SCHOOL . . . in one of the rooms of the Academy, where he means to teach Writing, Arithmetic and Geometry. Any person who has made a tolerable proficiency in Mathematical knowledge, if his curiosity prompts him, may, in the course of one quarter, learn the whole process of making an Almanack." Brackenridge's son, Henry Marie, was one of Taylor's pupils until he displeased his father by acting in a "genteel comedy" and was banished to Jefferson College in Canonsburg.*

In the 1790s, with the help of a public subscription and a $5,000 grant from the legislature, the trustees erected a brick building for Pittsburgh Academy. It was probably located on the corner of the lot at Third and Cherry, and it very likely provided a residence for the principal, as well as housing classes. The story that it adjoined the original log house of Pittsburgh Academy (if such ever existed) seems unlikely. Other more plausible references and illustrations suggest that a second brick building, adjoining the first, was constructed in the early years of the nineteenth century. (A version of the early buildings of Pittsburgh Academy and the major building of the Western University of Pennsylvania is seen on page 12.)†

---

*Henry Marie was to go on to a distinguished career as an author, traveler, jurist, and diplomat. Hugh Henry lost his bid for a second term in the assembly, partly because he was the only western assemblyman to campaign in favor of the proposed U.S. Constitution, which in the western counties was called "as deep and wicked a conspiracy as ever was invented in the darkest ages against the liberties of a free people." In 1793 he finished the third volume of *Modern Chivalry*, the satiric, picaresque novel for which he is remembered today. In 1799 his former enemies, the Jeffersonians, appointed him a judge of the Pennsylvania Supreme Court, whereupon, after almost twenty years in Pittsburgh, he moved to Carlisle.

In April 1804 the students took an examination in the presence of the trustees and in the evening in the court house "delivered orations, exhibited a dramatic performance embracing a great variety of characters, and spoke several dialogues on different subjects."

This being the first public performance of our young Students, there was a crowded audience, and the most lively interest was visible in their relatives and acquaintances who attended.

The exhibition far exceeded expectation. Many of the boys were not more than twelve years of age, some under ten: all, however, appeared to possess a correct idea of the parts assigned to them; their gestures gave appropriate effect to the sense; their pronunciation, manners, and deportment were highly commendable.

In the second decade of the new century it was apparent to anyone who thought about it that Pittsburgh needed and deserved something more to educate its young people than an academy. The borough had become an incorporated city in 1816. It had 7,000 inhabitants, served a far larger population in Allegheny County, and more than ever was the port of transit and supply for hundreds of thousands of settlers and travelers headed for the West. In 1818 a paved turnpike from Philadelphia to Pittsburgh was completed, and stage coaches and trains of Conestoga wagons came daily into the city all year around. By 1820 there was regular steamboat travel from Pittsburgh, the largest city in the west, to Louisville, the second largest. The city erected a toll bridge across the Monongahela in 1818 and across the Allegheny the following year. It was now an industrial city with boat yards, sawmills, breweries, distilleries, coal mines, iron furnaces, tanyards, brick yards, metal-working factories. It had made the cannon and the rigging in 1812 for ships of war on the Great Lakes. It had started a glass-making industry that within fifty years would be producing more than half the glass made in the United States,

---

†Readers who wish to pursue the elusive truth about the early buildings of Pittsburgh Academy should refer to the appropriate file in the Hillman Archives on this subject, under the 200th anniversary history.

University Archives

If the first building of Pittsburgh Academy was a log house, it probably looked like the structure in this 1936 drawing by Ward Hunter, based on a conjectural design by architectural historian Charles Morse Stotz.

including, incredible as it seems in a brawling center of heavy industry, pieces of extraordinary delicacy and beauty. A visiting Englishman said in 1818, even when the city was suffering from a postwar depression, "To this place is the attention directed of everyone, who speaks of America and her prospects. To it the emigrant looks; and if he asks, which is the most flourishing town, or where he is most likely to succeed, in almost any branch he may mention, 'Pittsburgh' is the answer."

But Pittsburgh had no true college. The trustees recognized that the Academy was "inadequate to the accommodation and complete education of the students," and they lamented that young people had to travel several hundred miles to the east to receive a higher education, thus falling prey to all the moral

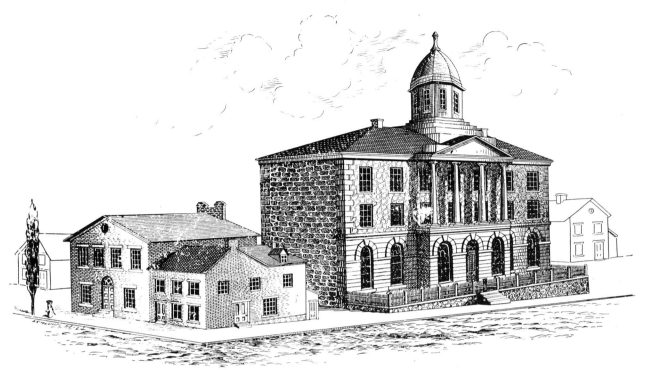

One reasonably likely version of the University's early buildings. The two adjoining brick structures of Pittsburgh Academy (left) face on Cherry Way, while the impressive first building of the Western University of Pennsylvania faces on Third Avenue. Today the space of all three buildings is occupied by the Allied Parking Garage.

dangers of living far from home in a strange city. Accordingly, late in 1818 they petitioned the legislature for a charter for the Western University of Pennsylvania. The new University would have twenty-six distinguished citizens of the community as its incorporators and trustees. The funds of the Academy would be transferred for the use of the University. Persons of every religious denomination were to be eligible to be elected trustees, nor could any person, either as principal, professor, or pupil, be refused admittance for his conscientious persuasion in matters of religion, provided, his demeanor be orderly and correct.

The charter was approved on February 18, 1819, and with it the legislators granted, for the maintenance of the University, forty acres of land in Allegheny City (Pittsburgh's North Side). Unfortunately, the citizens who pastured their cattle on that land claimed it on the ground that they had a constitutional right to a common, and the state supreme court ruled against the University. The legislature attempted to compensate the school for the loss, but its gift of $12,000 payable in four equal annual installments fell far short of what the sale of the land would have produced.

The trustees chose as the first principal of the University the Reverend Robert Bruce, born in Scotland, a student at the University of Edinburgh, professor of natural history, chemistry, and mathematics, a remarkable man and a fine scholar. He had four other professors on his faculty. All five men belonged to different religious denominations. One was a Roman Catholic.

Bruce's installation on May 10, 1822, was marked by an eighteen-section procession from the Academy buildings to the First Presbyterian Church on

The Reverend Doctor Robert Bruce. Portrait by John C. Darley.

Wood Street. It was led by "a Battalion of Volunteers," who were followed by the trustees two by two, the principal and his faculty, students, clergy, city officials, judges, officers of the courts, members of the bar, physicians, and finally by (17) Strangers and (18) Citizens. Dr. George Stevenson, president of the trustees, turned over to the principal two heavy keys as symbols of authority, occasioning some mirth among those in the audience who compared the size of the keys and the dimensions of the school's two buildings. Mr. Bruce responded with an inaugural address in which he said, among other things: Only a Pittsburgh college could serve the peculiar needs of Pittsburgh, the Gateway to the West; he hoped the University might soon own a rich library and apparatus for the teaching of science; he hoped further that it might soon set up a school of medicine. He also asked the faculty to live with moral habits and religious thinking that would "refine the taste, polish the manners, and uplift the conscience of themselves and their students." The reporter from the *Pittsburgh Mercury* confessed that he was unable "to do justice to this truly excellent address . . . evidently the production of a strong, vigorous mind, highly cultured."

Thomas A. Mellon, founder of the banking family in Pittsburgh, who entered the Western University in 1834 at the age of twenty-one, produced an autobiography fifty years later that gives a fascinating account of upward progress and earnest endeavor in a young, undeveloped country. Mellon had arrived in Baltimore in 1818 as a child of five with his Scots-Irish parents from county Tyrone. They had crossed the Allegheny Mountains walking behind a rented Conestoga wagon, preparing their food at campfires along the road and sleeping in the wagon. They acquired a "dry ridge" farm and a dilapidated two-room log cabin at a place known as Poverty Point, near Greensburg, some thirty miles east of Pittsburgh, and by strenuous effort and good management over the next fifteen years actually made it into a productive, profitable operation.

In the summer of 1834, having decided to continue his intermittent education full time, Thomas Mellon set out to look at Jefferson in Canonsburg, the most popular college in the area. Since the ride of almost twenty miles in a "hack" would cost him a dollar, he walked the distance and viewed the September commencement "in order to learn the course of procedure, with a view to entering."

There were some three or four hundred students at Jefferson then, and all seemed hilarious in anticipation of Commencement Day. [They] were formed in procession a short distance out of town, and headed by the faculty and trustees and preceded by a brass band, they marched through the town to the college. There assembled in the college hall or chapel which was crowded with spectators, the senior class . . . appeared on the platform; and after much parade of salutatory and valedictory and other addresses, the diplomas, profuse in sealing wax and blue ribbons, were delivered. . . . The whole performance struck me rather as an advertisement to attract students and tickle the fancy of the shallow public; but what discouraged me still more was the prevailing frivolity. The

"Imposing and stately," as the Pittsburgh Business Directory of 1837 described it, the first building for the Western University of Pennsylvania is shown here in a painting by Russell Smith.

spirit among the students was not of the nature which I expected; not at all in accord with the earnestness which the important purpose of training for life's serious work seemed to me to demand.

He walked home again, "not at all as much elated with the prospect as on my way out." He decided then to visit the Western University, "which had long been in operation and well known, but not with the same degree of eclat and notoriety as Jefferson." (The University then had forty-three students.) "Here I found a very different state of affairs. The numbers of students and professors were fewer, but what they lacked in numbers they appeared to make up in energy and earnestness. The purpose of all seemed to be work and progress, and accorded better with my own spirit and disposition on the subject. . . . It seemed to be just the place I had been looking for."

The University in 1830 had moved into a new building fronting on Third Street near Cherry, built with savings, private gifts, and an 1826 grant from the Commonwealth. (This was the last aid the state was to give for the next half-century.) It was a three-story freestone-fronted building with Ionic columns

C. Hax McCullough, One Hundred Years of Banking

An immigrant from Ireland at the age of five, Thomas A. Mellon became a student and then a teacher at the Western University of Pennsylvania. He founded the banking house of T. Mellon & Sons.

under a classic pediment, Roman arched windows, and a cupola, and for the next decade and a half it was considered the city's finest secular building. Mellon called it large and imposing and was pleased to find that it contained many vacant upstairs rooms, some of which were rented to students for living quarters. In a day or two he found several other students "as impecunious as myself and ready to join in a sumptuary club." He returned home and then,

with my trunk and table, bed and bedding and a few cooking utensils stowed upon a wagon loaded with farm products for market, my father and I made our way to the city. . . . The next day my companions of the club joined me with their furniture and bedding, and we soon had our rooms in snug and comfortable condition.

The arrangement was to procure the provisions at joint expense, and each to serve in rotation a week at a time, as cook. There were five of us, and the cooking was extremely simple. The labor was light and recurring only every fifth week. Our food was abundant but plain, and few dishes. . . . The cost of board on this plan at no time exceeded seventy-five cents per week to each.

Mellon spent five years and $500 at the University, taking time out now and then to work on the family farm (now moved to Murrysville, an eleven-mile walk) and to conduct a profitable summer "pay school" for children on the south side of the river. But at last, in September 1837,

our class was assembled in the college hall for the customary valedictory of our president. It was one of the few really impressive addresses of the kind I have ever heard. Its sentiments have influenced my life and still abide in my memory. . . . In after life I did derive benefit from the studies I had pursued, or some of them; but from the circumstance of having a diploma I never derived any benefit whatever. . . . In my forty years of subsequent experience in the legal profession it never occurred to any one among my numerous clients to inquire whether I had a diploma, or as to the kind of preliminary education I had received.

For a short time following his graduation and before his admission to the bar, Mellon taught classics at the University.

The new statutes of the Western University, printed in 1822, suggest that there were problems of discipline:

The students of this Institution will be expected to preserve that dignity which is due to their character, and to the objects of their pursuit. Every species of rudeness and vulgarity must be avoided. . . .

Dueling, or any concern in promoting or abetting it, shall be punished, in all cases, by expulsion.

No student shall be permitted to wear a dirk, or to carry any deadly weapon whatsoever.

The full course of study lasted seven years: four of preparatory work, called the classical section, and three years called the collegiate. Tuition for the classical course was twenty-five dollars a year, for the collegiate, thirty, one-half payable in advance. "Boarding" ran from one dollar to two dollars a week. The first class, graduated in 1823, had three members, all destined to be clergymen; the class of 1824 had five; the class of 1825 had eight. In the first twelve years, through 1835, bachelor of arts degrees (the diplomas written in Latin) were conferred on some eighty students. Almost all were to have notable or distinguished careers as clergymen, lawyers, merchants, teachers, physicians, or public officials—one as mayor of Pittsburgh and U.S. minister to Denmark. In a young country, their influence on their community and their country was considerably more powerful than their number would indicate.

On July 4, 1822, a faculty committee reported a new curriculum to the Board of Trustees. On the collegiate level, the first year was given over to Cicero, Vergil's *Eclogues* and *Georgics*, Horace, Demosthenes, Xenophon's *Cyropaedia*, Lucian, Homer, and other classic authors, antiquities, scansion, prose composition, geography, English composition and declamation, belles-lettres, geometry, trigonometry, and surveying. The second year was taken up with studies of Livy, Terence, Juvenal, Persius, Quintilian, Cicero's *De oratore*, Longinus, and other classic authors, Latin and Greek prose composition and scansion, philosophy, history, declamation, English composition and literature, trigonometry, navigation, astronomy, and natural philosophy. The third year brought Tacitus, Cicero's

De natura deorum, Epictetus, Xenophon's *Memorabilia,* scansion and composition, moral science, theology, ethics, rhetoric, belles-lettres, political economy, history, declamation, natural philosophy, natural history, chemistry, and geology. All translations of authors being read were prohibited either in the University building or in the students' quarters. The students were to commit to memory and recite striking passages of the Greek and Roman classics. There were regular exercises in Latin and Greek composition every morning except Friday and Saturday. Hebrew, French, German, Italian, Anglo-Saxon, and Spanish were offered as optional subjects.

In 1831 Alexis de Tocqueville wrote to a friend, a teacher in Paris: "The effort made in this country to spread instruction is truly prodigious. The universal and sincere faith that they profess here in the efficatiousness of education seems to me one of the most remarkable features of America." Until well into the nineteenth century, that faith in what "a system of education" could do for the young meant faith in a curriculum similar to the one developed at the Western University in 1822. The classical languages, one classical scholar says, "were taught for their theological, political, cultural, and social values. They provided educational tools for arriving at goals then regarded as useful, and they justified their existence . . . by creating and sustaining enlightened leadership." Thus, almost unbelievable emphasis (from today's viewpoint) was placed on classical literature and languages, on a curriculum inherited from the middle ages, in a society whose culture was dominated by theologians.

American life—especially on the western frontier—required something different, something more. By 1830 public sentiment was shifting to favor "useful learning," which meant placing more emphasis on the new practical arts and sciences needed to build roads, bridges, dams, and canals, to invent and discover and develop, to administer institutions and public affairs. Most Pennsylvania legislators understood this need far better than they understood why students should memorize passages from

Xenophon's *Memorabilia* or Vergil's *Eclogues.* Those legislators were now newly involved in a controversial program "to establish a general system of education by common schools" and to set up "normal schools" to train teachers for the new classrooms, with emphasis on courses that would prove to be useful in some trade or profession. They had authorized the program by passing the Free School Act of 1834, which for the first time in Pennsylvania acknowledged a responsibility for providing a free education for all children, regardless of the financial status of their parents. (Earlier state law had provided free education only for children of the poor; the parents were required to make public acknowledgment of their poverty.) Having voted an educational state subsidy to local districts and having created school boards, elected locally, to carry out the intent of the law, the legislators felt little interest in granting a subsidy to support the kinds of courses being taught at the Western University.

The trustees and the faculty had to make critical decisions. Should they modify their basic concepts and change their curriculum to meet the state's demand for what would now be called vocational training? Or should they continue to train a relatively small number of students for law, the church, and a few other professions with courses based on the classics, and in so doing lose state aid? The decisions were made, and carrying them out very nearly killed the Western University.

In 1831 the trustees asked the faculty to develop a reorganized curriculum for the three-year collegiate department. In 1832 they introduced a modified course of study. In 1835 they filled vacancies on the Board of Trustees with young replacements, and they appointed the Reverend Dr. Gilbert Morgan, given the new title of president, to replace Robert Bruce. Morgan's associates at Union College, New York, recommended him as "a man peculiarly suited to take part in the program of popular education opening up in Pennsylvania." The Alumni Association pledged its support to the trustees and to Dr. Morgan. Robert Bruce promised his cordial cooperation. A committee appointed by the trustees to raise funds for endowing professorships began by issuing a public statement: "The undersigned approve heartily of that part of Mr. Morgan's plan which would impart a more popular cast to the Institution, by enlarging the range of studies, and yielding a prominent place and consideration to such as may be turned to account in active life, in whatever sphere. Our citizens have had too much reason, perhaps, to regard it, heretofore, as something which stood apart, in lofty seclusion from their pursuits and sympathies. This erroneous notion will be discarded, and a deep interest claimed from all, in that which is designed for the common benefit of all."

In his inaugural address Morgan declared that a new motivation, which he called "General Education," should be brought into the classroom "to perfect the entire character of the individual and of society itself." He announced that he was selecting professors "whose talents were suited to the needs of the city." In recognition of the fact that culture gave man control over his material world, he would make changes in the curriculum: the University would teach methods of study and research; introduce a philological study of the English language; teach political science, "because so much of governing is left to the people"; start a system of training teachers for the public schools; and include courses in sacred literature and modern languages. He spoke of Pittsburgh as the Thermopylae of the Great Valley, standing as it did on a flow of thousands of miles of unbroken waterways at the time when steamboat navigation was growing rapidly. Small tests of Greek and Roman history were not enough in a country that had a history of its own. And yet he was firmly convinced that study of the classics must continue to have its place in the curriculum, for the classics stood like an open door into the souls of great men and into infinite and eternal experiences.

President Morgan's term was short and unsuccessful; he could not manage an effective compromise in the eternal conflict between theoretical and practical education. The state did not give money, nor did the city, nor did the alumni, nor did the community. By 1837 only two professors remained in the collegiate department. The school superintendent of Allegheny County stated in his report to the state superintendent of common schools, "The Preparatory School . . . is the only department at present in operation. . . . The Institute is destitute of means. . . . [The trustees] want to make a good *College now,* and may make a *University* hereafter." President Morgan advised that the institution be closed, and he resigned to accept a position in North Carolina in a school for young ladies. Many years later, at the age of eighty-two, he spoke of the futility he had felt in Pittsburgh and of his regret that the citizens there felt no need of a college. "Every man," he said, "was busy with industrial matters; state and city were agitated with Masonry, with Abolition convention and lectures, and with dividing churches."

With Morgan's departure, Bruce was reinstated to his former position. He now had a faculty of three. Despite the affection felt for him, unrest and dissatisfaction continued. There was recrimination in 1838 when the legislators declined to include the Western University among other colleges that were receiving grants, apparently because they felt that its courses did not yet meet community needs. Dr. Bruce again left the University, either in protest at the changes in the curriculum or because he was pushed out by reform-minded trustees. When he rented some rooms and set up a school, Duquesne College, under a charter granted "for the purpose of extending the facilities and diffusing more widely the influence and advantages of classical learning," a number of Western University students followed him. The charter of Duquesne College lapsed three years after Bruce's death in 1846. (Almost thirty years later, the seceding students were officially recognized as University alumni; nineteen survivors were awarded honorary master of arts degrees.)

Catastrophe struck the city and the University on April 10, 1845. At around noon an untended backyard fire at Ferry and Second streets spread to an ice house and then to several frame houses. By nightfall twenty squares in the most valuable part of the city—about fifty-six acres containing some nine hundred houses, all the great warehouses on the Monongahela River, and the Monongahela River Bridge—were in ruins. The University's hall at

Pittsburgh in the early 1840s.

Third Street and Cherry was destroyed, and with it all the Academy and University records, files, books, furniture, and scientific equipment.

Some trustees wanted to cease operations. Others wanted to sell the valuable Third Street lot, leave the downtown area, and relocate on cheaper ground outside Pittsburgh, perhaps in Allegheny City on the north shore of the river. A committee from the city's select and common councils called to "remonstrate" against removing the University from the city. Trinity Church offered use of its basement for temporary classrooms. That offer was accepted, and the money received from insurance and the sale of the Third Street property was used to erect a new building on Duquesne Way (on the site later occupied by Horne's department store). The *Gazette* called the building an architectural monstrosity, but it enabled the University to continue its operations without interruption for another four years.

Two years before the Great Fire, Heman Dyer, dean of the faculty, had been appointed to succeed Robert Bruce as principal. He was an effective administrator before and after the fire; he created a department and professorship of law, revived a professorship of chemistry, installed a professor of mechanical drawing, increased the enrollment as well as the strength of the faculty, began a training course for teachers, and was a more active civic leader than any principal had been before him.

In July 1849, only four years after the Great Fire,

The Great Fire of April 10, 1845. Painting by William Coventry Wall.

disaster struck again. In a fire in the lower part of town, the Duquesne Way building was destroyed with all its contents, including a valuable collection of fossils and minerals made by the state geologist and on loan to the University.

This time the disheartened trustees voted to suspend operations. The students were dismissed; the faculty departed. The charter remained. The trustees gathered the assets of the Western University of Pennsylvania—$26,000 in all, including insurance on the Duquesne Way building and lot—invested them in Allegheny County bonds, and waited for a new and brighter day.

2

"Great Diversity of Talent and Attention"

The value in every respect to our community of a large and well-endowed and well-equipped University is not understood. . . . The education acquired in a University will be the best means of opening up new industries, should those on which we now almost wholly depend languish. Intelligent men will devise and build them up.

George Woods, Chancellor, Report to the Trustees, June 1, 1875

The University's new main building at the corner of Ross and Diamond (Forbes) streets, the site of the present-day City-County Building.

THE WESTERN UNIVERSITY remained alive but dormant through many of the next six years. The trustees met from time to time to discuss plans for reopening the school. In 1853 they invested $1,000 of their capital in buying an excellent mineral collection from Jacob Henrici, second-generation leader of the religious sect that had settled at Old Economy, and they appointed a committee of four trustees to select a site for the university building. The four reported on February 14, 1854. They had inspected sites, compared prices, and "after mature consideration" recommended a city lot measuring 93 by 100 feet on the corner of Ross Street and Diamond (renamed Forbes Avenue, where the City-County Building now stands). The revival of the University, the committee concluded, was imperative. The new building should have a slate roof and be made as nearly as possible fire-proof.

A trustees committee "appointed to take into consideration the subject of opening the University" approved the choice. A fine new building located in a convenient yet quiet part of the city, it said, containing ample accommodations, owning an excellent mineral collection, and served by a competent and faithful faculty, would certainly attract 200 students, "which is as large a number as can be advantageously associated in an institution like ours." To think otherwise "would be a reflection little short of libelous on the parental interest and youthful aspirations existing among us." There was now, after all, a population of 100,000 within a radius of two miles around the University.

What will readily occur to judicious parents as a matter for their congratulation [is] that our youth may here be educated *at home;* with less expense for the entire course than a residence at college and board required for a single year; while all the hallowed influences and endearments of the domestic circle are maintained inviolate and parents are spared much distressing anxiety about the health and morals of their sons too dear to them to be needlessly imperilled by premature removal from home and exposure while young, ardent and inexperienced, to the contaminating wiles of the wicked and the follies of the indiscreet.

The proposed site had been occupied by the house of the late James Ross, lawyer, Federalist senator in the new Congress, author of a Latin grammar much used in the schools. His executors agreed to sell for $8,200 and to pay the cost of grading the land to meet city regulations. The cornerstone, laid on September 2, 1854, contained a copy of each of the city's eleven newspapers and a list of those working on the building. To their names they appended an exhortation: "God save the Union and abolish all slavery!" The sixteen-room building—brick with a slate roof—was completed one year later at a cost of $18,300, which was $5,000 over the estimate and necessitated a $5,000 mortgage from David Shields of Sewickley. School reopened with a strong preparatory department, two small classes of freshmen and sophomores, no juniors or seniors, and a faculty of five: a reverend minister as a teaching principal, three professors, and a tutor.

In August 1858—the year of the first Atlantic cable and the Lincoln-Douglas debates—a committee of three trustees, "in a very familiar and kindly way," interrogated the principal about disciplinary problems and the "depressed" state of the institution, after which they asked for his resignation. The trustees, stung by the threat of failure, set about to obtain a man—a scholar, a leader, one who understood business affairs—who could make a success of the institution for which they were responsible. They found him in George Woods, principal and part owner of North Yarmouth Academy, Maine. He had been educated in the country schools of Maine, worked his way through Bowdoin (Class of 1837), taught in a southern College, in a seminary, and in an academy in Maine, and had experience as a businessman in New England shipyards.

Woods accepted the post in November 1858 with the understanding that the board would make up deficiencies caused by wear and breakage of the chemical and philosophical apparatus and would attempt to raise money to buy additional pieces that illustrated recent discoveries in science. His salary was to be $1,500 per annum, "provided the income from the regular course of tuition amount to so much, and . . . in proportion if it does not." The trustees, as they admitted two decades later, in effect

George Woods, chancellor of the University, 1858–1880. Portrait by J. W. Vale.

put a faltering private school in the hands of professors who accepted all the responsibilities and risks of trying to make it succeed. "When I assumed charge of the University in March 1859," Woods wrote almost forty years later, "there were about thirty boys, no regular college courses, and but two professors, one of whom left in two months. There was no endowment, and the income to the professors for the first two years was about four hundred and fifty dollars each per year."

Woods set out to increase enrollment, maintain the classical courses, raise an endowment, and develop the scientific and engineering studies that were demanded by the times, the economy of the region, and the competition—that is, by the tax-supported Free High School and the colleges in the East. He intended to demonstrate what none of the eastern educators believed: that a college in what they perceived to be the Middle West should be taken seriously as a source of sound education in the sciences and classical arts. His first success was an almost immediate increase in the number of students. It has been suggested that this came about because of the confidence he inspired in the city and because of the streetcar line that was chartered in the autumn of 1859, on which day students—the backbone of this and of other urban colleges—rode to the city. For a five-cent fare, the students were transported from Manchester, Lawrenceville, and Allegheny City in cars pulled by horses over iron tracks embedded in the street. A *Gazette* editorial must also have helped increase enrollment: it urged parents to send their sons where "the discipline is mild and the teaching is excellent." No parent, it added, was now "forced to send his son away from the comfort of home and expose him to temptations abroad, to contract habits unknown until too late for reform, but fatal in their consequence to his happiness, success, and usefulness in life."*

The administration of George Woods lasted twenty-two years, the longest continuous tenure of any head of the institution until 1942. It ended in 1880 in bitterness and recrimination, but it was an

---

*"The devil seemed particularly interested in young men from Pittsburgh who attended a college outside the city." Arthur M. Young, *The Voice That Speaketh Clear*, 1957.

outstanding success. For in those years the school truly became a college, its first professional and technical training departments were started, and for the first time there was no longer any real doubt that the institution would survive as a permanent part of Pittsburgh life. During the University's first years, of course, the city was overshadowed by war and the threat of invasion by Rebel forces, under Generals John Hunt Morgan, J. E. B. Stuart, and Robert E. Lee, only 100 miles away. After the fall of Fort Sumpter in April 1861 and President Lincoln's call for an army of volunteers, the College and the city changed in appearance and in spirit. The students were given the largest room in the building as a gymnasium, and an army officer was stationed there to instruct them in drill and military tactics. Colonel Samuel W. Black (Class of 1834), hero of the Mexican War, former governor of the Nebraska Territory, took command of the Sixty-second Regiment, which was made up of three-year volunteers and was the first to leave the city. He was killed in July 1862 at the Battle of Gaines's Mill. Felix R. Brunot, grandson of one of the first physicians to practice medicine in Pittsburgh (1797), a civil engineer, later (1880–1898) a University trustee, raised money to buy two river boats. These he supplied with hospital stores and attending physicians and nurses and saw them sail down the Ohio to serve the troops fighting along the Mississippi and Tennessee River systems. He normally accompanied such relief missions, and on one occasion, in 1862, he was captured and sent to Libby Prison. He was released in an exchange of prisoners.

Pittsburgh was swarming with workmen throughout the war, for it was supplying the North with heavy cannon, small arms, armor plate, steamboats, steel pipe, steel and iron fabrication parts, and coal. The Fort Pitt Foundry alone furnished almost three thousand cannon, including the largest in the world, the fifteen-inch Columbiad, and 10 million pounds of shot and shell. Pittsburgh was also swarming with soldiers, 24,000 of them raised in what President Lincoln had called "the State of Allegheny." Most were headed down or returning up the Ohio Valley, for that route, by river or by rail, was recognized as the chief and safest artery of supply and transport

for the Union forces in the southwest, and Pittsburgh was the main shipping point and depot. The soldiers were paid thirteen dollars a month as privates; many of them were so very young as to be remarked upon. Especially for children, it was a patriotic duty and pleasure to wave and cheer when the soldiers passed by in or on top of freight trains. Margaret Wade, who was then not yet seven years old, on one occasion forgot her handkerchief and could not wave. Desperate, she unbuttoned and lowered her drawers, stepped out of them, and "waved them frantically—waved and screamed 'H'rah'" until she was apprehended by her horrified mother. She told the story in 1936 when she was Margaret Wade Deland, seventy-nine years old, and then one of America's popular novelists and short story writers.

Business virtually stopped in the city in the late spring of 1863 while some ten thousand workmen and ninety college students, wielding picks and shovels, threw up twelve miles of entrenchments across the city and twenty forts on the commanding heights, for which work they were paid $1.25 a day.* A trustees' committee at the University that was seeking an endowment for a professorship of natural science reported in July that "owing to the public excitement consequent on the Rebel invasion of Pennsylvania," it had not been able to make any progress. William B. Scaife, once a student at the Academy, then head of a sixty-year-old steel fabricating plant, and the future great-grandfather of a chairman of the board of the University, wrote in his diary in May, "Rebels are coming on us in 18,000 cavalry under Villain Stuart, Rebel thief. O! Lord! Thou art our help and our shield."

When the Confederate command surrendered on April 9, 1865, Pittsburgh was admirably equipped to supply the industrial products needed to build cities and expand across a continent. Its forty-six iron foundries were producing two-thirds of the country's iron; its blast furnaces and thirty-one rolling mills were turning out half its steel. A new industry had been born in 1859 in Titusville, 100 miles

---

*They dug a trench the length of the north hillside of the present-day campus.

The old Diamond, now Market Square, with the first Allegheny County Courthouse and the market stalls, about a quarter-mile from the Western University building. Lithograph by Otto Krebs, 1859, seven years after the Courthouse was demolished.

north of the city. Now, with fifty-eight oil refineries operating, it was searching for more efficient and new uses for its product. Accumulation of the first Pittsburgh fortunes began in this decade. In 1861 the wealthiest person in the city, William Fahnestock, died, leaving an estate of $171,000. So rapidly did conditions change that only two years later, in 1863, Andrew Carnegie, though only twenty-eight years old and still a salaried railroad employee, had an income from investments of $42,260.

On June 20, 1864, George Woods was pleased to report that "the present year has been very prosperous in all respects." The number of students at the University—166—was the highest in his term of office. There was now a well-furnished chemical lecture room, thanks to gifts of $2,200 from trustees William Thaw and Josiah King, proprietor of the Eagle Cotton Mill and later publisher of the *Pittsburgh Gazette*. A qualified man, a doctor of laws, had agreed to become professor of physical culture, anatomy, physiology, and hygiene. With such a lecturer on the faculty, and a chemistry professor prepared to lecture on chemistry, pharmacy, and *materia medica,* the University could think of establishing a medical school, "which we should have and would, were the members of the Medical profession united in its behalf. Other cities with one-third of our population and much less favorably situated than we are for such a school, are sustaining them."

But there were financial problems. Even if the University was to do no more than sustain the present standing, the expenses would be manyfold what they had been four years before. Incidental expenses had doubled; the professors were demanding increased salaries. The only answer was endowments. Pittsburgh had wealth and resources. Never had the city been more prosperous. "An endowment will remove one of the great difficulties now existing in retaining men of ability and learning in the position of teachers. It would cause the University to be respected and, as a consequence, its professors. And by increasing their incomes would enable them to live in such a manner as to secure a social position. Endow the University, and the serious evil now felt of a disreputable calling, elsewhere not so regarded, will be removed. Learning . . . will be raised to its true importance—a superior qualification."

These developments followed in the Woods administration:

1864

A committee of trustees went to Harrisburg to claim a share of the proceeds from the sale of 780,000 acres of western land. This had been donated to education in Pennsylvania by the U.S. government in carrying out the Morrill land-grant act. The trustees were unsuccessful; all the money went to the Farmer's High School, which became the Agricultural College of Pennsylvania and then, in 1874, Pennsylvania State College.

In October, trustees and friends of the University subscribed $20,000, which yielded an annual income of $1,446, to endow a chair of chemistry, geology, and mineralogy.

1865

A chair of military science and civil engineering was established.

In March, by an act of the legislature, the Allegheny Observatory and a frame house, with ten acres of vacant land surrounding them, were conveyed without cost to the Western University. The observatory had been built by a group of well-to-do businessmen who were astronomy enthusiasts and in 1857 founded the Allegheny Telescope Association. Thirty-one members headed by William Thaw, Josiah King, and James Park (all trustees of the University) set out to buy a telescope, "the magnifying power of which would bring the heavenly bodies near enough to be viewed with great interest and satisfaction." To their surprise, they somehow ended up with the third largest refracting telescope in the world, a Fitz telescope with a thirteen-inch lens, second in the United States only to Harvard's fifteen-inch lens. The telescope was mounted in a building erected for that purpose in Allegheny City on a hilltop henceforth called Observatory Hill. In addition to the observatory, valued at $102,000 (though there was a mortgage on it), the University received a $20,000 gift for an endowed chair of astronomy and physics.

1867

In August, Samuel Pierpont Langley was chosen director of Allegheny Observatory and professor of astronomy and physics. He was thirty-three. Since graduation from high school in Boston he had worked as a draftsman, architect, civil engineer, and for several years as office manager for the company that became Dun and Bradstreet. He traveled in Europe visiting observatories, spent three years building a seven-inch reflecting telescope, and became an assistant at the Harvard College Observatory. He was an assistant professor of mathematics at the U.S. Naval Academy, where he was in charge of a small observatory, when William Thaw persuaded him to take the post at the Western University.

Langley found that the observatory lacked basic furniture and equipment and, since it had only the great refractor telescope, the accessory instruments needed to make it a useful research facility. Maintenance of the telescope, moreover, had been so badly neglected that it had to be dismounted and shipped to Philadelphia to be reconditioned. The building itself required repairs that totaled nearly one-third of its original cost. Despite these troubles, Langley was able to invest $7,500, of which Thaw contributed $5,200, in a transit telescope, a clock, a chronograph, a spectrograph, and a micrometer. With these he scored a stunning success in his first two years: he invented a railroad time service, known as the Allegheny System, in which more than forty railroads had an electric connection with, and received precisely accurate time signals from, the observatory. The service produced an income of about $3,500 a year, which made the observatory very nearly self-supporting.

1870

Diplomas for scientific courses were henceforth to be written in English. The engineering course was extended to four years.

An attempt was made to revive the Law School, which had died with the fire in 1845. A two-year law course would grant the degree of bachelor of laws. Hill Burgwin was to lecture in practice and pleadings of common law and in law of real estate. W. T. Haines was to lecture in criminal law, domestic relations, insurance, commercial law, and Pennsylvania law. William Bakewell would lecture in equity, jurisprudence and practice, constitutional law, patent law, contracts and corporations, and U.S. law. The proposed course met with fierce resistance, however, from a number of the city's lawyers, including one who was a University trustee, who were unwilling to give up the traditional system by which aspiring lawyers were admitted to the bar by way of "reading law" and training as law clerks in the offices of already-established lawyers. Furthermore, the dissenting lawyers proclaimed that the faculty managed the finances of the University in their own interests and that the trustees exercised no control over fiscal matters. The University had no more claim on the consideration of the courts than any other private concern, such as Iron City Commercial College or Dr. Pershing's Female College. No special indulgence should be given in admitting the graduates of that institution to the practice of law.

Woods and a committee of trustees met with the judges in an effort to reach an agreement and "to correct any wrong impression that may have been made," but in time the three law professors resigned, and in 1873 the Law School was abandoned.

1871

At a trustees meeting on January 10, George Woods disposed of some routine business and then submitted a petition signed by all twelve members of the faculty. It asked the trustees to appoint a committee to investigate the condition of the University. The request was made because statements about the University had been voiced, either willfully or ignorantly, that served "greatly to impair its usefulness, to diminish the number of students, and [were] especially fitted to prevent us from securing funds. If these sentiments so frequently made are untrue . . . let the facts be made known, that the tongues of calumniators may be eliminated."

A ten-member investigating committee made its report on June 16, 1871.

Finances: Dr. Woods's statements of the financial history of the institution while in his charge were audited and approved; they were called "a testimony to the persistent, precise, and conscientious accuracy of Dr. Woods, in disbursing funds, acquired . . . in so large a measure by his vim, skill, tact, and diligence." His annual compensation received out of the tuition averaged slightly over $2,100.

Condition and management: The University had given promise of great usefulness, but in 1859 it had been "in a very depressed and feeble condition. From a boys' school with less than forty pupils it has advanced to a college ranking with similar institutions in the country." Credit for this progress was to be given mainly to Dr. Woods, "forever to be known as the real author and founder of the revised Western University."

The course of study: While the University could not

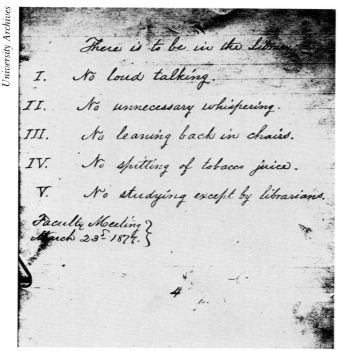

There is to be in the Library

I. No loud talking.

II. No unnecessary whispering.

III. No leaning back in chairs.

IV. No spitting of tobacco juice.

V. No studying except by librarians.

Faculty Meeting
March 23 1877.

Library Rules, 1877. The curious fifth rule—"No studying except by librarians"—meant that only those students who were acting as librarians were permitted to study in the room where the books were shelved. Other students had to take their books into the reading room.

compare with many institutions with respect to libraries, cabinets, philosophical apparatus, and lectures in some branches of science, the students "had opportunities to become proficient in the classics and mathematics, and indeed all the branches of a collegiate education equal to those in the most highly favored institutions in the country.

"The students were decorous and respectful, the teachers were kind but firm, and there was an air of earnestness and work about all, that were in the highest degree satisfactory." The classical course differed in no essential particular from that of the best colleges in the land.

On the other hand, the University was obliged "to receive pupils who were not sufficiently advanced

for even the preparatory department, as the poverty of the institution makes it necessary to replenish the treasury with their tuition fees." Some professors, moreover, "have had to teach subjects not in their line, and the President of the Faculty, besides managing the affairs of the University, has had to secure funds, solicit students, and converse with parents, perform all the correspondence, devise plans for the improvement of the University, examine and classify students, listen to excuses for tardiness and absence, and hear recitations in practically every study. This work, though very irksome, has been cheerfully performed by the Principal and Professors, not we are persuaded, from mercenary motives, but mainly from a desire to build up an educational institution which would be a credit to themselves, and an advantage to this city."

Suggested actions to be taken: The Board of Trustees should supervise the affairs of the University more closely. "It is difficult to get a quorum and impossible to keep them together except for a short time." The charter should be modified to allow the president of the faculty to sit on the Board of Trustees; to require the board to appoint an executive committee; to provide additional trustees elected on staggered three-year terms; to place the mayors of the cities of Pittsburgh and Allegheny on the board; and to change the principal's title to chancellor. The endowment was utterly inadequate. The preparatory department should be dropped. The board should be responsible for all "the pecuniary liabilities"; it should fix tuition fees and collect them, determine professors' salaries and pay them, provide funds for repairs, improvements, books, and equipment. "In a word, we recommend a complete separation of the professional and financial affairs of the University."

The committee said in conclusion that it was happy that the investigation had been made. The status quo of the institution was more satisfactory than expected. The University was aptly so called, well managed, and showed great promise. "Your committee takes great pleasure in stating that the deportment and industry of the students are found to be very satisfactory. Here, as elsewhere, of course,

William Thaw was the University's greatest benefactor in a time when benefactors were rare. Portrait by Charles Walz.

there is great diversity of talent and attention, but the general diligence, good conduct and progress of the students reflect both upon themselves and their professors great credit. There has not been anything approaching a rebellion in the university; nor, indeed, any serious resistance of authority. As to the morality and good conduct of the graduates of the university we can challenge comparison with the best institutions in the land."

While the investigating committee was preparing its report on the Woods administration, William Thaw astonished the city by announcing that, effective July 1, 1871, he would give the University $100,000 for its endowment fund—with two stipulations. One was that the people of Pittsburgh contribute the same amount to the University within three years. The other, not made public, related to what was to become a basic and perennial conflict in institutions of higher learning—the rivalry between the teaching and the research missions. Thaw asked the University to sign an agreement that Professor Langley "shall take charge of the Observatory and perform the duties pertaining to said charge, with the title of Director of the Allegheny Observatory. He shall not be required to attend at, or give instruction in the college buildings." He was to receive a salary of not less than $2,000 per year, together with the rent-free use of the house on the observatory grounds (for which Woods had made him pay rent). This was Thaw's way of resolving a festering animosity between Langley on the one hand and Woods, faculty members, and some trustees on the other. Thaw, chairman of the Observatory Committee, believed in the importance of scientific research, and he had freed Langley from his onerous teaching duties that he might devote all his time to his work at the observatory. Woods, whose first concern was to develop teachers and a curriculum for classes in science, had insisted that Langley fulfill his commitment as a teacher. Faculty members were angry that Langley, who did no teaching, should receive a higher salary than they did. ("What are we paying him for?") It seems that Woods was jealous of Langley's influence on Thaw, and he apparently attempted to replace Langley with his assistant, who thereafter was discharged.

The second Allegheny Observatory was erected in Riverview Park in 1912.

On October 13, 1871, the *Pittsburgh Daily Commercial* printed a feature article in which it reported on improvements made at the observatory and on some of Langley's research work. Langley had begun a program of measuring distances to and between the nearby stars that was bringing international recognition and honors to himself, the observatory, and the University. (The program is being carried on today with the aid of computers. The observatory has an invaluable scientific resource in its more than 110,000 photographic plates showing star positions over the past 100 years or more.) Langley was also measuring the intensity of the light and heat radiation from the sun, including the invisible and then little-understood infrared radiation. To accomplish this, he invented the bolometer, a finely tuned detector made of platinum wire that indicates resistance according to the amount of radiation that falls on it.

Langley had also begun research based on his conviction that it was possible to construct machines that could move bodies with inclined surfaces through the air with great velocity.

1872
The state legislators approved the changes in the charter sought by the trustees. The mayors of the two cities became ex officio members of the board.

Principal Woods became Chancellor Woods. The way in which the trustees were to be appointed was regulated, and their rights and duties pertaining to the operation of the school were clearly defined. The change was a landmark in the history of the University; it brought added support, a new stability, and a sense of permanence to the institution.

1875

The University received $25,000 from the estate of Charles Avery, a progressive clergyman, to provide free tuition for black students.

In December, Woods succeeded in raising the last of the $100,000 he needed to match Thaw's 1871 gift. (The deadline had been extended one year.) During these years, Thaw paid accumulated interest on the money he was holding in escrow for the University. Woods had said acidly a few months earlier, "The value in every respect to our community of a large and well endowed and well equipped University is not understood. What is sought and appreciated in other cities is regarded with indifference here. A sum which could be raised in most cities of the size and wealth of our own in a few weeks, after nearly four years is still in vain making its demands on our citizens."

1877

A second building was erected on the Ross Street site. The trustees had decided not to discontinue the preparatory department because it was needed as a "nursery" for the University; but henceforth that department would conduct all its operations in the new building, since it was not thought proper for children to be seen going in and out of the main University building.

During the strike and riots of railroad workers in July, in which forty people were killed and railroad property valued at $2 million was destroyed, citizens broke in the doors of the University and seized the weapons used by the students during drill. They intended to use them, they said, to suppress the rioters. When the crisis was over, they did not return the weapons. Cost of repairs to the doors: $58.59.

One hundred dollars was paid to each of several instructors who worked as "canvassers" to recruit students during the summer months.

1878

City guards asked permission to drill with arms in University Hall "in anticipation of trouble this summer of a communistic nature." They were refused.

The scientific course was extended from three to four years, and greater emphasis was placed on French and German.

The University rented a room to a group who wished to start a pharmacy college, gave it apparatus and the use of a laboratory, and awarded pharmacy degrees to its graduates.

1879

Chancellor Woods, in his annual report to the trustees, lamented that the Free High School in Pittsburgh, with its fine building, was harming the University enrollment, though its course was inferior to that of the University. He suggested that a committee report to the board once each year on conditions in the University and that a standing committee maintain close liaison between the faculty and the board. The University should try again to start a law school. It should start a technical school, "at least in a small way." A site for a new University building should be chosen. There should be still more emphasis on science and its applications. Greek should be dropped as a compulsory course, for it was a cause of some students leaving the University.

It was the chancellor's last report. Something had gone wrong in his relations with the board or the faculty, or both, and in the successful operations of the institution. The University, "for some reason or other," seemed to lack "tone and enthusiasm," and there was a lack of cooperation and a feeling of distrust between faculty and board members. The Committee on Instruction and Government declared that there was room for improvement in the departments. The Finance Committee declared that a large reduction in current expenditure was conclusively necessary, unless the trustees wished to draw from capital. In an effort to meet what was obviously a crisis, the trustees cut the preparatory school course from three to two years, thereby reducing the number of instructors. They lowered tuition and obtained more students but failed to increase earnings. They discharged all faculty members and then rehired "instructors to fill such departments, and at such compensation, as will form a total fully within the probable income of the institution." At the start of this three-year-long "thorough overhauling of the institution," they discharged Chancellor Woods, then agreed to accept his resignation, and then gave him $2,000 in severance pay. Six committeemen, including William Thaw, signed a statement on Dr. Woods that is wonderfully revealing of a variation on a classic theme: the conflict between the authority of the board and the power of the chancellor.

It should be kept in mind in behalf of Chancellor Woods, that he has had the leading place in the University for many years, and that in the earlier years of his administration, the University was in effect a private school transferred to the charge of four gentlemen who assumed all the risks and responsibilities of its financial results at a period when its very existence was in peril. He conducted all its affairs, and was the active instrument in every important step that has led to its growth and strength. He has been substantially supreme in governing all the details of his administration. It is not strange, therefore, that he should be slow to see that the University with its present numerous staff of Professors and Instructors, paid by the corporation, and of high personal and professional character, can no longer properly be conducted under the autocracy of a Chancellor, governing as to Board of Control, under rules and regulations practically obsolete or kept out of sight.

Eighteen years later, in 1897, a different chancellor of the University held a 110th anniversary celebration of the founding of the institution. He asked all surviving principals, presidents, and chancellors to appear beside him in an honored position during the ceremonies. George Woods on March 15 returned a hand-written reply on the letterhead of a large and successful enterprise he had founded, the Western Pennsylvania Agency of the Equitable Life Assurance Company of the United States. After one

brief sentence of thanks he proceeded to express a grievance he had carried with him from the campus.

While I was there I secured the endowment of a chair in chemistry, a chair in astronomy, the very valuable Watson library, cases for the cabinet, the telescope, the astronomy building, the dwelling house and eleven acres of valuable land all valued by the Board at ninety thousand dollars. There were when I left about two hundred students— about sixteen professors and regular college classes—and an endowment of five hundred thousand dollars. . . .

My work for twenty-five years, the results accomplished have been belittled and in fact almost entirely ignored. One who has performed such a work in building up an institution almost without compensation and rendered it such service cannot help desiring its complete success. Still, considering the attitude assumed toward me it would be an injustice to myself amounting almost to stultification were I to be present and to accept any position certainly any prominent one in the proposed demonstration. I have the honor Sir to be Yours Very Truly,

George Woods

Once again, in 1882, a fire caused the Western University to move to a new location, though this time no University building was harmed. Fire destroyed the Allegheny County Court House, and in their search for a quick replacement, the county commissioners decided to buy the buildings at Ross and Diamond. The trustees, who were staggering under the weight of a $20,000 deficit incurred over the past five years, asked $80,000 for the ground and both buildings. The commissioners refused to pay so high a price. The trustees were adamant. The commissioners capitulated and agreed to pay. There was a crisis, however, when the morning papers revealed that the money would be paid out of the Liquor License Fund. The trustees declared, also in the morning papers, that they would not accept such tainted money. The commissioners rescinded their action and paid out of general level taxes and insurance received on the destroyed courthouse.

The trustees thereupon moved the University across the river to Allegheny City, where they took over two buildings, the United Presbyterian Theological Seminary and the Reformed Presbyterian Theological Seminary, for an annual rent of $700 each. The buildings were on North Avenue, about three blocks apart, both facing the large grassy commons. There the University stayed for eight years.

The Reverend Henry Mitchell MacCracken, graduate of Princeton Theological Seminary in 1863, an experienced educational administrator and teacher of languages, succeeded Woods as chancellor on June 21, 1881. He spent less time and effort on his post than the trustees had hoped for. When he was questioned on this point, he explained that he had been called upon to do three times as much work for the public in lecturing and preaching as he had expected. Dr. MacCracken departed in 1884 for a post with New York University, where he presumably spent more time in his office and where he later became chancellor and achieved special distinction by fathering two sons who in 1915 became college presidents (Lafayette, Vassar). He was succeeded by Milton B. Goff, mathematician and graduate of Allegheny College, author of textbooks, professor of mathematics at the Western University since 1865, and the first faculty member to become chancellor.

This was not one of the more brilliant decades in the University's history, but important decisions were made, important actions were taken, and people important to the University arrived and departed.

Samuel Pierpont Langley stayed with the observatory for twenty-three years. In 1887 he became assistant secretary to the Smithsonian Institution in Washington, but for several more years, even after he was made secretary, he divided his time between Washington and Pittsburgh, doing so without pay from the University. In Washington he continued his researches in mechanical flight. In 1896 he sent unmanned planes driven by 1 h.p. steam engines on two flights over the Potomac River, each flight traveling thirty miles an hour over a distance of one-half to three-fourths of a mile at an altitude of nearly 100 feet. Of those flights one authority has said: "Never in the history of the world, previous to these attempts, had any mechanism, however actuated, sustained itself in the air more than a few seconds. He thus paved the way for others who have achieved success with man-carrying machines."

Samuel P. Langley, director of the Allegheny Observatory from 1867 to 1890.

William Thaw died in Paris in 1889. He left $100,000 to the University. The trustees resolved: "Our country has lost a noble and patriotic citizen, our community an honorable, enterprising and useful member, our religious and charitable institutions an interested, unfailing and generous friend, the University a wise counsellor and liberal supporter, and the cause of science one of its most zealous and unselfish benefactors." Christopher Lyman Magee, Class of 1864, political figure and philanthropist, offered a toast at an alumni banquet: "William Thaw, that man in the presence of whose memory every loyal friend of the Western University should stand uncovered."

William McCullough Darlington, a board member since 1880, also died in 1889. An attorney of means, he retired in 1856 and in the company of his wife, Mary Carson O'Hara Darlington (granddaughter of General James O'Hara), devoted his life to collecting books, pamphlets, letters, rare manuscripts, periodicals, maps, historical documents, and first editions of English novels and poetry. The Darlingtons were admired as a delightful couple; they would sometimes travel to New York to meet the ship carrying the latest installment of a twenty-four-part Dickens or Thackeray novel. Their two daughters, Mary and Edith, in 1918 gave the priceless collection of more than 14,000 pieces to the University, with an endowment of $1 million for a library in which to house it.

Enrollment reached a record high of ninety-five upperclassmen in 1890. Most were taking engineering and industrial chemistry courses, in which, by all accounts, they were receiving superior instruction from two outstanding teachers and from the instructors trained by them. The two teachers were Francis C. Phillips, professor of chemistry from 1875 to 1915, and Daniel E. Carhart, professor, later dean, of engineering and assistant to the chancellor from 1882 to 1908. Carhart, a national figure in the annals of engineering, retired from active teaching when he was sixty-nine; but until his death at eighty-seven in 1926 his students held an annual luncheon in his honor.

The minutes of the meetings of the trustees from 1880 to 1890 reveal in their own unique way the

A pioneer in aeronautics, Langley sent two unmanned planes on successful flights over the Potomac River in 1896.

flavor of academic life in the last years of the century:

● Professor Carhart, on arriving at the University, persuaded the trustees to buy him a complete transit, a level, two range poles, a leveling rod, an engineer's chain, a steel tape, a metallic tape, an aneroid barometer, a lock level, an extra plumbset, a set of marking pins, and a pair of beam compasses.

● In listing the desired qualities of a chancellor, the faculty put second "The ability to gain the confidence of persons of influence and means."

● In Resolutions Governing the Faculty, the trustees declared: "It is the sense of this Board that any gentleman occupying a position as teacher in the university should take pains to make his connection with the institution and his interest in its welfare known and felt throughout the circle of his acquaintance, and he should regard it as part of his daily duty to counsel and labor for the prosperity, usefulness and success of the institution."

● Asked why they had been so often absent from opening exercises (chapel service), Professor Carhart explained that he lived in Wilkinsburg and the train was often late, Professor Barber explained that his wife was ill, and Professor Gibbons said he was occupied during chapel services in teaching pupils outside of school hours.

• Professor Barber wrote to the board that his title in the catalogue should read Professor of Latin and of *English,* although he would rather not teach the English.

• The librarian reported that he needed more library space.

• A committee was appointed to make arrangements to have the University represented in the Educational Exhibit at the World's Columbian Exposition in 1893 at Chicago.

• A classification of the Corps of Instructors declared that professors' salaries were not to exceed $1,800; those of associate professors, $1,400; adjunct professors were not to receive more than $1,000; and instructors and tutors were limited to $800 "or less, as may be agreed upon." Four hours of recitation work each day were due from each professor and instructor.

• The librarian acknowledged receipt of a pamphlet issued by the Department of the Interior, *Coeducation of the Sexes.*

It was recognized from the first that the move into the crowded, badly ventilated seminary buildings in Allegheny was temporary and that eventually a permanent site would have to be chosen. A three-member committee advised that the University should be as near to the center of city population as possible *if* it was to continue to be a local institution supported by day students. If, on the other hand, there were prospects that at some time it would become "what we think it should become," a great University with state or national reputation, then it should be placed on an eligible tract containing forty or fifty acres, with a fine water frontage for aquatic sports and amusements, convenient to the two cities by rail and river, and yet "far enough away to give that quiet and retirement which is conductive to study." This, the committee pointed out, would remove the student "from the temptations and excitements of city life." A later committee of nine alumni tried to find a site along the line of the Penn-

sylvania Railroad to the east of the city, to which the center of population was shifting. The alumni looked at property at Roup's Station in Shadyside, in Wilkinsburg, and in Edgewood. It recommended a nineteen-acre tract in Swissvale that was "beautiful, healthful and commanding," 300 feet from the Swissvale station, five minutes' walk from the Monongahela River, and with a large two-story brick house that could be adapted to University work. The asking price was $50,000.

The trustees, having gone to such pains, ignored their own stipulations on the new location and chose to build in Allegheny, beside the observatory building on Observatory Hill. It was a major blunder. They already owned the land—ten vacant acres—and that consideration apparently outweighed the facts that the location in Allegheny had caused a loss in enrollment, that it was away from the main current of population growth, that there was no room on the property for expansion, and that it was perched on the top of a not easily accessible hill, even though there was now an electric trolley line on Perrysville Avenue.

The Search Committee made its report, and specifications were drawn up and submitted to "four of the principal architects of Pittsburgh." James T. Steen, Penn Avenue and Sixth Street, was awarded the contract. His plan embraced two structures. Science Hall was 83 by 65 by 40 feet. It had rooms for a foundry, a forge, woodworking, metalworking, pattern testing, and modeling, as well as a qualitative laboratory, a quantitative laboratory, a chemical laboratory, a private laboratory, and a gas laboratory. It had a darkroom and rooms for lectures, assorted apparatus, geological study, the mineral collection, "organic purposes," and balances. The estimated cost was $20,000. The Main Building, erected seventy-five yards west of the observatory, was a four-story stone and brick structure with hip roofs and gables, measuring 158 by 94 by 56 feet. It had a gymnasium in the basement, classrooms, lecture rooms, storage rooms, offices for the chancellor and the treasurer, drafting rooms, and a "society room." Its cost was estimated to be between $50,000 and $55,000.

In his sixth (and last) annual report, written June

University Archives

Science Hall and Main Hall, on Observatory Hill.

2, 1890, Chancellor Goff said that Science Hall was completed and occupied in September 1889, and Main Hall in January 1890. "I certainly shared with you many misgivings when it was resolved that the future home of the University should be Observatory Hill. But every day since the resolution was taken has shown me the wisdom of the decision. And I think I am safe in saying, that although under other circumstances, a better selection might have been made, that under the then existing circumstances, the one made was the very best." He reported that "in accordance with the action of the Board, all connection with and all responsibility for the former Preparatory Department ceased on June 30, 1889." (The school, renamed Park Institute, continued operations in one of the seminary buildings vacated by the University, using the furniture donated by the University. Park Institute continued to educate Pittsburgh children for nearly fifty more years.)

Milton Goff died in November 1890 as the result of an accident. He was escorting a group of engineers from England and other European countries through the great steel plant at Homestead when he fell and broke a leg. Pneumonia and death followed shortly thereafter.

The trustees elected as chancellor Dr. William Jacob Holland, a remarkable man with an extraordinary background, who was on the verge of becoming a nationally known writer, scientist, and personality. He was well equipped "to gain the confidence of persons of influence and means," and he was not likely to accept easily their refusal to give when he asked them to give. In the administration of George Woods the Academy became a college. In the administration of William Holland, the College was to become a university.

3

"The Greatest Work
I Have Ever
Undertaken"

Well, I am forty-three years old today. . . . The work I now have before me is the greatest I have ever undertaken. It fills me with no end of care and solicitude. If only the citizens of this great community will stand by me I shall be able to accomplish great things. I feel that I have their good will, but I need more than good words and kind prophecies of success. . . . There are many men of large means in this community, who could do much for us, but there are no end of small scrupulosities and senseless objections to be overcome. . . . If only I could get a good start with the pocket-books of our millionaires it would be an easy matter to do everything else that is necessary.

William J. Holland, chancellor of the Western University of Pennsylvania, to his parents, August 16, 1891

WILLIAM JACOB HOLLAND, Ph.D., Sc.D., D.D., LL.D., was born in 1848 on the island of Jamaica, West Indies, where his father was a Moravian missionary. He was graduated from Moravian College and Theological Seminary in Bethlehem, Pennslyvania, then from Amherst College, Massachusetts, and Princeton Theological Seminary. He worked briefly as a high school principal in New England, was ordained into the Moravian ministry at age twenty-four, served for two years as pastor of a church in Philadelphia, and in 1874 became pastor of the Bellefield Presbyterian Church, a substantial frame structure at Fifth and Bellefield avenues in Pittsburgh's Bellefield–Schenley Farms–Oakland district. Four years later he married Carrie T. Moorhead, by whom he had two sons. She was the youngest daughter of James K. Moorhead, pioneer Pittsburgh iron manufacturer (whose mansion stood on the present site of the Cathedral of Learning). In 1884 she had built a handsome gray stone house across the street from the church as a present for her husband. The wooden church was replaced in 1890 by a stone structure in Romanesque architecture that matched the house.* During these years Holland carried on parallel research in the biology of animals, insects, and ancient life. As a result of scientific articles produced on these subjects, he became nationally known as a zoologist, paleontologist, and entomologist. In 1887 he was chosen to accompany an expedition of the U.S. *Eclipse* to Japan; two years later he traveled in West Africa in search of butterflies and moths, on which subjects he was a recognized authority and carried on a worldwide correspondence. He had become a trustee of the Western University in 1886, and in March 1891 he was elected its chancellor.

Holland wrote regularly and often to his parents in Covington, Kentucky, enclosing a check for seventy-five dollars every month. On March 22 he wrote: "My election has been received with manifest expressions of pleasure by the press of the city and many of the alumni of the institution. I have the satisfaction of knowing that with the exception of two or three of my colleagues on the Board of Trustees I shall have the support of the entire body. The objecters are however men of no small weight and influence in the community and it may be that unless I am able to secure their hearty cooperation I shall decline to accept the nomination."

He wrote to his parents on April 23: "I never in my life have been so busy as I am now. There are a thousand things to be learned in regard to the institution, and there are a thousand wants that I am appealed to by the faculty and the students to supply. The institution needs the ardent efforts of a strong man to bring it up to the standard to which it is expected to come." On May 2: "The work at the University is getting along as well as could be expected, but we are a little crippled by the removal from us of several of our instructors, who have incontinently fled their posts. They yielded to the inducement of larger salaries in other stations and have rather left us in the lurch. I trust soon to be able to get successors for them. Men who thus cut sticks and go without any notice to us are not worthy of any confidence and I shall look out for such in the future." On September 21:

I have been so busy that it has been almost impossible for me to command time for my meals. The new term opened last Wednesday with the largest attendance in the history of the institution. We enter about fifty freshmen and a large number in the higher classes. The outlook now is that I shall be able to get through with the work of the year without a deficit. . . . The great trouble in the institution lies not in the faculty so much as in the Board of Trustees. Many of them are very inattentive to their duties. . . .

On last Saturday I began a new undertaking, viz.: the establishment of a natural history society among the students of the University. We went out and shot a few birds,

---

*The Hollands sold their house some time before 1912. It became a Knights of Columbus club, was given to the University in 1953 by Pittsburgh Plate Glass Company, was the first home of public television station WQED, and now houses the University's music department.

In 1967 the Bellefield Presbyterian Church merged with and moved to the First United Presbyterian Church at Fifth and Thackeray, which adopted its name. The old church was dismantled in 1985 except for its tower, which still stands as part of a new building.

and I gave them a lesson in the art of stuffing them, and besides gave them a lesson in practical botany. We had a very pleasant forenoon together and I hope in a short time to be able to awake a good deal of scientific enthusiasm among the boys. We are creating a good deal of spirit in the matter of the glee-club, a new departure. In a short time I think we shall have more of the true college spirit awakened here. . . .

Among the young men is a fellow from Cienfuegos in Cuba. I am going to teach him how to collect butterflies with a view to utilizing his services upon the island.

On January 18, following a student prank that disrupted morning prayers: "I succeeded after a short time in finding out the offenders, and as they are seniors made them do penalty by putting them under the care of the monitor of the Freshmen class. They will be treated as Freshmen during the rest of the term. This is mortification enough."

Holland wrote his first annual report in June 1892. Total enrollment, he said, was 137—a 35 percent gain over the previous year. His examination of the classwork, the lectures, and the recitations had convinced him that the instruction possessed high merit when compared with that imparted in other institutions of like grade. The course of "lectures extraordinary" he had introduced had been well attended, was a feature in the life of the university, and would be more extensive and more interesting in the coming year.* The physical training (which had been made compulsory in 1890) was producing good results. Holland wished to urge upon the attention of the board the extreme importance of using all diligence to raise money to remove the machinery in the basement of Science Hall to a new building specially planned as an engineering laboratory and erected on the campus. Knowing the need for such an addition, he had been laboring to enlist the sympathy and cooperation of the monied men of the community. He had in his pocket notebook subscriptions totaling a considerable sum of money, but the promises were conditioned on first raising

elsewhere the sum of $200,000. The trustees should also strive, he said, to acquire the 7½ adjoining acres belonging to the McGrew estate. Generous gifts had been made to the observatory, including a fine astronomical clock for the equatorial telescope and a spectroscope given by Mrs. William Thaw. The spectroscope was being made by Mr. John A. Brashear according to specifications furnished by Professor James Keeler and would probably be one of the very best in existence. He had found it necessary, with the approval of the Executive Committee, to discharge Mr. Heaslet, the assistant janitor, who had proved himself inefficient.

Despite the need to waste his time on such duties as discharging the assistant janitor, Holland never lost sight of his major objectives for the University. He was, one of his professors said forty-five years later, "the only man in Pittsburgh with a real vision of what a university ought to be, and he labored unceasingly to interest the public and to put the institution on a proper financial footing." Holland said in the *Western University Courant*, a student publication: "We know that this is the place for a [great] school, we know that there is a demand for it, we know the number of bright and promising young people who can be attracted to it is practically only limited by its ability to meet their wants, we know that the times are fully ripe for a great forward movement all along the line." He also understood perfectly that the University must have large sums of money. He knew how to go about raising it, and he was willing to perform the hard, slogging, disagreeable, sometimes humiliating work necessary to raise it. He began with an admonition to his trustees: "It is now my desire to take up this work and push it as rapidly as possible, but I desire in this enterprise the cooperation and assistance of the entire Board. I believe that if each member would consent to take in hand the work of solicitation in a very short time the entire amount [$50,000] could be raised in the community." He then asked the General Alumni Council to go to the graduates—453 degrees had been granted, exclusive of those from the new medical school—and raise $40,000 as an endowment for professorships. The council promised but did not raise the money.

---

*The 1893 lectures, open to the public, were given by nineteen different outside speakers. The subjects covered were education, folklore, Buddhism, hydraulics, engineering, socialism, Greek theater, birds of Allegheny County, mining, poetry, "The Beautiful and the Good," and "How to Choose a Wife."

He approached the state legislators—though the state had given nothing since the $12,000 grant in 1822—and asked them to give him $300,000, which he told his parents "they ought to do. I think I will get some of it at least." He got a promise of $50,000, payable in installments, to use in establishing the School of Mines and Mining Engineering—but only if he could raise matching funds from other sources.

He developed a bold three-part strategy for dramatically enlarging his enrollment and adding to the prestige and importance of the University, all without increasing his miniscule endowment ($268,854). First, he began a program of graduate studies that would result in postgraduate degrees. Second, he accepted two sisters, the Misses Margaret Lydia and Stella Mathilda Stein, into the College and, in what was called "a momentous decision of supreme importance to the higher education of Pittsburgh and the vicinity," announced that the University would hereafter be coeducational. Third, he brought into the fold three already established commercial professional schools that had expressed a desire to become affiliated with the Western University. These were the Western Pennsylvania Medical College, which became part of the University in 1892, and the Pittsburgh College of Pharmacy and the Pittsburgh Dental School, both joining the University in 1896. And in 1895 he contrived, finally, to establish a full-fledged school of law. He invited all the judges of Allegheny County to a dinner at the Duquesne Club (which he had joined the year before) and asked them to appoint a committee from among their number to act with the trustees in starting a law school as part of the University. The school was established smoothly that year and was an immediate success. The fees, tuitions, and gifts received by the pharmacy and dentistry schools did not benefit the University at first, since this income was kept "inviolably" for the schools themselves.

Now the University's various departments were scattered in four different places in the city: the Department of Medicine, with 300 students, was in West Penn Hospital; the Departments of Dentistry and Pharmacy were in a building on a hilltop at Pride and Bluff streets, overlooking the Mononga-hela River; and the Law School for two years occupied rooms of the Orphan's Court in the Old Allegheny County Court House and then moved to the former University building at Ross and Diamond streets. Thus was kindled Holland's burning desire to perfect the University by grouping all its component parts on one campus. It was a desire that was not to be satisfied for another four decades, but it took Holland only a few years to achieve the considerable feat of creating a true university and of increasing its enrollment from 95 students to nearly 500 (in 1895) and then to 691 (in 1898), all of whom were seeking degrees. The optimism he had expressed in a letter to his parents on October 30, 1893, was vindicated: "The work of the University appears to be prospering, and I am not without great hopes that the work of the present year will prove superior in many respects to that of former years. We have more students than ever and a good spirit seems to pervade the faculty and students. Gradually I trust we shall succeed in awakening these great cities [Pittsburgh and Allegheny] to a consciousness of the importance of the opportunity which presents itself to build up in our midst a true University."

While carrying out this strategy and during all his supplications for help from alumni, trustees, and the state, Holland was fully aware that his only hope for money in large amounts lay in those he called "the men in the community whom a good Providence has endowed with financial power." If, he said, "they would devote but a small part of the power which is entrusted to their keeping to the support and upbuilding of this great school, we shall in a few years be able to see marvellous results achieved."

He did have some success on what he called "my begging expeditions." Mrs. William (Mary Copley) Thaw, normally a generous donor, was angry at him over a now-obscure political matter, but she assured him in a hand-written postscript to her dictated, typed letter that she would be glad to see him when her anger subsided. In the meantime, her son Benjamin Thaw, the banker (B.A. 1878, a trustee since 1890), gave him $2,500—$1,500 for a profes-

The first women students to receive undergraduate degrees were the sisters Stella Mathilda (left) and Margaret Lydia Stein (right).

sorship, $500 to meet "current deficiencies," and $500 toward the $10,000 Holland was collecting (at the suggestion of William Thaw, Jr.) for a pension fund for faculty members who had served twenty-five years or more. And Isaac Kaufmann, merchant, gave him $10,000 to establish a chair at the School of Medicine. But these gifts were exceptions; there were no others so large.

There were good reasons why Pittsburgh in the 1890s should have been generous in supporting its University. For one thing, the city and a growing number of its people were becoming rich in the vig-orous industrial expansion of that decade. Within a few years, a team of twenty sociologists studying the city would report that it was "the most prosperous of all the communities of our western civilization." Pittsburghers, moreover, had a history of generous philanthropy. The Pittsburgh Sanitary Fair, an exposition held during the Civil War to raise money for the welfare and medical care of the soldiers, had set a national record for money given per capita. Pittsburghers were being generous in the 1890s to good causes in other cities. "Large gifts," Holland reported unhappily to his board, "are being made

The Class of 1898, twenty-eight strong. The Stein sisters were graduated with identical grades, the highest in the class.

constantly by Pittsburghers to institutions scattered all over the country, and hundreds of thousands of dollars are being spent upon enterprises which bring little or no return to the community." And in addition to all this, Pittsburgh had begun an ambitious and enlightened "betterment program" that would give the city a score of splendid new civic improvements. Pittsburghers might well have chosen to make the University one of their prize evidences of community spirit.

One circumstance that should have ensured Holland's success at fund raising was his acquaintance, and in some cases his friendship, with some of the city's rich families. He was a person of some importance and interest; he had an entrée into high circles; he was even, on occasion, a companion of the new giants of wealth. To his parents he had written in February 1890, before he became chancellor, "The past week was very interesting to me on some accounts because I was engaged for part of the time in discussing with my friend Mr. Andrew Carnegie, the method in which his magnificent gift of a million of dollars for the City of Pittsburgh might best be applied; it is his intention to build a grand library, and in connection therewith there will be provision made for housing the various learned societies which at present exist in the city."*

On February 15, 1893: "I am anticipating the arrival tomorrow of my friend Mr. [William Temple] Hornaday, the author of 'Two Years in the Jungle,' who is to lecture for us on Friday evening. I have arranged for a little dinner party to be given in his honor tomorrow night. Mr. Phipps, Mr. Walker, Mr. Brashear, Professor Keeler, and Mr. Lauder of Scotland are to be the guests.† All except Brashear and Keeler are partners of Mr. Carnegie."

And on February 12, 1895: "Friday evening I was in New York and spent the evening with some literary and scientific gentlemen, with whom I had an appointment, lunched at the Union League Club and met Mr. Chauncey Depew and came back to Pittsburgh with Mr. Andrew Carnegie; so you see I had my full share of lions on this trip."

Carnegie was close to Holland; he consented to serve on the University board and on at least one occasion went to some trouble on its behalf. But he pointedly gave the University no money. Whether Holland asked him and was refused, or was unwilling to ask him, is not known. Carnegie, of course, was at this time drawing up plans for the Carnegie Technical Schools, which he endowed and founded in the city in 1903. The historian J. N. Boucher said in 1908, "Mr. Carnegie founded his school as a protest against inferior and useless education. He does not believe that unless the student is preparing to enter one of the learned professions, much time needs be spent in acquiring a knowledge of the classics. When Matthew Arnold said in his hearing that 'no man could write good English without a knowledge of Greek and Latin,' Mr. Carnegie answered

William Jacob Holland, chancellor of the University from 1891 to 1901. Portrait by Leopold Gould Seyffert.

him by asking if Shakespeare and Burns had not written at least reasonably good English."

"Pittsburgh is a queer place," Holland wrote to his parents in October 1892. "Their philanthropy runs in very narrow channels. It is confined almost exclusively to hospitals and churches. Schools and colleges and things of that sort are apparently not regarded as of any particular importance by our

*Two months later, as a member of a Pittsburgh debating and social club called the Junta, Holland was assigned to talk on the question: "Are Andrew Carnegie's assertions 'that the college graduate is totally absent from every department of affairs and that his knowledge so far as business affairs are concerned is better adapted for life upon another planet than this' true either in fact or in principle?"

†Henry C. Phipps, John Walker, John Brashear, James E. Keeler, George E. Lauder.

University Archives

Chancellor Holland's office in Main Hall on Observatory Hill. The portrait of Robert Bruce (right) now hangs in the president's office in the Cathedral of Learning.

men of wealth, with perhaps here and there a few honorable exceptions." To his trustees he confessed, "I do not hesitate to say to this Board that I feel at times . . . a great deal of discouragement."

Samuel Black Linhart, who in 1906 became secretary of the University (and professor of the history of religion and ethics department), observed many years later: "Pittsburgh at that time was a large and prosperous industrial community with great wealth, with able leadership in industry, commerce, and finance, but as yet with no general realization of the value of higher education or of the potential value of its own university. The idea that a liberal education was a distinct asset in business or industry as well as in the professions was foreign to the thought of that period. Newspaper editors, business men, and leaders in industry generally subscribed to Horace Greeley's statement: 'Of all horned cattle, deliver me from the college graduate.'"

In 1893 Holland, on the recommendation of George Westinghouse, brought to the University a brilliant young scientist qualified to rank in stature with the astronomers Samuel Langley and James Keeler. He was Reginald Aubrey Fessenden, who was engaged to head the two-year-old electrical engineering department. Of New England parentage, Fessenden was born in Canada and had taught at age fifteen at Bishop's College School in Quebec, mastering a half-dozen languages there, including Greek, Arabic, Hebrew, and Sanskrit. He had worked as an electrical·engineer in the eastern branch of Westinghouse·Electric, as head chemist in Thomas Edison's machine works, and was professor of electrical engineering at Purdue University when Holland approached him.

Holland persuaded Fessenden to leave Purdue by promising him complete freedom in planning his department's curriculum and in selecting its laboratory equipment. Fessenden was a genius who played a major role in the development of American technology and became something of a legend, even a cult figure, among some historians of science. As the story is commonly told, he "spent seven happy and productive years in Pittsburgh." The long-buried minutes of the trustees' meetings in the 1890s reveal that this was not altogether true.

Trouble arose because Holland, with the best of intentions, promised Fessenden more than he could deliver. He told him that he had raised nearly $60,000 for the electrical laboratory in private subscriptions and was sure he would obtain $100,000 from the legislature. Fessenden accepted the post in Pittsburgh because of those promises. Through no fault of his own, Holland failed to obtain either amount. Fessenden wrote him a courteous letter on June 14, 1895, to tell the effect of the failure on himself and his work:

I have resigned a large and well-equipped laboratory, with four assistants, a salary of $2500 per annum, a grant of $1000 per annum from Mr. Westinghouse, and an income of about $2000 of consulting practice.

I now occupy a room in a damp basement, without any suitable equipment for scientific work, with no assistance, and no time for scientific work. Though my fees for consulting are $100 a day, I have not realized more than $1000 since I have been in Pittsburgh. My total money loss during the past two years therefore amounts to $6000, which you may verify by examining my accounts.

I have the most complete faith in the future of the Western University, and the utmost confidence in your ability to place it in its rightful position, but I feel that . . . it is not advisable that I should spend the next year in the same manner as I have spent the two previous ones.

He had asked for a salaried assistant in the electrical laboratory, for a means of providing a steady current suitable for electrical work, and for resistance boxes. Holland must have provided them, for Fessenden stayed another five years before he departed. He left the Western University in 1900 to work as a special agent for the U.S. Weather Bureau and in 1902 formed, with Pittsburgh backers, the National Electric Signalling Company. In 1906, on Brant Island, Massachusetts, he tested his theory—vehemently opposed by every other recognized authority—that transmitting human speech by radio waves was practicable if a continuous flow of high frequency vibrations was developed. He achieved success on a frequency of 50,000 cycles and on Christmas Eve, 1906, sent out what is generally accepted as the first broadcast of the human voice and of music—Christmas carols and a violin solo—ever made.

In a stormy career laced with legal battles (some involving patent suits) and accusations of piracy, Fessenden is credited with inventing or discovering heterodyne reception (a phrase he coined), the fathometer, the radio compass, the microfilming process, a coil circuit breaker that could detect tiny defects in steel armor plate, a submarine detecting device that enabled searchers to locate the sunken hull of the *Lusitania*, and, during his stay in Pittsburgh, a device he called "liquid barretter," a more sophisticated device than Marconi used for modulating radio waves. He died in Bermuda in 1932 at the age of sixty-six. An inscription on a marble tablet on his grave there reads:

By His Genius
Distant Lands converse
and Men sail
Unafraid upon
the Deep

These other developments took place during Holland's years at the Western University.

1894

Andrew W. Mellon was elected to the Board of Trustees.

David E. Park gave some two hundred acres of undeveloped land to the city of Allegheny on which to establish Riverview Park. The gift was offered on the condition that two acres were to be made available for an astronomical observatory.

1895

Andrew Carnegie and George Westinghouse were elected to the Board of Trustees. Carnegie agreed to serve. Westinghouse refused.

The Observatory Committee reported: "The Director of the Observatory, Professor James E. Keeler, has given to the world a most remarkable physical demonstration of the differential rotation of the rings of Saturn, a problem that has been proven by Clerk Maxwell, and others from a mathematical standpoint, but which has hitherto defied the attempts of astronomers to demonstrate by the most powerful instruments at their command. This elegant piece of work done by the Director of the Observatory, has not only added to the many important discoveries made at our Observatory, but it gives us a very high standing among the observatories of the world."

Chancellor Holland, having opened the University to coeducation, turned over his large office in Main Hall for use by the women students. (His working office was in downtown Pittsburgh.)

The Department of Legal Instruction, which was inaugurated in October 1895, had thirty-five students in the first year's class, "a very large percentage of them being graduates of colleges of repute," some of them "the sons of a number of gentlemen of eminence at the bar and on the bench." Within five years the Law School was invited to become a charter member of the Association of American Law Schools.

1897

Mrs. William Thaw, four other members of the Thaw family, and H. M. Curry gave $5,000 to start a fund for erecting a new observatory building in Riverview Park.

Chancellor Holland reported that some "athletic students," on being told that they would receive no allowance in fees or tuition, left to go to other colleges.

Three days in March were devoted to a celebration of the 110th anniversary of the University's founding and the 75th anniversary of the installation of the first University faculty in 1822. The ceremonies were conducted in a large building in downtown Pittsburgh. Alumni gathered. Delegates from other universities attended lectures on the problems and accomplishments of higher education. Dr. Holland delivered an address on the history of the University. Twelve hundred people, including the governor of the state and a number of college presidents, attended a banquet. President McKinley, the members of the cabinet, and the justices of the Supreme Court were invited, but they, unfortunately, could not come. The students paraded in a body through the downtown streets and across the bridges of the two cities, accompanied by elaborate floats. The chemistry department built a horse-drawn platform on which four students dressed as alchemists stood in a mysterious manner around a generator that emitted noxious fumes of hydrogen sulfide. It exploded in front of the court house, but no one was seriously injured. The engineers displayed forgings, castings, and other products of the University's shop and laboratory on a float supported by a steam tractor. The water in the boiler gave out in the middle of the Sixth Street Bridge, and the tractor had to be hauled away by horses. The *Courant* sponsored a large float carrying students dressed in every costume seen in the area throughout the 110 years of the University's history.

The football team in 1890, a squad of thirteen with a mascot. The players furnished their own uniforms and chipped in to buy the football.

Trustee John Brashear had urged at a planning meeting that the occasion be used "to advance the interests of the institution," meaning, to collect money. His advice was followed. A drive for funds produced $52,915 from 111 donors. Three people gave $5,000 each (two of them anonymously), 10 gave $1,000 (including Chancellor Holland), the Thaw family gave $5,500, and Christopher Lyman Magee surpassed all others with a gift of $10,000.

1898

The board thanked Andrew W. Mellon for taking charge of the University's funds and making good investments at a high rate of return.

Margaret Lydia and Stella Mathilda Stein were graduated with B.A. degrees in the "Latin scientific" course. Miss Margaret Lydia then obtained the master of arts degree, the first granted to a woman at the University. She later married John C. Fetterman, dean of the College. Also in 1898 Mary E. Hamilton was graduated by the affiliated School of Pharmacy. In 1900 Mary L. Glenn graduated from the School of Dentistry. (In 1895 Agnes Irwin, president of Radcliffe College, had received the first honorary degree, Doctor of Laws, granted by the University to a woman.)

An athletic committee was appointed with representatives from the board, the faculty, the alumni, and the students. It resolved to try to collect $1,500 "to promote interest in various athletic teams" and it permitted contests only with other educational institutions. The board expressed disapproval of those students who did not represent universities in athletics but were willing to sell their services to outside organizations. The Athletic Committee was given the power to assist students by paying tuition, in whole or in part, providing their class standing met requirements.

John Brashear notified the board that Professor Keeler had been offered a position as assistant director of Yerkes Observatory at Lake Geneva, Wisconsin. To stay in Pittsburgh, Keeler wanted $160,000 raised for building and equipping a new observatory in Riverview Park, a salary of $3,500 a year for ten years, and a free residence. A month later he resigned to accept another offer, that of director of Lick Observatory in California, "the highest position in his profession in this country." The Observatory Committee, having collected $153,000, voted to go ahead with the construction of the new observatory, with John Brashear as its director. The cornerstone was laid in October.

1900

Chancellor Holland testified on the good and successful work being done by the Department of Engineering and Technology. One of the largest employers of engineers in the city, he said, "who has in his establishment nearly a score of the graduates of the institution," told him that he "prefers them to the graduates of all other institutions, because of a certain practical cast of mind which they seem to have acquired as a result of their training."

At least as early as the spring of 1896, Holland had come to the unhappy conclusion that the University was badly sited. Alone on the top of a hill in Allegheny, away from the flow of traffic, out of sight and out of mind, it was receiving little attention from those who were expected to support it. In his report to the members of the board (meeting in the Common Council Chamber in Municipal Hall in Pittsburgh) on June 15, 1896, Holland said, "It cannot fail to be felt by those of us who have given the matter a careful and intelligent study, that there should have been in times past a more prudent and far-sighted policy as to the matter of a final location." He offered two alternatives: to stay on the hill and buy up adjacent property to keep from being "hemmed in and built about with inferior structures," or to sell the present site and building and secure "a site easily accessible in the eastern portion of the City of Pittsburgh and of sufficient size to allow of our massing thereon the buildings of the future." One of two proposed sites was in Oakland, on property owned by Mrs. Edward W. H. Schenley, formerly Mary E. Croghan of Pittsburgh, now living in London. Two Pittsburghers had visited her there in 1889 and persuaded her to give the city 300 acres and to sell 200 more for a park that would bear her name. (Other descendants of General James O'Hara, founder of the Pittsburgh fortune inherited by Mary Croghan, his granddaughter, say wryly that the name properly should be O'Hara Park.) At the entrance to the new Schenley Park, across from Mr. Carnegie's new library, nature museum, and art gallery, lay a stretch of open, undeveloped land admirably suited to hold new University buildings—the College, the Engineering School, the Department of Medicine, the Law School, the Department of Dentistry, and perhaps, as partners, the three theological seminaries situated in Allegheny. The new Carnegie Technical Schools (on which Carnegie was to expend $24 million by 1917) was across Junction (Panther) Hollow less than a half-mile away. The University really should be near the Technical Schools, for it was to be expected that a number of the Schools' graduates would go on to the University for advanced and postgraduate training.

The members of the board agreed, and on June 15, 1896, they appointed a committee to approach Mrs. Schenley to see if she would sell such a site and on what terms. In June 1897 Mrs. Schenley cordially received two members of the committee—Chancellor Holland and Andrew Carnegie—at her home at Number 14 Prince's Gate, Hyde Park, London. She said the property was for sale but that she intended it to be used solely for residential purposes. The locality, she felt, would not be improved by a multiplication of public institutions. She listened with interest, however, to "a full and careful explanation of the situation," agreed to read the documents they left with her, and said she would give her decision in a letter after conferring with Colonel William A. Herron, her agent in Pittsburgh. On June 28 she wrote Holland that upon reflection she had decided to hold to her decision to sell the property near the park only for dwelling houses.

Holland continued the correspondence, and on June 9, 1898, he was able to present to the board an offer from Mrs. Schenley, received through Colonel Herron, "to sell to the University ten acres of ground situated between Fifth Avenue and Forbes Street, and Bellefield Avenue and [Bigelow] Boulevard, for the sum of $400,000; or to lease the same, with the privilege of purchasing at any time, at a rental of three per cent upon this valuation." Holland also stated that his agent had secured options on adjacent property, making in all a little over thirteen acres, for $342,000. He presented, on behalf of the New Site Committee, a letter to Mr. Carnegie asking for his aid in buying the land and a petition to the state legislature for a grant of $500,000 to aid in the purchase.

"We could find nobody," Holland said, "to help us accept her generous offer."

Holland acquired a new, divisive commitment in 1899:

In the summer of 1899, while collecting dinosaurs in Wyoming . . . I received a heavy blow, and returned to Pittsburgh headed for my grave, as the physicians believed. I cheated the doctors, but for a long time I was physically very weak; and my friend, Mr. Carnegie, urged me to resign the Chancellorship and devote myself wholly to the interests of the Library and the Institute, of both of which I had been one of the original trustees. "The University can find a Chancellor more readily than I can find a man to aid and advise me in the work I have undertaken, and I need your services. You will never need from this time forward," he said to me, "to worry about finances, and you can devote yourself unremittingly to your scientific pur-

suits." In a moment of what I often since have thought was a great weakness, I yielded.

The members of the board accepted his resignation, scheduled to take effect in September 1901, "with profound regret."

First, because we know and recognize that he has done splendid things for our University during his nine years as Chancellor. When he took charge . . . in the spring of 1891, the total enrollment was seventy-five students, whereas . . . for the present year . . . we have an enrollment of eight hundred and twenty-two students. . . . While the University has increased tenfold in numbers, and new departments added from year to year, some of which have had almost phenomenal success, we also know that the Chancellor has been reaching out toward a higher, and ideal University, which would be the peer of any kindred institution in the United States.

In a special resolution of thanks, the trustees revealed that Holland had given over many years "a large proportion of his salary . . . in the shape of prizes to students who have passed the best examinations," to the athletic association, and to the medical department to meet pressing needs.

Holland's farewell report to the University was franker and more eloquent than such documents usually are.

That the good work will go on without me, I have no doubt; but I cannot . . . fail to emphasize what seems to me to be the one great necessity of the times in this Western Pennsylvania . . . and that is an awakening, in the minds and hearts of those who have the power to help, to the educational necessities of the times. . . . There is no other community in this country, of equal population and equal wealth, in which so little has as yet been done by men of wealth to promote the cause of higher education. The entire endowment and possessions of all the colleges, technical schools, and universities in Western Pennsylvania, though having a population of nearly two and a half millions of people, does not equal what is possessed today by many single institutions located in communities that have not one-quarter of the population, nor one-tenth of the wealth.

There have been some notable exceptions. . . . But in a community where wealth is reckoned by the hundreds of millions, and where there are so many who might help, if

A mechanical drawing class in the School of Engineering, about 1895.

they but would, it is discouraging to feel that it is necessary even to appeal for assistance. . . .

You cannot kill this institution. It will grow; it must grow. It is rooted deep in the affections of the men it has served and the community it has honored. I trust the day is coming when the rich men of Western Pennsylvania, and the poor men, too . . . will realize that to live and die without in some way having helped their University is to die disgraced.

William Holland served for the next twenty years as director of the Museum of Natural History and for ten more as curator and active director emeritus. He had two regrets in his later years. One was that he had never kept a diary. The other was that he never finished the history of the University he had always intended to write and for which he signed a contract in 1912 with G. P. Putnam's Sons, New York. His files show much research, much correspondence, and little writing. His *Butterfly Book*, however, published in 1898, sold 5,000 copies in the first few weeks. He followed it with *The Moth Book* (1903), *To the River Platte and Back* (1913), and *The Butterfly Guide* (1915). He directed the making of the casts of the museum's world-famous *Diplodocus carnegii*, and he traveled to ten national museums to supervise the installation of replicas, receiving at each yet another distinguished medal to add to his collection. He became president of the Carnegie Hero Fund and of the American Association of Museums. When a French combat regiment visited Pittsburgh in 1918, he addressed it outside the courthouse and its officers and diplomats at a banquet, both times in fluent French. He was a personage, an institution, renowned both in the city and in his various fields of activity. He was the portly gentleman with the luxuriant mustachios, the marvelous raconteur, the public speaker who swept the address system aside and could be heard in the last row of the top gallery, the former chancellor who at every Pitt commencement boomed out brilliant introductions for those receiving honorary degrees. Those who knew him still laugh at the stories told about him.* A line in his obituary read, "To everything to which he turned his hand he brought distinction."

---

*The present director emeritus of Carnegie Museum, M. Graham Netting, who was a young staff member when Holland was the director emeritus, has furnished several examples. In the 1920s a radio station telephoned the museum with a problem: "Do you have anyone there who can roar like a lion?" The curator who answered replied, "Yes, but he's in New York." Arriving at his office one morning, he told Elizabeth Courtney, his secretary, that he had a bad cold; would she please call the manager at the Schenley Hotel and have him send over a bottle of Large Whiskey (that is, a brand of Monongahela rye made at Large, Pennsylvania). Mrs. Courtney to manager: "Dr. Holland has a bad cold and wants you to send over a large bottle of whiskey." Holland booming from his adjoining office: "No, Mrs. Courtney, a bottle of *Large* Whiskey." Mrs. Courtney to manager: "Dr. Holland has a bad cold and wants you to send over a *very* large bottle of whiskey."

4

. . . And on into a Bright New Century

It was Chancellor Holland who changed the institution from a college into a university. It was ourselves who welded the several parts of the institution into a united whole, until now with a faculty of about five hundred, and a student body of more than six thousand, the University stands out as one of the real institutions of learning in America.

Samuel Black McCormick to the Board of Trustees, October 1, 1920

WILLIAM HOLLAND took a seat in 1901 on the Board of Directors, on the Executive Committee, and on the Search Committee named to recommend a successor. John Alfred Brashear, fifty-one, a trustee since 1891, was named to serve as acting chancellor until a permanent appointment was made.

Pittsburgh has never had any other public figure quite like "Uncle John" Brashear. He was courted, beloved, even revered to an extraordinary degree by all classes of society. In no way did he resemble his predecessors or his successors in the office of chancellor, nor did he fit the pattern of what a university chancellor then was expected to be—or to have been.

He was not a clergyman. His formal education consisted of six grades of public school in Brownsville, Pennsylvania, and four months at Pittsburgh's Duff's Mercantile College. He had been, in his forty-first year, a mechanic in a South Side rolling mill. But young Brashear had taken to working with telescopes as an avocation, and in the course of his efforts, while still a millwright, he became expert in making lenses, mirrors, spectrograph plates, and other astronomical apparatus. He developed a process for silvering lenses that was hailed and adopted in Europe. He wrote a weekly newspaper column on astronomy. When he called on Langley with one of his lenses, Langley made him a protégé, unofficial assistant, and consultant. William Thaw gave him $3,800 with which to pay a debt and to move the one-room Brashear Optical Works to Observatory Hill and provided him with a large house nearby on Perrysville Avenue. Henry Phipps sent him and his wife, Phoebe, to Europe (with Phipps's young son in their care), where Brashear visited and was welcomed by every observatory and scientific society in Britain, France, Switzerland, and Germany. In London he was an honored guest at the annual banquet of the Royal Astronomical Society. "While social ranks were drawn very close," he observed on his return, "science has no boundaries of this kind."

Brashear served three years, "with reluctance," as acting chancellor. To the office he brought one special quality: he was held in such high esteem that he was able to raise sizable sums of money for the Uni-

Allegheny Observatory

John Alfred Brashear became acting chancellor in 1901. Portrait by J. W. Vale.

versity, especially for the handsome new observatory in Riverview Park. Otherwise, in the words of a contemporary who knew him, "He was a sweet, lovely man who was utterly unqualified to be chancellor, and knew it."

The Search Committee, headed by board chairman George Hubbard Clapp (Bachelor of Philosophy 1877), nominated a chancellor with a more conventional background. Samuel Black McCormick, age forty-six, was a graduate of Washington and Jefferson, a clergyman, an educator, and a col-

University Art Gallery

Samuel Black McCormick, ordained Presbyterian minister and practicing lawyer, served as chancellor from 1904 to 1921. Portrait by J. W. Vale.

lege president. He was also a lawyer, having studied in the office of his uncle, the U.S. district attorney for Western Pennsylvania, and had practiced law in Pittsburgh and Denver for five years before entering the Western Theological Seminary in Allegheny. He taught English literature and rhetoric for a time at the University under Dr. Holland. From 1897 to 1904 he was president of Coe College in Cedar Rapids, Iowa.

McCormick accepted the chancellorship (at $6,000 a year) with firm conditions he set down in a letter to the trustees on June 4, 1904. He would not under any consideration accept the chancellorship of the University "as it is now, and where it is now," for its future in its present situation seemed to him to be hopeless. The institution must develop as a university in its several departments, according to an outline he and the trustees had agreed upon at a meeting in the Duquesne Club on June 1. Steps must be taken to secure a new site, preferably in the East End, not too far from Carnegie Library and the Carnegie Technical Schools. "With a new and desirable site, there can be no question that in time one of the finest institutions in the land can be built up in Pittsburgh. There is real need for a university in that center. A student body and financial resources are both at hand." Wisdom, energy, enterprise, and enthusiasm would be required on the part of both chancellor and board.

McCormick was inaugurated as ninth head of the institution on February 22, 1905, in a ceremony held in Carnegie Music Hall in Oakland. The next five or six years were the most important in the history of the school up to that time.

• The University purchased the Dental College and "through its proper officers assumed charge of the department and its property." In a complicated transaction, the proprietary shares of eight dentists were acquired with payments totaling $15,126.40. The value of the property (chiefly furniture and dental equipment) was inventoried at $7,372, thus reducing the cost of the purchase to $7,754.40. Four of the dentists would continue as professors in the Dental College for five years, "if their services are satisfactory," at salaries up to 4 percent of the school's gross income. Dr. H. Edmund Friesell was

to have an additional 3½ percent "as Dean, so long as he may serve as Dean."

• The University purchased the medical department and the stock of the West Penn Medical College "after long and tedious negotiations." Money for the payment was raised by placing a $100,000 mortgage on the real property, the appraised value of which was $85,000.

• A committee headed by William Lucien Scaife chose a new name for the Western University of Pennsylvania. Reasons were given: the old name did not give any hint as to location; W.U.P., pronounced *whup*, was not dignified; a shorter name was desirable; and (the ultimate indignity) some people actually thought the University was a western branch of the University of Pennsylvania. Two possible new names were considered: Pittsburgh University and University of Pittsburgh. The second was chosen because it sounded more dignified.

• Two new schools were established: the School of Economics, later named the School of Business Administration; and the School of Education, sometimes improperly called the Teachers College. A summer school and evening and Saturday classes were started.

• The Observatory Hill properties were sold to the Protestant Home for Orphans for $85,000.

• The University bought a new site of forty-three acres, held a nationwide architectural contest for the design of a campus with thirty buildings, started construction on three of the buildings, and moved from Observatory Hill and Allegheny to the new campus.

A "Betterment Committee" of six University officials, including Holland, McCormick, Andrew William Mellon, and Benjamin Thaw, considered five sites in the area extending eastward from Oakland to Wilkinsburg. (One was the Old Murdoch Homestead on Forbes Avenue, just east of Morewood Avenue, on land adjoining and later acquired by Carnegie Tech.) The site chosen was part of the Schenley Farms area in Oakland, where Holland and Carnegie had tried to buy land in 1897.

Mary Schenley had preferred to give long-term leaseholds on lots, in the English manner, rather than sell them outright, with the predictable result that the Schenley Farms area was an enclave of 103 acres of undeveloped farm and grazing land. In 1895, however, she sold some land to the city of Pittsburgh. The city resold part of this to a successful real estate developer from Cleveland, Franklin F. Nicola, who with his two brothers and some Pittsburgh backers hoped to acquire more land and make Schenley Farms into the city's civic center and choicest residential community. Nicola began by setting up the Bellefield Company, a stock company with fifty-eight blue chip shareholders. Through this company he built in 1898 a ten-story steel-frame luxury hotel, the Schenley, at the entrance to Schenley Park.

In 1900 there were a few scattered farmhouses in the area and only five major buildings: the Schenley Hotel; Carnegie Institute with its library, concert hall, and museums; Dr. Holland's Bellefield Presbyterian Church; a former streetcar barn at Fifth and Craig that had been converted into a very popular skating rink, sports arena, and theater; and, across the ravine, the fine Phipps Conservatory. In February 1905, in the biggest real estate transaction in Pittsburgh history, the executors of the Mary Schenley estate sold 103 acres of Schenley Farms to the Nicola syndicate for about $3 million. The land encompassed an area bounded by Forbes Avenue on the south, Center Avenue on the north, Bellefield Avenue on the east, and Bouquet Street on the west. In the next five years, Nicola built streets; laid down a single large conduit for water and gas pipes and telephone and electric wires; and sold about a thousand building lots for expensive houses (costing from $23,000 to $32,000), most of them built in a variety of Edwardian domestic styles. Now there were a dozen or more public or semipublic buildings, including the Soldiers and Sailors Memorial Hall; the First United Presbyterian Church; St. Paul's Cathedral; Logan Armory, used by the Eighteenth National Guard Regiment; the University Club; the beautiful new ballpark, Forbes Field; and the Pittsburgh Athletic Association (under construction). Nicola planned to have a huge town hall occupy the block bordered by Fifth Avenue and Ruskin, Bigelow, and Tennyson streets.

The University still fondly hoped to buy the 13 level acres in front of the Schenley Hotel, across from the entrance to Schenley Park, but Nicola had already sold 7.7 acres of that plot to Henry Clay Frick for $577,000; it was now known as Frick Acres. Instead, the University took what it was offered and what it could afford. It paid $537,000 for 45 acres on, along, and over the top of the unlovely hillside north of O'Hara and Terrace streets.

McCormick launched a drive in 1906 to raise $1 million by public subscription to pay this obligation and to construct the first of the new buildings on the new campus. He sent two-page, single-spaced letters to a number of the rich and mighty, explaining in earnest detail why the money was needed, what it would be used for, and how grateful he would be if he could have the privilege of presenting his story in a personal interview. John D. Rockefeller apparently did not answer. Henry Clay Frick, who had recently given $32,500 to Allegheny Observatory in a matching grant, declined in a two-sentence letter to see him. George Westinghouse replied: "Some few years ago I gave the Observatory an electric outfit at considerable cost, and felt then that that should be regarded as a contribution of some importance. I do not see my way clear to participate in your further plans. It seems almost extraordinary that you should ask me to assume the responsibility for the Electrical Department of the University and should make suggestions in such an offhand way involving such very large contributions. I am altogether too much occupied to be able even to discuss with you matters which you deem of such high importance. I wonder if you have any idea how many letters I receive making suggestions as to the manner in which I can appropriately make expenditures." He trusted, however, "that you may meet with success in your efforts." (McCormick's fund-raising attempts took place in the days before family or corporate foundations depersonalized such requests.) George Lauder, one of Carnegie's partners in the sale of the Carnegie Steel empire to United States Steel, declined to contribute because he had "no sympathy with the idea of bringing colleges into prominence by collossal [*sic*] buildings. On

Pittsburgh in the early 1890s.

the contrary, academic groves sacred to learning have always been associated in my mind with quiet and retirement. Students that are attracted by the outward trappings of colleges, are much better away both for themselves and their colleges."

Andrew Carnegie's male secretary replied, "Mr. Carnegie . . . can only repeat what he said to you and others, that he is not prepared to take the lead in this matter and now and then it comes into his head for a moment that people should feel that he should not be expected to do so." Three weeks later,

Carnegie wrote personally to McCormick to thank him for agreeing to serve as a trustee of his Carnegie Foundation for the Advancement of Teaching, which he was forming to provide pensions for college teachers and to which by 1917 he would donate $16.15 million. When they met, Carnegie told McCormick what he had told Brashear: he would present him with a list of nineteen other Pittsburghers, each of whom ought to give $100,000, and if they contributed, he would join them. He would, he said, always do his part.

A game at Forbes Field, about 1910, in the era of horse-drawn vehicles and early automobiles. St. Pierre Ravine, crossed by the bridge (center), was filled in about 1915.

McCormick's drive for $1 million was not a success; he got only $250,000 from the public—$50,000 less than Pittsburghers raised in three days for victims of the San Francisco earthquake and fire. From the state legislators he received $239,000 in 1906 for the School of Mines building and $325,000 in 1908 for the School of Medicine building, in return for which the University gave the state fifty free scholarships, one for each senatorial district. McCormick proceeded with his plans for the new campus. Using $7,700 donated for the purpose by

Frank Nicola and the state legislature, he initiated a nationwide architectural contest for the design and placement of thirty University buildings on the Schenley Farms hillside, on which he said $20 million would be spent over the next ten or twenty years. Sixty-one entries were submitted without identification of the sources. Nine architects or architectural firms received awards of honor, and four prizes of $1,000 each were given for "highly meritorious designs." Winner of the first prize ($1,500) was Number 40, which turned out to be

Future location of the Medical Center, about 1900. Photo from the corner of DeSoto Street (lower right) and Fifth Avenue, with Lothrop Street winding up the hillside (left). The building in the background (right) is the H. K. Porter mansion, used as a faculty club in the 1920s.

Palmer and Hornbostel of New York. (Henry Hornbostel had designed the buildings for the Carnegie Technical Schools and was now a member of the Tech faculty.)

In the Palmer and Hornbostel plan, the buildings stretched across the hillside, facing southeast toward Fifth and Forbes avenues. Alexander Moore's *Pittsburgh Leader* ("Not controlled by Politicians") said the design had majestic effects that reminded one of the Athenian Acropolis as depicted when it was still

intact. "The pillared facades, with their pediments highly adorned, rise one above another, the largest and most majestic being at the summit. To this the approach is by successive flights of stately steps, giving access to terrace upon terrace. . . . The plan includes other courts, an interior garden, widespread botanical gardens, greater and lesser assembly halls, halls for every department, scientific or academic, and dormitories, which, massed with artistic cleverness, are really imposing." The *Post,*

The "Acropolis plan," by Palmer and Hornbostel, won a 1908 nationwide architectural competition for thirty University buildings. The intersection in the foreground is that of O'Hara Street and Bigelow Boulevard.

citing the "indescribable beauty" of the winning design, told of a funicular or moving staircase at the entrance and of two gigantic smokestacks from the powerhouse and engineering schools, which, "like beautiful obelisks, will frame the entrance in great sweeps to the elevation of the campus more than 100 feet above."

The designs were exhibited at the Architectural Club in Pittsburgh and the T-Square Club in Philadelphia, where many architects favored the second choice ("modern Gothic" with pinnacles and towers, by Janssen and Abbott of Pittsburgh) over the winner. McCormick had Palmer and Hornbostel prepare sketches of several of their buildings "so that these may be exhibited to possible donors to excite their interest with a view to secure from them the gift of such a building."

On October 2, 1908, the cornerstone was laid for Henry Hornbostel's large, awkward, and inutile Soldiers and Sailors Memorial Hall. This ceremony took place near the close of the city's sesquicentennial, when distinguished guests from all over the world were gathered for a happy, successful, and beautifully managed celebration. Immediately after the Memorial Hall ceremony, the crowd walked fifty

feet to see the cornerstone laid for the first University building, that for the School of Mines. (The name was later changed to State Hall.) Short speeches were given by Dr. Holland, Dr. Brashear, the mayor of the city, the governor of Pennsylvania, the treasurer of Pennsylvania, and the vice president of the United States. Dr. Brashear squared off the stone, Dr. Linhart cemented it, and Chancellor McCormick tapped it with a hammer and said, "For the glory of God, for the uplifting of humanity, for the conquest of this earth, in the name of true science and sound learning, I now declare this cornerstone well and truly laid."

Nine months later, construction of the Engineering Building (soon to be renamed Thaw Hall) was started on what was to become O'Hara Street. The building was designed, with State Hall, to fit into the base line of the Acropolis plan. By the spring of 1910, those two buildings were finished, and the city had extended Bayard Street (under the name O'Hara Street) westward from the foot of Parkman Street to DeSoto Street. A medical building (Pennsylvania Hall) was going up near the top of the hillside. A gymnasium and playing field were being planned for a site on the crest of the hill, to be built

Participants in the laying of the cornerstone of State Hall and assorted onlookers pose for the camera, October 2, 1908. Chancellor McCormick is bearded and wearing a mortarboard. Behind him and to his left are his two predecessors: John Brashear and William Holland.

with $100,000 given by Joe Clifton Trees (M.E. 1895).

The actual move from Observatory Hill to Oakland was made in the summer of 1909.

The McCormick administration is best remembered today for changing the name of the University, moving the University to the new campus, and erecting six major buildings. It should be remembered as well for other less dramatic developments. That administration was one in which the deans of the schools and the heads of the departments wielded extraordinary power. They had, in fact, more authority to act and to command than faculty administrators were to have at the University of Pittsburgh for almost a half century. McCormick apparently felt no fear of being overshadowed by his faculty; he picked men with strong leadership qualities. He had a secretary of the University (his cousin Samuel Black Linhart), a registrar (Albert E. Frost), and a business manager (Frank Eckels). In the absence of a provost, assistant chancellors, and vice chancellors, he expected his deans and department heads to be executives—to run their operations by command decisions rather than by orders from above or through meetings, debates, and consensus of the teaching faculty. Dean H. E. Friesell was an extreme example; he ran the dental school for forty-two years almost as though it were still a proprietary school. John Thom Holdsworth (Business Administration), Will Grant Chambers (Education), John C. Fetterman (College), Frederick L. Bishop (Engineering), and Harry B. Meller (Mines) were deans with permitted authority and executive initiative. As such, they were regarded with respect and even, on occasion, with awe. Francis Newton Thorpe, head of a new (1910) Department of Political Science, a national authority on constitutional law, a prolific author of books, was looked upon as a giant in his field and an adornment to the campus. An alumnus of the Class of 1916 recalled years later that in those days personal relationships were easier between teachers and students. Some of the faculty (including Thorpe) "had large and ardent personal followings, because they not only won admiration in the classroom but had time to develop social contact with their students."

In June 1916 this faculty, the chancellor, and the trustees established a system of academic tenure. One-year appointments were continued for instructors and assistants, but assistant professors were henceforth to be appointed for a term of three years and subsequently for five-year terms; professors were appointed for an indefinite term. McCormick's successor did not rescind that advanced and enlightened policy; he simply ignored it.

The McCormick administration also was one that set out to save the College of Liberal Arts from extinction and in so doing produced an accommodation in the century-old conflict between proponents of technical training and those of liberal education.

In 1902 Acting Chancellor Brashear had reported: "Enrollment of collegiate students has fallen off fifteen percent in fifteen years, whereas the number of students in the technical and engineering departments has increased two hundred per cent." In his 1903 report he wrote: "Out of 55 freshmen, but one entered the Classical Course, and only three entered in the Sophomore Class. The tendency seems to be toward the Engineering and Scientific lines, and while we deprecate the diminishing interest in the Classical studies, the sooner we recognize

that we must give a first class engineering education, the better for us." In May 1904: "Remarkable decrease in attendance in Collegiate Department, only 21 students."

Between 1902 and 1908, the scientific and engineering courses were so popular that many persons, including some in the University itself, suggested that it might be wise to concentrate on such courses and drop classes in liberal arts. McCormick did not agree. He was committed to "a University—an institution of learning designed to give the people of the community instruction in whatever branch of learning they may desire. . . . Pittsburgh needs a University. . . . Not a little, dwarfed, imperfect University, but [one] finely equipped, largely endowed, splendid in all its departments."

Dean Fetterman concurred, as did at least three other powerful trustees—George Hubbard Clapp, Benjamin Thaw, and Daniel H. Wallace (who had recently made a gift of $50,000 to establish a chair of political science). Students, alumni, and some faculty members signed a petition in support of the College. A committee prepared a statement, published as a College bulletin, that liberal arts courses would continue to be given. Whatever the cause, enrollment in the College after 1908 rose progressively—from 108 in 1909–1910 to 649 in 1914–1915.

The McCormick administration also was one that found a roundabout path to national recognition and prestige, and through it, unexpectedly, to physical expansion and academic growth.

The most devoted alumnus would admit that the University, when it moved from Allegheny to Oakland, had very little national recognition or prestige compared with the traditional eastern universities or the great state universities to the west. One who was at the University in 1912 later testified: "Pitt was small in enrollment, small in faculty, small in dollars, small in traditions, and very much smaller in fame. It was too little recognized even to be credited with the few big things it *had* already produced." Recognition, expansion, and academic growth, he said, came to the University through athletics—specifically through intercollegiate football. "Pitt was not the first nor the only university whose history was affected by the success of its football teams, but it was certainly one that was benefited to a remarkable degree by increased alumni and public support based on that success."

The story seems to begin in the autumn of 1889, when students of the Western University, led by Bert H. Smyers (Class of 1893), organized a team to play American rugby, or football, a game first introduced on November 6, 1869, in a match between Princeton and Rutgers. The Western University team, known as W.U.P., began by losing a game with Shady Side Academy, Smyers, who weighed 131 pounds, playing quarterback. Penn State first appeared in 1893 and won 32−0, the first of six successive victories totaling 173 points to 4. By 1900 the Western University team was playing nine to twelve games per season, sometimes two games a week.

The teams had as few as eighteen men and seldom as many as thirty, each man, of course, playing both offense and defense. Sportswriters called them "lads"; second-team players were "scrubs." Substituting was rare, generally limited to replacing players who had to be helped or carried off the field and could not return. In several games the head coach of W.U.P. received permission to play, since no other substitute was available. Student managers scheduled the games, hired the officials, collected admission fees, and paid the bills. Officials wore street clothes and derby hats. Each player bought his own nose guard, helmet, shoes, and padded vest, and he contributed to a fund to buy the football for the first game. Observatory Hill had one playing field of cement-hard clay, smaller than regulation size, that ended in a drop down a steep hill. There were no athletic facilities other than the gymnasium, no season tickets, no students who went to the University because of athletic interest, and, until 1905, very little coaching.

In 1903 W.U.P. played nine games, lost eight of them, and tied one. It played the Geneva Covenanters of Beaver Falls, Pennsylvania, twice and lost twice, 57−0 and 32−0. It lost to Penn State 59−0. At the end of that disastrous season, the team and its supporters disbanded, leaving behind them a $500 debt to Penn State for unpaid guaranteed expenses. Trustee George Hubbard Clapp, chairman of the Gymnasium Committee, came to the rescue. He saw to it that Penn State was paid, and on May 19, 1904, he addressed a letter to the trustees: "Believing that nothing could help to advertise the school and to create good feeling among the students and the community at large so much as to have a first class college team, your committee has encouraged the organization of a football association. The Alumni have become interested and have guaranteed to raise a fund of $2,000; the students, with the exception of the Law School, have voted to pay an athletic fee of $5.00 each . . . and a schedule of games to be played on Saturday afternoons at Exposition Park has been arranged."

In an informal conference in July, the alumni spoke up for athletics: "It creates college spirit . . . it gives the institution a name and fame in the community . . . it makes all its alumni and students proud of their University." Dr. McCormick agreed: "I am deeply interested in the athletics of the W.U. and I am desirous that as long as intercollegiate games are played the university will play with our best colleges."

Important developments arose as a result of the decision to continue supporting a football team.

First, efforts were made to recruit some good players. In this Iron Age of intercollegiate football, there were few rules on eligibility, no residency requirement, and no regulations on what constituted a bona fide student. Arthur St. Leger Mosse, who had been persuaded to leave the University of Kansas to become head football coach at the Western University of Pennsylvania, induced a half-dozen of his sturdy young athletes to follow him. Several of these had been playing as mercenaries, and some others wished to attend the University's professional schools. The next logical place to recruit was at Geneva College, which had more first-rate players than it needed. The Reverend Guy D. Wallace, pastor of the First United Presbyterian Church in Braddock, Pennsylvania, in 1936 wrote a letter, only now uncovered, describing what occurred in 1904, when, as a graduate student, he was active in athletic administration: "We imported a group of players who had been very successful at Geneva: Jud Smith, Walter East, Joe Thompson, Joe Edgar, Arthur McLean. Dr. Waldron [Dr. Andrew Bennett Wallgren, physical education director at the University] manipulated the recruiting of some players and Mosse the rest, I think. Colonel Thompson had played years and years. At one of the games I heard someone ask, 'Is that old Joe Thompson, who used to play around here long ago?' The reply was, 'Oh, no, that is his grandson.'"*

In the second important development, the newly formed football association began to raise the $2,000 promised by the alumni for working capital. Donations were made with the agreement that no pledges would be callable until the entire sum had been subscribed. Andrew W. Mellon was the only person to subscribe $100, the largest amount. When $1,617.50 had been pledged and no more subscriptions were foreseen, several association members, including young Guy Wallace, "underwrote" the $382.50 balance, announced that the goal had been achieved, and called in the pledges. Wallace was treasurer of the drive, and in 1936 he asserted, "That financial campaign was the real beginning of the big football enterprise at Pitt."

Part of the money was used to set up the University's first athletic dormitory and training table. Wallace wrote, "We rented a house on Western Avenue [on the North Side] . . . and furnished it with cots and kitchen tables, etc., and hired a cook and began collecting our players."

Third, Mosse obtained from Barney Dreyfuss of the Pittsburgh Baseball Club an outright lease of Exposition Park for the fall months. The University paid him 20 percent of its gross gate receipts.

The Reverend Wallace described a typical home game in the 1904 season:

We made all our arrangements most efficiently and handled all our affairs skillfully. . . . On the day of a game we had a fair-sized parade through the down-town streets, of students, which led the way . . . to the park. . . . At the time advertised, the gong rang, which was used to start baseball games. . . . The team was *good.* They walked over

everything. On Thanksgiving day they played Penn State. The attendance was probably a record up to that time. It was about 13,000. As the [Fourteenth Regiment] band arrived at the park gates, leading the parade, I sat in the little office over the wickets, handing to the State manager a check for $500. . . . We had money in the treasury when the season was all over. We won from State (which had had a fine record among Eastern teams) by a score of 24 to 5. It was one of the cleverest games ever played.

The reinforced 1904 team indeed had an outstanding season: it played ten games, all against college opponents, won ten games, scored 406 points to its opponents' 5, and, in addition to beating Penn State for the first time, defeated West Virginia and, understandably, Geneva. The Western University of Pennsylvania claimed the championship of the western part of the state and second place in the entire state, behind the University of Pennsylvania, which was eastern collegiate champion that year.†

Now the community was truly aroused, as indicated by the pages and pages of press coverage of the games in the seven daily newspapers and by one of the typical headlines: "This Old Town Football Crazy." After victories over Penn State and Washington and Jefferson, some headings were "Crowd Goes Wild," "Spectators Become Hysterical," "Greatest Victory Ever," "The Most Enthusiastic Demonstration on the Downtown Streets in the History of Football."

That the team survived and prevailed owed largely to a small group of alumni who had passed the hat around, volunteered as assistant coaches, and recruited players. The most prominent of these, on their way to successful careers as business or professional men, were to play important roles in alumni and athletic affairs for the next three or four decades: Bert Smyers, Floyd Rose, Alfred R. Hamilton, Joe C. Trees, Wilbur D. Hockensmith, and Roy C. McKenna.

---

*Thompson was twenty-nine in 1904.

†The nineteen lettermen on the 1904 team had an average weight of 164 pounds, the heaviest man weighing 182 and the lightest 132. The tallest man was 6 feet 2 inches; the smallest was 5 feet 5¾ inches.

Of the eleven regulars, four became lawyers, four became physicians, one became a dentist, one a professor of engineering, and one (in the words of the annalist) "was the only failure in the crowd."

University Archives

The famous 1916 football team. H. C. (Red) Carlson is seated in the first row, third from the right. Captain Bob Peck holds the football in the second row, sixth from the right, and Coach Glenn L. (Pop) Warner wears a sweater and holds his hat at the end of the second row (left). Claude (Tiny) Thornhill is fifth from the right in the third row. Bill McClelland, later a force in Allegheny County politics, is fourth from the right in the back row. John B. (Jock) Sutherland, to become Pitt's most famous coach, is in the center of the back row.

The Reverend Wallace recalled what followed the glorious 1904 season:

Then the trouble began. Joe Thompson wanted Coach Mosse's job, Dr. Friezell wanted everybody's job, and there were plots and schemes and the worst of bitter feeling. Chancellor McCormick was very much worried by it all. My crowd lost out and Dr. Friezell was Czar. It did not bother me personally, for I had given my word to my father that I would drop out at the end of the year.

You would be surprised, I think, if I could remember and tell you all the scheming, plotting, lying and hating that went on that winter of 1904–5. Various fine men . . . tried to work out some harmonious settlement. And somehow they did go on.

The next season there was a squad of stars, but of course things did not go so well. . . . However, the big enterprise was started and has gone on grandly ever since. . . . *This is important:* The starting of the big team was most opportune. It came just when the University needed publicity badly, it made the University more popular in Pittsburgh than it had ever been within my knowledge.

At about this time, in 1906, Chancellor McCormick, in the words of a newspaper headline, took a "Firm Stand for Purer Athletics." He said, "We have joined the colleges of the country in the effort to eliminate from athletics, and especially from football, everything that justifies criticism upon the national game. This applies both to the playing of the game and its general management." To accomplish this at the University, he created an eligibility committee, consisting of faculty representatives, and gave it exclusive control in matters pertaining to the eligibility and conduct of players.

After graduating from the Law School, Joe Thompson became coach in 1908. His team in 1910 was the first to attract national attention when it not only defeated all nine teams on its schedule but did so without being scored on. While only four of the opponents were major teams, sportswriters and fans alike were impressed by—and did not forget—the remarkable feat of an undefeated 282–0 season.*

A development of major importance occurred in 1915 when Trees, Rose, A. R. Hamilton, and other alumni persuaded a new head coach to take over the Pitt team. He was Glenn Scobey (Pop) Warner, famous as one of the game's great innovative coaches, a national figure who had produced outstanding teams and upset victories at Cornell, Georgia, and the Indian School at Carlisle. He was known for the stars he developed, including, especially, the Sac and Fox Indian Jim Thorpe. Hiring a coach with the stature of Pop Warner, and his acceptance of the post, gave notice to all concerned that Pitt henceforth must be regarded as one of the top contenders in the country.

Warner's record was phenomenal: in his first four years (1915–1918), he produced four unbeaten, untied teams, 863 points to 17, and led three of them to national championships in 1915, 1916, and 1918. Eleven of Warner's players were first-team All-Americans. A sportswriter on the *New York Journal* said on November 1, 1916: "Warner has taught his . . . pupils a combination of team play that establishes a new standard of efficiency in football. . . . The great Pittsburgh gridiron machine is probably as smooth a running piece of machinery as was ever assembled. . . . Warner's pupils have time and again been termed the greatest squad of interferers of the

age. The long, sweeping end runs in which Pittsburgh excels, are nothing more nor less than a display . . . of a thorough course of instruction in the rudiments of the game . . . from one of the greatest master minds of football." Of the same team, Walter Camp declared, "This team play is perfect. They are a most wonderful team. Pitt is a marvelous combination."

In 1913 Pitt began a string of winning seasons that was to extend without a break for the next twenty-seven years, into another age. The University became a different institution in the first two decades of the century, still small in dollars but large in enrollment, large in faculty, and large in recognition. Football helped.

On January 18, 1914, the Pittsburgh Chamber of Commerce held a banquet that reflected the hopes of the time for a bright and peaceful future. The diners celebrated the 100 years of peace between Great Britain and the United States since the Treaty of Ghent in 1814. The main speaker was Sir Algernon Hawkins Thomond Keith-Falconer, Earl of Kintore, of Scotland. He predicted that "barbarous warfare" was on the point of being replaced by international arbitration. He was given a standing ovation.

McCormick's chief concerns early in 1914 were not war and peace but how to take care of the sharply increased numbers of students who were coming to an uncompleted campus. He was, someone said, a victim of his own success. Classes were too large and crowded, and there were no quarters for forming new sections. Dean John Fetterman complained that laboratories were so congested that instructors could not move about freely. Members of his faculty, he said, did not have offices (indeed, very few had desks) because the College had no building.

There were, to be sure, a few compensations. The state since 1913 had been giving the University regular appropriations amounting to $520,000 a year. The city was installing campus improvements, including new streets, steps, and a lighting system. The Council on Medical Education of the American Medical Association (AMA) had advanced the

---

*Coach Thompson became a lawyer, a state legislator, and a repeatedly wounded hero in World War I, winning the French Croix de Guerre, the British Medal of Honor, the American Distinguished Service Medal, and the Congressional Medal of Honor. He was inducted posthumously into the National Football Foundation's Hall of Fame in December 1971.

School of Medicine to the highest possible rating. The School of Mines had seven Chinese students, which suggested a possible new source of expansion and income. McCormick found that an automobile, a gift from Edward Vose Babcock, greatly improved his efficiency. A. W. and Richard Beatty Mellon had established a $15,000 fellowship for pathology research, and they were building an institute for industrial chemical research on O'Hara Street near Thaw Hall. It was a handsome structure that cost $230,000 to erect and equip, and the sight of it raised everyone's morale. The institute would be a graduate school managed and supervised by the University. And although donors usually prefer to ignore overhead costs, this gift came with $40,000 a year for five years for maintenance, after which the institute would be self-sustaining.

Nevertheless, the building program was lagging, the Acropolis plan was not progressing, the endowment was a disgrace, and impossible conditions simply had to be remedied.

McCormick's solution for the shortage of money was to make a renewed approach to Andrew Carnegie, a University trustee who had never attended a board meeting since his election in 1895 and had never made a financial contribution to the University. (He explained that he did not wish to "take the burden of the University off the shoulders of the people.") McCormick, board chairman George Clapp, and Samuel Harden Church joined forces in a bold and original proposition that they presented to Carnegie a number of times in letters and meetings in the years 1911–1914.

Colonel Church, a formidable figure, formerly a railroad executive, author of—among other works—*A Corporate History of the Pennsylvania Railroad Lines West of Pittsburgh* in thirteen volumes, was now president of Carnegie Institute—that is, of "Carnegie Museum." He proposed that Mr. Carnegie take charge of forming "a practical union" of the Carnegie Technical Schools, Carnegie Institute, and the University in a single institution. There would be, he said, great benefits for all.

The Technical Schools did not teach languages, literature, philosophy, and the arts, which meant that Arthur Arton Hamerschlag, president of the

Schools, could not confer degrees. He was "seriously embarrassed" at turning out his first graduating class in 1908 "without degrees which every other college gives its students, and without which our students . . . will be handicapped in making their business connections."

Carnegie Institute, created with $18.5 million of Mr. Carnegie's money, was a "splendid and brilliant piece of work," but it was "a slumbering, passive creation that needed "to multiply its educational powers."

The Western University, about to be renamed the University of Pittsburgh, would be "the bride of this marriage." It had (in 1908) endowments of more than $500,000; real estate and buildings worth $750,000; equipment worth $100,000; revenues annually of about $110,000; and seven departments with 1,037 students. It had just bought "an admirable site of forty-five acres . . . closely contiguous to the Institute." Of great importance, she "would bring with her, besides her unspotted reputation . . . her charter, giving us the right to confer degrees." The professors of the Technical Schools, moreover, who were debarred from the right to participate in Mr. Carnegie's own College Pension Fund, would enjoy that privilege with the new union. The students would "partake of the most comprehensive scheme of education which the world contains."

In a letter he signed "affectionately yours," Church estimated the cost of the union at $10 million. Of this amount, $6 million would go to the University, $1 million to Carnegie Institute (which was in dire need of money for maintenance and housekeeping), $1 million to the Carnegie Art Department, and $2 million to the Technical Schools. It was proposed that Mr. Carnegie agree to duplicate all sums of money bestowed upon the new institution "up to a total amount on your part of $5 million during a five-year period."

There was a suspicion at the time that Mr. Carnegie donated no money to the University because he had expected it to be given his name. McCormick had addressed this problem in a letter to Mr. Carnegie in 1906. The University, he said, really ought to bear the name "The University of Pittsburgh."

But Mr. Carnegie's name would be connected with it forever with its full title: "The University of Pittsburgh upon the Andrew Carnegie Foundation." Colonel Church suggested a possible variation: "The Pittsburgh University upon the Carnegie Institute Foundation."

Mr. Carnegie was not receptive to any of the proposals. He responded in January 1912:

Dear Mr. Church:

To rival the charm and attractions of Princeton, Hamilton, Harvard and other Eastern Universities would be difficult, if not impossible, for any Pittsburgh University, just as it is impossible for the East to rival Pittsburgh's Technical Schools. Here lies her power. Her high position in art and annual exhibitions now in the lead, are exceptional becaus* we hav the funds to bring celebrated artists there as judges and the rite system of awarding prizes. Money draws. New York must soon become preëminent in this, however. A modest university is all we can aspire to and I understand this is steadily being attained. Be comforted. Always yours.

Church, writing to McCormick to express his disappointment, closed with, "Adversity is always a source of strength."

Faced with this rebuff, McCormick set out to raise $3 milion in a broad-based "canvass." To conduct the drive he engaged a man who had first conceived the idea of a professionally planned and managed campaign. He was Charles S. Ward, international secretary of the YMCA, whose plan for financing its buildings had raised $60 million since 1905, half of it under his personal direction. Ward was on loan from the YMCA for the great 1914 endowment campaign. He was pleased with the program he developed for Pittsburgh—especially the electric signs twelve feet high and thirty-six feet long that blazoned "PITT 1787–1912" on hillsides, including Mount Washington and the campus ridge. "Never anywhere," he said, "have I seen such great enthusiasm as is shown by the big business men of Pittsburgh in this campaign. Not only are men of wealth interested in the movement, but the newspapers have shown praiseworthy zeal in promoting this big civic undertaking. Most Pittsburgh citizens feel it is a

matter of local pride with them to subscribe the $3,000,000 in the time allotted." Unfortunately, the campaign raised only $1.8 million. Howard Heinz and Babcock made a trip together to New York to call on Henry C. Frick and Carnegie, but they returned empty handed. The picture was brightened somewhat by a Heinz gift of $100,000 with which to build a wooden structure for student activities.

McCormick visited European universities in the spring of 1914 in the hope that he might introduce into his curriculum courses in foreign trade, European economic and sociological problems, and international relations. His secretary, George Ketchum, a student who knew shorthand and could type 155 words a minute, kept him apprised of developments on the campus. ("Mr. Howe, of the History department, will be married on Friday, I believe, to a Miss White. I shall congratulate him in your name. . . . I enclose a digest of the various reports. Each year it seems more difficult to obtain the reports from the deans, and even yet some of them are lacking. Imagine you are quite interested in the Irish troubles, which seem to be worse than ever just now. The Serbian trouble has awakened considerable interest in the foreign population here.")

McCormick was in Italy on June 28 when a Serbian terrorist assassinated the heir to the Austro-Hungarian throne and his wife. He was in Zurich on July 28 when Austria declared war on Serbia, and in Berlin when the Germans declared war on Russia and prepared to march into Belgium.

Pittsburgh, with its large numbers of immigrants and children of immigrants, was emotionally involved with the terrible events in Europe during the years of American neutrality. There were large numbers of Italians, Irish, Poles, Russians, Hungarians, Serbians, Czechs, and Slovaks, and some of them had associations with an irredentist or revolutionary movement. (The groundwork for the Czechoslovakian republic was to be formed in 1918 in an agreement between the Czechs and the Slovaks in a meeting hall in Pittsburgh.) There was a sizable German population. (It had staged a victory parade in October 1870 at the close of the Franco-Prussian War.) Thus the political life of the community and

---

*Carnegie was an advocate of simplified spelling.

the campus reflected the struggle to reach conclusions on the passionate issues of the day: neutrality, nonintervention, pacifism, military preparedness, anger at loss of lives by German submarine warfare, and the slow shift from nonbelligerence to support for sending aid to Britain, France, and Italy.

There were, at the same time, important and exciting domestic issues and events: the newly imposed federal income tax; the opening of the Panama Canal; Henry Ford's $5.00 wage for an eight-hour day replacing $2.40 for nine hours; the Woodrow Wilson–Charles Evans Hughes presidential campaign; the first transcontinental telephone call, from New York to San Francisco; the first wireless message from a moving train; the bomb explosion at the San Francisco Preparedness Day parade, which killed ten and wounded forty; the Black Tom explosion in Jersey City in July 1916, caused by German saboteurs, which killed two and caused $40 million in damage. There was impassioned debate on the campuses in 1915 when the University of Pennsylvania, in a still-famous case, discharged Scott Nearing, economist and sociologist, for his Socialist and pacifist opinions. All these events were experienced in the shadow of continuing horror at the monstrous loss of lives in the bloodiest battles in human history, at Vimy, Arras, the Marne, Ypres, Cambrai, Verdun, Passchendaele, Jutland, the Somme.

Everything changed on April 6, 1917.

In an unusual development, the University School of Medicine had a field hospital unit ready for service the day after the United States declared war on Germany. This came about because of actions taken earlier by private citizens who opposed President Wilson's neutrality policy and did so by privately training an officers corps. Believing the United States would become involved in the war on the side of Britain and France, they used private contributions to establish a camp at Plattsburgh, New York, for training officers at their own expense and on their own time. Dr. Thomas S. Arbuthnot, dean of the Pitt School of Medicine, and Dr. James D. Heard, senior professor of medicine, adopted the Plattsburgh Plan; they raised $75,000 in private funds to erect a building, enlist and train personnel from surgeons to nurses and orderlies, and equip a complete unit that became famous as AEF Base Hospital 27. The unit was already in service in France, in a school room in Angers, when the first American troops were deployed in France. It started the war with 500 beds and concluded it with 5,000; it treated 19,582 cases that resulted in 277 deaths.

Congress, aware of the trouble caused by a delayed conscription act in the Civil War, enacted a draft law quickly in 1917. All male college students were subject to military training, which at the University of Pittsburgh, for the first year of the war, meant little more than one hour of close-order drill six days a week, without uniforms or weapons, conducted by faculty members who had had some experience in the National Guard. (The students were issued regulation army uniforms on May 26, 1918.) All faculty members were, pro forma, dismissed until a decision could be made on which courses should be retained. In the meantime, 100 faculty members chose voluntary enlistment, 58 of them from the School of Medicine.

On April 11, 1918, the University began to train students as automobile and gas engine mechanics for war-related industrial work; within six months it had classes of more than 2,200 men. On the hillside north of O'Hara Street, the army built seven frame barracks for housing 1,000 men, a mess hall seating 2,000, an administrative building, and a YMCA Hospitality House. The campus was as busy as an anthill. Some classes continued throughout the war. Women students made surgical dressings, knit socks and wristlets, compiled scrapbooks for mailing to soldiers away from home, fashioned a huge service flag, and some, at their own insistence, participated in close-order drill. Celebrities appeared to sell Liberty Bonds. Football heroes—airman Jimmy DeHart was one—returned in uniform to the campus or to Camp Hamilton, the training field at Windber, to visit and swagger a bit.

On September 3, 1918, McCormick was summoned to a two-day conference at Plattsburgh, where he and 524 other college presidents were told that the government was taking over their institutions for the training of officers and technical specialists in the Student Army Training Corps (SATC)

Student soldiers in formation on the lawn before Soldiers and Sailors Memorial Hall, May 17, 1918. In the left background is State Hall, demolished in the early 1970s.

University Archives

program. The presidents and chancellors were to cooperate with the army in erecting barracks and mess halls and in procuring as much as possible of the necessary equipment from civilian sources.

The students already being trained in technical courses were called Section B of the SATC. A second contingent of 1,359 men, called Section A, was to be trained as officers. Some of these men were housed in the barracks, but most were lodged in various rented buildings or parts of buildings in the area: in Logan Armory, a German turnverein, Soldiers and Sailors Memorial Hall, an office building, a large rooming house, and in the fraternity houses, which the brothers had vacated and turned over to the University and the government. Both sections were formally inducted in a ceremony on the steps of Memorial Hall, 6,650 men from three colleges. Chancellor McCormick, who presided, called it the most impressive event since the Civil War.

The next day all class work at the University was

abruptly stopped by a quarantine—a preventive measure taken against a worldwide epidemic of influenza that struck 23,268 persons in Pittsburgh and killed 548,000 in the United States and in its armed forces. The quarantine lasted forty days, during which nothing but outdoor drill was permitted and all but four of the scheduled football games were canceled. The Department of Health lifted the quarantine on November 11, the day Germany surrendered. On November 26 orders were received to cease operations and disband the SATC. By December 21 all the student soldiers were out of the service.

The final count showed 167 faculty members in military service, 930 students, and 1,404 alumni; 5,031 were in the SATC.

The chancellor, the deans, and the department heads made an effort to compress a whole school year into the six months between January 2 and July 1, 1919. Holidays were omitted and spring vacation shortened, but the effort was less than successful, partly because of the complications that came with the return during that period of faculty members and 915 students from the nineteen-month war.

Now the congestion was far worse than it had been in 1914, and the sudden enlargement of the student body brought with it a whole new set of problems. The one alleviating circumstance was the half-dozen army barracks on the campus, which were easily converted to classrooms. These were used for years to come, some of them for several decades, identified always, euphemistically and hopefully, as "temporary."

In 1920, in an unprecedented development, the University's alumni set about to remedy the agonizing shortage of space. They proposed to build on the hillside a large hall that would have thirty-six standardized, identical classrooms, four lecture halls, and sixteen faculty offices. Accordingly, they created an organization with a letterhead: The Alumni Building Campaign; chose a slogan: "Build a Bigger, Better Home for Alma Mater"; set a campaign goal: $600,000; and established a campaign policy: to direct the solicitation solely at graduates and former students. They chose as chairman Colonel Joseph H. Thompson of "The Fighting Tenth,"

who was chairman of the General Alumni Association; Bert H. Smyers as treasurer; Carlton G. Ketchum, who was handling University publicity, as campaign manager; and J. Steele Gow as his assistant. They persuaded thirty or forty alumni to serve on committees for the ten schools, and they named a committee to supervise construction, headed by Floyd Rose.

There were three good reasons why the campaign should not have succeeded. First, the very high percentage of the 8,000 alumni who were under thirty years of age and the high percentage that had been in military service signified that their contributions would be small, since they had not had time to build up their economic strength. Second, it was discovered that the hillside was undercut with coal mines, and some of these began to emit smoke from long-burning fires when the digging started. Third, the campaign managers proposed, with McCormick's consent, to alter the famous Greek Acropolis plan to which the University was committed. Benno Janssen, the runner-up in the architectural competition, designed a long, low building that cut across the axis of Hornbostel's masterpiece. It was also of simpler design, with less fealty to Hornbostel's concept. Hornbostel was furious at this departure from his plan and told Floyd Rose as much. Rose felt that Hornbostel was a great innovator who tended to overlook things like restrooms, and he responded in kind: "Horney, you gave us an eight-story building towering up on the side of a hill that's hardly strong enough to hold what we do have, a flat building. You were going to hold it together with ivy."

Ground was broken on January 26, 1920; the cornerstone was laid in June; the dedication was held on March 31, 1921. The mines were filled while construction progressed. (The last fire was extinguished about a year after Alumni Hall was completed.) The campaign was a success: more than $670,000 was raised, $70,000 over the goal. A bronze plaque in the building reads: "This building was erected by the alumni of the University of Pittsburgh and presented to their Alma Mater as an expression of deepest devotion and as a symbol of their faith in her ability to provide in the fullest measure for the higher training of the young of the nation." Several classrooms were individually dedicated as memorials—for example, to George Alexander McKallip Dyess, professor of history (1906–1913); to Francis Clifford Phillips, professor of chemistry (1875–1920); to Albert Ellis Frost, professor of mathematics and registrar (1895–1917). Other classrooms were presented by prominent alumni and still others by entire classes. There was fierce rivalry for the sixteen offices; those faculty members who were chosen had to double up, including even the venerable Francis Newton Thorpe.

One campaigner attributes the success of the campaign in considerable measure to alumni and former students who for the first time were excited about the University. "I am certain," he says, "that if it had not been for the Pitt athletic development from 1910 on, we would not have come anywhere close to raising what we did. For one thing, we had only one large contribution, one in six figures. It came from the Athletic Committee. It came out of football receipts. $100,000."

Alumni Hall was crowded and noisy from the day it opened, but it provided recitation and lecture space for as many as 2,500 students at a time, and it was to remain for the next fifteen years the University's one major teaching facility. It now (1986) houses the new Surface Science Research Center.

McCormick had intended to serve as chancellor until 1923, when he would be sixty-five, but now he found he had neither "the vital force nor the mental enthusiasm" that he had in earlier years. He was exhausted by his labors, frustrated by some of his disappointments, and appalled at the work that lay before him. The buildings were in disrepair because of overuse and neglect during two years of war. The University was $1 million in debt because of its lands and buildings. One of his faculty, William Charles White, M.D., who, it was thought, wished to be chancellor, was challenging the efficiency and organization of his administration, and he seemed to have the ear of some of the trustees.

And so in July 1919 Dr. McCormick asked for retirement, to take place in January 1920. While his general health was not impaired, he said in a graceful letter of resignation, "I find that I do not have the physical strength to carry on the burden and the responsibility of the chancellorship. . . . It is advisable to secure a younger man, who will both initiate and carry to completion the next state in the development of the University."

To the man who succeeded him he wrote a short note: "I am sorry to miss you, both yesterday and today, when I dropped in to say goodbye.

"I also wanted to bid you to be of good cheer. If things do not move as rapidly as you wish, or the way you wish, stand by, be patient, be wise, be persistent, and in due time the way opens and everything is right again. So it will be with your work at the University. Goodbye and good luck."

As chancellor emeritus, McCormick had an office in State Hall. William Holland would call on him there from time to time, and in voices that could be heard the length of the outside hall they would discuss the policies of their successor. In January 1921 McCormick was trying to raise, "without publicity," a fund of $2 million, which was necessary if the University was to continue its work. In 1927–1928 he spent the winter in Florida in an effort to regain his health. He started to drive north in the spring, was marooned in a blizzard, contracted pneumonia, and died as a result. William Holland conducted the funeral service.

THE PANTHER
FORMED BY THE FACULTY AND STUDENTS OF
THE UNIVERSITY OF PITTSBURGH

In April 1920, on an unknown occasion, the students and faculty form the Pitt Panther.

Alumni Affairs

Book II
1921-1946

It was characteristic of the Jazz Age that it had no interest in politics at all.

F. Scott Fitzgerald
The Crack-up

We are the first nation in the history of the world to go to the poor house in an automobile.

Will Rogers

Admiral Husband E. Kimmel, Commander-in-Chief, U.S. Pacific Fleet on December 7, 1941, at Pearl Harbor: "I knew right away that something terrible was going on, that this was not a casual raid by just a few stray planes. The sky was full of the enemy." Gazing toward his beloved ships with bombers and fighters swooping over them like vampire bats, he saw the "*Arizona* lift out of the water, then sink back down— way down." History had swept past Kimmel with the speed of a movie out of control, beyond human capability to see or comprehend.

Gordon W. Prange,
Donald M. Goldstein,
and Katherine V. Dillon
At Dawn We Slept

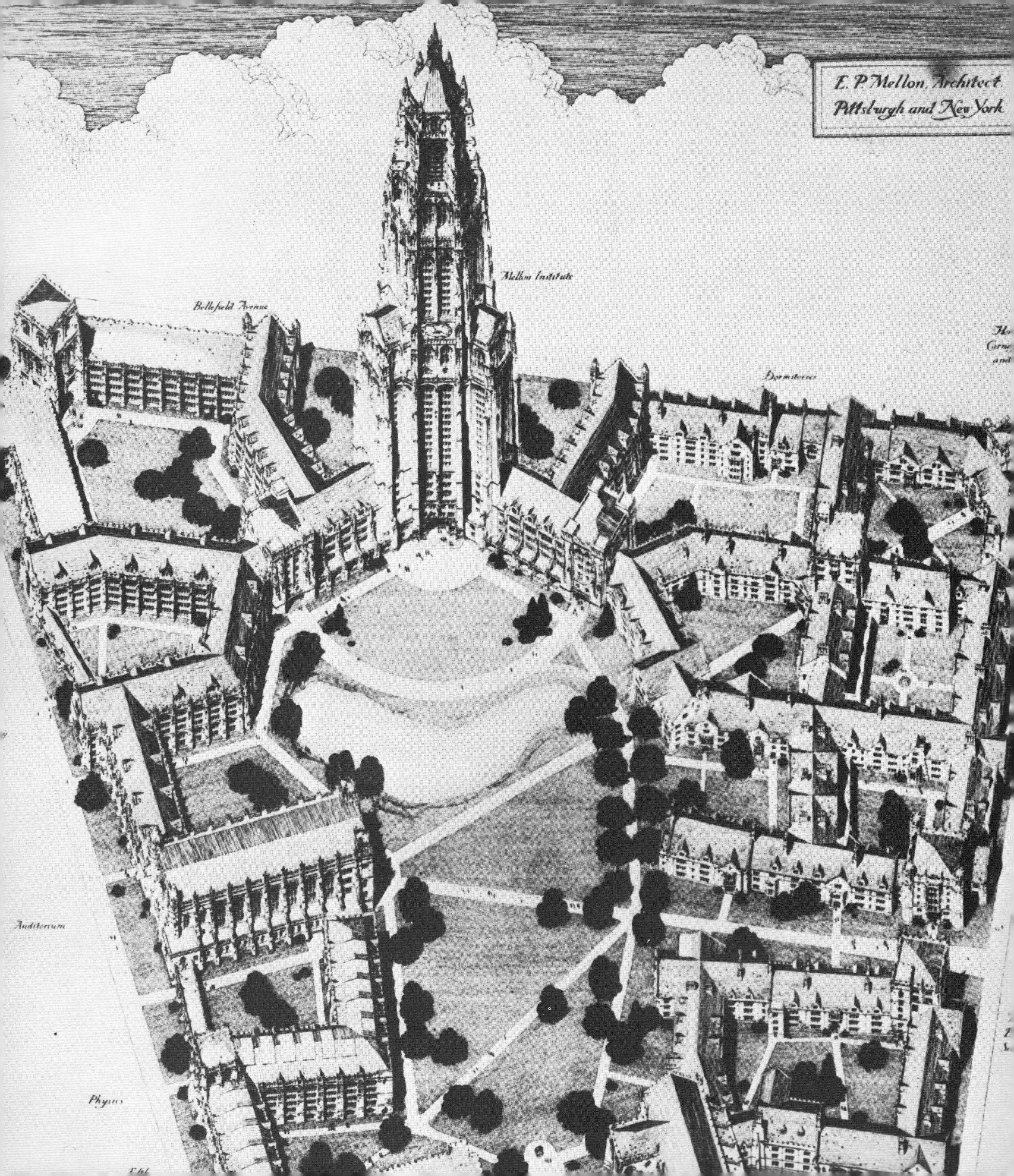

Bellefield Avenue

Mellon Institute

Dormitories

The
Carne
and

Auditorium

Physics

5

"A New Kind of Schoolmaster"

He was a man of great intellectual gifts, tremendous self-confidence and an exceptional imagination, but had very little understanding of people. He was an unusually introspective man, a lonely genius.

Carlton G. Ketchum, Class of 1916, "Pitt: The Adolescent Years," 1971

John Gabbert Bowman, chancellor from 1921 to 1945. Portrait by Elizabeth Shoumatoff.

University Art Gallery

THE trustees began to compile the lists and to make the discreet inquiries that are part of a quiet search for a chancellor. They wanted a man who would develop a modern university, who would bring their institution nearer to the level of the older universities in the East and the large state colleges in the West. They had no feeling that he should be, like almost all his predecessors—McCormick, Holland, MacCracken, McLaren, Riddle, Dyer, Morgan, Bruce—a minister of the gospel.

In October 1920 two of the trustees attended a two-day hospital meeting in Pittsburgh. They were Andrew Jackson Kelly, Jr., president of the Commonwealth Realty Company, and Alfred Reed Hamilton, owner of extensive coal-mining interests in Pennsylvania and West Virginia and publisher of one of the industry's leading trade magazines. They were there to observe and report on the qualities of one of the speakers: John Gabbert Bowman, LL.D. Dr. Bowman—his doctoral degree was honorary—had been president of Iowa State University at age thirty-four—the youngest college president in the country—and now, at forty-three, was the first director of the American College of Surgeons. He talked before various small groups at hospitals, and on the evening of the first day in Pittsburgh he addressed a public meeting in the ballroom of the William Penn Hotel. About seven hundred people were present, some dozens of them laymen on hospital boards. Bowman and the Pittsburgh chapter of the College of Surgeons were promoting a reform program, one point of which was to persuade hospital trustees to accept responsibility for the competence of their hospital staff.

Kelly and Hamilton apparently were favorably impressed with what they saw and heard, for they asked Bowman to dine informally the following evening "with a group of men."

They met in a private room of the Duquesne Club, with about fifteen men present. Bowman knew none of them; he later said he assumed they were probably hospital trustees interested in the financial and medical problems of their institutions. He sat between George Hubbard Clapp, an officer of the Aluminum Company of America, and Andrew W. Mellon, a banker. Neither man, as he remembered, said much. The others from the beginning asked questions—not about hospitals but about education. Is a college education good for everybody? To what extent do colleges accomplish the purposes they set for themselves? What, perhaps, is their greatest weakness? What should be done about it? What did he think about the business sense of college administrators? Specific problems were presented—what would he do about this or that? "The meeting became so lively," Bowman said, "that I missed most of the dinner.

"At about ten o'clock one of the men at the table asked me to step into the hall with him. We went out of the room and walked down the hall toward a window hung with heavy draperies. We had covered only half of the distance to the window, however, when another man of the group opened the door and asked us to come back."

At the table again, Clapp said to him, "These men are trustees of the University of Pittsburgh. For some weeks we have been gathering information about you. If it is agreeable to you, we would like to talk with you about becoming chancellor of the University."

The work of a university president "held no illusions" for Bowman, and he replied that he did not think he would be interested. The conversation continued for another half hour or so. The compensation, he was told then or later, would be $35,000 a year, which he must have known was one of the highest academic salaries in the country. He asked for four or five days to consider the offer.

He struggled with his decision that night on a train ride to Montreal. Three days later he had an appointment with Dr. William James Mayo, who, with his younger brother, had developed the famous Mayo Clinic and who had just retired as president of the College of Surgeons. At an early breakfast at Mayo's house in Rochester, Minnesota, Bowman told "Dr. Will" about the meeting in Pittsburgh. Mayo made no comment, and the talk turned to medicine and hospitals. That afternoon he asked Bowman to take a ride with him. "When we were among the corn fields he said, 'I have been thinking about Pittsburgh. If you were my son I would make you go to Pittsburgh. Do you realize

George Hubbard Clapp as a young man. He was chairman of the Board of Trustees for forty-two years, 1907–1949.

that Pittsburgh is the last place in the United States where there is not a great university and where there could be one? The people, the wealth, the stability—everything is there. You could build there one of the greatest universities of the world. God made you for the job. You must go.'"

Bowman took the train that night to Chicago. As he recalled the event forty-three years later in his *Unofficial Notes,* he was surprised the next morning to see Dr. Mayo walk into his office. "You did not say that you would go to Pittsburgh," Mayo said brusquely. "I decided, as you left, to take the next train and to settle this matter today. Here I am. Here I stay until you agree to go to Pittsburgh." Then, in a "firm but friendly" voice, "Call Pittsburgh on the telephone." Since a round trip between the two cities involved a journey of 770 miles, one may assume that Dr. Mayo must have had other business to conduct in Chicago.

Bowman arrived in Pittsburgh, ready to begin work, early in January 1921. He took a cab to the Pittsburgh Athletic Association, where a room had been reserved for him. Before going to his office, he headed up the steep hillside that was the University campus. "On the way," he said,

I came to one old frame building after another, all Army barracks left from the World War. They needed paint. Many of the wooden steps leading up to the buildings were broken. Working my way through a group of laughing, chattering students, I edged into one of the barracks. There in the floor were several holes big enough for a cat to jump through. A gas stove without a flue hummed with a low tone. Sometimes between classes I introduced myself to a member of the faculty, sometimes I talked with the students. The morning was gone before I got to the top of the hill.

In his office in State Hall he asked to see the treasurer and requested that he bring the budget and the balance sheet with him. Dr. Samuel Black Linhart, treasurer, secretary, and professor of sacred history, appeared with papers in his hands. "He was a rather slight man somewhat stooped, hair almost white, and only by a swift occasional glance would he look at me. Depression was on his face." From Linhart, and later from others, Bowman learned about the problems the University faced.

It was $1.024 million in debt, and the 1920–1921 budget called for expenditures that were $302,015 greater than projected income. The budget had not been in balance since 1916. Enrollment had doubled with the introduction of professional schools and a wave of students that began in 1916; some six thousand of them were crowded into four main buildings and the unplastered pine "temporary" barracks Bowman had inspected. The University needed classrooms, laboratories, offices, equipment, a meeting place for students, more faculty members in the important schools, and more income for larger salaries. It needed an athletic field; it had outgrown its small field house on top of the hill and the very small swimming pool contained therein. Books were needed and a proper place to hold them; in the one-room library in State Hall students sat around long tables with elbows touching elbows. An arrangement had been worked out with the nearby main branch of the Carnegie Library for special use of its facilities, but the Carnegie people wished to see it ended. Convocations, commencements, chapel services, and any other meetings calling for an assembly of students were held in Soldiers and Sailors Memorial Hall. An alumnus of that time recalled, "During the war, we held classes on the steps of buildings when the weather permitted and called some of them off if it rained. We met in the furnace room, literally, of State Hall."

McCormick's drive to bring all the schools and departments to the Oakland campus had not been realized: the Law School was on the tenth floor of the Chamber of Commerce Building downtown, and the School of Pharmacy stood on a bluff some three miles away, overlooking the Monongahela River. The School of Dentistry, fifth in the nation in enrollment, the training place of more than half of all the students studying dentistry in Pennsylvania, was on the campus but in three widely scattered buildings. One bright development was Alumni Hall, which in March of that year would bring into use a number of small faculty offices, four large auditoriums, and thirty-six classrooms—recitation areas for 2,500 students hourly. In a rare, almost unique, tribute to a contribution from the alumni, Bowman declared in his first report to his trustees,

"Both as an expression of the goodwill and cooperation on the part of the alumni and for its intrinsic worth in the headway of the University, the value of the gift seems beyond estimate."

Bowman carried these problems with him when he made a round of visits to his leading trustees. He called first on A. W. Mellon, president of Mellon National Bank. "I was surprised," he said, "to see the bank housed in half a dozen old adjoining buildings, two to four stories high on Fifth Avenue. To the rear of the bank was Andrew Mellon's tiny office." He introduced himself to Mellon as he entered, despite their earlier meetings.

He rose from behind a small desk, a man slender and straight; eyes blue and direct; hair and short moustache gray; and although his face and hands with long slender fingers suggested sensitiveness and inherent fineness, he stood there with a dominant over-all rocklike quality. . . . He shook hands. He did not ask me to sit down. I said that I would like to have some talk with him about the University. In a soft voice but with amazing finality he said that he was busy, that he was not interested, that he did not care to talk about the subject. Any more talk, it seemed then, would make only for more finality of the same sort. I changed the subject and in a short time left the office.

The man was so well dressed that you would not notice his clothes. He had not been unfriendly in that talk; he had not been cordial. Austere, alone, serious—I had not seen so much of these qualities in any man before. He had said, in effect, no; but it seemed somehow to be a revisable no.

He called next on Henry Clay McEldowney, president of the Union Trust Company (a Mellon bank).

He was a short, heavy-set man who looked straight at you. He seemed, as I sat across his desk from him, to be much farther away than a yardstick would tell. "I notice by the records," I told him, "that in the last five years you have not been present at a meeting of the trustees of the University. I wish you would tell me why."

He made no answer. We talked of other things for a minute or two. Then I said, "I asked you a question a moment ago. I want an answer."

"Do you want the truth?" he asked with no smile.

"Yes," I said.

"Well," he said, "the University is so unbusinesslike in financial matters that I do not care to go. The place is run

In the 1920s students crowd the only reading room of the library located in State Hall.

in such a slipshod way that I'm ashamed to be seen inside it. I think that the sheriff is about to take it."

"I understand the words," I told him, and then made some statements about the value of a university to a city. He interrupted—

"You seem to think that if the sheriff took the college it would make a difference in Pittsburgh. We wouldn't even know that the place was gone."

We sat for a rather long time without words. Then I said, "I'm not thinking just now about the finances of a university. I am thinking about the people of a city who

might realize the values of their own heritage, let us say, in medicine, in music and in poetry; who might be more loyal to their government and to their city, more loyal to each other and to those few principles of honor and of decency which we need. I'm thinking that these matters are all banking problems and . . .

"I take back what I just said," Mr. McEldowney interrupted. We both laughed.

He called on the president of a large foundry. The man told him "with a good-natured smile, 'I'm the dog that wears the brass collar. Where's the money for the next payroll? Does your college have a course in that? No, a college is no good to business.'"

He called on Homer D. Williams, president of Carnegie Steel Company, "a tall man of medium weight, his face smooth and tanned, his hair black, his eyes steady, and when he spoke his voice made him your friend." They talked about Pittsburgh, the University, steel mills, and what steelmen thought about a college education. Williams took him that afternoon on a tour of his Duquesne Works. "What hope," Bowman asked, "did these steelmen share with their wives for their children? Would some of their boys become workers in the mill? Yes. Would some of them become physicians, dentists, teachers, metallurgists, attorneys, and engineers? Yes again." Bowman became eloquent. "Why not a steel-mill Robert Burns? Or a steel-mill Bach and a fugue of the mill folks' own in which their griefs, frustrations, joys, hopes, and strength would rise, fuse, glow in victory, like the Bessemer converters at night?" Homer Williams agreed that a steel mill needed a university and a university needed the dynamic force and creativeness of a steel mill.

He called on E. V. Babcock, owner with his brother of extensive lumbering operations, now serving as mayor of the city of Pittsburgh. Babcock fell into the role he affected of a tobacco-chewing roughneck with a vocabulary fitted to a logging camp. "He condemned in a loud voice and with profanity 'the whole damned nonsense of culture.' No, he did not believe in any of it." Bowman protested that culture was not so bad, using profanity quite as earthy "or worse." Where, Babcock asked, had he had a college course in that kind of talk? Bowman told of some work he had done on a Mississippi lumber raft. Babcock forthwith took him to spend the night at Vosemary, his farm at Gibsonia, Pennsylvania, where they sat on the porch and talked until midnight about cows, stars, trees, Wordsworth, and how children see things. On his plate next morning Bowman found a check for $50,000 made out to the University of Pittsburgh.*

John R. McCune, president of Union National Bank, and not a trustee of the University, summoned Bowman to his office and requested that he pay, without delay, principal and interest on an overdue note for $350,000. Bowman pointed out that if the University defaulted and the sheriff took over, the bank would get only a small part of its loan, perhaps 5 percent. "If, however, you and the other creditors stop talking in a harsh way and turn in and help to make a real university in Pittsburgh, you will get payment in full. It is nonsense, all just pure nonsense, that there is not a great university here, a great university out of debt." McCune leaned back in his chair and laughed out loud. "That," he said, "is the most sense, the most business sense, that I've heard come out of the University." He never mentioned the debt again.

In due course the trustees held a formal dinner at the Pittsburgh Athletic Association to introduce the new chancellor to the board. George H. Clapp, chairman, presided. Howard Heinz was there, in charge, since his father's death a year earlier, of the family food processing company. Richard Beatty Mellon, younger brother of Andrew, was there; Mayor Babcock; William Lucien Scaife, whose company, one of the oldest in Western Pennsylvania, manufactured iron and steel tanks. Two leading attorneys were there; two presidents of steel companies; the president of a glass manufacturing company; one Presbyterian minister; and the Right Reverend Courtland Whitehead, bishop of the Protestant Episcopal diocese of Pittsburgh, born in 1842, in the administration of John Tyler, the tenth president. Bowman's description of this event reveals a peculiar flaw in his perception; he seems to have found in the meeting what he saw before he went there. These were business and professional associates of long standing; they belonged to the same clubs; some of them, like Chairman Clapp, were men of varied interests and remarkable accomplishments; some of them had been meeting as trustees years before the University changed its name and

---

*E. V. Babcock was known as the father of the Pitt band, which he had supported for many years. In his will he left a handsome legacy to the band, with the request that between the halves of a home football game it play Stephen Foster's "Beautiful Dreamer" in his memory.

Richard B. Mellon, Class of 1876, younger brother of Andrew and also a trustee.

moved from Allegheny City. Their past investments of time and money, their dutiful service on various committees as shown on the record, indicate that they cared somewhat more about the University than Dr. Bowman believed. But as he saw it, this was a stolid, ill-at-ease group of men. "Dignity," he said, "came in with them." There was none of the "lively talk" of the October meeting. The conversations during the dinner "did not get much beyond the weather." The men, the setting, and the formal manners "might all have come out of a Victorian picture book."

He sat between Clapp and R. B. Mellon. The table was cleared and Bishop Whitehead opened the meeting with a prayer. One of the trustees, "the spokesman for the occasion," gave a ten-minute address. "Excellent reports," he said, "have come to me about the impression Chancellor Bowman is making in Pittsburgh." He mentioned a talk the chancellor had made to the students; it had been well received. Then, turning directly to Bowman: "If in the next year or two you could raise, let us say, $100,000, the future of the University would be assured."

Bowman rose to respond. After the usual amenities and some talk about the meaning of a college education to a boy and a girl, he said, "I had not expected that the subject of money would come up at this meeting. On that subject I do not know my way around at the University. Talk about dollars, however, is up. A specific amount has been stated, $100,000. That sum would about pay the interest on the University's debt for one year. Looking forward, would that sum be enough? From what little I know, the least sum that could be rightly mentioned as our present need is, let us say, $15,000,000."

He felt several small jerks on his coat. This, a signal from R. B. Mellon, clearly meant *stop*. He ended his talk and sat down. "More dignity settled around the table. The whole room seemed to grow cold. The meeting quickly came to an end."

The next morning he called on R. B. Mellon at his office. He was greeted, he said, with a happy, cordial smile.

"What was the matter last night?" he asked. "Do you think $15,000,000 is too much for a fresh start at the University?"

"No," Mellon said. "But there's no use to talk about sums such as $15,000,000 to those men. They don't understand your *educational* language." Some silence followed.

Bowman: "Please, will you keep on talking?"

Mellon, with a laugh: "Talk about a plan—a plan, not money. Get a plan."

"As I was leaving the office a little later he repeated with an even more cordial smile, 'Get a plan for that fresh start. Talk about a plan.'"

Bowman wanted to know how much space he needed for classrooms, laboratories, and undergraduate social activities—how much now and how much more in ten years' time. He asked John Weber, professor of mechanical engineering, to find out. Weber (his nickname was "Heinie" and he always carried with him a pocket-size volume of classical literature) was thirty-six years old and looked to be about twenty; he was to play an important administrative role at the University over the next quarter of a century. He and Bowman made a list of eight universities that should be visited and measured: Ohio State, Chicago, Michigan, Illinois, Northwestern, Syracuse, Harvard, and Columbia. Weber was gone for three weeks. He returned with graphs on enrollment and physical facilities of those institutions and the median space they provided for each student in the various departments. Pitt was substantially behind them; its science laboratories, for example, were operating in about one-sixth the space of the others. Weber estimated the need for space for corresponding departments at the University and then projected the needs ten and twenty years ahead. Pitt needed about 13 million additional cubic feet for undergraduate courses. The cost would be about $11 million, exclusive of the price of land and equipment. Bowman concluded that for physical improvements he must raise $15 million, the amount he had named at the January dinner. He wrote the various figures on small cards and carried them with him as he proceeded to rebuild and reform the University of Pittsburgh. They would be ammunition he would use to carry out the plan he was trying to formulate.

The plan. Thirteen million cubic feet of space . . . $15 million for buildings and land. Seeking to discover the causes of the University's poverty, he asked himself questions. Why had the city, a community of wealth and industry, been so indifferent to the University's need for money? "Have the people of Pittsburgh forgot that men for thousands of years have searched for means to train youth into clear thinking and responsible maturity? Have they lost interest in the strategy of human progress?" Almost every day for more than a month he talked with R. B. Mellon and was helped by "his smile and his words of encouragement. He was a natural man with natural, strong, intuitive sense."

He hit upon the plan early in March, after hardly more than two months at the University. "There it was," he wrote, "natural and simple, and, as it

seemed to me, the inevitable thing. . . . It was like a psalm, a psalm that would tell of the courage and spirit of Pittsburgh." And again: "Sometimes the plan brought a tremble of ecstasy as it stood out in sunrise colors and, as it seemed, in elemental rightness." The plan was not an accident, not "a flare up." It was born out of his experiences, "from the woods and the river [in Iowa], part of it from the talk . . . of Prospero on 'an uninhabited island' and from the mystery of lyrics such as 'John Anderson, my Jo.'" Part of it arose, too, from his early interest in and "slight acquaintance . . . gathered mostly from Ruskin" with Gothic architecture.

"An architect could make stones talk. . . . Why not record in stone what Pittsburgh, an Inland Empire, really is? Why not put up a building which itself will tell of the spirit of Pittsburgh? Such a building, if it were to express intense emotion, would necessarily be high. A high building, a tower—a tower singing upward that would tell the epic story of Pittsburgh. A tower—why not build a tower?"

He sought more information, presumably from John Weber. Would 13 million cubic feet be enough space for a tower five to six hundred feet high? The answer was yes.

He asked himself: Where is the site? Such a building obviously could not be erected on the hillside campus. He would abandon once and for all the McCormick-Hornbostel plan for the hillside Acropolis.

For weeks he had been prowling the areas that surrounded his campus, walking with a gait that is remembered today as somewhat like that of a not-ungraceful long-legged bird. He returned always to the undeveloped, level, rectangular plot known as Frick Acres. It lay one long block south of the campus at the heart of what was becoming the city's new Civic Center, between Fifth and Forbes avenues, two main arteries of traffic that ran east and west. Some 150,000 people passed that site daily. On its fourteen acres were several houses, two run-down Victorian mansions, two truck gardens, some tennis courts, the rest open fields. A ravine or gully ran the length of the eastern end, along Bellefield Street; it would serve admirably to take the earth excavated by a crew that would dig the foundation for a tall building. Around and across from the block stood imposing public and semipublic structures: the Schenley Hotel; the Pittsburgh Athletic Association; the Masonic Temple; two churches; Carnegie Institute with its museum of natural history, art gallery, music hall, and library; and the plaza leading into Schenley Park.

This land had belonged to Mary Schenley and then to Henry Clay Frick, who had died in 1919; it was now in the hands of the trustees of the Frick estate. It was unquestionably the most valuable unused land in the whole city. Bowman walked around it almost every day, around and across, across again and around and across.

He asked A. J. Kelly, Jr., the expert in real estate: Is the land for sale? If it is, for how much? Kelly replied: the lot is not spoken for; the price is $1.5 million. And later: There are plans to place the Schenley Apartments there, five large buildings, companion pieces to the Schenley Hotel. The Frick trustees, however, would consider with him what purpose he might have for the land before they sold. They would "dally" the sale for a while.

Now more questions arose—about design, about building materials. "Stone? What kind of stone? Did a suitable bed of rock for a foundation exist under the surface of the lot? If so, at what depth? How do you know? What would a high wind do to such a tower unprotected by other high buildings? Would a tower function as well for a college as would a low building? What about noise and crowding of students around the elevators? Or noise anywhere in the building? Could calm and inspiration live in a high building? Could a tower be a home of good manners rather than a pushing and a shoving among students and teachers?"

He needed a drawing of the tower. For that he needed an architect, "a sunrise type of man who could put such great adventure into a picture that Pittsburgh would say—'yes.'" He wrote to the deans of seven schools of architecture, described the kind of building he wanted, and asked for the names of architects best qualified to design it for him. The men most often named in the replies were Ralph Adams Cram of Boston, Bertram Grosvenor Good-

hue of New York, and Charles Zeller Klauder of Philadelphia.

Goodhue was ill (he died within three years). Bowman called at Klauder's office at 1416 Chestnut Street, Philadelphia. Klauder was civil, he listened, and he asked questions, but he hardly concealed his skepticism and lack of interest. In Pittsburgh a few days later, R. B. Mellon produced a letter from Klauder. A man named Bowman, Klauder wrote, had called on him and "talked about a rather impossible building. What sort of man is he? Is he responsible? Will people follow his lead?"

Bowman explained that he had asked Mr. Klauder for some help in connection with a plan for the University. How, Mellon asked, should he answer the letter?

"Tell him," Bowman said in one of his rare flashes of humor, "that I am the greatest man in Pittsburgh and that people here will do whatever I want." Mellon laughed and said, "I'll do just that."

R. B. Mellon was the first Pittsburgher to whom Bowman described his dream of erecting a tall building, a skyscraper, in the middle of Frick Acres:

A building . . . to rise 500 feet or more above the grass; to rise and to express by parallel lines and sixty degree arches the heart and soul of education. Courage and spirituality—stones could be made to express such values of character. Parallel lines going up and up—they would express courage, fearlessness. The building was to be cut off flat at the top—that would suggest that the lines could go higher if they wanted to. They were not afraid. By lines, arches, and great height, the building, with open space all around, would suggest, by its outside, the character that ought to be in an educated man. The building, perfect in all details of material and of design, would be a symbol of life on the campus. It would tell Pittsburgh every day of these values. It would unify Pittsburgh into a community conscious of its character. A workman or a doctor or a banker would look at the building and take off his hat and say, "Whatever that thing means, I want it in my boy!" And no student could be so dumb but that he would at some time feel the lines and arches cry out to him a powerful note of victory and adventure. Yes, it could be done!

As I grew a bit intense in the story, [R. B. Mellon] chuckled a little. He said, "You might have an idea there." He sent for the Pittsburgh Plat Plan Book and studied the

Frick Acres in 1924, from the roof of the Pittsburgh Athletic Association on Fifth Avenue. Carnegie Institute is in the background.

fourteen-acre site. He asked, "Can you think of any reason why classes and laboratories should not be in a high building?"

"No."

"I think that's right. Are the buildings at Oxford good buildings for a college?"

"Yes, wonderfully good for their day. They told a story in stone of what medieval England wanted—escape from confusion, war, rats, poverty. Those low, ivy-covered buildings interpret an era that is gone."

They talked of Oxford, the meaning of college to the young man and woman, the meaning of a college to Pittsburgh. Bowman told Mellon that he had come to him sooner than he had intended because some white stakes had been placed at various points on Frick Acres. The Frick trustees could not be expected to wait forever. R. B. Mellon made no promise.

He next called on Homer Williams and "with as much fire as I could put into the plan I told him about it." When he stopped talking, Williams put his feet on top of his desk and leaned back with his hands clasped behind his head. After a considerable silence he said, as though talking to himself, "God, why not!" Sitting up, he added, "Do you want to make a headache for youself all the time? That's what you're doing."

Bowman said, "Yes or no?"

Williams said, "Yes. There's enough sense and drama enough in the idea to put it over. That's how it strikes me. What a drama! Nothing else that I can think of would so stir Pittsburgh. Industries, business, individuals, associations, clubs—all would help. They couldn't afford not to help!"

In these interviews, Bowman realized, the idea, the plan, was merely a theoretical one. "It was all off yonder; something for the imagination to play with, not much more." With A. W. Mellon the proposition would be different. To start with, it would involve a gift from him of $1.5 million for the land. "The 'feel' of the project, when I saw myself presenting it to him, was not good." He saw A. W. Mellon several times a week, discussing University business, There was some increase in cordiality, but Bowman still did not consider his plan "talkable."

One morning early in 1921, Mellon said, "Mr. Harding has asked me to become Secretary of the Treasury. I've been thinking about the matter. The idea is attractive. To end my career in the service of the country seems like the fulfillment of a long wish." Some days later he said, "I've decided to go and I'm busy putting the house here in order." He would turn the bank over to his younger brother and would resign from the boards of fifty-one companies and corporations, including the Aluminum Company of America, the Carborundum Company, Gulf Oil, Koppers, and Pittsburgh Coal. While he was in the service of the government, his pay would be $12,000 a year.

In the meantime, in his office as chancellor, Bowman was following a tireless, dynamic, and effective course of reorganization and reform:

● He closed six departments in the School of Education: nature study and gardening, music, fine and industrial arts, household economy, teacher training in physical education, and commercial education. Some 170 courses were thereby discontinued.

Through an arrangement he made with Carnegie Institute of Technology (so renamed in 1912), that school took over much of the work of those courses and many of their instructors.

● He discontinued many courses of small registration, especially in the College.

● He reduced the salaries of part-time faculty members of the School of Medicine, lowering his payroll cost $16,500. The members, he said in his report to the trustees, "accepted the reductions in good spirit."

● In his first year he called for and received the resignations of fifty-three faculty members.

● He made reforms in curricula and in organization. Among other changes, he transferred the first two years of engineering, mines, economics, and education—all professional courses except dentistry and pharmacy—to the College. He made a bachelor's degree a requirement for admission to the Law School. He created the position of dean of men.

● The state legislature appropriated $900,000 for the University for the years 1921 and 1922, an increase of $147,000 over the amount given for the previous biennium. R. B. and A. W. Mellon made a gift of $35,000 for current expenditures. With this added income and savings of more than $200,000, the budget for the school year 1921–1922 had a small surplus.

None of these economies was done on A. W. Mellon's advice. He was aware of the debt and the deficit, of course, remarking on one occasion with distaste, "It is all unbusinesslike!" When he was told of the new budget and its black-ink balance, "he showed some interest." The interest caused him to discuss with Bowman his problems with the Mellon Institute of Industrial Research, which, he said, was losing about $100,000 a year in its association with the University. (The loss, Mellon said, "was not in accord with my agreement.") He asked Bowman to take over management of the institute. When Bowman did not accept, he "insisted that I see what could be done." Bowman "made some study of the situation" and appointed as director Dr. Edward R. Weidlein, who had been acting director during and since the war. In 1921, as part of Bowman's reorganization plan, the institute was transferred to the control of the University. It had a balanced budget at the end of that year. Mr. Mellon was pleased.

With money from some source that is not known, Bowman bought the Porter estate in September 1921—twelve acres along the north side of Fifth Avenue, a westward extension of the campus. He paid $182,500 for the land, intending it from the first as the future site of a complex of hospitals—a medical center.

The chancellor's record of accomplishment in those first months appears all the more remarkable when an extraordinary circumstance is considered—a development that was not widely known then and is now long forgotten. Beginning in April 1921 and continuing for the next year and a half, Bowman spent several days of each week in Washington. He was there on a special assignment for A. W. Mellon that had nothing to do with the affairs of the University of Pittsburgh.

He had received a request relayed to him by R. B. Mellon to meet with A. W. on the morning of March 16 in his office in the Treasury Building. The secretary of the treasury explained that the Sixty-sixth Congress had just passed Public Act 384 with an appropriation of $18.6 million. The act called for a program of hospitalization for soldiers disabled by tuberculosis and mental and nervous disorders. The program was to be carried out under the direction and supervision of the secretary of the treasury. The secretary was appointing a committee of four "Consultants on Hospitalization." He had named three very distinguished physicians, choosing as his chairman William C. White, former professor of medicine at the University of Pittsburgh, McCormick's opponent there, now medical director of the Tuberculosis League of Pittsburgh.

"I made considerable inquiry," Mellon said to Bowman, "to find the right men with experience in such work. From various quarters your name was recommended, but I did not realize until a few days ago that that man was the same one I knew in Pittsburgh.

"There is great pressure that additional hospital facilities be provided without unnecessary delay. Would you serve as one of a committee of four to help me in this matter?"

Bowman weighed the added work against the advantages of the assignment. He had huge responsibilities at his new post in Pittsburgh, but he would be doing a service for a person important to the University, one who was only now being recognized nationally as one of the two or three wealthiest men in America. Fortunately, under the circumstances, he had no interest in anything but work—no hobbies, little social life, few friends, few obligations in a marriage that was being maintained minimally for the sake of appearances. He accepted the assignment.

Unfortunately, on the other hand, two of the consultants were passive members of the committee, and so the work devolved almost entirely on Bowman and White. For the next eighteen months Bowman saw Mellon frequently, sometimes in company with other members, sometimes alone.

"Time and again," he said,

I saw Mr. Mellon, but none of the occasions offered even half of a right opportunity to talk about the University. After about ten days I determined to make an occasion for the talk; and although the mission seemed to me as bad as poison, one afternoon at about four o'clock I went to his office.

As I entered the office, Mr. Mellon looked up from his desk. His hair was gray, grayer than usual, it seemed; his face was gray; and he looked very tired. . . . Over his desk were a dozen or more piles of letter-sized papers. Usually he kept his desk clear. I walked close to his desk, looked at him and then at the papers. "I wish I could help you," I said.

Mellon said, "You can," and asked him to write answers to some important letters for his signature. Bowman distinguished himself as a letter writer, exactly catching Mellon's style and thought processes, and he found himself with a new duty. But he did not raise the matter of the purchase of Frick Acres nor the plan for a high building.

"Word came that Mr. Mellon wanted to see me. I went. 'Perhaps,' he began, 'you could help me find a man whom I need.' Then he stated in detail the qualities he wanted in the man.

"'A large order,' I said. 'May I have a few days before I answer?'

"'No,' he said. 'What I want is that you come here and live close with me in this work. They can get another man at the University. It will be to your advantage to come—much to your advantage.'"

Bowman was pleased at the invitation and expressed his thanks, but he declined to abandon his post at the University.

In the months of 1921 and 1922, when Bowman was constantly in and out of his office in Washington, A. W. Mellon was troubled by one of the deep emotional experiences of his life. In 1912 he and his wife, Nora McMullen Mellon, daughter of a prosperous family of brewers in Hertfordshire, England, had been divorced after twelve years of marriage. Andrew Mellon had lately reestablished a friendly relationship with Nora—a partial reconciliation carried on by letters and telephone calls. Now he was begging "dearest Norchen" for a complete reconciliation leading to remarriage, putting much of the blame for their "years of contention" on himself, asking and offering forgiveness. A letter to Nora of this period, recently revealed, is an astonishing document, a beautifully written and still moving expression of love and contrition. ("I have been sadly wrong. . . . The old love was in my heart even while I was so obtuse and blind, and it makes me heartsick to think of you in all this time suffering so sadly alone. . . . I want to be helpful to you now and always.") Readers of Bowman's various reminiscences have tended to discount the philosophical discussions, the high-level exchange of abstract ideas, he claimed to have had with A. W. Mellon; they were quite out of character; they were simply not credible coming from the ice-cold banker and businessman Mellon was known to be. This one letter to Nora, published in 1978 but apparently little noticed, gives credibility to Bowman's text. It also would seem to call for an overdue reassessment of Andrew W. Mellon, despite his reserved, austere appearance, as a sensitive, warm-blooded, troubled, decent man.

One afternoon Bowman at last brought up the subject of the high building and the need to buy Frick Acres. Mellon listened, but after less than a minute he interrupted. "What," he asked, "is the cost of the lot?" Bowman told him.

"How much is the university debt?" Bowman told him.

"How much would the building cost?"

"About $11,000,000."

"The whole matter is so impractical," Mellon said, "that I ask you not to mention it to me again."

"I am a bad salesman," Bowman said, "but I have an idea." He spoke of the meaning that could be put into a high building.

You grasp the financial side. That is important. But it is only part of the story. If the plan gets off on the right foot, the people of Pittsburgh will pay the bills.

If the youth of Pittsburgh grow up with commonplace abilities and commonplace loyalties, what is the future of Pittsburgh?

A boy needs to have little examples of the good life about him: the parallel lines that express courage, and arches that call out to him the victory of understanding and the joy of adventure in a non-material world. He needs a teacher who says good morning to him in a way that means, "Thank God that you are here." The boy, before he gets to the far end of the hall, will feel kindness grow within himself; fresh kindness and a wider view.

He talked, standing, for at least half an hour. Mellon listened. He did not say yes or no.

During the next three months he talked about twice a week with Mellon about the University and about Pittsburgh and about the Lot. He saw him sometimes at breakfast at the Willard Hotel, sometimes at lunch, sometimes at his office.

He seemed to attach no importance to the probable sale of the Lot. I did not think of it at the time, but I believe now that he had arranged that the sale be further dallied.

On one occasion at his office I had pushed rather hard for an answer. . . . Mr. Mellon said, "You want to put up a high building. Colleges have never been built that way. You want me to be a pioneer or a frontiersman in college building. I do not want to be a frontiersman in anything. In business I always let the other man have that part."

"Well, anyway," I said, "the idea is not wrong or it is not right because it pioneers. To your statement, however, there is no answer."

Usually he would plan for hours what he would say to Mellon at their next meeting. Then he would put on cards various facts, dates, and figures in

Andrew W. Mellon, financier, secretary of the treasury, art collector, trustee of the University.

order to answer questions he thought might be asked. "The idea," he said,

was not bad. On one occasion, Mr. Mellon spoke of his interest in chemistry. "How many chemists have been graduated from the University?" he asked. I gave him the exact number for as many years back as we had records. Then I took from my pocket a card which listed the number of Pitt chemists employed in each of the laboratories in the Pittsburgh District. He looked at the card for a long moment. "How did you happen to have this card in your pocket?"

"Because I thought you might ask the question," I said. . . .

Days wore into weeks and months. Try as I would, I could get no conclusion—at least not the one I wanted—from Mr. Mellon. Finally, I made an appointment to see him one Thursday afternoon at four o'clock. He knew what the appointment was about. All day the preceding Wednesday—morning, afternoon, and evening, at the Cosmos Club—I thought about the interview. I made an outline of what I would say; made the outline on cards. . . .

Four o'clock came. Mr. Mellon looked up, tired. I reviewed quickly most of what, on various occasions, I had told him. I talked about the desire to live and the mystery of it; about the necessity of art in life and about the necessity of faith and intelligence. . . .

"Education," I went on, "is poor stuff at best when carried on among ugly surroundings. . . . I want classrooms with master-made chairs in them; chairs not arranged in rows, but grouped informally about a teacher's chair; doors, door-knobs, and hinges that tell that workmen left their souls in these things; and a fireplace with a fire in it. . . .

"You are talking impractical extravagance," he said. . . .

Hours went by. How the time went, I don't know. Mr. Mellon walked back and forth by the windows. . . . Finally he took out his watch by the window and said, "Eight o'clock—I was to be a guest at dinner tonight. It is too late to go."

He walked to me and put his hand on my shoulder. "I will give you the Lot," he said. Without taking his hand from my shoulder he added, "You are the most persistent man I ever met."

"I'm sorry," I said, "about the dinner and about being so persistent. But tell me, if I had not been persistent would you have given me the land?"

"No," he answered. Then, taking a few steps backward, he continued, "I know now that I have done the right thing. But tomorrow, when I try to explain what I have done, I can not explain. . . ."

When Mr. Mellon said that he would give the Lot, that meant that he and his brother, R. B. Mellon would give the Lot. They did. But Mr. A. W. was not in accord with the idea of the high building. There was too much pioneering in it, and to this he held.

In December 1921 Bowman asked A. W. Mellon to pay the debts of the University. "I told him that I wanted a chance to start 'not from a hole in the mud.' I said that 'only a man who wants no thanks for such a gift would pay the debts. You are the only such person there is.' Mr. Mellon did not seem to appreciate this compliment. Some days later, however, in Pittsburgh, I was talking with R. B. Mellon. He said, 'What did you do to Andy? He came here and went around to the various banks and signed his name on the backs of all the University's notes.' This cost the brothers about $600,000."

6

The Campaign

My life is tied up in the idea that the proposed structure will be the most beautiful and outstanding building ever erected. I am confident that Pittsburgh will build it.

John Gabbert Bowman, in a letter to Charles Zeller Klauder, December 2, 1924

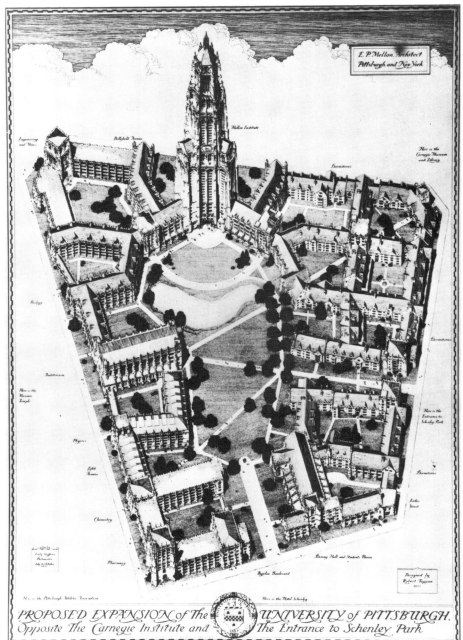

An early (1923) conception of John Bowman's "tall building" as cathedral, with connecting buildings handled in the quadrangle tradition of Oxford and Cambridge. The architect was Edward Purcell Mellon, nephew of A. W. and R. B. Mellon. Bowman rejected the plan.

JOHN BOWMAN now had Frick Acres for his tall building . . . he owned additional land on which to build a medical center . . . the University debt was paid . . . student enrollment was up . . . and his expenditures were within income. These achievements he had worked in his first eighteen months in office, but they were like foothills compared to the mountain that lay before him. In his projected building program he was setting out to do something that had never been done before: to erect a fifty-two story structure of Gothic design, one-eighth of a mile high, the tallest steel-frame masonry building in the world, in the middle of an empty field. He was erecting it, moreover, for the uses of education, not of commerce.

To accomplish this goal, he would first have to develop a design that would satisfy him, satisfy his architect, and startle and capture the imagination of anyone else who saw it. He would next have to prove that the structure could be built, that its engineering was sound, and that it would serve the purposes of a proper schoolhouse. He would then have to raise $10 million to build it.

To accomplish this, he would need the support of his alumni and his trustees. But he had alienated many of his alumni, including the most powerful, because he had been too busy to see them or attend their meetings. And a number of his trustees, perhaps even a majority, were saying that his plan was impractical, unacademic, or dangerous, the cost was too high, the maintenance too expensive, and the size of the building monstrous. The trustees were conservative businessmen and professional people, and they had an understandable dread of failure and of being made to look foolish.

And to accomplish this, he would have to mount a fund-raising campaign (the phrase was a new one at the time) that would collect more money than any American community had ever voluntarily contributed at one time to a civic project. Every movement of the campaign would have to be perfectly planned and carried out to sustain interest and to achieve maximum effect on the people of Western Pennsylvania.

He began with three resolves. He would not go to the Mellons for the money; they had given enough and should not be asked to give more until others had shown their interest in the project by contributing to it. He would not build with borrowed money and so would not start anything until the cash to pay for it was in hand. And he would make this a city-wide, even a regional, undertaking. The tall building would be "an inspiration, a witness to the spirit of hope and achievement of Pittsburgh, both to itself and to the world." It would be a great central symbol that would unite the community in a massive common effort.

The chancellor traveled again to Philadelphia on February 12, 1924, talked with Charles Z. Klauder, and retained him as his architect. Klauder had never designed a skyscraper, but he was, after Ralph Adams Cram, the foremost American student of collegiate Gothic design and, at forty-nine, the country's leading architect in college buildings, with well-known works at Yale, Princeton, Cornell, Brown, Wellesley, and the whole complex of new Gothic buildings at Duke University. He agreed to prepare "exhibition drawings" for $6,000 and to follow Bowman's charge "to concentrate his thought, skill and imagination on design for the high building." He thought he could "show how stones could be put together with the dignity of a temple" and yet in such a way that, rising to the sky, they would "sing of courage and give delight."

Bowman some weeks later saw Klauder's first design in a drawing about five feet high. "It struck me," he said, "as a picture merely of a tall apartment house with an overhanging roof. It was neither a temple nor an expression of courage." He restrained himself for a few minutes before he expressed his disappointment. He described all over again the whole history and idea of the great plan. At the end of an hour Klauder said he would try again.

The next meeting was equally empty, though Klauder insisted that his drawing was "most excellent architecture." "It may be excellent architecture," Bowman responded, "but it is not a thing I can offer Pittsburgh. It is nothing that Pittsburgh would buy. You still haven't got the idea."

The trial attempts, the meetings, the rejections, the discussions continued throughout 1924. John

E. P. Mellon's design for the campus included this "proposed chapel on Fifth Avenue as Viewed from the Campus." It would have stood close to the street, midway between Bellefield Avenue and Bigelow Boulevard.

In 1932 Charles Z. Klauder proposed that this half-Gothic, half-Renaissance structure—for administrative offices and classrooms—be located on Forbes Avenue, south of and between the Cathedral and Heinz Chapel.

Weber spent much of his time in Philadelphia working with Klauder and consulting with other engineers and with contractor-builders on the East Coast—so much time, in fact, that Bowman wrote him, "I am afraid now that you will visit Pittsburgh only on occasional weekends." Klauder, at Bowman's suggestion, spent some months traveling in Europe in search of ideas and perhaps of a little peace. Albert A. Klimcheck, one of Klauder's associates, later the resident architect of the University of Pittsburgh, said in 1954, "None of us was ever hopeful of satisfying Dr. Bowman."

After still another disappointing session, Klauder asked Bowman to have dinner with him at his home in a suburb near Germantown.

After dinner we sat on the floor in his living room, he

with a big drawing board with a pile of paper on it. The man had exceptional ability to draw freehand. He drew a picture of a building, just the barest outline of it.

"Does your building look like this?" he said.

"No, I'm sorry, that is not it." He threw it away.

"Well, how would this do?" he asked, making another sketch.

"He kept that up until 1:00 or 2:00 o'clock in the morning. The floor was pretty well covered with sketches. He was getting pretty cross, and so was I. We both stood up. He walked to a phonograph and put on a record that happened to be on the top of the pile. It was the Magic Fire Music from *Die Walküre*.

The orchestra was filling the room with sound. The music went up to a climax very soon, until it seemed that it could go no higher. But it did go higher, and higher again, and came to climax after climax. Was it possible the music could go on? The music answered by going on. On and on, the music finally rose to the burst of the Magic Fire. Tired, we both had listened.

"One climax after another!" I said. "The music is the building. And it did not get its height, its meaning, its awful power by one leap. It took many. Isn't each leap a buttress, a buttress on a tower?

No. 103

"Spread the bottom buttress way out so that it looks like a big, solid stone, strong, heavy, substantial. And then the tower goes out of that."

We had been sitting on chairs through the Magic Fire, but we went to the floor again. Mr. Klauder drew a shaft with buttresses. Hours went by. We were excited.

About 4:00 o'clock it was time I got home. I walked about a mile to the station at Germantown. I was not tired. For the first time after two years of effort and discouragement it seemed to me that we had really made a start.

Bowman had also asked Klauder to design near the center of the main floor a Commons Room roughly to be 100 feet by 200 feet by 60 to 70 feet high with stone arches overhead, the whole room to be of stone. "The room was to be the heart and soul of the building. It would be too large for crowding and confusion. It was to be the home of simplicity and of good manners." Klauder was to draw a room "with walls opening on corridors of the first three or four floors. On the other side of the corridors are to be classrooms. Put into the stone arches the spirituality that belongs with education. Draw a room that will so grip a boy that he will never enter it with his hat on." When Klauder produced no design of the room, Weber was told to spend even more time in Philadelphia "to answer questions and, with tactful insistence, to keep the work in motion."

After a week or two, Bowman went east to see the first drawings of the Commons Room. Weber advised him at breakfast that Klauder had expended much effort on them and believed they were just the right solution for the room. "If you do not approve this plan," he said, "I think he will refuse to try again."

Bowman did not approve Klauder's drawing. The room was designed to be seventeen feet high and the floor was cluttered with pillars. He tried to say calmly that the room was not at all what he had in mind.

"What you want," Klauder said, "is the waiting room of a mid-western railroad station."

"What you want . . . seems to be the cloistered basement of the chapel at Assisi. We need spaciousness—60 to 70 feet of height."

"There's no use to discuss such a room," Klauder said. "The engineering problems would be too difficult."

John Weber was sent forthwith to New York City with a set of plans to consult H. G. Balcom, a leading structural steel engineer. (He would, in time, do the engineering for the Empire State Building and Rockefeller Center.) He returned with Balcom's word that, yes, a Commons Room seventy feet high could be put into a building, but it would be very expensive. Two concrete and steel pillars about twelve feet in diameter would have to be built into the earth down to solid rock. A heavy steel plate would rest at ground level on the top of each pillar. From each plate the heaviest steel beams probably ever put into construction would rise and carry the weight of the vault and the rooms above it.

Klauder agreed to try to design a Commons Room sixty to seventy feet high. He was not, Bowman observed, in a happy mood.

The drawing was nearing its final form in the summer of 1924. No public announcement had been made about the building or the plans for use of Frick Acres, though interest and curiosity were fairly high. Finding among his trustees a diminishing enthusiasm for his plan, Bowman on March 24, 1924, formed a citizens committee "to implement the strength of the trustees" in considering their building program. It had thirty-five members and an executive committee of eighteen that had on it four or five persons, mostly younger men, who favored his plan.

The members of this committee proposed, and the trustees concurred, that the time had come for action. They authorized $50,000 for the start of a

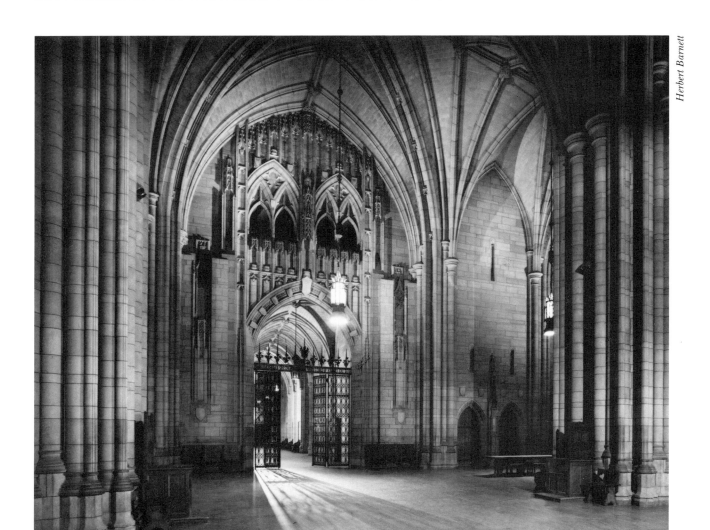

Herbert Barnett

The Commons Room, Bowman told his architect, "must be the heart and soul of the building. . . . Draw a room that will so grip a boy that he will never enter it with his hat on."

fund drive, but they knew that no drive was possible without an announced purpose and goal, and so they decided to hold a large announcement dinner on the evening of Friday, November 6. For this occasion, which was to take place in the University Club, Klauder and Weber produced a one-foot-high plaster model of the tall building. They mounted drawings for display and prepared "lantern slides" for projection on a screen. Bowman wrote a pamphlet about the building and prepared a nine-page press release for use the morning after the dinner, complete with pictures of the tall building and the names and positions of all members of the Executive Committee of the Citizens' Committee. The first copy of the pamphlet was inscribed and sent to President Calvin Coolidge. All the trustees were invited, as well as the members of the Citizens' Committee, the professors on the faculty, members of the press, and as many other leading citizens as the room would accommodate.

The dinner itself went off well, with the maximum number of people present. When the tables were cleared, Bowman rose to tell his guests about the plan, the location and purpose of the tall building, and "its meaning in education." He described the building: 260 by 360 feet at the base; fifty-two stories high (twenty-seven stories higher than the Oliver Building, Pittsburgh's tallest); with four entrances 39 feet high, 11 million cubic feet of space served by thirteen elevators, and capacity for 12,000 students at once (3,000 more than the current enrollment). The cost: $10 million. He asked and answered the questions he had previously been asked about the building. It would not sway in high winds. It would cost less to heat than conventional buildings because it had only one cold roof and one cold cellar floor. It would occupy less than two acres of the whole block, thus leaving more than twelve acres open for other buildings. It would provide good light, good ventilation, and great flexibility in use of space for various educational functions. It would admit little noise and dust.

"Pittsburgh is known as a center of wealth and of industry," he said.

It is known for the making of steel, glass, aluminum, and machinery. The idea of Pittsburgh's vast tonnage is in the minds of millions of people here and over the country. But tonnage is only one phase of Pittsburgh. There is a way of thinking here, a way of doing, an inward spirit and imagination. Out of things of the spirit, out of imagination, the tonnage has come.

The new building is to express that spirit of achievement with such force and sublimity that the whole world will understand. The building is high. It is not high, though, just for the sake of being high. It is only with height that stones can talk the language of courage and sublimity. Such a building belongs in Pittsburgh.

The lights had been lowered gradually, and with Bowman's last words, a series of pictures of the building flashed on the screen. "Silence followed," he recalled, "as though something unbelievable had happened." The lights were turned up.

William J. Holland, former chancellor of the University, still one of its trustees, director emeritus of Carnegie Museum and now its curator, was the first to speak. He had been a most vocal opponent of the plan as a member of the Citizens' Committee, and he rose now to voice his opposition with all the majestic dignity of his seventy-six years, his commanding presence, his shock of white hair, and his flowing moustache. In doing so he walked straight into a trap.

"Oh! Ho!" he began in his booming voice. "I feel forced to tell what I know about the ground chosen for this building. I am speaking as a geologist. Under the surface where it is proposed to put up this structure there is a deep bed of quicksand. No such building could be erected there." He added, after a pregnant pause, "It is lucky the quicksand is there. The whole plan is nonsense."

Bowman rose again, apparently in distress. "I apologize to Dr. Holland," he said. "I forgot part of what I had planned to say. We had a test boring made at each corner of the building location, each 170 feet deep. The quicksand is there. The layer, near the surface, is eight feet thick. And I forgot something else." He held up a flat piece of rock, round, with a diameter of about four inches. "This is a disc taken from the core drill, about 60 feet below the surface. It is a little piece of the hard rock, a slab 40 feet through, on which the building will stand. I have under the table here a bushel of these discs. They are for you as a souvenir of this meeting. They will make good paperweights." Two young student assistants lifted the basket onto the table and began to pass out the pieces.

Walter J. Rome (Class of 1926), later acting dean of men at the University, still later chief probation officer of the Juvenile Court and then for many years executive director of Children's Hospital, was one of the young aides. He remembered Dr. Bowman with admiration and gratitude for kindness shown him, both as a student and as a member of the staff, and fifty-eight years later he recalled the November 6 dinner as a moment of dramatic triumph. Dr. Holland, he said, looked like a man who had been whipped.

Holland rose again and said, "I am very sorry that I said a word. I made a mistake. Perhaps I made a mistake, too, in opposing the plan at all."

Lawrence E. Sands, president of the Peoples Pittsburgh National Bank, broke the tension. "The plan came to me as a shock," he said. "After getting over that shock, I am much in favor of the plan. A man must feel new pride in Pittsburgh as the idea of the building, noble in its art and in its purpose, grows upon him." Charles D. Armstrong, president of Armstrong Cork Company, a man of considerable influence, declared that if Pittsburgh supported remarkable developments like this one, there would come a day when it would be just as much an honor to be a citizen of Pittsburgh as it was in ancient days to be a citizen of Rome. Marcus Aaron, a manufacturer who was also president of the Pittsburgh Board of Public Education, expressed approval, and Senator David Aiken Reed, and several others. No one else rose to object. The party broke up. The guests departed, taking with them the stone discs from the test boring.*

Press coverage of the dinner was splendid. The five daily Pittsburgh papers used banner headlines and pictures on page one. Editorial comment was generally favorable. The story appeared in newspapers from coast to coast; the *New York Times* ran a picture of the building as tall as the *Times* page itself. Then followed a backwash of adverse criticism and doubt. The trustees of Carnegie Institute passed a resolution condemning the building on the ground that it would destroy the beauty of the new Civic Center. An engineer living in the area circulated a petition charging that the development would ruin the neighborhood and property values. A move was started to have city council change the zoning laws to prohibit a high building in the area. Fears were expressed that the building would sway in the wind and probably collapse, and that students, being students, would fall out of the windows. A trustee of the University wrote R. B. Mellon that the project was making the trustees look ridiculous. A good many people felt that if four-story Georgian buildings covered with moss and ivy were good enough for Harvard, Princeton, Yale, and Dartmouth, they should be good enough for Pitt.

Bowman had another problem that was somewhat more pressing. He was committed to begin a money-raising program early in 1925, but his plans for that had collapsed in October. The firm he had retained to run the campaign resigned.

The University's own fund-raising programs had been managed out of the General Alumni Association's office downtown, in the Commonwealth Building. Karl E. Davis (Class of 1910), secretary to the association, handled alumni affairs; Carlton Ketchum, his co-director, handled fund raising with the help of one assistant, J. Steele Gow (Class of 1916, *cum laude*). When making his budget for 1922, however, Bowman dropped the fund-raising department and told Gow he was henceforth to work out

---

*Bowman used the phrase "the Cathedral of Learning" for the first time in his speech on this occasion. In *Unofficial Notes* he says the name was first used by one of Klauder's associates in Philadelphia, a Scotsman who said, "It's a Cadral [*sic*] of Larnin', that's what it is." Carlton Ketchum, however, said Bowman told him that it was first used by Charles D. Armstrong at a trustees' meeting.

Bowman disliked the term and intended to abandon it, but on

August 4, 1925, he wrote to Klauder: "As you stated, the title 'Cathedral of Learning' is one which does not much please me. It has proved to have great publicity value, however, and in as much as this fall we must go through another campaign 'for the Cathedral of Learning' it may be as well to place this name of the building on the drawings." Once in a jocular moment Bowman referred to "The Learning Tower of Pisaburgh."

of the chancellor's office. Gow's first assignment was to tell Ketchum that he was no longer on the payroll. He delayed two weeks before he could bring himself to carry out that unpleasant duty. Carlton Ketchum thereafter devoted his attention solely to Ketchum Publicity, the company he and his brother George had founded to provide services in advertising, public relations, and fund raising.*

Bowman had retained the John Price Jones Company of Nassau Street, New York, to help him run his 1925 campaign. John Price Jones, then and for some years thereafter, was the best-known and most successful company engaged in the new art of raising money for worthy institutions, but it did not distinguish itself on the University of Pittsburgh account. Bowman found himself with rooms full of pamphlets pleading the cause of the tall building. A pamphlet was written specifically for each of more than a dozen interest groups in the community— businessmen, steelworkers, teachers, physicians, housewives, and so on—on the dubious theory that each of these had a special and different interest in seeing a Cathedral of Learning rise on Frick Acres. Bowman did not know what do do with these, though one might suspect that they were his idea (he eventually burned them in a secret operation), and some heated words followed. John Price Jones's letter resigning the account, and Bowman's reply, are uncommonly revealing, both on the agonies of mounting a major fund-raising campaign and on the personalities of the principals involved.

October 16, 1924

Dear Dr. Bowman:

After a careful review of the year's work and consideration of the circumstances affecting it including your attitude both to Mr. Tucker and myself, we desire to withdraw from the building campaign project of the University of Pittsburgh. Our reasons for this decision are as follows:

*The company later split into two parts. George Ketchum headed Ketchum, MacLeod and Grove, Inc., which in 1985, renamed Ketchum Communications, Inc., with $420 million in billings, was the nation's twenty-third largest advertising company; Carlton Ketchum headed Ketchum, Inc., which since 1958 has been the world's largest company in what has come to be called institutional finance, otherwise known as fund raising.

1. The failure of your mind and my mind to meet on what we consider important questions.
2. The absolute disregard of any work that we do with the comment that "This is rotten" or "This is not what I wanted;" whereas that piece of work should have been the basis for a discussion and further elaboration.
3. Your absolutely unjust and thoroughly dictatorial attitude to which we cannot submit except with humiliation.
4. Your policy of ignoring both Mr. Tucker and myself in regard to your plans and the plans of the committee.

Please understand that we appreciate the fact that you hired us and that you hired us for our counsel and advice, which you would have a right to reject at any time, and that you hired us to do certain things. We do say, however, that your attitude has been humiliating in the sense that you have refused to cooperate with us in developing a policy and that you have been insulting us in your attitude in the past few weeks.

It is with the greatest regret that I am forced to write thus, and it is with the keenest regret that we submit our resignation. It was only because I had a deep conviction that your sense of fairness would bring you to realize your attitude towards us that I have submitted to these conditions so long and have permitted Mr. Tucker to do so.

Sincerely yours,
John Price Jones

October 21, 1924

Dear Mr. Jones:

I have your letter of October 16. I am sorry to have it. I think you wrote out of a mood rather than out of conviction.

We have disagreed on a good many matters of opinion. You have been right stubborn about insisting that your views were correct. I admit that I have been positive, perhaps too much so, on the other side. But after all, when I have thought things were not right, I have not wanted to go through so much argument in the matter as you have forced upon me.

Personally, I have liked you and Tucker and Fuller. I wish you success in everything you try to do, and I am sorry that you are not to go ahead with the work here.

Faithfully yours,
John G. Bowman

In the middle of December 1924, Dr. Bowman

swallowed hard and called unannounced at the office of Ketchum Publicity in the Park Building. He asked to see Mr. Carlton Ketchum, and when Carlton Ketchum appeared Bowman sat down with him and told him what had happened. Did Mr. Ketchum think he could take over the campaign? George Ketchum was called in, a discussion followed, and the brothers asked for a couple of days in which to study the problems. They found that the campaign had no chairman, other than John Bowman, no headquarters, other than John Bowman's office, and no usable literature, except perhaps a letter of encouragement from President Calvin Coolidge. Carlton Ketchum called on Dr. Bowman to say that, under certain conditions, he and his brother thought they could help, and so they would be willing to direct the campaign. They settled on a flat fee for their services. (It was established early in this new profession, and holds true today, that no ethical fund-raising firm will take a percentage of the amount it helps to raise.) Bowman balked at the idea of having a "campaign manager," and so Carlton Ketchum agreed to work under the title Assistant to the Chancellor. Bowman also balked at the idea of signing a contract, stating simply, "My word is good." (It was: in an association with Bowman over the next fourteen years, the firm's bills were always paid promptly.)

They agreed on a goal of $10 million to be raised in three campaigns—$3.5 million in the spring of that year, 1925, and the remainder in two campaigns to come in intervals of two to five years later. Carlton Ketchum recalled:

I went to work on a couple of things before I left his office. We opened up a campaign headquarters on February 1 in an empty bank building on Fourth Avenue and began the operation. We told Dr. Bowman that the first thing he had to have was a campaign chairman. He could not go on being chairman himself. He agreed. He didn't know anybody much in town except his board and his faculty. We looked over the list of trustees and picked Homer D. Williams. Bowman wouldn't ask him, so I did. He was head of Carnegie Steel, which was then merging with United States Steel, and he said at first that he couldn't possibly give enough time from his duties to do all we told him he would be called on to do. My policy has

always been to tell a man who takes the chairmanship of a campaign, "It's going to be a damned hard job and you'll have to give it a lot of time." You never get anywhere with this business of telling somebody, "It isn't going to take much of your time." Williams agreed to serve.

On March 5, 1925, Bowman sent Williams the names of 1,179 Pitt graduates and 1,028 Pitt students who lived in communities where United States Steel had plants. The University, he said, probably trained more young people from homes of industrial workers than any other in the country. This training, he pointed out, was "an insurance against radicalism." The students were learning "sound conservatism." This, he said, was an added reason why industry should contribute to the building fund.

Carlton Ketchum continued: "I had met a man by the name of Hamilton Stewart, a Scotsman who was vice president of Harbison-Walker Refractories Company, a very able and popular businessman. He was not connected with the University, never had been. I proposed him as vice chairman. He agreed, Williams was pleased, and we built the whole campaign on Williams and Stewart."

The Cathedral of Learning campaign today is considered a landmark in the field—a classic example of a very large early campaign that used pioneering methods and had striking results.

The campaign headquarters on Fourth Avenue made lists and lists of names. It created an organization with captains, lieutenants, and "brigades" of working solicitors. It gave each brigade a goal to meet and the names of people to call on. It sent out daily boxscores to the newspapers on amounts received, the names of the generous and civic-minded persons who gave them, and the names of the brigade captains who brought them into the fold. It put banners on streetcars bearing the campaign slogan "It's Our University." It placed plywood silhouettes of the Cathedral of Learning in store windows, banks, and hallways. These were six feet high, they were painted to resemble stone, and they bore such inspiring legends as "A gate for boys and girls to useful and satisfying careers" and "Industry and spiritual fineness live in Pittsburgh."

The people of the community began to become interested and involved. Thirty children at the Colfax School kindergarten fashioned a reproduction of the Cathedral of Learning with their building blocks. (Picture in the papers.) The Federal Baking Company at 435 Wood Street displayed in its window a fifty-six-inch-high model of the building made of baked cake dough, the icing serving to represent the Indiana limestone. (Picture and story in the papers.) The C. D. Kenny Company, a grocery at 214 Federal Street, exhibited "one of the most unique window displays seen in the city for some time": a model of the Cathedral made of 500 cans of milk, with loose coffee and sugar tastefully arranged to represent the ground. (Picture and story in the papers.) Purveyors of building supplies for the project made their gifts in kind—67,000 square feet of roofing, 1,700 doors, 75,000 square feet of window sashing, as well as cement, glass, plumbing and heating materials, elevators—and mentioned their contributions in their advertisements.

The campaign was carried to towns in twenty outlying areas, each with its own campaign chairman and team of solicitors. A figure often mentioned in solicitations was $1,040, payable in five yearly installments of $208. This would provide space in the Cathedral of Learning for one student for all time. Editorials on the campaign were friendly: "Many More Must Give," "A Work Worth Doing," "$10,000,000 and 52 Stories Not Too Big for Pittsburgh," and "Pittsburgh Leads the Way." When foreign papers picked up the story and ran the widely distributed Associated Press pictures (*"Die Kathedrale der Wissenschaft"*), Pittsburghers were deeply impressed. Press coverage would have been better, Carlton Ketchum said, if Dr. Bowman had not rewritten so many news releases. "I would give him a beautiful piece written by one of our staff, skilled men like Vince Drayne or C. V. Starrett or Harry Stanley, and he would completely rewrite it, with considerable loss in intelligibility and in the space it received, if any."

On the third day of the campaign, Marcus Aaron declared a recess of classes for an afternoon and filled the auditorium of Syria Mosque with some three thousand elementary school teachers. They were there to learn how they could help. Bowman asked them what they thought of an idea he had. Suppose a certificate were to be printed up with a small picture of the Cathedral of Learning, a simple statement of its purpose, and a certification that the child who received the certificate—his or her name and the name of the school to be written in—had earned and given ten cents toward the construction ("a brick") of the building. The child's name would be written in a book of parchment containing the name of every donor that would last for at least 2,000 years. The teachers approved. It is not known who thought of this gambit, but in time some ninety-seven thousand schoolchildren contributed their coins and received certificates "signed" by R. B. Mellon testifying that they were "Builders of the Cathedral of Learning." Carlton Ketchum observed, "You don't put up much Cathedral with 97,000 dimes. It took a great deal of work, cost more than $9,700, and broke a basic rule of the business, which is that you have wasteage and lower your standard of giving if you make a major effort to collect small amounts. But it did dramatize the project for people. And for years afterward I kept running into young people who chose Pitt as their college because they had once 'bought a brick' to help build the Cathedral of Learning."

There had to be, of course, a big kickoff dinner to start the campaign. Who would be the speaker? Homer Williams proposed his boss, Elbert Henry Gary, who was chairman of the board, chairman of the Finance Committee, and chief executive officer of United States Steel Corporation, a one-time county judge who had left the practice of law to manage the nation's largest steel company. Williams and Bowman hastened to New York and there were given a quick and gruff refusal; Gary said he had not done anything of the sort for twenty-five years and he did not intend to start doing it now. Williams went about other business. Bowman took the train back to Pittsburgh, but he did not accept refusal easily; he returned to New York the next day with fire in his eye, and in a ten-minute exhortation he persuaded Judge Gary to change his mind.

Bowman, R. B. Mellon, and Homer Williams met Judge Gary on the morning of January 29 at Pittsburgh's East Liberty Station (of fondest memory) and escorted him to breakfast at R. B.'s mansion at 6500 Fifth Avenue. Gary held a press conference there ("Gary Says Steel Supremacy Will Stay Here") and then was driven to Braddock to inspect the Edgar Thomson Works. Bowman accompanied him. On the way he gave the judge some information he needed and no doubt welcomed: "Sometimes steelworkers get sick, and then what do they do? They go to doctors who are graduates of the University of Pittsburgh. Or they get toothaches and go to dentists who are graduates of the University. Their children go to schools whose teachers were educated at the University. Many of the engineers, chemists, physicists, metallurgists, and pharmacists in these steel towns were trained at the University. Steel and education ought to be in one grand partnership." He presented Gary with some cards on which were recorded the number of such men and women—University graduates—in each of the surrounding towns.

A committee had reserved the ballroom of the William Penn Hotel, agreeing to pay double the cost of the meals on the guarantee of fast service provided by double the usual number of waiters. This time the plaster model of the Cathedral of Learning was 3½ feet high, scaled ¹⁄₁₆th of an inch to the foot, and accurate in every detail. (Klauder was embarrassed to have to tell Bowman it had cost $15,000.) The Pitt Band played the "Star Spangled Banner" from the gallery while a large silk flag opened and fluttered in the breeze of strong fans. A motion picture about the University was shown on two screens, one on the east and one on the west side of the room, so that no one among the 750 guests had to crick his neck. An enormous picture of the model of the tall building appeared on the screens. It had clouds (produced for the camera by cigar smoke) around the top to emphasize its height.

Judge Gary used a melodramatic device in opening his address. He held up the manuscript of "the speech I wrote before I came to Pittsburgh." He thought it was a good speech. But it was not good enough. The University's plan for Pittsburgh seemed almost too great for him to talk about. He elaborately discarded the speech and appeared to speak extemporaneously from the heart. He gladdened his audience by informing them that the world was growing better and that education was responsible for its improved morality. He closed with a soaring endorsement of the University's proposed building: "There has been adopted a plan which will provide an educational home for 12,000 or more students at one time. The capacity is very large. The form is monumental; it is unique. To be built largely of steel and stone, it will be massive, permanent, and beautiful in its architectural symmetry and proportions. It will receive the admiration and wonder of the world. Its physical height is limited . . . but the height and breadth of its influence can never be measured by figures or words. . . . Throngs of people will come to Pittsburgh to gaze upon this remarkable tower of solidity and grandeur. Here in this populous city, this cathedral of learning will stand for ages as an example and an inspiration."

A few days later Gary announced that U.S. Steel would contribute $250,000 to the University's building campaign, to be given in steel rods, bars, girders, and beams. At the going rate of $35 a ton, this represented a gift of 7,142 tons of unfabricated steel. It also represented something considerably more important than that. It was a pioneering event, a breakthrough in corporate philanthropy. Gifts from corporations to colleges and universities were virtually unknown in 1925, for such use of the stockholders' money was considered improper, and even some of the recipients of the gifts would have distrusted support from such a source. In fact, when John D. Rockefeller, Sr., made large gifts as an individual to the University of Chicago in 1910, indignant protest was heard up and down the land. To the protesters, this marked the beginning of the decline of academic freedom, intellectual integrity, and honor among academicians. The 1925 U.S. Steel gift set a precedent and cleared the way for a long and honorable tradition of corporate giving.

The biggest solicitor in the campaign, aside from Bowman himself, was David Lindsay Gillespie. He had started out in Pittsburgh in the lumber business, invested his earnings in a new enterprise, Standard

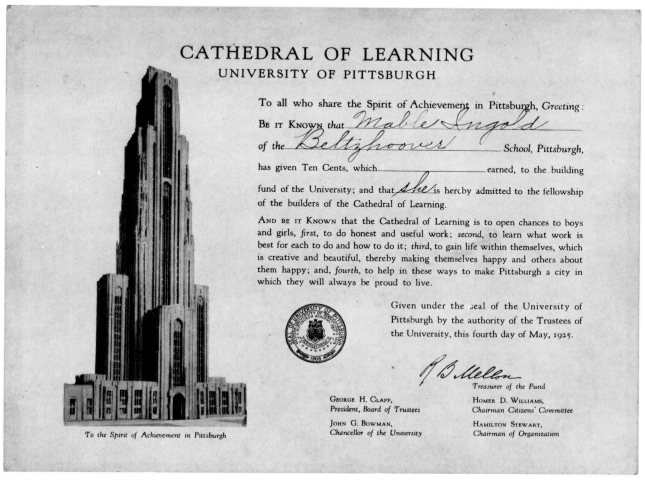

CATHEDRAL OF LEARNING
UNIVERSITY OF PITTSBURGH

To the Spirit of Achievement in Pittsburgh

To all who share the Spirit of Achievement in Pittsburgh, *Greeting:*

BE IT KNOWN that *Mable Ingold*

of the *Beltzhoover* School, Pittsburgh,

has given Ten Cents, which_____ earned, to the building

fund of the University; and that *she* is hereby admitted to the fellowship of the builders of the Cathedral of Learning.

AND BE IT KNOWN that the Cathedral of Learning is to open chances to boys and girls, *first*, to do honest and useful work; *second*, to learn what work is best for each to do and how to do it; *third*, to gain life within themselves, which is creative and beautiful, thereby making themselves happy and others about them happy; and, *fourth*, to help in these ways to make Pittsburgh a city in which they will always be proud to live.

Given under the seal of the University of Pittsburgh by the authority of the Trustees of the University, this fourth day of May, 1925.

R B Mellon
Treasurer of the Fund

GEORGE H. CLAPP,
President, Board of Trustees

JOHN G. BOWMAN,
Chancellor of the University

HOMER D. WILLIAMS,
Chairman Citizens' Committee

HAMILTON STEWART,
Chairman of Organization

By giving ten cents, Mable Ingold, of the Beltzhoover School, was "admitted to the fellowship of the builders of the Cathedral of Learning." She was one of 97,000 children who contributed.

Oil Company, and then invested his earnings from that in still another new enterprise, which became the Aluminum Company of America. Early in the campaign, Gillespie visited the headquarters and volunteered for an assignment to look for prospects—people he knew who might give to the University. As Carlton Ketchum told the story fifty-five years later:

He came to the name Woods. Edward A. Woods was pres-

ident of the highly successful Equitable Life Assurance Agency.* . . . His face lit up. "Aah," he said, "that Woods is for me. I am his biggest customer. He's got more insurance from me than from anyone else, and I want to see him."

Then he went to the phone and got Woods. Gillespie said: "Ed, this is Lin. Say, I understand that you have a sales meeting every Monday morning, and have all your salesmen in from all over the area." Woods replied that

*He was a son of Chancellor George Woods.

that was so. Gillespie: "What time?" Woods: "8:30." Gillespie then said, "Could I come over and give them a little talk?" Woods said: "We'd be delighted to have you over, if you wanted to do that it would be perfectly marvelous."

Gillespie went over to Woods's and gave a little talk covering all the points we had given him—why donating to the University would be a good thing, what it would do for the city, and what it would do for the school. He did a good job. Then he continued, "Now, I am counting on you to be good citizens, patriots, the kind of people to help good things along. I know every one of you is going to contribute to this, aren't you?" A good number of people said yes. "Hold up your hands," Gillespie said, and everyone held up his hand. "That's wonderful," he said. "I just happen to have a few hundred subscription cards here, which I am going to pass around to you. You can fill them out and we'll pick them up. And I have a piece of good news for you. Ed Woods is going to match everything you give. Ed is an alumnus of the University and he loves it, and Ed is going to match all your gifts." Gillespie turned to Woods and said, "You are, aren't you, Ed?" Woods gulped twice and agreed. Gillespie came back to the campaign headquarters with pledges for $15,000 and a note from Woods committing him to match this and any further gifts from employees of his agency.

In March 1924 the University had opened a new educational radio station, and in the course of a series of five-minute, 600-word talks ("Hello, radio folk!"), Dr. Bowman spoke of his dream for a Tower of Learning in Pittsburgh. KDKA, "The World's Pioneer Broadcasting Station," sent out this particular talk on its own wavelength. An elderly woman in Rutland, Vermont, heard the talk and mailed a letter and a one-dollar bill to the chancellor. One dollar was only one dollar, but somebody at campaign headquarters saw in the woman and her contribution the glint of pure gold. An attorney associated with the University, Minnie Z. Buckley (Class of 1915, LL.B. 1918), was dispatched to Rutland. She liked what she found, brought the lady to Pittsburgh as the University's guest, and put her up at the Schenley Hotel. Miss (Rosamund) Elizabeth Watson agreed to appear on May 5 at a luncheon of some three hundred campaign workers. She was cast perfectly for the role she was to play. A retired school teacher, seventy-five years old, she was living in a

home for the aged. Bodily infirmities, including failing eyesight, had kept her from teaching for the past five years. She had been reared by her dear grandfather, a Civil War veteran. The small two-tube radio on which she heard the chancellor's address had been a gift.

Hamilton Stewart, general chairman of the campaign organization, opened the May 5 luncheon meeting (held at the University Club) with a report that subscriptions had now reached $3,287,229. Attaining the goal of $10 million, he declared, was an assured fact, but it was secondary to getting the entire community's undivided and wholehearted support for, and belief in, the project. Dr. J. H. (Hube) Wagner announced that additional gifts from alumni had brought the total of their contributions to $776,031. Captain Greer Coolidge was pleased to hear that his brigade had collected $32,107; Captain Charles Donley was chagrined to hear that his had collected only $1,625. Dr. Carl Wallace Petty, pastor of the Bellefield Baptist Church, an orator of some distinction, looked at Miss Watson, seated beside him at the head table, when he began his talk with the words, "I take my text today from the first chapter of the Gospel according to St. Elizabeth, patron saint of the Cathedral of Learning."

Miss Watson had never addressed a large audience before, but her speech was a sensation. She talked of her childhood yearning for a college education, which she could not afford. In her community "there were no men who had the vision of this wonderful great 'Cathedral,' and while they were dear, good people, and hard-working people, they did not believe in education. . . . I love the thought of this 'Cathedral' as I have never loved anything of the same kind before. I have been so anxious that the vision will become a great reality for the boys and girls, that they may have the chances I never had, and carry the glory of the good news out into the world, not only in Pittsburgh and Western Pennsylvania, but far away to other cities and other nations, that the world may see that you here, in Pittsburgh, have made the vision a reality for the world." She pleaded with the campaign workers to do their utmost "to insure the realization of the university's hope of guaranteeing an education to every boy and girl of this community who is willing to work for it." The *Gazette-Times* printed the speech in full and told of her "seventy-five years of an excessively lonely and poignantly hungry life spent among barren New England hills. . . . Tears welled in the eyes of hundreds who felt honest sympathy when they heard the story of the battle against dire poverty, ill health and the unconcern of those about her."

The first campaign ended on June 8, 1925. There are, for understandable reasons, differing accounts of how much money was raised, Bowman claiming the highest figure, $9,178,871; but a check with the records and with the campaign manager reveals the following. A total of $8.1 million was given in cash and signed subscriptions in the five-month January–June drive. Of that amount, five pledges totaling $2,457,091 could not properly be used for the tall building. The Heinz family, for example, gave $650,000 toward the construction of Heinz Memorial Chapel. The department stores and some specialty shops contributed $458,091, but in order to forestall appeals for aid from other colleges, they specified that the money be used to set up a research bureau for retail training. Miss Helen Clay Frick gave $75,000 to establish a department to teach appreciation of the fine arts. Miss Mary O'Hara Darlington gave $1 million, the bulk of her estate, to build a library to house the Darlington collection of rare and precious books. (Bowman was seeking court permission to assign the Darlington Library bequest to the Cathedral of Learning building fund.) Several corporations and one individual donor who had given $274,000 had changes of heart and ordered that their money be paid into the University's general endowment fund. After these five amounts had been deducted, there was a remainder of $5,642,909 that could actually be put toward the Cathedral of Learning. This was $2,142,909 more than the $3.5 million goal set six months earlier for the first campaign; but the papers had placed such emphasis on the $10 million goal that the public and some trustees tended to forget the other two planned campaigns and to think that the goal had not been met.

A victory dinner was held on June 10, 1925. Hamilton Stewart reported that almost $7 million had been collected and that the drive to collect an additional $3 million would continue. Board Chairman Clapp announced that the trustees had appointed a building committee "to investigate all matters concerning construction and to get estimates," Clapp to serve as chairman and Homer Williams as vice chairman. Bowman announced the gifts from Mary O'Hara Darlington and Helen Clay Frick, a gift of $100,000 from Mrs. Henry Rea of Sewickly in memory of her father, Henry W. Oliver, and a gift of $500,000 from Dr. and Mrs. Ogden M. Edwards to found the Edwards Laboratory in the School of Medicine. The construction of the Cathedral of Learning, Bowman said, would begin around the middle of October. Despite rumors to the contrary, it would be fifty-two stories tall, as orginally planned.

7

The Tall Building, and Some Others

No architect in all history was ever before given such an opportunity. The use of mass and proportion is unlimited; ornamentation is scarcely needed at all; and the whole structure is unhampered by its surroundings.

Charles Zeller Klauder, January 5, 1925

Bowman called the months that followed the campaign "the summer of confusion." He and those who worked with and for him had raised more money for the University in five months than all the money all the private donors had given the University in the past 138 years. His tall building was creating national, even international, excitement. Klauder was winning prizes and commendations for his design. But despite these triumphs, there was opposition to the tall building from several of the trustees and from some other leading citizens; and now, after the excitement of the campaign had cooled and only $5.6 million had been raised that could be used solely for the building, the opposition hardened. Some trustees simply refused to commit themselves to an undertaking that was larger than the available resources. Some feared that the skyscraper project, like the famous Acropolis plan, would peter out, leaving them with huge obligations. Some had emotional objections: they feared that ridicule would be directed at them, the University, and the city. Some resented what they came to believe was the chancellor's proclivity for pushing ahead arrogantly on his own, some leagues ahead of his Board of Trustees.

A. J. Kelly, Jr., the realtor who had "scouted" Bowman in 1920, called at Bowman's home at 155 North Dithridge Street and all but ordered him to give up the tall tower and cover the fourteen acres with buildings no more than four stories high, erected one at a time. Bowman refused, declaring he could not have collected even a half million dollars on such a commonplace plan. Howard Heinz, conscious of the "great responsibility resting on the trustees to put up the right kind of building," offered to pay the full cost of getting the advice of the best engineering consultants, who would advise them whether or not to go ahead with the plan exactly as adopted. Unlike Kelly, he recognized that the University was committed to a high building "because the money had been raised for that purpose." Joseph B. Shea, president of the Joseph Horne Company, a member of one of the three families who owned that department store, wrote a polite letter to Bowman expressing his utter aversion to putting up a high building of any design. He

did not like skyscrapers; the building would not look the way it was made to look in the imaginative drawings; it would not work; and the University had no right to erect such a building.

During these weeks, several more large donors ordered that their gift or pledge be used solely for endowment or for other purposes not related to the tall building.

The situation was further complicated by the lack of consensus, and even of a stable majority opinion, among the trustees on the design and construction schedule of the building. The trustees disagreed among themselves on the height and number of floors. One faction wanted to delay construction until the entire $10 million had been collected; another wanted to erect in stages only as much building as could be paid for with the money in hand. In desperation, the Building Committee made a proposal for a halfway house: "It is proposed to build the first five floors of the high building, . . . work to start as soon as satisfactory bids are obtained for excavation and foundation. This portion of the building will include the entire four-story quadrangle with its permanent roof and five stories of the central section. The sixth floor slab properly waterproofed will serve as the roof of the five-story central section. Blue prints are submitted herewith."

As a result of such vacillation, shifts, and changes, the board at different meetings in 1925 and 1926 voted yes . . . voted no . . . maybe . . . build . . . don't build . . . go ahead . . . wait.

July 15, 1925. The board approved contracts with Klauder and with Stone and Webster. Klauder's contract specified that the building was not to cost more than $9 million. His commission was 5½ percent of the cost of the building, out of which he was to pay for all structural and mechanical engineering services. As consulting engineers and general contractor, the company of Stone and Webster was authorized to erect a building costing $10.25 million; it was to receive a 4 percent commission on the cost of the building, the cost to include all building materials, wages, salaries, and expenses. The trustees added an escape clause: the University might delay or cancel either contract without penalty, provided it paid for any work actually done when it gave notice of such a delay or cancellation. Klauder managed to get a resolution clearing up the difference between $9 and $10.25 million.

September 14, 1925. The trustees approved Klauder's plans "in accord with the original drawings and instructed Klauder and Stone & Webster to proceed to complete their plans so that the foundation of the building could be started in October 1925."

September 29, 1925. "It was decided that a vote should be taken by ballot of those present expressing their choice as to whether the proposed University building should be a high building (with tower as designed by Mr. Klauder) or a low building. Of the 23 members present, 15 expressed a preference for a high building, 7 for a low building, and 1 member did not vote.

"After a full and detailed discussion of the matter it was decided that the beginning of the construction of the proposed building should be deferred until the Board of Trustees should take action at a later meeting fixing the time when the construction of the building should begin."

October 27, 1925. George Breed Gordon (Class of 1883) presented "a resolution which, if approved, will put an end once and for all to talk about building a tower on the campus of the University." He accompanied the resolution with a reading of a prepared statement listing all the objections previously brought up and adding a few new ones of his own. ("The proposed building would be a center of confusion, noise, and general bedlam.") This was very formidable opposition indeed. Gordon was one of Pittsburgh's few authentic aristocrats (he was descended from a famous Scottish family by way of Virginia), he had founded the prestigious law firm of Gordon, Smith, Buchanan and Scott, he selected his clients carefully, he had been president of the Pennsylvania Bar Association, and when he spoke he was heard with respect.

Bowman heard him out and then answered each of his charges with solid technical information, of which by this time he was a master. He closed with: "Mr. Gordon, do you know what is the matter with Pittsburgh? There are too many George Gordons in

it—too many men who decide offhand that all new things are wrong. If you [the trustees] want to make yourselves ridiculous in the eyes of the people of Pittsburgh, just pass Mr. Gordon's resolution. The people and the corporations of Pittsburgh gave money without precedent for the construction of a school building in the form of a tower. Are you with your present information to act as obstructionists? Won't you consider the plan without the foregone conclusion that it is wrong?"

Bowman then offered a substitute motion calling for approval of the tall building as designed by Klauder. The chairman (with calm disregard of proper parliamentary procedure) asked for a vote on Dr. Bowman's motion. Three or four trustees voted aye; a smaller number voted nay; a majority of the trustees, confused by these developments, did not vote at all. Chairman Clapp announced, "The *ayes* have it," and adjourned the meeting.

Bowman found a letter from George B. Gordon on his desk the next morning. One may imagine the perturbation with which he opened it. Gordon again stated his unalterable opposition to the tower. He could not support the chancellor in his plan, but he did not wish to see the chancellor placed in an impossible situation. Therefore he submitted his resignation from the board. With the letter he enclosed a check to the University for $10,000. When they next met, the two men shook hands. The other trustees refused to accept Gordon's resignation.

One who was there remembered that Gordon's letter had an electric and quite unexpected effect on the wavering trustees. Their respect for Gordon was such that they concluded that they must make a decision—they must either wholeheartedly support the tall building or declare their opposition to it openly and, like Gordon, resign from the board. Faced with this choice, they tended to give their support to Bowman.

October 30, 1925. A meeting was called to see drawings and sketches; ask questions of Klauder and A. L. Hartridge of Stone and Webster, present by invitation; and pass on a recommendation of the Building Committee. The committee said it had assumed at the end of the campaign of the previous spring that the campaign would be renewed in October. It had assumed further that "there would be at this time some announcement which would have both news value and power to renew confidence in the whole project. The starting of the building with a ground-breaking program . . . would serve as such a start." (The original wording, altered by Bowman, had declared, "If the situation stays the way it is, interest of people, particularly contributors, will turn to disgust. Few payments on subscriptions will be collected. . . . The failure of the trustees to unite in the effort last spring cost the University at least $2,000,000. To begin again, we need a ground-breaking program, a starting program, and the letting of contracts.")

A resolution that the Building Committee be authorized to contract for the foundation of the Cathedral of Learning was adopted with a majority of two. "In view of the small majority in favor . . . it was moved to reconsider the action. . . . The resolution was then voted on a second time and failed to receive a majority of the votes of those present." Another resolution was proposed to the effect that no building on the fourteen acres should ever be more than 100 feet high. To Bowman's consternation, that resolution was passed.

Two days later Bowman went to R. B. Mellon's office. "I've come on an unusual errand," he said. "I'm asking no questions. I do not expect a reply. I bring merely some information. I'm going ahead at once with construction of the high building."

Mellon looked at him for a long pause. "That is all," Bowman said and headed for the door.

Mellon: "Wait a minute. Do you mean what you say?"

Bowman: "Yes."

Mellon, laughing: "*You* might get away with it."

Bowman called on Charles A. Stone of Stone and Webster, a friend of some years' standing, showed him the trustees' resolutions of October 30, told him the names of the trustees, and asked him if he was willing to go ahead with the building. Stone was (he said later) frightened by the question and even more by his answer. He said yes. Bowman knew that Stone was at that time chairman of the board at the Massachussetts Institute of Technology and had con-

structed the new buildings there. He said, "Will you take the building and subject it to the sharpest engineering criticism you possibly can as to whether or not it will function and, as far as you can, to an educational criticism?" Stone's report was affirmative. But when the size of the steel beams was being considered, Bowman ordered that the strength of the steel be increased about 40 percent over and above what the engineers thought adequate.

Bowman did not begin building at once. There was a lull. No mention was made, at least on the record, of the tall building at any board meeting between the session of October 30 and that of June 8, 1926, save only a brief reference to a conversation on the subject with A. W. Mellon in Washington.

During this time, A. W. and R. B. Mellon, both of them trustees, refused to take part in discussions about the tall building. Their silence was taken by a good many people as an evidence of their opposition. Actually, their attitude was one of neutrality; they would not say yes or no, though they did permit corporations they controlled to make gifts to the building fund.

Carlton Ketchum recalled: "For a long time during the battle to win support for the Cathedral of Learning, it was widely believed that the Mellons had given and would give nothing to it, and it was a matter of common opinion that they disapproved of the whole project. For some reason they had made the gift of the land, a $1,500,000 contribution, without public announcement, and while a few people were aware of that fact, it took a long, long time for the knowledge to become common. This added to the difficulty of the campaign, because folks who wanted an excuse to abstain could and did say, 'It hasn't a chance of success, the Mellons are against it.' The two brothers, Andrew and Richard, always avoided discussion of their beneficences. Bowman was afraid that publicity might annoy them, and he would not allow us to run a story regarding the land gift. Finally, someone, I wouldn't have any idea who, 'leaked' the story to the press, with a benign effect on the campaign."

June 8, 1926. At the annual meeting of the board, Bowman presented photographs and blueprints "with modification in the height of the proposed building" and with drawings of five other low buildings to be placed on the site: Heinz Chapel, Stephen Foster Memorial, a library, a gymnasium, and a science hall. The plan to have faculty houses on the roofs of the low sections of the Cathedral was dropped, as well as the plan for the large dining room in the Cathedral itself. The trustees resolved to build "a high building of the general form and design as that originally approved, the dimensions of said building, however, to [be] so reduced that the estimated cost of construction shall not exceed the amount paid or pledged to the University for the purpose." The Building Committee was instructed to draw up revised plans.

September 21, 1926. The trustees passed a resolution approving plans for construction of a building "not over 400 feet high [twenty-nine stories]." The cost was not to exceed $7 million, including all fees.

September 27, 1926. At 11:15 on a rainy Monday morning, work began on the tall building, the Cathedral of Learning. A steam shovel at the western end of Frick Acres scooped up a load of earth and shale and poured it into a dump car pulled by a small, squat locomotive. The car was emptied into the ravine on Frick Acres about two hundred feet to the east. John Bowman was present, and John Weber, but not many others. Bowman had been advised to make a ceremony of the occasion, with at least the major contributors present or represented, but he decided to act quietly, perhaps not to antagonize his opposition. He was in a hurry, and he ordered the work to continue around the clock. On the second day, the manager of the Schenley Hotel called to complain. His guests, he said, could not sleep because of all the noise. Bowman agreed to cut the work schedule to two shifts, sixteen hours.

Bowman had no intention of following the September 21 directive to reduce the height of the building from fifty-two to twenty-nine stories. He had earlier agreed to lower it to forty-two stories because of the recommendation of Stone and Webster engineers and because of a court decision that the Darlington Library bequest could not be used in the building fund. Forty-two stories he could accept, but he simply refused to cut down to twenty-nine

stories. The trustees became aware of his determination to ignore their instruction. Bowman tells of an exchange at the next board meeting:

George Clapp, as usual, called the meeting to order and as usual I started to make some report to the board. I had scarcely started to talk, however, when John H. Nicholson, president of the National Tube, a division of the U.S. Steel Corporation, interrupted me.

"By the way," he said, "we notice a building up out there. Would you mind telling us what that is?"

"That's the building we've been talking about all these years," I said.

"How high is it going?" someone else promptly asked.

"Let's face the facts," I said. "You know them as well as I do. Last September, with little encouragement, we started to build. Here we are."

"Did you get the plan the way you wanted it?" another trustee asked.

"Yes," I said. (Laughter.)

"I'm glad of it," said another in a loud voice. (More laughter.)

Arthur E. Braun rose to say that he, for one, was delighted for Pittsburgh and for the University to see the high building go up. In doing so, he praised the chancellor. His talk was followed by a burst of applause.

Klauder had designed a "steel frame" or "column-bearing" building. This, a product of the marriage of the structural engineer and the architect that has been called the most momentous step in the history of architecture since the days of Rome, was then a relatively recent development: the first great example, the Woolworth Tower in New York, 792 feet high, still the tallest building in the world in 1925, had been built only twelve years earlier. It too was of Gothic design, and Klauder, of course, had studied it. Gothic, the only architectural style designed for verticality and upward thrust, was naturally adaptable to tall buildings.

In Klauder's design of the central tower, seventy-six columns of steel girders rose 535 feet from ground level. These were to be riveted to horizontal steel beams at the floor level of each of the forty-two stories. The whole skeleton, before it was encased in masonry, would resemble an enormous rectangular steel cage set on end. The columns, bearing all the dead weight of walls and floors and the live weight of people and furniture, would carry the load directly to the foundation bed. (A 500-foot structure built with load-bearing stone walls would have walls so thick that they would occupy much of the floor space of the lower stories and would be too heavy for their bases to bear.)

Klauder made the seventy-six columns of the central tower forty inches square at the base, some of them designed to bear a maximum load of 1,841 tons. Since it was impossible to get a single rolled section forty inches square, the columns were formed in several sections and riveted together. These were the largest and strongest columns ever used in the Pittsburgh district up to that time. They diminished in size and weight, of course, as they rose to the higher stories, where there was less overhead weight. The steel framework was covered with pitch made of pine resin, then with twelve inches of concrete, and finally with limestone.

Klauder originally specified Kentucky limestone block cut to exact measurements to face the steel frame of the entire structure. (He later changed his mind and specified the use of limestone mined in the vast quarries in southern Indiana.) The blocks, far heavier than the facing tiles or sections now used for cladding in most steel-frame buildings, were to be tied and bonded to the frame in such a way that they would be practically an integral part of the structure. The stonework was sawn and tooled so as to exhibit a varied and strong texture when seen from close up. Most of the stone was laid on-bed (that is, with the strata horizontal, or as it was taken out of the ground), but some was laid off-bed (strata upright), so that what appears to be iron, which turns brown on weathering, and random horizontal and vertical streaking add to the vigorous surface effect.

Such high buildings absolutely must be based on a foundation bed that will bear not only the direct vertical force of the enormous weight resting on it, but also the increased compression caused by the force of the wind pushing against the exposed vertical surfaces of the structure. It was to the founda-

tion bed that the first months of work were directed in 1926 and 1927. Frederick H. Crabtree, Stone and Webster's field engineer in charge of erecting the building, called it "quite an interesting engineering and construction problem."

The site was originally thought to be an unusually favorable one, and as the work progressed that belief was strengthened. The core borings showed an overburden at the surface of layers of sand and clay about twenty feet deep. (The clay was found to be excellent modeling clay.) Below this was a layer of mixed sandstone and shale about fifteen feet thick, then about twenty-five feet of red shale. At a depth of sixty feet lay a bed of rock thirty-eight to forty feet thick on an almost horizontal plane—a very hard red rock the geologists call Birmingham shale.

When the sand and clay had been shoveled away to a depth of twenty feet, workmen began to sink sixty-eight vertical shafts or caissons. These, varying in diameter from five to ten feet, were dug and blasted through the remaining forty feet to bedrock. Two rectangular caissons ten feet by seventeen feet were centered under the tower. Men were lowered into the shaft after each blast to shovel the spoil into buckets, which were then hoisted to the surface on a powered windlass. The work was slow, for water poured from the seams of the rock in some caissons and had to be pumped out. It was also dangerous, for some parts of the shaft had loose shale that might fall on the men below, and these had to be cemented.

When the caissons had been dug to bedrock, tests were made to make sure they rested on a solid base. Laboratory testing showed that the rock could withstand from 200 to 400 tons per square foot before any signs of failure. The actual load would not exceed 25 tons per square foot. The caissons were filled with reinforced concrete almost to the level of what would be the floor of the lower of two basements.

Each caisson, now a concrete pier, was topped with a huge steel billet plate. The plates were round; the largest of them was more than eight feet in diameter and almost fourteen inches thick. The plate received and supported the base of the steel column, and in so doing distributed the load evenly over the whole top of the caisson.

The foundation for the columns in the low sections of the building, receiving a much lighter load, was simpler to design and build.

When the foundation was finished in the spring of 1927, work stopped and another long delay followed. No steel was raised. People began to ask, some impatiently, "When are you going to begin building?"

The trustees' minutes are uninformative on the building program for 1927, partly because the chancellor canceled as many board meetings as he could, but there seem to have been three reasons for the extended delay. There was still no real agreement among the trustees on the design and construction schedule for the building. Secondly, the excavation and foundation had been started too early, before plans and drawings that the engineers and steel mills could work from had been completed and approved. "We had a very good reason for starting the excavation when we did," Bowman told his trustees. "It was necessary to show the public that we meant to put up a building. The foundations are now completed. The public knows that we intend to keep faith with them." Finally, Bowman was still struggling with Klauder for plans and drawings he was willing to accept and give to the trustees. Many studies of the exterior designs, he told his trustees in mid-1927, had been submitted. The trustees had seen only a small fraction of these. Mr. Klauder "did not relish the idea" of making so many design changes, but now he was satisfied that it was the best thing for the building. He had written, in fact, that his lastest design was the best thing he had ever done. He had prepared more than thirty perspectives of the Commons Room, in addition to the necessary structural studies. He designed rooms of various sizes, heights, proportions, and styles. Now the Building Committee had approved the general proportions and structural features of the Commons Room. The interior treatment had yet to be studied, but Mr. Klauder's first recommendation was now about ready.

In explaining and justifying the reasons for delaying construction of the building he had at first

High above Oakland, workmen on a scaffold during construction of the tall building. The campus of Carnegie Institute of Technology (now Carnegie-Mellon University) is in the background.

rushed into production, Bowman found himself in an unaccustomed position. He did his eloquent best.

We are building the Cathedral for all time. We hope it will be the outstanding landmark of the city for centuries. When the building is finished, the question will not be, "Was it finished in 1928 or 1930?" but rather, "Does the building meet the expectations of the people who contributed to it? Does it fulfill the purpose for which the University intended it?" In the end, we will be forgiven for taking the necessary time to do our best. Never will we be forgiven if we spare any effort to make the building what it should be. . . .

The community has been told to expect something superlative. The obligation to the community which I feel most keenly is that we should spare no effort to give them a superlative building.

(On the typescript of this address the author added a postscript: "At this point all trustees present should be instructed to shout 'Amen!'" The author or someone else then crossed it out with a severe stroke of a red pencil.)

On the eighth of May, 1928, in the eighth year of the Bowman administration, the steel skeleton structure of the Cathedral of Learning began to go up.

The Cathedral of Learning is probably what it has been called, the most important single event in the history of the University, but other developments were taking place and other structures were going up under Bowman's administration in the 1920s. The first of these (in sequence, if not in importance) was Pitt Stadium, erected in 1924–1925 on the hillside slope of the upper campus. It was a remarkable undertaking on at least three scores. It was completed twenty days ahead of schedule, in only thirteen months. It exceeded its estimated cost of $2.1 million by only $100,000, despite overtime and a speed-up to finish it. And it was *immense*—one of the biggest stadiums in the country at that time. Pitt Stadium: an oval arena 791 by 617 feet, covering ten acres. Outer circumference, one-half mile. Sixty-seven thousand seats, seventeen miles of seats in fifty-five rows. A quarter-mile running track with a 220-yard straightaway. A basketball court, a turf tennis court, equipment for rifle practice and gymnasium work. Called justly (if ungrammatically) "one of the most complete, substantial and finely equipped athletic plants in the world" and "one of the most unique and interesting structures of its kind ever built."

The stadium was not a Bowman, nor even an administration, project; it was, rather, the brain child of what have been called "football-crazy alumni and other fanatics." Pitt had won national recognition for its great 1915–1918 teams under Glenn Warner. Now his successor, John Bain Sutherland, one of Warner's All-American heroes, had returned to Pitt as head coach, hired on the strong recommendation of the Athletic Council. Despite a slow start, a 5–3–1 record in 1924, and narrow escapes from defeats by Allegheny and Grove City, he showed promise of continuing

Warner's successes, though it was thought that he of course could never equal them. After sixteen years of games in Forbes Field, which was a baseball park with only 32,000 seats, the University needed room for the crowds that wanted to see the Panthers play football. Pitt now had 11,000 alumni and 9,000 students, each of them entitled to two seats. Subtract those seats, subtract the seats allotted to the opposing college, and how many do you have left for the general public? Especially for the big games against Washington and Jefferson, Penn State, Carnegie Tech, West Virginia?

And so in the summer of 1923, the Athletic Council bought the nine-acre Bailey estate at the upper end of DeSoto Street, joined it to some land that the University already owned, and had a site for an athletic stadium. The seven-man Stadium Committee, headed by the old faithfuls, Homer Williams, Hamilton Stewart, and A. J. Kelly, Jr., had architect W. S. Hindman (Class of 1898) design the stadium, making its foundation and walls strong enough to support an upper deck, to be installed a year or so later, that would hold 30,000 additional seats. In October 1924 the trustees authorized an issue of 6 percent first-mortgage bonds to pay for the land and to erect the stadium. Volunteer solicitors directed by Carlton Ketchum and Norman MacLeod (Class of 1917) sold the bonds. Subscribers were enticed to purchase bonds by the promise that they would be able to buy tickets for seats in preferred space during the life of the bond. The sale was such a striking success, the entire issue being oversubscribed within nine days, that the committee, to its infinite regret, had to return half a million dollars to subscribers. A happy feature was that bonds worth some hundreds of thousands of dollars were bought by friends like E. V. Babcock, Leon Falk, the Mellons, and George Hubbard Clapp, who might be expected one day to endorse them and present them to the University, as indeed they did.

Ground was broken for the stadium on August 7, 1924 (at the same time that Bowman was finally extracting from Charles Klauder a satisfactory design of the tall building). Construction was completed on September 1, 1925, three weeks before the opening game against Washington and Lee (Pitt 28,

Historical Society of Western Pennsylvania

Pitt Stadium under construction, 1924–1925.

Opponent 0). To show off its new arena, to attract large crowds, and to pay its stadium bonds, Pitt scheduled all thirty-six games at home through the 1928 season, and all but six in the two seasons after that. Three games in those years drew more than 40,000 to the stadium: those against Penn State in 1927, Ohio State in 1929, and Notre Dame in 1930 drew 45,000, 44,000, and 60,000 fans, respectively. (There was a saying in those days: "Everybody has two favorite teams: his own alma mater and whoever is playing against Notre Dame.")

Coach Jock Sutherland, said one-time athletic director Frank Carver (Class of 1931), was a master

tactician and technician rather than a strategist and innovator, and it took a while for his precision-built teams to get rolling. But in the six years between 1925 and 1930, his teams had a phenomenal 47–7–5 record in regularly scheduled games. Pitt beat Penn State six straight. In 1928 Pitt tied Nebraska in a historic 0–0 battle in which it did not give up a first down or make a substitution. These were powerhouse teams, and yet heights of 5 feet 9 inches, 5 feet 10 inches, and 5 feet 11 inches were common. We are surprised, too, at the weights, many of them in the range of 165 to 180 pounds. The stated weights, however, are not to be trusted.

It seems that around 1915 coaches began to understate the weight of their players in order to deceive the opposition and to generate sympathy as an outweighed underdog. By the mid-1930s the custom had become so ridiculous that the coaches quietly agreed to drop it.

The 1927 team went to the Rose Bowl as eastern champions in the days when there was only one postseason bowl game instead of twenty. The temperature on the field was ninety-five degrees, and Pitt had a squad of only twenty-five men. Glenn Warner, who now coached at Stanford, had a large squad, and yet it was a close game until Pitt lost,

7–6, on a disputed play. What happened was, with fourth down and goal to go, a Stanford back threw a lateral pass, the receiver dropped the ball, another Stanford player picked it up, and he scored the winning touchdown. Now, every Pitt man and woman in the stadium, clear-eyed and impartial, saw at once that beyond any possible question of doubt, the pass was incomplete, the ball dead, and the touchdown not valid. But the official ruled otherwise. He said the pass was complete, the ball fumbled, the fumble recovered, and the touchdown valid. And besides that, there were twelve penalties against Pitt and only one, for five yards, against Stanford. (But the

Stanford lads gallantly refused to accept a penalty they felt they were not entitled to.) The Pitt players were heroes on the West Coast after the game, and they were privileged to go to Hollywood and meet such immortals of the silver screen as Jack Mulhall, Clive Brooks, Rod La Roque, Billy Dove, who was beautiful and nice but had little to say, Lon Chaney, and Douglas Fairbanks.

The upper deck of the stadium with the 30,000 additional seats was never built. Wiser heads prevailed, pointing out that a crowd of 97,000 football fans in Oakland at one time could be caught in a gridlock and might never get near the stadium, or leave it if they did. Nevertheless, everyone was delighted with the stadium as a great community asset. Everyone except a succession of athletic directors who, when Pitt athletics fell on hard times, had trouble finding opponents who would fill half of those 65,000 seats, and more trouble paying for bond interest, debt retirement, maintenance, heat, light, insurance, paint for thousands of feet of exposed steel, and the repair of thousands of broken seats. And everyone except Raleigh Russell Huggins, dean of the School of Medicine, who had objected to the stadium from the start. For some reason, Dr. Huggins could never understand why anyone would build a 65,000-seat stadium next door to a complex of hospitals.

Dr. Raleigh Russell Huggins had a healthy dissatisfaction with the School of Medicine of the University of Pittsburgh, with which he had been associated as professor of gynecology since 1912 and of which he became dean in 1920. To the public, of course, he made the best case he could for his school:

● It is the only medical school between Philadelphia and Cleveland.

● It serves a population of some 6 million.

● It is rated in class A by the American Medical Association.

● It has an enrollment in 1920 of 154, exclusive of premedical students.

● It limits its freshman class to sixty students, its other classes to fifty students each.

● It requires a four-year standard high school

course and two years of college work for entrance.

● Its students and faculty gave 31,942 patients free clinical and dispensary treatment in 1919.

● More than 60 percent of its graduates—a high percentage among medical schools—hold bachelors' degrees.

● More than 82 percent of its graduates are practicing in the Pittsburgh district.

● In 1922 it will introduce graduate courses.

So much for the best that could be said in 1921. Dr. Huggins knew that much more was needed. He was seriously handicapped by a lack of space for teaching and research. Pennsylvania Hall, only thirteen years old, was in a sad state of disrepair; a skylight, for example, was leaking rain on the students in the dissecting room.

No university medical school, moreover, was adequate unless it had at close hand a hospital that was a part of its teaching facilities, with patients whose ailments lent themselves to research and teaching. Pitt had no such hospital.

Students spent the last two years of their medical course working in hospitals. To use their time efficiently, they should have been working in hospitals closely grouped about the medical school. Pitt did not have that grouping. The small building called the School of Medicine—in reality only a group of teaching laboratories—was situated on the campus, but the hospitals and dispensaries with which it was associated were scattered about the city. In 1921 the Pennsylvania State Board of Medical Licensure notified the University that if this condition was not improved, Pitt could not continue as a class A school—which meant that its graduates would not be accredited in their own state.

The growth of specialization among physicians, moreover, was making it increasingly difficult for the laboratory, the clinic, and the practicing physician to work together, even though it was now more essential than before that they act as a unit.

The answer, of course, was that relatively new development in medicine, the medical center. Far more thorough training could be given where a university was linked with a group of hospitals, and where hospital and university medical staff cooperated. "Medicine," said Dr. Huggins, "advances most rapidly where there is a close relationship between the general practitioner, the research man, the specialist, and actual hospital work. This is possible today only within a medical center group." A Carnegie Foundation survey made in 1919 declared that the population in Western Pennsylvania and Pittsburgh's geographical location made it "almost necessary" that a modern medical school and medical center be developed there. Dr. Huggins, of course, agreed, and, fortunately, so did his predecessor, Dr. Ogden M. Edwards, professor of children's diseases and chairman of the Medical School Committee of the Board of Trustees, and Dr. William S. McEllroy, assistant dean of the School of Medicine.

John Bowman was also aware of the problem and the need. He had reorganized the medical school at Iowa State. He had watched his friends Charles and William Mayo develop their famous medical center in Rochester, Minnesota. In his six years as director of the American College of Surgeons, he had seen the medical centers developed or developing in St. Louis, Cleveland, Cincinnati, Boston, Ann Arbor, New York (by the Rockefeller Institute), and Baltimore (in 1899, the first in this country, by Johns Hopkins University). It was for the purpose of building such a center that he had bought the twelve-acre Porter estate in his first year in office. "Practical success of the medical school," he declared in his first report to the trustees, submitted on June 30, 1922, "means the development of the medical center in Pittsburgh." The full text of the report, probably written by Huggins, called for a group of teaching hospitals having a total capacity of at least 1,000 beds; laboratory and lecture room facilities for at least 400 medical students; an out-patient department; clinical and diagnostic laboratories for advanced study and research; a nurses' training school and nurses' home; and dormitory facilities for medical students, interns, and house officers.

Medical science, the report reads, had made great advances in the preceding fifty years.

Medicine has changed from an empirical art to a biological science. Mystery and guesswork have given way to scientific facts upon which is laid the whole structure of curative and preventive medicine. Didactic lectures no longer suffice as a means of instruction. In their stead have come the laboratory, the clinic, and the teaching hospital. . . .

The meaning and value of medicine today are beyond the grasp generally of the present generation. . . . Diphtheria, for example, which a generation ago used to sweep away the children from thousands of homes, is now little more serious than a "cold." Consumption, which used to cause one third of the deaths between the ages of 20 and 30, is now under control. Infant mortality, typhoid fever, scarlet fever, malaria, and venereal diseases are upon the program of prevention. And the problem of teaching medicine, also, as it should be taught, is difficult to grasp. For this purpose nothing less than the development of a great medical center in Pittsburgh will do.

Committees were formed: they studied the matter, listed problems, wrote a set of rules, drew up plans, specified the working relationships among the hospitals and the University, signed agreements, and raised money. Within a remarkably few years, a medical center had taken shape and was functioning. The School of Medicine was the nucleus around which a half-dozen other institutions assembled:

The Elizabeth Steel Magee Hospital, 175 beds, which devoted itself to the care of women, was the first to agree to join the Medical Center. It added 150 beds, took over the department of obstetrics and gynecology in 1921 and made its wards a part of the teaching facilities of the University. Magee continued to occupy its old location at Forbes and Halkett, a few blocks from the University campus.

Children's Hospital (chartered in 1887) signed an agreement of affiliation on June 20, 1922. The University gave it a plot 240 by 200 feet in the southeast corner of the Porter tract for a payment of $20,000. The trustees of the hospital raised $1.5 million and erected a new building, which opened its doors in March 1926. While building was progressing, Children's agreed to make its clinical facilities available for teaching, to house the Department of Pediatrics of the School of Medicine, and to continue broadening its scope in serving as a general hospital for children, rather than limiting itself to orthopedic services.

A house being moved from Frick Acres after the Cathedral of Learning was well under construction.

The Presbyterian Hospital (chartered in 1893) was to be the central unit in the complex. Its design was to be consistent with the other hospitals in the center. In 1930 its design and construction were under contract.

The Eye and Ear Hospital (chartered in 1895) was to occupy the left wing of the building it would share with the Presbyterian.

The Falk Clinic, founded in 1928 by Maurice and Leon Falk with gifts of $900,000, was a permanent medical and surgical outpatient dispensary, to be conducted as part of the School of Medicine. It was scheduled to open late in 1931.

The Falks turned over their clinic as an outright gift to the University, but otherwise each of these institutions retained its own individuality and independence, with autonomy over its own affairs. Each owned its building and grounds and had its own board of trustees, who were responsible for the finances of the unit. Each had representation on a joint administrative board that controlled matters concerning the Medical Center as a whole. The institutions' great early contribution to the University was in providing faculty for the School of Medicine and, by slow degrees, in opening up their wards to its students as teaching hospitals.

Perhaps the best-known segment of the new Medical Center in the 1920s was the University's School of Dentistry, which had grown to be the largest and one of the best in the country. It had 1,038 students at the end of the 1924–1925 term, of whom 19—an extraordinarily large number for that era—were black. Its first-year class in that term, consisting of 403 students, was called "the largest single class in the history of dental schools." The faculty consisted of 102 teachers; 46 of these were full-time, and 11 of these were full-time professors. The Dental Educational Council of America consistently rated the school as class A, one of the hardly more than a dozen in the United States and Canada so classified.

Despite its reputation and its success, the School of Dentistry suffered grievously from the need for more money and more space. The Upper Dental Building was too small, and the steps taken to provide more space were obviously temporary and inadequate. In 1920 the University bought a former German clubhouse at Thackeray and O'Hara streets and converted it into a clinic. In 1921 it took over one of the wartime frame structures on O'Hara Street near the old Mellon Institute and remodeled it for classroom use. In 1924 Dean H. E. Friesell organized a campaign to raise money from his faculty, alumni, and students. Between 1924 and 1928, every student then enrolled in the School of Dentistry was asked to sign a pledge to pay $250.00 to "a fund for the erection of a new building for the School of Dentistry," payable at the rate of $12.50 every three months. Friesell managed to raise some $200,000 in competition with the Cathedral of Learning campaigns. Dr. Bowman borrowed this money to pay construction bills on the Cathedral and as security on bank loans. (The loan was repaid in due course.)

Thus the University of Pittsburgh Medical Center was a promising but an unfinished story in 1930. The School of Pharmacy, which had hoped to move into new quarters in the center, was still three miles

Edward B. Lee, Jr.

Some people did not like the tall building. For Christmas 1929 the architect Edward B. Lee and his family sent a card lamenting the passing of their house, which had stood on Frick Acres. The card shows the house superimposed over the towering framework of its successor. The Lee house is in the lower right hand corner of the picture of Frick Acres on p. 87.

away on the bluff overlooking the Monongahela. The School of Dentistry and the School of Medicine would wait forty more years before they moved into proper modern quarters suited to their needs and their importance to the University and to Pittsburgh.

In October 1929 steelworkers fitted the last beam into place and raised the American flag atop the Cathedral of Learning. Dr. Bowman drove the last rivet. Only a few workmen, construction officials, and newspaper reporters and photographers were present to watch him.

The building was forty-two stories and 525 feet high.*

Earlier that morning Bowman had set the first stone into place in an interior light court, thus signifying that the facing of the steel would now begin. Six carloads of limestone blocks had been received from Bedford, Indiana, and sixteen more were ready to leave.

That evening Dr. Bowman was the guest of honor at a dinner given at the Keystone Athletic Club by the president of the construction company that erected the steel structure. Officials of the University were present, as well as all the foremen and workmen involved in the project. The president of the company stated that the Cathedral of Learning could be classed among the most accurately and efficiently constructed steel structures in the world. A steel worker presented the chancellor with a chromium-plated rivet engraved with a suitable inscription. There was an exchange of compliments and congratulations on no one's having lost his life or being seriously injured in dangerous and difficult work lasting a year and a half. A spokesman for the workers, Vincent McCarthy by name, took a deep breath and delivered a declamation in one remarkable sentence: "As we climbed and worked our way to the lofty peak of this great structure, which is to be used for the advancement of education, so we hope that the young men and women who will occupy it will climb to greatness, and that some engineer of genius may be developed who will devise new methods of steel construction that will eliminate the hazards and lessen the labors of those engaged in our occupation."

This celebration took place on Monday, October 21, 1929, three days before Black Thursday, when the market collapsed on the New York Stock Exchange and the nation began the longest, deepest, and most painful economic depression in its history.

---

*The heights of some later Pittsburgh buildings: U.S. Steel, sixty-three stories (841 feet); One Mellon Bank Center, fifty-four stories; Oxford Center, forty-six; Gulf, forty-four; PPG, forty; Oliver Plaza, thirty-four.

8

The 1930s:
Fulfillment and
Good Fortune

They shall find wisdom here, and faith. In steel and stone, in character and thought, they shall find beauty, adventure, and moments of high victory.

John G. Bowman

"Here is eternal spring; for you the very stars of heaven are new."

Robert Bridges, "Ode to Eaton College," inscribed on Samuel Yellin's iron gate in the Commons Room of the Cathedral of Learning

I T was a decade of fulfillment and frustration, of achievement and failure, of advance and retreat, of pride and humiliation. At the beginning of the 1930s, John Bowman's goals for the University were in sight. He was recognized as one of the most dynamic and successful educators of his time. He was respected for courage that had accomplished a miracle against opposition, indifference, and long odds. He then guided the University safely through seven years of depression without incurring debt, to a triumphant 150th birthday celebration held in the almost-finished Commons Room of the almost-finished Cathedral of Learning. But he ended the decade with an irreparable quarrel with his organized alumni; with a vote of no confidence by his trustees; with a widely publicized censure by his peers in other universities. He wrote an angry letter of resignation that he was persuaded not to send.

This chapter covers the episodes of fulfillment, achievement, advance, and pride.

February 1930. John Bowman, working like a man obsessed with running the University, raising money, and building his Cathedral of Learning, pushed himself to his limits physically and emotionally, and early in 1930 his physician ordered him to rest for six months. He telephoned J. Steele Gow, who had recently resigned as his dean of administration. Gow had just become executive director of the new $10 million foundation established by Maurice Falk in memory of his wife, Laura, and he was inspecting at the time the foundation's new offices in the Farmers Bank Building. Bowman told him he was leaving immediately for Europe and explained why. Would Mr. Gow be willing to resume his post at the University during that time? Gow, with the approval of the Falks, agreed to do so. He did not move into his foundation offices until late in July, when Bowman returned from a long stay in the seaport town of St. Ives in Cornwall.

September 1930. Enrollment for the school year 1930–1931 was 14,372. This was the highest it had ever been, more than double what it was when Bowman took office in 1921, and higher than it would be again until 1940–1941. The increase reflected a national trend that was caused, in part,

by the unprecedented numbers of women who were going to college to prepare themselves for careers.

February 28, 1931. The first classes moved into the Cathedral of Learning. Electric lights and concrete floors had just been installed on floors five to eight. An engineering drawing class and the small office of the dean of men, which had been housed in one of the old residences still standing on Frick Acres, moved to those floors. These *avant coureurs* walked up and down four to seven flights of stairs for almost a year, and they worked in rough-finished, unplastered rooms that until March 1935 were heated by kerosene heaters and electric stoves. For a time during the first winter, the nearest toilet facilities were at the Schenley Hotel, on the other side of Bigelow Boulevard. Walter Rome, acting dean, and William Morrell, University editor, one day filled out a month's expense account itemizing with date and hour the nickles they had expended in the hotel men's rooms. They presented it to Dr. Bowman, who was not amused.

April 1, 1931. All contractors stopped work on the Cathedral of Learning. The piles of stone were stored in the building and further shipments were canceled. Pitt workers covered the unfinished construction and the scaffolding to protect them from the weather. Bowman ordered the halt because he had used up his money and could not collect more in these lean times. The stonework began in the light wells on the first floor, but it was not visible from the street until it reached the fifth floor, where it could be clearly seen. This gave rise to the assumption that the stonework began on the fifth floor and to the legend that Bowman did not begin the stonework at the bottom floor and work up because he feared the trustees might order him to put a roof over the fifth floor and forget the rest of the building.

Cathedral of Learning, about 1970. Forbes Field is in the left background. Hillman Library and David Lawrence Hall (then the Common Facilities Building) are to its right. The William Pitt Union (then the Schenley Union) and the Schenley Quadrangle Residence Halls are in the right background.

While operations were being halted, a number of newspapers, including the *Shanghai Times* of August 9, 1931, ran a press service drawing of the Cathedral of Learning, hailing its successful completion.

During the lull in the work, a Pitt crew dug the lawn to a level approximately seven inches below finished grade, installed French drains and a sprinkler system, and then spread five to six inches of "fairly good top soil" and over this two inches of compost. To each sixteen cubic feet of compost were added five pounds of bone meal, one pound of ammonium sulfate, and one-half pound of arsenate of lead. A mixture of grass seed followed: South German Bent, 30 percent by weight; Kentucky Blue Grass, 50 percent; Pacey English Rye, 10 percent; and Red Top, 10 percent. Because of a continuing flood of inquiries about the beautiful lawn that resulted, the administration had to produce a pamphlet: "Specifications for Building Lawns."

September 1, 1931. The University entered into a five-year agreement with two other institutions to sponsor the Historical Survey—a program of collecting, researching, and writing in the field of Western Pennsylvania history. Pitt contributed $5,000 a year for five years; the Buhl Foundation made a grant of $20,000; the Historical Society of Western Pennsylvania, then in financial distress, was unable to pay its commitment of $10,000 but supplied office space and research services. Solon J. Buck moved to Pittsburgh from the University of Minnesota to serve as director and editor of the Historical Society, as a professor of history at Pitt, and as director of the Historical Survey. On August 31, 1935, he went on to greater scholarly pursuits in government service in Washington, and Leland D. Baldwin, lecturer in the Pitt history department, took over editorial direction of the survey.

Twelve historical works were commissioned, and by August 31, 1936, when the Buhl Foundation grant expired, nine completed manuscripts were on hand, waiting for a publisher. (Another was near completion; two authors did not finish their books.) Out of these circumstances was born the University of Pittsburgh Press. Paul Mellon told Dr. Bowman on September 18, 1936, that the A. W. Mellon Educational and Charitable Trust would give the University $30,000 in three yearly installments to establish a university press. Lawrence E. Irwin (Class of 1925), experienced in printing, was made manager of the operation.

The first volume published—not one of the twelve originally commissioned works—was written by Agnes Lynch Starrett, then an instructor in the Pitt English department (Class of 1920): *Through One Hundred and Fifty Years: The University of Pittsburgh.* This, a 600-page illustrated history of the University up to the year 1937, was released at the start of the school's 150th anniversary celebration. Then ten Historical Survey books appeared over the next five years:

Pittsburgh: The Story of a City, 1937, by Leland D. Baldwin. It went into a second printing within four months.

Pen Pictures of Early Western Pennsylvania, 1938, John W. Harpster, editor. A collection of excerpts from early diaries, journals, and other documents.

Early Western Pennsylvania Politics, 1938, by Russell J. Ferguson, then associate professor of history at the University.

With Rifle and Plow, 1938, by J. Ernest Wright, Elisabeth M. Sellers, and Jeannette Shirk. A compilation of sixteen stories and legends of the Western Pennsylvania frontier.

Whiskey Rebels: The Story of a Frontier Uprising, 1939, by Leland D. Baldwin.

The Planting of Civilization in Western Pennsylvania, 1939, by Solon J. and Elizabeth Hawthorne Buck. An account of the development of agriculture, industry, education, religion, social customs, and law and order on the Western Pennsylvania frontier.

Council Fires on the Upper Ohio, 1940, by Randolph C. Downes. The story of the conquest of the region told from the point of view of the Native Americans.

Pioneer Life in Western Pennsylvania, 1940, by J. Ernest Wright and Doris S. Corbett. The story of daily life on the colonial frontier.

The Keelboat Age on Western Waters, 1941, by Leland D. Baldwin.

Guidebook to Historic Places in Western Pennsylvania, 1938, compiled by the Historical Survey.

The first nine of these books are not only significant contributions to scholarship and to an understanding of events on the colonial frontier, but are highly readable works on a colorful period of the nation's history as well. (The tenth, the guidebook, was replaced in time by better and up-to-date versions.) The books are clean typographically, error-free, and printed on good stock with sturdy bindings; six are admirably illustrated by original commissioned art. The prices, even for the time, were low, from $1.50 for the guidebook to $5.00 for the most scholarly work, *The Planting of Civilization*, a classic book in its field.

The Buhl Foundation bought 1,250 copies of each book at discount to pay the cost of printing; it distributed them without charge to public libraries and to the libraries of local colleges and universities. In 1986 six of the ten works were still in print, in paperback. They have in some degree offset the truism of American letters: "Pennsylvania had the history, New England had the historians."

Despite the success of these works and the prestige they and their successors brought to the University, the Press at the beginning of the 1940s was in an uncertain position. Its function, its status, its relationship to the University were undefined and, it would appear, misunderstood. Bowman sent copies of the books with his card to friends, supporters, and potential supporters, and he used the Press to produce handsome promotional pamphlets, making no distinction between publication for public relations purposes and the publication of scholarly and semipopular books after careful evaluation by impartial judges. He had little interest in the selection of scholarly books, and he was indifferent to the broader potential of the Press. Today one of the major goals of a university is, along with teaching, research and the dissemination of research through publication. But to Rufus Henry Fitzgerald, his provost, Bowman suggested that ways should be found "to stop the men around here rushing into print." The function of the Press, he observed, "is to publish historical books on Western Pennsylvania, not to encourage the faculty to publish." George Carver, English professor (to whom this writer owes fealty as his preceptor), had a broader vision. He proposed in 1938 that the Press should encourage the production of books other than those on local

history; that it should have "a revolving fund sufficient for the Press to take some chances in its selections"; and that an editorial board of faculty members, their identity secret, should be created to pass on the value of manuscripts proposed for publication. Bowman thought such a board "would not be wise."

September 9, 1931. The Fanny Edel Falk Elementary School opened its doors as a private school on the crest of University Hill. The building was an outright gift to the University from Leon Falk, Jr., and his sister, Marjorie Falk Levy of Paris, in memory of their mother, whose name it bears. The cost was $125,400 for construction and $200,000 for endowment.* Known from the first as "progressive," "experimental," "a model observation school," and "a laboratory school," the institution in its first year enrolled 78 children and had as staff a principal, seven full-time teachers, and a part-time teacher in physical education from the University. (It had a capacity for 155 students.) Pupils were accepted from the ages of 2½ to 12 years. They were admitted to a nursery school, a kindergarten, and the first six grades. Tuition was $200 a year for the three lower grades, $275 for the upper grades. The classrooms were open, movement was free, classes were not graded in the conventional way, and teachers sometimes worked as teams. Corporal punishment was banned. Parents were considered equal partners with the teachers in the education of children. "Experiences" were organized to give the child a chance to express his or her personality in some form of creative activity.

In its seventh year, the school expanded to eight grades, giving full preparation for high school. In time it introduced full-day kindergarten, courses aided by tape recorders and computers, and other advanced methods of teaching that have become

---

*The building resembles an English country house of fine stonework design. When the construction cost rose to $180,125, some $55,000 more than the Falks subscribed for that purpose, the University made up the deficit by "borrowing" from the endowment subscription. The Falks, on learning this, not only restored the endowment to its original figure but paid the University $17,354 in interest the deficit payment would have earned if it had been working as endowment.

commonplace. Its teachers are considered Pitt employees; some of them also teach education courses at the University.

September 28, 1931. The Falk Clinic was dedicated and opened on this date, when Maurice Falk presented the key to Dr. Bowman in an informal ceremony. A part of the Medical Center of the University, it was soon treating 80,000 outpatients a year at no cost or at a nominal rate, in accordance with their needs. Some 125 juniors and seniors in the School of Medicine performed clinical duties there under the guidance and instruction of the medical faculty.

October 25, 1932. Almost six thousand students attended classes in the Cathedral of Learning. For the first time in more than a decade, the University did not have to schedule classes during the noon hour.

December 16, 1932. Dr. Charles Glen King, young professor of chemistry at the University, told the Chicago Section of the American Chemical Society how he and his associates had for the first time isolated and identified vitamin C. After five years of patient and intensive experimentation, after elaborate precipitations and crystallizations, he had produced in 1932 the crystalline substance that scientists the world over had long been striving for: a compound of carbon, hydrogen, and oxygen—a hexuronic acid. The following year he synthesized vitamin C, the preventive of scurvy, one of mankind's oldest diseases.

January 2, 1933. Pitt, eastern football champions again, played the Southern California Trojans in the Rose Bowl at Pasadena. Most fans from Pittsburgh who went to the game traveled by train, a three-day journey, while others spent a week or more driving. A select few, by paying a round-trip fare of $248.30, were able to travel by Transcontinental and Western Air *in less than twenty-four hours!* Their all-metal Ford high-speed trimotor left the City-County Airport at midnight and made the first of many stops the next morning at Kansas City. After a second day of transcontinental flight, they arrived in Los Angeles shortly after 9:00 P.M.

July 26, 1933. The University gave the city a strip ten feet wide of its Frick Acres tract with which to widen Fifth Avenue between Bigelow Boulevard and Bellefield Avenue from sixty feet to eighty feet.

August 10, 1933. The General Alumni Association, defunct for the first three dreadful depression years, was revived and reorganized. The University had some 20,000 living alumni.

December 3, 1933. Congressman Henry Ellenbogen of Allegheny County revealed a plan he had helped to develop by which the University would receive $2.8 million in federal loans and gifts for continuing work on the tall building. The Public Works Administration would turn over $840,000 (30 percent of that amount) as an outright gift and would lend $1.96 million (the other 70 percent) at 4 percent interest. The University, in return, would (1) spend $360,000 of the gift to build a dormitory near the Cathedral and (2) become a "public institution." That is, Pitt would amend its charter to have a majority of its thirty-two trustees appointed by the governor, the mayor, and the courts.

Chancellor Bowman and Chairman George Hubbard Clapp rejected the proposal as politely as they could. They were unwilling to become a public institution, and they recognized the obvious: that a $1.96 million debt would be impossible to pay off with private grants and gifts, since donors prefer to give their money to erect buildings or start programs, not to pay off back obligations—especially to the government. Bowman and the trustees were reluctant to impugn the public spirit of donors and potential donors by pointing this out, and so they simply declared that they were unwilling to go into debt. Bowman, unfortunately, was quoted as saying that if the government held a mortgage on the Cathedral, it might foreclose.

The newspapers had been kind to Pitt, and they would be kind again, but on this occasion there was a fierce editorial outcry. ("A Strange Attitude," "The public will register both disappointment and surprise," "The naked skeleton of the lower floors is becoming an eyesore," "The Cathedral of Learning . . . was to have been an emblem of the greatness of this district and the accomplishments of higher education. In its present unfinished condition it is neither. It stands as the monument to a dream that didn't work out, to an ambition that was a little too extensive." This last editorial appeared under the heading "Gross Indifference.")

December 23, 1933. The federal Civil Works Administration (CWA) announced that it was giving a $300,000 labor grant for work on the Cathedral. Pitt contributed $520,000 in materials. Until the program ended on April 30, 1934, a force of 1,259 previously unemployed stonemasons, ironworkers, plumbers, electricians, engineers, and carpenters worked at the site twenty-four hours a week. There were unforeseen complications when it was discovered that the code numbers chalked on some of the shaped limestone blocks had been weathered away.

During this time, Bowman remade the top of the tall building. He had ordered a blunt, flat top on the tower, thinking that it would convey the idea that the building's upward thrust of straight Gothic lines might have continued on to heaven. He changed his mind when he saw it. He told Albert Klimcheck, who had become the University architect, to add a forty-foot Gothic turret at each of the four corners.

January 23, 1934. On this date a scandal was unearthed in the work on the Cathedral. Before they could obtain employment, jobless carpenters had to sign a contract with the Pittsburgh Central Labor Union that called for payment of 50 percent of their CWA wages ($1.25 an hour) to the union to make up for dues they could not pay during their jobless years. In the brouhaha that followed, the University, an innocent bystander, wisely said nothing.

February 28, 1934. The University began an all-out, professionally directed campaign to raise $1.65 million by public subscription. Dr. Bowman (who had cut his own salary from $35,000 to $31,500) told 1,000 alumni at the annual Charter Day banquet that if this amount were collected, the CWA would add $950,000 in federal funds. The total, $2.6 million, would make it possible to complete and equip the lower twenty floors (of which only seven were finished and in use), to rough-finish the upper half, and to buy the materials needed immediately by the CWA workers. This would bring all students into classes in the main building except those studying medicine, dentistry, pharmacy, and

chemistry and, of course, those attending the three regional junior colleges at Johnstown (established in 1927), Erie (1928), and Uniontown (1928).

The campaign started off well under the slogan "Finish the Cathedral." Homer D. Williams again was general chairman, and he had five outstanding vice chairmen. The tall building was thrown open for a week-long open house and public inspection, its tower illuminated with floodlights from the thirty-second floor buttresses; 12,243 visitors came. There was a big dinner on the top floor of the Cathedral and another in the unfinished Commons Room, which had been cleared of building materials for this occasion. Lowell Thomas gave one of his nightly newscasts from the top of the tower. Good publicity arose from a program for choosing 100 great Pittsburghers, for whom 100 memorial rooms would be named. A publicist invited George Gibson, manager of the Pittsburgh Pirates, to choose a player who would catch a baseball thrown from the forty-second story of the Cathedral. Gibson refused. "Not by a damn sight," he said. Newspaper comment was quite favorable. Editorial heads included: "The Pitt Cathedral Deserves Popular Support Because It Serves the People," "Complete the Cathedral—The Beautiful Building, if Finished, Will Be a Joy Forever," "The City Should Welcome the Opportunity to Get the Cathedral Finished."

The campaign was not a success. It raised only $635,000 by subscription—$1 million short of its goal. Times were bad, and perhaps people remembered that the University had turned down what they thought was a good offer from the federal government. But the last exterior stones—eight two-ton blocks—were put into place in October 1934. From the outside, the Cathedral of Learning was finished.

June 6, 1934. Hervey Allen, Pitt Business Administration graduate (1915), author of the 500,000-word romantic novel *Anthony Adverse*, which had sold one million copies since its publication one year earlier, was given the doctor of letters degree.

March 31, 1936. John Bowman had asked Andrew Mellon for $500,000 with which to finish the Commons Room, the last major construction work on the Cathedral. On this day Mellon told him to go ahead on the program and finish "the big room." He said that for the present, at least, there was to be no publicity about his gift.

April 1936. Campus enrollment was increased by 2,317 students when the downtown division of the University was moved to the Cathedral of Learning. All night school classes were now held in the tall building.

May 1, 1936. The Law School closed its downtown offices and classrooms and library and moved into the fourteenth, fifteenth, and sixteenth floors of the Cathedral, though they were finished only in the rough. It was the first school of the University to move as an entire unit into the building.

May 4, 1936. The University librarians moved their books and desks and chairs and card catalogues to the fourth, fifth, and sixth floors of the Cathedral. There was now room, they announced, for 730 students to use the library at the same time—six times the capacity at State Hall. There were even separate reading rooms for men and women.

August 4, 1936. John Woodruff, Pitt middle-distance and cross country runner (Class of 1939), won the 800-meter event in the eleventh Olympic Games held in Berlin. An Olympic gold is the highest honor an amateur athlete can attain. Woodruff, called "one of the greatest natural runners of all time," won it as a freshman, as a relatively unknown contender, and in a race the United States had not won since 1912. He had three more years in an outstanding career at Pitt, winning a string of Intercollegiate Association of Amateur Athletes of America (IC4A) and National Collegiate Athletic Association (NCAA) championships and setting school and stadium records that held up for years after his graduation.

Woodruff became a career army officer. At the 1972 Olympics held in Munich, he was a guest of the German government—a kind of atonement for Hitler's rudeness to winning American black athletes in Berlin in 1936.

November 6, 1936. The University announced that work was being pushed forward rapidly on the Commons Room, with nearly one hundred men employed and Indiana limestone arriving at the rate

of two carloads a day. Only 10 percent of the limestone, or approximately forty carloads, had been shipped to date. The remainder of the 4,500 tons was expected by January 1937. In Bedford, Indiana, three mills were preparing the stone according to specifications.

February 28, 1937. On this day, Charter Day, began four months of celebration of the 150th anniversary of the founding of the University. A stream of publicity was released, most of it beginning with the story of the University's founding in a three-room log house on the western frontier. Some of it emphasized that Pitt was the nation's twelfth-oldest university, with seventeen schools and divisions embracing nearly every phase of modern education.

The day began with an academic procession marching into a student convocation in Soldiers and Sailors Memorial Hall, where more than 1,000 persons witnessed the annual Scholars Day ceremony; watched a "Book of Scholars" weighing forty-five pounds being carried in, "which henceforth will bear the names of Pitt students who distinguish themselves in scholastic pursuits"; and heard "a stirring address" titled "Training for Freedom." The day continued after lunch with an official inspection tour of the Cathedral of Learning, now 90 percent finished. The visitors, escorted by members of Mortar Board, a senior women's honorary sorority, looked at the new library, the Law School, the faculty club on the seventeenth floor, and the partly completed Commons Room, "the largest room of its kind in the world."

The day ended with a banquet in the main ballroom of the Schenley Hotel. The whole first floor was reserved for this occasion; more than 1,500 alumni were present. The national commander of the American Legion, Harry W. Colmery (Class of 1916), spoke, as did Pittsburgh mayor Cornelius D. Scully (Class of 1904), Agnes L. Starrett, University historian, and Chancellor Bowman. The chancellor chose this occasion to call for an end to mediocre teaching, mediocre thinking, and mediocre living, to be replaced by a birth of real intellectual life on the campus. The Pitt band played and the Pitt glee club sang.

But the major event of the evening took place

John Woodruff, called one of the greatest natural runners of all time, had a distinguished four-year career, 1935–1939.

while thirty minutes of the proceedings were being broadcast coast to coast over the NBC Blue Network to 25,000 alumni, 40,000 former students, and other interested listeners. When Coach John B. Sutherland was introduced as a speaker, the alumni, despite the rule against applause during the carefully timed broadcast, began to cheer, stomp their feet, and whistle. They were, it seems, expressing their allegiance in a dispute, fully reported in the press, between the chancellor and the coach over athletic policy. Only with difficulty could they be quelled and the broadcast continued.

May 6, 1937. The new $8 million Mellon Institute of Industrial Research building was dedicated. Its sixty perfect Ionic limestone columns, said to be the largest solid stone columns in the world, carried one by one from Indiana strapped to two flatcars and brought to the site on special trucks after midnight, were an architectural wonder of the time.

Andrew W. Mellon spoke at the ceremony. It was one of his last public appearances, for he died on August 26, 1937. To John Bowman he had said, "All these years I have thought that you were wrong in what you wanted to do. I have changed my mind. I think now that you were right and that I was wrong."

June 4, 1937. Chancellor Bowman, wielding a silver trowel, laid the cornerstone of the Commons Room at 4:00 P.M. on a Friday afternoon. It was a large, hollow stone, suitably inscribed, a gift of the 1937 graduating class. In it was sealed a mélange of documents, some of them printed on special paper warranted to last 500 years, the expected life of the building. Among the documents were the signatures of the graduating class and of the faculty of the schools of the University, a University catalogue, a copy of the 1937 *Owl*, a copy of the *Pitt News*, the names of those who gave money to build the Cathedral, progress photographs of the construction, the names of the craftsmen and workmen "whose skill and energy built it to last time out of mind," Agnes

Starrett's history of the University, a sesquicentennial medal, an engraved plate to commemorate the gifts of seventeen Nationality Rooms, and a "cornerstone statement." ("The Cathedral of Learning expresses for Pittsburgh a desire to live honestly in a world where kindness and the happiness of creating are life.")

June 6, 1937. At a Sunday afternoon open house, 6,200 people visited the Cathedral. Guides told the impressive figures on the tall building: 9 million cubic feet of space, 87 classrooms, 113 laboratories, 71 graduate research laboratories, 11 medium-sized lecture rooms, 12 large departmental lecture rooms, 80 conference rooms, 19 libraries, 1 faculty club, and 1 Commons Room, 175 by 128 by 52 feet high.

June 7, 1937. In a culminating event of the sesquicentennial celebration, the trustees gave a banquet in the Commons Room for 1,125 graduates receiving degrees and for all the faculty and administrators. Food was relayed from the Schenley Hotel kitchens to steam tables set up in rooms off the first floor corridor.

June 9, 1937. At commencement exercises, an honorary degree (doctor of science) was conferred on John Weber in appreciation for his services in the building of the three Gothic structures on the campus (the Cathedral, the Stephen Foster Memorial, and Heinz Chapel). The commencement speaker, Walter Albert Jessup, president of the Carnegie Foundation for the Advancement of Teaching, called the Cathedral of Learning "the most daring and the most beautiful thing ever attempted on a university campus."

September 1938. The School of Applied Social Sciences was established as a professional school on the graduate level. Its purpose was to meet the growing need for properly qualified people to administer social welfare services. A Buhl Foundation grant of $194,740 later made it possible for the school, already one of the four largest of its type in the United States, to strengthen its program and to build a library on social work.

January 28, 1939. The chancellor, in an effort "to learn the pulse of the undergraduate student body," held the first of a series of fireside chats. Ten stu-

dents outstanding for classroom work and campus activity were invited to his office on Thursday afternoons for what came to be called "charm teas." The chancellor, struggling not to be stiff and formal, asked the students about themselves and their ambitions; the students asked him how he built the Cathedral of Learning.

May 9, 1939. The old Mellon Institute building on O'Hara Street was given to the University. It was remodeled and equipped to provide laboratories and additional classrooms for the School of Medicine. These increased facilities made it possible to admit 70 percent more students to the freshman class in medicine.

September 1939. The School of Nursing was established. Its mission was "to coordinate and strengthen the instruction already being given in hospitals and in the University's undergraduate schools" and to provide courses leading to the bachelor of science in nursing degree and to graduate work.

Three striking and lasting achievements of the Bowman administration fell into place in 1937 and 1938: the erection of the Stephen Collins Foster Memorial and the Heinz Memorial Chapel (the second and third, and last, buildings added to the Cathedral campus), and the presentation to the University of the first four Nationality Rooms.

The idea for a memorial to Foster had been conceived in 1927 by the ladies of the city's Tuesday Musical Club. They approached Dr. Bowman and asked his advice and support in putting up a bronze statue somewhat like that of Robert Burns in Schenley Park. Bowman proposed that they put up a building instead, perhaps a small theater for chamber music. Foster, he pointed out, was born in Pittsburgh, almost within sight of the University campus, lived in Pittsburgh, wrote most of his songs there, and married a Pittsburgh girl, possibly "Jeanie with the Light Brown Hair." He offered to donate a site near the Cathedral, to maintain and operate the building, and (in a casual agreement that caused some difficulties later) to give the musical club certain rights in using it. The ladies formed a memorial

The Stephen Collins Foster Memorial, dedicated in 1937.

building committee, the governor of the Commonwealth proclaimed a Stephen Collins Foster Day, and for some years after that not much happened.

Late in 1932 Dr. John W. Oliver, head of the Pitt Department of History, had told Bowman that Josiah Kirby Lilly, Indianapolis pharmaceutical manufacturer, had been collecting art and articles associated with Foster. Oliver urged the chancellor to call on Mr. Lilly. Bowman did so, and in time he was able to report that Mr. Lilly was giving his entire collection, on which he had spent $162,000, to the University. It contained manuscripts, first editions of sheet music, rare books, letters, and personal possessions of the composer—his flute, portable melodeon (3½ octave range), the pocketbook he was carrying when at the age of thirty-seven he died after a fall in New York City, and the thirty-eight cents in paper money and coins found in it, with the piece of paper bearing the haunting phrase in his handwriting, presumably the title of a song he did not live to write, "Dear Friends and Gentle Hearts." And of course his 189 vocal and 12 instrumental pieces, including the sheet music of his songs: "My Old Kentucky Home"; "Massa's in de Cold, Cold Ground"; "Old Folks at Home"; "Old Black Joe"; "Camptown Races"; "Oh! Susanna"; "Beautiful Dreamer"; and "Come Where My Love Lies Dreaming." In accepting the Foster Hall collection the University was to serve as "trustee for America."

With such a treasure promised, $500,000 was raised: half of it from Josiah Lilly and his son Eli; $125,000 from A. W. Mellon and the estate of R. B. Mellon (who had died on December 1, 1933); $50,000 from the Buhl Foundation; and the balance through the efforts of the Memorial Committee and the Tuesday Musical Club. Some 2,160 persons in twenty-six states made contributions, and once again the schoolchildren of Pittsburgh gave up their candy money and contributed $7,000. The Lilly Endowment thereafter made an annual contribution for operation of the collection, beginning in 1937 with $15,000, and has made grants for special publications and renovations. Fletcher Hodges, Jr., came from Indianapolis in 1937 to supervise installation of the collection and stayed on at the Memorial as curator and director.

Charles Klauder designed the Foster Memorial in Gothic style in harmony with the Cathedral. It was built as a steel frame structure with hand-cut Indiana limestone blocks. Samuel Yellin of Philadelphia, called the greatest worker in wrought iron since the Renaissance, fashioned the decorative ironwork, and Charles J. Connick of Boston designed and made the stained glass windows. The building has an auditorium-theater seating 600, a stage, a social room, a kitchen, an office for the Tuesday Musical Club, and, in a separate wing, an office for the director, a library and storage rooms, and a twelve-sided shrine and museum holding the Lilly collection. Incredible as it may seem in 1986, the Memorial was built for $550,000. Ground was broken on January 13, 1935, the seventy-first anniversary of the death of Foster. The dedication ceremony, with Josiah Lilly delivering the main address, took place as one of the last events of the University's 150th anniversary celebration on June 2, 1937.

The first four Nationality Rooms—Swedish, German, Russian, and Scottish—were presented to the University by their sponsoring committees on July 8, 1938. On this occasion, on a Friday evening, nearly one thousand people bearing tickets of invitation assembled in the Commons Room. Some were wearing colorful national dress. An academic procession of University officials, trustees, deans, and members of the faculty entered the room at half past eight. George Hubbard Clapp made an address of welcome. Chancellor Bowman thanked the committees of nationals and children of nationals whose work had made possible the first four rooms. Now, he said, they were all "ex-officio members of the Pitt faculty"; they had given the University their own hearts "in a manner no other university had ever known." The four rooms were presented, one at a time, and accepted. Two bagpipers played. A German *männerchor*, a Russian choir, and a Greek tabor chorus sang. The rooms were opened for public inspection the following Sunday afternoon.

The concept of the Nationality Rooms, one of the striking achievements of the Bowman administration, evolved when two people, two problems, and a set of serendipitous circumstances came together in the mid-1920s.

John Bowman was driven by the problem of making the interior of the Cathedral of Learning worthy of its dramatic exterior. He said over and over, "People who see the tall building from the outside must not be disappointed when they enter." The vaulted Commons Room, of course, fifty-two feet (four stories) high and almost a half-acre in extent, would certainly be worthy, but he worried about the classrooms. They must be different. They must be better. He startled his trustees with talk of classrooms with oriental rugs, wood-burning fireplaces, and chairs in circles rather than in rows. He thought of designing and furnishing rooms to represent fields of study, such as mathematics, geography, history, and philosophy, but he found that too difficult to express.

John Bowman's second problem was that of persuading the entire community to support his great undertaking. In the Pittsburgh district—Allegheny and the six adjoining counties—in the 1920s, the

Herbert Barnett

Nationality Room committees presented the first four rooms to the University on July 8, 1938: German (above), Russian, Scottish, and Swedish.

entire community meant a mixture of peoples from forty-three foreign countries. Of a total population of 2,117,000 in the district, 425,000 were foreign-born. These included, in rounded numbers, 66,000 Italians. 53,000 Poles. 51,000 Austrians. 37,000 Czechoslovaks. 36,000 Germans. 29,000 Russians. 26,000 Hungarians. 23,000 Irish. 23,000 Yugoslavs. 11,000 Scots. 5,000 Lithuanians. 5,000 Swedes.

4,000 Welsh. And smaller numbers of Danes, Dutch, Norwegians, Armenians, Belgians, Swiss, French, Finns, Spaniards, Romanians, Bulgarians, Serbs, Greeks, Turks, as well as 678 Asians and 2 Portuguese.

These were the foreign-born. Some 513,000 more inhabitants were American-born of two foreign parents, and 158,000 more were born of mixed parents.

Herbert Barnett

The Russian Room.

Thus one-fifth of the population of the Pittsburgh district were foreign-born and one-third were children of immigrants. And thus every other person living in the district was an immigrant or the child of an immigrant. At the University of Pittsburgh itself, one of every three students was foreign-born or the child of an immigrant.

Dr. Bowman set out to persuade these various nationality groups to help him pay for his tall building. He visited their communities in the city and in the Ohio, Allegheny, and Monongahela valleys, and he talked there of his program at churches, clubs, and social halls. Unaccustomed to attention except when they were sought out as a source of labor and votes, these people were receptive when he spoke about their national heritage and the need to preserve their Old World cultures. His first purpose was to raise money, but he was genuinely moved by the distress of parents and grandparents of young people—including those attending the University—who were ashamed of their national origins, bored by talk of the homeland, and embarrassed by broken English, foreign dress, and old-country customs. Thus it came about that Bowman conceived the extraordinary idea of asking each nationality group if it would be willing to work to build and pay for some kind of special room in the Cathedral that would be dedicated as a memorial to the art, religion, and culture it cherished. The groups he talked with were pleased at being asked to put rooms in such a building. Bowman asked one of his faculty members to consider the matter and represent him in negotiating with the nationality groups.

The person he chose was Ruth Crawford Mitchell, a thirty-five-year-old member of the Department of Sociology. After graduating from Vassar in 1912 and from Washington University with a master's degree in 1915, she had worked with the national YWCA in organizing international institutes for foreign-born girls in New England, New York, and New Jersey. After the war, the YWCA sent her to Prague as director of a team of American social workers to make a social survey for the Czechoslovak Red Cross. When she went to Pittsburgh in 1923 with her husband, a Westinghouse engineer, J. Steele Gow put her on the faculty as a lecturer on the history of immigration and the problems of immigrant assimilation. Bowman then had her research and write a three-volume study on the national origins of students at the University.

Out of their meetings and discussions, John Bowman and Ruth Mitchell developed the idea of having each ethnic group sponsor a "nationality classroom." These would be on the first floor around the Commons Room. A committee from each nationality group would be responsible, through its own efforts, for the planning, design, decoration, and furnishing of its own room. There would be certain guidelines. The content of each room would express the best of its nation's culture and history. All work and materials must be honest, authentic, and of the best possible quality. Only one political reference would be permitted: a symbol

University Archives

Ruth Crawford Mitchell worked for more than three decades to create the Nationality Rooms. She is shown here in 1935.

carved on the stone shield in the corridor above the entrance. No living person would be portrayed. The room's design should represent a period predating the American Constitution and the founding of the University in 1787. The architects and designers should be, save in exceptional circumstances, natives of the country represented by the sponsoring committee. The rooms must be working classrooms, not museum pieces.

Mrs. Mitchell began by making a survey of the nationality leaders in the city. "By asking around," she recalled, "I compiled a list of doctors, lawyers, businessmen, and leaders in both men and women's nationality benefit organizations—organizations that dealt with illness and death. Dr. Bowman invited these people, nationality by nationality, to spend an evening at the old Faculty Club—on the hill above Fifth Avenue, about where Scaife Hall is

Herbert Barnett

The Scottish Room.

today—to discuss the project and his dreams for the new building."

By the autumn of 1926, six separate Nationality Committees were meeting in one of the vine-covered frame houses still on the Cathedral grounds. By 1936, seventeen committees with some six hundred elected members were at work. They had collected $151,000 and were trying for $200,000. They raised money by bake sales, church events, benefits at an amusement park, and by soliciting individual donors, fraternal unions, and social groups—by a Swedish Christmas smorgasbord, a Polish festival, a Czech concert, an exhibit of Lithuanian sculpture.

They arranged to form counterpart committees in their countries abroad, and from them they received guidance on choice of design, materials, architects, artisans, and craftsmen. Some of the artists and artisans worked in their own studios; others traveled to Pittsburgh to work at the site. Polish artists, for example, came from Cracow to paint the beamed ceiling of the Polish Room with informal

Herbert Barnett

The Swedish Room.

geometric Renaissance decorations. In preparing their colors, they required delivery of one dozen fresh eggs every morning. When the colors were being mixed, visitors were asked to leave and the doors were locked.

Not infrequently an overseas committee would obtain gifts from its own government, generally through the ministry of education, of money, furniture, rugs, books, even the services of architects, artists, and artisans. Sometimes the gifts would be rare or unique—a part of the Polish Room cornerstone, for example, from the twelfth-century Jagiellonian Library in Cracow; and Lithuanian wall frames made from black oak that had been buried for decades in a peat bog. And, later, linenfold paneling from Britain's bombed-out House of Commons. In 1936 Ruth Mitchell spent four months in Europe, traveling 14,667 miles, to discuss final plans for decoration of the various rooms with architects and counterpart committees.

"The depression," she said, "helped us in the long run. It gave us time to plan and think."

Four more Nationality Rooms were completed and dedicated in 1939: the Yugoslavian, Czechoslovakian, Hungarian, and Chinese. Two more were dedicated in 1940: the Polish and the Lithuanian. Eight others were in progress, with much of their contents completed and in storage.

By this time the Nationality Room program had clearly demonstrated that it would fulfill the purposes for which it was intended. A stream of visitors began to call to see the rooms. The rooms did indeed bring the ethnic communities into the mainstream of University affairs, and thereby deeper into the life of the city. They were eminently successful as expressions of the values of ethnic culture, customs, history, and thought.

"The creation of the Nationality Rooms," Mrs. Mitchell said, "was the first time that any university in the United States recognized the immigrant groups as bringing something other than industrial brawn—that they, too, had a cultural heritage which they would like to share." Andrey Avinoff, director of Carnegie Museum and designer of the Russian Room, declared, "The Nationality Rooms hold that unwritten curriculum which is the real teaching force of a University. . . . It lives in the teaching which stirs the student to vitality, to honest thinking and doing, to appreciation, to his own best." Someone else has called them simply "the classrooms that teach."

In the 1970s revised guidelines were introduced by Director E. Maxine Bruhns that permitted important Pittsburgh groups, formerly excluded by the "nation" principle, to build classrooms. A new generation of rooms will eventually join the Early American Room on the third floor. They will represent African Heritage, Israeli Heritage, Armenia, Ukraine, and Austria.

On a Sunday afternoon, November 20, 1938, with 450 invited guests present, the third and final building on the Cathedral of Learning campus was dedicated: the Heinz Memorial Chapel.

The idea of building a small nonsectarian chapel on the campus was conceived by Henry J. Heinz, who had been a trustee and who in his will in 1919 gave the University $100,000 for that purpose. His original intent had been to dedicate the chapel to students past, present, and future, but his children decided to double the bequest 2½ times over and build a larger chapel to the memory of Anna Margaretha Schmitt Heinz and Henry J. Heinz, mother and son.

In September 1928 John Bowman wrote to John Weber, "Mr. [Howard] Heinz, at his home last evening, agreed for the family and himself to go ahead with the proposed chapel. . . . The total cost is not to exceed $570,000. This does not include the organ, for which he will make an allowance of $50,000 additional, this sum not to be included in the figure on which architectural and building fees are based." Mr. Weber was to confer with Mr. Klauder in Philadelphia and then accompany him to meet Mr. Heinz at the chapel on the campus at Princeton. No announcement of the Heinz Chapel should be made until approved by the trustees.

Ground was broken in August 1933, the cornerstone was laid in February 1934, and the building was completed in November 1938. In the meantime, the cost had risen to nearly $1 million, of which some $200,000 was for twenty-three stained glass windows. Howard Heinz delivered an address in turning over the Chapel to the University, and John Bowman delivered an address in accepting it. The principal address was made by the famous Reverend William Sloane Coffin, who had been Howard Heinz's roommate at Yale and best man at his wedding in 1906. A few days after the dedication, Thanksgiving services were held at the Chapel; 450 people filled every seat, and several hundred others had to be turned away.

Charles Klauder was not present to see the third of his buildings dedicated on the University campus. He had died one month earlier.

Klauder built the Chapel of gray Indiana limestone, inside and out, in a thirteenth-century Gothic style that suggests the Sainte-Chapelle in Paris. It is 146 feet long, 55 feet wide at the transept, and 100 feet high at the nave. It is 256 feet from the ground to the top of the lead-covered spire, which reaches the level of the seventeenth floor of the Cathedral of Learning 110 yards to the west. The four main columns are 43 feet 7 inches high. The high-pitched

(above)
Heinz Chapel under construction, 1934.
(right)
Heinz Chapel completed.

vaults, the pointed arches, the long, thin stone buttresses, the tall windows, all give an illusion of great height.

In a symbolic union of education and religion, carved stone arms or academic shields decorate the outside walls; they are of the oldest European and American universities in the order of their foundings. Samuel Yellin fashioned the ornamental ironwork and hardware. Joseph Gattoni of New York, master in stonework, hand-carved the stone, using flora and fauna supplied him by the botanical and zoological departments of the University. The very names of the materials are intriguing: English pollard quartered oak, Appalachian mountain oak, crab apple stone, Vermont green slate, Numidian marble imported from Egypt.

And then there are the twenty-three stained glass windows. James Truslow Adams called them "vast windows filled with glass that possibly cannot be equalled by European examples created later than the 14th century." The statistics are astonishing. The windows depict 319 figures famous in religion, history, and the arts; the four transept windows, depicting Courage, Tolerance, Temperance, and Truth, are seventy-three feet high, and each contains more than 25,000 pieces of glass. Charles J. Connick, the Pittsburgh-trained master of a lost art, worked for seven years planning, designing, and assembling the windows. The light, tone, and color of stained glass change throughout the day and with the passing seasons, and they had to be harmonized in such a way that no one window at any time or season will outshine the others. Connick placed the cool colors, the blues and greens, on the southern and sunny side of the Chapel, and the warm colors, the reds and golds, in the northern windows, thus bringing about a balanced warmth to the interior.

The windows are beautiful in and of themselves, but, like a symphony or an opera or a poem, they become more beautiful as they are better understood. There is a rich multiplicity of iconography—of symbols and emblems, of themes and characters—that demands, or at least deserves, interpretation. A passage from a guidebook suggests a complexity in one window that is typical of all twenty-three: "The south [choir window] shows the great masters of religious music, Palestrina and Bach, here symbolized as composers and directors accompanied by small figures playing instruments and singing. Palestrina's patron, St. Charles Borromeo, is represented by his symbol, and the arms of Bach's patron, Frederick the Great, are displayed. The growing form is articulated with flowers and birds. The central tracery piece represents Jubal, traditional inventor of the harp and the organ (Gen. 4:21). The text is 'Praise Him with stringed instruments and with organs, praise ye the Lord' (Ps. 150)."

The Heinz Chapel has entered into the life of the University and, indeed, into that of the community, especially in recent years, when its functions and uses have broadened. It is a favored place for weddings and christenings; the waiting list is long. Of the Heinz Chapel John Bowman said in 1940: "The Chapel is not a church. It is not connected with a church. It is a chapel on a university campus. It is part of the education on that campus. . . . Aside from a place of service for the religious groups at the University, it will be open as a center for meditation. . . . The Chapel serves by its presence. Through it high values, such as kindness, faith, courage, and reverence . . . are made vivid."

On March 20, 1939, because of mounting criticism of his conduct in administering the affairs of the University, Chancellor Bowman asked a seven-man committee of the Board of Trustees to "study the situation at the University in all its phases and to report to the Board as early as possible." The secretary of the committee was J. Steele Gow, executive

The nonsectarian chapel on campus was the idea of Henry J. Heinz, founder of the H. J. Heinz Company. After his death in 1919, his children—Howard (above), Clifford, and Irene—increased the gift and built a larger chapel in memory of Henry J. Heinz and his mother, Anna Margaretha Schmitt Heinz. Howard Heinz served as a trustee of the University from 1906 until his death in 1941.

director of the Falk Foundation. Gow first asked if Bowman had any objection to his taking the post. Bowman said no. He felt he could depend on Gow, his friend and one-time protégé, to conduct a fair (and presumably favorable) hearing.

9

The 1930s: Dissension in the House

An outstanding person in the history department and certainly one of the U. top-notchers. . . . He is dogmatic and you will do well not to quarrel with him.

The Campus Index, a student assessment of faculty and courses, on Ralph E. Turner, 1934

THE first wave in a sea of troubles in John Bowman's administration had come on April 22, 1929, back in that period when the steel was going up on the tall building. The causes were trivial, the effect was calamitous, the lessons imparted were clear.

There was on the campus at that time an organization known as the Liberal Club. It was one of 134 chartered student organizations, and its purpose, as set forth in its constitution, was "to conduct open-minded investigations of pressing social problems." It claimed sixty-two undergraduate members and had four faculty advisors. Its chairman, William Albertson, was a sophomore in the College.

On Thursday, April 18, Albertson asked the registrar of the University for permission to use a room in which the club could discuss one of the pressing social problems of the day. He had obtained the approval of his faculty advisors, and the permit was routinely given: Room 118, Alumni Hall, 3:30 P.M. on Monday, April 22.

On Friday, April 19, printed placards appeared on the campus announcing that the purpose of the meeting was to demand the UNCONDITIONAL RELEASE of Tom Mooney and Warren K. Billings, who had been tried and sentenced to life imprisonment "on a trumped-up charge" of throwing a bomb into a patriotic parade in 1916. These two labor leaders, the placards said, had already spent almost fourteen years in jail for a crime they did not commit. Two students and a member of the Mooney-Billings International Labor Defense would speak.*

A great many people in 1929, including Judge Franklin A. Griffin, who presided at the trial, thought that the Mooney-Billings case was what the *Pittsburgh Press* was shortly to call it: "One of the worst miscarriages of justice in the history of the United States." University officials may have agreed with that, but they perceived certain aspects of the situation that they felt they could not ignore. As they saw it, in the cast of thought common to college administrators in the unenlightened 1920s, the Liberal Club was something less than open minded on the subject; it was holding a meeting to spread propaganda; it was using the name and facilities of the University to advance a political end. On Friday, April 19, the permit to hold the meeting was withdrawn. Albertson and several other leaders of the club were ordered to report to the dean of men at the hour the meeting was to have begun.

On Monday, Albertson chanced to meet Harry Elmer Barnes, who was in town speaking to the Hungry Club, a downtown luncheon discussion group. Apparently on the spur of the moment, Albertson asked Barnes if he would appear that afternoon at the Mooney-Billings meeting. Barnes was a great and famous scholar: professor of historical sociology at Smith College, a man with seventy-four lines in *Who's Who in America,* the author of nineteen books, three of them being used as textbooks at Pitt, and a member of the national Free Mooney-Billings Committee. He agreed to speak. Albertson did not tell Barnes that the permit to hold the meeting in a room at the University campus had been withdrawn, nor did he tell the club's faculty advisor, Dr. Phineas Westcott Whiting, associate professor of zoology, who agreed to introduce Barnes. Albertson thereupon notified the newspapers that Barnes would address the meeting.

When the speakers, a scattering of spectators, and reporters and cameramen appeared at 118 Alumni Hall at 3:30 P.M., the door was barred. It was guarded by an assistant to the dean of men, William Daufenbach (any mention of whom was almost invariably accompanied by the helpful information that he had once worked as a prison guard). The permit for the meeting, Daufenbach explained, had been revoked three days earlier, and no meeting could be held in a University building or on the campus. The speakers, the audience, the newspaper reporters, and the cameramen thereupon followed Albertson to the steps of Thaw Hall, attracting people along the way. Albertson then left to keep his appointment with the dean of men. Dr. Whiting made his introduction. Dr. Barnes began to speak

---

*Ten people were killed and forty injured in the bombing. Mooney was condemned to die, but President Wilson intervened to have the sentence changed to life imprisonment. Both men were freed in 1939.

and Mr. Daufenbach interrupted him; the meeting could not be held on University property. Barnes joked at being stopped from speaking, which was a new experience to him, and everyone laughed. The crowd, now grown to perhaps a hundred people, walked a short distance to the parking lot of the Concordia Club. There, standing on the running board of a parked car, Whiting again introduced the speaker. Barnes delivered his plea to free Mooney and Billings and was followed by the representative of the International Labor Defense and the two students. One of these was Frederick Enos Woltman, a *magna cum laude* graduate of Pitt, now a graduate student, a graduate assistant in psychology, and secretary of the local chapter of the American Civil Liberties Union (ACLU). And so the meeting ended. From the point of view of the Liberal Club, it could not have been a greater success.

Later that afternoon, Dr. John Oliver, head of the Pitt history department, happened to see Dr. Barnes, welcomed him cordially to the University, and persuaded him to take part later that afternoon in his seminar course called the History of Science and Technology.

The newspapers played the story for laughs, but condemnation in several local editorial columns was scathing. ("How Chancellor Bowman can reconcile his expressions of idealism with what has happened at the university this week is beyond comprehension." "Whether the university officials acted on their own responsibility or at the initiative of outside interests, they are guilty of the same spirit of injustice which put Mooney and Billings behind the bars and which had kept them there . . . in defiance of all right and honor and decency.")

The story expanded and grew and continued on and on:

• The administration, quoting the signed pledge of chartered organizations that they would abide by all rules and regulations of the University and citing warnings it had given the Liberal Club before, revoked the club's right to function as an activity of the institution and forbade it to hold meetings on University property.

• The club's officers spoke darkly of "some greater power than the school heads that is the directing force" in the effort to silence them. They said, and apparently really believed, that the University of Pittsburgh had dissolved the Liberal Club in order to curry favor with powerful financial interests that wanted to stop the club's effort to free Mooney and Billings. In any event, they declared that they would continue to hold meetings on the campus with or without permission from University authorities.

• University authorities announced that if they did, they would be expelled.

• Frederick Woltman held a press conference in which he said that the trouble had arisen because of an article he had written with William L. Nunn, instructor in economics, for the December issue of H. L. Mencken's *American Mercury*. It was titled "Cossacks" and it criticized the conduct of the state police in the recent coal strike. Governor John S. Fisher, Woltman said, was "mad as a hornet" over the article and was threatening to veto the University's pending appropriation. He added that he and Nunn had been severely rebuked by Dean L. P. Sieg and J. Steele Gow, secretary of the University. He had kept notes each time he was admonished, with a faithful copy of the dialogue and by-play, and he gave these to the press. The interview was reported in one paper under the headline "Free Speech Gag at Pitt Bared by School Faculty" and began, "While the controversy . . . approached a crisis . . . fresh revelations of long-existing scholastic tyranny rose from the campus."

• Members of the Liberal Club held a meeting on April 26 in an empty classroom in Alumni Hall. The acting dean chased them out of the building. The members regrouped on the lawn outside the building, where they passed a resolution, ten votes to five, condemning the *Pitt Weekly* for suppressing news in their case and truckling to the administration. Albertson declared that an official meeting of the Liberal Club had now been held on campus. Arthur McDowell, a member of the Executive Committee, announced that another meeting would be held on May 5. The meeting adjourned.

• The trustees approved the recommendation of

the chancellor that William Albertson and Arthur McDowell be expelled from the University, and that Frederick Woltman be expelled as a student and dismissed as a graduate assistant, his salary to be paid to the end of the year.

Chancellor Bowman refused to make any comment or to be interviewed on the Liberal Club affair, but on April 24 on a visit to Erie he was cornered by a persistent reporter from the *Pittsburgh Press*. The reporter read fifteen questions aloud, one by one, and one by one Bowman refused to respond. Examples: "Do you believe that liberal thought has no place in the university?" "Does the disposal of the Liberal Club meeting have any connection with the canvass for funds for the Cathedral of Learning?" "Is your administration governed by your own ideas or by fear of displeasing men who might be sources of contributions to the school's program?" "Do you believe that a university should encourage its students to think for themselves or that it should try to hold their minds to a pattern set by the administration, perhaps as a reflection of outside influences?" "Do you understand that a continuance of your course of suppression will leave with the entire country the impression that Pitt is under the domination of reactionary influences, and that the power rests with you to correct such an impression?"

In the face of continued silence, the reporter said, "You know that the university is not a private enterprise, but a public institution and that the public is entitled to a knowledge of your policy in these matters." The chancellor murmured an affirmative answer but otherwise would not respond. His only comment, given at the end of the interview, was, "You have certainly thought these [questions] out well."

On May 3 Bowman made a statement in the *Post-Gazette:* "The issue was that the club, with its president known as a Communist and aided by organizations or individuals outside of Pittsburgh and in Pittsburgh, was using the name of the University to advance its propaganda and publicity." Thereafter he was silent again, pleading that since the issue was in pending litigation he was not free to speak. (The ACLU represented the expelled students in an unsuccessful attempt to have them reinstated.)

Twenty-six faculty members signed a petition asking the chancellor to call a faculty meeting and explain his action. Dr. Ralph Edmund Turner, associate professor of history, was elected to present the petition to the chancellor. He presented it, but no meeting was called.

The American Association of University Professors (AAUP) sent two professors to visit the campus and look into the Liberal Club affair. The AAUP took no official action on their report but printed it as an article, "Academic Freedom at the University of Pittsburgh," in the December 1929 issue of the *AAUP Bulletin*. Most accounts of the affair misreported it (and still do so today) by saying that the great Dr. Barnes was denied permission to speak at the University and was escorted off the campus by a University policeman because he was unfit and held radical views. The two AAUP reporters told a factually correct story. They did not find the three students faultless: all three had clearly broken the rules of the University, Woltman by violation of confidence in releasing to the press notes of his interviews with University officials. They bore down on two points that Chancellor Bowman might well have considered more carefully than he apparently did: (1) University authorities displayed an unreasonable fear that the University would be involved by the action of a student organization; and (2) Woltman was dismissed solely on the decision of the chancellor, without a statement of charges, without a hearing, and without recommendation by the dean or faculty of the department in which he performed his duties. The administration, the article said, urgently needed to legalize its relation with the faculty as a body and to recognize the faculty's right to participate in the administrative procedure.

Aftermath: Albertson and McDowell brought a proceeding to compel the University to reinstate them. At the hearing given them by the Board of Trustees, according to Charles F. C. Arensberg, University counsel, "Albertson's chief concern was to take the entire responsibility upon himself and exculpate McDowell, his fellow student, a young Methodist who wanted to become a minister so that he could continue his studies. I admired Albertson very much but his attempted self-sacrifice did no good. Both were expelled and the expulsion stood the test of two court proceedings."

Albertson, who was (or soon became) a card-carrying member of the Communist party, was active for a time in the trade union movement in New York City and then returned to Pittsburgh to become organizational secretary for the Party in the Pittsburgh district.* He was tried and convicted in federal court in 1953 under the Smith Act of "conspiring to teach and advocate the duty or necessity" of the overthrow of the government by violent means. The conviction was overturned by the Supreme Court in 1956.

Frederick Woltman went on to become a top investigative reporter on the *New York World,* later the *World-Telegram,* where in 1931 he won a Pulitzer Prize for the paper and in 1933 an honorable mention for himself. He became a specialist in exposing Communist "Red-front," and "fellow-traveler" movements in the United States, carrying a crusade even to the point where some commentators charged him with Red-baiting. In 1946 he was awarded a Pulitzer Prize for a series of articles on a broad front of Communist activities, including infiltration of and influence on the labor movement.

Those who were inclined to believe that John Bowman was opposed to freedom of speech were encouraged to think so by a second incident, which came on June 8, 1932, during commencement exercises. The speaker on that occasion was General Douglas MacArthur, army chief of staff, a hero of the World War, undoubtedly a "militarist," and for this day a guest of the University and the city. (This was before the famous occasion when he used tanks and federal troops to drive the Bonus Army out of Washington.) The commencement was being held in Pitt Stadium, and the man responsible for seeing that the crowd was handled efficiently was W. Don Harrison, former teacher of English, later dean of men, and now director of athletics.

Having made arrangements with the superintendent of police to see that traffic regulations were

enforced and that policemen were on hand to take care of the crowd, Harrison was riding around on Commencement Day in the radio car with the police lieutenant in charge. They encountered four young men carrying cardboard signs, two of which read "Generals Die in Bed" and "Down with Heinz, Mellon and Dupont." Harrison astutely surmised that the young men were on their way to stage some kind of antiwar demonstration during the ceremony. The signs, he said later, "were insulting to the University and to General MacArthur."

When the police car stopped near them, the young men ran with their signs into the YMCA hut. (It was that day closed to students, having been assigned to the School of Pharmacy as a place for seniors and faculty to keep their belongings and to don academic robes.) Harrison and the police lieutenant followed and found that the four had locked themselves in a small inner room. They summoned a caretaker, who opened the door. The signs were confiscated. The young men were told to leave. One departed and is heard of no more. Three refused to leave, and they were arrested by the police officer on a charge of disorderly conduct. Two were Pitt students; one was a Pitt graduate who was attending Columbia Law School. As soon as the commencement exercises were over, Harrison said, he asked the police to release the young men. Though the University made no charge against them, they were held in jail five hours, then were fined five dollars each by a magistrate and released.

As the young men told it, they were quietly making their signs in the activities room of the YMCA when the police lieutenant charged in and, on Harrison's order, arrested them. Either way, there was a wave of bad publicity—once when it happened and again three months later when an appeals judge, ruling that the arrests were illegal and unwarranted, reversed the conviction and discharged the defendants. "It is utterly amazing to this court," the judge said,

*He is so identified by Steve Nelson in *Steve Nelson, American Radical,* pp. 573–74.

that these three youths should have been subjected to a criminal prosecution on so trivial and so insignificant an infraction of the rules of the university and proprieties of campus conduct, if any there were. . . . This court exceedingly regrets that the university authorities permit sensationalism to arise out of incidents which otherwise would pass unnoticed.

The University of Pittsburgh is a laudable institution and should waken the pride of every person in Western Pennsylvania interested in higher education, and the court repeats that it is regrettable and blameworthy on the part of the authorities that they permit themselves to lose a sense of proportion and indiscriminately cause arrests which can only result in bringing the good name of that splendid university into disrepute.

Aftermath: One of the arrested students received a University scholarship the following year, and another caused a brief news item when he passed out handbills to freshmen about to register at Pitt and Carnegie Tech, protesting the presence on the campuses of the Reserve Officers' Training Corps (ROTC). "War is certain," the handbill proclaimed, "as long as war preparations go on. The responsibility for causing war rests with those who prepare for war. The R.O.T.C. prepares you for war. That is its only excuse for existence. Freshmen, why be cannon fodder? Don't join the R.O.T.C."

In 1942 Agnes Starrett, editor, reprinted MacArthur's entire speech in *Pitt Magazine.* Somehow it seemed to make more sense in the grim world of 1942 than it did on June 8, 1932.

Editorial writers felt obliged to chastise the University again only one week after the judge's lecture. This time Bowman took steps that he thought would scourge any radical sentiment from the campus. It was revealed on September 24, 1932, that the University was requesting all students to sign the following pledge before registering: "While I am a student at the University of Pittsburgh, I pledge, upon my honor, loyalty and allegiance to the Constitution of the United States of America, and to the constitution and laws of the state of Pennsylvania; and I pledge upon my honor loyalty in spirit and in action to the purposes and regulations of the University of Pittsburgh." Those who refused to sign the pledge or who questioned why they should sign it were being asked to write out their reasons, Only four students out of 7,000 protested, and a call to the students to mount a demonstration against the loy-

alty oath failed when nobody showed up. This was cited as proof of the loyal attitude of the students. Secretary of the University John Weber spoke for the chancellor, who was out of the city: "We know the students are a good loyal body and we are giving them a chance to show it. Half a dozen students who crave publicity have, by posing as representatives of the student body, made the university appear as a hot bed of radicalism." The Student Council, in its first meeting of the new term, voted unanimously to support the administration in the matter. The *Pittsburgh Press* wrote a long editorial that ended, "We recommend to Chancellor Bowman the thought that the tallest building will never make the best college and that the severest restrictions will never make the best citizens."

Aftermath: The loyalty oath was quietly dropped— so quietly that there is no record of any action taken.

The Liberal Club affair, the MacArthur arrests, and the bad reception of the loyalty oath were minor episodes compared with what occurred in 1934 when Chancellor Bowman dismissed Dr. Ralph E. Turner from the faculty. The Turner case had a prolonged effect on the University during a period of growing pains. It was important because of what University trustees, faculty members, and administrators, including the next chancellor, learned from a major administrative blunder and because the Turner affair is a historic landmark in the determination of faculty-administration relationships in American higher education.

Ralph Turner received his college training at the University of Iowa, studying there when Bowman was president. He joined the Pitt history department in 1925 as an assistant professor, teaching a new freshman-orientation course known as the Survey of Social Sciences and using his own book, *America in Civilization* (Knopf, 1925), as text material. He also offered two advanced courses in alternate years: Western Civilization and Contemporary Civilization, in which he attempted to correlate social and intellectual development. In 1927 he was made associate professor. In 1933 he was placed in charge of English history classes and taught a course in modern English history. His classes were not required, but they were large, enrollment running from 290 to 400 students. Senior students in 1932 voted him the most popular professor in the College. An anonymously edited student publication, *The Campus Index: Comments on Faculty, Courses, Organization,* called him one of the top teachers in the University and advised that it would not be wise to pick a quarrell with him. "His attitude is original, his lectures pointed. Exams are difficult. . . . Sometimes he gets bogged down in theory . . . but don't miss him." (Of Bowman it said, "He has never made himself known to or liked by very many of us; he has never come before the student body in any way to explain himself and ask us to go along with him. If he has principles or opinions, we have not heard them. He does not have our affection. . . . In public tests he has stood, by inference, for everything alien to the university spirit. . . . He has failed to lead as an educator, and he had not even been an admirable failure.")

Turner was interested in political reform and in labor and social legislation. It was an interest that created some concern in the minds of Pitt administrators and produced some criticism from people who were not in accord with his views or with his right to express them. He became state chairman in 1933 of something called the Pennsylvania Security League, which worked to enact a legislative program (written by Turner) for such radical causes as unemployment insurance; old age pensions; adequate relief for the poor; minimum wages for women and minors; and abolition of child labor, sweatshops, and "starvation almshouses." The league distributed *Black News,* a one-sheet paper that recorded the attitudes and votes of assemblymen on such measures. Turner was reported in the press as presiding at a meeting of the Friends of the Soviet Union. In a lecture at a Presbyterian church he said the U.S. Constitution should be rewritten, and he criticized the churches for their lack of social consciousness. And on April 24, 1934, he made a speech at the Historical Society of Western Pennsylvania that, he later testified, was the "last straw" that caused his dismissal. This lecture, "History in the Making in Western Pennsylvania," was never published, and it has been ignored in the several million words writ-

ten about the "Turner Case." More clearly than any other document, it tells what Turner was thinking and saying in the spring of 1934 that caused so much trouble, and it reveals, perhaps, something of his controversial classroom conduct.

The lecture was an attack on the Mellon family—though the name was not used—as a typical dominant entrepreneurial group whose chief pursuit was making money on invested capital. Its proposition was that governments were largely under the control of the dominant group. In the society created by such a system, there was no economic liberty or security; talents were frustrated; education was wasted; science was perverted; and there had been no fundamental amelioration of the basic conditions of life in the past 150 years. There was in Western Pennsylvania, as elsewhere, a pressure for change backed up behind walls of conviction, which, when they gave way, would release a flood of change over society. Undoubtedly, this "out-working" would occur through much travail. But if the change did not come, if conditions continued as they were, then the present industrial system was doomed.

John S. Fisher, ex-governor of the state and president of the Historical Society, and several others who were present at this exegesis, were displeased, and they expressed their displeasure to the chancellor and to some of the trustees of the University. Such complaints were not uncommon; Dean Sieg, Secretary Gow, and Dr. Oliver had warned Turner a number of times that protests had been received about his economic views, his political activities, and his classroom conduct. Turner's style was to rouse and stimulate his students by jarring them with provocative remarks and ideas. A few of the 2,900 students who had attended his classes at Pitt complained that he was flippant and sneering.

In the spring of 1933, Turner failed to receive a renewal of his contract. (All faculty members were on one-year contracts, which, unless renewed, terminated at the end of the school year.) Turner conferred with Steele Gow, who told hin that his work was highly regarded and that it was regrettable that his energies were being divided. Did Dr. Turner intend to make his career in scholarship or in politics? Scholarship, of course. Turner said he would resign from the Security League and make no more speeches, and his 1933–1934 contract was renewed.

The following year his contract was renewed on May 9, but on June 30 Dr. Oliver relayed the information to him that the chancellor had decided to pay him one year's salary in advance and not to allow him to teach. The chancellor, Oliver said, "is not hostile to you personally, but rather he feels that he is helping you by asking you to go somewhere else, where he thinks you will be happier." Turner asked for a meeting with Bowman, and for the first time the two men sat face to face in conference. According to Turner, Bowman was vague about his reasons for dismissal and said, "There is discontent in the community," and then added, "Turner, I want to talk with you as a friend." Turner replied, "No, Dr. Bowman, this is official. Dr. Oliver and Dean Sieg referred me to you for an official explanation and I want it." According to Bowman, Turner was in an emotional state.

On July 5 Turner sent a four-page letter to Bowman in which he asked for a full explanation of the decision to dismiss him and for a clear statement on "what happened between May 9, when his contract was renewed, and June 30, when he was dismissed."* Two issues, Turner said, were involved. One was "the right of a university instructor to teach his subject in the light of the body of facts which he has mastered and according to the convictions which he believes that body of facts to justify—in other words, the principle of academic freedom." The other was "the right of a university instructor to exercise his full rights of citizenship as he sees fit—in other words, the principle of democracy." He concluded, "In regard to whatever complaints and criticisms arose as a result of my public activities . . . I assert that the persons who made them had no moral right to make them and that you have no moral right to dismiss me from my position

*Turner partisans held that Bowman renewed the contract on May 9 and delayed canceling it until June 30, after school had closed, in order to avoid a student protest demonstration on the campus. Bowman said that he delayed because of the bad effect the announcement would have had on the 1934 Cathedral of Learning fund-raising campaign then under way.

because of them. I claim the full rights of every American citizen." Turner gave a copy of the letter to the press.

On July 9 Congressman Henry Ellenbogen of Allegheny County asked the chancellor to explain the dismissal. In a two-page reply Bowman gave his first extended statement on the now-notorious case of Dr. Turner. "It seemed," he wrote, "a matter of ordinary kindness to Dr. Turner at the beginning of this incident, to make no statement except this: 'We believe that the purposes of the University can be better fulfilled with another man in his place.' I should be sorry to cause Dr. Turner any unnecessary hurt." Two hundred words followed on the character required in a good teacher and on the policy of the University "in illuminating a path toward a happy, useful and good life" for "impressionable boys and girls." Dr. Turner did not adequately fulfill the requirements. Bowman then revealed, somewhat belatedly, that Dr. Turner's dismissal had nothing to do with his political views, but rather was caused by his flippant attitude toward religion and by his ridicule of students known to be religious. He quoted at length from a complaint by a local minister on that matter. The effect was somewhat diminished by the fact that the minister's letter was written some days after Turner's dismissal had been made public.

From this time forward, events followed hard one upon another:

● Dr. Turner denied that he had ever attacked "religion, as such."

● Gifford Pinchot, Republican governor of Pennsylvania, fired off a letter to Bowman and the trustees declaring that he would demand an investigation of the state of academic freedom at Pitt. "If the Mellons want a school to teach their ideas," he wrote, "then let them support it. The Commonwealth cannot."

● David L. Lawrence, state Democratic chairman, later to be mayor of Pittsburgh and governor of the Commonwealth, issued a statement: "Institutions which seek to punish those advocating the New Deal in economics and in social relationships have no right to support from public funds." He promised an investigation when a Democratic legislature and administration began its tenure in Harrisburg the following January.

• A group of students at the University of Michigan were so outraged by the dismissal of Dr. Turner that they formed a branch of the Liberal Club, drafted a resolution of condemnation, sent it to the press and to Chancellor Bowman, and dissolved the club, all on the same day.

• Andrew W. Mellon wrote a gentle disclaimer that he was responsible for the dismissal of Dr. Turner and in so doing set Dr. Bowman straight on the meaning of academic freedom:

My affection for the University of Pittsburgh and my confidence in the University's value to our people prompt me to make this statement. . . . I have reached the time of life at which controversy or misrepresentation about myself does not greatly affect me. But I am disturbed when an institution serving the public welfare and with which my name happens to be linked is the subject of harmful criticism. . . .

Out of a loyalty and an affection growing from [my] long contact with the University, I make the following statement of facts bearing upon the Turner incident so simply and briefly, I hope, as to leave the way open for no misunderstanding.

1. I had never heard the name of Dr. Turner until I saw it in the newspaper following his dismissal.

2. At no time have I discussed with Dr. Bowman, nor have other trustees to the best of my knowledge discussed, the personal beliefs or public statements of faculty members.

3. I am not an expert in education nor upon universities, but I have a slight acquaintance with the philosophy which has guided them. I recognize that only under conditions of academic freedom can truth be discovered and impartial knowledge disseminated.

4. If it were Doctor Turner's political beliefs or statements which caused his dismissal, I should be heartily in favor of his immediate re-instatement.

The statement was not made public.

• The Pittsburgh Chamber of Commerce, the Federation of Patriotic Americans, and representatives of twenty-one churches in Wilkinsburg congratulated the chancellor for having dismissed Dr. Turner. Public feelings by now were perhaps

running a bit ahead of knowledge; one letter congratulated Dr. Bowman for having dismissed Harry Elmer Barnes.

• A *Pittsburgh Press* editorial said, "There cannot but be a realization that [Dr. Bowman's] departure would be an excellent thing for the institution. . . . In view of the sincerity of his vision, it is tragic that the end should not have been more impressive."

• Some three hundred people paid honor to Dr. Turner on August 14, 1934, at a farewell dinner. In his address, Dr. Turner did not mention Dr. Bowman, except obliquely. He had apparently decided since April 24 that the present industrial system was not doomed after all, for he urged all liberals to support the New Deal "as the first administration which has given any consideration to the converging forces which are bringing about the changes in our society." And he announced a monumental new revelation: "We have made this discovery: that man is moulded into the pattern of his social order—that human nature can be changed." He left the next day to spend time with his family in Iowa and then to live for some months in England working on historical research.

• A committee of three AAUP professors was in the city, but they did not attend the farewell dinner. They were engaged in their investigations of Dr. Turner's dismissal and of the tenure practice and policy of the University of Pittsburgh.

The AAUP committee, representing 10,844 university professors, was headed by Ralph E. Himstead, professor of law at Syracuse University. The other members were an economist from Ohio State and a pathologist from the University of North Carolina. They were cordially received by Dr. Bowman, who had informed the AAUP that the committee was "satisfactory" to him. The committee spent six days on the campus in August, and two members of it spent three more days in November. With Bowman's cooperation, they had "unhurried conference" with 117 persons, some in small groups, and with a number of other persons in written testimony.

The committee completed its report, some twenty thousand words in seventy-two pages of typescript, in February 1935. As was the AAUP practice, the general secretary sent a draft of the report to Bowman, giving him "an opportunity to point out what might seem . . . to be errors of fact." He was told that the draft was confidential and was not to be made public.

The report, beautifully written and carefully reasoned (except for one paragraph), was a shattering attack on Bowman and on his administrative policies and practices. When Bowman recovered from the shock he must have felt, he saw that in one passage the professors had made an incredible blunder. He or one of his advisors was both shrewd enough to recognize how he might use it to his own advantage and knowledgeable enough to realize that the passage would probably be deleted from the final printed version of the AAUP document. Acting on this belief, he released the entire draft of the report to the press. With it he sent a copy of his letter to the AAUP:

I regret to note that the unrestrained hostility of your report has extended to the City of Pittsburgh. In violent language you hold up to scorn a people, a community, which as much as any other, has expressed for a century and a half the best in American progress. To quote from your report:

"In the world of the existing Pittsburgh, with its extremes of riches and poverty, its unrelieved dirtiness and ugliness, its ruthless materialism and individualism, its irrepressible industrial conflicts, its lack of any integrating principle other than the sign of the dollar, the Chancellor moves with one immediate driving motive: to wring from the community the money essential to the development and support of the kind of university which his mind conceives as the ideal for this particular city."

Do you think it within your scope, or worthy of your association, to attack the good name of the city, which is not the issue? It is evident that such a gratuitous attack reveals an animus which removes your report from the realm of judicial consideration.

The report was still shattering, but its effect had now been dulled, and there was a noticeable swing of support and sympathy to the University as part of the public anger at the insult to the city. Andrei Avinoff, director of Carnegie Museum, expressed the feeling of a good many angry Pittsburghers when he wrote to Bowman, "Permit me to congratulate you upon your excellent reply to the despicable assault of a few irresponsible radical agitators." As for the general secretary of the AAUP, he was shocked at Bowman's violation of trust in releasing the preliminary draft of the report without permission and for quoting a passage from the report "out of its context."

The AAUP had the last word. It released its official report in mid-December 1935, and in it found the defendant guilty on all counts.

The AAUP did not accept Bowman's statement that Turner was dismissed for his antireligious utterances to students. It held on this point that the letters of complaint from ministers and parents had been collected in an *ex post facto* operation. (In this it ignored the testimony of Dean Sieg and Dr. Oliver.) They found nothing in the Historical Society lecture that would offend any open-minded person, though they did feel that Turner was wrong in giving such a speech to listeners "who were not expecting that sort of thing and were not used to critical historical analysis." Dr. Bowman, they discovered, had abrogated a code governing academic tenure that had been in effect for four years when he took office. They deplored a situation in which an autocratic chancellor was able to terminate employment of his faculty members simply by not renewing one-year contracts. Bowman did this, they held, in a manner inimical to academic freedom and tenure, without charges or a hearing, often without even a notice of dismissal, and sometimes by whim or caprice based on intense personal dislike. The report concluded that Turner's dismissal was an unjustifiable termination of his services.

Members of the AAUP at their annual convention in St. Louis concurred unanimously with these judgments, though two officers of the Pittsburgh chapter of the AAUP went there to plead the University's case. The University of Pittsburgh was removed from the AAUP "eligible" list and placed in the category of Censured Administrations. It joined four other proscribed institutions: Brenau (women's) College, Gainesville, Georgia; De Pauw, Greencastle, Indiana; Rollins, Winter Park, Florida; and the U.S. Naval Academy.*

The AAUP, as Bowman had surmised it would, dropped the "gratuitous insult" to the city from the official report. That paragraph now read: "In the world of the existing Pittsburgh, with its extremes of riches and poverty, the Chancellor moves with one immediate driving motive, to wring from the community the money essential to the development and support of the kind of university which his mind conceives as the ideal for this kind of city."

An investigating committee of the State House of Representatives began its hearings on the state of academic freedom at the University on April 5, 1935: five Western Pennsylvania Democrats under Eugene A. Caputo of Ambridge (Business Administration 1923, Law 1925), all members of the House Appropriations Committee. Pittsburghers may have thought they had heard enough of that story, but this time there was a difference. Two differences. First, the hearings were held in city council chambers, with press and public present to see and hear all. Second, Pitt was represented by its counsel, Charles F. C. Arensberg, and it had the right to defend itself before the committee by cross-examination of witnesses, rebuttal, and submission to the record of documentary evidence.

With a budget of only $5,000, the committee members met for ten days and four nights, including two weekends. Their report ran to 1,500 pages in eight volumes. They heard eighty-one witnesses, six of them stars: Frederick Woltman of the Liberal Club incident; W. Don Harrison of the MacArthur affair; Dr. Ralph Himstead, author of the AAUP report; J. Steele Gow; Ralph Turner; and John Bowman. A Pitt publication wrote of the hearings,

"They were charged with drama. There were occasional moments of levity when facetious quips, intentional or otherwise, furnished comedy relief, but most of the investigation was conducted in an atmosphere of tension. However, the judicious attitude of the committee and the tact of Chairman [Eugene A.] Caputo maintained a high level of dignity throughout the proceedings."

The first witness, Professor Colston E. T. Warne of Amherst, testified that he was dismissed for—among other sins—saying in his classroom, "The Pennsylvania Railroad is not well managed."

Dr. Turner told his story in six hours of examination and cross-examination. He stood up well on the charge of religious prejudice, but he damaged his credibility with a statement on the twenty-six faculty members who had signed the petition to Bowman after the Liberal Club expulsions. "It was recognized by the faculty," Turner said, "that every man who signed the petition was a marked man, and one by one the men who signed the petition have left the University, for various reasons, but they have gone." Arensberg, however, had the records of those who signed, and he established clearly that fourteen had received recognition from the University by increases in salary or by promotions in rank, or both, after they signed the petition. Only two of the signers were asked to leave. One of these was Phineas Westcott Whiting, who was dropped "because of a necessary reduction in the department budget." (Whiting confirmed this in testimony at the hearing.) The other was Dr. Turner.

Arensberg started his cross-examination of Turner near the end of the day and had time to confront him with the names of only a few of the faculty signers who were still at the University. "The next day," Arensberg said, "we waited in vain for Turner—he never came. He left town without my completing his cross examination."

The findings of the legislative committee were mild and on some points indecisive—so much so that they pleased neither friend nor foe. The committee:

● commended the chancellor for increasing the material assets of the University;

● found that the Liberal Club members had vio-

---

*It was generally reported at the time (and still is) that the so-called blacklist "forbade its 12,000 members on pain of expulsion to accept a job at the designated institution." That is not true. The only restriction was that faculty members at Pitt who were not already members of the AAUP could not join it as long as they were at Pitt. There was no effect on those eighty-one Pitt faculty who were already members of the AAUP; nor on those AAUP members from other universities who wished to join the Pitt faculty.

Arch-enemies in the Turner case, a classic confrontation about academic freedom: Ralph Turner, associate professor of history (above) and John Bowman (opposite). They are testifying in Pittsburgh City Council chambers before a committee of the State House of Representatives in April 1935.

Pittsburgh Press

lated the rules of the University but felt that the punishment was too severe and drastic;

● found that the MacArthur pickets did not show proper regard for Commencement Day activities but felt that their arrests were not justifiable, since no disturbance had yet occurred;

● declared that Turner's charge that the twenty-six signers of the petition had left the University "was found to be erroneous";

● found that there had been no interference with Dr. Turner's classroom activities;

● in the matter of Dr. Turner's dismissal, was "unable to arrive at any conclusion, due to the fact that the testimony touching this point is hopelessly vague, indefinite and conflicting";

● found no other evidence of the suppression of academic freedom except in one "comparatively isolated case";

● advocated the restoration of the tenure rules of 1919, which Bowman had replaced with a one-year contract system;

● called the AAUP's definition of academic freedom ideal but felt that "consideration should be given to certain factors such as location, environment, financial resources, and the size of the Institution, all of which may make the ideal situation unobtainable in totality."

Aftermath: Ralph Turner taught history for a time at the University of Minnesota and the American University and then, during the war, served as a government official for the Board of Economic Warfare, for military intelligence, and for the Department of State as principal divisional assistant of the Division of Cultural Relations. He became Durfree Professor of History at Yale University, helped to found the United Nations Educational, Scientific, and Cultural Organization (UNESCO), and following his retirement as professor emeritus was in charge of a multivolume history of mankind, for which UNESCO put up $400,000 and other interests added $200,000. He died at seventy-one in October 1964.

On June 31, 1941, Rufus H. Fitzgerald, provost of the University and Bowman's designated successor, dictated a passage in a journal he kept. He had just talked with a dean who was having problems with a troublesome left-wing professor.

"He had with him a document which had to do with the running of the English department. He thought he should take the matter in his own hands and fire [the professor]. I told him I admired his courage but there was no good reason for repeating the Turner case if it could be handled in some other way. I suggested that he have his committee in the English department come together to consider the complaints [and get] their reactions, and if they recommended dismissal that it be taken to the College committee. He thanked me and said that is the way he would proceed."

10

Code Bowman and "The Most Discussed Controversy"

Dear President Bowman:

The purpose of my writing you is to get your confidential opinion of Jock Sutherland. . . . Our coach has resigned. . . . Some have suggested that we should consider Dr. Sutherland.

John J. Tigert, University of Florida

Dear President Tigert:

Dr. Jock Sutherland was coach . . . from 1925 [1924] to 1939. He decided about a year ago that he was not satisfied, either with the set-up of football at the University or with the athletic policy here. In this decision I have felt he was given an unusually large supply of bad advice.

I know nothing detrimental about his character. He is a rather silent man who was held in high respect here by his friends.

John G. Bowman

Dr. JOHN BAIN SUTHERLAND. Jock Sutherland. In the first months of 1939 he was everywhere rated the best head coach in college football. With 111 victories, 20 losses, and 12 ties in 15 years at Pitt, he was the winningest coach in the school's history. He never had a losing season. His teams won the eastern championship 7 times; they won the national championship 6 times (by one count); they were near the top in most of the other years. They went 4 times to the Rose Bowl; they fielded 21 official All-Americans; they beat Penn State 12 straight times; in 5 victories over Notre Dame they held that team to 15 points.

Sutherland was in varying degrees admired, idolized, and venerated by his players, the students, the Varsity Letter Club, the Athletic Council, the General Alumni Association, the alumni at large, and a million or so football fans in the area. A *Saturday Evening Post* article called him "a national hero" and really meant it. He had friends everywhere, and he broadened his friendships in the 1934 fund-raising campaign when he served as chairman of all the Nationality Room committees. Chester Smith, *Pittsburgh Press* and Scripps-Howard sports columnist, who was a friend and dedicated supporter, wrote of Sutherland: "His influence on the campus and as a good will man for Pitt was among the University's greatest assets."

In October 1938 the team with the "Dream Backfield" (Goldberg, Cassiano, Stebbins, Chickerneo) met a great Fordham team in a game that has been called the peak of the Golden Age of Pitt athletics. The two teams had played three successive scoreless ties. Fordham led 7–3 late in this, the fourth game, but Pitt scored 21 points in ten explosive minutes in the final quarter to win 24–13. The game set an all-time Pitt Stadium record with 68,918 spectators.

The game also marked the summit of Sutherland's career as a college coach. He was already caught up in a contest for control of the University's athletic program—in a struggle between the alumni groups, Sutherland supporters, who held the dominant position; and the administration-faculty people to whom, in the inevitable course of events, the control would eventually be given. (Faculty control of athletic programs is today an NCAA rule.) It was a struggle in which both sides were partly in the right and no one was wholly to blame, but it would change careers, cause resignations, blemish reputations, disturb campus amity.

The story, called "the most discussed controversy in the history of the University," has been told and retold. It has always been seen, however, through the eyes of Sutherland's supporters, some of whom wrote the articles, the columns, and the histories of the controversy. To them, the issues were simple: the chancellor and some of his closest administrative aides, for whatever reasons, made conditions unbearable for Jock Sutherland and in so doing ruined the University's position in the word of intercollegiate athletics. The administration was not free to defend itself against that charge, nor could it give the reasons for the course it followed. And so, in the words of Frank Carver (with the athletic department from 1931 and athletic director from 1958 to 1968), no effort was made to explain "what forces made it necessary for intelligent, well-meaning, honorable men to publicly disembowel the University's athletic program."

They did it because, despite the great teams, superb coaching, and winning seasons, there were deep-seated problems and troubles in the athletic situation.

One problem was finding opponents who would fill a substantial percentage of the 65,000 seats in Pitt Stadium. (It was and is a problem common to other urban universities, many of which have difficulty with attendance figures.) Pitt was not a member of a conference, and it had close ties and long-standing rivalries with only three other schools: Penn State, Washington and Jefferson, and Carnegie Tech. With many seats available, the customers did not buy tickets in advance. Attendance records show that, except for one or two games a year, people stayed away from the stadium in large numbers. In the twelve years from 1927 through 1938, only ten games attracted more than 40,000 paying customers. Selling enough seats to pay the stadium bond requirements and maintenance costs was a heavy burden successive athletic directors had to bear.

Another problem was recruiting adequate foot-

Dr. John (Jock) Sutherland, a great and controversial name in Pitt athletics, at a sesquicentennial alumni dinner in 1937.

ball talent. Pitt was competing against rural campuses at Penn State and Duke, against great facilities at Ohio State, against a famous tradition at Notre Dame. Those schools and others had dormitories and dining halls. "What," Frank Carver asked, "did our one recruiter have to sell?"

A few brick buildings on the side of a hill, an unfinished Cathedral of Learning, some wooden barracks converted to classrooms, a mammoth stadium. Rooming houses in Oakland instead of dormitories.

The bottom line, of course, was how the athlete was to eat and where he was to sleep. Way back, Pitt had found a way to even up for the lack of dormitories and messhalls. Somewhere in the chain, the athlete met an alumnus to whom he was to go, once a month, and pick up an envelope with money for his board, room and books. Supposedly the money came from the alumnus.

We had one advantage: a long history of athletes making good in professional schools, particularly dentistry, where Jock Sutherland had an appointment as Assistant Professor of Crown and Bridge. The hope, the chance to be a professional man was a lure, especially to youngsters coming out of mill and mining families, with parents who wanted them to be somebody.

W. Don Harrison, a former English teacher who had become dean of men, was made athletic director in 1928. Alumni groups felt this was a Bowman move to bring athletic activities under full control of the administration; but Harrison clearly saw the problems of his new post and began an honest attempt to find some solutions and to give the University a first-rate, modern athletic department. He closed the suite of rooms in a downtown bank building where the graduate manager of athletics was running the department. He had a large office built for Sutherland in the crowded stadium quarters above the dressing rooms, allowing himself only a small walled cubicle in one corner. He brought in Carl Olsen as full-time track and cross country coach. He made the position of freshman football coach a full-time job, with responsibilities for seeing that the young men attended classes regularly. He brought in James (Whitey) Hagan, the blocking halfback on the great 1927–1929 teams, as assistant athletic director and recruiter of football talent. He helped Sutherland to build up a coaching staff. He knew the value of personal contacts in scheduling and made friends in athletic circles, especially in the Big Ten area. In his campaign to win friends at other schools, he would sometimes accompany Henry Clifford (Doc) Carlson and his basketball team on its annual swing through the Big Ten country in December. Dr. Carlson had built up some close personal relationships there; he was called "a perfect good will ambassador whose teams, to whom he taught manners as well as basketball, made a fine impression." The teams he coached won two national championships in the late 1920s and in 1927–1928 established a record as the first major college team to have an undefeated season (21–0).

Football and basketball were (and are) the only teams that make money; as such, they give sustenance to other varsity sports, from track and field and swimming to wrestling, gymnastics, baseball, volleyball, soccer, and a half-dozen others, including sports for women. These do not pay their way in terms of revenue, but they excite the interest and participation of students; each has a small but devoted following, and when the teams are outstanding, they shed glory on both the players and the University. Pitt would have such glory in 1939, when it made athletic history before 30,000 track fans in Philadelphia: its relay teams, for the first time in the forty-five years of Penn Relays competition, won the four major events—the quarter-mile, half-mile, mile, and medley relays. Pitt would achieve it again in 1975–1980, when the men's swim team won six consecutive Eastern championships.

The combined efforts of Sutherland, Harrison, and Hagan began to show results in the 1930s. Harrison's schedules improved, with a steady increase in competition with big name schools. Hagan brought in talent. Sutherland, probably the game's finest technician, produced teams whose players were so nearly perfect in their assignments that they looked like professionals. There was a temporary setback when the newspapers revealed that four of Pitt's senior players were married, which was not only contrary to what was then expected of a college athlete but was also interpreted to signify that Pitt paid so well that its star players could support wives.

(Actually, they were working wives who were supporting their husbands.) Pitt bowed to propriety and established a rule against married players on its teams, thereby losing the services of several first-rate players who were on scholarships.

One more problem arose: Sutherland and Harrison found as early as 1930 that they disliked each other. They had a quarrel that—though trivial in itself—made national news, caused both Harrison and Sutherland to resign, produced a trustee investigation of the administration, and irreparably harmed Chancellor Bowman.

Sutherland had Old World courtesy and a Scottish reserve that was sometimes chilling. He could be charming, especially with sports writers, who tended to become his advocates, and he could be tough. He focused such powers of concentration that he occasionally forgot about human feelings. For example:

• Pitt opened Duke's new stadium in 1929. Duke was making a first bid for the big time. Pitt won by a score of 52–7. Sutherland ran up the score unmercifully, calling for forward passes in the final minutes of the game. His opponent as head coach was Jimmy DeHart, an old-time teammate.

• Penn State was outclassed by Pitt in the late 1920s and early 1930s (playing games with scores like 30–0, 26–0, 20–7) and was dropped from the Thanksgiving slot to a midseason game. When Pitt played at Penn State in 1931, Sutherland did not use his first team in the entire game and won 41–6. While embarrassed Penn State people were still leaving their stadium, he had his first team practice signals after the game. Penn State dropped Pitt in the 1932–1934 seasons.

• When Pitt played Iowa at Iowa, Howdy O'Dell, a Pitt halfback from Sioux City, was not used in the game. Sutherland had him carrying the first-down chain for the head linesman.

The trouble between Sutherland and Harrison was first made public with an exchange of words in Pasadena, California. The Panthers had just won a glorious victory on New Year's Day 1937 over the University of Washington Huskies before 87,000 spectators—the only Pitt victory in four trips to the Rose Bowl. The players had gone to the coast in style, wearing the first traveling uniform issued to

University Archives

Following defeat by Southern California at the Rose Bowl in 1932, the team meets comedian Joe E. Brown (center, hat in hand) and twenty-five-year-old Barbara Stanwyck on a motion picture set. Sutherland is to Brown's right.

any team—gray slacks and gray shirts with a Pitt monogram, provided at Pitt expense by a top outfitter. They traveled in a special Santa Fe Railroad train that included the club car Alf Landon had used in campaigning for president, which had been exhibited at the Chicago World's Fair as the ultimate in luxury. The Santa Fe put the chef of its Super Chief on duty. The team worked out at a famous spa in San Bernardino until it went to Pasadena, where

it stayed at the Huntington, a luxury resort where the bellboys changed the guard every afternoon in a manner worthy of Buckingham Palace.

But after the game, some unremembered person on the athletic staff gave each man $7 for pocket money for a night on the town. Pitt players had been away from home for several weeks; they had sacrificed their Christmas and New Year holidays for the trip; they heard that the Washington players were being given between $75 and $125; they knew that Pitt would get upward of $95,000 from the Tournament of Roses people; and they were angry. So was Sutherland, who gave the players somewhere between $450 and $600 of his own money. The story continues in newly uncovered and released testimony Sutherland gave in April 1939 before a special committee of the Board of Trustees—his only known recorded statement on the affair.

Our players had been invited to be guests at a banquet that evening at which the Reisman Cup was to be presented to us as victors of the Rose Bowl game. My players and I were under the impression that this banquet was under the auspices of the Rose Bowl Committee. At 10:30 that evening I learned that our boys were being neglected at the banquet, that waiters were paying no attention to them and that they were very disgruntled by the affair. I then got in touch with Mr. Harold Reynolds, chairman of the Rose Bowl Committee, and asked him to give the problem his attention. He then told me that the Rose Bowl Committee had no authority over the banquet and that the banquet was an affair of a Mr. Reisman, who was a clothing merchant and used the banquet for advertising purposes.

I then asked Mr. Reynolds if he would be willing to make that statement to our Director of Athletics, Mr. Harrison, who had arranged for our team to attend the banquet. . . . We found Harrison and Mr. Reynolds made the statement. Mr. Harrison turned to me and said that he would take care of his end of affairs and that I should confine my attention to coaching. Mr. Harrison then told me that he had made me and that he would break me.

This was the thing that set off the sparks.

The story, relayed from Chet Smith to Joe Williams when it happened in 1937, made national news, and, among its other effects, it created the false impression that Pitt had treated its players shabbily from the start of the trip to the coast.

As the feud between Sutherland and Harrison developed, they became the front figures in a larger struggle between Bowman and his deputies, Harrison and John Weber, on the one hand, and the members of the Athletic Council and the General Alumni Association on the other. These held opposing views on how the athletic program should be conducted and who should conduct it. Their disputes inevitably involved the struggle for athletic excellence and for academic excellence, with all the tension resident in that continuing classic situation. The conflict between academic values and athletic values was to dominate Pitt programs for the next thirty-five years, until a reconciliation was accomplished in the 1970s under a new administration.

In a letter to the Athletic Council in March 1937, Bowman declared that football and the other sports at the University "shall be conducted primarily for the benefit of the students. They should have fun at the games. This fun should not be dependent too much on the winning of games. I can not express too strongly my desire that the University shall discourage the giving of special help to students who have nothing to recommend them but athletic ability. In other words, you are charged with the responsibility to discourage any subsidies, from whatever source, to students merely because of athletic ability."

The alumni and athletic groups, of course, did not agree. They wanted winning teams. They wanted a voice in any changes the University made to concur with the policy "that the progress of athletics shall be conducted in accord with the best traditions of intercollegiate athletic practice." They insisted that Pitt must not adopt restrictions unless equivalent restrictions were also imposed on the competing schools. Knowing Bowman's attitude toward competitive team athletics, which was somewhere between indifference and hostility, they did not trust him; they feared he would disarm unilaterally. They recognized and sometimes admitted that subsidization of athletes had got out of hand in all the larger competing colleges and that some reform was necessary. Pitt, they said, was no worse than some of the others and was actually not one of the schools where athletics were most heavily subsidized. The percentages of Pitt's varsity athletes who graduated, who took postbaccalaureate degrees, and who became outstanding figures in many fields other than athletics were exceptionally high. But Pitt, its sports-minded proponents said, was a big name in football, its successes made it a target for criticism, and it was the one college that a number of feature writers and columnists chose to expose. (Pitt,

In this 1937 cartoon, the Pittsburgh Post-Gazette's *Cy Hungerford leaves no doubt about his opinion of Bowman's plan to purify Pitt athletics.*

in fact—a charter member of the NCAA—has never been publicly sanctioned or reprimanded by that body.)

The changes proposed by Bowman grew out of demands and trends that were larger than, stronger than, and beyond the control of both the Pitt administration and the alumni partisans. For one thing, a widely publicized Carnegie Foundation report had condemned the manner in which intercollegiate sports, particularly football, were being conducted, and its charges made a deep impression. For another, some colleges were shying away from playing Pitt. Pitt was not particularly good at drawing

crowds; its academic and amateur statuses were being questioned; and it was likely to give any opponent a sound thrashing. Frank Carver recalled, "Some of our players said things that indicated they were getting tremendous amounts of money to play. Well, they weren't, but they made it sound good. And suddenly we developed a bad name. We began to lose opponents. People who were scheduled to play us called up and cancelled." Carlson told how, on a basketball trip in 1936, Harrison went to his hotel room, sick at news he had just received: Notre Dame, a main financial support to the whole season, had dropped Pitt from its schedule. The trustees themselves were given official notice by the Commission on Institutions of Higher Education of the Middle States Association that if they did not tighten their code on aid to athletes they could forfeit the University's accreditation. In 1936 all members of the Big Ten agreed to eliminate the University of Pittsburgh as a competitor in all sports.

John Weber, testifying to a trustees committee behind locked doors in May 1939, stated that the University was paying its athletes $65 per month for their room and board, with free tuition for all and extras for some. This expenditure, he said, was listed on the department budget as "special equipment," and it totaled about $36,000 in 1930–1931 and the same in 1931–1932. The free tuition totaled about $25,000. "With employment of players for pay," he told the trustees, "we were confronted with the charge that we were conducting a business for profit and for several years we were threatened with taxation on that basis. Another spectre was that in case of injury of a paid player we were in position of forfeiting our freedom from liability which a charitable institution is given."

Bowman, Harrison, and Weber believed that the long-range interests of the University demanded a radical change in athletic scheduling. If Pitt football was to survive financially, the administration would have to turn west or south for opponents. It could not turn east because the Ivy League colleges were not receptive and Fordham was Pitt's only friend. West was the better choice. It would provide good opponents in a good geographical relationship. Ohio State, Northwestern, Indiana, Michigan, Michigan

State, and Purdue were all within an overnight train ride. There was a new situation in the Big Ten, moreover, that offered a possible opportunity for Pitt to join that league if it reformed its athletic practices. Chicago had withdrawn from intercollegiate athletics, leaving a vacancy. Some schools that were eligible to fill it were not interested, and they were pushing Pitt—if Pitt met the requirements of the Big Ten code. It was a long shot, but the administrators felt they should take it.

In February 1937 the Executive Committee of the Athletic Council undertook to mediate the dispute between Sutherland and Harrison. It met with Sutherland and obtained a statement of his complaints. Among other things, he charged that he was permitted no part in the scheduling of games; he did not learn what teams he was to meet in the coming season until he read it in the newspapers. He had too few assistant coaches, no voice in how much they were paid, and only one recruiter, who was not permitted to proselytize inside the high schools. He had no scout. In the Bowman-Harrison-Weber decision to try to take the place of Chicago in the Big Ten, his teams were being overmatched, having no freshmen good enough to stand up against such competition.

The Executive Committee submitted these charges to Harrison. He reviewed them, said he would reply in writing for the record, and then decided that he could best serve the University by resigning. His letter of resignation was graceful. ("The problem in the department of athletics is one of personalities. It is not for me to pass on the merits of either side. But this I know: Such a situation should, under no circumstances, exist in any department in the University.") He transferred to the English department at the University's extension school in Erie and then to Johnstown. So far as is known, he never released any public statement defending himself or his record. A day or so after Harrison's resignation, Sutherland said to Weber that he was very sorry that the controversy had turned out as it did, and that if he had known the outcome he would not have been involved in any part of it.

James Hagan succeeded Harrison as athletic director on May 3, 1937. Sutherland approved of his appointment. He had been handling the scheduling of games since Harrison's departure, and he at once turned his correspondence over to Hagan, requesting that he be consulted on the selection of opponents his team was to play. Hagan, according to Sutherland, refused to accept the correspondence, put it back on Sutherland's desk, and declined to consult with him on the scheduling of games, feeling that would be the equivalent of giving Sutherland a veto power over his selections.

Hagan had been a subsidized star at Pitt, but now he was placed in a situation where he had to be an advocate of the Bowman-Weber-Harrison athletic reform program. After two months in office, accordingly, he sent to the Athletic Council, at its request, what came to be known as the Hagan Plan. Henceforth, athletics at Pitt were to be on a strictly amateur basis. Special grants to students, if made solely because of athletic ability, were to cease. Students with such ability, however, would be given paid work "on the same basis such help is given to other University undergraduates whose resources limit their chance of completing their education." Sutherland was not consulted and did not see the Hagan Plan before it was released.

The author of the Hagan Plan wrote, "The execution of this policy will bring about a great appreciation on the part of the student of his educational opportunities and a greater sense of loyalty to the University." Weber (who had never participated in competitive organized athletics) assured a trustees committee, "We think we will get enough good athletes without such plans [for recruiting]. We think we can handle our usual type of football schedule without recruiting. We will have good teams and we will be able to compete with teams that will attract crowds to the Pitt stadium." It did not turn out that way.

The Hagan Plan was absorbed in February 1938 by a totally uncompromising set of regulations called the Code for Conduct of Athletics, Code Bowman for short. Henceforth there would be no athletic scholarships at all, no loans or remissions of tuition awarded on athletic skill, and "no financial aid . . . with the purpose of subsidizing the athlete or of promoting athletic success." Thus the one loophole that had made the Hagan Plan bearable to alumni was closed: the new code specifically prohibited alumni and other friends of Pitt athletics from giving private assistance to worthy athletes. The Athletic Council of the Alumni Association was to be dissolved and replaced by a faculty committee. Bowman now had greater control over a program he had called "a thorn in the side of the administration."

Bowman presented his code at a trustees meeting without advance notice and requested a favorable vote on a take-it-or-leave-it basis. Norman MacLeod protested that the trustees should have at least a month to study such a revolutionary step. Another trustee said that the issue was so complicated that he could study it for six months and still not reach a conclusion. The trustees approved Code Bowman because they felt that the athletic set-up needed to be reorganized and that its supervision should be placed on the same basis as that of other undergraduate extracurricular activities, with finances of athletics under control of the University's officers. The trustees, moreover, were conscious of the threat to their accreditation voiced by the Middle States Association.

On November 17, 1938, a five-man committee of the Varsity Letter Club (more than 900 members) called on Chancellor Bowman in an effort to "straighten out the Pitt athletic situation" and "to assist in working out a plan which will restore good will toward the University." The committee presented him with a 750-word memorandum that proposed that he approve "a competent, impartial and responsible committee to make a thorough investigation":

In recent years our athletics have been in a terrible muddle—one embarrassing episode after another has discredited the University and its athletes, and we say sincerely, Dr. Bowman, that we letter men have had to hang our heads in shame. . . .

In the past two years, athletic affairs have been so badly bungled and the resulting publicity has been so vicious that the University of Pittsburgh has become the most shamefully maligned institution in the country. . . .

We cannot understand how even ordinary horse sense would permit such mistakes. . . .

We like you, Dr. Bowman. We believe you are sincere. We want to help you. But we ask you, for God's sake, take hold of this mess and clean it up. Set our athletic house in order.

November 21, 1938. A delegation from the Pittsburgh Chamber of Commerce called on Dr. Bowman to persuade him to support strong and winning football teams for the good of the city. Floyd Rose said that the chancellor "received us in a friendly way," though in professing his desire for strong and winning teams "he made some misstatements which I didn't want to contradict in the presence of the non-Pitt men who were there," such as the claim that he brought Sutherland to the University, which was not true. One of the delegates was George David Thompson, industrialist, investment broker, one of the century's greatest collectors of modern art, and, as a fellow Scot, a close friend of Jock Sutherland. As Thompson saw it, the delegation got a "chilly reception," though he admitted that an "unbridled speech" by Robert Waddell did not help the delegation in what it was seeking. Everyone agreed that there should be no publicity about the meeting.

November 22, 1938. Chancellor Bowman gave his annual address to the student body at Soldiers and Sailors Memorial Hall. In an unusually fervid speech, he attacked "outsiders," "downtown alumni," and "unofficial football managers." These men, he said, "want to sit in the press box and go down between halves to the dressing room to hobnob with the players. They are a damned nuisance." Addressing any freshman players who might be in the audience, he said, "Don't do anything those damn unofficial managers asked you to do." He explained that he had learned such profane language when he was a young man working on a Mississippi river boat. He said he was in favor of winning football teams.

A dozen groups, including the Varsity Letter Club, the Athletic Council, the Alumni Association, Pitt clubs in various cities, and the Chamber of Commerce took the attack as one directed at them.

November 30, 1938. Rufus Fitzgerald, the new provost, acting as Bowman's representative on the faculty athletic committee, telephoned Thomas E. French, Ohio State trustee who was attending a Big Ten meeting in Chicago. He conveyed the message that Pitt hoped to replace Chicago in the Big Ten and that to accomplish this it would do whatever was necessary.

January 23, 1939. A committee of seven graduates chosen by the Alumni Association delivered a report on athletic and publicity problems at the University. It had worked more than two months, held thirty meetings in the Schenley Hotel, interviewed seventy-five witnesses, and amassed 100,000 words of testimony. Its findings were not unexpected:

• The administration had failed to make Code Bowman known to alumni and other Pitt followers before it was adopted. It was imposed after insufficient study of what it meant and how it would be administered.

• There was no great difference in the way sports were handled at Pitt as compared with other institutions.

• Other teams—Michigan, Notre Dame, California, Minnesota, Dartmouth, and Cornell—had dominated football through extended periods without being subjected to the abuse Pitt was getting.

• In nine meetings with teams of the Western Conference, Pitt had lost three games, won five, and tied one. So why were the Western Conference teams complaining that the Panthers were so heavily subsidized that other teams could not compete with them?

• The faculty committee had no authority; it was a "puppet body" dominated by John Weber, who was dominated by Dr. Bowman.

• Weber was trying to do too many things and had become a bottleneck.

• Unfavorable publicity had not been the fault of outside agencies. Pitt had made its own bad news, which the newspapers, though they generally wished to be friendly, had no other recourse but to print.

• Public opinion was in favor of giving some assistance for athletes, providing they maintained scholastic standards.

• Unless some plan was worked out to take care of at least a nominal amount of scholarship aid, Code Bowman would restrict the flow of manpower essential to maintain athletic teams of high caliber. A team that did not compete for high school talent and was forced to depend solely on its regular student body for its material was on the way to athletic disaster.

Dr. Bowman never acknowledged, commented on, or acted on the Alumni Association report.

In the course of these events, Sutherland came to some hard and unpleasant conclusions. He saw Code Bowman as a one-school code with probably the most drastic set of restrictions imposed on any athletic program in the country; it was athletic evangelism run wild. Unless Pitt adopted a liberal, practical interpretation of the code—specifically in granting athletic scholarships and allowing some financial aid from alumni—he would never get the football material the team needed to carry out a major schedule. He had been given no reason to believe that the code would be so interpreted. Instead of frankly reducing the caliber of the teams to be played, the administration, in leaning toward the Western Conference, was making a fatal mistake. It was preparing a suicide schedule with some of the strongest teams in football—Washington, Ohio State, Nebraska, Purdue, Missouri, and Minnesota. This meant that he would have to send young men onto the field who would be physically outclassed. He could not ask them to make such a sacrifice.

On Friday night, March 4, Sutherland decided to quit. He typed a letter of resignation. It was, he said, the most difficult decision he would ever have to make; the whole episode he would always regard "as the most distasteful I ever experienced." He wrote to Bowman:

Since our meetings . . . I have tried to find some hope for the solutions of the problems we discussed. Frankly, the future athletic course is so indefinite and vague that I have concluded it will be for the best interests of all concerned if I ask you to accept my resignation, effective at once. I know from our conversations that you have no desire to have me stay on under conditions which cause me great worry and unhappiness. . . .

The present system of athletic administration has

resulted in conditions which, for me, are intolerable. . . . I make this decision with genuine regret because I have been associated with the University as a student and as a member of the faculty for twenty-five years.

With every good wish for you personally and for the University which means so much to both of us.

Sutherland placed the letter on Bowman's desk on Saturday. He had typed his name at the end of the letter but did not sign it, which led some observers to believe that he did not mean actually to resign. Bowman's mail was picked up that day and carried 100 miles east to his farm in Bedford. Bowman said that after reading the letter, he called a number of his strongest trustees for a meeting on Sunday. "Six of them attended—I believe the others were out of town. I showed them Dr. Sutherland's letter, asked them for advice. They asked me what I would do without their advice. I said that from my conversations with Sutherland, and from this typewritten statement, I would think that the man wanted to resign, and that I would be inclined to accept a resignation. The trustees told me that I was running the university, to use my judgment, and that whatever I did was all right with them."

Sutherland called at Bowman's office on Monday morning. Bowman was not there; the unsigned letter was not on his desk; and the last chance for what may have been planned as a final discussion was lost. One theory has it that Sutherland's alumni backers, feeling that he had the University in a bind, advised him that he could use a threat to resign as a means of moderating Code Bowman. If so, they were wrong. Bowman wrote:

I had thought that by our recent talks . . . we had ironed out the differences of opinion. These differences are evidently more deeply rooted with yourself than you stated in any of our talks.

The result [of our talks] was, I thought, a set-up in which we could go happily ahead. I tried to meet you half way, more than half way. . . .

I feel confident that you have given full and deep thought to the whole problem. With real regret, therefore . . . I accept your resignation. . . .

Let me add a personal word. I hope that you will be very happy in your new work. You have my good will and my wish always that many victories will be yours.

Pittsburgh Post-Gazette

Hungerford on the resignation of Jock Sutherland. His cartoons of this period frequently personified the Cathedral of Learning as John Bowman.

The news had a stunning effect on the University, the city, and the sports world. A group of dental students organized a protest demonstration and a one-day strike, but only a hundred or so students paraded. When some strikers invaded a classroom and Dr. James C. Charlesworth, professor of political science, ejected them by force, the strike collapsed. Two of the signs drew attention and appeared in the newspapers and the *Saturday Evening Post*: "We Will Trade Our Iowa Poison for a Wee Bit of Scottish Heather Any Day" and "Big John [Bowman] and Little John [Weber] Must Go." Two thousand students and faculty members gathered in Memorial Hall on April 19 to give Sutherland a farewell ovation. He spoke for ten minutes and urged the students to support the University.

Some fifteen hundred alumni and varsity letter men gave a farewell testimonial dinner at the William Penn Hotel. Telegrams were read and tributes delivered. When the program went on radio, Floyd Rose, master of ceremonies, introduced the affair to a coast-to-coast audience as "the celebration of a calamity." In his address Sutherland made his only public allusion to Bowman during these days: he said that he could see "no place in this city of dynamic poetry of noise, strong muscles and great courage" for "the verse of daffodils, pink sunsets and milky moonlight mixed with anemic idealism."

Charles W. Bowser (Class of 1922), a former Sutherland aide not currently employed in athletics, was named head coach. Athletic Director Hagan told Bowman and Weber, somewhat optimistically, that Bowser "was superior to Sutherland when it came to knowing his football and getting his men whipped into line on fundamentals." Sutherland's four assistant coaches resigned. W. Don Saunders, editor of the *Alumni Review* and executive secretary of the General Alumni Association, resigned. (Bowman was holding up $8,000 of Saunders's budget, complaining that about the only thing Saunders was doing with the magazine was running a campaign to serve Sutherland.)

A peculiar statement in the 1937 Hagan Plan read: "A football game is no longer a game when teams as powerful as ours run roughshod over the teams of schools which under normal conditions do not attract an abundance of football material." This was a problem that gave Pitt very little trouble for the next several decades. Pitt had a losing season in 1940—the first since 1912—and eight more years were to pass before it had a winning season. In the fifteen years between 1940 and 1954, Pitt had twelve losing seasons. It lost eight of nine games in 1947 and again in 1950. Coaches came and went. The team lost twenty-four straight games to Big Ten opponents. Some scores were 69–0, 58–0, 47–0, 46–0, 41–0 (twice), 40–0 (twice), 39–0, 33–0 (three times). There is no record of how much fun and benefit the students and the players had at these contests, or whether they ceased to be too much dependent on the winning of games, as Bowman had hoped, or whether they felt a greater sense of loyalty to the University, as the Hagan Plan said they would. Pitt lost thirteen of fourteen games with Ohio State, six of six with Minnesota, three of three with Michigan State, five of five with Illinois. There were good players in these difficult years, a few fine victories, spectacular plays, great stars, some College All-Stars, even some All-Americans. These teams and their players deserve as much respect as the players on the Sutherland championship teams—certainly more sympathy. But they lacked depth, reserves, and staying power. In eleven games with Notre Dame, Pitt scored 58 points and won one game. Notre Dame scored 377 and won ten. Pitt played two games with Michigan and lost both with a total score of 109 to 0. Attendance dropped off at Pitt games, gate receipts paid less of the interest on the stadium debt, and a drive was launched to persuade alumni investors to turn back their bonds as gifts. The most pessimistic forecasts of the opponents of Code Bowman were more than realized.

11

The Ordeal of a Chancellor

Faculties are always more or less unhappy and the problem is to appease this unhappiness as much as is humanly possible. To this end we need a more democratic form of administration in the University. Such a form of administration may lead to odd things sometimes, but it is the price we would have to pay.

Charles S. Tippetts, dean of the School of Business Administration, to the trustees' Special Investigating Committee, March 24, 1939

On Tuesday morning, March 20, 1939, a day of crisis at the University, John Bowman called Rufus H. Fitzgerald to his office. Fitzgerald kept a record of this and of four other meetings held on that day:

He started out by saying that he had been thinking about the present situation in the University and the series of some events over the past years—unfavorable publicity, a bad student attitude, rotten alumni attitude—and that he had come to a conclusion. He passed a paper across the desk and said, that is it, there is no use discussing it or talking about it, that is all there is to it. The paper contained his resignation to be presented to the Board of Trustees at the 6:30 meeting.

I told him that it could not be, that this was not the time to inject a personal attitude into it. He knew that I felt very strongly about it. I told him that besides all that, he could not leave the thing that he had given his life to in his present frame of mind.

Bowman said there were three things that troubled him personally. The first was the loss of twenty-five pounds since his return from China.* The second was "the way he had to get sleep." The third was discreetly left blank in Fitzgerald's notes. One may surmise that it concerned family problems: a wife to whom he seldom spoke and never took to social events, though she longed for company, or a son who was a brilliant but erratic scientist, who suffered from a bad stutter, and whose salary at Mellon Institute Bowman was paying privately and personally.

Fitzgerald told Bowman that he, too, was discouraged and had been for about a month. He said he might as well put all the cards on the table and tell what he thought. His work with committees was not going well. Then there was the chancellor's opposition to a code of permanent faculty tenure. "We set the highest standards in the country with our code in football; and failed, when it came to our faculty, to adopt the plan which is adhered to in 75%

to 80% of the schools in the United States."† Fitzgerald told Bowman of sitting across the table from a vice president of Gulf Oil, who said that universities had to do this for their employees. Fitzgerald had agreed with him: "I said that this thing of taking care of the faculty was just a part of the operations of the University." Bowman asked him whether Iowa had adopted a code of tenure. Fitzgerald's notes: "I told him, 'Yes, we had it there.' He seemed surprised. Then I told him . . . that we needed to appoint some important men in this faculty and we ought to do that soon. He indicated that he knew where the trouble was and something had to be done about it right away."

Fitzgerald went directly from that meeting to consult Dr. Hugh Thomson Kerr, pastor of the Shadyside Presbyterian Church and a University trustee.

I told Dr. Kerr that the Chancellor was terribly depressed and in a very serious frame of mind. . . . I told him that, as I saw it, this was no time to inject personal attitudes. . . . Then I mentioned the question of tenure. We might as well look at it frankly, that was something which is in the minds of the faculty and I was not critical up to this time, but it seemed to me that we might well think, without any emotion, about adopting the same principles of tenure that other institutions adopted.

He said that Dr. Bowman had consumed too much of his own smoke and that it just made it terribly hard on him and we must all try to help him, and that he would stand by to do everything he could.

Fitzgerald was called from his lunch to the chancellor's office. Bowman asked him to take the agenda and handle the 6:30 P.M. meeting with the board. He said that neither he nor Weber would be there. He went over the agenda and asked Fitzgerald to do two things: to recommend the appointment of a special committee to investigate the administrative operations of the University and

---

*Bowman, traveling with his nephew and son-in-law, Theodore Bowman, had left for China from Vancouver on August 8, 1938, and returned on October 16. His small book *Notes Along the Way*, illustrated with drawings by Theodore Bowman, is an account of the trip.

†Fitzgerald's notes contain a number of accounts of his fruitless attempts to persuade Bowman to end his practice of giving only one-year faculty appointments and to introduce a code of tenure. Bowman had ignored a code painstakingly drawn up and presented by a faculty committee in 1936.

to present his resignation. Fitzgerald said he could not do that. He said he had talked with Dr. Kerr, and Dr. Kerr had said that the men on the board would be behind him and wanted to be helpful. During this conversation, Kerr called and asked for an appointment; he wanted "to give him moral courage. That got under Dr. Bowman's skin."

Fitzgerald went from Bowman's office to the city, where he saw Arthur Braun.

I told Mr. Braun that I did not know the whole situation here, but that I was convinced of two things. First, that the Chancellor was a great administrator—that he could go as low and as high as any man I ever saw, and that he was low today. I said that he was not well and that he was in a serious frame of mind and I was worried about him and the outcome.

I [said] that I was going to handle the evening meeting . . . because Dr. Bowman was not feeling well and did not think it was the thing for him to be there. Mr. Braun was greatly disturbed about that. He said that the Chancellor must be there.

Braun telephoned Leon Falk, who came to his office and said at once that the chancellor should attend the meeting. "It appeared that Mr. Braun and Mr. Falk had been in a meeting some time during the day and knew what all this was about and where things were. Both of them felt . . . that this situation was bad and that it ought to be cleaned up and cleaned up by a committee. Mr. Falk said that he had just been discussing that committee with the Chancellor and he indicated that he was going along with it."

Fitzgerald now went back to the University and told Bowman that both Braun and Falk thought it would be a mistake for the chancellor not to attend the meeting—he should be there on his own behalf. "Then I said, this resignation business is out, we simply have to go through this thing—you take the order of business and go through this meeting. He began to yield and said that he would carry through on it."

Bowman did attend the meeting, during which seven trustees were appointed to serve as a special committee "to study the situation at the University in all of its phases and to report to the Board as early as possible."* For the sake of appearances, it was recorded that this step was taken at the request of Chancellor Bowman. Fitzgerald finished his notes on a hard day's work: "Dr. Bowman came to my office after the meeting all lighted up and smiling. . . . The resolution for the committee was adopted. Dr. Bowman said that he was sorry he had been so far down during the day and was glad that he went through with the meeting, as I told him I knew he would be."

Shortly after the meeting, Ernest T. Weir led five of the other six committee members into Fitzgerald's office, where he and Bowman were talking. Fitzgerald's notes for that day read: "Mr. Weir was their spokesman. They had just had a meeting and had talked it over. They were of the opinion that they needed somebody to help lay out the program and advise with them. They had decided upon the man and wanted to know if Dr. Bowman would approve his serving with them as Secretary of the Committee. The man was Steele Gow. Dr. Bowman said—go right ahead, that is a good setup, I think he would be a good man." Fitzgerald then added the cryptic observation, "It appeared, after the Committee had gone, that lances are to be crossed."

J. Steele Gow, who had served successively in the 1920s as Bowman's assistant, executive secretary, and dean of administration, called on Bowman a few days later. He had accepted the assignment, he said, only after hearing that the chancellor approved. If for any reason the chancellor did not wish him to serve, he would gladly withdraw. He hoped there would be no misunderstanding about his part in the investigation or about his motives.

The investigation of "the situation at the University in all of its aspects" was a model of its kind: a

---

*Those named were Arthur E. Braun, president, Farmers Deposit National Bank; Leon Falk, Jr., chairman, Maurice and Laura Falk Foundation; Norman MacLeod, partner, Ketchum, Inc.; Charles W. Ridinger, president, Iron City Electric Company; A. W. Robertson, chairman, Westinghouse Electric and Manufacturing Company; Edward R. Weidlein, director, Mellon Institute of Industrial Research; and Ernest T. Weir, chairman, National Steel Corporation. Braun was committee chairman.

painstaking, probing, productive study of the operations of an institution in trouble. The members of the special committee went directly to the heart of the University's problems. They made surprising proposals that opened the way for a revolution in procedure and style. They conducted the investigation in a manner that reflected credit on themselves—the seven trustees who asked the questions—as well as on the administrators, faculty, and alumni who answered them. And they produced an invaluable document in the history of the University in the years 1921 to 1939.

Work began at once, with the first meeting held on the afternoon of March 22. The committee held eighteen meetings in all, totaling a little over forty-seven hours. Thirteen of these were interview sessions held in the boardroom of the new Mellon Institute at intervals of two to four days. They generally began at 3:30 P.M. and lasted 2½ to 3 hours. The members took their assignment seriously. All seven were present at two sessions, six were present at seven sessions, and there were never fewer than four present at any meeting. MacLeod and Ridinger attended all thirteen meetings; Braun, the chairman, missed one meeting; Weir missed two.

The committee interviewed a cross section of the University's family: forty-three officers of general administration, deans, professors, instructors, and representatives of student organizations and alumni groups. The record of information contains 408 typewritten pages. Steele Gow gave each member an agenda before the meeting, the names and titles of the persons who would appear, the nature of their work or their departments, and a list of appropriate leading questions.

Some of those invited to testify called on Fitzgerald for counsel on how to respond. His advice was simple. He thought it was time for every man to speak exactly what he had in his mind and soul to say. It was not, he told one professor, "a question of whether or not you stick your neck out. Until the leading men of the University did what they thought in their souls should be done for the welfare of their individual schools and the University, and stopped trying to do the expedient thing, they would never build a great institution."

Faculty members, administrators, and alumni, interviewed with the committee's promise of secrecy, did speak their minds with extraordinary freedom and candor. Their testimony and the drama of the trustees' investigation, as played out to the end, give a fascinating picture of Bowman's relationship with those who worked closely with and for him.

Even those who gave him full credit for his great accomplishments of the past eighteen years described, in the words of Vincent Lanfear, his dean of men, "more than a usual amount of dissatisfaction, discontent, and confusion." There was complaint by consensus that the chancellor did not consult his faculty in running the University and that the faculty had almost no part in academic and administrative decisions. Everyone agreed that the University needed a university council and a code of tenure by written contract. Elmer D. Graper, professor of political science and head of that department, declared, "On the few occasions when Dr. Bowman has addressed the faculty, the teachers felt that he read the 'riot act' and scolded them. They got the feeling that he thought the faculty was 'no good.' The Chancellor's ineptitude on such occasions hurts faculty morale."

Graper added, "The faculty feels that the Chancellor puts too much stress on factors that are unique and highly emotionalized, and that he thinks that somehow such things will perform acts of magic. The faculty is a hard-headed bunch and they believe that nothing will succeed except good hard work intelligently done." Don Saunders, secretary of the General Alumni Association and editor of the Association's *Alumni Review*, also opposed emotionalism. The chancellor, he said, "favored articles which stressed esthetic values . . . and poesy," which, as editor, he found lacked reader appeal.

Indeed, there had been considerable comment and some bewilderment or amusement among the trustees at parts of Dr. Bowman's biennial reports, which were printed, bound, and widely distributed as University bulletins. His first report for 1921–1922 had dwelt at some length on the character of the ideal teacher, who, "young and enthusiastic and filled with high motives . . . vitalizes his students. Together they rise to a high plane where sheer existence is a sort of rapture." When he achieved this, the teacher "is free, and inarticulately, blindly happy." The characteristics of a bad teacher were quite otherwise: "His mind runs in ferment and waywardness rather than in reason. . . . Sometimes he swings clear through to the revolutionist. Then he gives way more completely to discontent and fault-finding." Sometimes the chancellor's reports began with parables, written in a false-naive, fake-simple style that reads like a parody of the prose of Sherwood Anderson. The 1922–1924 report began with three pages about "Red," a master workman in a sawmill, whom Bowman said he had known in Iowa. ("He was tall and lean, and he looked straight at you. . . . He created a few simple, strong habits. . . . That is a wonderful thing to do.") The 1930 report contained a page on a parent ("dad") buying his son's first long trousers. The 1932–1934 report to trustees began, "After the body of this report was put together, I spent some days on a farm in the mountains near Pittsburgh. Swallows, bluebirds, and an occasional thrush were new friends. Quail whistled in the wheat. Wild mallard ducks were at home along the creek in the pasture." Students were always "boys" and "girls," including the young men who had seen military service in 1917–1919. Parents were advised, "If you have sent your child here so he will make money later in life, take him out now; our purpose is merely to teach him to enjoy a fuller meaning of the things of life."

One faculty member, after leaving the University, observed, "Pittsburgh businessmen wanted an administrator, and they got a poet." One critic pointed out that the chancellor, raised as a farm boy in Iowa in the 1880s, had had only eight years of training in academic life (1902–1907, 1911–1914) at Columbia and Iowa State before arriving in Pittsburgh. Everyone agreed that this was a complex man, a puzzle even to his closest associates, a man constantly misunderstood and easily ridiculed and who did not take criticism well. He had been a liberal at Iowa State but was an extreme conservative in Pittsburgh. He was pathologically shy, but he personally handed back a large check to a donor because it was not large enough. He would not use a bell to summon his office help, because no one should have to answer a bell; but he not infrequently gave a workman or a colleague a scalding dressing-down in public. If Dr. Bowman had been a different person, he undoubtedly would have shown better judgment in some things, would have had more congenial human relationships, and would have avoided a great deal of trouble for himself and the University. And if Dr. Bowman had been a different person, he undoubtedly would not have accomplished the remarkable achievements against long odds and strong opposition for which he is remembered and honored by later generations.

The Gow committee met in interview sessions until May 9, when it concluded with a seventy-five minute interrogation of Rufus Fitzgerald and an hour with James Hagan. It then retired to meditate and write its report. Rumors cascaded about the campus. It was said that a high-ranking administrative official (John Weber) would be asked to resign. It was said that a wealthy alumnus, influential in University politics (probably George Hubbard Clapp) was threatening to withdraw a bequest of several million dollars from his will if the trustees permitted any further embarrassment to Chancellor Bowman. Elmer Allen Holbrook, dean of the School of Engineering and of the School of Mines, reported after his interview, "They are much interested in the Turner Case." The Reverend Hugh Thomson Kerr heard that they would call for the University to adopt a code of tenure. Was it true that the committee had not talked with Chancellor Bowman, and if not, why not? Would the report be friendly and constructive? Or would it be unfriendly with a view to causing embarrassment?

On September 5—this was four days after Hitler's troops invaded Poland and started World War II—George Clapp met privately with Bowman and gave him "the sum and substance" of the report that the committee would present to the trustees in ten days. On the whole, he said, it was a criticism of Dr. Bowman and his administration. Bowman warned Clapp that he "would say his piece and say it to the papers in headlines if that kind of report was made to the board." To Fitzgerald he said a few hours later that the report apparently had been written in the negative by one man (J. Steele Gow) and he would "go into it hard."

Twenty-four of the thirty-one trustees met at 5:00 P.M. on September 15 in the Red Room of the Duquesne Club in what the press assumed was "a tension-filled session." Copies of the forty-nine-page committee report were given to the trustees and to John Bowman. (The committee, for reasons never expressed on the record, had never interviewed Bowman or given him an advance copy of the report.) The press people, who were not admitted into the room, received a mild six-page abstract of the report, but not the report itself; that was to be a secret document for thirty days.* Arthur Braun read the report aloud. It appears that Bowman forthwith made a slashing attack on the committee, for Dr. Kerr later reported to Fitzgerald, "The committee were important men—some of them had been badly hurt by what the Chancellor said." At the end of the meeting, the trustees, rather than carry the report past waiting newsmen, turned their copies over to Bowman, who was to return them by mail. No action was taken on the report at this meeting.

The report was indeed a criticism of Dr. Bowman and his administration, though it began with praise for his accomplishments.

In the past 20 years the University has achieved a rapid growth in enrollment, a remarkable enlargement and improvement of physical facilities, and a wide expansion of educational services. The Administration of the University is to be commended without stint for its achievements along these lines. The record is one not paralleled by many universities in a comparable period of time. Further, the financial structure of the institution has been kept sound throughout the period, which was marked by many years of a severe depression.

However, the strength of the University in other respects has not been developed in pace with its growth. The result is that the University now suffers from an acute case of "growing pains." That this should not become a

*The report did not include or quote from Gow's transcripts of the interviews, nor identify those who testified, since they were covered by the pledge of secrecy.

chronic condition, it is now vital that steps be taken without delay to make the University as sound as it is large. . . .

The Administration of the University is not . . . well organized. The officers who are charged with the over-all administration of the institution do not function along lines of clearly defined responsibility and authority. The same function is ofttimes divided haphazardly among several officers, and a single officer's roster of duties may comprise an almost impossible heterogeneity.

One of the most noticeable results of this confusion in organization is an excessively heavy concentration of administrative work in the hands of one man [John Weber], the Business Manager and Secretary of the University. . . . He has an overload of duties which affects the University's work adversely. . . . An excessive amount of heavy volume of administrative work is forced into a bottleneck in his office; decisions and actions are greatly impeded. . . . His volume of duties is so heavy that it constitutes a barrier against his taking the time to consult the advice of those whose official interests are affected by his decisions and actions. . . .

There has never been a clear arrangement of the relationship of the work of the new Provost [Fitzgerald] to the work of the Business Manager and Secretary. The result has been confusion. . . . Work is poorly distributed, often delayed, and sometimes inexpertly managed. . . .

There is less than adequate consultation by the University's chief officers of administration. In recent years the Administration had held few meetings of its deans as a group. . . . Valuable sources of information and guidance are overlooked . . . and there is left a trail of feeling among the deans and faculty that their interests are passed upon by an inadequately informed, and sometimes arbitrary, authority. . . .

The Administration formulates objectives, makes decisions and takes action not only without adequate consultation but also without "following through" to make sure that all members of the official family are acquainted with what has been done. . . .

The combination of (1) a loose administrative set-up, (2) neglect to bring all segments of the institution into a consultative partnership, and (3) failure to keep all parties advised of decisions made and actions taken is responsible . . . for many of the difficulties currently besetting the University. . . .

Two devastating paragraphs followed:

"Many specific situations and problems now needing attention might not have arisen had the University's Administration followed the methods recognized everywhere as essential for sound institutional management. . . .

"Certain specific conditions and situations . . . if given constructive attention, would go far toward fully regaining for the University the esteem in which it has been held in the past by its students, faculty, and alumni, by the academic world at large, and the general public."

The administration, the trustees said, had not succeeded in developing a library worthy of the institution. That circumstance was a major factor in preventing the University from getting a chapter of Phi Beta Kappa. The administration had given little attention to providing "club" (student union) facilities for the students; the available facilities were pitifully short.

The report gave nine pages to tenure and academic freedom.

The absence of official recognition of a code of tenure by the University appears definitely to hurt the University's reputation at other universities. It is difficult for other institutions to understand why a policy which they have been able to put into practice successfully should be resisted here, especially since the result is hurtful to the University's academic standing. Absence of a code was a chief factor in putting the University on the blacklist of the A.A.U.P. Many members of the University's faculty are sensitive about the University of Pittsburgh's being one of the two colleges currently on this blacklist. . . . The University appears to practice security of tenure in its appointments even though it avoids official recognition of a code. This way of handling the matter is unwise and leads inevitably to distrust. A more open and definite treatment of this problem would go far to cure a sore spot. . . .

The committee made especially careful inquiry concerning [academic freedom] of all the University's people whom it interviewed. Practically without exception, these people answered that they do not feel their academic freedom is infringed. The very few who were not clearly definite on the question made no greater protest than to say they "felt" that they had to be "careful" in expressing their opinions on public issues "outside the classrooms." However, none of these persons claimed that the Administration ever took him to task for anything he did or said.

The committee feels thoroughly justified in concluding, therefore, that academic freedom in the University of Pittsburgh is not violated and that every individual in its family is permitted to express his views on issues quite as freely as are the teachers in other institutions.

The committee observed that members of the faculty appear to have a fine sense of their responsibility to be competently informed on issues about which they speak, and to speak always in a manner becoming scholars and gentlemen. . . .

The University's Administration was justified in the change of athletic policy it affected. This change was . . . necessary to bring the University into line with established practices at the best institutions. However, it does appear that the management of the transition from the old policy to the new was inept and that this factor accounts, in large measure, for the ill-will which has grown up among many of the groups interested in athletics.

One of the most regrettable results of the controversies which arose out of the athletic situation was the resignation of Dr. John B. Sutherland. . . . The committee feels, in common with the deans, faculty members, students, and alumni whom it interviewed, that Dr. Sutherland's resignation was a distinct loss to the University.

The committee found that the University's relations with the press were not good. The administration appeared not to realize the importance of cooperation in reporting its news. While the University was often shown in a worse light than it deserved, the fault lay more often with the University than with the press.

The committee recommended that:
- the chancellor reorganize the University offices to achieve a better distribution of work and responsibility and promote understanding of school aims among deans and faculty members;
- the chancellor take into greater confidence the head of the University News Service in order to patch up public relations troubles;
- the deans of the various schools convene periodically as a cabinet for offering advice on school affairs and educational policies;
- a University council of faculty members be established for the expression of faculty advice on educational policies and procedures;
- a code of tenure be drawn up "representative of

Forbes Avenue, west of the Cathedral of Learning, in the 1930s.

the principles and practices in force at institutions which have had successful experience with codes of tenure";

● salary cuts be abolished; the salary scale for instructors be raised; library, laboratory, and recreational facilities for students be enlarged;

● the athletic code of the Western Conference (Big Ten) or some similar conference be followed.

The committee is thoroughly convinced that the University of Pittsburgh is a very much better institution than its current reputation suggests to some. Further, its potentialities are immeasurable. It is still in a plastic condition and can be quickly moulded into a leading institution of higher education if the problems now confronting it are competently attended to without delay. . . .

There is much in the University that is good and the committee wishes not to fail to recognize that the present Administration, whatever it has slighted, has given the University in the past 18 years or so an advancement exceeding that of any comparable period in its history.

Forbes Avenue, east of the Cathedral of Learning, in the 1930s.

Archives of Industrial Society

Bowman had one month in which to study the report, and to write a reply to it if he wished, before it was released to the public and given to the Executive Committee of the board for action. He did indeed wish to comment; he thought of little else for the next thirty days. His plans, feelings, and drafts of his reply he conveyed almost daily to Fitzgerald, who recorded them daily in his notes.

It seems obvious today, some forty-six years later, that Bowman, his back to the wall, had only two fitting courses to follow. He could consider the report a vote of no confidence and resign. Or he could thank the committee members for their praise, welcome their sage advice, take advantage of their commitment to provide expanded facilities, and throw himself into carrying out the long overdue and reasonable reforms. He followed neither course.

He did intend to resign, Fitzgerald noted, the day after the meeting.

He talked for quite a bit in the afternoon. He was pretty quiet about it. Finally, he said that he had made up his mind. He had worked over this thing until about daybreak and he was going to write a fairly reasonable report answering the report of the Committee, taking about two weeks to do it. With his report would go his resignation. He said that he intended at that time to recommend that I be made Acting Chancellor with the thought that I would be put in at the end of this year. I told him I was greatly pleased by his thought of me, but that . . . if he passed in his resignation at this time he would cease almost immediately to have power and that his recommendations would not go through. I reminded him that Dr. Sutherland had power one day and when he handed in his resignation it was all over—he was a different man.

Fitzgerald also said that in the normal course of events these people would not want an independent person like himself.

The decision to resign was soon dropped, and so was the "fairly reasonable" answer. Bowman felt impelled to express his indignation at the "loose statements" in the report, at "a small group of alumni" who were keeping the trustees "in a state of agitation," and most especially at the indignity of not having been interviewed by the committee.

Bowman was goaded still further in these spring months of 1939 by two other unpleasant developments. The American Historical Association canceled its 1940 convention scheduled to be held at Pitt; it did so, according to the news stories, because of protests among its 3,000 professors and historians against meeting on the campus of a university that had been blacklisted by the AAUP "for violations of the principles of academic freedom." And on April 3, 1939, twelve very prominent alumni leaders sent a letter to the Gow committee proposing a step they believed was "the only one that assures the restoration of confidence and general good will toward the University." They recommended that Dr. Bowman be relieved of all administrative duties and put in charge solely of fund raising. He would be replaced by a president responsible for educational policies and for all relationships with students, faculty, alumni, and the public. Dr. Bowman, they wrote, "is obviously too egocentric and too lacking in a sense of organization

for the position he now holds."* The letter was not made public, but one may assume that since it involved twelve or more persons, it was talked about.

Bowman worked slowly on his reply to the trustees' investigating committee, sitting up all night at his desk (he said), showing Fitzgerald the next day what he had written, and asking him and Weber to assemble statistics that would support his points. "Now is the one time to come back," he said, "and to come back strong, in regard to certain opposition that has been slowing down the University for some time." He felt that he could handle this in such a way that the trustees would ignore their six months of work and withdraw their report. Fitzgerald pointed out to him that he had on the committee a group of men who had had to meet opposition to be where they were—they had been in battle before. Bowman thought he could handle it. He was thinking of "going after several members of the board very strenuously."

One after another of his advisors begged him not to challenge the committee or the board. Fitzgerald: "I said that he could write his answer in such a way as to salvage the best things from their report and incorporate them into the policies of the institution." Again: "I cut loose then stating that I thought the thing to do was not to answer this report in a controversial way but to use it to build a picture of the next step in the development of the University."

Fitzgerald wrote that Dean Tippetts was of the opinion that the chancellor "would find it possible to go along with several of the things that the committee had suggested, although his [Tippetts's] sympathy was with the Chancellor in the whole affair." Tippetts "said that the Chancellor had indicated that he was going to hit back strong. He then said that he did not know who was advising the Chancel-

*The signers were Allen K. Collingwood, Wilbur D. Hockensmith, Carlton G. Ketchum, R. A. McCrady, Roy C. McKenna, P. V. McParland, Harbaugh Miller, John B. Nicklas, Jr., Norman C. Ochsenhirt, Floyd Rose, Bert H. Smyers, and W. Arch Weldin. All had been presidents, chairmen, or vice presidents of the General Alumni Association, Alumni Council, or Varsity Letter Club.

lor, or if anybody could, but that he was of the opinion that the issue between the Chancellor and the Board was much more serious than he, the Chancellor, might know. He said that he had met one of the very influential members of the Committee last week and that he had indicated that the Committee had had its say and they were back of it and it was too bad if the Chancellor could not see it their way, but they all sincerely hoped that he would. He indicated that that was the attitude that one bumped into practically everywhere. He has some misgivings about the outcome."

Stanton C. Crawford, dean of the College, the next day echoed Tippetts's attitude and said that "he felt very deeply about it." Hugh Thomson Kerr told Fitzgerald that the only thing for the chancellor to do was to swallow his pride and work out with the Executive Committee the forward steps that he wanted to accomplish, based on the report, and present them to the board in December. Walter Albert Jessup, president since 1934 of the Carnegie Foundation for the Advancement of Teaching, was called on for advice. (Bowman and Fitzgerald had known him when he was dean, later president, of Iowa State University from 1912 to 1934.) Above all, Jessup said, Bowman should not "become enmeshed in controversy with the board. If we start scrapping around we will just get into trouble." Every college president he knew who started a fight with his board got into a mess. Fitzgerald told Jessup that the committee of prominent men had chosen as secretary a man (Gow) who had been in the administration and that there was no doubt that he had used a sharp pen. Jessup said, "Forget it."

Bowman held a "reading" of his reply on October 15 before Fitzgerald, Weber, Professor James B. Blackburn of the Law School, and Robert R. Gaw, a trustee friendly to Bowman. (He had previously read it to Dr. Kerr.) Everyone agreed that "modifications" should be made. Weber thought that the reply should be softened and the parts removed that pertained to the committee members, also the "rather sharp questions at the end of the sections."

Bowman later gave Fitzgerald that part of his reply that explained why he opposed a code of ten-ure. He asked what Dr. Fitzgerald thought of a passage about monastic orders: "Let me suggest that you read the history of the rise and fall of the orders of monasteries in the Middle Ages. The story of each order is a story of fine desire, of idealism, and of struggles; then come luxury, and security to the monks; and then fatness, desirelessness and the end of the order. What you will see here in long perspective is that ease and security are associated with decay." Instead of telling Bowman that what he had written was nonsense, Fitzgerald, worn down by days of discussion, told Bowman that he "thought his philosophy was all right, but that [his] idea would be to keep the reply out of the controversial realm and be more factual."

Bowman finally read his rebuttal—nineteen pages—at the regular trustees meeting held on Tuesday, October 17. He began:

At a meeting of the trustees, on September 15, I learned, for the first time, the content of the report of your Committee of investigation. The Committee spent six months on its report. During this period I was consulted in no way about the matter.

Much of the report tells that the administration of the University is less than adequate. If this were all, I should make no reply. It interests me, however, that I could have given your Committee more convincing evidence to the point than is in the report. Other parts of the report, however, do harm to the University. To some of these I reply.

Judgments are made in the report sometimes on little or no data. If more information had been at hand, some of the conclusions, I think, would have had a different color. Good as the intent is, the effect is to hurt the University, both in Pittsburgh and over the country. . . .

I am at a loss to understand the tone of the language of the report, although I am sure that the Committee as a whole is loyal to the University.

In the next five pages Bowman corrected the trustees in a number of details, such as the size of the library collection, and he devoted four pages to salary scale and academic standards and a half-page to the charge that the University's relations with the press were "far from satisfactory." ("Much of the publicity about the University has a habit of wanting

myself in it. Good or bad, I prefer to be out of it. . . .
I hereby agree as best I can . . . to try to improve
our relations with the press. I should much value
suggestions from the down-town newspaper men
themselves on this matter. I should like to ask, too,
for a bit of special and kindly consideration at the
start because of a probably-incurable lack of joy at
being in the news.")

On permanent tenure of office:

The teacher [who has overcome obstacles] is now the
designer of his own life-plan. He is self-respecting and
gives expression to the wealth of his mind and of his
heart. There is not, I believe, a more glorious road open
to anyone.

Now comes a kindly-disposed board of trustees and says
to him, "We are proud of your success. We want to help
you. Here is our pledge for your safety of tenure."

The teacher will value the message for its kind intent. If
he is of full stature, however, he will by his innate nature
resent the idea of cushioned ease for himself in a world
where others find contest and struggle. He will wonder at
the message in that it proposes to take from him one of
the chief means by which he arrived at and maintains his
present state. What he will probably think, in a lighter
vein, but not say, is this: "Have you noticed that I sometimes play baseball? Should you not suggest that I play
from now on with a large soft ball, a big woolly one, for
safety's sake?" His friend, the doctor, holds his practice
because he gives good service to his patients. His friend,
the engineer, builds bridges because the bridges he has
built stand up. He had thought that he was in a class with
doctors and engineers. But will they think so, he wonders,
when they learn that he holds his position perhaps by
virtue of special protection. Something inglorious has
come to him; and in spite of all excuses he can make for
his protection, his self-respect takes a tumble and, if this is
true, the value of his teaching goes down, for his old
desire is somewhat in decay.

A conclusion and a countercharge: "Projects are
most difficult [to accomplish] under the best of conditions. But when athletics, the faculty, the students,
the newspapers, alumni clubs, the legislature in
Harrisburg, and now the board of trustees itself are
kept in a state of agitation by a small group of
alumni, progress is impossible. Time will make all of
this, with its motives, clear. In the meantime and as

always the target for fault-finding and for disdain is
broad."

The special committee's report and Bowman's
reply to it were given to the press after the meeting.
Each appeared almost in full in the pages of the next
day's papers. Editorial comment on Bowman's presentation was scathing. The *Pittsburgh Press:*

Chancellor Bowman Is Resentful
Chancellor John G. Bowman . . . showed by his reply that
he does not intend to pay any attention to the recommendations contained in a report made by a group of seven
university trustees following a long investigation. . . .

Instead of accepting these suggestions in a spirit of
goodwill and co-operation, Chancellor Bowman's reply
shows that he is irritated because trustees presumed to
give him advice. He even questions the motives prompting
the inquiry and charges that conditions which finally led
to it were inspired by a small and hostile group of alumni.

This is another case of everybody out of step but Mr.
Bowman.

It is becoming increasingly obvious that the University
of Pittsburgh will either continue to be run as the private
and personal institution of Chancellor Bowman or else
there will have to be a new chancellor. There does not
seem to be any middle ground. . . .

It is regrettable that instead of taking this advice in the
kindly and helpful manner in which the trustees gave it,
Chancellor Bowman should have displayed a resentful
attitude. It is a bad situation when any state institution is
conducted as if it were the private property of a single
individual.

The University of Pittsburgh is a great and important
institution, contributing much to the welfare of Pittsburgh. Chancellor Bowman has made many important
contributions toward its development. It would be very
unfair to ignore or discount his personal part in its
growth. But at the same time, there have been unpleasant
and, we believe, unnecessary conflicts. . . .

It is impossible to believe that there is no reason for the
unfavorable publicity which Pitt has received and that the
trustees in seeking to correct the situation were hood-
winked by a little group of wilful alumni.

The *Pittsburgh Post-Gazette:*

Constructive Tone Rules
Pitt Trustee Report
The administrative set-up is criticized, and in the light of

the executive training and ability of those who made up the committee, it would seem that the University officials could hardly question the competence of their critics to speak with authority. . . .

Perhaps the sharpest clash between the committee and the Chancellor comes on the question of adopting a recognized system of tenure. In conjuring up visions of medieval monasteries where luxury killed enterprise, it would seem that Dr. Bowman builds a fictitious picture in order to tear it to pieces. There is no suggestion of rigid tenure before teachers have proved their qualifications; it is quite a different matter to say that professors of established standing should be protected from executive whim. To follow the example of most comparable institutions will not give Pitt faculty members the "cushioned ease" which the Chancellor deplores.

If the Board as a whole puts into effect the committee's recommendations, or the majority of them, it is probable that the stir of recent years will fade out entirely and that Pitt's splendid accomplishments will be matched in others.

Writers have speculated from time to time: What made John Bowman follow the course he did in administering the affairs of his University? What were his motives? For whom was he acting when he ordered or condoned "illiberal" policies? When he broke up the Liberal Club, caused Harry Elmer Barnes to be escorted off the campus, and expelled three students; when he condoned the arrest of three students for preparing to picket General MacArthur; when he imposed a loyalty oath on his students; when he dismissed Ralph Turner without consulting his faculty; when he imposed censorship on the *Pitt News* in September 1937? Was he acting independently, because of his personal convictions? Or was he carrying out policies his trustees wanted him to follow?

The political left was quite certain that Bowman was following orders given him by "Pittsburgh industrialists," each of whom, cast in an identical mold, fitted their stereotype of how a Pittsburgh industrialist looked, thought, and acted. Democratic Chairman David L. Lawrence (some ten years before he acquired the stature of a statesman) declared in 1934, "When a Democratic legislature

and administration starts functioning at Harrisburg next January . . . I am quite sure that the charges of persecution of liberal teachers by the reactionary board of trustees at the University will be investigated." A *Time* magazine writer charged that to build the Cathedral of Learning, Bowman "has sacrificed . . . the liberal principles he once held [as president of Iowa State and director of the College of Surgeons]. His Board of Trustees is packed with the reactionary industrialists who gave him money. One liberal professor after another has walked Pitt's plank." Raymond Howes, a disaffected instructor in the English department in the middle 1920s, wrote as late as 1972 that Bowman's problem "was the extent to which [he] was willing to bow to what he thought were the desires of Pittsburgh industrialists." Howes had written in the *American Mercury* in 1930 that Bowman faced a clear choice of two courses. He could uphold academic freedom, but if he did he would offend his donors and risk losing his Cathedral of Learning. Or he could support the donors of his Cathedral, but if he did he would risk losing academic prestige.

A somewhat more sophisticated analysis was given by C. Hartley Grattan, a liberal essayist, in *Survey Graphic* in 1936: "The minds of some university administrators assimilate pretty much to the pattern characteristic of the business leaders. There is, therefore, relatively little point in seeking to establish whether a given university official takes orders from a conservative board of trustees or acts in harmony with their express, implied, or deducible interests from personal conviction of their essential rightness. In such instances, it is sounder psychology to assume the identity. Liberals frequently overlook this psycho-cultural identification, apparently feeling that no one can possibly hold such views except direct participants in the power, prestige and financial benefits accruing from them, and radicals go still farther in disbelieving in the honesty of conservatives, putting the whole matter on the plane of buying and selling. For them it is sufficient that Chancellor Bowman draws a salary of $31,500 a year even after depression cuts." The basic premise of all discussion of such matters, of course, including

Thrysa W. Amos, dean of women from 1919 to 1941.

Grattan's, was that all businessmen-trustees were conservative and therefore wrong.

If the report of the special committee of the board was indeed a vote of no confidence in John Bowman, then it would seem that a third possibility might be considered. Perhaps Bowman was following illiberal administrative policies that his businessmen-trustees did not expect or want. He may have been acting independently, or he may have followed a course he assumed his trustees wanted him to follow; but either way, he gave the trustees a set of policies that they did not approve, and in the summer of 1939 they ordered him to stop, change, and follow a more liberal course. It was an action for which they have never received recognition. Such

unorthodox behavior is confusing. How can the dogmatist possibly explain the act of Ernest T. Weir, the very embodiment of ultraconservatism in the 1930s, in calling for a council of faculty members, abolishment of pay cuts, a pay raise for instructors, and a code of permanent tenure for the faculty? Ernie *Weir?* Did these men have a sense of what a university meant that was lacking in John Bowman?

There is other evidence—not conclusive but intriguing—that Bowman formed his political opinions independently and acted on his own initiative without prodding from his trustees, and, indeed, against their wishes.

When Andrew W. Mellon died on August 26, 1937, a signed column appeared on the *Pitt News* editorial page attacking Mellon for "retaining control of his corporations" by setting up the multi-million-dollar Educational and Charitable Trust. (In its lifetime it was to give almost $200 million to good causes—$43,866,372 of it to the University of Pittsburgh.) Bowman demanded and got a front-page apology. He imposed censorship on the paper, and Leo Koeberlein, the editor (not the author of the offending column), resigned in protest, as did the rest of his staff. Faculty members put out the issue of October 4.

On September 30, Alan M. Scaife, a trustee, R. B. Mellon's son-in-law, wrote a letter to Dr. Bowman:

At today's meeting of the Board of Trustees when you discussed the unfortunate incident regarding the publication of an article derogatory to Mr. Mellon, you said that you had taken steps to see that a repetition of this incident would not occur. . . .

In thinking this matter over I am going to suggest to you that you do not have faculty censorship of the publication. I think that such a move on part of the officials will merely intensify the efforts of the radicals to create trouble for the University in Harrisburg and elsewhere. If there is any method by which a sense of responsibility can be generated in the minds of editors of the Pitt News, this should be done. To my way of thinking strict censorship will be much worse than risking the continuance of the paper's publication after appealing to the better side of the editors and allowing them to proceed on the promise that they will not allow such an incident to occur again.

On October 4, Paul Mellon wrote Dr. Bowman:

Please accept my late but none the less sincere thanks for your kind letter of sympathy on the death of my father, and for your kindness in accepting the duties of an Honorary Pallbearer.

In reference to your visit to my office the other day, please do not feel that I have any resentment toward the author or editors of the paper, who are only misled and strangely bitter: or toward the University in any way. Such things are unpleasant, but I don't think they do much harm: and one forgets quickly.

I am very glad to be a trustee and thank you very much for the honour.

On October 6 censorship of the *News* was somewhat modified. Controversial articles would henceforth be submitted to an advisory board consisting of three faculty members and ten senior students "who are known for intelligence, fair-mindedness, and loyalty to the University." The advisory board's decision in a matter would be final. Such an arrangement would be considered stark oppression today, but Koeberlein was satisfied that freedom of the press had been preserved; he agreed with the administration that every effort should be made to conduct the *News* on a high plane, "especially in the matter of courtesy toward individuals and institutions"; and he returned as editor—the first rung in a distinguished career in journalism in Pittsburgh.

These were important issues, but attention was being directed more and more to the war in Europe and America's part in it, if any. On October 18, the day the special committee report and Bowman's reply appeared side by side in the *Pittsburgh Press,* the headlines read: "Germany's Big Push Nears," "Hitler Expects to Knock Out British Navy with Series of Lightning Blows," "Nazis Jubilant over Victories."

12
The University at War

We must fight, and now. Only by losing themselves in helping to win the war can universities and colleges find themselves. Only by sacrifice can they help save the values for which this nation fights.

Pitt Magazine, Spring 1942

University Archives

"Soldiers belong here," commented a booklet published by the University during World War II. Thousands were trained by Pitt between 1942 and 1945.

In the history of the University, December 1941 is a watershed between the old and the new, a Great Divide between the past and the future. Doubts were quelled and uncertainties resolved by the Japanese attack on Pearl Harbor, and for the students there was relief and unaccustomed excitement in the common national purpose. Throughout the United States the need for trained personnel, civilian as well as military, was sudden and urgent. In a flurry of activity, the University prepared to make its contribution to the war effort.

The first military contingent to arrive on campus was a squadron of cadets in the Air Cadet Training Program. In all, 4,135 cadets would pass through the University from early 1943 until the program was ended late in the summer of 1944, receiving five months of preflight training in science, history, English, civil air regulations, medical aid, and basic sanitation. To accommodate them, University crews altered parts of the Cathedral of Learning, installed toilets and showers, and moved classrooms and offices to higher floors or to other buildings. They made the empty classrooms into 100 dormitories, each with chairs, a table, five double-deckers (made in the University's own carpentry shop), mattresses, pillows, and bedclothes. In a subbasement sixty feet down they built the largest kitchen in Pittsburgh, equipped with huge refrigerators, six-gallon kettles,

Wartime on the campus.

stoves, ovens, steam cookers, and coffee urns. They set up a bake shop, a butcher shop, and an enormous mess hall.

The cadets wore khaki, received the service pay of privates, and were quartered ten men to a room. They entered and left the Cathedral by the door facing Bellefield Avenue, which was reserved for the military, and they marched between buildings, frequently at double time, sometimes in gas masks, and occasionally at double time in gas masks.

The cadets shared the University facilities with a large enrollment of civilian students—11,961 of them in 1942–1943. These were women, young men not yet eighteen or not physically fit for military service, and some thousands of male students in engineering, physics, chemistry, geology, geophysics, medicine, and dentistry who were registered on the University's quota of those entitled to draft deferment. In addition there were the participants in some thirteen other programs of wide range and

varied purpose. Many of these were units of the Army Specialist Training Program (ASTP), which had been developed by the army, the American Council on Education, and the colleges. All ASTP trainees had already undergone thirteen weeks of basic training. Among the specialists the programs aimed at producing were:

Specialists for military government. Pitt was one of six universities chosen to offer courses in area and language study to train army officers for duty in occupied countries. Called civil affairs specialists, the officers studied the languages, politics, agriculture, industry, education, and social forms of countries in a specific geographical region. The Civil Affairs Training School at the University of Pittsburgh, given the endearing acronym CATSUP, was assigned the area of central and southeastern Europe. Number of trainees: 175.

Psychological technicians (as the army chose to call personnel officers) were a select group of men, some of them former college professors, instructors, or principals of public schools. They were trained at the graduate level to become personnel psychologists. Number of trainees: 121.

Area and language trainees. Specially selected enlisted men studied language and related geographical material as preparation for service with combat units in certain theaters. With twelve to seventeen hours of instruction a week by the army's intensive method, the soldier in two to three months (longer for Russian and the Asian languages) could converse below the level of abstract ideas. The University turned to its Nationality Room committees and asked them to find people in the community who were qualified to teach the required tongues. John Geise, director of Area and Language Studies, soon decided that the languages were being taught with too much refinement, and he asked for some truck drivers, bartenders, and artisans to teach the slang and profanity of everyday life.

Medics. The School of Medicine and the School of Dentistry were crowded with students in uniform. Most of these were medical and dental students who had been drafted and then had returned under the ASTP to complete their medical training in uniform. Number of trainees: 978.

On July 19, 1942, General Hospital 27 went into active service. The unit was assigned 500 enlisted men and was sent to Fort Lewis, Washington, for preliminary training. It was ordered to the Southwest Pacific Theater and from July 1944 to July 1945 ran a hospital in Hollandia, New Guinea.

By mid-1943 the Cathedral of Learning was at the center of a large, important, and efficiently run military installation. The classrooms, the halls, the Commons Room, the lawn, and the sidewalks about the building were crowded with young soliders—2,895 on September 8, 1943; 2,671 on February 23, 1944. A contingent of 200 trained Air Crew Cadets now left the station the first Saturday of every month, and 200 untrained cadets arrived the following Monday to replace them.

Foster Memorial was taken over completely by the air force as a rest and recreation facility. The people of the city, and particularly of the adjacent commu-

nities, were friendly and helpful. The trainees were given free tickets to see Pirate and Steeler games. The Schenley Hotel set up a lounge for air cadets. There were Saturday night dances at the Masonic Temple. Some thirty women volunteers set up a canteen in the Young Men's and Women's Hebrew Association building. They mended tears in uniforms, sewed on insignia, and lengthened or shortened trousers. They served ice cream, candy, and cigarettes, and they gave dancing lessons. Helen Pool Rush, dean of women, set up a service for finding jobs and living quarters for women who had come to the city to be with their husbands during training. She confided to Fitzgerald on October 12, 1943, that the problem of young female students and the soldiers was quite "serious." The women, she said, could not turn around without causing comments, and they could not go into the Commons Room without being called to and having notes thrown to them from the two upper floors. But an order went out, the soldiery apparently obeyed it, and on November 10 Miss Rush was pleased to report that the relationships between civilian students and army students were rapidly improving.

Soldiers who were taught at the University and the professors who taught them speak highly today of the 1943–1945 experience. The seriousness and discipline in the classrooms were hitherto unknown on many campuses. The students marched to their classrooms to the cadence count of a section marcher, who was distinguished for the day by a blue band around his upper left arm. They stood at attention when the professor entered. The marcher reported his section all present and accounted for, holding his salute until the professor returned it. The professor, in the capacity of a surrogate officer (in the classroom only), saluted and said, "Seats, gentlemen." (One young instructor was mortified when he realized that he had been giving a three-finger Boy Scout salute.) The professor addressed the students as "mister," and the students used "sir" or "ma'am" in responding. After the bell, the students stood at attention until the professor left the room.

The campus situation changed early in 1944. Casualties were heavy in the Pacific Theater and in Italy, and hundreds of thousands of trained troops were joining the forces that were to invade Normandy. The college training programs, therefore, were reduced in size, number, and relative importance thoughout the year. On August 29, 1944, the University was notified that it would receive no more assignments of ASTP students or other professional trainees. At the same time Selective Service reduced the number of draft-deferred undergraduates in all colleges to 10,000. It was now the responsibility of the college to determine, within its assigned quota, the students to whom deferments would be given. Under the curtailed figures, Pitt had in February 1944 a quota of 150 deferments. It gave 129 of them to undergraduate engineers, the others to students in chemistry, physics, and geophysics. The AST medical program was not terminated until July 1, 1946.

On September 8, 1943, Pitt had a peak enrollment of 2,895 trainees; on September 19, 1944, it had 755. The air cadets were all gone, the CATSUPs, the psychological technicians, the area and language specialists. Most of those remaining were medical or dental trainees; 135 were seventeen-year-olds in preinduction training.

By the end of World War II in the late summer of 1945, the University of Pittsburgh had given specialized training to 6,850 army and 201 navy men. It did so at no profit to itself, recovering only its costs.

It supplied the professional people to staff and run a 1,000-bed military hospital. It increased the enrollment in the School of Nursing from 281 to 1,286. Under the Engineering, Science and Management War Training Program, it gave technical training to 24,948 civilians. Its spectroscopy laboratory trained 600 workers in spectroscopic testing of materials, the trainees coming from thirty war plants in the area. The Department of Chemical Engineering trained 190 college women as technical operators for government plants built and run by the Koppers Company for the manufacture of butadiene and styrene, the ingredients of synthetic rubber. Its faculty conducted an extensive wartime research and development program.

A total of 9,508 University people served in the military forces during the war—graduates, undergraduates, women (260 of them), faculty and staff members (286 of them). Of the total, 249 died in the service.

With the end of the war on August 14, 1945, the University turned its attention to new and happier problems. Now and for some years ahead it would be necessary to process, enroll, and find room and teachers for a flood of veterans—4,796 in the second semester of the 1945–1946 term. John Bowman declared in his biennial report, "Everyone who comes in contact with this group of students is impressed by their intelligence and by the strength of their purpose. They are eager, disciplined, and, the faculty say, a joy to teach."

Book III
1947-1955

Pittsburgh is worried. It is worried about the shift of steel to the West and the decentralization pattern of post-war industry. It is worried about the dwindling markets in bituminous. It is worried about its continued imbalance of heavy industry and its failure to attract more diversified, lighter industry to the area. It is haunted still by the memory of the late great depression, the idle men in the streets, the streets greasy with river damp. . . . This may be Pittsburgh's last chance. . . . [The city] is the test of industrialism everywhere to renew itself, to rebuild upon the gritty ruins of the past a society more equitable, more spacious, more in the human scale.

Fortune
February 1947

More than any other U.S. city, Pittsburgh has demonstrated how a community on the downgrade can arrest its slide, reverse the trend, and build anew.

Engineering News Record
November 1959

13

The Peacemaker

The University prepares young men and women to be: doctors, bacteriologists, linguists, engineers, historians, chemists, teachers, psychologists, metallurgists, dentists, writers, aviation specialists, social workers, mathematicians, biologists, personnel directors, astronomers, political scientists, lawyers, statisticians, X-Ray technologists, public health specialists, economists, bankers, seismologists, geographers, pharmacists, retail experts, research workers, sociologists, translators, social administrators, physicists, geologists, accountants, surgeons, pathologists, botanists, nurses, journalists, cartographers, business leaders, spectroscopists. . . .

If you are not convinced of the value of this University to Pittsburgh and Western Pennsylvania, just take out of it the 25,000 students enrolled . . . for this year and see how it will affect this modern complex industrial society. Eliminate the School of Medicine and see what happens to the health of your family.

Rufus H. Fitzgerald, in an address to community leaders, June 3, 1948

A T A BOARD MEETING on February 16, 1945, John Bowman asked the trustees of the University to accept his resignation as chancellor, effective on July 1. He had been engaged for forty years, he said, in educational administrative duties, and he now felt it was time to be relieved. After making the request, he rose and asked to be excused so that the board could consider what action it wished to take. When he returned he was told that his resignation had been accepted, but he had been elected president honorarius, a new position and title that would terminate when he relinquished them. He would carry no administrative or teaching load; his duties would be "related to the growth of the University and to the maintenance of those spiritual and cultural ideals which have always had a central place in his thoughts."

Bowman would be sixty-eight on May 18, three years past retirement age. He had held his office longer than any other living American college president save only Nicholas Murray Butler, eighty-three, who had presided over Columbia since 1901. When the news of the resignation spread, there was an upwelling of good will for him. The controversies, misfortunes, and mistakes of the 1930s, of course, were all recorded in indelible ink, but now there was a remission of animosity. This, after all, was the man who built the Cathedral and the Nationality Rooms, conceived and started the Medical Center, kept the University solvent and brought it safely through the Great Depression, headed the University for a quarter of a century, and told Pittsburgh that it could be one of the great and beautiful cities of the world. This was the leader with whom Pittsburgh and denizens of its University had traveled through good times, bad times, and war. He was an institution, a survivor.

Dr. Bowman now spent most of his time at Waterbrooks Farm in Bedford County, 580 acres of low-cost, marginal land that he had made into a productive, working, modern operation with a sizable flock of sheep, sixty-five Jersey cattle, and contracts to supply Bedford with milk. He suffered a severe cerebral hemorrhage not long after his retirement

Parry/University Archives

Rufus Henry Fitzgerald, chancellor from 1945 to 1955.

and for some months was a hospital patient in Bedford, but he managed a remarkable recovery.

He was succeeded as chancellor in 1945 by Rufus Henry Fitzgerald, fifty-four, to whom Bowman had personally promised the position in 1941. A graduate of Guilford College in North Carolina, he had been a general secretary of the YMCA at two colleges and athletic director and coach at the University of Tennessee. Before joining Pitt in 1938, he had spent fourteen years at Iowa State University, part of it as head of the Department of Appreciation and History of Fine Arts, for which he had raised $1 million for a new building. Fitzgerald was favored by several circumstantial advantages when he took over the chancellorship in 1945, and to those advantages he added certain strengths of character, personality, and experience.

First, he inherited an institution that was almost free of debt and was about to enter a ten-year period of unprecedented demand for higher education, much of it subsidized by federal support for veterans in a booming economy.

Second, he had in fact been competently managing the affairs of the University during the last five years of the Bowman administration, since the shattering impact of the trustees' investigation in 1939. (Fitzgerald joined the University as provost. In 1942, he asked to be made a vice chancellor, because, he said, no one in Pittsburgh knew what a provost was.)

His colleagues, moreover, respected, liked, and were comfortable with him. Almost everyone who knew and worked with Fitzgerald spoke favorably of him; he is remembered today as a considerate person with gentlemanly manners. One of his colleagues called him "the peacemaker." Another claimed to have heard a great sigh of relief rise from the campus at the news of his appointment. A third likened his role at the University to that of Dwight Eisenhower in the White House during the years between 1953 and 1960, and he believed that, like Eisenhower, who for a time was underrated as a president, Fitzgerald had been underrated as a chancellor.

Fitzerald already had one major achievement when he took office: he had caused a code of permanent tenure to be written and on March 31, 1944, had it approved by the trustees. (He would revise and strengthen it in 1947.) As chancellor he began subtle negotiations to have the University's name removed from the AAUP blacklist. Dr. Guy Everett Snavely, executive director of the Association of American Colleges, telephoned Fitzgerald in April 1946 to report that he had been talking with Dr. Ralph Himstead (who had written the AAUP report on Pitt). As Fitzgerald reported the conversation, Snavely told Himstead that "Pittsburgh should be off their list." Himstead agreed. He said he was very fond of Fitzgerald but added that the AAUP was disturbed by several phrases in Pittsburgh's tenure policy. Snavely advised Fitzgerald to drop in and see Himstead. He thought the whole matter might be straightened out in that way.

Fitzgerald called on Himstead on May 6 in Washington. There was an amusing delicacy in the situation, owing to the disapproval Bowman and Himstead had expressed of each other. Fitzgerald explained that he was there as a result of a long-distance call from Dr. Snavely, who had suggested that he drop off in Washington and have a talk. He was there unofficially, not representing the University, though of course he could not separate himself from his position and in one sense he *did* represent the University. He was there unofficially to discuss Pitt's tenure policy and to be sure there was nothing about the policy that the AAUP had misunderstood.

Himstead, attended by his assistant, Mr. Lundrum, said that the Pittsburgh tenure policy was not good from their standpoint because it tied tenure and rank together, and he asked for clarification of a paragraph on finances.

Fitzgerald said there were no jokers in the paragraph. It was drawn in good faith and it represented their best thinking.

Himstead: The AAUP would like the University to be much more critical of teachers during the first six years of their employment, before they achieved tenure. It should investigate, go to the classrooms, and take great responsibility in approving these instructors at the end of the six-year period.

Fitzgerald: This was a point of view he had not gotten before.

Himstead: Did Dr. Fitzgerald think the University would go in the next few years in the direction indicated?

Fitzgerald: He could not commit the board, but his record in regard to this matter, he felt, was good and not far out of line with good practices.

Himstead: Their only justification, if they took favorable action, was that, though they did not agree in detail with the University's policy, yet they did feel that the University was going in the right direction and therefore should be taken off the unapproved list.

The tenure code was modified to meet Himstead's objections and to accord with codes at other universities, and on February 23, 1947, the University of Pittsburgh was restored to academic respectability.

Fitzgerald at the same time had begun to work to persuade Phi Beta Kappa, the nation's oldest and most famous honorary scholastic society, to accredit a chapter at Pitt. It was not an easy task. The society considered the University's library inadequate, and it had on its record a shocked adverse report by its last investigating committee. The delegation of professors, calling on a Monday in November 1937, was shocked to find the campus in an unseemly uproar. Pitt had won a glorious 21 to 6 victory over Notre Dame two days earlier, and a large body of students was celebrating the event by derailing a streetcar. Fitzgerald worked for another six years before he saw Xi Chapter of Phi Beta Kappa accredited to the University in September 1952.

In several reports he made to his trustees for the years 1945–1948, Fitzgerald gave a lucid, detailed account of what life and work, people and problems were like on the postwar campus.

For the academic year 1947–1948, he reported, there were 25,700 students under University instruction—an enormous increase over the wartime and prewar figures. Of these, 13,268, or 51.5 percent of the student body, were veterans of the late war. They were attending under the Servicemen's Readjustment Act of June 22, 1944, otherwise known as the G.I. Bill of Rights, which provided tuition and a monthly cash allowance to some millions of World War II veterans who had served more than 180 days of active duty. "We are determined," Fitzgerald declared, "to do our utmost to take care of every possible veteran." His deans approved a policy under which all veterans who had been graduated from high school were admitted; all veterans twenty-one years of age and over were admitted as "adult specials"; and those under twenty-one who were not high school graduates were accepted if they passed the tests prescribed by the University admissions committee. Preprofessional applicants were admitted in accordance with the regulations of the Pennsylvania State Department of Public Instruction. Theodore W. Biddle (Class of 1929), dean of men (1942–1958), and four assistants worked long hours to handle all the interviews and registrations, which were running between fifty and seventy-five a day. Biddle felt that some of the men coming in as "adult specials" were "scholastic tramps and no good," but of the veterans as a whole Fitzgerald said in his report, "Their work is excellent, far better than anyone had reason to expect."

Fitzgerald was "quite disturbed about the quality of teaching of some of our new instructors," and he asked the students at one of his fireside meetings to talk to him frankly about the instruction they were receiving. "One of them made an observation with which the others seemed to agree, namely, that the young instructors presented their material better than some of the older men. When I asked how he explained that, he said that many of the younger men had had experience in presenting their material as officers in one of the armed services. They, therefore, knew how to organize and present it. Then another student observed that while the younger men presented their material better, they did not have the content of the older men. I rather think that these students have made shrewd observations of present-day university instruction."

One outstanding fact about the postwar expansion on the campus, Fitzgerald said, was the improvement in the quality of the student body, not only in the veterans but also in the able high school graduates. Increased use of admission tests and interviews, coupled with the opportunity of selecting from among large groups of applicants, had given the University "the most able student body in [its] history." Most of the students now came from the upper two-fifths of their graduating classes and were admitted without examination. The University, however, followed a policy of accepting as well those students from the lower fifths who qualified by examination. Freshman classes in 1946–1948 performed well above the national average on the American Council on Education examinations. In the 1946–1947 academic year, 257 of the 317 colleges involved had average freshman scores that were lower than Pitt's. In the Graduate Record Examination (GRE), which was given to college seniors opting for graduate work and to other seniors willing to take it, Fitzgerald said that Pitt students "usually perform above the national norms in the fields of mathematics, physics, chemistry, biology, social studies, literature, and vocabulary. They tend to fall below the national norms in their knowledge of the fine arts and in effectiveness of expression." In April 1947, 97 percent of the seniors took the GRE, though it was so extensive that it took eight hours to administer. (In the 1980s the test was reduced to three hours.)

The high quality of the students, Fitzgerald added, "has stimulated the teachers, with the result that standards have been raised all along the line." Faculty morale was "very good," in part, perhaps, because of a 10 percent salary increase made in December 1946. The deans were working harder than he had ever before seen deans work.

The two overriding problems of the University in the postwar years were the struggle to find qualified teachers and the need for classroom space for the avalanche of students. The competition among universities for teachers, Fitzgerald reported, was "terrific." The University of Illinois was receiving from the state for this biennium $63 million, "which enabled it to raid almost any campus in the country." To meet the shortage, he authorized the employment or retention of professors past the age of seventy and suspended the rule against employing two members of the same family. He was taken aback when, in attempting to get an outstanding head for the physics department, he found that neither of the two men he wanted "would budge," though he offered a high figure: $9,000 a year. Pitt was fortunate, he said, in that it was an urban university, for it was very much easier to find both teachers and space in a large city. Universities expanding in small towns were buying trailers and were moving temporary wartime buildings to their campuses for classrooms and to house students and faculty. Pitt, on the other hand, situated as it was in a large residential area, was able to take all the qualified students it could possibly handle without building one additional room for living quarters. And being in a center of science and industry, it was able to recruit engineers and scientists with teaching experience from industrial companies and research

laboratories of the Pittsburgh area—often men and women who had been selected for employment some years earlier from the University's roster of graduates.

For classroom space, the University expanded upward in the Cathedral of Learning; of its eighty classrooms, only eighteen were plastered and usable in the spring of 1947. It also borrowed and rented space in Soldiers and Sailors Memorial Hall, in the Young Men's and Young Women's Hebrew Association (YM and YWHA), in several nearby churches, and, about a mile to the east, in a building on Ellsworth Avenue formerly used by Shady Side Academy, a preparatory school, which had moved to a new campus in the suburbs. Pitt had rented the building and grounds in 1941 for one dollar a year, bought them outright in 1942, used them during the war to train ASTP engineers, and in 1947 set up Ellsworth Center, a kind of junior college. In 1947–1948 more than 700 men, 60 percent of them veterans, carried a full schedule of classes there in their freshman and sophomore years. (The Winchester-Thurston School now stands on the site.)

Fitzgerald documented his years as provost, vice chancellor, and chancellor with some thousands of pages of daily notes that recorded his conversations, thoughts, decisions, and orders. The notes provide a rounded characterization of the chancellor and reveal the surprising information that he could be rough and even, on occasion, deliberately ruthless, especially with several of his deans who, he thought, were performing inadequately. The notes give an invaluable account of events of this period. They depict in some detail the problems—large or small, complex or simple, puzzling, time-consuming, sometimes humorous, sometimes painful, always infinite in their variety—that face anyone doing "the impossible job" of trying to run a large urban university.

Up to 1949 the notes reveal a man who could not delegate authority, who insisted on making decisions that could have been made by his staff, who accepted telephone calls and visits that might have been handled by others, and who consequently overburdened himself with excessive detail and too much work. In his first years as chancellor, he seems simply to have added the responsibilities of the new office to the heavy duties he had carried out as vice chancellor, including the approval of small expenditures. The dean of women went to him for permission to buy two lace tablecloths, to hold a Santa Claus party costing between $25 and $50, and to travel with some of her staff to meetings in Harrisburg and Washington at a cost of $100. He authorized the dean of the School of Social Work to pay the cost of a luncheon for a civic committee and to give one of the employees in his office a $10-a-month raise. He heard and turned down the request of the Heinz Chapel organist to take down the organ curtains before his concerts because they muffled certain tones. He told the athletic director to clean up the profanity that was being heard around the athletic office. He sent word to Fletcher Hodges, curator of the Stephen Foster Memorial, that the evening programs were running too late. Thirty-five separate departments were reporting directly to him, including the manager of the University's food service. He continued to administer personally the A. W. Mellon scholarship fund. He prepared the annual budget himself, on an adding machine, working with the "green sheets" submitted by his deans and department heads. Decisions and permissions were so slow in coming from Fitzgerald and Weber that administrators sometimes risked using the device of last resort: "If I do not hear from you I will assume that I may proceed."

Chancellor Fitzgerald went for six years without a vacation, and he confessed in October 1948 that he "was running on a pretty narrow margin physically." He observed that the introduction of democracy into University affairs was a good thing and paid off in better spirit and morale, but lamented that it was time-consuming and kept him from giving as much time as he should to the trustees and "the people downtown." Because he felt a sense of obligation to participate in the Pittsburgh renaissance then gathering momentum, he for several years held the civic post of chairman of the city's Public Parking Authority. When Dean Biddle asked for a meeting to discuss one of his projects, Fitzgerald replied, "My interest is perennial, but my time is not," and asked

him to bring up the matter the next time he had a scheduled appointment.

Fitzgerald's daily record of important conferences, large plans, and weighty decisions is interspersed with trivia. This was no doubt regrettable from an administrative point of view, but a historian must be grateful, because the trivia give an unusual, amusing, and curiously revealing picture of a college president at work.

● James Patterson, clerk of the city of Pittsburgh, called the chancellor to congratulate him enthusiastically on the fine address he had given to the Freedom of Religion Committee the previous Sunday. After several compliments on the talk, he asked a favor: would the chancellor help him to get four tickets to the Pitt–Notre Dame game?

● A student leader complained to the chancellor that a most deserving female student had been left off the Hall of Fame award list. He could, he said, have 500 names on a petition in short order about the injustice of it. It was one of the worst things that had happened at the University since he was a student. "He wanted to know what I would do about it. I told him I was quite busy and did not know that I could do anything about it." But he asked Dean Biddle to look into the case. Biddle advised him to abide by the decision of the award committee.

● A mother whose son had been dropped by Carnegie Tech became "quite hysterical" when Fitzgerald told her that the University could not admit a student who had not made good at another college. She thought that was not democratic.

● Frank Vittor, a local sculptor, called to say that he intended to make a group statue for the city's Point State Park. One figure was to represent education. Could Dr. Fitzgerald suggest what object the figure should be holding in her hands to represent the best idea of education? Dr. Fitzgerald suggested a torch.

● Fitzgerald sent word to the custodian in charge of housekeeping that he had walked down from the twenty-seventh floor in the Cathedral and found that lights were out along the way, that the condition of the building was bad and dirty, and that the hall on the fifth floor was full of wooden boxes. The custodian said the lights had been checked the evening before and any that were out must have gone out during the night. He could not help the condition of the walls. The only time the window washers could wash the classroom windows was on Saturday, and it always rained on Saturday. (Presumably he did something about the wooden boxes.)

• Mrs. Jay Ream called from Somerset to say that a girl in the town had been named the Maple Sugar Queen, which entitled her to Senator John Walker's senatorial scholarship to Pitt. But the girl wanted to attend West Chester State Teachers College. Could the scholarship be transferred to the Teachers College? Fitzgerald said he would find out. He reported back that senatorial scholarships could be given only to Penn, Temple, Penn State, and Pitt, and that Senator Walker said he had never tried to give a scholarship for the Teachers College because the Teachers College was state-owned and did not charge tuition, only fees.

• A sophomore asked if the chancellor would help get him a job in England so that he could join his English wife. The chancellor said he was sorry but he could not help him.

• William Block, publisher of the *Pittsburgh Post-Gazette,* had just learned through a friend how low professors' salaries were, and he thought the public should be told what a Ph.D. was expected to work for. Neither Pitt nor Tech, however, would give him a list of the salaries it paid. Fitzgerald pointed out that there was quite a range in salaries because of the market—that is, a professor of English and a professor in the Law School would have quite different salaries. If Mr. Block did succeed in getting and publishing the salaries, he said, the next meeting of the University's Senate "would be a humdinger."

• Fitzgerald attended a civic luncheon in the city and by chance sat beside the treasurer of a large corporation headquartered in Pittsburgh. The treasurer informed him that the University had recently turned down his daughter for admission to a summer course.

• The president of the Student Congress led a delegation to the chancellor to request that dances be permitted in the Commons Room—a limited number of them, held on special occasions, under faculty supervision. The chancellor reversed a long-standing policy and gave permission. (The student is now dean of the Law School of New York University.)

• Fitzgerald asked John Weber to delay the carving of the panel for the English Nationality Room. The quotation to be carved was from Richard II, act 2, scene 1:

This royal throne of kings, this scept'red isle,
This earth of majesty, this seat of Mars,
This other Eden, demi-paradise,
This fortress built by Nature for herself
Against infection and the hand of war,
This happy breed of men, this little world. . . .
This blessed plot, this earth, this realm, this England.

One of the friends of the University had called to suggest that the phrase "this little world" might give offense to the English and perhaps should be deleted.

• The Pitt Marching Band was invited to play at the Steelers football game on September 23, 1946. Someone objected, and the matter was referred to the chancellor. After serious consultation and deliberation, he ruled that it would not be proper for the band to open the season and "put in its first stellar performance for another organization."

• On a trip to Minnesota with the football team, Fitzgerald entered a fishing contest at Otis Lodge in which each of nineteen men put one dollar in a pot. He won. Back in Pittsburgh, he had his secretary send each of the other eighteen men a receipt from the University for one dollar contributed to the endowment fund.

In April 1947 Fitzgerald persuaded the trustees to create a committee on planning and development. He then asked Alan Magee Scaife in a private conversation if he would accept the "important post" of chairman of that committee. Scaife, forty-seven, the fifth-generation scion of an old Pittsburgh industrial family and a graduate of Yale's Sheffield Scientific School, in 1927 had married Sarah Cordelia Mellon, daughter of Richard Beatty Mellon and sister of Richard King Mellon. Scaife had been a trustee since 1931 and was a working member of the Medical Committee.

He was, Fitzgerald wrote in his notes, "quite excited and said he would be glad to serve as a member of the committee or chairman. He felt greatly honored to be part of the committee." The two men liked each other and worked well together. As George Clapp was in his late eighties, Scaife became unofficial acting president of the board, the relatively young trustee on whose "energy, organizing ability, and planning" the chancellor drew for advice and help. In working with Scaife, Fitzgerald rose to meet the broader demands of his office. Together they started the University on an ambitious expansion and building program.

The already acute need for new buildings was exacerbated when the University felt obliged to sell the site of Trees Gymnasium to the federal government for a veterans hospital. The loss of Trees Gym meant that in order to qualify to teach physical education, the University would have to erect a field house or gymnasium elsewhere on the campus. And on Memorial Day in 1948, a fire destroyed the World-War-I temporary wooden building on the upper campus in which chemical engineering classes were being held. The flood of students was so heavy that Fitzgerald permitted himself in a public speech (and in Western Pennsylvania usage) to express the hope that "enrollment will go down some."

Scaife told Fitzgerald that Richard King Mellon was interested in the University and wished it well. Fitzgerald called on Mellon, talked about his building plans, and found him "quite enthusiastic, especially in the way they would tie into the city plans they are working on."

In luncheon meetings in the Mellon Room of the Duquesne Club and in George Clapp's home in Sewickley, Fitzgerald, Scaife, the other members of the Committee on Planning and Development, and campaign manager Norman MacLeod drew up plans for raising a very large sum of money. On the evening of June 3, 1948, some 250 business and civic leaders attended a banquet in the main dining room of the Duquesne Club. Alan Scaife presided. "I have never found a city and a university," he said, "better to live in, to think in, and to work in; and I have never found a city and a university better to think for and work for." Fitzgerald told of the phe-

nomenal increase in numbers of students and applicants. ("For the 96 freshman places in dentistry for next fall, we have had something like 1800 applications. For the 86 places in medicine there have been 2300 applicants.")

He then addressed his main subject: "the buildings we need" and the program that had been developed to get them. The program called for eight new buildings. It would cost some $20 million. It would raise to twenty-five the number of permanent buildings and—if carried out successfully—would virtually double the cost-value of the University's holdings:

1. A $3.2 million ten-story medical school building.

2. A $2.25 million medical building to house clinical wards and clinical laboratories.

3. A residence hall with accommodations for 650 student nurses, costing $4.05 million. Of that amount, $1.2 million was already in hand and it was believed that $2 million could be obtained from the state and federal governments.

4. A $3.7 million science building to be named George H. Clapp Hall, which would house the Departments of Physics, Chemistry, Biology, Metallurgy, and Chemical Engineering. This building had the highest priority; it was hoped that ground could be broken by the end of the year.

5. A $2.5 million University library with space for 1.5 million books. "We cannot house more books in the stacks of the Cathedral of Learning; our librarian has notified me that 100,000 volumes are stored in attics, basements, and corridors, space which is dirty and dark and inaccessible. Estimates show that in large universities the aim should be to provide seating space for at least 25 per cent of the student body. Our main library seats 650. One student in twenty can find a place in the library at a given time. The reserve book room in the main library has 50 seats. In this room are required reading assignments for over 100 different classes. Do I need to go further?"

6. A $1 million student activities center. This would serve as headquarters for student publications, organizations, and government and would have facilities for relaxation and recreation.

7. A $3.25 million gymnasium. This would be a

large, low building with facilities for undergraduate athletics and physical education courses, a large pool, and seating capacity for 6,000 spectators.

8. A $300,000 field house. This would be the size of a football field—160 by 300 feet. It would be a shell built of cement block and would be placed at the top of the hill above the stadium, and it would resemble the stadium in texture. (The University had considered building a combined gymnasium-field house capable of seating 10,000 persons and had obtained the city's approval to build it behind the Neptune Fountain at the entrance to Schenley Park; but the project was abandoned because of prohibitively high costs.)

The student center, gymnasium, and field house would be financed by a $5 million revenue bond issue sponsored by the First Boston Corporation. The plan included the refinancing of $1.2 million in Pitt Stadium bonds, due in 1949, with 3 percent bonds.

Four of the buildings would be placed in the open space beside the Cathedral of Learning. Their architecture would be "of the general neo-Gothic tone" and would blend with the three other buildings on the site. Clapp Hall would stand on Fifth Avenue facing the Masonic Temple. The student center would be on Bellefield Avenue in line with and south of Heinz Chapel, across from the YMHA. The gymnasium would extend along Forbes Avenue across from Carnegie Institute, and the library would stand in the center of the complex of buildings, seven in all.

Fitzgerald paused in his speech for dramatic effect. Then, "Now I come to the most important part of what I have to say. I hold in my hand a letter, the most important letter that I have ever received. It will speak for itself." He read the letter aloud. It was from a donor who wished his name not to be revealed.

I am desirous of joining with others who are interested in providing funds necessary for you to proceed with your plans for the erection of a new School of Medicine. . . . I agree to contribute in cash or securities a sum equal to gifts made by others, within three years from this date . . . up to a total contribution by me of three million ($3,000,000) dollars. My understanding is that such gifts

aggregating approximately six million ($6,000,000) dollars would cover the estimated construction cost of the new School of Medicine, possibly with some surplus for equipment. . . . By this agreement I intend to be legally bound.

Fitzgerald closed by imagining a society in which four powerful forces—education, religion, government, and industry—cooperated in making great individuals and a great society. He asked: "Why not here? *Why not here?*"

The anonymous donor was George Hubbard Clapp, the University's oldest alumnus (Class of 1877), a trustee for the past forty-six years (since 1902), and president of trustees for the past forty-one years (since 1907). He was truly a venerable figure, respected nationally as a scientist, admired for his pioneering contributions to two new industries (aluminum and scientific industrial testing), and honored as a philanthropist, collector of coins and mollusks, and patron of art and learning. His letters in the University archives reveal him as a man of admirable sympathies. His pleas over a fifteen-year period to be relieved of his position as president of the trustees—always refused—were obviously sincere. As the 1948 fund-raising campaign progressed, Norman MacLeod begged Dr. Clapp to allow his name to be used, and he finally agreed, "if you think it will do the University any good."

On January 16, 1949, Dr. Clapp sent a complaint to Dr. Fitzgerald. Whenever the large wrought-iron gate in the Commons Room was mentioned, he wrote, it was said that George Hubbard Clapp had given $200,000 to have it made. He would like that to stop. The gate was designed and made by Samuel Yellin. It was Mr. Yellin's name, not his, that should be used when the gate was mentioned.

George Hubbard Clapp died on March 31, 1949, three and one-half months after his ninetieth birthday. In his will he left his American coins, considered the finest private collection of its kind in the country, subject of a monograph he had written, to Carnegie Museum.

He was succeeded as president of the Board of Trustees by Alan Magee Scaife. "I told him how pleased I was," Fitzgerald wrote on June 22, 1949, at the new appointment. "He replied by saying that one of the fine things about it from his standpoint was the fact that we would be working closer together and suggested that we drop the formalities in regard to names, which was agreed upon. He said that he did hope I could get some help. Perhaps I would want a provost so that I could get away from things. I explained that would be highly desirable if we could get the right man. That he could also work on budget as well as educational policy, for the two went together."

Fitzgerald did not take the help that was offered him, possibly because, having done everything himself for years, he did not really want it. At the same time, his duties increased under the new building program and his problems multiplied. He was faced with a half-dozen particularly annoying, time-consuming difficulties at this time.

A problem in community relations arose over the use of Ellsworth Center. The building was providing much-needed space for overflow classes from the main campus, including night classes. The field beside the building was useful for ROTC drill; for outdoor classes for men and women majoring in physical education; for freshman football practice; for intramural sports activities; for spring festivals; for victory celebrations; and, during the summer, for a special supervised recreational program for students (softball, volleyball, horseshoes, and badminton). The field was improved early in 1951 with the addition of eight sixty-foot light towers, which made it possible to use the facilities at night. At that point, residents of the area formed a save-our-neighborhood committee, obtained a widely publicized hearing in court, and won an injunction. The University capitulated. It issued a news release announcing a new schedule for Ellsworth Center. Henceforth, use of the building and grounds would be limited to research and laboratory work in civil engineering, surveying, physical education, biology, and chemistry. In addition, the Pennsylvania Forensic and Music League would be located there. The reason given for the change was the drop in enrollment under the G.I. Bill and the high cost of flood-lighting.

A more difficult problem arose when opposition surfaced against the decision to place four of the new buildings—Clapp Hall, the library, the gymnasium, and the student activities center—in the open space around the Cathedral of Learning.

The siting seemed to be logical. The land was open, paid for, available, and in a sense unused. The addition of four buildings on the Cathedral campus would create the traditional academic quadrangle. Some ten thousand students would be able to walk from building to building in the normal ten-minute interval between classes. And there appeared to be virtually no other land available for expansion in the immediate Oakland area.

Opposition came from those who liked open space and a vista and held that both were so rare and precious in the city that they should be preserved. The *Post-Gazette*'s William Block and Westinghouse Electric's chairman A. W. Robertson spoke up for protecting the open, green lawn. When he saw the flags set out along Fifth Avenue to mark the dimensions of Clapp Hall, Charles M. Stotz, architect, chairman of the City Art Commission, co-designer of Point State Park, sought a resolution of opposition by the Pittsburgh Chapter of the American Institute of Architects. William R. Oliver of Ligonier carried a protest directly to his friend Richard King Mellon.

General Mellon, it was at once discovered, had a firm opinion on the matter of placing additional buildings on the Cathedral campus. He was against it. He, too, favored open space and a vista—especially the long, open vista in the approach to Mellon Institute from the west. When queried, John Bowman revealed that in the early 1930s he had agreed with the Mellons that no buildings should impede that striking view. Indeed, legal papers had been drawn up and placed on the record, effective until 1976.

Construction of the nurses' residence on Lothrop Street at Fifth Avenue was under way in 1950, because it was out of the contested area, in the Medical Center. Construction on the gymnasium and the field house had been started, because they were at the top of the hill on the upper campus. But no

Eric Schaal

University Archives

Helen Pool Rush, Class of 1919, helped to run the University in the administrations of eight chancellors, as assistant dean of women, dean of women, dean of students, and vice chancellor for student affairs.

Agnes Lynch Starrett, Class of 1920, taught English, wrote the first history of the University in 1937 (Through One Hundred and Fifty Years), *edited* Pitt Magazine, *and directed the University of Pittsburgh Press.*

buildings were started on the lawn around the Cathedral, though $11 million was available for new construction.

Extraordinary efforts were made in 1950 to find room for expansion on the periphery of the Cathedral campus. University administrators made overtures, through Leon Falk, Jr., and Edgar J. Kaufmann, to buy the YMHA on Bellefield Avenue at a price high enough to enable the association to build an equivalent or better building elsewhere. Discussions were held but they came to nothing at that time.

The University paid $7,500 for a ninety-day option on Duquesne Gardens, a huge, outmoded sports facility at Fifth Avenue and Craig Street.* It had approached the officers of the Masonic Temple with the proposal that Pitt would pay $5 million for their building and throw in the Duquesne Gardens land (bought at a cost of $325,000) as the site for a new and better temple. Pitt would then remodel the original temple, perhaps as a library, at a cost of "somewhere between $500,000 and $5,000,000." Or

*The University Square Apartments now stand on the site.

perhaps the temple could be lifted from its foundation, moved north to Bigelow Boulevard—maybe even to the far side of Bigelow—and set down on a new foundation. There was also talk in May 1949 and again in October 1953 of somehow making use of the deep, unoccupied valley known as Panther Hollow that lay south of the campus between Pitt and Carnegie Tech—perhaps by erecting buildings on its near hillside.

These nebulous proposals were being discussed at a time when the Allegheny Conference was advocating a Master Plan for Oakland and for control of the University's expansion therein. The negotiations between University and conference officials were complicated, tedious, and at this time indecisive. Fitzgerald described one meeting as "very unsatisfactory" and as "almost a knock-down and drag-out" with "a good deal of heat." In another meeting, Scaife "was worked up to a high pitch" and was "white" after a sharp clash.

The situation was complicated by strong views from a surprising source—John Bowman. Fitzgerald and Scaife found that his deep involvement with University architecture did not end with his retirement. Recovered from the effects of his stroke, he volunteered his emphatic disapproval of the plans for Clapp Hall. Bowman had presented a design for the building to the board in 1944. Changes were made in the design in the late 1940s. It appeared that Bowman approved them.

In a later meeting with the architects there were, in Fitzgerald's words, "some clashes which in my opinion . . . started Dr. Bowman in a somewhat different direction architecturally." Bowman worked out "a nice building" but added thirty-five cents per cubic foot to the cost. Scaife and Fitzgerald agreed that the increase was too high. Bowman was "very much worked up" that the board somehow had been given the impression that he had approved the original plans. "He stated officially that he had not done so. . . . He would write a letter to Mr. Scaife stating that he had not approved the plans, and would send copies to all members of the board."

On May 10, 1951, in a meeting with the architects, Bowman was shown the latest designs of Clapp Hall and its positioning on the campus. "Dr. Bowman glanced at them and started his rebuttal before he had even looked at them well." He retold the story of building the Cathedral and stated that Mr. Scaife, Mr. Fitzgerald, Mr. Jackson, and Mr. Trautwein did not understand what it was all about and what Gothic architecture was. He said he would not argue his case before the Executive Committee of the board, "because it was already stacked." He proposed that a committee be formed: twenty faculty members, twenty trustees, and twenty citizens at large. He would appear before them in a debate on the design and would abide by their decision. Fitzgerald advised Scaife that the business of the University should not be conducted in a public forum. Scaife agreed, Richard King Mellon agreed, the trustees agreed, and Bowman was so informed.

All this time, much of the University's expansion program was blocked. There could be no decision on when and where and how to build until the board definitely decided whether or not to build on the Cathedral campus. And if not on the Cathedral campus, where?

Richard King Mellon provided the solution. There was on the north side of Fifth Avenue, across from the eastern half of the Cathedral campus, a three-acre plot remembered as the town hall site, between Ruskin and Tennyson streets. The few buildings on it, except for the Ruskin Apartments, were undistinguished. Mr. Mellon had reason to believe that the land could be purchased, and on June 27, 1950, he proposed that one of the Mellon family foundations buy it for the University. The A. W. Mellon Educational and Charitable Trust bought the land for $675,000 and gave it to the University, which at once designated it as the site for Clapp Hall. Alan Scaife made a public announcement for the board in April 1953: "There will never be any more buildings on the Cathedral lawn than there are now." For the next ten years the University had "a new axis to the north."

14

The Letters of Gift

It is worthy of record that when the instrument outlining the magnitude of the gift was presented to the Board . . . by the Chancellor, it was received in awed silence and sensitive awareness of the confidence it implied and the responsibility it imposed. It was an unforgettable moment of pride and gratitude and this resolution of appreciation seeks to convey what words are too weak to express. . . . The Board is aware that this is a great moment in the history of the University.

Extract from the minute of a special meeting of the Board of Trustees, September 21, 1948

I T all began in 1946 with an incident that might have been borrowed from the plot of a popular novel. Paul Mellon wrote to six prominent Pittsburghers and asked them what they would recommend if they had $40 million to give to good causes in the community. His letter led to a development that added a new dimension to the University's plans for expansion and improvement of services in the Pittsburgh area.

The A. W. Mellon Educational and Charitable Trust, founded in 1930 to support undertakings that "shall be in furtherance of the public welfare and tend to promote the well-doing and well-being of mankind," on occasion went beyond the normal routine of receiving, investigating, and responding to requests for money. On these occasions it performed a creative role by calling attention to a shortcoming in the community—educational, social, medical, or cultural—and by proposing a program to help remedy that shortcoming. It did so in 1946 when it commissioned Adolph W. Schmidt, forty-two, a trustee, the treasurer, and later executive vice president of the charitable trust, to conduct an investigation and devise a plan on "the most urgent and long-range needs of Pittsburgh," whatever they might be. Schmidt (who was also a governor and vice president of T. Mellon & Sons) conceived the idea of requesting six "knowledgeable" Pittsburghers to write memoranda outlining the community's most serious needs as they saw them and to suggest possible solutions. The idea was approved, and on August 2, 1946, Paul Mellon, chairman of the trust, sent a confidential letter to each of six selected citizens. They were Charles F. Lewis, director of the Buhl Foundation; J. Steele Gow, director of the Falk Foundation; Edward R. Weidlein, director of Mellon Institute; Edward T. Leech, editor of the *Pittsburgh Press;* Robert E. Doherty, president of Carnegie Tech; and Rufus H. Fitzgerald, chancellor of the University of Pittsburgh.

The six consultants worked individually and independently; their answers were lengthy and mentioned a variety of problem areas; but all six cited public and occupational health services as a pressing need. Several ranked it first.

Schmidt submitted a proposal early in 1948 to the

Morris Berman/Pittsburgh Post-Gazette

Paul Mellon, trustee of the A. W. Mellon Educational and Charitable Trust from its establishment in 1930 until its termination in 1980.

Mellon trustees for creating a school of public health. They liked the idea and asked him to explore means and forms for creating the school, perhaps as a part of the Medical Center of the University of Pittsburgh. Schmidt set out at once to learn all he could about public health, its institutions, and its nine university-affiliated schools in North America. Among other things, he found that the Commission on Public Health and Preventive Medicine had just declared that Pennsylvania ranked forty-second among the forty-eight states in the quality of its public health services.

He also found that others were recognizing the need for a school of public health in Pennsylvania. Five medical schools in Philadelphia, in fact, were talking about sponsoring a center of public health in that city. It was apparent that the need for fast action in Pittsburgh was urgent, not merely because of intercity rivalry but because there seemed reason to believe that the American Public Health Association intended to accredit only one school of public health in Pennsylvania. "Professional acceptance and professional sponsorship," Schmidt wrote to his trustees, "is the all-important matter in this field."

He had been working with an assistant, Philip S. Broughton, and with him decided to push ahead with careful planning and "strategic methodology." He interviewed five leading authorities in public health in search of advice and information, and he asked Lowell J. Reed, vice president of Johns Hopkins University and in charge of medical sciences at that institution, to develop "a sound operating proposal backed up by facts." Dr. Reed drew up a series of proposals and programs, revising them as he progressed to meet the particular policies of the community, the University, and the charitable trust. None of the nine public health schools, he said, had as yet developed industrial hygiene "to anything like the extent that this important subject deserves."

On January 29, 1948, Schmidt, Broughton, and Reed called on Chancellor Fitzgerald, revealed their interest in establishing a school of public health in Pittsburgh, and gave him a preliminary survey of a school "probably connected with the University of Pittsburgh." The charitable trust would provide a $4 million endowment, the income from which would

pay faculty salaries and "attract eminent men." The trust would also give $1.6 million for operating capital and developmental expenses, and when the school was accredited the trustees would give $5 million for a building and equipment. Within five years they would "re-examine the whole project, and if it appears that the School is a successful undertaking and that it has or will become an institution of a comparable quality and standards with the best in the United States," they would add another $3 million to the endowment. The total amount the University could receive under the proposal was $13.6 million.

The school could not be considered established, the trustees specified, until the University had appointed a dean. Fitzgerald, already alerted to this need, had persuaded six leaders in the field of public health and preventive medicine, who would not themselves be considered candidates, to serve as a nominating committee. Their immediate and unanimous choice was Thomas Parran, who was about to retire, at age fifty-six, as surgeon general of the U.S. Public Health Service.

Dr. Parran, an honors graduate in medicine from Georgetown University, had been commissioned a public health officer in 1917. In 1936, after a six-year stint as health commissioner of New York State, he began the first of three four-year terms as surgeon general. He was an international figure and was especially well known in Pittsburgh for a program he had started there in 1940, with the financial backing of the Buhl Foundation, to expose and stamp out the scourge of syphilis. That was then a word, a subject, that could not be mentioned in public, let alone discussed, with the result that its prevention and treatment had been obstructed. The Pittsburgh program made history by putting the word and the subject on the front pages of the newspapers.

When President Truman did not reappoint him, Parran let it be known in February 1948 that he had made no plans for the future. Within three days, Broughton wrote him a letter conveying the hope of the Mellon trustees that he would become dean of a new school of public health in Pittsburgh; he would shortly receive a formal proposal from the chancellor of the University. Fitzgerald in his letter asked

Parran to accept the deanship and also to serve as a consultant to the University on the development of its total medical science program. He would not be expected to raise money. The University would help him to find a suitable house and would pay a salary of $20,000. After a visit to Pittsburgh and a meeting in Washington with Paul Mellon, Schmidt, Broughton, Reed, and Fitzgerald, Parran accepted the offer.

At a special board meeting called for September 21, 1948, Fitzgerald gave his trustees the full details on these stirring events—the $13.6 million grant and the selection of Dr. Parran as dean of the new school. To Paul Mellon he wrote, "I wish you could have been in the Board meeting to see and hear the reaction of the twenty-one members when I read your letter. It had the effect of an electric charge. One of the older members said later that he had never seen anything like it."

Parran was introduced to Pittsburgh on September 28 (his fifty-sixth birthday), and he began two years of spade work to assemble a faculty, write a teaching curriculum, develop a research program, find a building, draw up a budget, establish a working relationship with the seven hospitals and four other schools in the Medical Center, obtain accreditation, and hold the first class. He had described the school to reporters: "For a medical student, the hospital is the clinical center where he studies the patient. For the graduate student of public health, the community is the patient and the field training center."

In September 1949, work began on remodeling one of the underused hospitals in the complex of buildings in the Medical Center. This was the Pittsburgh Municipal Hospital, which was constructed in 1941 on land the University had given to the city. (It is now known as Salk Hall.) It was intended to be used primarily to treat communicable diseases, but when sulfa drugs and antibiotics virtually eliminated the need to quarantine such patients, the building had become something of a white elephant, with fewer than 50 of its 225 beds occupied in a typical week. The School of Public Health took up temporary quarters in the remodeled building under a five-year lease with the city. The school was ac-

credited on April 6, 1950. It was the first instance in which a school of public health was granted accreditation before it had admitted a class. In September 1950, two years from the date of the Mellon grant, the first class convened: twenty-nine full-time and five part-time students.

Those who founded the School of Public Health were convinced that it must be integrated into a strong medical center—that its administration must be coordinated with that of the other components of the center. Lowell Reed put himself on record on this point in a letter to Adolph Schmidt in June 1948: "As I have told you in our conversations, the school of public health cannot in the long run be stronger than the medical center with which it is associated. It is therefore important that the Trustees bend every effort to the improvement of the medical school." Thomas Parran emphasized it in his first published progress report: "First and last, the Graduate School of Public Health is part of a larger organism, the University and its Medical Center. No school of public health can become great unless it is integrated with a great university and a great medical center."

Such statements clearly called for the reorganization of the administrations of the five schools related to medicine—Medicine, Dental Medicine, Public Health, Pharmacy, and Nursing—in coordination with the seven affiliated hospitals and Falk Clinic. Schmidt had submitted such a proposal and a tentative plan in 1948. Accordingly, the University trustees in September 1949 appointed a committee to confer with the deans of the medical schools and the board members of the hospitals of the Medical Center. Together they were to decide on a form of reorganization of the center.

Reorganization would require the appointment of an administrative officer with authority over the deans of the schools and with enough stature to deal with the hospital officers, staff, and trustees. Scaife, Falk, and Fitzgerald undertook the search for a vice chancellor for medical affairs. They had a formidable assignment. They faced a sellers' market in a prosperous economy. The profession knew that the School of Medicine was indeed what Scaife called it in conversation with prospects: below the median. It had an endowment of only $1 million, virtually no basic research program, and no long-range plans for development. There were, moreover, relatively few full-time teachers on the medical faculties of the schools; there was, in fact, a preponderance of practitioners, and most of them objected to being replaced by full-time salaried professors and to losing their perquisites, including the control of an allotted number of beds in the hospitals.

When a young epidemiologist named Jonas E. Salk took a post in the School of Medicine in 1947, he found that "the faculty consisted almost entirely of part-time instructors who earned their living in the private practice of medicine and had neither time nor inclination for basic research." Parran wrote in a confidential report to the Mellon Trust, "I have stressed the obstacles to the integration of our School into the Medical Center, the chief block being that there was no such center but an agglomeration of weak schools and individualistically inclined hospitals." The hospitals, he wrote, for the most part owed only a secondary allegiance to the University, and they were dominated by staffs of part-time appointments in the School of Medicine. Schmidt describes the situation as he saw it in 1948, when he was president of Presbyterian-University Hospital: "The hierarchy of professors in the School of Medicine saw some kind of threat in the founding of the School [of Public Health] and bringing professional teachers of public health into their midst." Their fears were heightened, he said, by a proposal in 1950 that all the full professors in the School of Medicine be placed on a fixed salary of $25,000 per annum, and that all fees collected in the course of their full teaching load be turned into a common pool for the financing of the budget of the School of Medicine.

It must be remembered, of course, that the University could not possibly have paid the salaries of a full-time medical school faculty before 1950, and that without the part-time faculty there would have been no teaching and no School of Medicine. These physicians, many of them distinguished figures in their fields, had given their services for decades for a token salary combined with certain perquisites.

On this complex issue, the establishment of the School of Public Health, with its full-time salaried teaching faculty, paid an unexpected and unintended dividend. It helped to produce the change in the School of Medicine to a core of full-time faculty for all departments, while (in the words of a Mellon Trust report) "retaining the essential place of some part-time physician teachers in the program." That reform was clinched when Schmidt called the administrators of the affiliated hospitals to the boardroom of T. Mellon & Sons and told them there would be no more grants from the Richard King Mellon foundations until the control of the hospitals by medical practitioners was ended.

During the search for an administrator to head the Medical Center, Alan Scaife proposed that Dr. Parran be appointed "Vice President of the University in Charge of Medical Sciences." Parran was not popular among the physicians—he was charged with believing in socialized medicine—and Fitzgerald said that the time was not ripe for such a move: the classification could cause "a revolution in the Medical School." Fitzgerald, in fact, was not using his consultant to the chancellor on medical sciences as he had promised he would during the courtship; he was consulting Parran almost solely on those matters relating to the School of Public Health. When Parran requested that either his duties and responsibilities to his office as consultant be clarified or he be relieved of them, Ernest Fiedler, the Mellon Trust attorney, fearing that Parran might resign, sent a chilling note to the trust officers: "If Dr. Parran should decide that others could do the job better in Pittsburgh, it would be a good indication to institutions and foundations everywhere that possibly Pittsburgh was still not ready for the big-leaguers. It might also be a signal to younger men who wish to try out for the big leagues to go elsewhere than Pittsburgh." (Parran remained at his post until 1958.)

A vice chancellor for medical affairs was appointed on January 1, 1954. He was Robert A. Moore, M.D. fifty-two, a nationally prominent medical educator, administrator, and pathologist, dean since 1947 of the School of Medicine at Washington

University in St. Louis. He accepted the new post with a number of conditions. First, he asked and received satisfactory answers to two questions: "Are the traditions of the health professions in Pittsburgh so ingrained and strong that an attempt to change them would destroy the objective which is being sought? Is it possible to obtain the objective in a reasonable period without bitterness that might last for a generation?" Second, he stipulated that the proposed program at Pittsburgh be more than administrative integration of the schools of the health professions and more than development of the medical school only; it must be a true educational integration of the five schools. Since a significant integration of the health professions could not be accomplished if each of the five schools was maintained in a separate physical and intellectual environment, the trustees must erect a single coordinated building for all five schools. He would need at least five years before his plant would be operating. He must have an operating budget of "hard money" income. The trustees must assure him that the entire program, estimated to cost $75 million, would be supported.

He did not for one moment, he said, doubt the sincerity and the determination of men like Mr. Scaife, Mr. Falk, and Mr. Schmidt. Yet he was not certain that even they fully realized what the future held in the creation of a modern health center. He told what his fourteen years' experience at Washington University had taught him could happen.

The deans and faculties of each of the schools may question moves that might impinge on their autonomy. The dentist and the nurse are suspicious of the physician. The dental and nursing professions will support their deans and faculties. The heads of the departments and faculty members will be reluctant to assume administrative and teaching responsibilities beyond those they now have. The medical profession will oppose full time unless the full time faculty in the clinical departments has a sharp limitation on the right to practice medicine. The medical profession will oppose necessary changes in the admission policy of the Falk Clinic. The hospital staffs will oppose necessary changes in staff organization and in professional responsibility. The local professional societies may pass resolutions or exclude the full time faculty from membership as they have in other cities. Interested parties will question the wisdom of admission policy when a relative or friend is rejected. All of this opposition will funnel up to the university and hospital boards through their friends and private physicians. The accumulated pressure will be very great.

Dr. Moore's comprehensive development plan for the Health Center, "a detailed prospectus," was presented to the world on January 18, 1954, at a formal dinner held in the Commons Room. Fitzgerald then announced to the 350 guests the stunning news that three Mellon family foundations—the A. W. Mellon Educational and Charitable Trust, the Richard King Mellon Foundation, and the Sarah Mellon Scaife Foundation—would each contribute $5 million in a joint grant of $15 million to the School of Medicine. It was the largest gift ever made to the University in its 167-year history, and possibly it was the largest made up to that time to medical education in this country. None of the money was to be spent on construction of buildings; it must all go to endowment.

A letter from Paul Mellon, similar in substance to letters received from the other two foundations, was read. Moore outlined the three objectives of the Health Center, all advanced by the grants: education of practitioners; research to acquire new knowledge of the cause, prevention, and cure of disease; and patient care. He said that the gifts would enable the University to increase its number of medical undergraduates by 50 percent at a time of national shortage; the total capacity would rise from 400 to 600 students.

Within the span of three years, three Health Center buildings were completed or were under construction:

In May 1953, the $4.5 million nurses' residence was completed and dedicated.

On June 29, 1954, Mrs. Alan Magee Scaife (Sarah Mellon Scaife) turned the first spade of earth for the ten-story, $15 million School of Medicine building that four years later would bear her husband's name.

On March 3, 1955, with no ground-breaking ceremonies, on a site facing Fifth Avenue at Bouquet

Street, a power shovel began work on the nine-story building that would house the Graduate School of Public Health. The building was completed in 1957. At the dedication ceremony in that year, Thomas Parran introduced his "senior team," the full professors of his faculty. Paul Mellon spoke:

The School . . . has in nine short years become the worthy colleague and recognized peer of the leaders in its professional field. . . .

The fight for quality cannot be won in any single School or Department. The University as a whole must find greatness. Fundamental to that greatness in any university must be The College. Without first attention to the basic liberal arts and disciplines there can be no professions worthy to be called learned. . . .

As for this building, the instruments and equipment, these are merely the work shop and the tools—essential though they be. The tangible is hardly real. What is real is the quest, the opportunity to know more of man—his body, his mind, his physical and social environment and the dynamic interrelationships which we call "human ecology" or Public Health.

15
The Pitt Vaccine

Once we got momentum and it looked like we were going to be able to develop a safe vaccine, it got very exciting. You can't imagine the excitement of seeing this come to pass under your very fingers.

Julius S. Youngner, Sc.D.

Dr. Youngner was the senior member of the Pitt research team that developed the polio vaccine. He is now professor and chairman of the Department of Microbiology, Biochemistry, and Molecular Biology, School of Medicine, and president of the American Society for Virology.

DURING the flourishing activities on the campus in 1948–1955, a development was unfolding that was of immeasurable importance to the University and of measurable benefit to Pittsburgh, the nation, and, indeed, the world. It was one of the most dramatic stories in the annals of medicine: the discovery of a means to conquer one of mankind's cruelest diseases.

Poliomyelitis—infantile paralysis—was an infectious and contagious disease that attacked people of all ages but preferred children, especially those under five years of age, striking most commonly in summer and autumn, in the "polio season," the "season of fear." It destroys the motor nerve cells in the spinal cord and brain that control muscular action, including the muscles of respiration, and it causes crippled limbs, brain damage, or death. It is a worldwide natural infection at least as old as civilization, but in a bitter paradox, it became a widespread menace because of improved sanitation, sewerage, and other public health measures introduced after 1800. In earlier centuries everyone was exposed to the virus, which, as it passed through the blood stream and the digestive tract, stimulated the system to manufacture immunizing antibodies. With improved standards of hygiene, however, there was less exposure to the virus in early childhood, and less exposure meant reduced immunization and a rising incidence of paralytic polio. The United States, the nation most afflicted by the disease, suffered a terrible epidemic in 1916 in which there were 27,363 cases with 7,179 deaths, 2,448 of them in New York City. The year 1952, when polio killed more American children than any other contagious disease, was the worst on record, with some 57,000 cases, 21,269 of them fatal.

There seemed to be no way to avoid the disease, whose causes were unknown, and no effective way to treat the patient. Enter now William Swindler McEllroy, graduate of the University of Pittsburgh School of Medicine in 1916, its dean since 1938. A professor of physiological chemistry, co-developer of the Folin-McEllroy test for urinary sugar, Dr. McEllroy was not entirely reconciled to having become an administrator instead of a medical researcher. In 1944 the Buhl Foundation gave him

grants to establish the Division of Research in Natural Sciences in the School of Medicine, and in 1946 he received a $15,000 grant from the Scaife Foundation with which to establish a virus research program and to buy major equipment for a virus research laboratory. He made an agreement with the city of Pittsburgh to put the laboratory in the basement of the Municipal Hospital for Contagious Diseases, which stood on the steep hill on the northwest edge of the campus, and with Dr. Max A. Lauffer, professor of biophysics, he began looking for someone to head a virus research program and run the laboratory as an associate professor. Some friends recommended Dr. Jonas E. Salk as a bright, ambitious worker whose field of research was flu vaccines. McEllroy called on him at the University of Michigan at Ann Arbor.

Jonas Edward Salk, born in Manhattan in 1914, son of a designer of women's garments, had intended to study law but shifted to medicine and science on entering New York University. He interned at Mount Sinai and in April 1942 went to the University of Michigan to work under Thomas Francis, Jr., an outstanding microbiologist who had been one of his favorite professors at New York University. He was an assistant professor of epidemiology when McEllroy called on him in 1947.

"I didn't have much to offer him," McEllroy said. "A lab that wasn't even finished. A moderate salary. A promise to give him a free hand and to help get any financial assistance he might need. Really, I think Jonas came here on faith."

Salk came as associate research professor of bacteriology and head of the Virus Research Laboratory, half of the funding for which came from the School of Medicine budget and half from National Foundation for Infantile Paralysis grants. He was made a professor in 1949. Occupying the laboratory in the basement of the Municipal Hospital, he continued his work on influenza virus and began also to work on "the polio problem." Everybody else, he said, "was fooling around with the polio thing, so I thought I'd play around with it too, to gain some experience."

Hard research had produced important discoveries and a good running start in the quest for the cause, prevention, and cure of poliomyelitis. In 1949, in what is called "the great breakthrough," three Harvard doctors (John F. Enders, Thomas H. Weller, and Frederick C. Robbins) discovered that live polio virus could be made to grow in test tubes in cultures of ordinary, nonneural tissue. (They used the kidney of the rhesus monkey as their medium.) Living tissue could thus be infected with the polio virus in quantities great enough to be used in a vaccine. Enders was given the Nobel Prize for Medicine for his work. He refused to accept it until his two associates, Weller and Robbins, were included.

Late in 1947 Harry Merwyn Weaver, director of research at the National Foundation for Infantile Paralysis (headed by Basil O'Connor and famous for its March of Dimes campaigns), called on Salk and asked him and the University of Pittsburgh to accept a contract of $200,000 a year for polio research. Pitt and three other universities (Utah, Southern California, and Kansas) would work on classifying all known strains of polio virus into types according to their immunological differences or similarities. It had been discovered in the 1930s that an animal immune to polio infection caused by one strain of virus had no immunity to infection caused by another strain. It was necessary, therefore, to determine how many different strains there were and how many vaccines would be needed to give immunity against all strains.

Salk knew that this was work the more experienced polio experts would be reluctant to take on, for it was a tedious, routine assignment that would confer no distinction and yet would make great demands on time, laboratory space, manpower, and animals. He accepted the contract because "it was an opportunity to learn something about polio, get facilities that I could do other things with, and assemble an adequate staff."

McEllroy and Salk persuaded Mayor Lawrence to give a great deal more space in the Municipal Hospital to the Virus Research Laboratory and obtained another grant from the Scaife Foundation to buy equipment, build animal cages, and collect a staff. The entire classification program took three years, cost the National Foundation $1.9 million, and

established that all strains of polio virus belong to three main types. This meant that to confer immunity, one strain of each type—but no more—would have to be included in a vaccine. That had been established part-way through the program by work done at Johns Hopkins by David Bodian and Isabel Morgan, and so the conclusion was more or less academic. Salk, undisturbed, told the foundation that he was now ready to step up his work on finding a means of preventing polio and that he was willing to accept its financial support in the work.

Salk believed that human beings could be immunized by a compound of polio viruses killed in a solution of formaldehyde but retaining enough strength to stimulate protective antibodies in the blood stream. In this analysis he was opposed by most other medical researchers. One group held that polio could not be prevented by a vaccine, since polio, they believed, was a disease of the nervous system, not of the blood stream. Another group, citing the preventive and curative effects of the new "wonder drugs," called for a major research effort to find a chemical solution. A third group held that a vaccine could be effective, but only if it contained attenuated ("live") virus, as in smallpox and yellow fever virus vaccines. The leading advocate of this theory was Albert B. Sabin of the Children's Hospital in Cincinnati, who would become an antagonist Salk battled through the next several decades.

In 1951 the University began a three-year research program, under the direction of Jonas Salk, which sought to find a practical method of preventing paralytic polio. Harry Weaver of the National Foundation described Salk's manner and method of working:

There was nobody like him in those days. . . . His approach was entirely different from that which had dominated the field. The older workers had all been brought up in the days when you didn't accept a grant of more than four of five hundred dollars from an outside source without having a long conference with the dean. Everything was on a small scale. You made do with one or two laboratory animals because you couldn't afford to pay for the twelve which were needed. Jonas had no such psychology. He thought big. He wanted lots of space, was perfectly comfortable with the idea of using hundreds of

Jonas Salk (left) and Julius S. Youngner, senior scientist at the Virus Research Laboratory.

monkeys, and running dozens of experiments at a time. He always wanted to expand his program so that it would encompass as much of the subject as possible. He was out of phase with the tradition of narrowing research down to one or two details, making progress inch by inch. He wanted to leap, not crawl. His willingness to shoot the works was made to order for us.

"There was so much excitement," recalls Elsie N. Ward, a zoologist on Salk's staff, that "it was pure joy to come to work in the morning. Every day brought new progress. To look into the microscope and see what we saw was a great thrill. Dr. Salk was in the lab morning, afternoon, and night. He couldn't wait to see what was going to happen."

One of the unknown factors was the level of antibodies a person needed to be immunized against polio. William McDowell Hammon, professor of epidemiology at the new Graduate School of Public Health, who was working on the fourth floor of the Municipal Hospital, contributed an answer to that problem in 1952. He used gamma globulin—a protein component of blood plasma containing antibodies—as an immunizing agent against polio. It provided only brief and temporary protection, it was costly, and it could not be produced in great volume, but it was of possible value in a community threatened by an epidemic, and it did reveal that even small amounts of antibody in the human blood stream would protect against paralytic polio. Hammon received widespread recognition and heavy National Foundation support for this discovery.

By 1954 Salk had recruited a staff of five key research scientists for the Virus Research Laboratory. Senior among these was Julius S. Youngner, assistant professor, who had been educated at New York University and the University of Michigan and came to Pitt in 1949, at age twenty-nine, from the National Cancer Institute at Bethesda. Responsible for production and for developing procedures for safety testing, Dr. Youngner developed cell culture methods for growth of polio viruses, isolated and characterized the virus from fecal specimens of paralytic patients, created the color test used for large-scale testing of pre- and postvaccination antibody titers, and carried out antibody tests of serum specimens.

L. James Lewis, research associate, carried out all testing of polio virus vaccines in monkeys for antigenicity and for safety.

Byron L. Bennett, research associate, carried out all experiments using mouse-adapted polio viruses of Type 2. He characterized the virulence and immunogenic potency of these viruses. He participated in the work of isolating polio viruses from fecal samples of patients with paralytic poliomyelitis.

Percival L. Bazeley, research associate, recruited in 1953, developed large-scale production techniques necessary for scaling up vaccine preparation. He worked on model systems for the pharmaceutical manufacture of vaccine.

Ulrich Krech, research associate, recruited in 1954, participated in local field trials, inoculation, and bleeding of volunteer vaccine recipients.

Salk was one of five University research physicians who on May 12, 1952, spoke at a dinner held in the Mellon Institute, the purpose of which was to persuade some eighty top business and industrial leaders to give $10 million to erect the long-needed School of Medicine building (later named Alan Magee Scaife Hall). In an interview before the dinner, Salk almost casually made a memorable announcement: he said he would soon begin tests of a polio vaccine on human beings. John Troan, Scripps-Howard and *Pittsburgh Press* science reporter, in a story sent around the world, called this "the first indication that science is so close to its goal of wiping out the scourge of infantile paralysis by vaccination—the way smallpox has been eradicated." The vaccine, Salk revealed, had already been tried on monkeys at the Virus Research Laboratory with excellent results. It would next be given to chimpanzees, then to volunteer children. "Whatever is tested on human beings," he said, "will have been demonstrated through laboratory tests to be absolutely safe."

One month later, on June 10, having made tests on chimpanzees, Salk was satisfied that he now had a vaccine he could give to human beings. He paid a call on Jessie Wright, medical director of the D. T. Watson Home for Crippled Children. She was a remarkable woman, a Pittsburgh institution, a nurse-physiotherapist who had become famous for her "magic fingers" in hands-on medicine and had been sent through the University of Pittsburgh School of Medicine (Class of 1934) by a group of physicians. Dr. Wright agreed to work with Salk in the Watson Home.

The administrator of the Watson Home, Lucille Cochran, recalls Salk's first visit.

Dr. Wright and Harry F. Stambaugh, who was chairman of the board, brought him here for lunch. He was charming and gentle—we have never seen him otherwise—and obviously he was not just a scientist on an experiment but a man deeply concerned about the human importance of the experiment. He explained the scientific basis of his work with great care. The first thing he wanted to do was take blood from polio patients, find out the type of antibodies they had, and then inoculate them with vaccines of the same types to see if the vaccines would raise their antibody levels. Since the subjects already had antibody and were immune to another paralytic attack from the one type of virus, the experiment would be as safe as it could possibly be. We all were very much in favor of trying it. So were the parents of the children. It may seem peculiar, but we had no sense of making history. We just enjoyed being part of the project.

Salk and his associates took blood samples on June 12 from forty-five resident children and from twenty-seven members of the Watson Home staff. They typed the antibodies in these samples and returned on July 2 to inoculate forty-three children with their type of vaccine. They returned again to inject all three types into subjects who had no detectable antibody count to begin with. They next extended the tests to persons with no history of poliomyelitis, inoculating sixty-three children and adults ranging in age from four to thirty years at the Polk State School near Franklin, Pennsylvania. They returned again to the Watson Home and the school to check on the condition of the subjects. "When you inoculate children with a polio vaccine," Salk said, "you don't sleep well for two or three months."

There were no adverse reactions in any of the volunteers. None developed polio. Those without polio antibodies now had antibodies, and those who had had antibodies now had a higher level. The

antibodies rose to a level where they killed virulent polio viruses in test tubes. The vaccine worked, and it was safe. "It was," Salk said, "the thrill of my life. Compared to the feeling I got seeing those results under the microscope, everything else that followed was anticlimactic."

Salk and his associates published an account of their work in an eighteen-page article in the March 28, 1953, *Journal of the American Medical Association* (JAMA): "Studies in Human Subjects on Active Immunization against Poliomyelitis: A Preliminary Report of Experiments in Progress." In these tests with human beings, they reported, the vaccine did produce immunizing antibodies for all three types of polio. Indications were that the protection lasted for at least 4½ months and probably much longer. Before the vaccine could be licensed for general use, however, important questions had to be answered. The authors invited other scientists to join in perfecting a safe and sure polio vaccine as quickly as possible. They hoped that "others might repeat our experiments" even before the team could complete its own vaccine studies.

From the beginning, Jonas Salk had generated controversy. His idea of creating a vaccine from dead virus was untraditional. His organization of a research team at the University of Pittsburgh was effective, but he was to be accused of failing to give the other members of the team credit for their accomplishments. And at the time the JAMA article was published, Salk through the medium of a brief radio broadcast became a public figure—and the target of much criticism from his peers.

The results of any scientific experiment are published in a specialized journal first so that other scientists may criticize and test the work, before it is described to the general public and possibly arouses false expectations about a new "cure" or other medical breakthrough. Two days before the JAMA article appeared, Salk broke this taboo. He addressed the nation about the vaccine on a special prime-time CBS radio broadcast entitled "The Scientist Speaks for Himself."

The broadcast was Salk's idea. He hoped to have what he described as "a moderating effect" on "premature enthusiasm" about the vaccine. (One of several references to the vaccine was in Earl Wilson's Broadway gossip column under the headline "Big Hopes Seen.") Whatever his motivation may have been, the broadcast was a serious misjudgment by Salk the scientist, if not by Salk the emerging public figure.

Salk had thrust himself forward as the spokesman for the attempt to develop a vaccine against polio. In the wake of criticism following the broadcast, he asked Basil O'Connor to order National Foundation people to keep his name out of the news, which O'Connor agreed to try to do, and to stop all reference to a "Salk vaccine," which O'Connor said was now impossible. (Undoubtedly, the foundation found it more convenient to raise money around a single heroic scientist than around a team of scientists.) The University made an attempt to change the name to the "Pitt vaccine" and used that phrase in its press releases, but no one followed its lead.

The vaccine was the result of a collaborative effort involving the team of University of Pittsburgh scientists: Youngner, Lewis, Bennett, Bazeley, and Krech. They were a fine staff, recruited by Salk, and he knew how to use them. He did a certain amount of scientific work himself, collaborating in the design of the procedure for developing experimental batches of vaccine, organizing and carrying out local field trials, and supervising, but his major contributions were imagination and administrative ability. He had vision and charm and the good executive's gift of getting things done.

One scientist who has criticized Salk for failing to give the proper credit to his staff—for consciously avoiding giving them credit—says, "The vaccine would not have happened without him." Nor would it have happened without the efforts of his associates, and Salk's later failure to mention them in a key speech has fueled the controversy that surrounds his name.

The talk at the National Foundation was now directed mainly to planning a national field trial—a conclusive test in which a million or more children would be inoculated with the Salk vaccine beginning early in the spring of 1954. The Advisory Vaccine Committee was formed, and in its meetings over the next year were fought the battles of conflicting and irreconcilable scientific schools of thought—notably in the bitter contest between proponents of the Sabin vaccine and those who favored Salk's.

Salk was authorized to precede the national field trial with a trial conducted by the Virus Research Laboratory. In February 1953 he and his associates set out to inoculate 1,000 consenting children and adults in and around Pittsburgh. He began at the Arsenal Elementary School in the Lawrenceville section of the city, where, in the school gymnasium, he personally inoculated each of 137 children with one cc of the Pitt vaccine, produced on a nonprofit basis by one of the commercial pharmaceutical houses.

Salk said, "The position I took was that I'd give every one of those . . . vaccinations myself and would put the responsibility in nobody else's hands." Among those he vaccinated were himself, his wife, Donna, their three sons, and several top officials of the National Foundation who had come to Pittsburgh for that purpose.

The new subjects suffered no bad effects, and they produced a gratifying increase in their antibody count.

A number of responsible people, however, including some county and state health officers, felt that 1,000 subjects were not enough to prove that the time had come for a mass program of inoculation. They recommended that further trials of 10,000 and 50,000 subjects be made before starting the national field trial. That would delay the trial one year, pushing it back to the spring of 1955. To convince the doubters and to avoid that delay, the Salk team in less than two months vaccinated 6,500 more school children in the Pittsburgh area. On the basis of continued affirmative results, and despite opposition from adversary groups that favored the Sabin vaccine, the Advisory Vaccine Committee elected to proceed in 1954 with the nationwide inoculation and evaluation trial.

The National Foundation persuaded Thomas Francis, Jr.—Salk's former teacher at New York University and his department head at the University of Michigan at Ann Arbor—to take charge of collecting, compiling, and analyzing the statistics.

Dr. Francis was an authority with experience in this field; during a flu epidemic in 1943–1944 he had conducted a much-admired controlled field study involving inoculations of an experimental flu vaccine. For the polio test he wrote his own rules and conditions.

In the spring and summer of 1954, in what was called "the biggest field testing program in the history of preventive medicine," 1.830 million children in the first three grades in twelve states were vaccinated. Some 20,000 physicians and public health officers; 14,000 school principals; 50,000 teachers; 40,000 registered nurses; and 220,000 nonprofessional volunteers from local chapters of the National Foundation and from various women's organizations took part in the work. The children were to receive three injections in five weeks, and with the third dose they would be given a "Polio Pioneer" button to wear. It was a "double blind" study. Half the children were injected with the vaccine commercially produced; the other half were given an inert liquid—a placebo. (Children in a third group, chosen solely for use in a comparison study, were simply listed and got no injection of any kind.) The small bottles of vaccine and placebo were identical in size and appearance, and those giving the injections did not know who got which. That information was available only to the staff that decoded the numbers and evaluated the results in Ann Arbor. The vaccinations began on Monday, April 26, and ended in June. Dr. Francis and his staff, 132 at its peak, had 144 million pieces of information recorded on punch cards for machine evaluation.

The attention of the world was focused on Ann Arbor on Tuesday, April 12, 1955. Rackham Hall was jammed with people: 500 biological scientists, physicians, and public health officers who had been invited to a scientific meeting held in conjunction with the release of the Francis Report; 150 press, radio, and television people; representatives of pharmaceutical companies; staff members from the National Foundation; and anyone else who wanted to see history made at first-hand and could get into the building. William Lawrence of the *New York Times* wrote, "The formal verdict on the Salk vaccine was disclosed today amid fanfare and drama far more typical of a Hollywood premiere than a medical meeting."

Francis spoke for one hour and thirty-eight minutes. What he said was summarized in a news release that opened with the words, "The vaccine works. It is safe, effective and potent. . . . There can be no doubt now that children can be inoculated successfully against polio."

At the scientific meeting that followed that afternoon, Salk was to read a paper entitled "Vaccination Against Paralytic Poliomyelitis." He was greeted by applause and a standing audience when he entered the auditorium. He corrected Dr. Francis on two points in his report on the vaccine and he thanked more than a score of people and institutions for their help and support over the previous eight years. He thanked Dr. Francis, Basil O'Connor, the five pharmaceutical manufacturers, the Advisory Vaccine Committee, the Watson Home, Jessie Wright, Harry Stambaugh, and Lucille Cochran, the Polk State School, Chancellor Fitzgerald, Dean McEllroy, and the trustees of the University of Pittsburgh. He mentioned the group of helpers whose role was so often taken for granted, but who gave so much more than they received that he confessed inability to express his gratitude. He presumably included his laboratory staff in this group, but he did not mention their names. Some of them were in the audience, and some—perhaps all—whether present or not were stunned by the avoidance of recognition of their work and their names. One of his associates recalls the day of the Ann Arbor press conference: "The world is listening to Salk along with us. The *whole world* is listening. He seems about to give us credit for our work. But it never comes."

Salk signed the paper he read "From Virus Research Laboratory, School of Medicine, University of Pittsburgh," and in a preface he paid tribute to "the joint efforts of many." But with some justice his biographer writes, "He seemed to have forgotten that, in the academic world, self-effacement is a luxury but enforced anonymity a hardship."

Even while Dr. Francis was still speaking, churches in some towns began to ring their bells. During the following weeks Salk was assaulted by an onrush of well-wishers, grateful strangers, reporters, and photographers; by people with awards to give, grants to offer, and favors to ask; by program chairmen in search of a speaker. The public relations director of the University had to install a special telephone in his home to handle the off-hours calls from around the world concerning Dr. Salk. Magazines bid for the story of his life. Five Hollywood studios wanted to make a movie about him; Marlon Brando had agreed to play the title role in one of them.

A tragedy struck the inoculation program in midcourse when vaccine produced by Cutter Laboratories in Berkeley, California, mistakenly containing live virus, caused 204 cases of polio, 150 of these involving paralysis, and eleven deaths. The program was stopped and then, in an agonizing decision, was resumed with even stricter, triple-test procedures. There were no more vaccine-induced polio cases. In February 1957, thirty inoculation teams began operating in the Commons Room of the Cathedral of Learning, giving free injections to students, faculty members, staff personnel, and their families. In the meantime, the vaccine had been licensed for use. Foreign countries, including Canada, Denmark, and Sweden, began programs of their own. The names of children who had received placebos were sent to the public health departments so they might be given the true vaccine.

In June 1959 a group of women in Pittsburgh's Bethel Park area initiated a program to inoculate every unvaccinated child in Allegheny County. Some 360 clinics were established, staffed with volunteer help from physicians, public health nurses, fraternal societies, neighborhood business associations, and parent-teacher groups. More than half a million injections were given at minimal or no cost. As a result of that effort, Pittsburgh became the first major city in the United States to rid itself of polio.* In 1961 and 1962 there were no cases of polio reported in Pittsburgh.

By 1959 some seventy million Americans under

*The last reported case of poliomyelitis in Allegheny County occurred in 1967.

forty had received one or more injections of the Salk vaccine. By 1961 polio cases had dropped almost to zero, not only in the United States but in other countries using the vaccine. In the 1960s, however, the orally administered "live virus" vaccine developed by Albert Sabin began to replace the Salk vaccine in the United States. Sabin had been unable to obtain financing in the United States to field test his vaccine, but he found it in the Soviet Union, and the results there were so spectacular that they were accepted in this country without field tests and even without licensing by the federal government. The case for the Sabin vaccine was and is supported by the belief that live virus—as in smallpox and measles vaccines—is more effective in producing antibodies. The Sabin vaccine also has the advantage of being far easier to administer: a few drops of a sweetish liquid are dropped on the tongue, while the Salk vaccine requires three separate injections.

The Sabin vaccine, on the other hand, causes a few cases of polio each year—about one case for every 3.2 million doses distributed. The situation presents medical authorities with a delicate problem of medical ethics. They believe that acceptance of the Salk vaccine would be low in the absence of epidemics and large-scale organized programs, especially among the poor and the uneducated, because of the three injections required. If that was true, more polio cases probably would result—and each case would carry with it the danger of other cases caused by contagion. On the basis of a calculated risk-benefit ratio, medical authorities favor the Sabin vaccine, despite the polio cases it causes.

The Salk vaccine, however, has remained the favorite in some foreign countries, notably in Scandinavia, which uses it exclusively and year after year has no cases of polio to report. In 1984 a new and more potent Salk vaccine, developed at the Salk Institute and in Europe, was being field-tested in India and in other developing countries in Africa and the Middle East, where the Sabin vaccine has been ineffective because of problems in storage and handling (it must be kept frozen) and because the effectiveness of the live-virus vaccine is interfered with by the presence of endemic enteroviruses in the intestinal tracts of people in tropical climates.

In 1962 Jonas Salk left the University, amid headlines, to build a research institute at La Jolla, California. He had talked of forming the institute as an affiliate of the University of Pittsburgh, using $10 million pledged to him by the National Foundation for Infantile Paralysis "to support multidisciplinary studies on the problems of man." However, Edward Litchfield, chancellor at that time, simply could not accept the condition Salk laid down, which was virtually total independence from the management and administration of the University. The chancellor and others worked hard to persuade Salk to stay in Pittsburgh, arguing that he would be involved in a sterile operation if he cut himself off from the academic association. They were not successful.

On April 12, 1965, the tenth anniversary of the great announcement at Ann Arbor that the Salk vaccine was "safe, effective, and potent," the National Foundation for Infantile Paralysis issued a tenth-anniversary progress report.

Today, it said, "all forms of poliomyelitis . . . have virtually vanished from the United States. There will always be a few cases scattered over the face of the land. But the fear-haunted days and nights that parents endured, the frantic rush of teams of doctors and nurses to areas savagely hit by this plague, the shuttered schools and churches and theaters, the barricaded beaches, the mounting polio casualty lists—those horrors and terrors all belong to the past."

The report estimated that in the ten years since 1955, no fewer than 230,000 persons in the United States had been spared paralysis as a result of vaccinations.

16

"The Athletic Situation," or, Days of Rage and Anguish

Sick of its noble experiment in football de-emphasis, the University of Pittsburgh is once again fashioning a gridiron powerhouse. But is there a middle ground in athletic subsidization?

Subtitle of an article by Harry T. Paxton, in the *Saturday Evening Post*, November 19, 1949

CHANCELLOR FITZGERALD was plagued throughout his administration by a problem that drained his energies and consumed an inordinate amount of his time. It was an inherited, ever-present, ever-troublesome, but sometimes amusing and possibly solvable problem involving athletics. A Pittsburgh sports editor called it "the annual dissatisfaction over the football situation."

During the four war years, 1942–1945, the University had played a full football schedule, fielding teams made up of young men under eighteen (almost all of them freshmen), or exempt from military service for physical reasons, or deferred because of their war-related studies. The main purpose of the wartime teams was to keep the game alive. Pitt played thirty-seven games, won thirteen, and lost twenty-four, failing to score in six games. The long football rivalry between Pitt and Carnegie Tech ended in wartime with a 45–0 Pitt victory in 1943. Under President Doherty, Tech dropped to lower-level competition, having endured twenty-three successive losses in three winless seasons and a year (1946) in which it did not score a point.

Charles Bowser, Coach Sutherland's successor, retired after the 1942 season when he saw that his material was beginning to run thin. He was succeeded by Clark D. Shaughnessy, who, after twenty-nine years of college coaching, left the University of Maryland to take on "one of the finest football coaching opportunities I have ever had." Shaughnessy brought with him his famous T formation, in which the quarterback stands directly behind and close to the center and handles the ball, with the three backs forming the top of the T behind him. For this and for other accomplishments he was granted a full professorship. Shaughnessy stayed three years, had a 10–17 record, and resigned late in 1945 after his team dropped six games in a row, the last four of them shutouts. Contributing reasons for his resignation were the threats of three of his assistant coaches, a dozen of his players, and Carl Olsen, track coach, to leave if he stayed; and publication of the fact that he was also working part-time as an advisory coach for the professional Washington Redskins.

Athletic director Hagan pulled a ten-strike in per-

suading Wesley Fesler, one-time All-American end at Ohio State, to leave Harvard, where he was an obscure end coach, and take over at Pitt. What he did in one year, 1946, and a 3–5–1 season, was sensational. He took 100 players, about 70 of them freshmen, to fall camp high on a hill above the Kiskiminetas Springs School. The training was rough and the camp even rougher, the players living in tents and walking a half-mile down the mountain side for meals. Each night a few young men packed up and left, generally without saying goodbye. Pitt opened against Illinois (which a few months later would beat UCLA 47–0 in the Rose Bowl) with 8 freshmen in the starting lineup. The score was 7–7 at the half, but Illinois power and experience in the second half took the score to 33–7. Pitt beat West Virginia, Marquette, and Penn State, tied Temple, and lost to Notre Dame, Indiana, and Purdue (by two points in the last thirty seconds), and Ohio State. The team looked so good in losing to Ohio State that Pitt authorities decided Fesler was a potentially great coach. Unfortunately, Ohio State officials formed the same conclusion and planned a campaign to make him head coach at Columbus.

Fesler liked Pittsburgh, felt an empathy for its ethnic population, and worked hard at a successful recruiting program. It was largely owing to his enthusiasm that a group of prominent and devoted alumni founded the Bellefield Trust, a scholarship fund carefully and correctly managed. The Bellefield Trust, formed in 1946 (and renamed the Panther Foundation in 1968) solicited funds from alumni and other friends of the University for three purposes. It provided low-interest loans to student athletes who wished to continue their education in graduate and professional training at the University. It made grants to the University for improvement in athletic facilities. And it underwrote scholarships, mostly but not exclusively for students participating in athletics at the University. Under the foundation's rules, the individual contributor could designate which sport his money would be spent on but otherwise had no voice at all on how, where, or on whom it was spent. That was the University's decision; the University spent the money.

Fitzgerald was genuinely interested in and cared

about athletics, including the winning of football games. When he became chancellor in 1945, he told Hagan to begin a recruiting program aimed at rebuilding the football team as a power that would win at least half its games, acting within the eligibility rules imposed by the agreement with the Western Conference and the NCAA. It was to that end that late in 1945 Fitzgerald had installed a new faculty committee on athletics. At an end-of-season dinner honoring Coach Fesler, he declared that steps would be taken to improve the fortunes of the Panthers and to put Pitt's athletic facilities on a par with those of other major colleges. A local sports columnist wrote that the chancellor's speech was "electrifying" and that it stole the show. Fesler's pay was raised to $13,000, but shortly thereafter, to the regret of one and all, he departed to become head coach at Ohio State.

Now, in the spring of 1947, the Panthers, the athletic director, the chancellor, and the University had problems.

The first problem was to find a football coach who would take over a losing team, knowing that he would always be compared with and would always work in the shadow of Jock Sutherland.

The second problem was that training facilities, after five years of wartime and postwar neglect, were inadequate and in a lamentable condition. The windows of the basketball court were broken, there was no heat, and rain was damaging the floor. The track squad had no indoor facilities, and the stadium running track was in worse shape than usual. The baseball team after one month of outdoor drill had to leave the stadium to make way for the staging of a summer light opera program. The football players had been given no season-end banquet and no sweaters on which to wear their letters.

The third problem was that in the postwar economy, athletic costs were rising faster than gate receipts. The federal tax on tickets was larger; medical and hospital bills were higher; laundry bills for a larger squad were higher; fees for game officials had risen from $2,900 to $4,315 per season; ticket printing and ticket takers cost more, and so did police and ushers. To pay these costs, Pitt had to draw large home game crowds to the stadium. With

Sutherland and his winning ways, that had been a manageable problem, but games played by a losing team did not draw large crowds, especially when played against small time opposition. The powerhouse teams from the Middle West did indeed attract larger crowds, but the cost in team morale and public regard was also large, for those teams invariably beat Pitt, often by lopsided scores.

Finally, despite "Pitt's strange flirtation with the Western Conference" (the words are those of the *New York Time*'s Arthur Daley), the Big Nine declined a Pitt request: to be admitted to membership in place of Chicago. According to Frank Carver, Pitt came very close to being accepted, but Michigan State was chosen.

The situation was worsened in 1947 by a schedule that would have frightened Jock Sutherland in his prime: Illinois, Notre Dame, Michigan, Indiana, Ohio State, Minnesota, Purdue, Penn State, and West Virginia, in that order. Fitzgerald told Hagan, "There is a lot of talk going around to the effect, 'Do you think they will win one game?'" He added, "That is not good."

Fesler had suggested that Walter (Mike) Milligan, his line coach at Pitt, be made head coach, and his advice was taken. Two good things happened in 1947, Milligan's first season. Pitt did win one game in a stunning upset at Pitt Stadium against Fesler's heavily favored Ohio State team, thus stopping at twenty-four the string of successive losses to the Big Nine and producing a memorable jubilation on the streets of Pittsburgh. And Notre Dame filled the stadium with 64,000 spectators, which helped the athletic director to end the year with an unusual $70,000 surplus.* The rest of the season was sheer compounded disaster: eight loses in nine games, Pitt 26 points, Opponents 267. The ultimate indignity came on successive weekends in October, when Pitt

---

*The stadium could no longer hold the maximum 68,000 it was built for. New safety rules imposed by the city fire marshal now prohibited temporary bleacher seats both on the rim of the stadium and in the track area. The Department of Athletics, furthermore, discovered that the new, bigger generation of spectators had increased in breadth of beam. It therefore widened seats from sixteen to eighteen inches. Full capacity in 1986 is 56,500.

lost to Notre Dame 46–0 and to Michigan 69–0.

Mayor David L. Lawrence, during a trustees' meeting, officially protested Pitt's declining athletic fortunes. Fitzgerald had just reported that Pitt now had 21,000 students and was looking forward to an enrollment of 25,000 by the end of the school year. When he finished, Lawrence responded: "Pittsburgh has always been accustomed to high-class athletic teams, particularly at Pitt. I am talking as a fan who likes to see good athletics and good teams here in Pittsburgh. Wherever I go, people ask me what has happened at Pitt. Why the decline? I think the time has come for Pitt either to play good football with the present heavy schedule, or cut the schedule and play teams in their own class. . . . I think it's a mistake to make these boys take such a beating Saturday after Saturday."

On October 24, following the 69–0 loss to Michigan (and one day before the unexpected victory over Ohio State), Fitzgerald admitted in an address to Pitt lettermen and alumni that the University's athletic policy had been at fault. He called for a reexamination of Code Bowman to determine "if we are not leaning over backwards" in the direction of simon-pure athletics.

A football banquet was held at the end of the unfortunate 1947 season, and it was graced by a bittersweet commemoration of past glory. Members of Pitt's 1927 squad were there to mark their twentieth anniversary—Jock Sutherland's Eastern Champions, his first team undefeated in regular play, the first Pitt team to go to the Rose Bowl. Sutherland was not there. He was now, following three years' military service during the war, head coach of the Pittsburgh Steelers. In a breezy letter to Fitzgerald, E. V. Babcock had reported on a recent meeting with him: "While attending the Dapper Dan sports-loving Americans' celebration in Johnstown Saturday night, sat beside Sutherland. He was very chummy with me. Sutherland likes you. He likes Dr. McEllroy. Thinks Bowman did not treat him right. Said he had not been on the campus since he left Pitt." But Sutherland sent word through Babcock of a prospect, "a splendid student and marvelous football player in Johnstown who ought to go to Pitt. He wants to study medicine." Babcock wrote, "I practically promised him entrance into the Medical School if he would join Pitt."

A few months later, in April 1948, John Bain Sutherland went south on a recruiting trip for the Steelers. He disappeared from view for several days and then was found walking along a country road, suitcase in hand, near Bandana, Kentucky. He was intermittently incoherent and lucid. His friend G. David Thompson borrowed a corporate plane and with John Michelosen and Dr. Ralph Daugherty brought him back to Pittsburgh and to the West Penn Hospital. A young doctor on duty remembers that the patient said as he was being taken down the corridor to a room, "I think I have been in this school before. I gave a talk here." Brain surgery revealed that he had an inoperable malignant tumor. He died the next day. He was fifty-nine. A number of his former Pitt players stood as an honor guard at his funeral. He left an estate—thanks largely to the investment advice given him by Thompson—of one-half million dollars.

Two investigating committees were involved in the spring of 1948 in studies of the athletic situation at Pitt. One was a faculty committee. The other was an alumni committee dominated by lettermen and remnants of "the Sutherland faction." The alumni committee declared that athletic director Hagan had failed and should be asked to resign; head coach Milligan, on the other hand, should be retained. It recommended that if Pitt was to play major rivals in the future, it should subsidize the athletes who played them. Otherwise, Pitt should adopt a deflated schedule. The faculty committee advised that Coach Milligan resign and that Mr. Hagan stay. It felt strongly that professionalism in any form must not be allowed in Pitt intercollegiate athletics and that programs must be continued on a strictly amateur basis. Pitt should maintain its association with the midwestern teams but should increase its efforts to meet those teams on a more equal basis. Certain eastern schools, however, like Penn, Yale, Cornell, Army, and Navy, "would be very desirable additions to our schedules." The faculty committeemen felt that "calm, constructive thinking and co-operation can solve our athletic problems, but destructive criticism and disharmony will only add to the difficulty." They called for "co-operation between all parts of the University and its alumni and friends in informing the athletic youth of opportunities at Pitt." A *Press* reporter asked Dr. William McClelland, one-time star back on Warner's teams and an Allegheny County commissioner, what he thought of these sentiments. McClelland replied, "The Faculty Committee is just plain stupid."

The trustees, however, took things calmly and in full stride. They met for an hour and appointed a five-man administrative committee from their own thirty-four members to report on the reports of the other two committees. This committee disbanded the two earlier committees, scrapped their reports, and placed the athletic situation in the hands of still another committee—a standing committee of eight members chosen from the faculty, the Alumni Council, the Varsity Letter Club, and the Student Congress. The chairman was Norman C. Ochsenhirt, a sports-loving surgeon and team physician of the Pittsburgh Pirates, who had been president of the Varsity Letter Club and a leader in the 1938–1939 fight against Code Bowman. Fitzgerald told him: "I want you to draw up a liberal code. But stay within the rules of the Big Nine and the N.C.A.A. And once you set up your code, stick to it. Don't let anyone cheat on it."

When Ochsenhirt's committee held its second meeting without asking athletic director Hagan to be present, Hagan anticipated their next move. He resigned quietly and with dignity, went on a month's vacation with his wife and children, and took a peaceful, uncomplicated job in the Department of Industrial Relations of Carnegie-Illinois Steel Company. A *Post-Gazette* headline on June 9 read: "Pitt in Turmoil as Hagan Quits Post." Frank Carver, sports publicity head, highly regarded by working newspeople, was asked to serve as acting director until a new man was chosen.

Hagan closed his twenty-year career at Pitt with a special accomplishment: the best squad of freshman football candidates in a decade.

Fitzgerald concluded that what the athletic situation needed was a strong athletic director, a man of experience and stature in his own right, a leader who could take charge, work with the faculty and the alumni, and free the chancellor from the turmoil of the past several years, He found him in Annapolis in the person of Thomas J. Hamilton, Captain, U.S.N., athletic director of the Naval Academy.

Tom Hamilton was something of a national figure: former All-American quarterback for Navy in the mid-1920s; Navy football coach during 1931–1937 with a 19–8 record; originator and director of the navy's outstanding wartime preflight physical program; and for a time executive officer of the aircraft carrier *Enterprise* in the Pacific. In the navy's shortsighted policy of rotating its coaches and athletic directors—a vestige of the military principle that any commissioned officer is considered competent to perform any assignment satisfactorily—Hamilton was due to be sent on another tour of sea duty. Having logged twenty-one years of service, he elected instead to take retirement and go to Pitt, with full faculty status, as director of physical education and intercollegiate athletics. Fitzgerald, who conducted the negotiations with Hamilton, wrote in his daily log, "I was deeply impressed by him as a man of brains, ability and character." Hamilton reported on board on February 1, 1949.

In the meantime, Coach Milligan had distinguished himself in 1948 by giving Pitt its first winning season since 1939: a 6–3 record with victories over West Virginia, Marquette, Indiana, Western Reserve, Purdue, and Penn State. The sports world was beginning to take an interested look at Pitt to see if it could really come back from its long experiment in self-flagellation, rebuild, and regain athletic status, and if so, how it managed to do it. The *Saturday Evening Post* sent Harry T. Paxton, an associate editor, to Pittsburgh to find out. His article, which appeared in the *Post* on November 19, 1949, retold the story of the rise of Pitt as a football colossus under Warner and Sutherland; of the charges of professionalism ("The free-ride system was no monopoly, though Pitt was the first to have it exposed to public view"); of the Bowman-Sutherland confrontation; and of the unhappy experiences during the drastic de-emphasis program, which he described as "days of rage and anguish." He told of the postwar shift under Fitzgerald to recruiting, scholarships, and subsidy practices within the permissible limits of the NCAA code. Paxton reported that on the 1949 squad of fifty-five men, most had scholarships or job assistance, or both. "Five get a full free ride because of their high scholastic standing—an exception permitted under the code. Another 20 do well enough in the classrooms to get tuition plus $300. Most of the others get tuition only. Against its program of aid to athletes, Pitt can point to the fact that more than 2,000 non-athletes get scholarship assistance at the University, and many more get job help." The article also told of an argument newly emphasized in Pitt recruiting: "Get your education and your football publicity in the section where you are going to live and work. What good will it do you to get your name in the papers out West or down South? Everybody back here will have forgotten you by the time you get out of school."

It was a fair article that brought no discredit to the University, but its effect was distorted by a title—"Purity Dies at Pitt"—that caused much comment, implied certain conclusions, and was simply not supported by the text. Pitt officials felt that the *Post* had hoped to come up with a sensational exposé, and that since Paxton found no evidence of such, the title was devised to make up for the lack of sensationalism in the story. Tom Hamilton suggested that the title must have been written by the circulation manager.

Hamilton was a popular figure in Pittsburgh and at Pitt: on the campus among players, students, and faculty; in the Duquesne Club as well as in a neighborhood bar. He threw himself with energy and imagination into improving the athletic plant and broadening both the intercollegiate and the intramural athletic programs. He added freshman and junior varsity teams in most sports and took Pitt back after a long absence into intercollegiate wrestling, in which it won an eastern team championship and a number of individual national titles. He made repairs to the stadium and the old gymnasium. When he discovered that Pitt had on its hands two mess halls and some hundreds of double-decker bunks left over from World War II, he put his football squads in the University's first true dormitory—

a training table and living quarters at the Ellsworth Center during the season.

When he saw the plans for the meager new field house, Hamilton had them redrawn to provide a complete, proper, and expensive facility. Asked where the money was to come from, he suggested that it should come from the General State Authority (GSA). That, he was told, was impossible: it would violate GSA rules and conflict with the University charter. He replied that he might be able to persuade the authority to make an exception in the cause of developing strong and healthy young Americans. He was right. An exception was made; the redesigned field house was built with GSA money and dedicated in December 1951. It had a basketball court that seated 6,000, expandable to 8,000. It had a wrestling room, eight squash courts, a 220-yard dirt track, a gymnastic room, training rooms, locker rooms, and offices for the entire athletic department. "The field house," Fitzgerald said in showing it to the press, "is a monument to Tom Hamilton's foresight. We had planned little more than a roof over a patch of ground before he came into the picture. Tom raised our sights, and as a result we have a field house of which we can be proud." Long-time administrator Edison Montgomery says: "This GSA exception set a new pattern for university financing of state building. Under the pattern, the state borrows the money, constructs the building, and owns it; the university uses it. This has had an impact on all Pennsylvania universities. They owe a debt to Pitt and Tom Hamilton."

Hamilton became a friend and hunting companion of Alan Scaife, the new chairman of the Board of Trustees. Frank Carver, who was Hamilton's graduate manager of athletics, his sounding board, and his "no-man," recalled, "Scaife would telephone Tom at noon and say, 'Let's go duck hunting,' and they would take off in one of the private planes Scaife had available and fly to New Jersey or somewhere, shoot a few ducks, and come back that same evening." Together they devised a program in which people who were important to the University—such as community leaders, major industrialists, educators, and state legislators—would be taken on weekend trips in the Gulf Oil Company plane to inspect the athletic plants of other colleges. A trip sometimes coincided with a football game Pitt was playing at the place being inspected. Whether this happened by chance or design, it created good will and improved the understanding of the University's problems and goals in the minds of those who made the trips.

Hamilton was an amiable and "clubbable" man at Pitt, but he had two personality traits that caused administrative complications from time to time. Despite his military training at working through channels, he preferred to deal solely, directly, and at length with the chancellor rather than with the administrative officer to whom the chancellor had delegated athletic affairs. And he made the mistake of taking seriously what student reporters wrote in the campus publications. Everyone else understood that allowances had to be made for a young person eager to make a name for himself by attacking and insulting a member of the establishment; this was recognized as one of the hazards of an academic career. Captain Hamilton could not accept this. He made few allowances, and he became angry at unfriendly stories, especially when they impugned his honor and were picked up and reported by other news media. On one occasion—March 5, 1952—in a letter to Edward Jensen, editor of the *Pitt News*, he wrote of "demanding satisfaction" from one of the reporters.

Sometimes the effect of the two traits merged, as when he requested a meeting with no one but the chancellor to report some offense in the campus press and to explain why the offender should be subject to "disciplinary action on a high University administrative level." On November 19, 1952, a *News* reporter had telephoned a member of the Orange Bowl Committee to discuss the chances of Pitt receiving a bowl bid. Hamilton, understandably outraged, wrote Fitzgerald, "It is impossible to represent the University properly if the 'freedom of the press' gives students such uncontrolled privilege." He added a postscript: "Since this was written, the attached article appeared in today's *Pitt News*. This indicates a flagrant disregard of my request to the *Pitt News* that its writers stay out of Athletic Department affairs."

Fitzgerald wrote an answer on December 8: "We wish to provide *News* staff members adequate opportunity to gain experience in handling stories and publishing a student newspaper; however, the experience of 'learning through errors' is frequently painful. I am glad you brought the matter to my attention and shall urge that it be resolved in the interest of all concerned." Fitzgerald then decided not to send the letter. His secretary wrote to Hamilton: "I regret that your letter of November 19 was not acknowledged, but it has come during an especially busy period for Dr. Fitzgerald." On the bottom of her copy she wrote lightly in pencil: "12/15. Dean Biddle said he and RHF talked about this on 12/13. RHF indicated he wanted to let the matter rest. If anyone brings it up, he will indicate that he simply hasn't had time to go into it."

Hamilton had both bad and good luck with his football teams. He clashed with Coach Milligan, despite Milligan's second 6–3 record in 1949, and offered him a one-year contract rather than the two-year contract that Milligan had wanted. Milligan resigned, and Pitt lost a coach who gave every evidence that he would continue to produce winning seasons.

Hamilton persuaded Len Casanova to come from a winning record at Santa Clara, and in 1950 they suffered together through another 1–8 season. When Casanova resigned in July 1951, a few weeks before the opening game, Hamilton, at the request of the trustees, stepped in as coach for one year. He lost the first seven games, most of them by close scores, but ended the season with successive victories over West Virginia, Penn State, and Miami of Florida. He then hired Lowell P. (Red) Dawson, assistant coach at Michigan State, who took the job with the declaration that he would need three or four years to rebuild the team. Dawson had a respectable 9–12–1 record in his first two years and excelled in recruiting, but he suffered a heart attack in 1954 after losing the first three games. Hamilton again took over as coach. He began on Tuesday; coached his team against Navy on Saturday, possibly with mixed emotions; and won 21–19—Navy's only loss that season.

Hamilton then signed John Pollock Michelosen to

a three-year contract. The new coach was an extremely popular choice, especially among disgruntled old grads and Sutherland admirers. Michelosen, thirty-nine, a native of Ambridge, had been quarterback and blocking back on the great 1935–1937 Sutherland teams. As Sutherland's friend and protégé—his youngest child was named Jock—he had coached the "Dream Backfield" on the 1938 team, and when Sutherland went to the Brooklyn Dodgers and the Pittsburgh Steelers, Michelosen followed as his assistant coach. He had succeeded Sutherland as head coach of the Steelers,

1948–1951, and became Pitt's defensive coach under Dawson. Michelosen was the eighth Pitt coach in seventeen years.

In 1955, Michelosen's first year, Pitt achieved total redemption with a 7–3 season; victories over California, Syracuse, Nebraska, Duke, Virginia, unbeaten West Virginia, and Penn State; and a trip to the Sugar Bowl in New Orleans—Pitt's first bowl game since 1936. Fitzgerald's ten-year effort to rebuild Pittsburgh into a football power was realized a few months after he ceased to be chancellor.

17
Farewell, a Long Farewell . . .

Ten years is a short period in the life of a university, but it is a substantial period in the life of a chancellor. There is a happy coincidence of my age, my best judgment and the readiness of the university to embark on a new era of development which gives me compelling reasons to arrange at this time for an orderly transfer to a successor next year.

Rufus H. Fitzgerald, July 12, 1954

On a Friday afternoon early in July 1954, John J. Geise boarded a plane in Washington bound for Pittsburgh. A long-time professor of history at the University of Pittsburgh, he was on loan to several of the military services as chief historian and head of a program to write their training manuals in language that could be understood by any sergeant or second lieutenant in the field. He had spent the week at his office in the Pentagon and was returning to spend Saturday at the University and Sunday with his family. He chanced to meet Rufus Fitzgerald on the plane. "I was already seated when he came in. He greeted me and sat down. I commented at once on how well he looked, how relaxed he looked. He said, 'Yes, John, I am. I'll tell you—it's not going to be announced immediately—but I decided today, definitely decided today, that I'm going to resign the chancellorship.' I said, 'Well, that's too bad for the University, but I think it's going to be—from the looks of you—it's going to be fine for you.' And that was that."

The trustees released the announcement of Fitzgerald's retirement on July 12, to take effect a year later, on July 1, 1955, at the end of the 1954–1955 academic year and on the tenth anniversary of his induction as chancellor. His letter to the trustees read:

It seems to me appropriate that I tender my resignation as the University completes one great era in its development and is ready to move forward to an even greater era. My successor, whoever he may be, will be able to grasp responsibilities and carry them uninterruptedly through the next phase of development which I should have to leave in midstream in any event.

The University has just had the guidance of the exhaustive survey by the Middle States Association of Colleges. We have just completed a comprehensive study of our administrative structure. We are well into a building program without parallel in the history of the University. The programs of almost every individual School have been subject of study, and new development programs are under way in many areas.

Fitzgerald's announcement produced an uncommon number of tributes from friends, colleagues, and the press. Trustee Edward Weidlein said, "Dr. Fitzerald neglected no phase of the complete university program. Every department had received careful attention, not only in terms of physical facilities but also in terms of building a strong teaching and research staff. . . . He has brought great distinction to the University." A *Sun-Telegraph* editorial lamented the loss of a "gallant and gentle-mannered" chancellor who "has guided the University of Pittsburgh through many turbulent and changing events. . . . He has seen massive enrollment, due to World War II and an accelerated program, sweep like a tidal wave over the University. . . . As the Chancellor bows out . . . a new and shining era has already dawned at Pitt." The Junior Chamber of Commerce named him Pittsburgh's Man of the Year for 1954; the American Association of Colleges elected him as its president; and President Eisenhower appointed him chairman of the U.S. Advisory Commission on the International Exchange of Students.

At the same time, there were rumors and persisting conjectures about the real reason for Fitzgerald's resignation, based on the inevitable assumption that the reasons he gave could not be the true ones. Why should he make himself a lame duck chancellor for a whole year? Perhaps he resigned because of poor health? People had commented on his stooped appearance, even as he played tennis on the University courts. Perhaps he was burned out by the overwork he endured during World War II, or by the turmoil of postwar growth, or by his role as buffer between an obdurate John Bowman and a critical Board of Trustees. Perhaps, like Chancellor McCormick before him, he simply did not feel up to the requirements he knew would be imposed on him in the next several years. There were demands, he knew, for a division of his responsibilities among three or more vice chancellors, which would require him to do what he was reluctant or seemed emotionally incapable of doing: to delegate authority.

There is, in fact, hard evidence that Fitzgerald resigned because the trustees wished him to resign, and that the means they used to accomplish this was the "comprehensive study of our administrative structure" Fitzgerald referred to in his letter of resignation.

This was a study carried out by Cresap, McCormick and Paget (CMP), Management Engineers, of New York City, financed in part by a $28,000 grant from the Ford Foundation. Fitzgerald handled the mechanics of retaining the firm in July 1953. A few months later he recorded in his notes a somewhat abrasive grilling he received from two CMP consultants on the outmoded procedures he used in preparing the budget.

Edison Montgomery, then a member of the CMP staff, said in an interview in 1971:

My particular area of responsibility was business affairs of the university—checking out their efficiency and effectiveness. I discovered after about a month of survey work that I had misunderstood the purpose of the survey. I was finding that the business operations were organizationally not very clear-cut but were working reasonably well, and I made my report to that effect to Mr. Walter Vieh.* It was then that he revealed that the purpose of the study was to develop the University of Pittsburgh as a great national university and that the study had been conceived not by Chancellor Fitzgerald, but by the trustees. When I made my report that things worked reasonably well, sure, there were a number of things that could be improved, I found that I was not following the party line. What was needed was the condemnation of the University which would provide material for the trustees to replace Chancellor Fitzgerald. They viewed the chancellor as a man who was getting a little bit along in years, but more importantly, a man who did not have the vision of a great national university. . . .

The report itself is probably not nearly so revealing as a meeting held on the thirty-ninth floor [at 525 William Penn Place] with the community leaders. . . . I don't remember many of the people who sat around the table, but I am sure the leader was Alan Scaife, and the other person who seemed to take most of the initiative was Steele Gow, Sr. At that time the management consultants, with their great objectivity, said in order for you to become a national university you must replace your chancellor. Now the other recommendations that were made were major changes in organization and many, many procedural improvements, but that really wasn't of interest to these people. What they were interested in was a justifica-

*Vieh, head of the CMP team, and Montgomery both became vice chancellors of the University.

The relatively peaceful administration of Rufus Fitzgerald made him a less frequent subject for cartoons than John Bowman. Here Hungerford recognizes his election as Pittsburgh's man of the year in 1954.

Pittsburgh Post-Gazette

tion to go after Chancellor Fitzgerald. As a result of this, indeed, Alan Scaife did ask for the chancellor's resignation. It was done on a very easy basis, and I think he was permitted full salary for two or three years after he left the place and a very generous retirement allowance. He continued to attend all of the board meetings throughout the Litchfield administration until he ultimately passed away—never said a word during all of the subsequent board meetings. I'm not sure he ever understood actually what had happened.

When it was completed, the seven-part Cresap, McCormick and Paget report, *Survey of Administrative Management,* criticized the chancellor on several major points. It charged that he had become inaccessible to his faculty and staff and that, forced to consider and act on a multitude of details, "he sometimes has been unable to discharge his responsibilities as promptly as he would have wished," the most common delay being in the late approval of the annual budget. It pointed out that the University in the past seven years had had a net deficit of expenses over income of $409,000; that it had succeeded in only one year during the past five in operating within its income; and that recent years of deficit operations had exhausted the surplus account of the general fund and had forced the University to encroach upon its capital to the extent of almost $385,000. The message was clear that the chancellor must keep the fiscal affairs of the institution under control. He should, moreover, create an organized and coordinated development program. He should restructure his administration, delegate administrative responsibility to five principal officers, and devote most of his energy to comprehensive planning and development.

The trustees should declare a moratorium on all future construction unless such buildings were of a self-liquidating nature, such as dormitories, or there was sufficient endowment to provide adequate maintenance and operation, with no additional drain on existing funds.

The report was given to the chancellor and the trustees in April 1954. Fitzgerald submitted his letter of resignation two months later.

The CMP report was never made public, and Fitzgerald enjoyed a heightened popularity throughout his last year as chancellor. Much was written and said about the accomplishments of his ten years as chancellor.

He ended the AAUP blacklist of the University, introduced a code of permanent tenure, and saw a Phi Beta Kappa chapter brought to the campus. He increased the size of the endowment more than eight times over, from $3.5 million to $29 million.

In his administration, student enrollment increased enormously, reaching a peak of 26,494 in 1948–1949. The University successfully accommodated the surge of veterans of World War II and of the Korean War. The faculty was enlarged to 725 members. Some 2,700 degrees were being awarded annually. It was estimated that the University had granted 70,752 diplomas since 1883 (the earliest date of record in the registrar's office) and that Fitzgerald had signed 29,000 of these—more than 42 percent—as chancellor.

Fitzgerald started the University on its greatest building and expansion program, projected to cost $50 million. Two buildings had been completed: the 650-room nurses' residence and the Memorial Field House. Four more were under construction: the engineering building between Thaw Hall and the old Mellon Institute, the building to house the Schools of Public Health, the School of Medicine (Scaife Hall), and the Science Building (Clapp Hall). Four more were in the planning stage, with a considerable part of their cost already in hand: a student union, a gymnasium, a dormitory for men, and a parking garage. Fitzgerald acquired land for these buildings, expanding the University on its "new axis to the north" of Fifth Avenue.

He took the University into a new relationship with the community, which, for the first time, worked with the City Planning Commission and the Pittsburgh Regional Planning Association. Out of this evolved the beginning of the Oakland Plan to accommodate the University's expansion in a planned, orderly, and acceptable manner. Consideration was given in 1949 and again in 1953 to the construction of buildings on the hillside of Panther Hollow, the deep valley at the south edge of the campus.

Under the Fitzgerald administration, the complex of medical facilities developed into a health center, with construction of three major buildings and first use of the Municipal Hospital (Salk Hall), scene of the University's greatest research achievement. The Falk Foundation gave $300,000 for the acquisition of a first-rate medical library. The teaching faculty of the medical schools and hospitals was recast to a higher standard. Of all living medical alumni of the University in 1955, more than one-third were graduated in the Fitzgerald decade.

These achievements of the Fitzgerald decade were, to be sure, largely measured in bricks and mortar and body counts. Educators both within and outside the University did report advances in scholarship and scholarly research, in standards of educational programs in various disciplines, and in teaching and learning in the classroom. But how are such advances measured? Indeed, how are they to be described? The year-end reports made by schools on their new developments are almost always general, innocuous, and weak on specifics, even where significant advances have been made. Some thousands of words in an educational journal, and long-term comparison studies made under nearly identical conditions with similar subjects, are needed to quantify the improvements of a changed educational procedure or the results of a new core curriculum. Hence the inevitable emphasis is on measurable highlights: increased enrollment; the listing of research projects, awards, and grants; new departments, positions, duties, and titles; new physical facilities; raised standards of admission; and higher scores on standardized exams, accompanied by mention of the less-measurable "many new and diversified programs established" and the "new system introduced for orienting junior students." Deficiencies are seldom mentioned publicly, and certainly they are not stressed: in Pitt's case in 1955, for example, that the library was inadequate or that the faculty had no endowed professorships; no distinguished "name" professors outside the medical school; no published, productive, nationally known poet, novelist, playwright, essayist, or historian.

Examples of scholarly advance in the decade, nevertheless, can be given. Though some are minor and relatively unimportant, cumulatively they indicate an upward trend, and they deserve to be reported as significant developments in the administration of Rufus Fitzgerald.

In the autumn of 1948, (Margaret) Storm Jameson, a distinguished and prolific English novelist since the publication of her first book in 1920, arrived at the University to serve for nine months as a visiting professor, the first literary celebrity and writer of international reputation on the campus. In her two-volume autobiography, *Journey from the North,* 1970, she describes her life in Pittsburgh and her work as a teacher of creative writing at the University.

She began by hating the apartment the University had arranged for her to rent and by deciding that she had made an unendurable nine-month blunder. She then concluded that her boredom and despair were "atrocious and shameful." Pittsburgh was a beautiful city. "Built, like Rome, on hills, with two magnificent rivers, the Monongahela—five liquid syllables—and the Allegheny, meeting in the city to become the Ohio, it has a strange, awful, and at times overwhelming beauty."

Even Americans had made derisive comments when I said I was going to Pittsburgh, and even in my first unreason I knew they were wrong; it is one of the finest cities in the world, the fable of the present as the Parthenon was the fable of Greece.

Also, it is . . . the city which has not yet resolved—dissolved—its European elements. It has more "nations" than medieval Paris. This . . . may be a source of its magnificent energy. Czechs, Poles, Hungarians, Syrians, Greeks, Jugoslavs, heaven knows what more, formed resistant knots in the pattern. . . .

The university in Pittsburgh is like no other I have seen. Imagine the masons of a Gothic cathedral deciding to do without statues and, to make amends, elongating the tower to an enormous height. . . . It ought to be absurd . . . and is in fact very impressive, at night even charming. To look down into the great hall called the Commons Room when it is filled with students sitting about reading, arguing, drinking coffee, is to be reminded—distantly, but without any sense of incongruity—of a medieval refectory or chapter-house.

She faced her students for the first time in a lecture room on one of the upper floors of the Cathedral of Learning. The students sat on tiered benches "and looked at me with polite curiosity." She said that she would give each of them a tutoring hour every week and would discuss anything they were working on and cared to show her. Tutoring sessions were held in the Early American Room on the third floor.

[It] had been fitted up as an early American kitchen, with small leaded windows, low ceiling, beams, a vast open fireplace in which an iron pan swung from a hook. . . . With my student of the hour I sat at a long table, he on a narrow backless bench, I on a chair so low I had to sit on the only two books in the room. . . . Sometimes during a tutoring hour I was disturbed . . . by a conducted party of tourists.

I may have been lucky in my ex-soldiers, but I was never bored. Nor conscious of the gap between their age and mine, their attitude to life and mine. There were moments when, glancing up as the door of the colonial kitchen opened, I should not have been startled to see any one of the young men my friends in 1914. These young Americans had a natural self-possession, a lack of pretentions, a liveliness, that made it easy for them to be friendly: it did not occur to them to think of themselves as *the young*. . . .

This escape from diffidence and boredom . . . is, of all the pleasures of my American year, the most exhilarating, the one I miss.

Storm Jameson was the precursor of a number of outstanding writers and scholars who have since taught at the University, some of them as visiting or permanent Andrew Mellon Professors in a program started in 1958 by the A. W. Mellon Educational and Charitable Trust.

National committees—Norwegian, Italian, and English—added three more Nationality Rooms during the Fitzgerald decade. The rooms were used, of course, for their primary purpose: the teaching of classes. They continued to attract visitors—more than 20,000 a year. And they still served as an inspiration for national pride and ethnic studies. But now the University and the national committees broadened the concept and scope of the Nationality Rooms. The committees, having worked for twenty years to complete their basic purpose, did not wish to disband, nor did the University wish them to do so. In 1946 they reorganized. Other groups, including the Women's International Club, augmented the original committees; a national council was formed of the four officers of each room committee. The new organization began a program concentrated on international cultural and educational exchange. It has provided (since 1948) more than 280 scholarship grants for University of Pittsburgh students and faculty members to study abroad, and it has helped to bring some hundreds of foreign students and distinguished international visitors to the University.

Storm Jameson, despite her difficulties with the Early American kitchen, was deeply impressed by the Nationality Rooms. She was not unfamiliar with international relationships, having served for eight years as president of the English PEN Club, the association of "Poets, Playwrights, Editors, Essayists, Novelists," which had strong international relationships. To her friend Ruth Mitchell and in her autobiography she wrote that the Nationality Rooms were "a splendid stroke of sanity and imagination . . . worth a thousand treatises on world government."

The University of Pittsburgh Press in 1945 had published twelve volumes; by 1955, under the directorship of Agnes L. Starrett, it had published seventy. Among the seventy was one of the rare and beautiful books of American art, printing, and publishing: *Wildflowers of Western Pennsylvania and the Upper Ohio Basin*, 1953. It was cited by the American Institute of Graphic Arts as one of the fifty best books of 1953, and a noted botanist called it "probably the most comprehensive study of a single botanical region yet made."

The author of the text was O. E. Jennings, director of Carnegie Museum, professor of botany and head of the Department of Biological Sciences at the University of Pittsburgh. Jennings began collecting the plants in the spring of 1941, in his sixty-fourth year, and over the next two years he and his wife, Grace, traveled some six thousand miles in the region searching for specimens. He brought the plants to the artist at any hour of the day or night, and the artist would drop everything to paint them at once in watercolor, in the condition in which they arrived. Two hundred of his pictures, showing 253 plants, were reproduced life-size and in color in the book.

The artist, who estimated that he worked 1,600 hours on the pictures, was probably one of the most versatile, exotic, and talented personalities ever to live and work in Pittsburgh. Andrei Avinoff, born in 1884, a Russian nobleman of impeccable pedigree, had been a gentleman in waiting to Czar Nicholas II. He was fluent in seven languages (especially English, thanks to a childhood governess from England) and read in ten others. He was an accomplished pianist and artist. Pittsburgh-born John Walker, director of the National Gallery in Washington, D.C., called him the finest flower painter of this century. He was a world-renowned collector of and authority on butterflies, with more than 80,000 specimens in his collection in Russia, one of the largest ever assembled privately by a single person.

Avinoff left Russia with most of his family and several family servants just before the Bolsheviks took over in 1917; he came to the United States as an official representative of the Kerensky Provisional Government, on behalf of which he deposited in a New York bank several million dollars worth of Russian funds. In 1922 he met William J. Holland, "the dean of American entomologists," whose *Butterfly Book* and *Moth Book* he had studied and used as a child of fourteen in Russia. When Holland invited him to join Carnegie Museum as an associate curator of entomology, Avinoff accepted. He became director of the museum in 1926. A year later he joined the faculty of the University of Pittsburgh, teaching the history and appreciation of art. He lived in the Schenley Hotel, was for some twenty years an ornament of Pittsburgh society and intellectual gatherings, and was thought to be the only active member of the Russian Orthodox church who was also a member of the Rolling Rock Club. His sister, Mme. Elizabeth Shoumatoff, visited the city from time to time to paint portraits of prominent Pittsburghers, including George Hubbard Clapp and John Bowman.*

In 1927 Edwin L. Peterson, having just graduated from the University of Pittsburgh, was engaged as one of its graduate assistants (at eighty dollars a month) and assigned to a class few teachers like, the lowest rung on the academic ladder, freshman English composition. He was a protégé of Percival Hunt, head of the department, whose freshman class Peterson called "a profound course."

Peterson was now teaching in what some academicians today call one of the best teaching schools in the country. John Geise, who was part of it, declared three decades later: "The top 7 to 10 percent of the graduates of the College were able to go to any graduate school and be on even ground with the top graduates of colleges far more prestigious than Pitt. To be sure, Pitt was a streetcar college, but there was a large cadre of professors, associate professors, assistants, and instructors who worked very, very effectively with all types of students. They spent untold hours in their offices and in consultancies with the student organizations in personal contact with the students. The rapport between teachers and students was excellent and, in my opinion, went far to counteract the relative lack of equipment, books, and research materials." Dr. Geise had reason, perhaps, to be biased, but Professor Walter Evert, who had trained and taught elsewhere, declared of the English department in 1981: "It is considered historically, retroactively, one of the founding writing programs in the country. Back in the 1920s and 1930s, this was a seed bed."

Edwin Peterson taught English composition at the University for forty years. In that time he introduced new teaching methods that attracted national attention. The education editors of the *Christian Science Monitor* and the *New York Herald Tribune* wrote feature articles on him and his work. Edward Weeks, editor of the *Atlantic*, singled him out for praise as one of the best teachers of writing in the country and called one of his techniques "an audacious discovery" and "a breakthrough." A *Post-Gazette* feature writer called him "a miracle man" in his ability to get the work of his advanced students published for pay in national magazines. Quality in teaching is hard to assess, and perhaps the saying is true that creative writing cannot be taught; it can only be learned. But here is one instance where a great teacher and great teaching were clearly identifiable and measurable.

In 1938 there were three major literary contests conducted each year for college students: by *Harper's*, the *Atlantic*, and *Story*. In 1939 a Peterson student won sixth place in the *Story* contest. In 1940 students of his won a first and a third honorable mention for poetry submitted to the *Atlantic*. In 1941 two of his students won first prize and an honorable mention for short stories submitted to the *Harper's* contest (500 contestants entered); another won sixth place in the *Story* contest; and three others won hon-

*Madame Shoumatoff was painting a portrait from life of Franklin D. Roosevelt at Warm Springs, Georgia, in 1945 when he suffered his fatal stroke.

orable mentions (one for poetry, two for short stories) in the *Atlantic* contest.

By 1962 his "writing majors" had won *Atlantic* awards every year of his tenure but one (the year he was on leave of absence). In 1960 three of his students published novels: Peter Beagle, *A Fine and Private Place* (Viking), written for the most part while the author was still an undergraduate; Robert M. Brown, *A Different Drummer* (Harcourt, Brace); and Lester Goran, *The Paratrooper of Mechanic Avenue* (Houghton Mifflin).*

Peterson made his "audacious discovery" in 1959. In analyzing his teaching methods, he had found that he was spending too much time with his back to the class writing on the chalkboard. "As soon as you turn your back to write something," he observed, "you lose their interest. Then you scrawl something and they can't read it, especially in the back row." He thought there must be a better way.

He was also disturbed that he was *telling* his students how to write, revise, and edit, not *showing* them. "Students of writing," he said, "have to feel and see good writing, not simply be told about it in a lecture. . . . If I read a piece of writing to the class— perhaps William Faulkner's *The Bear*—and say, 'Did you notice those wonderful verbs?' they'll be polite and say, 'Sure,' and of course they didn't notice any verbs.

"I have to see a manuscript to tell whether it is any good, yet for all these years, writing teachers— myself included—have been trying to tell students about writing. It's no wonder it hasn't worked. We have been asking our students to do something we can't do ourselves."

He experimented with thirty-five millimeter film and slides but found them, for his purpose, slow, inflexible, and expensive. He wanted a graphic technique in which the class as a whole could see him editing a student's theme or writing comments in the margin of a passage from a great book. He found it in a relatively new $400 machine called an overhead projector. With this device, he stood beside a compact box, facing his class. Without dimming the lights, he laid a page from a theme on a glass plate, from which it was projected to a ten-foot-by-ten-foot screen on the wall behind him, in full view of the class. He placed an acetate transparency over the page, and on this, using a grease pencil, he proceeded to edit the copy, explaining at the same time what he was doing and why. "I can do this," he said in an early interview, with a note of lingering incredulity in his voice, "not just for one student who sits beside me at my office desk but for hundreds of students at the same time."

With the help of an artist, he experimented with multicolored transparencies. Now the passive verbs in a chosen passage appeared in a vivid color, the active verbs in another color, the pronouns in still another. He added animating devices, and now the passive verbs appeared in a flashing color, and adjective blinked on and off, a comma wiggled its tail. He coined a phrase for the editing and writing he had developed: word processing, a term that would take on a different meaning in the age of the computer.

Peterson estimated that his students learned almost twice as fast as they had learned previously in his classes. "I am amazed," he said, "to find that I never once had to call the class to attention. In this generation there is a kind of sanctity about a screen. These young people believe that as long as there is anything up there on that screen, they've got to look at it."

Stories were told and articles written about the Peterson method. High school and college teachers came to study his class work, and colleges coast to coast invited him to demonstrate his technique for them. The U.S. Office of Education gave him a $22,839 grant for teaching his visual method to other college people. Science Research Associates of Chicago packaged and marketed the Peterson method in twenty-four books containing 510 multicolored transparencies, good for two full semesters, accompanied by an instructor's guide with each book and student manuals containing exercises and assignments.

After Peterson's retirement in 1967 interest began

---

*It has been said over and over, in Pitt publications and elsewhere, that Gladys Schmitt (Class of 1931), author of *David the King* and eight other novels, was a Peterson student. She was not, a fact stated to the author in the 1960s by both Peterson and Schmitt.

to wane. In 1971, under the pressure of greatly increased enrollment and a trend to "curriculum reform," freshman English composition was discontinued as a compulsory course. There was a successful revival of creative writing courses in the University in the late 1970s and early 1980s, but not with the Peterson method. In 1981 his beloved "magic lanterns," his overhead projectors, were stacked in a storeroom in the Cathedral of Learning. An instructor with an office on that floor, chancing to see them, wondered what they had been used for. A custodian had asked him, "What do you want me to do with these? We need the space."

In assessing Fitzgerald's ten-year record, one must examine his conduct during a strange period of academic history: the Time of the Loyalty Oath.

In Washington and in the state capitol in Harrisburg, certain legislators were alarmed at Communist advances in Europe and Asia, frightened by the unexpected development of Soviet nuclear weapons, and shocked by revelations of Communist conspiracy and espionage. Inspired by the public attention being given to Senator Joseph R. McCarthy, they decided that members of the academic community should be given the opportunity to express their loyalty to country and constitution by swearing an oath that they were not subversives.

A leader of the movement in Pennsylvania was Senator Albert R. Pechan of Ford City, assistant Republican floor leader, author of Senate Bill Number 27, Session of 1951. His bill would decree that all those persons in the employ of any school that received state aid should make a written statement under oath or affirmation that they did not advocate the overthrow of the government of the United States or of the Commonwealth by force or violence and that they were not and would not become members of any organization that advocated such an overthrow. In making the statement, they were subject to the penalties of perjury and to immediate dismissal if they refused to take the oath. The state attorney general would have the power to decide what organizations were subversive and would hear the appeals of those persons who were

discharged from their positions. The bill had passed the Senate 42 to 7 and would next be taken up by the House.

The heads of Pennsylvania's four state-aided universities—Milton S. Eisenhower of Penn State, Harold E. Stassen of Penn, Robert E. Johnson of Temple, and Rufus H. Fitzgerald of Pitt—had met some months earlier in Stassen's home in Philadelphia and agreed to work to defeat Pechan's bill. They were supported in their stand by the heads and faculties of other Pennsylvania colleges and universities not affected by the bill, including Carnegie Tech, Bryn Mawr, Haverford, and the Pennsylvania College for Women (Chatham College). There seemed little chance, however, that the bill could be defeated or sidetracked, for the pressure on assemblymen from veterans and patriotic groups to pass it, and from much of the press, was intense. (Two of the three daily papers in Pittsburgh favored the bill.)

As a second recourse, the heads of the four universities hoped to modify the bill into something they and their faculty could accept. To accomplish this, they agreed to offer the legislators a compromise. They would accept the oath that the Commonwealth already required of all its legislators and all judicial, state, and county officers: to support and defend the constitutions of the Commonwealth and of the United States. Charles Nutting, dean of the Pitt Law School, and Stanton C. Crawford, dean of the College of Arts and Sciences, conducted meetings of faculty and administrative personnel of thirteen schools and departments. Of the 1,265 persons eligible to vote on the issue, 1,159 voted in favor of accepting a lesser evil in order to avoid an intolerable indignity.

In his testimony before the legislative committee, Fitzgerald made three strong points.

• State-aided educational institutions were prohibited from employing persons who advocated subversive doctrines by a Commonwealth law passed in 1941. Senate Bill 27, therefore, was redundant and unnecessary, since ample legal authority for preventing subversive activity already existed.

• The real purpose of the bill was to require the dismissal of persons belonging to or affiliated with organizations declared by the attorney general to be subversive. The wide discretion vested in him would make it possible for him to exercise control over research and teaching in universities. If this power were improperly exercised, it would do irreparable damage to higher education in the Commonwealth. (Fitzgerald put it more strongly in a public statement: "Individual attorneys-general might have the power to destroy basic freedoms which all Americans prize. The bill goes far beyond a loyalty oath and has a dangerous tendency to give to an administrative official power of definition amounting to thought control.")

• In states that had adopted loyalty oath bills, notably in California, institutions had experienced serious losses in personnel and in academic standing, and highly competent educators of unquestioned loyalty had left the institutions and gone to other states. The morale of the faculty who stayed could suffer, since they might fear the loss of their positions if they engaged in the explanation of political, social, and economic subjects.

His faculty members, Fitzgerald said, were in accord with the desire to prevent the spread of Communism everywhere, including institutions of higher learning. The faculty of his nine schools had stated their willingness to subscribe to an oath to support and defend the constitutions of the United States and of the Commonwealth.

It was a tempestuous and sometimes confusing period. A *Post-Gazette* editorial called the Pechan bill "more a symptom of our frenzied times than a reasoned safeguard against subversives." The state legislature, which had excoriated Chancellor Bowman in 1932 for his illiberality in imposing a loyalty oath on his students, was now demanding that his successor impose a loyalty oath on his faculty. The editor of the *Pitt News* wrote a letter to the editor of the *Pittsburgh Press* demanding that he apologize to the chancellor for the "sneering tone" used in a *Press* editorial entitled "Rufus Says ——." Louis Budenz, former editor of the Communist *Daily Worker* but now reborn, published an article in the *American Legion Magazine* in which he supported the Pechan bill and attacked the record of a Pitt professor who had departed a year earlier to take a position at

another college. A Penn State employee, a marine officer in World War I and a member of the American Legion, who was in charge of the layout and production of the college's publications, refused to sign a questionnaire about his loyalty and made President Milton Eisenhower discharge him and start a test case of his right to do so. Senator Pechan declared that the fight against his bill was being engineered by Communists and subversive elements. Robert E. Woodside, state attorney general, said he did not seek and did not desire the power to list subversive organizations, nor did he wish to sit in judgment in the appeals of those discharged from their jobs; his office was not equipped for such work. A dean of a graduate school in an address to the annual Phi Beta Kappa dinner declared that the teaching profession was insulted and hurt at being singled out to be watched specially and checked periodically; he asked why loyalty oaths did not apply to radio commentators, ministers, bank presidents, members of school boards, and university trustees. The four heads of the state-aided institutions spent much of their time telephoning each other and exchanging resolutions passed by their faculties.

The Pechan bill passed the House, was signed by Governor Fine, and became law, but in a much-altered form. The educators opposing it succeeded at the last moment in making deletions and adding amendments that rendered it a somewhat less offensive bill. The attorney general was not given the right to name organizations that he considered subversive, and the faculty members of the four state-aided universities were not required actually to sign a loyalty oath. Instead, each university was required to send to the governor an annual statement of compliance setting forth what procedures it had adopted to determine the presence of any subversive person and what steps it would take to terminate his or her employment. The four presidents conferred and agreed that since the bill was now law, it must be complied with. Compliance consisted of the dean or head of each school or department sending to the chancellor a statement that to the best of his knowledge there were no subversive persons responsible to him. These statements were then

Commencement on the lawn between the east entrance to the Cathedral of Learning and Heinz Chapel, June 1955.

sent to the governor. This time-consuming, paper-mounting procedure continued well into the administration of Fitzgerald's successor. Senator Pechan in the 1960s expressed regret to at least one academician for having sponsored the bill, and in 1965 he proved to be a staunch and useful supporter of the University when it needed help. The state Department of Justice declared the act unconstitutional on January 11, 1975.

The trustees on June 23, 1955, gave a farewell dinner for Chancellor Fitzgerald. More than 400 close friends and associates gathered in the Commons Room to honor him for his work over the preceding eighteen years, ten of them as chancellor.

Among those present was Leon Falk, Jr., who at Fitzgerald's suggestion had been chosen to head a committee of trustees to find a new chancellor. The committee, appointed on October 7, 1954, had expressed the hope publicly that it would make a recommendation by the end of the 1953–1954 academic year, but the hope had been overly optimistic. Charles Nutting, dean of the Law School, agreed to serve as acting chancellor until a successor was named. The search committee would work with an administrative committee headed by Stanton Crawford and a faculty committee headed by George W. Crouch, chairman of the English department and secretary of the University Senate. The three groups had industriously exchanged letters setting forth the main qualities they were looking for in the new chancellor. ("Age under 55. Rugged physical and nervous health. Known ability in raising large sums of money and in managing them. Preferably an earned doctor's degree. An entrée to the circles of social, business, and industrial leadership, local and national. A wife able to carry her share of the position. Recognized executive skill, including tact [and, in an obvious reference to Fitzgerald,] good judgment in selecting persons to share administrative responsibility, and willingness to delegate responsibility."

The searchers had looked to the Cresap, McCormick and Paget *Survey* for guidance, and they took seriously its warning: Questions must be asked and resolved. Should this continue to be essentially a university for the city of Pittsburgh, or should it seek actively to recruit students from other parts of the country? What should be its enrollment goals? Should greater or less emphasis be placed on the graduate program? And the committees were inspired by the survey's enthusiasm about the future. "The University of Pittsburgh," it said,

has reached a point in its development where it is about to undergo extensive growth in measuring up to the opportunities before it. . . . the University possesses an unusual opportunity to develop further as an outstanding institution of higher education. The exceptional character of the opportunity springs largely from the University's location in a community anxious to improve its position as a center of industry, business and culture.

In civic development and improvement, Pittsburgh is pressing enthusiastically in all directions. Its redevelopment program of the past decade has produced outstanding civic improvements. The citizens of the community and the leaders of its industry have indicated that they are willing and able to provide necessary support for development of Pittsburgh and its university.

Book IV
1956-1965

We stand today on the edge of a new frontier—the frontier of the 1960s, a frontier of unknown opportunities and perils, a frontier of unfulfilled hopes and threats.

John F. Kennedy
July 1960

18
The Twelfth Chancellor

This is a very far-reaching proposal. Indeed, I would suspect that it has not been paralleled either in this country, or perhaps, in the world, since the great period of development at the University of Chicago.

Edward H. Litchfield to Alan Magee Scaife, June 1, 1955

IN the early summer of 1954, the dean of the Graduate School of Business and Public Administration at Cornell University called on J. Steele Gow in the offices of the Maurice and Laura Falk Foundation. His name was Edward Harold Litchfield, and he asked Gow for a grant to pay the cost of publishing a book titled *America Votes: A Handbook of Contemporary American Election Statistics*. His presentation was so striking that Gow asked Litchfield to submit the proposal in writing. "I was afraid I was being mesmerized by the man," he said. A day or so later the document was on his desk. "It was a strange experience. I found that as soon as a question popped into my mind, the answer would come along a paragraph or two later. It was the most complete and effective presentation we have ever had." Gow had only moderate interest in a study on election statistics, but as the right-hand man of Leon Falk, the chairman of the committee searching for a new chancellor, he was very much interested in the person who proposed it.

On October 19, 1954, Gow sent two letters to Litchfield in Ithaca. In one he turned down the request for a grant, using the phrases of foundation executives everywhere to explain that earlier commitments must have prior claims on the foundation's resources. In the other letter he wrote:

When I was asked recently to submit a list of persons I would suggest for consideration for the chancellorship of the University of Pittsburgh, I took the liberty of including your name in the list. In the past few days I have learned that the University's trustees are now making a preliminary review of some fifty persons. . . . It may have been an undue liberty on my part to submit your name without your knowledge but I felt it was best that way. Only the trustees and I know that I have sent in your name. I shall be grateful if you will, therefore, hold the information in the strictest confidence.

Litchfield answered five days later. He deeply regretted that the foundation board had not looked favorably on his proposal. He would try elsewhere—perhaps it was all for the best—and let Mr. Gow know what developed. "It was kind of you to think of me in connection with the chancellorship. . . . To be considered would be flattering but I am more pleased that you felt you could make the suggestion."

Following more correspondence, Litchfield agreed, "purely as a matter of courtesy," to go to Pittsburgh for preliminary discussions. As Gow expected, the committee members—especially Alan Scaife and Leon Falk—were favorably impressed. "When we met him," Falk says, "we could see that he had everything we wanted: contact with business, experience in administration and government. Pittsburgh is an industrial city and the chancellor has to meet with the leaders of business here. Litchfield fit any blueprint you could find." Said Peter Gray, professor of biology and a member of the faculty committee, "Litchfield arrived with a strong recommendation from Gow. We met him and were enchanted."

On April 19, 1955, Litchfield sent two letters to Pittsburgh. To Leon Falk he wrote: "After the most careful consideration I must ask that you give no further consideration to me as a candidate for the chancellorship of the University of Pittsburgh." Two circumstances, he said, made the request unavoidable. One was Mrs. Litchfield's health, which was such that he did not feel that he could assume the responsibility of the position in a fashion that would meet either the University's needs or his own standards.* And he owed Cornell more than he had yet provided. The president and the trustees had supported him generously, and he felt a deep obligation to lay "a clear foundation" for his school's program before departing. To Steele Gow he expressed his thanks for "a very great honor and a mark of personal confidence which I shall never forget" and his regret at being forced to turn down an opportunity such as he might never again have.

Falk, Scaife, and Gow saw in Litchfield's letter an invitation to continue negotiations. They and their colleagues on the two search committees were apparently willing to delay the assumption of the chancellorship until July 1, 1956, at which time Litchfield's wife's health might no longer be a prob-

---

*Anne Muir Macintyre Litchfield was afflicted with cancer of the spine, a terminal illness. She was paralyzed from the waist down.

As chairman of the Board of Trustees until his untimely death in July 1958, Alan M. Scaife worked closely with Litchfield.

Leon Falk, Jr., now trustee emeritus, served on the University's board from 1931 to 1974. He established Falk Clinic and the Falk Library of the Health Professions.

lem and he would have discharged his obligation to Cornell. In any case, the sequence and content of the exchange of letters that followed are important in their relationship to problems that arose and questions that were asked ten years later.

June 1. Following another visit and meetings in Pittsburgh, Litchfield wrote a 1,500-word letter to Scaife (a copy going to Falk) in which he set forth his "understanding of [their] discussions." It appears today as a formal statement for the Board of Trustees, almost a warning, about the resources the University would need to reach the goals set forth by Scaife, Falk, and Gow, and what they might expect of Litchfield if he became their chancellor.

If he interpreted their conversations correctly, Litchfield wrote, Mr. Scaife, Mr. Falk, and their fel-low trustees hoped to make their institution into one of the nation's outstanding universities. With this in mind, they intended to continue the present development in the health sciences, to improve substantially the academic program in the other professional areas, and to upgrade the University's work in the basic disciplines comprising the social sciences, the physical sciences, and the humanities. In each instance, the development was to include both undergraduate and graduate work.

Litchfield believed further that they agreed that this broad objective would require strengthening of the financial structure, including a raise in tuition and "additional endowment of from ninety to one hundred million dollars." The roles of the trustees, the chancellor and his staff, and the faculty should be clearly defined. He visualized the Board of Trustees functioning in much the manner of the board of directors of a well-managed corporation. He closed his letter: "One seldom has the opportunity to contemplate the horizons which your objective suggests. Whatever the outcome of our discussions, I want you to know that it has been a great personal pleasure and professional privilege to explore these dimensions with you."

June 3. Scaife told Litchfield that he had read his letter and that his first impression was exceedingly favorable. He would confer with Mr. Falk "in an effort to determine the best way in which such a comprehensive program might be 'sold' to the trustees."

June 7. In his reply to Scaife, Litchfield wrote: "I do hope that we are agreed that the 'comprehensive program' of which you speak is not my proposal to you, but rather my understanding of what you and Mr. Falk and others had said represented your objectives. At this point it does seem to me quite important that your colleagues understand that I am not making a proposal, for my knowledge of the situation would not warrant my preparing such a suggestion for you." He enclosed a press release he had written at Mr. Falk's request on the University's plans for improvement and expansion. He also enclosed "a brief outline of the immediate policy issues which are brought out by our conversations." In the statement on policy he made these main points:

● The city of Pittsburgh and the whole Western Pennsylvania–Eastern Ohio region was clearly in need of a cultural center that the smaller and more specialized educational institutions could not provide. Hence, the University of Pittsburgh had both the opportunity and the responsibility of providing that focal point.

● A genuinely top-ranking university could not be built around a purely regional concept. It would be difficult to obtain the high-quality standards that the trustees had in mind unless the sights of the University were national and worldwide in scope.

● There was a tremendous opportunity in this country for a top-ranking university with new and uncommitted funds to make a great national contribution and to develop a worldwide concept of service and a worldwide reputation.

● The program's most fundamental issue related to the growth of the disciplines that comprised the social sciences, humanities, and natural sciences. In many cases, the present offering appeared to be below the high-quality standards that would be required and that the trustees had in mind. Certainly the faculty was understaffed and underpaid in many of these areas.

● "We should see the University as an integrated whole, with the basic disciplines closely related to the professional fields. We must not see the University as a collection of fragmented colleges brought together largely for purposes of administrative convenience. In this respect, Pittsburgh has a tremendous opportunity to demonstrate to the country and to the world that it is possible to construct a university in the fullest sense of the term, that is, one which seeks all knowledge and sees knowledge as a whole or as a universal thing."

June 10. Scaife informed the trustees that the search committees were now ready to nominate a chancellor. He enclosed Litchfield's memorandum on plans and policies, asking each trustee to study it in advance of the annual meeting on June 14.

June 14. Leon Falk reported at length to the trustees on the work of the committees and on their choice of a nominee. He distributed and read aloud a series of resolutions setting forth the basic objectives of the University, as written by Litchfield, and moved that they be adopted. Following a discussion, the trustees unanimously approved the resolutions.

Scaife wrote to Litchfield after the meeting: "Everything went off very smoothly. Leon Falk made a splendid presentation of a policy statement that was adopted by the Board of Trustees after full discussion."

June 17. The University News Service released a four-page announcement revealing plans for a ten-year program of educational development: "This is the first and basic step," Dr. Scaife said, "in a program to make Pitt one of the world's foremost universities. We are fully aware of all that this will require and we intend to provide it. . . . It is perfectly clear to both the Board and the faculties that we must provide resources as ample as our purpose." He went on to note that the program would involve "many millions of dollars over the next decade."

The press release contained two pages of "interpretation" based on extracts from Litchfield's letters and documents. (His name and the announcement of his nomination as chancellor were withheld.) A reporter who interviewed faculty members after they had read the release posted on the faculty club bulletin board declared that they were "electrified."

June 29. Scaife wrote a formal statement of the terms of Litchfield's employment as chancellor. He was to receive a salary of $40,000 a year. He was to have the use of the chancellor's residence, the former William Penn Snyder, Jr., house at 651 Morewood Avenue, which would be remodeled and furnished by the University. (He later found it too small.) He was to have an expense account not to exceed $10,000 a year for "entertainment, etc." He would, in addition, be reimbursed for normal traveling expenses incurred in discharging his duties as chancellor. He would be supplied with a car and a chauffeur. On his retirement at age sixty-five he would receive a lifetime pension of 50 percent of his salary.

July 18. The announcement of the election of Edward Harold Litchfield as twelfth chancellor of the University of Pittsburgh was made at a press conference held in the Duquesne Club. The chancellor-elect stood between Alan Scaife and Leon Falk. In his introduction Scaife said: "Dr. Litchfield has been named chancellor at a critically important time in the University's history. We have completed ten years of unprecedented development under the leadership of Dr. Fitzgerald. Now the trustees have set forth new goals, which, when realized, will place the University of Pittsburgh among the leaders of the world's great universities."

Richard King Mellon rose to express his approval. "Dr. Litchfield," he said, "will bring to Pittsburgh experience in and understanding of the partnership of education, business, and government which is so essential to success in our modern society. His election underscores our belief that the University of Pittsburgh must undertake the role of building a great cultural and educational center for the region, a center without which no industrial city can become and remain great."

The announcement received national attention, and in succeeding months a dozen magazines wrote articles on Litchfield, including *Time* ("Dynamo at Pitt"), *Newsweek* ("Business in Education"), *Saturday Evening Post* ("$100,000,000 to Work With"), and *Fortune* ("The All-Purpose Executive"). People in Pittsburgh and elsewhere were curious about this meteoric young man—who he was, where he came from, what he stood for, what he had done, how he operated.

EDWARD HAROLD LITCHFIELD
Curriculum Vitae, July 18, 1955

Date of birth
April 12, 1914
Place of birth
Detroit, Michigan
Height
Five feet nine inches
Weight
180 pounds
Father
Adelbert Leigh Litchfield. Subject says that to the best of his knowledge, the small Litchfield clan is all descended from Lawrence Litchfield, who migrated from England to Massachusetts in 1632
Father's occupation
Employee of U.S. Postal Service, Detroit
Mother
Ethel Blanch McKim Litchfield, born in Canada
Subject's religion
Protestant
Political affiliation
None
Elementary schooling
Detroit public school
Secondary schooling
Northwest High School, Detroit, 1928–1932
High school activities
Class president; editor of the yearbook; overcame a speech impediment and became a member of the debating team
College
University of Michigan, 1932–1936, B.A. degree in political science

Edward Harold Litchfield, chancellor from 1956 to 1965.

Pittsburgh Press

College activities

Made the varsity debating team in freshman year. Was a member of the team that won the Big Ten debating championship in 1936. Won a national intercollegiate public-speaking championship in that year. Winner of the William Jennings Bryan Award. On graduating, ran for the Michigan State Senate in the Democratic primary, finished seventh in a field of eleven

Postgraduate work

University of Michigan, 1936–1940, as a Carl Braun Fellow in political science and public administration. Ph.D. 1940. Dissertation: *Voting Behavior in a Metropolitan Community* (Detroit)

Military service

None

Marital status

A first marriage of short duration. Second wife, married on September 11, 1940, Anne Muir Macintyre, who was born in Glasgow of a family of shipbuilders. Came to the United States as a child. She was for a time an instructor in history at Michigan State University

Children

Peter Macintyre, 14; Janet Macintyre, 12; Anne Roberta, 8

Hobbies

Sandlot baseball on the semiprofessional level (payment of nine dollars per game); flying private plane; spectator sports, especially track meets

Publications

Governing Post War Germany (editor), 1953; several small volumes published by the University of Michigan Press on political parties and public administration; articles on general governmental subjects in *National Municipal Review, Public Personnel Review, American Political Science Review,* and *Public Opinion Quarterly*

Employment record

1937–1938: Helped to write the Michigan civil service law and, while taking postgraduate work, served as executive secretary of the Michigan Merit System Association, a citizens' group that protected the law from political attack by having it written as an amendment to the Michigan constitution

1940–1941: Instructor in political science at Brown University

1941: Personnel training specialist with the Panama Canal civilian administration

1942–1945: Lecturer in public administration at the University of Michigan; deputy director of the Michigan State Civil Service Commission

November 1945–October 1949: Served with the U.S. Office of Military Government for Germany successively as chief of the Governmental Structures Branch of the Civil Administration Division, with responsibility for establishing and maintaining a democratic and administratively adequate structure in all levels of German government in the American Zone; as deputy director and then director of the Civil Administration Division; and as advisor to General Lucius DuB. Clay, U.S. military governor

1950–1953: Was concurrently executive director of the American Political Science Association; founder and president of the nonprofit Governmental Affairs Institute in Washington; and visiting professor and then professor of administration at the Cornell University School of Business and Public Administration. Became dean of the school in 1953. Converted it into a graduate school, doubled the size of both faculty and student body, and made it self-supporting

When Litchfield became dean of the School of Business and Public Administration, he brought to the job his own concept of what administration meant. "Administration and the administrative process," he said, "occur in substantially the same generalized form in industrial, commercial, civil, educational, military, and hospital organizations. Administration, therefore, should be looked upon as a profession as such. A person who competently manages a corporation should be able to make the change easily to a university, and vice versa."

One may assume that the author of this radical and controversial principle based it in some degree on his own successful careers in disparate fields. He had been a civil servant, a teacher, an executive director of a professional society, and had held a high civilian post in Occupied West Germany. He was now at once a teacher and the dean of a graduate school at Cornell; founder and chief executive officer of a flourishing research and service corporation in Washington; and the next chancellor of the University of Pittsburgh. He had lately become an active member of the boards of directors of two major industrial corporations. One was Victor

Emmanuel's Avco Manufacturing Corporation, an early industrial conglomerate. The other was Smith-Corona (later Smith-Corona-Marchant), maker of business machines, which he was advising in a reorganization of the company and in its defense against an attempted takeover in a proxy fight.

Edward H. Litchfield in the spring of 1955 was obviously a man on the way up. Those who wondered about his decision to accept the post at the University of Pittsburgh assumed that he would do an outstanding job there and in perhaps five years—when he was forty-six—would move on and up to a high elective or appointive office as a senator, a governor, a cabinet officer, and possibly even higher. Or, if he so chose, to the presidency of one of the major corporations. This seemed to be the destiny of a leading authority on administration, as demonstrated in principle and performance and in public and private enterprise. The more so when the person had an unusual capacity for long hours of hard work.

In giving the reasons for taking the new post, Litchfield cited the advice of his friend Lucius Clay, who told him, "You have no choice." And of his wife, Anne, who, though gravely ill, urged him to sell their house in Ithaca and move to Pittsburgh. He was fond of quoting Jonas Salk, who had called Pittsburgh "the last frontier east of the Mississippi." "Nobody," Litchfield said, "ever had such an opportunity in all educational history." Pitt was made to order for an expert in administration, for it was then what one Pitt professor called the most under-administered institution in American education. As soon as Pitt's administrative, physical, and intellectual metamorphosis was firmly on course, he told friends, he might move on.

After the announcement of his election, Litchfield began to work one day a week at the University and to spend time at his McGraw Hall office at Cornell drawing up a new organizational structure and recruiting an administrative staff for the new post. He first appeared before a large audience in Pittsburgh on September 12, 1955, when he spoke at the annual dinner of the Allegheny Conference on Community Development (ACCD). This was the organization of business executives that Richard K. Mellon had conceived, created, and subsidized to chart and direct the course of the Pittsburgh renaissance. The dinner was held, as always, in the elegant foyer of the Carnegie Music Hall, with more than 400 people present. Among them were ACCD officers and University trustees, some of whom were both. Litchfield delivered a major address in a serious manner on an important subject. He took the opportunity to state what he had been asked to do at the University and how he intended to do it and to disclose how much it would cost. His speaking style was a revelation to that audience, for he had the diction and timing of a trained lecturer and a voice of uncommon clarity, resonance, and persuasiveness.

The trustees, he said, had recently announced the goal of upgrading the University of Pittsburgh into one of the foremost universities in the world. "Eight of the better American institutions of learning spend an average of $2,761 per year per student. Pitt spends an average of $1,560—some $1,200 less." Multiply that $1,200 by the school's 10,000 students, he said, and you have an annual cost of $12 million.

To excel other schools in teaching and research, the University should henceforth admit only those students who were capable of higher education. Of the present crop of students at Pitt, he said, some were not qualified and should not be there, while some others who were not there should be there by reason of superior ability. The answer was to raise the University's entrance requirements so that only the most capable students would be admitted, and at the same time to expand the scholarship and fellowship programs so that competent students need not be turned away because of lack of money. Dormitories should be built so that in its search for brilliant students, the University need not be confined to area residents.

To pay top salaries to teachers and administrators and to take all the other steps that would be needed to raise Pitt to the desired preeminence would require an additional investment of $125 million over the next ten years—$25 million more than the trustees had originally suggested.

It is said that there was some muttering at Litchfield's proposed denial of admission to inferior students at home while recruiting better students from other regions. According to one report, the trustees were not at all dismayed by Litchfield's estimate of cost. They didn't even blink at the figure. According to another report, the ACCD audience was stunned at hearing the price of attaining preeminence.

Litchfield's first address following the ACCD dinner was a full-scale formal presentation on December 13 to the trustees assembled in the chancellor's office in the Cathedral of Learning. Twenty-four trustees and four top administrators were present. Trustee Richard Mellon, who doubtless would have been interested in the figure given for the cost of the program, unfortunately could not be present.

In a step-by-step progression and with the aid of charts thrown on a screen, the chancellor outlined the factors involved in the announced intention of the board to make the University a top-ranking institution. He listed six outstanding needs, and he showed what it would cost to meet the trustees' goal. Pitt, he said, would have to establish academic standards comparable to those then existing at California, Chicago, Columbia, Cornell, Harvard, Michigan, Princeton, and Yale. To do that would require an additional annual expenditure of $10 million.

In visualizing the possible sources of that new income, Litchfield showed $3.5 million coming from increased tuition; $1 million from increased legislative appropriation; $500,000 from increased alumni and other annual gifts; and $5 million as income from increased endowment. The endowment, he hoped, would be raised to $125 million, which at 4 percent per year would yield the $5 million in income.

But the University, Dr. Litchfield pointed out, could not attain the desired improvement in quality of instruction and at the same time try to absorb the prospective pressures of increased enrollment. He called upon Harbaugh Miller, trustee, chairman of the Committee on Curriculum and Faculty, to speak on this issue.

Mr. Miller said he had reviewed the situation with Dr. Litchfield and was heartily in accord with his views. He moved a resolution: that the chancellor be requested to apply new financial support to the improvement of the University's educational offering rather than to increasing enrollment.

The question was put to the board and was adopted with a unanimous vote, and thus the program Litchfield had announced to the ACCD on September 12 was legitimized. Scaife said that it was one of the most important actions ever taken by the board. The vote, however, was one of general endorsement of intentions and goals. There was no specific approval of any of the various dollar amounts that were being cited as necessary to raise the endowment from $29 million to $90 million, or to $100 million, or to $125 million, which would help to provide "an additional annual expenditure of $10 million," or of $12 million, or "$100 million to work with," or "many millions of dollars over the next ten years." There was no target date for producing the money, no date for beginning a campaign, no fixed responsibility for conducting it.

The trustees made two other important decisions at the December 13 meeting: to raise academic salaries and to approve a general reorganization of structure recommended by the new chancellor. The following day Scaife wrote to Litchfield, "This is just a line to tell you how thrilled I was at your presentation of the problems with which Pitt is confronted. In my long experience on the Board of Directors I never saw a group so enthusiastically aroused as they were during the meeting. We are proud to have you with us."

In the six months remaining before he took office, Litchfield made trips to the city to speak before each of the other "publics" of his constituency: the alumni, the faculty, and the students. His wife died on January 7 in a New York City hospital and was buried in Ithaca. He set off alone on an extended cruise in the Caribbean and thereafter came to Pittsburgh more often, driving himself harder and frequently working beyond his normal eighty-hour week. At his request, Helen Pool Rush, dean of women, helped him to find a live-in housemother to run his new household in Pittsburgh. (His son, Peter, was at the George School, a Quaker institution in Bucks County; his two daughters were registered for the 1956–1957 term at the Ellis School in Pittsburgh.)

To the Century Club, an association of alumni who have given at least $100 that year to the University and who meet annually at a dinner on Charter Day, he delivered an address televised by WQED. He was careful on this occasion not to express dissatisfaction with the past, "for, while I am a newcomer I share as jealously as you do the pride in what the University has been in the past." It was high time, he said, "that this country had another great university that will compete with and . . . push aside some of those who for so long have claimed the position of America's most distinctive and best-quality institutions." He said that faculty salaries should be raised, but he spoke emphatically on the need to improve the quality of personnel where it was not as high as the new role of the University required.

Leland Hazard, a corporate lawyer known as the intellectual spokesman of the renaissance, the next day wrote Litchfield a letter in which he commented on their pleasant conversation at the speakers' table, complimented him on the clarity with which he expressed creative concepts, and cautioned him: "You probably frightened rather badly both good and bad faculty by the declaration of intent to weed out the bad. Of course you have to do that, but many sensitive and effective people do not really have any inner assurance as to whether they are good or bad." Litchfield replied that he realized he was touching on a sensitive point but he hoped to keep the process in proper balance.

Addressing the assembled faculties publicly for the first time, speaking at considerable length in the auditorium of the Stephen Foster Memorial, Litchfield spelled out a three-part salary program "designed to put Pittsburgh in a position to compete nationally for the best minds in higher education." The present salaries "can be defined as being from quite low to incredibly low. And of all the disciplines, the humanities, as usual, suffer the most." With the approval of the Board of Trustees, who agreed "with considerable enthusiasm—and I want to stress that—considerable enthusiasm, because the Board feels this problem critically," he revealed that all faculty members would receive a flat 10 per-

cent salary increase retroactive to February 1. Another $75,000 was being allocated for additional salary increases to encourage and recognize outstanding attainment; and within five years, finances permitting, faculty salary scales in each of the University's schools would be brought up to a par with salaries in the best universities. The trustees had instructed him to do this within five years, but he hoped to do it in three, because he knew that "a great university is measured by the calibre and by the morale of its faculty."

The trustees were aware, he told the faculty, that accomplishing the directive they had given him might require raising as much as $100 million in the next ten years, "in order to win for the University a distinctive national role in meeting the contemporary problems of our society." He described Pittsburgh as one of the few universities that were working in close relationship with the communities in which they served.

The chancellor was given a standing ovation. Putnam F. Jones, dean of the College, acting dean of the graduate school, and professor of English, declared, "That was a wonderful speech—a statement that will simply put us on fire to carry the University to the point where the chancellor and trustees agree it should go. It is wonderfully stimulating and a clear-cut call to our destiny."

In the course of recruiting his new administrative staff, Litchfield wrote on March 31, 1956, to Albert C. Van Dusen, vice president of Northwestern University, Evanston, Illinois, and asked him to become his assistant chancellor in charge of planning and development. The trustees, he said, concluded a year ago "that they wished to build the University into a genuinely distinguished institution. . . . At the same time, they committed themselves to a very substantial change in the amount of financial support available for the new program. When I was invited to come as chancellor, they spoke confidently of new endowment in the amount of better than one hundred million dollars. Since the Board includes Leon Falk, Richard Mellon and Alan Scaife, as well as presidents and board chairmen of Westinghouse, Pittsburgh Plate Glass and similar organizations, it was apparent that this was not idle conversation."

19

Toward Higher Ground

His ambition has proved contagious. "Ever since he came," says one facultyman, "the university has been in a ferment. There is a terrific amount of soul-searching going on."

"Dynamo at Pitt," *Time*, January 7, 1957

FROM the day he took office as chancellor on July 1, 1956, Edward Litchfield's overriding problem was time: how to find enough of it to do all he had to do and to be where he had to be on a given working day. His second problem was to divide his working time equitably among the different positions he held. He developed a pattern in which he gave about 70 percent of his time to Pitt. Fifteen percent he gave to the affairs of Smith-Corona in Syracuse, Avco in New York, and still another large company of which he had become a director and member of the Executive Committee, Studebaker-Packard in South Bend, Indiana. He gave 10 percent to the Governmental Affairs Institute in Washington and the remaining 5 percent to several charitable and welfare foundations of which he was an unpaid director. *Fortune* magazine in 1958 estimated his annual earned income from these occupations at $90,000 "in cash and in kind."

On August 28, shortly before the start of his first fall term, he departed on a sixteen-day trip abroad. He went to Geneva to attend the annual meeting of the Board of Governors of the International Political Science Association, and thence to Teheran, where he prepared for a general study on the reorganization of the government of Iran being undertaken by the Governmental Affairs Institute. A day or two after his return he accepted the post of chairman of the board of Smith-Corona. At this point Scaife, Falk, and Gow expressed some uneasy concern about the time and talent Litchfield was devoting to activities other than those taking place on the Pitt campus. Litchfield wrote to Scaife on October 3 "about something which I think is troubling us both."

I was prompted to do this by a call from Steele Gow, who had apparently talked to you this afternoon. As we both know, Steele has the University's interest at heart above everything else, and I am therefore most grateful that he was kind enough to call this matter to my attention. It concerns my Smith-Corona board chairmanship immediately and my outside interests more generally. . . .

I regard this question as a matter of principle, and I know that you must regard it as a matter of grave consequence as well. Permit me, therefore, to set forth my views on the matter with the utmost candor, for if I have misun-

derstood the situation, or if we are in clear disagreement in principle I think it best we know it now rather than to drift into further difficulties. I much prefer to deal with these matters in absolute frankness, regardless of their consequence.

He argued that business affairs "are just as important [as], if indeed not more important than, public service undertakings." In any event, he had asked Mr. Scaife and Mr. Gow during their early discussions if he might retain his business connections, and they had assured him that he could do so. ("Frankly," he wrote, "I would not have come had the answer been in the negative.") He had, moreover, discussed the desirability of his taking the Smith-Corona chairmanship. Mr. Scaife had said that the post was suitable, since it was not an executive position, but that it would be best not to give it extensive publicity. Mr. Falk felt it would be better if Dr. Litchfield did not accept the position but said his opinion was a suggestion only and that Dr. Litchfield must make his own decision. Other university presidents he had consulted, Litchfield said, and his own colleagues on campus, felt that his acceptance of the position would be helpful to the University. He also pointed out that he had resigned from more than half of his editorial boards, officerships in professional organizations, and similar appointments.

Litchfield ended his letter with a blunt statement that may have made Scaife and Falk reflect on the strong will of the man they had sponsored for the chancellorship:

Finally, may I say that I cannot remain at the University of Pittsburgh unless I am judged in terms of the results I obtain. The hours which I may work and the methods which I employ, I feel are mine. If I am ever derelict in my responsibilities I would wish to know about the dereliction. If you ever feel that we are not moving forward, I hope you will tell me. I assume complete responsibility for any failures which this administration may produce. But I think you will agree that I must find my own ways of pursuing our objectives. One of these includes the allocation of my own time.

The issue was dropped, although the chancellor's outside activities and frequent absences from campus caused an undercurrent of gossip throughout his administration. In time he consolidated his activities into something called Litchfield Associates, Inc., a Pennsylvania corporation of which he was the president, treasurer, and principal stockholder. In 1959 John Funari, Litchfield's new young administrative assistant, expressed offhand annoyance that the chancellor was not in the city to make a decision on some matter or other. Stanton Crawford, secretary of the University and more than twice Funari's age, chided him: "John, Edward Litchfield in three days at this University gives it the kind of administrative leadership that might take anyone else seven days to do."

Litchfield depended on a first-rate staff and his own administrative skills to create an operation that would run with superior efficiency whether he was present or absent. He relied heavily on Alan C. Rankin, forty-one, a faculty colleague at Cornell's graduate school and his closest friend there. He had placed Rankin on the Pitt campus late in 1955 as his executive assistant, giving him extraordinary responsibilities, including the management of his office.

By the start of 1957, the chancellor had five secretaries: one who managed the office, a receptionist and appointments secretary, a correspondence secretary, an executive assistant secretary, and a personal and social secretary. He carried a Dictet and blank belts with him on his travels and customarily dictated letters and memoranda in cars and planes.

He was considerate in bringing back presents for his staff from his trips abroad. He could be severe, as when he wrote to one of his secretaries: "One thing I expect you to do is to read incmg & outgoing mail. Here I failed to correct all of the letter & you apparently did not read it. How could you let me say I cld not see him [Henry M. Wriston] & then say I hoped to discuss meetg w. him while he was here. Why shld I catch these thgs *after* the fact. That's your job! Call him pls and say there was erro etc." He could be generous, as when he wrote a short, unsolicited letter to a former associate: "I want you to know that if at any time I can be of help to you, I should be happy, indeed, to hear from you. Never hesitate to use my name if it will be of assistance or to call on me if some more active help would be of value to you."

In answer to a letter from a boyhood friend, he wrote: "I spend rather more time traveling than I would like. I am in Syracuse, New York, and Washington every week covering my responsibilities to Smith-Corona, Studebaker, Governmental Affairs Institute and other things I am involved in. I enjoy the movement but sometimes it becomes a little overwhelming."

To cope with the movement, Litchfield decided in the autumn of 1956 to buy his first private plane. He chose a twin-engine Piper Apache that cost him $34,000, rented hangar space at the county airport, and took out blanket insurance of $150,000 on each passenger. He employed Major Leroy Smith, commander of the county's Air National Guard, as his pilot. One year later he sold the Apache and bought a Beechcraft, an all-weather Beech 65 named the Queen Air, with greater carrying capacity.

While he was establishing a manner and style of conducting routine administrative operating procedures, Litchfield was more deeply and seriously concerned with his primary missions: to improve the quality of the entire academic program and to reorganize completely the University's administrative structure. After months of study and consultation, he created a "central piloting system" of five administrative chiefs. Three of these were new assistant chancellors brought in from other campuses.

In addition to Alan Rankin as executive assistant, he retained Stanton C. Crawford as secretary of the University and dean of the faculties. Walter F. Vieh, the Cresap, McCormick and Paget partner who had conducted the management survey, became assistant chancellor for business affairs. Edison Montgomery, a member of the CMP survey team who had been an official for twelve years with the U.S. Maritime Commission in Washington and then for three years with the Office of Price Stabilization, became Vieh's program analyst, budget director, and executive assistant.

Albert C. Van Dusen, a naval aviation psychologist for four years during World War II, associate professor of psychology, a vice president and director of public relations at Northwestern University, became assistant chancellor for planning and development. Charles H. Peake, a faculty member and administrator for fourteen years at the University of Michigan, a wartime graduate (at age thirty-six) of the Infantry School at Fort Benning, assistant dean of the College of Literature, Science, and the Arts and then dean of Knox College since 1950, became assistant chancellor for student affairs. In his restructuring, Litchfield also created three academic vice chancellors: Elvis J. Stahr for the professions; Robert A. Moore, M.D., for the professional programs in medicine; and a vice chancellorship, not yet filled, for the humanities and social and natural sciences.

In this table of organization, the chancellor had only seven administrators reporting to him, as contrasted with the thirty-odd deans, department heads, and directors who had reported to Fitzgerald. Beneath Litchfield's seven were a dozen deans of schools or divisions, the presidents of the regional campuses, and various department heads and directors. The top administrators were linked by a custom-built electronic system, controlled at a walnut intercom panel with blinking buttons, that could produce instant ten-way (later fifteen-way) conferences. His seven-man administrative committee or cabinet—the vice chancellors, assistant chancellors, the executive assistant, and the secretary— met with him every Wednesday at lunch to determine Universitywide policy in both academic and administrative areas.

In the course of carrying out his commitment to achieve new salary objectives, Litchfield looked into the pensions that were being paid to retired professors, and he found instances where "substantial injustices have been done." Pensions were shockingly low in almost all colleges and universities in this country before World War II. In 1905 Andrew Carnegie had created a funded organization, the Teachers Insurance Annuity Association (TIAA), for paying pensions on a contributory basis to "decayed college professors," but the amounts paid, despite his enormous contribution to the fund, were necessarily small. They tended to be somewhat smaller at Pitt, because Samuel B. Linhart, secretary of the University for decades before his retirement

as secretary emeritus in 1936, had "turned aside" some of the professors who approached him about joining the TIAA, presumably because it would have cost the University money. Thus in 1956 a former head of the English department was receiving an annual pension of $688 and a former head of the history department was receiving $689. A veteran professor of English, the only member of the department with a Ph.D. degree in the 1920s, was told at age seventy, after thirty-five years of service, that for the twenty-one years he had served before he joined the TIAA, his supplemental annuity would net him $38.11 monthly. "This news," he said, "crushes me."

Litchfield, in an act of decency and compassion, asked Crawford to draw up a list of all pensioned faculty members and the amounts they were being paid. He asked Edison Montgomery to calculate what it would cost to bring the sixteen worst cases to within 40 percent of their salary at the time of their retirement. The required amount was $1,566.67 per month. On January 8, 1957, he persuaded the Executive Committee of the board to authorize an expenditure of $20,000 "to take care of the increased costs . . . while more permanent financing was arranged." Each of the sixteen recipients wrote moving letters of thanks. "It makes me feel," one said, "that the days of miracles are not past." Litchfield expressed regret that the payments could not be higher. As an added gesture, he increased the number and the privileges of retired faculty members who bore the title of professor emeritus or dean emeritus—a rank to be conferred only by the chancellor and never automatically. Henceforth they were to be honored by invitations to attend meetings of their departments, schools, or divisions as well as University ceremonies, and they were to have office space if they wished it.

Other changes and reforms followed in 1957.

The promised 5 percent salary increase for the academic staff (following the 10 percent increase in February 1956) was accompanied by a major increase in health and retirement benefits, group life insurance, and catastrophe medical protection.

Teaching loads were reduced in order to leave

faculty more time for research and writing.

The University Senate and the trustees adopted a new faculty tenure plan.

A Senate Council was organized to give the faculty representation on policy matters.

The Office of Cultural and Educational Exchange was organized for operation in foreign countries.

The chancellor began his program to raise the level of all the professional schools by no longer admitting undergraduates.

Faculty research carrels were opened in Dithridge House to be used until a general library could be built. Land was acquired for the library building.

The University entered into a tuition-exchange program with some two hundred other colleges and universities, under which children of full-time faculty members could attend those colleges without payment of tuition or fees.

The University worked out an arrangement with local banks so that it could provide inexpensive second mortgaging for faculty housing.

Litchfield introduced a program for granting a limited number of sabbatical leaves for qualified faculty members. The leaves were to be granted to professors or associate professors who had held tenure in that rank for at least six years. They were subsidized at half salary for one year or full salary for six months. Nine sabbaticals were given in the first year, 1957–1958, three of them for a full year. Four professors granted sabbaticals were in the humanities, two were in engineering, two were in the natural sciences, and one was in the social sciences.

The most protracted and difficult operation Litchfield undertook in his first two years was "a comprehensive faculty development program directed toward bringing about a rapid but orderly change in the quality of the faculty." To do that, he first had to evaluate the competence of the 725 full-time faculty members he had inherited. To make the evaluation he took a step unprecedented in higher education. He set up a review committee to grade his faculty on their effectiveness as teachers, their research and scholarship, their professional stature. In so doing, the committee was to identify those who had made no effective attempt to keep abreast of the rapid scientific, social, humanistic, and political advances of the time. This came to be known as Litchfield's "up-or-out program."

This was not a gentle or painless affair—it could not have been. It was, however, considerably less brutal than it was reported to be. For one thing, Litchfield named as members of the review committee prominent and respected professors on the faculty itself. For another, he sweetened the operation by combining it with a program for giving "merit increases" in salary to all who deserved them. He called his faculty judges the Committee on Faculty Merit Increases and gave them the help of several distinguished outside educator-consultants. The dominant consultant was a major figure in higher education, Henry Merritt Wriston, sixty-six, who had retired after twelve years as president of Brown University and was now executive director of the American Assembly, an adjunct of the Columbia Graduate School of Business. The University of Pittsburgh, Wriston declared, was badly inbred. It had "obviously and obnoxiously prostituted rank. Faculty members have been prematurely promoted to associate and full professor since adequate salaries were not possible in the lower ranks. This should be corrected by withholding promotion except in cases of clearly demonstrated merit; although salary increases should be awarded, even beyond the established ranges, to keep promising assistant professors in line."

In April 1957 Litchfield sent "letters of merit" to each of 434 professors, associate and assistant professors, and instructors who were to receive full- or half-merit increases. The letters in each of the categories were delicately shaded to express an exact degree of approbation or measured caution. ("In the future, I hope you will be able to accomplish still more than you have found it possible to do in the past. This expression of professional esteem should be taken as encouragement for you to put forward still greater efforts." "As you know, a university of standing must maintain constant emphasis on creative scholarship without sacrificing teaching excellence. In the years ahead I shall look to you for important contributions to the academic excellence of the University. Your future merit increases will depend on the degree to which you fulfill these expectations." "Your name was called to my attention as one who has served the University for many years with outstanding fidelity. . . . I regret that the pressures of the past year have prevented me from becoming better acquainted with you. . . . Please accept the gratitude of the University with my good wishes.")

Litchfield thanked the members of the committee and praised their work but told them that they had not given him the rigorous evaluation he wanted and expected. In the late spring of 1957 he added several members to the committee and renamed it the Committee on Faculty Evaluation. In a six-page letter to that committee he specified "the important things that I should like to see accomplished":

All members of the faculty should be reviewed and placed in one of the following categories:

a. Distinctly superior persons who would be a credit to any faculty in this country and whom we want to keep under any circumstances.

b. Persons about whom we have reservations, who may have the capacity to be placed in the first category, but who, because of circumstances in which they find themselves, have not yet definitely proved themselves either distinctly superior or, on the other hand, as less than the caliber we ultimately want on this faculty.

c. People who are known to be of less than our new standard but whom we must keep for the time being because of inability to find replacements. [The next sentence was crossed out in the draft: "These people should never be promoted."]

d. People who are distinctly below standard and whom we intend to replace just as quickly as superior people can be found to replace them.

Accordingly, the Committee on Faculty Evaluation made a review of its first survey. It corrected some "truly grave injustices" in the first survey. It amended its judgment on teachers with the declaration: "The Committee found a number of faculty members with established reputations for teaching excellence who have either written nothing or very little and who are unlikely to write in the future. We recognized this superior teaching in every such instance as indicative of genuine distinction." And it added three new categories, noting "with varying degrees of regret a number of cases wherein the best interests of the University would be served by the individuals' transfer elsewhere."

In 1958 the committee was renamed again: the Advisory Committee on Faculty Personnel. In all, 660 full-time nonmedical faculty members were evaluated. Of these, 434 received merit increases and 202 persons were identified as clearly not meeting the new criteria for appointment. By the 1961–1962 school year, 43 of the 202 were considered to have upgraded themselves, 38 were still employed, and 121 had departed. They were replaced by newly recruited faculty members, only 4 percent of them Pitt graduates, with Harvard, Columbia, and Oxford the three major contributors.

In 1954, three years earlier, Litchfield had been in Djakarta on the island of Java with his wife and Alan Rankin, conducting a Cornell–Ford Foundation survey for the Indonesian government. There they met Mary Carolyn Morrill, an American who was posted to the International Cooperation Administration (ICA). Miss Morrill was what in 1954 was called a career girl. A graduate in 1946 of the University of Kansas, where she was a member of Phi Beta Kappa, she had worked for the State Department in Washington for four years. She then joined the ICA, with which she was to spend 3½ years in Indonesia. She was the daughter of Frank Nash Morrill, retired board chairman of his family's bank in Hiawatha (a county seat in northeast Kansas, pop. 3,238), and the granddaughter of Edwin Needham Morrill, banker, businessman, member of Congress and anti-Populist Republican governor (1895–1897). In Indonesia she was the press officer; a writer of articles, press releases, and radio scripts on ICA work; and the liaison officer between the ICA mission and the Indonesian Ministry of Information. In traveling about the islands she had learned to speak Bahasa Indonesia. In 1954 Mary Morrill was thirty-one years of age, five feet ten inches tall, slender, strikingly beautiful, an heiress, and unspoken for.

In December 1956, while visiting his aunt's home in Hutchinson, Kansas, Alan Rankin picked up a copy of the University of Kansas *Alumni Magazine* and read a full-page article with pictures titled "The Most Popular American in Indonesia." It told of Mary Morrill's return to the United States on a leave of absence during which she would study for a master's degree in political science at Columbia University. It quoted Mr. Harjoto, secretary general of the Ministry of Information: "Among us Miss Mary Morrill is . . . nearly an institution."

Back in Pittsburgh, Rankin laid the article on Litchfield's desk with a brief covering note. Litchfield called him in and asked him to get Miss Morrill's address. "Dear Mary," he wrote. "Alan showed me the very flattering story in the University of Kansas alumni magazine. Congratulations. I should be interested in your plans for the time after you complete your present studies. If I can be of any help to you, you know that you may call on me. With best wishes, I am, Cordially yours."

Litchfield had been living in the chancellor's suite in the newly acquired Schenley Apartments—a five bedroom, four-bath suite on the twelfth floor of what is now called Bruce Hall. In November 1956, a widower of ten months, he moved with the children and Mrs. Peter McCrae, their governess, into a thirteen-room white brick house at 1129 Beechwood Boulevard, 2½ miles east of the campus, that had been bought and redecorated as a new chancellor's residence.* In the meantime, he had been corresponding with and visiting Mary Morrill in New York. In due course friendship blossomed into something more serious, and a proposal of marriage followed. On February 20 Mary Morrill paid a visit to Pittsburgh and inspected the Beechwood Boulevard house. She then continued on to Hiawatha, Kansas, to complete plans for her marriage to Edward Litchfield.

The wedding took place with a minimum of publicity on Saturday, March 20, 1957, at the home of the bride's parents. The Reverend Hobart Hildyard of the First Methodist Church of Hiawatha per-

formed the ceremony in the presence of the immediate families. Alan C. Rankin served as best man. For their honeymoon the couple flew to Harbor Island in the Bahamas, where they spent one of their afternoons at the Richard King Mellon home, Conch Rest, at Cabel Beach, Nassau.

The new Mrs. Litchfield was a success from the start. The wife of a Harvard professor enticed to Pitt recalls some of her appeal to faculty people: "She was a charming and considerate hostess. She used to tell us before Women's Association meetings, 'If you don't have a baby sitter, bring the children and park them in the nursery we have set up on the fourth floor.' At Harvard, when there was a gathering of faculty people, you knew what the refreshments would be: crackers, cheese, and a glass of sherry. That was standard for Harvard. At a Litchfield reception you had a repast, a spread—caviar, shrimp, fruit, sliced beef, sliced ham, sauces, hors d'oeuvres, a bar."

Despite the salary increases, the improved benefits, the sabbatical years, and the upgrading of the University's academic goals, there were doubters and detractors on the campus in 1956 and 1957. Some of the teaching faculty still suspected that Litchfield would try to run the University like one of his corporations, to the detriment of its academic needs. Some felt that the merit increase and faculty evaluation committees were a barrier between them and the chancellor. Others said the committees had given too much emphasis to long lists of published work, many of them simply "bibliography-making" out of "patently thin material, clearly recognizable as the gleanings from earlier meritorious work or as a rehash of someone else's original material." More than a few Pitt people on and off the campus resented the chancellor and his people for criticizing what had happened at the University before they arrived in 1956. The damage was not lessened by politic, routine praise of what had gone before; it was the more severe when it appeared in magazines of national circulation. It was at its worst in a *Time* article on Litchfield on January 7, 1957. In that article, Pitt "had long been doing a competent job [but] it was, in comparison with other U.S. cam-

---

*The Bruce Hall apartment had been occupied for some years by Frank R. Denton, vice chairman of the Mellon National Bank. The Bigelow Boulevard house had been the home of Albert Horne Burchfield, president of Horne's department store.

puses, a mediocre place in danger of stagnation." Litchfield was quoted for the world to read: "Our teaching is not as good as it should be. In fact, some of it is poor. Our research is not as good as it should be." Except for medicine, he continued, none of Pitt's eleven professional schools was in the first rank, and in spite of Pitt's traditional emphasis on engineering, it lagged behind its neighbor Carnegie Tech as a technological school. Pitt's work in anthropology was inadequate. Pitt's library was not in good shape. The University was suffering from a severe case of provincialism. Deadwood faculty would have to be weeded out.

Steele Gow wrote to Litchfield that the *Time* article had "created some irritations locally" and that he had been doing all he could to "assuage those of which I heard." Litchfield replied that there were indeed unfortunate aspects to the *Time* story, but that on balance there were also some very considerable advantages nationally in the message it carried. "We've had a number of applications for faculty appointments from good institutions, from people we find to be of considerable reputation. We had a university president here last week who said that there was a good deal of conversation within his faculty about what was developing at Pittsburgh, and indicated that they based their information on the *Time, Newsweek* and *Saturday Evening Post* stories. . . . I've had letters from our own faculty members who are on leave from as far away as Tokyo. In each case their reaction was that they were pleased to read in *Time* about the aspirations which the University had set for itself. These are but illustrations of quite a wide reaction throughout the nation which has been distinctly to our advantage."

Litchfield was right. The authors of feature stories on the new chancellor and the new Pitt praised Litchfield's ideas, accomplishments, and promise; but in searching for an "angle" to make their pieces readable and, if possible, shocking, they depicted Litchfield as a brash, too-brilliant, too-ambitious character in too much of a hurry. Such articles did him permanent damage. At the same time, they made him nationally famous, and they conveyed to an enormous audience the essential story of what was happening at the University of Pittsburgh: its determined attempt, backed by the power and wealth of the community, to make itself a great institution of learning. Pittsburghers, of course, were more impressed by the articles in the big magazines, some of them with well-known bylines, than they were, or would have been, by similar stories in the local press.

As Litchfield's programs began to move forward, faculty resentment was bottled up, or left the campus, or changed to applause. Robinson Miller Upton, president of Beloit College, was exaggerating only a little when he said, "The other universities throughout the nation consider the rebirth of the University of Pittsburgh as one of the phenomena of our age."

20

"New Dimensions of Learning in a Free Society"

He brings to the University qualities of intellect and understanding that should make a brilliant mark in education. . . . Certainly, there can be no higher calling than the one to which Dr. Litchfield has set himself. The University has been a great resource to Pittsburgh, producing so many of the trained people who have helped to make it what it is. The larger role charted for it now will benefit all of the free society in which we live.

An editorial on the inauguration of Chancellor Edward H. Litchfield, the *Pittsburgh Press*, May 10, 1957

EDWARD LITCHFIELD had a strong and abiding sense of the ceremony to be accorded the chancellorship. He instructed Alan Rankin that he wished always to be accompanied to meetings on campus and that when he entered the room everyone should rise as a mark of respect—not for him, but for the office he held. For his inauguration on May 10, 1957, he caused to be designed and crafted a chancellor's medallion with a heavy gold chain, which Alan Scaife placed around his shoulders during the ceremony, declaring, "I believe you are to be for many years our leader toward a greater destiny for the University." Litchfield wore a specially designed gown of "antique gold faille of the best quality," with four navy blue velvet bars on the sleeves. The bars represented a combination of the academic tradition embodied in a doctoral robe and the administrative authority vested in the chancellor by the trustees. He laid aside his conventional gold-tassled mortarboard to wear a jaunty velvet "beefeater" hat, a kind of large beret, such as the marshalls were wearing.

His inauguration was held in Syria Mosque, but within a year or two he was using a large and elaborate covered platform for the chancellor's party and trustees at major outdoor ceremonies. It stood on the open lawn just east of the Cathedral of Learning. It resembled the canopy sheltering a medieval king watching jousting games, and perhaps it led to the sobriquet "King Edward," by which Litchfield came to be known by some in the Pittsburgh community. The platform and its ramps required several days and a crew of workmen to erect, but it served a good purpose, since it sometimes rained on commencement day and the roof kept the chancellor and the trustees dry. The students and the audience, unfortunately, were exposed to the elements.

The title of the chancellor's 8,000-word acceptance speech that closed the three-day-long ceremonies was "New Dimensions of Learning in a Free Society." Its most important feature was a plan by which the University made it possible for students, if they so elected, to complete the equivalent of a four-year undergraduate liberal arts program and a full course in law or medicine in five years, or complete a liberal education plus two years of graduate work in business administration in four years. This, the "trimester plan," would call for a regular academic schedule of three fifteen-week units in each year, instead of the usual thirty-four-week schedule. It would eliminate the traditional summer vacation for college students. Trimester was not new; it had been used during both world wars, and it was constantly being advocated, with almost no success, by proponents who were disturbed by schoolrooms that remained empty three months of the year. Litchfield's move received voluminous attention—tentative, watchful, but mostly favorable—from the press and the academic community.

The most important influence on U.S. education in these years, perhaps in this century, derived from the events of October 4, 1957, not in this country but in the Soviet Union. Russian scientists on that date launched Sputnik I, the first man-made satellite, a sphere that weighed 183.6 pounds, circled the earth every 96.17 minutes in an elliptical orbit 140 to 560 miles high, and in so doing opened the space age. Sputnik I was followed one month later by Sputnik II, a 1,120-pound satellite carrying the first space passenger, a dog named Laika. The response in the United States was consternation, chagrin, and anger. Especially anger—and most of that directed at the nation's high schools and colleges. An educator said in February 1958: "Today there is a civil war in education. . . . The schools are being blamed for juvenile delinquency, the popularity of rock and roll music, the low intellectual content of television commercials, and the fiasco of the Navy's Vanguard rocket."

As a result of Sputnik, there was a reexamination of education in the United States, accompanied by an increase in federal aid to strengthen instruction in science, engineering, and mathematics. A 1958 federal program authorized expenditure of $900 million for education over the next four years, and another program made $295 million available for student loans. Pennsylvania's General State Authority and various departments of the federal government made grants for college buildings, especially for research in science and medicine, but often including libraries, dormitories, and physical training and general-purpose facilities. The grants had one thing in common: they paid for the building, seldom for its equipment and furnishings, and never for its maintenance.

In Litchfield's first three years, 1956 through 1959, the University had undertaken or was committed to a dozen major new capital projects, some of them made possible by the largesse that resulted from the rivalry between the United States and the Soviet Union in the exploration of space.

The first project was a surprising push ahead in a residence-hall program, conceived and carried out in late 1955 and early 1956, when the chancellor-elect was still commuting back and forth between Cornell and Pitt. The University bought the five grouped buildings called the Schenley Apartments, a residence of well-to-do Pittsburghers that stood just west of the Schenley Hotel, between Fifth and Forbes avenues. Built in 1924 at a cost of more than $4.5 million, the five buildings had 1,113 rooms in 238 apartments. Pitt paid $3 million (financed by revenue bonds subsidized by a surcharge on student tuition) and raised a volley of protests from tenants when, most inappropriately during Christmas week of 1955, the takeover was announced. By the opening of the 1957–1958 school year, 101 female students were in residence in Building F, now renamed Brackenridge Hall. They lived there under quaint regulations, supervised by a couple stationed on the premises. Freshman women had to be in their rooms by 8:30 P.M. weekdays; sophomore, junior, and senior women were permitted to be out until 12:30 once a week. (Male students in a nearby dormitory could come and go as they pleased.) It cost about $1 million to convert the apartments to residence halls, of which $450,000 was paid by an anonymous donor.

The second project, announced a month later, was the purchase of the Schenley Hotel directly across from the Cathedral of Learning and adjacent to the apartments. The Schenley, 217 rooms, fifty-eight years old, had a glamorous past and was still a busy Pittsburgh institution in 1956. Eleonora Duse died there; Lillian Russell married Alexander Moore there; Enrico Caruso had once rented an entire floor; Andrew Carnegie, Woodrow Wilson, Theodore Roosevelt, William Howard Taft, and Diamond Jim Brady had eaten there (separately); Maude Adams had danced in the ballroom; Spencer Tracy called late at night on Katherine Hepburn (in Pittsburgh in 1942 in the play *Without Love*), wearing dark glasses in the hope that no one would recognize him. Pitt bought the hotel for $1.8 million, which it paid by transferring the Ellsworth Center property, valued at $300,000, to the former hotel owners, by paying $200,000 in cash (supplied by another anonymous donor), and by assuming a $1.3 million mortgage. Pitt took possession in August 1956, sandblasted the brick exterior, made changes in the interior, and on October 9, 1957, moved all major student activities there. Twenty rooms, including the famous lobby, were remodeled to provide space for student lounges, meeting places, a cafeteria, and a publications office. Floors six to nine were made into dormitory quarters for 204 men.

Acquisition of the hotel and apartments added five acres to the campus. Pitt now called itself "a twenty-four-hour educational enterprise" and "a campus community." Dr. Litchfield was quoted: "By making it possible to develop suitable living facilities for students, we will be enabled to build a student body representative of all sections of the country. This wider representation will further enrich our whole education process."

The Schenley complex was followed in succeeding months by nine other projects constructed, acquired, or committed:

Salk Hall, known at the time as the Municipal Hospital, was acquired in October 1957. With the decline of contagious diseases it had become a financial burden to the city, and after studying the estimate that $1 million would be required to remodel it as a 250-bed general hospital and $2 million annually to maintain it, Mayor Lawrence offered the building to Pitt for $1.3 million. Litchfield obtained $500,000 from the A. W. Mellon Educational and Charitable Trust and the balance from three other foundations. For a time the upper floors of the building, renamed Jonas Salk Hall, served as a residence for students. In 1961–1962, using a GSA grant, Pitt remodeled it to house the School of Dentistry and the School of Pharmacy.

The eight-story *Ruskin Apartments,* a hundred yards or so northeast of Clapp Hall, became University property in February 1958. Pitt bought it for $2.25 million as an investment, with the intention of using it eventually for faculty residences. Litchfield held a tea there for its 189 tenants, many of them elderly, well-to-do widows, told them that no one would be asked to move, promised that the present staff and management would be retained, and then sat back and waited for apartments to become vacant in the normal course of time. Ten years later ninety of the tenants who had attended that meeting were still living in the Ruskin.

The *E. V. Babcock Memorial Room,* built on the top floor of the Cathedral of Learning with a Babcock family grant of $327,000, was dedicated in November 1958 for use as the trustees' boardroom.

Construction began in 1958 on *Trees Hall,* which held a 165-by-75-foot swimming pool, called at the time the largest indoor pool in the country, with seats for 3,000 spectators. This was built on the "upper campus" near the stadium.

In 1957 and 1958 the University acquired the land and money for the *Hillman Library,* its long-needed "general library" and its first separate main library. It bought four plots of land and the buildings thereon (including the Schenley Theater and the Park Schenley Restaurant) on the south side of Forbes Avenue just west of the Cathedral campus. In so doing it assembled enough land to build a structure that would serve as the keystone for its projected Social Professions Quadrangle. The library as designed was large enough to hold 2.5 million bound volumes on self-service open stacks; to serve 2,400 readers at one time; and to contain administrative offices, student and faculty carrels, rooms for reading, conferences, conversation, smoking, and contemplation, and departments to hold periodicals, rare books, special collections, large research collections, files of government documents, archives, and audiovisual equipment. The GSA gave $7 million for the building; the Hillman family and the Hillman Foundation gave $3 million as a memorial to J. H. Hillman, Jr., for whom the building is named. The oriel windows designed by Max Abramovitz, placed at a bay-window angle,

The Hillman Company

Henry L. Hillman served on the board of the University from 1956 to 1984 and is now trustee emeritus. He is the son of J. H. Hillman, Jr., for whom Hillman Library is named.

Hillman Library.

Ray Cristina/News & Publications

provide light but are inconspicuous on the plane surface of the outer wall. (Because of delay in demolishing buildings on the site and changes in plans and design, construction was not started until June 1965.)

Samuel P. Langley Hall, the second unit in the Natural Science Quadrangle, following Clapp Hall, was started in 1959. Construction was made possible by a $2.4 million grant from the GSA. University income was used to equip the building.*

---

*On January 20, 1977, two women were killed and several people injured in a gas explosion that destroyed part of Langley Hall. Coroner Cyril H. Wecht, after a two-day inquest, ruled the explosion an accident. Langley Hall was rebuilt and then reopened in 1982.

As early as November 1956, the University had a commitment from Miss Helen Clay Frick that she would construct a building in the style of the Italian Renaissance to house the Department of Fine Arts, which she had been supporting for the past thirty years. The *Henry Clay Frick Fine Arts Building,* named in honor of her father, would contain a museum of art works with exhibition rooms, the Frick Art Reference Library, an auditorium, offices, and studios. Negotiations were started and continued for several years to agree upon an architectural design and to obtain permission to place the building on city land on the southern edge of Schenley Plaza, with the understanding that the facilities would be open to the public. Work was started on the building in September 1962.

In July 1955 the University's total investment in buildings, land, and equipment was $34,663,767. At the end of fiscal year 1958–1959, it was $79,176,748—an increase of almost $45 million in a five-year period of moderate inflation. University accountants estimated that the actual replacement cost of the University's plant in 1959 would be more than $200 million. They recognized it as a pointless figure, since the Cathedral of Learning, the Nationality Rooms, Heinz Chapel, and Foster Memorial could not have been duplicated at any price.

In one of his earliest actions, taken several months before he became chancellor, Litchfield obtained permission from the trustees to retain the advisory services of Max Abramovitz, architect and planner, recommended to Litchfield by Henry Wriston. Abramovitz, a senior partner of Harrison and Abramovitz, designers of Rockefeller Center, the United Nations buildings, and in Pittsburgh the Alcoa Building and 525 William Penn Place, was asked to make a "comprehensive study of directions for the University's future physical growth." He took a personal interest in the Pitt assignment and in 1956 was frequently on campus developing models.

Litchfield's directives to him were to proceed under a comprehensive plan rather than on an ad hoc basis; to establish more unity of arrangement for a "reasonably centralized campus"; to point out areas and directions where the University could expand its physical facilities (Litchfield always avoided the words *expand* and *expansion,* using *develop* and *development* instead); and "to make of the campus an academic island not much interfered with by Oakland traffic or Oakland business." The last of these goals was one Litchfield felt strongly about and returned to frequently. In "A Confidential Conference with Mr. Abramovitz about Overall Plans," he said, "A change is intended in the general nature of the University, from one with a scattered campus with frequent interruptions of noise and movement of traffic and persons, to the quiet type of campus such as is often found in a rural location or small town. Ideally, there should be a general atmosphere conducive to intellectual and physical relaxation, seven days a week."

Abramovitz proposed various ideas, some of them unrealistic, others mutually conflicting, but all intriguing then and now. Fifth Avenue and Bigelow Boulevard, he said, were the main traffic arteries at the campus, and "perhaps both of them should be made to disappear from the campus scene, though this operation would be very expensive." Perhaps Forbes Avenue traffic could be made to disappear by taking advantage of the elevation on which the Cathedral of Learning and Heinz Chapel stood and "by the simple expedient of raising the level of the lower Cathedral campus and of the [Schenley] parking plaza beyond Forbes Street. Thus the street itself could be bridged over rather easily." He exhibited a preliminary chart in which Fifth Avenue, the other main east-west thoroughfare, was "depressed" and decked over, "so that it would run underground with many resulting opportunities for uninterrupted campus traffic movement in the 'green' areas between buildings." This would cost between $850 and $1,500 per lineal foot. The chart also suggested the elimination of Bellefield Avenue and Craig Street, with traffic diverted to Neville Street, thus making it possible to expand the campus to the east beyond the Mellon Institute. Perhaps Pitt Stadium and Forbes Field should be moved to the outskirts of the city, which would make it possible to expand to the west. Perhaps the University itself should acquire and dispose of Forbes Field. Dr. Litchfield said, "It is a very exciting prospect," and he asked Albert Van Dusen, assistant chancellor for planning and development, to look into the Forbes Field matter. Abramovitz said that one distinctive quality, the green area around the Cathedral, should not be destroyed by placing other buildings there. It was inevitable, he said, that the Cathedral of Learning would continue as an outstanding symbol of the University's significance in the community; "it is one of the finest buildings in the country."

In August 1958, the Municipal Stadium Study Committee, appointed some months earlier by the Lawrence administration, submitted a report. It recommended that Forbes Field be replaced by a

Trees Hall.

municipal stadium to be built on the north shore of the Allegheny River across from downtown Pittsburgh. Pitt had been negotiating with the Forbes Field Company and the Pittsburgh Baseball Club and was about to sign an ingenious purchase agreement. Pitt would buy Forbes Field for $3.045 million and then lease it back to the previous owners for use as a ballpark as long as they wished to stay there. The Pittsburgh Pirates would be guaranteed a playing field until the new stadium was built on the North Side, and Pitt would waive the rent as a substitute for part of the down payment. The agreement was signed in November 1958.

In the meantime, the University had completed its long-range campus development plan, and when it first learned that Forbes Field would be put up for sale it decided to release its plan, in toto, to the public. Pitt announced that it hoped to occupy the entire

area between the Cathedral campus, Oakland Avenue four blocks to the west, Fifth Avenue on the north, and the far edge of the Forbes Field site to the south. It would build high rise dormitories west of the Schenley complex; the general library at the Schenley Plaza; and structures on the Forbes Field site, when and if it became available, to house six professional schools: Business Adminstration, Retailing, Law, Education, Social Work, and Public and International Affairs.

To make this development possible, the University would ask for two major street changes. That part of Bigelow Boulevard between the Cathedral of Learning and the former Schenley Hotel—one long block running from Fifth to Forbes avenues— would be vacated; the boulevard, coming downhill from the north, would dead-end at Fifth. And the quarter-mile stretch of Forbes Avenue running from Oakland Avenue almost to Carnegie Music Hall would also be vacated. It would be diverted at Oakland Avenue to swing southeast, running in an arc on the hillside behind Carnegie Museum and reconnecting with the original Forbes Avenue at Craig Street.

The presentation of this plan to city council and Mayor Lawrence in September 1958 produced an explosion of protest, particularly among Oakland merchants. In a continuing campaign called Stop Pitt, the *Oakland News* charged, among other things, that too many residential and business properties were being removed from the tax rolls for University use and that much of the benefit of the expansion "is going to foreign students whom the Chancellor is trying to attract to spread his fame around the world." Rege Cordic, Pittsburgh's favorite early morning radio humorist, repeatedly did a piece in which, against the soundtrack of a Nuremberg *Sieg Heil! Sieg Heil!* rally, he shouted in a shrill voice, "Give me Forbes Field and I won't take Carnegie Tech!" And in a variation on the theme: "Today Oakland—Tomorrow the World!"

University administrators were upset by the strong position taken in a two-column article, "Pitt's Ambitious Expansion Plans," in the *Pittsburgh Press*. "Pitt has now proposed a sweeping program," it read, "which would close Bigelow Boulevard between Fifth Avenue and Schenley Park and wipe out an entire section of Forbes Avenue between Craig Street and Oakland Avenue. . . . The Cathedral of Learning, envisioned as a skyscraper schoolhouse, was poorly located when it was constructed 30 years ago, between two of the city's main thoroughfares and in an area which was rapidly becoming congested. The present administration wants to redeem this mistake and give the university a country-like campus in the heart of the civic center—by taking over much of that civic center."

The administrators were ready with a set of previously prepared and rehearsed answers to the objections. Among them:

● Through traffic would move much more quickly around Oakland under the new street pattern; Forbes Avenue would have only one traffic light instead of seven.

● The safety hazards of Oakland-area traffic would be reduced.

● The University would construct dormitories for 3,500 students and provide housing for almost one thousand other students and faculty families. These students and faculty would bring greater purchasing power into the area; they would create extensive and varied opportunities for other kinds of business enterprises and an upgrading of shops.

● Many other improvements carried out as part of the Pittsburgh renaissance had resulted in properties being taken off the tax rolls of the city without major objections.

● The property the University hoped to acquire, including Forbes Field, had a taxable assessment of $2,180,446. That was only 0.3 of 1 percent of the city's total assessed valuation.

● The land Pitt was buying was being purchased on the open market. The University had no power of eminent domain, nor did it seek it. The sellers were under no duress in arriving at a price. They were under no duress to sell.

● The University wished to point out that "it has been an integral part of the community for more than 170 years; that it provides employment to more than 3,000 faculty and service people; that its annual payroll is more than $17,000,000; and that rather than injuring the Oakland civic area, it is adding immeasurably to it by improving its appearance, by providing more all-year-round purchasing power and helping to improve traffic conditions."

The controversy was not settled soon or easily; it dragged on intermittently for thirteen more years. Pitt discovered that it could put up its buildings without closing off main thoroughfares. Then another chancellor in another era called a truce and signed a peace treaty in the long war between Town and Gown.

Early in 1958 Litchfield decided to go to the Soviet Union on a fifteen-day tour to study that country's system of higher education. He arranged to go as chairman of an official delegation from the State Department under the recent U.S.-U.S.S.R. agreement for the exchange of visits by persons in scientific and cultural fields. His delegation consisted of five other college presidents, including Deane W. Malott of Cornell, as well as H. Phillip Mettgar, who was running the Governmental Affairs Institute; and Alan M. Scaife, president of trustees of the University of Pittsburgh. Sarah Mellon Scaife accompanied her husband and with him "sponsored" the visit. Mary Litchfield, who on April 28 had mothered a son, Edward Harold, Jr., to be known as Teddy, also accompanied her husband.

Arriving in Moscow in June, the Litchfield delegation was given a State Department escort as an advisor, interpreter, and aide in dealing with Soviet officials. He was Cole Blasier, thirty-three, a political scientist who held a certificate from the Russian Institute, had earned his Ph.D. at Columbia, and as a foreign service officer had served in Belgrade, Bonn, and Washington. During the next week he was with the group sixteen hours a day at visits, receptions, and dinners at Soviet institutions of higher learning in Moscow, Leningrad, and Tiflis.

Blasier felt that Litchfield's "imperial style" may have irritated some of the delegation and their Soviet hosts,

yet I found him consistently warm, generous-spirited, and thoughtful. I recall a short taxi ride we took alone to a dinner in Leningrad, during which he described his coming to Pittsburgh. He gave what seemed to me an objective appraisal of Richard King Mellon, described the latter's leadership, and gave me a sense of what was . . . his own productive, if not intimate, collaboration with Pittsburgh's civic leader.

Mary was friendly and easy to talk to. She was fresh, high-spirited, and tactful, providing the social lubricant that held the large group together. Her light touch concealed shrewd judgment of human character and a personal reserve not easily penetrated.

Our long hours together in airplanes and automobiles made it easy to become acquainted also with Alan and Sarah Scaife. Alan was charming, almost courtly, and consistently sweet-tempered. There was a kind of boyish quality about him, especially in contrast to the Chancellor's heavier manner. Alan seemed to take great zest in life, looking forward with keen satisfaction to his forthcoming shooting expedition in Spain. . . .

Sarah Scaife was an intensely private person. She conducted herself throughout the visit with dignity and sen-

sitivity. An occasional wry remark reflected a salty sense of humor.

Blasier learned at Tiflis that a local news service planned to tape an interview with Litchfield at the airport and so informed him. On the ride out to the airport Litchfield took two or three minutes—the only time available—to make notes. "This interview was a remarkable demonstration of extemporaneous speaking. The Chancellor delivered a five-minute personal message to the Georgian people, a model of clarity, balance, and relevance. For over a year I had followed events in Georgia as best one can from Washington and knew many of the political issues in the region. It was remarkable how Litchfield was able to speak directly and persuasively to what I believed to be the yearnings and interests of his Georgian audience."

The Litchfield delegation separated in Stockholm. At the last dinner together, Litchfield proposed a toast to Alan Scaife, who "was like nobody else as a board chairman. He could understand clearly the difference between policy and management. He was very creative and imaginative without losing sight of practical realities. He could see new problems constructively, not negatively, a quality that is essential to build a great university. And he had the ability to bring all parts of the University up to him, dealing with all departments on the basis of equality, as man to man."

The Scaifes returned to Pittsburgh by way of Spain after a cheerful parting in Stockholm, during which they spoke of their hopes of visiting China and its educational institutions in 1959. The Litchfields flew to Paris, where Litchfield gave the *New York Times* the text of his "Preliminary Report on Higher Education in the Soviet Union" (it was published on July 14) and appeared on a thirty-minute special NBC news program conducted by Chet Huntley titled "How Good Are the Soviet Colleges?"* Then they flew to Iran, where Litchfield

---

*He published his thirty-two page *Report on Higher Education in the Soviet Union* (University of Pittsburgh Press) later in 1958. The *New York Times* said in 1964 that it "led to serious re-evaluation of American methods in colleges." Cole Blasier called it "the best and most perceptive statement about Soviet higher education that I had read up to that time."

conferred with the shah as a representative of the Governmental Affairs Institute and, as chancellor, completed negotiations with the University of Teheran for the exchange of faculty and students with Pitt.

On July 24 Alan Rankin placed a call to Litchfield at the Darband Hotel in Teheran. He was told that the Litchfields were at the Apadana Hotel in Persepolis. Rankin could not reach them there and left an urgent message in care of the U.S. Embassy in Teheran, following it with a telegram. Alan Scaife, he said, was gravely ill from a sudden heart attack.

The Litchfields canceled all other plans, left Iran on the first plane they could get, and for the next three days traveled or waited at airports, almost without rest. They got a direct flight from Vienna to Idlewild.

Alan Scaife, fifty-eight, died in Magee Hospital on Thursday, July 25. At the funeral services at Calvary Episcopal Church on Saturday afternoon, University trustees and administrative officers, forty-four in number, sat together in a body. Richard K. Mellon was one of the pallbearers. Burial was in Allegheny Cemetery. The Litchfields could not reach Pittsburgh in time for the funeral.

21

An Episode in the Life
of a Chancellor

Nor, sir, are we afraid of competition. I think we are happy that you have introduced the concept of competition, for competition is the dynamic that we believe to be essential to our society. We build institutions about it. Competition of opinion leads to a free press, competition of ideas leads to a conviction about freedom of speech, competition among programs leads to a concept of a two or multi-party system.

Edward H. Litchfield, in an address at a luncheon, September 24, 1959

On September 24, 1959, Dr. and Mrs. Litchfield had out-of-town guests for lunch on the campus—husband, wife, three of their children, and several other people. They arrived at the airport in three U.S. Air Force jet transports and were accompanied by four ambassadors and 325 American and foreign news correspondents—"such a horde," one local reporter said, "as this city has never seen." Batteries of teletype machines, telephones, and typewriters were set up in the Venetian Room of Schenley Hall. Classes were canceled between 1:20 and 3:00 P.M., and thirty-five television sets were placed in campus buildings so that the students might see the luncheon. They were warned not to appear at windows during that time. While the visitors were in Pittsburgh—seventeen hours altogether—every available policeman was on duty, with all leave days canceled. No comparable event had ever been held on the Pitt campus, nor has one been held since.

Pittsburgh was the last city Nikita Khrushchev visited on his eleven-day transcontinental tour of this country before he returned to Washington to spend three days in conference with President Eisenhower. Many people were fully aware of Khrushchev's complicity in the purges and the terror of the Stalin era and of his part in sending troops and tanks to put down uprisings in Poznan and Budapest; but even they accorded him a respectful welcome for other actions taken since his rise to power in 1955. He had made a historic speech in February 1956 at the Twentieth Congress of the Soviet Communist Party in Moscow—a four-hour midnight address to a closed meeting, never published in the U.S.S.R., in which he exposed the monstrous inhumanities in the years under Stalin. He had started the "thaw" in which censorship was eased and had introduced some economic reforms. The Berlin Wall, built to prevent the escape of Communist subjects to the West, and the placing of nuclear missiles in Cuba were yet to come.

The Khrushchev party, arriving at 10:45 Wednesday evening, entered Pittsburgh by way of Mount Washington in order to see the brightly lighted Golden Triangle. Khrushchev said, "Wonderful! Wonderful!" and other members avowed that it was the finest thing they had seen in America. They spent the night at the Carlton House Hotel, occupying the entire eighth floor. Next morning Khrushchev and some of his entourage were driven to West Homestead to visit the Mesta Machine Company plant, whose steel-manufacturing products he had seen as lend-lease goods in his own country during the war. (It was a nonunion shop and one of the few plants not closed in a nationwide steel strike.) He returned to the hotel at noon, being driven in a white Chrysler Imperial convertible through an enormous crowd of people in the downtown streets, for whom he alternately wore and waved a large cowboy hat.

Mrs. Khrushchev (who spoke a little English) was accompanied throughout the morning by her two daughters, by Mrs. Litchfield, and by Mrs. Andrei Gromyko, Mrs. Henry Cabot Lodge, and a train of followers and security people. They first visited an observation deck on Grandview Avenue, drove around Mount Washington at a leisurely pace (no sirens), and then headed for Children's Hospital. Walter Rome, the hospital's executive director, met them at the door and gave them a conducted tour of the emergency floor and the orthopedic, surgery, and infants' rooms. At the University they visited the Russian, Norwegian, and Yugoslav Nationality rooms. A Spanish class was in session at the last of these, and a moment after leaving it Mrs. Khrushchev returned to apologize to the teacher for the interruption. (She had been a teacher herself when young.) Looking out at the city from the top of the Cathedral of Learning, she said it reminded her of Kiev, where she had lived many years.

There had been some difficulties about a "civic luncheon" for almost five hundred people that was scheduled for that afternoon in the Schenley Hall ballroom, sponsored jointly by the state, the city, and the University. The State Department had canceled the luncheon when it learned that a clergyman would deliver an invocation; it held that a prayer would not be appropriate for the occasion. It rescinded the cancelation when the University stood firm and one of the trustees, calling the decision "terrible," threatened to take the story to the newspapers. The State Department had also insisted that the governor of the state or the mayor of the city preside, but David Lawrence declined the honor and Thomas Gallagher, who was in poor health, felt the task was beyond his strength. Litchfield, therefore, presided. The State Department's Henry Cabot Lodge, Jr., who was Khrushchev's escort, declared that the arrangement was the most unusual he had ever seen.

Alan Rankin, in charge of the luncheon for the University, had been up all night working on the seating arrangement. Shortly before the guests arrived, he observed the Soviet security people switching all the salads at the head table. Soviet and U.S. agents together took a position above the grillwork in the ceiling that looks down on the ballroom.

The guests entered by the east door. The press people, except for thirty selected correspondents, ate together in the cafeteria and watched the happening on television. Thirty-two people sat at the head table, seventeen of them Russian. Other Russians, including the forty news people on the tour, were distributed among the other tables, as were twelve student leaders from the city colleges. These tables were placed in a semicircle in such a way that no one was closer than thirty feet to the principals at the head table. Richard Boswell Finn, foreign service officer, had given a select few of the Americans a list of thirteen questions marked "Confidential" and headed "Any information on the following topics would be appreciated." Mr. Finn wanted to learn of Khrushchev's relationships with the various other members of the delegation—particularly Gromyko, Adzhubei, Shuisky, and Shevchenko. The status of Khrushchev's health; signs of fatigue or depression; eating and drinking habits; the role of his personal physician. Remarks by Khrushchev or members of his party on internal Soviet affairs, on Chinese-Soviet relations, on Laos and the Taiwan Straits. Information that would help determine the exact size of Khrushchev's family—particularly the number of daughters and the names of their husbands. What were the mechanics in the composition of one of Khrushchev's speeches? With whom and to what

extent did he consult with respect to his public statements?* The Russians were not very outgoing during the meal; one man even refused to divulge his name.

The luncheon opened with the prayer—the first time that happened on the tour. Khrushchev observed what the others were doing and bowed his head in silence. Howard C. Scharfe, pastor of the Shadyside Presbyterian Church and a University trustee, spoke for one minute: "Almighty God . . . we know that where there is strife, Thou wouldst have peace; where there is despair, hope; where there is fear, faith; where there is error, truth. Inspire us, we pray, to continue to seek those lights that dispel shadows and overcome darkness." The menu was cold crème vichyssoise, trays of relishes, breast of chicken suprême, parsleyed potatoes, green beans amandine, tomato and cucumber salad with French dressing, rolls, butter, ice cream with peach sauce, and beverage. Mary Litchfield, seated between Khrushchev, who was in a jovial mood, and Gromyko, who was courteous but stonefaced, asked Khrushchev if he would like a second cup of vichyssoise. He told her, "I could eat two or three bowls more, because it is good peasant Russian soup, but my doctor would not allow it." She asked him if the Russians used a word like *cheese* to produce a smile when being photographed. He said he was not aware of any such word, but when the photographers filed by at the front of the table to take their one permitted photograph, he greeted each of them with the word *cheese*. One observer watched Khrushchev's face as he and Mary Litchfield spoke and concluded that he was obviously having a good time and was being charmed.

*On Litchfield's copy is written: "9/25—EHL talked to Mr. Finn by phone."

Arcady Shevchenko, on whom Finn particularly wanted information, had a senior post with the Soviet Department of the Interior in 1956–1963 and was a member of Khrushchev's personal secretariat on the 1959 visit. He is the Soviet diplomat and K.G.B. agent who for some years gave secret information to the C.I.A. He defected to the west in 1978, the highest-ranking Soviet official ever to do so, wrote a book about his experiences (*Breaking with Moscow*), and is now an authority in the United States on Soviet affairs and on other Soviet defectors.

During the meal, a young lady from Cleveland, accompanied by a newspaperman from that city, approached the head table, presented a written petition, and asked Khrushchev to allow her mother and brother, from whom she had been separated seventeen years, to leave Lithuania. He said, "Little girl, you can expect your mother back very soon." Litchfield introduced the "nonworking" guests at the head table, using, for the Russian names, a pronunciation guide the State Department chief of protocol had distributed: Mrs. Nina Petrovna Khrushcheva (Nee-na Pet-*rov*-na Khroo-shch-*ova*), wife of Chairman Khrushchev; their two married daughters; M. A. Sholokhov, the famous Russian writer; Alexei Ivanovich Adzhubei, editor of *Izvestia* and son-in-law of the Khrushchevs, among others. When Litchfield said he would not at this time introduce the guest of honor, Khrushchev called out in Russian, "That's discrimination!" Litchfield then introduced Mayor Gallagher, who welcomed the guests briefly, and Governor Lawrence, who spoke for ten minutes on the theme that this is not a one-party nation.

The audience rose and applauded when Litchfield presented His Excellency Nikita Khrushchev, chairman of the council of ministers of the Union of Soviet Socialist Republics. Pittsburgh reminded him, Khrushchev began, of the distant past, of his childhood, of the days he worked in the Donetz coal fields. He liked to meet serious-minded people, and so he had those two reasons for being pleased to be at this meeting. At this point he stopped, said he would not inflict his Russian on those in the audience who did not know his language, and asked his interpreter, Vladimir M. Sukhodrey (a Dartmouth graduate), to continue with his prepared address in English. He stepped from the lectern—a much shorter man than the audience had expected—and stood before his chair at the table, sometimes smiling, as the speech was read. The address developed the two main themes he had emphasized on his trip across the country: that the Soviet Union would surpass the United States in production within a few years; and that the two most powerful nations on earth should cooperate

Nikita Khrushchev, chairman of the Council of Ministers of the Union of Soviet Socialist Republics, emphasizes a point during his address at a luncheon on campus in September 1959.

Burt Glinn/Magnum Photos

for peace and compete for production without bloodshed.

The Soviet people, he said, have always admired American efficiency.

Your country has attained a very high level of industrial development. . . . Formerly you did not have a worthy partner in the pace of development and power, but now you have one in the Soviet Union. At present we are already overtaking your country in some respects. Speaking figuratively, we are now having an exchange of whistle calls. You will hear that our whistle is becoming even louder and clearer. It will be heard even better with every coming year. And the day is not far off when we shall draw even with you, at the same station, salute you, and move on. Then it will be us who will be ahead, not you. . . .

Neither you nor our people want war, so let us live like good neighbors. . . . Under conditions of tension the cold war may easily turn into a hot war, into a very hot one, a nuclear war which could not only burn but incinerate. The surest way to avoid this unenviable proposition is to destroy the means of war. . . . We propose that the cold war be outlawed everywhere and for all times to come.

The speech was long; the room was hot from television lights; people, including Mrs. Khrushchev, began to fan themselves with their programs; and the audience became a bit restless until it ended. Then in an unexpected development, Khrushchev returned to the lectern and for the next twenty minutes continued with a lively extemporaneous talk and with verbal exchanges with the other speakers. He offered his thanks to Bishop John Joseph Wright, who, he was told, had appealed to all believers to welcome him to the city and show themselves good hosts. He congratulated Mr. Lodge, on whom had fallen the burden of accompanying him on his trip, and who would now feel a sense of gladness. "You are probably saying, Mr. Lodge, 'My dear departing guest, I am seeing you off with the greatest of pleasure.'" (Lodge shook his head negatively and said over a burst of laughter, "I enjoyed every minute of it.") Khrushchev continued, "What is wrong about that, Mr. Lodge? Don't you want to see me off? [Laughter.] Or do you want to have a bad sending-off party?"

He congratulated Governor Lawrence on his well-prepared speech, and especially the part at the end about how the two parties were united in foreign policy.

But what the difference is between the two parties, I don't know. Perhaps you do. It is all the same to me. . . . Our people are united. They support our Communist party, the one party, but the best party of all the parties in the world. [A wave of laughter.] That is my opinion. What do you expect me to say? Your party is better? Then I would join it.

Well, God be with you. That is up to you, and if you want to continue developing under your old system that is up to you to decide, but we are going to gallop ahead on our new Socialist course. If you continue progressing in the old way we will surpass you. Let us live in peace and let us have sincere competition, in which in any case there will be no bloodshed. . . . We are ready to render you fraternal assistance.

The audience rose again and applauded, as for a fine performance, when he finished and, thinking the luncheon ended, began to leave. Litchfield, in some agitation, asked them please to return to their seats. He concluded the proceedings at 3:40, one hour over schedule, with a short but powerful declaration for which he later received much acclaim:

I would like to say to you, Mr. Chairman, on behalf, I think, of all the ladies and gentlemen here, that we do appreciate the frankness and friendliness of your comments. I think I can also say for them that none of us would seriously challenge your right to set a slogan of "overtake and pass." We just challenge your ability to do it. . . .

I would like to respectfully broaden your proposal of a competitive relationship, sir, by talking about some of the things that are more fundamental than even our ideologies of socialism or capitalism. . . . I would suggest that we compete in establishing societies in which all men find opportunity to develop their knowledge and their abilities in accordance with their capacities. Societies, both of ours, in which men's minds are free to explore the universe with no limits imposed upon them beyond those of their own abilities. Societies in which the search for truth is our mutual and constant objective. I suggest, sir, that the winner in such competition will not be your country, or ours, but all mankind.

Pittsburgers talked for days about the famous Khrushchev visit. A *Press* editorial regretted that the chancellor's closing reply to the Russian leader "was largely overlooked in the confusion," quoted it at length, and ended with a two-word paragraph: "Well said." And in New York, in a story headed "Pittsburgh Stop Warmest of Tour," the *Times* commented that Khrushchev "basked in the warmest reception of his American tour." Edward Litchfield commented that Pittsburgh was also the city where Khrushchev's challenge to the United States was greeted most firmly.

Mrs. Khrushchev won high praise from everyone who met her. One woman said, "She's nice, but whatever did she see in that man she married?" Reporter Ann Zurosky, who spoke a broken Russian, wrote, "You've seen her counterpart many times. Smiling and serene, pushing a cart in the supermarket or calming a child." In the car on the way to the airport and to Washington, Mrs. Khrushchev made a request to Councilman Frederick G. Weir: would he be so kind as to send her a copy of the minister's opening prayer?

22

The Golden Glow

The trouble at Pitt has been that, until a few years ago, Pitt was just about cut off from the scholarly world where reputations are made. The big change is that Pitt has now joined the scholarly world.

Putnam F. Jones, September 1962

By the beginning of Edward Litchfield's fourth year, July 1, 1959, the University had made substantial progress in pursuit of its goal: to attain a level of distinction in its faculty, its student body, and its programs that would ultimately provide the region it served with a quality of higher education equal to the best in the nation. Every development in the program—except one—had been carried forward more or less as planned.

Faculty salaries were now at the median level of those at the dozen leading universities. The faculty had been winnowed, upgraded, and enlarged; it had a rising percentage of those holding the Ph.D. degree at a time when the percentage elsewhere was declining. Classes were smaller, teaching loads lighter. Some sixty marginal courses had been or were about to be dropped. New courses, programs, departments, schools, and interdisciplinary centers, some of them on the frontiers of knowledge, were flourishing. The University was publishing several new scholarly journals. Better qualified freshman students with higher median Scholastic Aptitude Test scores, more of them—65 percent—from the top one-fifth of their graduating classes, were entering the University. Sponsored research programs had increased sixfold in three years. Perhaps the greatest change was at the graduate level, where the numbers of students were larger and the standards for admission—particularly at the doctoral level—were higher.

In a tone of measured approval, an evaluation team sent by the Middle States Association of Colleges reported that the Litchfield program "has sharply clarified the University's goals and has markedly accelerated progress toward them in many sections of its economy. In few if any areas has the University achieved 'equal to the best' academic stature yet, but in some it has closed the gap far more than would have seemed likely five years ago."

The one exception in the litany of accomplishment had to do with money—specifically, with money for endowment.

Litchfield's program from the first had called for an increase in the University's nonmedical endowment from $30 million (in 1955) to $100 million—

later $125 million—within ten years. In 1959 the endowment was only $42 million when, under Litchfield's schedule, it should have been close to $70 million. The loss, or absence, of income from that expected but missing $28 million was something of an embarrassment. Litchfield had operated with balanced budgets in the first two years, owing largely to new income realized from a 43 percent increase in tuition. He had a deficiency of $159,000 in 1958–1959, which was not considered alarming in view of the large development program under way and of the accumulated surpluses of close to $1 million. For 1959–1960 he faced a deficiency of almost $2 million, which would absorb the remainder of the surplus and leave the University almost $1 million in the red. "The coming year," he wrote to his faculty and administrative aides in 1958, "will be a difficult one in terms of meeting an increased budget. In approving the new budget the trustees acted with courage and faith in the future."

In February 1958 Litchfield and Scaife had discussed the need to raise additional endowment. Scaife wrote the next day that he was disturbed "that we have been unable to broaden our base for support . . . and are entirely too dependent on a very few foundations." The University's trustees, he said, had committed themselves in 1954 to attempt to obtain endowment "looking towards a goal of $50 million." It was at that time, he said, that the Mellon family had made grants of $15 million to the School of Medicine for endowment, but the University had not initiated a broadly based campaign, "in all probability due to the fact that the committee on gifts and endowment had been entirely inactive. I have nothing to recommend at this particular time except that continuing attention be given to the development of a program which will solicit gifts for endowment funds and bequests in wills."

Inevitable questions must be asked. Why was nothing attempted? Why was the board's committee on gifts and endowment "entirely inactive" when the board had agreed with Litchfield in 1956 that the endowment must be raised from $30 million to $100 million, or perhaps $125 million? The answers will be developed at some length in the chapters that follow, but these preliminary points must be made now as an aid to understanding the surprising developments of the next several years.

First, money in large amounts was actually coming in during these years. In the fiscal year 1959, Pitt was ranked first nationally in grants it received ($6,358,435) from various foundations. This was about one-third more than foundation gifts to the second-ranking school, Columbia University. Pitt ranked eighth among American colleges in gift income from corporate business, with $1,331,875.

Second, most of the money received was for capital plant or specified academic or research programs—and most of that was for the Health Center. Very little was collected for general purposes or endowment. Vice Chancellor Charles Peake spoke to this aspect of the problem in an interview years later: "A fundamental problem was the preoccupation with the Health Center in raising money. What you have to see is that the great thrust of development, of redevelopment, the changed Pitt, was going on in our area, not in medicine. While medicine was relatively good, their capacity for absorbing and using money was infinite. Every time we wanted money from the foundations to help the academic disciplines, engineering, the sciences, and the other professional schools, it was always going into health. There was, of course, a predisposition on the part of the donors. For R. K. Mellon and other people, medicine was the thing."

Peake cited as an example "of the kind of thing that happened" the construction of Scaife Hall in the 1950s. There was, he said, a cost overrun of several million dollars. "They were adding this and changing that. We were chafing at the bit. As soon as they had paid for Scaife Hall, then they started talking about a drive for the entire Health Center, including the six affiliated hospitals. They set up a supervisory office downtown. I myself had to mark time practically for about five years in fund raising for the prior claim of the Health Center. I could not go and ask for money from any Mellon foundation."

Third, in approaching the local foundations and corporations, Pitt was competing against Carnegie Tech, which early in 1957 began a $24.3 million

capital development program. That drive, led by co-chairman Benjamin F. Fairless, president of United States Steel, and Gwilym A. Price, president of Westinghouse Electric, raised $22 million by the end of Phase One in December 1960.

Fourth, Pitt was woefully weak in contributions received from its alumni. They gave only $184,019 in the fiscal year 1958–1959. (Carnegie Tech, though a much smaller school, received $526,375 that year from its alumni.) Alumni giving was an area where Litchfield was free to act himself, even if he was unable to persuade his trustees to do so; but he mounted no alumni campaign until 1965.

Finally, Litchfield, though talented and aggressive in obtaining support for specific academic and research programs, was lax, even derelict, in his effort to raise money for general purposes and endowment. John Bowman's colleagues described the painful hours he spent preparing himself—"psyching himself up"—before going to the city to call on a potential donor. Litchfield was disinclined to endure that indignity. Peake said of him: "Litchfield wasn't a really good fund raiser. From his accustomed administrative point of view, he assumed he could get able people and delegate that responsibility. He would set the goals and they were to go ahead and perform. He applied the same methods to fund raising, and it doesn't work there. In the final analysis, you can't delegate that responsibility. The Number One Person must go."

In this situation and with this temperament, Litchfield neglected the bricks-and-mortar of capital development and relied too heavily on a very few but very wealthy sources—mostly on the Mellon family—for foundation grants and personal gifts. Here, in the summer of 1958, he suffered a major disappointment. A letter he wrote to Richard King Mellon in August, addressed to Long House, Woods Hole, Massachusetts, reveals that Scaife and Litchfield had counted on receiving a very large grant for endowment—how many millions is not known—from the A. W. Mellon Educational and Charitable Trust:

I have just had a long talk with Schmitty [Adolph W.

Schmidt, president of the Charitable Trust] about a matter which disturbs me greatly. He tells me that Paul [Mellon] has decided that instead of liquidating the [Trust] it will be continued indefinitely. This means that a substantial portion of the capital which they had planned to give to the University will now be retained. This removes one of the substantial sources of endowment on which Alan and I had always counted. It raises serious questions as to whether or not we will be able to make this into the distinguished university which was the objective when I came here. I am afraid this means some rather thorough reconsiderations

The trustees of the foundation had indeed decided not to liquidate but rather to continue operations on a reduced scale. The principal was to be conserved at its present level of $20 million, and only $850,000 would be distributed each year. It was Richard Mellon who brought about the decision to continue, rather than to liquidate, the foundation. According to Adolph Schmidt, vice president, later president, of the trust, he persuaded Paul Mellon to change his mind. He said, in effect, "Paul, you cannot leave me alone with the largest foundation in this city, unprotected against the appeals of all the seekers of grants and contributions."

A few days after Litchfield's conversation with Schmidt and his pained letter to Richard Mellon, he received a request from Philip S. Broughton to describe for the charitable trust "the extent to which early actions and conversations contemplated substantial increases both in endowment and in capital plant fund." On October 14 Litchfield sent a three-page letter and five attached exhibits in submitting "the written record and my own recollection of events." The exhibits included the five-page letter he wrote to Alan Scaife on June 1, 1955; the three-page "Memorandum—General Policy Questions" he wrote for Scaife on June 10, 1955; two newspaper clippings reporting his speech to the Allegheny Conference on September 13, 1955; and a *Press* editorial on that speech titled "Dream for a University." He summarized his own conclusions in four points:

1. The Board of Trustees clearly and deliberately determined [in 1956] that it would embark upon a very substantial change in the institution's character.
2. From the time I first became involved, it was clear

that responsible officers of the Board were aware of the tremendous financial costs involved in such a policy move.

3. In subsequent times I confirmed my conversations regarding them [the costs] to Mr. Scaife during our negotiations as to my coming here. They were publicly outlined and confirmed by the Board before I actually did come here and they have been repeatedly presented to the various elements of the University community.

4. Stated negatively, it should be clear that no one ever committed these funds in his own or any one else's behalf. On the other hand, it is equally clear that everyone was aware of the amounts involved and committed to an effort to realize the funds requisite to this major educational undertaking. I am personally committed to doing everything I possibly can to raise these funds and I will make the effort.

Three days later Broughton asked Litchfield's secretary to send him four sets of good copies of the newspaper clippings. She surmised that he intended to give them to the directors of the trust.

Some ten years earlier, when plans were being laid for the Mellon trust grant of $12.5 million that created the Graduate School of Public Health, the trust's consultants had raised and reraised a question: was Pitt's undergraduate College of Arts and Sciences strong enough to support the high quality of faculty and curriculum that the trust was demanding for the Schools of Public Health and Medicine? Discussions were held throughout a decade between officers of the trust and the University on how to establish a high level of teaching and curriculum in the basic liberal arts and disciplines of the undergraduate College. In January, March, and December of 1958, the University presented plans to the trust that emphasized the need to obtain and support individual scholars of high reputation at both the undergraduate and graduate student levels. The trustees responded affirmatively to these proposals.

Litchfield made the great announcement on December 16, 1958, at a convocation of faculty members, administrators, trustees, student leaders, and alumni representatives. It was, according to Stanton Crawford, a magnificent presentation. The A. W. Mellon Educational and Charitable Trust, Litchfield said, had just made a grant to the University of $12 million for the advancement of the basic academic disciplines—the humanities, the natural sciences, and the social sciences. The gift would be used for three purposes:

1. $350,000 to planning the activities incident to developing the new program. This would go to the newly created College of the Academic Disciplines, the organizational unit that encompassed the humanities, the natural sciences, and the social sciences.

2. $5.5 million to establish and endow ten distinguished Andrew Mellon Professorships. Six of the endowed chairs would be established in the humanities: classics, English, fine arts, modern languages and literature, music, and philosophy. Two would be in the natural sciences: mathematics and physics. Two would be in the social sciences: history and sociology (which then included anthropology).

3. $6.15 million to support fifty predoctoral fellows and six to nine postdoctoral fellows, to be awarded primarily, though not exclusively, in the specific disciplines in which the professorial appointments were made. The fifty predoctoral Mellon Fellowships would pay an annual stipend that, with free tuition of $700 or more, would have a value ranging from $2,700 to $3,700 each. The postdoctoral Mellon Fellowships would pay $6,000, plus supplements for dependents, travel, and incidental costs of research.

In a letter read by Litchfield to the convocation, Paul Mellon wrote: "This grant is made with the understanding that the University will agree that salaries paid to the Andrew Mellon Professors will be such as to attract eminent men capable of distinguished scholarship in their fields and will be commensurate with or superior to the best salaries paid in like fields in any other American university. This principle will apply also to the stipends for holders of Andrew Mellon Fellowships."

Stanton Crawford relayed to Litchfield a dozen or more comments he heard after the convocation broke up. They ranged from overwhelmingly favorable ("Even the people in Business Administration were pleased") to a few that were unfavorable ("It won't do me any good").

The Mellon gift changed the reputation of the University of Pittsburgh. A faculty member returning from a meeting of the American Economic Association reported that everyone seemed to be talking about Pittsburgh, and members who attended meetings of the American Philosophical Association, the Modern Language Association, and others gave similar reports. Charles Peake, who was placed in charge of the program, was delighted to hear it said that people around the country were telling their bright young men and women, "Why not go to Pitt? That's where things are changing, that's where you can get ahead." Alvin Eurich, vice president of the Ford Foundation's Fund for the Advancement of Education, wrote in the *Atlantic* of the pioneering of the University of Pittsburgh under Chancellor Litchfield. James W. Wiggins, chairman of the Department of Sociology and Anthropology at Emory University, wrote Litchfield to volunteer the information that, according to his researchers, "Your maximum predoctoral fellowships have stipends almost as high as those at any institution of higher learning in this country."

In running the program, Peake worked with a committee at the University and with eminent advisors in various fields in this country and abroad. There were ninety-four applicants for the first fourteen Mellon Fellowships; eleven were found worthy and were signed on. In practice it was found advisable to bend the rules a bit and "to give higher stipends even to first year students if they are exceptionally well qualified and if by this means we can induce them to come here rather than to go elsewhere." Peake's most satisfying duty was that of traveling about and offering Mellon Professorships that paid $20,000 to $25,000 per academic year, with supplements, to distinguished scholars. He was cordially welcomed everywhere, for even those who had no interest in his proposition had a friend or two who would be.* The original plan had been to

---

*His fine arts advisor in England was Sir Anthony Frederick Blunt, K.C.V.O., F.B.A., graduate of Trinity College, Cambridge, director of the Courtauld Institute of Art, and Surveyor of the Queen's Pictures, who some two decades later was discovered to have been a long-time Soviet espionage agent. He turned down the offer of a Visiting Mellon Professorship at Pitt because, he said, he had an ulcer.

give five-year contracts to the Mellon Professors, but that had proved to be impractical, and so the contracts were made permanent. A new category, however, was added with the permission of the trust: that of a Visiting Mellon Professor who stayed for a year or two while permanent tenure was being negotiated with him or someone else.

In assessing the results of the program twenty years later, the Mellon Educational and Charitable Trust declared in a report: "Of the approximately 150 Mellon Fellows to date, most have gone on to teach and conduct research both in this country and abroad. Many have already achieved distinction in their respective fields. Almost half are already listed in the *Directory of American Scholars* or in *American Men and Women of Science.*"

Of the Andrew Mellon Professorships the report said, "It is evident that the Mellon Professorships have been a central influence in the development of scholarly programs in the Arts and Sciences at the University of Pittsburgh. For example, the first two appointments in Anthropology and Philosophy made possible the development of those departments into leaders in their fields throughout the United States. Other appointments have similarly served to create significant academic communities in those disciplines in which they have been made."

The anthropology appointment went to George Peter Murdock, professor of anthropology at Yale since 1939 and one of the world's outstanding anthropologists. Murdock built the department, and in 1964 and 1965 the American Anthropological Association elected two successive presidents from the University. One of the presidents was John P. Gillin, research professor of anthropology and dean of the Division of Social Sciences, author or coauthor of seven books, and specialist in Latin American studies and research into the disintegration of complex sociocultural systems. The other president was Alexander Spoehr, specialist in and author of works on North American and Pacific ethnology, social anthropology, and archeology. With George Murdock as a recent past-president, the University became the only institution besides Harvard with three presidents of the sixty-eight-year-old association on its staff.

The Mellon Professorship that started the Department of Philosophy on its path to preeminence was awarded in 1960 to Adolf Grunbaum, a brilliant young (thirty-seven) pioneer in a new field—the philosophy of science. The philosopher of science is described as a scholar who is two parts philosopher and one part scientist. Although he has been scientifically trained, he is not a scientist in the practicing, professional sense. Instead, he is interested in scientific ideas and theories as they influence or contradict or dovetail with ideas in other areas of thought.

Grunbaum brought with him a Lehigh colleague as the associate director of the new Center for the Philosophy of Science: Nicholas Rescher, an internationally recognized authority on the theory of knowledge and a prolific author (he now has over forty books to his credit).

Late in 1962, Yale University attempted a raid: it invited Adolf Grunbaum to set up a center for the philosophy of science at New Haven, making what Charles Peake called a most appealing offer. Grunbaum's strongest advocate at Yale had been Wilfred Stalker Sellars, a star of the department. When Grunbaum declined the Yale offer, writing a letter "painstaking in its presentation of the many considerations" that swayed him in his decision, the Yale department head bowed out gracefully. ("We have lost a great opportunity and I am sorry, but I wish you well. . . . We tried hard to get the best man we knew.") Grunbaum thereupon proposed that since he could not join Sellars at Yale, perhaps Sellars would like to join him at Pitt. Sellars agreed to come early in 1963. The Yale philosophy department held an emergency meeting on a Sunday morning and, after a unanimous vote on the matter, made a dramatic telephone call to Grunbaum. They appealed to him not to take Sellars on the ground that his departure would wreck their department. Grunbaum refused to withdraw the offer. Sellars said that the decision had been made and that the subject was closed. To Litchfield he wrote, "The prospect of joining in a cooperative effort to make the University of Pittsburgh a major center of philosophical activity is an exciting one."

With him Sellars brought a magazine he was coediting, *Philosophical Studies,* and the manuscript of a book he was completing, *Science, Perception and Reality*. Three of his outstanding young colleagues followed him to Pittsburgh and to the Pitt faculty: Alan Ross Anderson, whose special interests included mathematical logic—especially modal logic, deontic logic, and entailment; Nuel D. Belnap, Jr., authority on the logical relations of entailment; and Omar Khayyam Moore, a philosopher-sociologist, who had created the "talking typewriter," which combined an electric typewriter with an early computer and speaker, through which children could learn the various language skills early in their development. Still another Yale colleague, Jerome B. Schneewind, joined the Department of Philosophy about a year later.

The department's claim to preeminence was fortified in 1962 when Kurt E. Baier, forty-five, head of philosophy at the Australian National University in Melbourne, became chairman. Norwood R. Hanson, professor of philosophy at Yale, wrote on June 10, 1965, "You people are doing something which is invaluable to the future of my professional discipline. . . . All we professionals look to Pittsburgh now as the virtual heart of the serious metabolism in Philosophy of Science within this hemisphere."

Late in 1982 the Conference Board of Associated Research Councils evaluated the Pitt philosophy department as among the top five in the country. It ranked second in its effectiveness in educating scholars and third in the quality of its faculty. It was the only institution with two distinct programs ranked in the philosophy category: philosophy and the history and philosophy of science. Pitt's faculty in the history and philosophy of science is generally recognized today as the most powerful in the world.

One of the duties of each Mellon Professor, permanent and visiting, was to deliver at least one evening lecture, free and open to students, faculty, and citizens at large. Henceforth Pittsburgh was to hear some of the great scholars of their time speak in the field of their life's work. Mario Pei, greatest of living philologists, on linguistic forms of the modern world. L. C. Knights, Shakespearean scholar, on Shakespeare and politics. Rhys Carpenter, classical archeologist, on archeology and the humanities. Ernest T. DeWald, scholar of medieval art and Italian painting, on the roles of mysticism and Neo-Platonism in determining the style and contents of the works of Fra Angelico and Michelangelo. Jean J. Seznec, professor of French literature at Oxford, on Ernest Renan and the religious crisis in the nineteenth century. Wilfred Mellers, musicologist and composer, on whether there is a crisis in modern music. Max A. Lauffer, Permanent Andrew Mellon Professor of biophysics, on water, virus, and life.

The University was helped in its search for top-ranking new faculty members by the presence of the Mellon Professors, since professors tend to go to a university because of the quality of its faculty in their disciplines. The University was helped further by two magnificent grants from the Ford Foundation, which had recently reduced its $3 billion in holdings by giving huge sums to scores of colleges and universities. Pitt received $1.5 million for medical education and $1.617 million for general purposes. Litchfield promised some of his more distinguished recruits that henceforth he would "maintain the status of University professors on a level with that of the Mellon Professors." The recruiting was eminently successful, but there were lapses of judgment that surviving administrators have forgotten or, perhaps, wish they could forget. One involved a brilliant young naturalized citizen from Poland, a political scientist with a Harvard Ph.D. He was an assistant professor in Harvard's Russian Research Center and Center for International Affairs, which already had several brilliant young Poles and so offered this one to Pitt. Pitt was not interested, perhaps because of the man's unpronounceable name, Zbigniew Brzezinski.

These developments at the University were accompanied by administrative changes, beginning with the choice of a chairman to succeed Alan Scaife. As early as January 1957, Litchfield had asked the alumni groups to consider nominating Gwilym A. Price, chairman of Westinghouse Electric, as their trustee. Nothing came of the suggestion at the time, but the following year Harry B. Higgins, recently retired chairman of Pittsburgh Plate Glass, asked Price to join him on the Pitt board. There were some negative minds about Litchfield on the board, he said, but he thought the chancellor was a brilliant man who deserved all the help he could get.

Price, born in Canonsburg, Pennsylvania, in 1895, was the son of Welsh immigrants. "I was a very poor boy. I wanted badly to become a lawyer, and I started to go to night school. I went to Pitt a couple of times, Duquesne a couple of times, and I figured, 'My God! I'll be fifty years old before I get into law school.'" He was tutored for three years in a law office while going to high school, and in 1914 passed the preliminary bar examination, which permitted him to enter Pitt Law School without the two years of college then otherwise required. He graduated in 1917, served 2½ years as an army officer, became president of Peoples-Pittsburgh Trust Company (now Pittsburgh National Bank) in 1940 and president of Westinghouse in 1947, chairman in 1959.

Price was receptive to Higgins's invitation to join the Pitt board, but there was one complication: he was already serving on the Carnegie Tech board. He called on Dr. John C. Warner, president of Tech. "I explained as best I could that the LL.B. from Pitt was the only degree I had, the only earned degree, and that I felt greatly indebted to the University and wished to serve it. He said, 'You know, Bill, Ben Fairless is not going to be around too long, and I was hoping you might take his place as chairman of our board.' But I resigned, and I think Jake always resented it a little." His nomination to the Pitt board was endorsed by Richard K. Mellon, and he was elected to fill the vacancy caused by the retirement of Arthur Braun, who at eighty-three became trustee emeritus. Price became chairman of the Pitt board on March 21, 1959.

Within three months Price and Litchfield together made a call on Frank R. Denton, chief executive officer of Mellon Bank, and persuaded him to fill a vacancy on the Pitt board. Litchfield had sought out Denton when he first came to Pittsburgh as chancellor-elect. Early in 1957 he flew his plane to Tucson, where Denton was vacationing, to ask his advice on some matter. His fiancée, Mary Morrill, was with him. She and Denton became good friends at once; they had the bond of having been born and reared in Kansas, and, in Denton's words, "We had things

in common out there." Of Litchfield, Denton said, "He had a brilliant mind, he was an excellent speaker, and he improved the University. I thought him attractive and I quite liked him."

Price had told Litchfield before becoming board chairman that he would not "go to the 39th floor for you"—would not intercede for him with R. K. Mellon. With Denton's acceptance of a place on the board in June 1959, Litchfield and Price had with them a man who was one of those closest to Mellon.

The Hillman archives contain seven letters from Mellon to Litchfield. Although there is in their correspondence an underlying formality and reserve, the letters are cordial, and the two men were on a "Dick" and "Ed," "Connie" and "Mary" basis. In December 1958 Mellon sent regrets on an invitation: "Ed, between now and the end of the year, there just isn't time for me to do anything but sit and hold on to my desk and lunch from its corner. This year-end closing and with additional responsibilities which I have temporarily assumed since Alan's death, has made this particular December unusually burdensome." In November 1958 he had written, "I was delighted to hear that the newspaper editors and representatives of both radio and television were so impressed by your magnificent plans for the development of the university and particularly the re-routing of Forbes Avenue."

In that month Litchfield sent Mellon a very worried letter. In it he told of "a profile story" about himself as chancellor, titled "The All-Purpose Executive," that was to appear in *Fortune*. It was something, he said, that they had asked to do. He tried to resist it, "but they insisted they were going to write it whether I wanted them to or not. Under the circumstances, we had no choice but to cooperate. . . . There were many parts in it that made me most unhappy, and, indeed, at one point I was so angry that I threatened to sue them if they printed some of the material they proposed to include. After a great deal of effort . . . we finally eliminated some of the most unhappy parts. However, we weren't able to get them all out and I thought I should tell you about this before the story appears."

Litchfield sent identical letters to ten other people

Richard King Mellon, prime mover in the Pittsburgh Renaissance of 1945–1960, featured on the cover of Time *magazine, October 3, 1949.*

on the same day: to Frank Denton, Joseph D. Hughes, Mrs. Alan Scaife, Leon Falk, Gwilym Price, William Penn Snyder, J. Steele Gow, and to associates at Cornell and Smith-Corona. *Fortune* had sent him three copies of the article in typescript for "your correction of inaccuracies and your opinions on questions of interpretations." Stanton Crawford told him at once that the article would be "disturbing to trustees and other supporting interests, since it might be interpreted as implying a threat [to leave] quoted from you. Further, the possibility of your departure might be a serious deterrent to recruitment of new faculty and administrative persons."

Mellon's letter of reply was the warmest and most open of the seven he wrote to Litchfield: "I felt rather sorry for you after reading your letter, but let me give you this much sympathetic advice. These rather peculiar magazine writers, well, in fact, all authors and editors, never quite tell the whole truth and although they guarantee you can read the galley proof, that usually is received the day before the magazine is placed for sale on the newsstand. I don't think you should worry too much about this situation as you and I can do so little when the article is edited and printed." Litchfield replied with relief, "I cannot tell you how happy I was to return from a speech to the Penn, Temple, Pitt alumni in Allentown last night, in an effort to raise money, and find your good letter. . . . You are most understanding and most consoling and I want you to know how deeply I appreciate it."

The University was a much larger and more complex operation under Litchfield than it had been under his predecessor, and this change in scale was inevitably reflected in the size of the administrative staff. A faculty member complained mildly in 1962, "I have trouble identifying all these vice chancellors and assistant chancellors." His trouble was understandable. There were six such offices in 1962, they were relatively new, some of the officers departed and were replaced by others, and some of them traded positions and titles.

New schools and departments, and new buildings to hold them, also proliferated in the early 1960s.

• In April 1962 the University began a drive to win a share of the billions of dollars that were being sluiced into the nation's aerospace program. Litchfield set out to sell the region's preeminence in metals and nuclear energy, its complex of research laboratories, and the need for an institution that would channel the "spin-off" of space technology into industrial and commerical use. Working with Pittsburgh civic and political people, and obtaining a number of corporate grants, he made repeated trips to Washington to meet with congressmen, senators, officers of the National Aeronautics and Space Administration (NASA), and on one occasion with President Kennedy himself. He obtained NASA grants of several hundred thousand dollars for predoctoral fellowships and $1.5 million to erect the Space Research and Coordinating Center for studies in the natural sciences, social sciences, engineering, and health areas concerned with the aerospace field. This was hailed in Pittsburgh, somewhat prematurely, as the first step of "what could be a move into the forefront of the space renaissance."

• The Department of Physics, competing against Yale and Stanford, among others, was awarded a $2 million, three-stage, 18-million-volt Van de Graaf nuclear accelerator by the National Science Foundation. Sarah Mellon Scaife made a gift of $1 million to erect a three-story structure beside the old Mellon Institute on O'Hara Street to hold the 160-foot-long machine, which bends a proton beam upward through an opening in the ceiling into a "target room" on the second floor.

• The most ambitious of the new schools grew out of Litchfield's experiences at Cornell. In 1957 he appointed a group under the direction of Alan Rankin to develop a graduate school that would provide both instruction and research in preparing executive leaders for public administration at all levels of government. A name was chosen: the Graduate School of Public and International Affairs (GSPIA). The Falk Foundation gave $100,000 as a starter; the A. W. Mellon Educational and Charitable Trust, $125,000; the Howard Heinz Endowment, $100,000 for support of a Heinz Associate Professor of International Affairs; the Richard King

Mellon Foundation, $100,000; and the Ford Foundation, $500,000. Donald C. Stone, president of Springfield (Massachusetts) College, who had had a thirty-year career in public service and administration, became the founding dean.

• In September 1962 the University opened the Graduate School of Library and Information Sciences. This venture grew out of the Carnegie Library School, which had been founded in 1901 as a training school for children's librarians. As part of Carnegie Tech since 1930, it had trained most of the professional librarians in the area. Now it had a class of about fifty students, half of them part-time, and it could not renew its accreditation from the American Library Association unless it could become part of a university with a broad liberal arts program. Carnegie Tech, deciding it could not meet that requirement and that it should no longer support the school financially, asked Pitt to take it over. Pitt accordingly undertook to train librarians for public, educational, and special libraries in a one-year, three-trimester program leading to a master's degree in library science. The first dean was Harold Lancour, who had been associate director of the Library School at the University of Illinois. By 1965 his school had twenty-two faculty members and an enrollment of 397, and it was one of only nine schools in the country that offered a doctorate in library science.

• The Department of Modern Languages was reorganized and took on sixteen new faculty members in entering upon what it called a new and propitious era. It changed its name to Department of Modern Languages and Literature and changed its emphasis to graduate and advanced undergraduate programs. Divided into four sections, it taught Romance, Slavic, German, and Far Eastern languages and literature.

• In a convocation address in 1960, Litchfield pressed for a broader program of international studies. A Ford Foundation grant was awarded to Pitt two years later, and in 1964 the Latin American Studies Center was founded by Cole Blasier. The Russian and East European Studies Program was established in 1965 under the direction of Carl Beck.

The East Asian Language and Area Center had been begun by James Liu in 1960, based on a program established by Liu in 1951.

Since 1979, the Latin American Center has been designated by the U.S. Department of Education as one of the ten best centers in the country, and another outside evaluation ranks it as the best center in the Northeast. The Russian and East European Studies Program is building America's most comprehensive research tool for the study of the Soviet government—a computerized inventory of Soviet government officials from the Russian Revolution to the present. The East Asian library, housed in Hillman Library, now ranks fifteenth among the one hundred major East Asian collections in the United States.

• After making a one-year feasibility study, the University created two-year colleges in Greensburg, Titusville, and Bradford to meet the problems of rising college costs and the flood of students expected in the mid-1970s. (Pitt's junior colleges at Erie and Uniontown had been closed in the 1940s.) These were to emphasize freshman and sophomore training that would lead to enrollment on the main campus in the third year. The University of Pittsburgh at Johnstown, founded in 1927, would move in 1967 to a 635-acre wooded campus and become a four-year undergraduate college with six academic buildings, a library, a student union–physical education complex, and five residence halls.

• In August 1962 Litchfield and four faculty members left on a journey to Ecuador "to explore a long-term cooperative development program" with Central University at Quito. This was the forerunner of other such trips to other such countries, sponsored and largely paid for by the U.S. Agency for International Development.

• The University Book Center opened in January 1960 on the ground floor of one of the Schenley Quadrangle buildings, facing on Fifth Avenue. It was called at the time the largest college bookstore in the country; it cost $495,000; and it had sales of $401,000 in its first six months. The Middle States Association evaluation team described it as "truly magnificent."

Book Center.

Lynn Johnson

Morale was running high in these years. It was a glittering time; there was a golden glow resulting from solid accomplishments, new educational adventures (extending even into developing countries), and progress toward the goals that had been set in 1956. This chancellor had turned out to be dynamic, a leader, an authority on administration, a success in the world of business and yet absolutely sound as an educator. There was a feeling among some of the faculty and staff that on this campus they were part of a special situation—that here the capacity of an educational institution to raise itself to a level of excellence was being demonstrated before an interested national audience. Charles Peake re-

called two decades later, "It was an exciting atmosphere here. I felt it myself."

There were problems, of course, most of them, annoyingly, having to do with money. But Litchfield's philosophy was reflected in his comment to a faculty member, "It's nice to have a problem"; and he took care of the big one—money—with characteristic decisiveness and largeness of thought.

He held a two-day meeting of trustees and top administrators at the Rolling Rock Club in January 1961, and there he presented what appeared to be a carefully developed financial program for the University that would solve all problems for the next ten years. He showed by charts and graphs that there would be planned operating deficits of $1.6 million for 1960–1961 and $1.9 million for 1961–1962, after which there would be annual budget surpluses. The first surplus, in 1962–1963, would be $370,000; in 1966–1967 it would be $2.5 million. For the whole ten-year period the surplus would be $7.3 million.

In order to carry the University through the deficits of the next two years, the chancellor asked the trustees to approve a $10 million loan from the Equitable Life Assurance Company. The interest rate would be 5¾ percent per annum; principal would be repayable with interest in quarterly installments beginning in 1962–1963, the year of the first surplus. He called the loan the means of making "a great educational leap forward." He had discussed it with Equitable, with the University's two largest banks, Mellon and Pittsburgh National, and with the Finance, Executive, and Educational Policy committees. A new comptroller, hired in October 1959, said that $10 million was inadequate—that at least $20 million would be needed to carry out all the programs that were being planned—but his report was ignored.

Some of those present at the January meeting remembered it two decades later as a magnificent presentation. The trustees, including Frank Denton and Gwilym Price, both trained as bankers and both relatively new trustees, concluded that the plan was forward looking and constructive. The chancellor's past record gave them no reason to question his assurance that the two-year imbalance was temporary. It was not unusual, in their corporate operations, to make loans to realize an advantageous development. The audience applauded when Litchfield concluded, and there was a general note of appreciation and optimism.

On the basis of the chancellor's forecasts and recommendations, the trustees on March 13, 1961, voted to borrow the $10 million from Equitable for the great educational leap forward. If anyone questioned the chancellor's figures, or thought that perhaps the trustees should raise the $10 million by public subscription rather than by borrowing, he did not express his views at either of these meetings.

The evaluation team of the Middle States Association warned that the 5¾ percent interest rate on the proposed loan was above the national average for institutions and that repayment of debt and interest would recur each year after 1962 as a constant cash drain. In its view, "the philosophy of letting the future pay for current requirements may be an acceptable, calculated, fiscal policy, but it must always be fully recognized as such by all responsible people with complete knowledge and with adequate supporting financial accounting reports available." The team, however, was reassured on these points by what it conceived to be the high quality of the current personnel in the business and institutional planning offices. The presence of an assistant chancellor for business affairs in the budget-making process, it felt, "insures adequacy of information for the Chancellor, administrative officials, and the Board of Trustees to enable them to project properly good fiscal planning, not only for the immediate operating areas, but also for long-term commitments."

On December 3, 1962, at six o'clock in the morning died John Gabbert Bowman, president emeritus of the University, in the eighty-fifth year of his life.

His wife had been struck and killed by an automobile in October 1950 while she was crossing the street from the Schenley Hotel to the Cathedral of Learning. The following year Bowman sold his farm to the state for $180,000, to become part of a state park, and he bought a large 125-year-old house at 341 South Juliana Street in Bedford.

On March 8, 1956, on the thirtieth anniversary of the ground-breaking for the Cathedral of Learning, he attended a cermony in the Commons Room in which that building was dedicated to him. A stone tablet embedded in the wall carries these carved words:

THE TRUSTEES OF THE UNIVERSITY OF PITTSBURGH DEDICATE THIS BUILDING TO JOHN GABBERT BOWMAN CHANCELLOR 1921–1946 MAY THE BUILDING STAND FOR CENTURIES A SYMBOL OF HIS VISION A SIGN OF HIS FAITH THAT YOUTH WILL FIND HERE MOMENTS OF GREAT VICTORY

In May of 1957 Bowman wrote Dr. Litchfield that

he could not, on his doctor's advice, accept the invitation to attend the chancellor's inauguration. "You are making a fine start," he said, "but you will come on discouraging days in which you will need the patience of Job and immeasurable wisdom."

The newspaper obituaries, in telling Dr. Bowman's career, emphasized his achievements and the paradoxes in his character, and, in a final irony, gave much space to his troubles with Ralph E. Turner and John B. Sutherland.

23

The Colodny Case

Thank God for fair-minded citizens with the courage and ability to defend a free society against the misguided and ill-informed zealots no less than against subversive elements. Such a defense comes most appropriately from a great institution of higher learning. Long may the spirit of truth and inquiry flourish at the University! For should it falter there, we would have lost one of the strongest bulwarks of freedom.

Editorial in the *Pittsburgh Post-Gazette*, June 15, 1961

On March 7, 1959, Charles Peake, vice chancellor for the academic disciplines, announced the appointment of Robert Garland Colodny, forty-four, as an associate professor of history at the University. Dr. Colodny, the news release said,

is currently a member of the faculty at the University of Kansas and has taught at the University of California, San Francisco State College, and Wesleyan University (Connecticut). He was for two years a research fellow in the Institute for Philosophical Research under the direction of Dr. Mortimer Adler and is a contributor to the recently published volume *The Idea of Freedom*.

From 1941 to 1945 he served in the United States Army and is co-author of the War Department book *Battle of the Aleutians*. He also has published the book *The Struggle for Madrid* and numerous reviews and is currently writing a book on the philosophy of history.

Dr. Colodny's career was more varied and interesting than the press release indicated. He was a student of chemistry at the University of Chicago in 1937 when he elected to join some thirty-two hundred other young Americans who had been seized by a passionate cause. With them he went to fight in the Spanish Civil War on behalf of the elected republican government of that country, which was under attack in an uprising led by right-wing military officers under General Francisco Franco. When Mussolini sent some eighty thousand regular army ground troops to fight in Spain, and Hitler sent air and sea forces, a great many people of many persuasions in many nations felt that this was the start of World War II and that Hitler and Mussolini must be turned back at all costs. As a member of the Abraham Lincoln Brigade, one of a number of international brigades recruited in fifty-three countries with the help of the Soviet Union, Colodny saw heavy fighting for almost a year around Madrid, until he was severely wounded by a bullet above his right eye. The Nazi-Fascist incursion in Spain was victorious; the government fell and resistance ended in March 1939—the same month that the Nazis dissolved what was left of the Republic of Czechoslovakia, five months before the invasion of Poland and the beginning of World War II.

In 1941—before the attack on Pearl Harbor— Colodny enlisted in the U.S. Army, serving four years, two of them in the Aleutian Islands. He received security clearance to serve in a unit controlled by army intelligence, assigned as a technician fifth grade to monitor Axis radio communications. During that time he coauthored *The Battle of the Aleutians*, for which he received the Army Commendation Medal. (His coauthor was Sergeant Dashiell Hammett, U.S. Signal Corps.)

In 1950 Colodny received a doctorate in history and philosophy from the University of California (Berkeley) and began his teaching career. He came to Pitt warmly recommended by his latest employer, the chancellor of the University of Kansas. On his appointment forms Litchfield wrote, "Let's congratulate ourselves."

In Pittsburgh in 1960, Colodny became a supporter of the Fair Play for Cuba Committee and was one of some thirty people who signed an advertisement in the *New York Times* on April 6, 1960, largely paid for, it was alleged, by R. Roa, Jr., son of Fidel Castro's foreign minister. In 1961 Colodny became vice chairman of the Pittsburgh Committee for a Sane Nuclear Policy.

In January 1961 a *Pittsburgh Press* reporter named William Gill interviewed Dr. Colodny about his political views and his affinity for left-wing causes and organizations. The result appeared on the front page of the Sunday *Press* on January 13. In a peculiar technique, the author interspersed parenthetical notes in italics to explain editorially, in what purported to be a news story, the significance of what had just been said and to link Colodny's comments with events and facts not immediately germane to the interview. The article amounted to a charge of subversion against Colodny because of his association with the Abraham Lincoln Brigade twenty-three years earlier and with other organizations labeled un-American by the attorney general.

At this point, a member of the state legislature, John T. Walsh, denounced Colodny on the floor of the House and introduced a two-part resolution. He called for a legislative investigation of Colodny and for an investigation of what he called "pro-Communist leanings" and "anti-U.S. sentiment" in all stated-aided colleges. As an aside, he threatened the University with loss of its state appropriation and said that other Pitt professors were also suspect.

Litchfield ignored the original *Press* article, but he at once issued a statement defending Colodny against a legislative attack. "By law, by charter, and by conviction," he said, "the University is committed to resist Communism in every possible way. . . . At the same time, we deplore all forms of unfair and defamatory accusations leveled against any man. Such attacks are in reality attacks on our democratic processes and freedoms, and have no place in a society such as ours. . . . We have attested to Dr. Colodny's loyalty to democracy, and we have found nothing substantive to date which would cause us to doubt his loyalty now."

Colodny denied that he had defended Cuban actions in the Gill interview. He said he had merely expressed his objective views as a historian when asked, and charged that his words had been "misquoted in every important aspect." The *Post-Gazette*, in an editorial titled "Fair Play for Professor," said, "The administration at Pitt is to be commended for coming promptly and forthrightly to the defense of Dr. Colodny. . . . The House Rules Committee in Harrisburg, to which the Walsh resolution was referred, should tell the legislator it has no intention of launching an educational witch-hunt on the flimsy evidence he has offered. This is not Cuba, this is America. And in America there is still room for dissent. When there ceases to be, God help us all."

Thus was born what has been called "the last national case of anti-Communist witch-hunting." The Gill article set off a chain of events that involved, among other organizations, the Pennsylvania State Legislature, the House Committee on Un-American Activities, the Senate Internal Security Committee, the American Association of University Professors, the American Civil Liberties Union, the American Legion, and the Veterans of Foreign Wars. It led to an editorial battle between the *Pittsburgh Press* and the *Post-Gazette*.

● The *Pittsburgh Press* reported that the proposed state investigation was gaining support, and it carried an exclusive story out of Washington quoting Francis E. Walters (Democrat, Pennsylvania), chairman of the House Committee on Un-American

Activities, who disclosed that his committee's files contained "many mentions" of Dr. Colodny, although the professor himself had never appeared before the committee. Walters cited the names of seven listed organizations with which Colodny's name had been linked, including the Veterans of the Abraham Lincoln Brigade, which was put on the list long after Colodny joined it.

● The *Pitt News* ran two front-page editorials defending Chancellor Litchfield, who more usually had been the object of its attacks.

● Sixty-eight of Colodny's students signed a letter to the *Press* supporting him.

● Representative Walsh said he had discovered that Colodny did not get the army medal, as he claimed, for his services in the Aleutians.*

● The *Post-Gazette* printed a statement by the chairman of the Pittsburgh branch of the American Civil Liberties Union in which he charged that Dr. Colodny had forced the *Press* into acknowledging an inaccuracy in a story about him and printing a retraction, and *that* was why the *Press* had declared a personal vendetta on Colodny.

● The *Press* disproved this charge decisively and asserted that the attacks being made on it by the defenders of Dr. Colodny had reached a new low in the *Post-Gazette*.

● The *Post-Gazette* said that a legislator was heard to shout, "Why should we support a publicity stunt of the *Pittsburgh Press?*"

● The AAUP chapters at Pitt, Carnegie Tech, Chatham, Mount Mercy, and Duquesne passed resolutions supporting Colodny and Litchfield.

● The *Press* quoted a boast by Earl Browder, head of the Communist Party U.S.A. (before he was expelled from the party), that 60 percent of the members of the Abraham Lincoln Brigade were Communists (which, of course, indicated that 40 percent were not).

● The Reverend Charles Owen Rice of the Church of the Immaculate Conception wrote in his

---

*He was wrong. The medal was given on a letter of commendation dated July 29, 1944, signed by Lieutenant General Delos C. Emmons, U.S. Army, Commanding General, Alaskan Department.

column in the *Pittsburgh Catholic* that Colodny's service in the Abraham Lincoln Brigade should not be held against him, because he was probably in a hospital with his head wound when the Communists took over the brigade and purged it of anti-Communists. "The university," he wrote, "should be trusted to handle the matter and to settle it with justice and wisdom."

● The newspapers expanded their letters-to-the-editor sections to handle the flood of correspondence, pro and con, on the Colodny affair.

Litchfield in the spring of 1961 was in a difficult position. The Colodny case clearly raised basic questions of a most serious nature about academic freedom, the right of free expression, the meaning of loyalty, and the nature of an academic community. Is a professor to risk reprisal if he opens his mouth on a controversial subject? Is he to be forced to defend himself every time a politician or reporter attacks him for expressing an unpopular opinion? Would not the community be intellectually poorer if he were? Is the professor to be held responsible—is there no statute of limitations—for ideas he held and actions he took twenty-five years earlier? Is not the best protection against subversive doctrine a healthy atmosphere with free and informed discussion? Should not an educational institution accept the expression within it of differing points of view, some of them unpopular?

On the other hand, should a newspaper be expected to censor itself, curtail its freedom of the press, and withhold what might be damaging information about an educator? And is academic freedom absolute and without boundaries? Was the Pittsburgh chapter of the AAUP justified in announcing, as it did at the start of the Colodny case, that it would defend any professor, regardless of his associations, against any attack upon his expression of ideas, from whatever source and however unpopular those ideas might be? Suppose the teacher was passionately dedicated to an ideology of the extreme right instead of the far left—say, to repulsive concepts of Aryan racial purity and supremacy. Would the faculty rally around to defend his right to express his views? Would his teaching be permitted for a second week on any American campus? *Should* it be permitted?

In this troubled situation, Litchfield elected to appoint an ad hoc fact-finding committee of three University people who were *sans peur et sans reproche*. He chose as chairman Philip H. Powers, assistant chancellor for development of the University, who for ten years had been president of the West Penn Power Company. The other two members of the committee were Dr. Robert E. Olson, professor of biochemistry at the Graduate School of Public Health; and George D. Lockhart, Law School alumnus and trustee of the University, a prominent attorney and a member of the boards of various corporations, including the H. K. Porter Company, the Dollar Savings Bank, and Lockhart Iron and Steel. They would review the allegations made by Mr. Walsh and deliver a report to the chancellor. The law firm of Eckert, Seamans, and Cherin was retained "to help determine the relevance of all findings and to assure the proper regard for the legal rights of all parties." The chancellor's report would be given to the press and the state assembly, but the papers and the findings of the committee itself would remain classified in order to protect Colodny's right to privacy and the confidentiality of those who testified.

In the meantime, opposition to the Walsh bill was being led by K. Leroy Irvis, the black legislator whose district included the University campus. The Walsh bill was killed by a vote of 125 to 69, with a dozen abstentions, thus leaving the matter in the hands of the University.

In the last week in May, after more than four months of work, the Powers Committee turned over its findings to the chancellor. Included were the records of legal counsel, the report of the committee, and several thousand pages of testimony in four volumes more than two feet high.

On June 1 Colodny appeared as a subpoenaed witness before the House Committee on Un-American Activities in Washington, where he testified for five hours in connection with a request he had made for a grant (which he did not get) to a left-wing tax-exempt foundation. The hearing was closed to reporters, but information about Colodny's appearance and his testimony was leaked to the *Pittsburgh Press.* Colodny admitted he had been a member of a half-dozen organizations listed by the attorney general as Communist fronts, but he swore under oath that he was not and never had been a member of the Communist party. The committee did not cite Colodny or take any other action.

Litchfield had been working for several weeks on the report he had to make. He began by sending the Powers Committee report and the counsel's findings to three trusted friends for their review and comment. They were Dexter Perkins, recently retired as emeritus senior professor of American civilization at Cornell; Maurice T. Moore, senior vice president in the New York law firm of Cravath, Swaine and Moore; and Deane Malott, president of Cornell University. Perkins found the committee's report entirely convincing. Moore said, "In my opinion you are justified in relying upon the investigation of the Committee and its findings of fact." Malott found some documented cause for concern about "Mr. Colodny's participation in the Spanish Civil War and subsequent related events" but found no justification in the document either for Colodny's removal or for other punitive or corrective measures.

Litchfield prepared his report—the only one that would be made public—in the form of a letter to Gwilym Price, chairman. In it he protected his right flank by stating in several places the evils of Communism, the University's pledged opposition to the threats of international Communism, and the danger "of admitting to our fellowship those who would subvert a society which postulates multiplicity of values, pluralistic institutions, and the constitutional framework designed to protect them."

He began with a graceful essay on the meaning of academic freedom.

An American university is by definition a place of free enquiry. It is not a government bureau, nor an industrial corporation nor a church. Its role in society postulates question, criticism, controversy, debate and doubt in all matters, social as well as scientific. The university embraces and supports the society in which it operates, but it knows no established doctrines, accepts no ordained patterns of behavior, acknowledges no truth as given. Were it otherwise the university would be unworthy of the role which our society has assigned it.

In the last analysis, the university must be free to think as its members will, to the same extent that the press must be free to comment as it will, as one branch of government must function independently of another, as the churches must be free to offer doctrinal sanctuary, as the corporations must have opportunity to pursue product and market with an absolute minimum of outside direction. . . .

As staunch defenders of a democratic system we must also be concerned about those who would over-zealously "defend" our social system in such a way as to destroy it. If I rise and damn my fellow man, I should be prepared with clear and incontrovertible evidence. I should first have conferred with his peers, should have tried established channels for just consideration of my claim, and otherwise should have exhausted all the vehicles and remedies of an orderly society.

He described the steps he had taken "in the peculiar situation which has caused so much public comment"—the caliber of the fact-finding committee he had appointed, the procedures the members had followed, the principles under which they had performed their distasteful task. He then gave the unanimous conclusion of the committee on the essential question addressed to it: "Is Dr. Robert Colodny a subversive person as defined by the Pennsylvania Loyalty Act of 1951?" The answer was no.

Litchfield told of the distinguished persons who had advised him (without mentioning their names) and said they held unanimously that the committee's decision was just, fair, and principled. He too agreed that the findings were valid. Therefore, in the matter of the allegations concerning Dr. Colodny, no action on the part of the University was warranted and none would be forthcoming.

The *Post-Gazette* greeted the decision with an editorial titled "The University Finds for Inquiry and Truth." It began: "Like the welcome rain that washed away the city's heat, the University of Pittsburgh's report on an investigation of one of its faculty members has a cleansing and refreshing effect, It shows that the spirit of inquiry and the defense of freedom still flourish where they should—in the

Robert G. Colodny, professor of history and of the history and philosophy of science.

groves of academe." A long editorial by the *Press*, "On Teachers and Red Fronts," began, "Of the Litchfield report on the case of the University of Pittsburgh's history professor, Dr. Robert G. Colodny, this much can be said—that Chancellor Litchfield has examined Chancellor Litchfield's administration and found it to be without fault."

The investigation cost the University about $100,000 and what the chancellor called "an inordinate amount of the institution's time." He received some hundreds of letters from around the country, from friends and strangers, some from prominent figures, all preserved in a sheaf in the University's archives. Almost all were favorable. His letter/report appeared as the lead article in the Phi Beta Kappa organ, *The Key Reporter,* under the title "A Defense of Freedom of Inquiry and Expression." The magazine printed two critical letters. Both writers held that Litchfield had evaded the basic issue—that of fully protecting the faculty member's right to do, be, and say whatever he pleased, subject solely to the criteria of professional competence and intellectual integrity.

Of the verdict Colodny said, "A university can never be more certain that it is properly functioning than when its faculty is accused of subversion, because then some entrenched idea is under assault and some traditional holder of power feels the tempest of new and renewing ideas." The statement was quoted on his retirement in 1985.

The academic community as a whole honored the University. Litchfield's handling of the Colodny case had a profound effect on his own faculty; his standing with that body was raised. There is always something of an adversarial relationship between faculty and administration; but in this controversy, with the wide world of academia watching, both were drawn to the same side of the barricade to stand off a common assailant. For what was called his unhesitating and courageous defense of one of his faculty members on the issue of academic freedom, Litchfield gained the approbation and trust of his entire faculty.

"The Colodny case," one faculty member said, "showed that a great university cannot be intimidated." Another said: "At a critical moment when fundamental issues of academic freedom were at stake, Litchfield came down on the right side, and he stated the case not only correctly but elegantly. The statement he made ought to stand almost as a classic in the defense of academic freedom." A third said, "If anything good can be said to have come out of a battle like that, it was that our reputation was reestablished in the profession. In an odd way, I suppose we were lucky it happened."

24
Trouble

In 1955–56 the administration was faced with two alternatives—to expand or not to expand. It elected to expand. Again there were two choices to be faced—should the University expand only when it had the money in hand for this purpose, or should expansion be undertaken on the basis of what it is assumed the University should be doing? The second choice was taken, and the University embarked upon an expansion program without the money in hand to back it. The reasons for this were mainly—

1. It would be unlikely that the large sums of money needed to support expansion would be forthcoming from corporate and other sources until the University had demonstrated that it had a worthwhile program which would justify financial support.

2. Students from outside the area would not be interested in coming to the University until a well developed program could be offered them.

In other words, it was necessary that the University spend more money than it had to develop an academic program which was wanted and needed, in order to bring students from outside the Pittsburgh area, and to bring corporate and other support which was not here in Pittsburgh. Eventually expenditures exceeded revenues as was expected.

Edward H. Litchfield to the Council of Deans, January 17, 1961

THE triumphs, achievements, and applause of the first four years of the Litchfield administration continued into the early 1960s, but now they seemed to be outnumbered, if not outweighed, by a mounting succession of problems, troubles, and frustrations.

• In 1960 Chancellor Litchfield was charged with impropriety in a congressional hearing in Washington, a story that was covered in the local press with such headlines as "Litchfield Group Accused: $100-a-Day Pay for Pitt Chancellor" and "Million Given Litchfield Group: What Iran Advice Costs U.S." All this arose from testimony before a House Appropriations Subcommittee that Litchfield's Governmental Affairs Institute had received $1.113 million in U.S. funds for rendering management and technical services to the government of Iran over the previous three years.

The money was paid to the institute by the International Cooperation Administration (ICA), the government's foreign aid agency, for maintaining twelve staff members in Iran who received average salaries of $92,730 each for the three-year period, with an added cost of $148,710 for transportation of personnel and their automobiles and $228,530 for overhead. As a member of the "senior committee" on the Iran contract, Litchfield received $6,925 at the rate of $100 a day for time he had spent in Iran during the three-year period. He informed the press that he had turned back his Iran fees to the institute as gifts to cover the cost of activities there, as he had been doing with most of his other fees and "a good share" of his $10,000 annual salary. He said that personally he had lost money by being affiliated with the Governmental Affairs Institute.

There was no accusation of fraud; the University was not involved except as Litchfield was involved; and the head of the ICA defended the contract as a good one with "a very fine organization" that did work for which the ICA had no manpower. But several Democrats in the Congress, including the gadfly Otto Passman, called the affair outrageous, and that judgment was no doubt what people remembered the longest.

In 1962 Litchfield wrote to a friend, "I have abandoned the Persians."

• In 1962 Jonas Salk left the University of Pittsburgh to build his research institute at La Jolla, California. The chancellor and others, having failed to persuade him to stay in Pittsburgh, found some solace in the fact that Salk "is not going to another university, but rather to an entirely different kind of situation" and in Salk's agreement to retain ties to Pitt with a formal appointment as professor-at-large and visiting lecturer. He promised, moreover, "to speak of the La Jolla deal only in a positive way, without reference to his position in Pittsburgh."

• Another resident celebrity, Captain Thomas J. Hamilton, had resigned as athletic director in June 1959 and moved to the West Coast. He did not like Pittsburgh winters; he had been insulted by Walter Vieh, vice chancellor for business affairs, who negotiated the purchase and lease-back arrangement on Forbes Field without consulting him; and he had clashed with Litchfield, who wrote a blistering Memorandum for the Record on Hamilton's excessive demands on his time and unwillingness to talk to anyone but the chancellor.

• In June 1962 Dr. Edmund R. McCluskey, vice chancellor of the Schools of the Health Professions, died at the age of sixty-two. His death was lamented by medical people and University administrators, who saw in him a hope that he might master the discord and the personal rivalries that were afflicting the Health Center.

• In 1962–1965 Litchfield was subjected to unpleasant and undignified publicity about the taxes that were not being paid on his thirty-six-room mansion.

In December 1958 Mrs. Clifford S. (Vira) Heinz, daughter-in-law of the founder of the H. J. Heinz Company, gave the University her private residence, which stood in a cluster of other mansions on Morewood Heights about a mile east of the campus. In 1961 H. J. Heinz II, grandson of the founder, followed suit: he gave the University the Howard Heinz mansion, thirty-six rooms on five acres, also on Morewood Heights. These gifts sparked a Litchfield plan: "We sell the Vira Heinz house to Carnegie-Tech at something less than a fair value for use by President Warner as a residence; the Jack Heinz house is converted into a residence for the

Jeffrey Cepull/UCIR

Built by H. J. Heinz in 1924, this residence at 5090 Warwick Terrace was given to the University in 1961 by H. J Heinz II. It served as Chancellor Litchfield's residence.

Chancellor of the University; the Arthur Braun house and any other houses that we acquire up there will be used for the Arden House kind of concept."* Arthur Braun, trustee emeritus, indicated that he might give his house, some furnishings, and an endowment for that purpose.

The Howard Heinz mansion stood empty and idle for two years while this plan was developed and discussed. Dr. Warner was not interested in buying the Vira Heinz house for Carnegie Tech, the neighbors

---

*Arden House, the former Harriman mansion at Harriman, New York, was converted by Columbia University into a famed off-campus center for high-level meetings of scholars, business leaders, and public officials.

vigorously opposed the idea, and the City Board of Assessors refused to change the residence-only zoning requirement.

The University dropped the Arden House project and attempted unsuccessfully to find a single-family buyer. Rather than destroy a Pittsburgh landmark and turn the land over for residential development, the University then decided to sell the chancellor's residence on Beechwood Boulevard (thereby returning it to the tax rolls) and to go ahead with the plan to convert the Howard Heinz mansion into the official residence. This would cost less than leaving the house empty; there were two funds devoted solely to rehabilitating the building; and it would provide the chancellor with better facilities for holding University meetings. Litchfield took pains to record in the minutes of two Executive Committee meetings that this was not his proposal. He said that he and his family were not eager to move, but they were willing to live wherever the trustees directed him to live. If it should ever be found possible to use the property for nonresidential purposes, he and his family would move at once to other quarters.

The University spent $100,000 remodeling the Howard Heinz mansion for the chancellor's use, and the Litchfields used it with gusto and style, receiving more than 3,300 guests there in 1964. When the University filed for a tax exemption, however, the Board of Assessors balked, announcing that they would tax that portion of the house and grounds "serving no apparent educational purpose." To defend himself against rumors and bad publicity, Litchfield produced a "fact book" about the house and his use of it. The house, he said, really had fifteen rooms; only by counting such things as coal bins, fruit cellars, and partitioned attic areas could anyone say that it had thirty-six. Six students, he revealed, lived on the third floor, receiving free rooms in return for household chores and maintenance work.

In the final ruling, 40 percent of the assessed valuation of the house was declared taxable.

● In 1963, in one of the most dismal episodes in the school's athletic history, Pitt had a team of championship quality that won nine of ten games played, all against first-rate opponents, but did not receive an invitation to a major postseason bowl game.

Coach John Michelosen eight and nine years earlier had restored Pitt football to respectability with two bowl games (1955, 1956). In the first bowl game, Pitt had struck a celebrated blow for racial equality when it took Bobby Grier along as the first black athlete to play in the Sugar Bowl. It did so on a decision of Charles Nutting, dean of the Law School, who was serving as acting chancellor until Litchfield took over. He sent a four-word ultimatum to the governor of Georgia: "No Grier, no game."

At the start of the 1963 season, Chancellor Litchfield, to the delight of sports writers everywhere, publicly ordered Michelosen to use "a daring, imaginative, wide-open style of game" and to

play football that was "more interesting to the spectators." Michelosen obliged with a stunning season: by mid-November his team had beaten UCLA (20–0), Washington, California, West Virginia, Syracuse, Notre Dame (27–7), and Army (28–0). It had lost only to Navy and Roger Staubach (27–12), when quarterback Fred Mazurek had a sore toe. Two teams remained to be played—Penn State on Saturday, November 23, and Miami of Florida the following week.

John F. Kennedy was assassinated on Friday, November 22. After much soul searching and telephone calls to some twenty college presidents and athletic directors, Litchfield, despite the 57,331 tickets sold, elected to pay proper respect to the memory of the dead president by postponing the Penn State game. (It was rescheduled for December 7.) The bowl committees, running scared, refused to await the outcome of the delayed game. Fearing that Pitt might lose to Miami and Penn State and that they would lose gate receipts, they chose other teams. Pitt's last hope, the Gator Bowl committee, picked Penn State.

The Panthers beat Miami 31–20 and beat Penn State 22–21 a week later. Penn State played Florida State in the Gator Bowl and lost. Nebraska, which had not postponed its game on November 23, got the Orange Bowl bid. Pitt, with its splendid 9–1 record, had no bowl game. Al Abrams, sports columnist, expressed his contempt for bowl committees and colleges that profited by not appropriately honoring the assassinated president. He wrote, "And they criticize the pros!"*

These problems were insignificant compared with the one that overshadowed all others.

The trustees had approved the ten-year financial program presented by Chancellor Litchfield at the Rolling Rock Club in January 1961. They borrowed $10 million from Equitable Life Assurance Com-

---

*The players on the 1963 team had even more success off the field. Of the 61 players, 57 graduated, 34 of them with advanced degrees. There were 15 dentists, 3 physicians, a chiropractor, 6 educators, 5 engineers, 3 lawyers, 4 business executives, a banker, 2 National Football League coaches, a college coach, 2 stockbrokers, and a bookmaker.

pany. This, the chancellor had said, would pay for the planned deficits of the next two years and carry the University through an era in which there would be annual surpluses in the next eight years. But the program was not turning out as planned and promised.

Later inquiry revealed that the 1961 loan of $10 million, which was to have lasted through 1970, had been spent in 2½ years. It had gone to pay current operating expenses.

At the Rolling Rock presentation, the chancellor had estimated the planned deficits for the first two fiscal years ending July 31, 1961 and 1962, at $4 million. The actual deficits were $5.8 million—$1.8 million more than was planned for.

Faced with the failure of his planning, Litchfield in January 1963 asked the nine members and the chairman of the Executive Committee to ratify another loan from Equitable Life—this one for $5 million. The request came as a complete surprise. Because the need was immediate, the committee had no choice but to approve the loan. Some trustees felt that the chancellor had unfairly asked them to make a serious decision with the least possible notice, on the assumption that they would have to do what he asked because they had no time for another choice. The $5 million loan was taken out at 5½ percent. The University had to pay Equitable a total of $187,000 each quarter beginning in April 1964, and it would have to pay in full a large balance at the end of twelve years or renegotiate the loan at the prevailing interest rate. The University now had five of its buildings mortgaged as security: the Cathedral of Learning, Clapp Hall, Stephen Foster Memorial, the nurses' residence, and Falk Clinic.

For the year ending July 31, 1963, the chancellor had estimated a budget surplus of $370,000. He later revised his estimate and asked the trustees to approve a budget deficit of $2.7 million. The minute of the January 8, 1963, meeting—about half-way through the fiscal year—contains the statement, "The Chancellor said there is some expectation that the University will do better than break even this year rather than show a modest loss as was predicted." The actual deficit was $3.4 million.

What went wrong? How did the University run up operating deficits totaling more than $11 million in the five years between 1959 and 1963? Who was to blame? Did the chancellor, or the trustees, or the comptroller, or the independent auditing firm, realize what was happening? If so, why did they not act on the situation earlier?

There were conflicting stories at the time about the significance and seriousness of these unhappy developments. There were heated opinions—and they are still warm after more than two decades—about who was responsible, who should have done what, and when they should have done it. These questions were to occupy the energy and main attention of the administration for the next three years; they were to produce a crisis of the most serious proportions at the University.

In October 1959 Walter Vieh hired a new comptroller, Jesse T. Hudson, Jr. When he left the University six years later, Hudson prepared for the chairman of the board a detailed report on what he had seen during his tenure in office. It is a useful source in understanding the Litchfield fiscal crisis. Hudson was initially surprised to find that the comptroller he had been hired to replace had not been relieved of his duties nor told that he was being replaced. Vieh asked Hudson to serve for an interim period as his assistant. Hudson's duties were to make an evaluation of and recommendations for improvement of the Comptroller's Office. He discovered that the department was behind in its work and that interim financial reports had not been issued in some time. Reports that were issued were neither accurate nor complete. After he had brought the workload up to date and operations became normal, an analysis revealed that the University was headed for a large operating deficit for the first time, in the fiscal year ending June 1960. Hudson wrote:

In attempting to find out the reasons for the deficit, I discovered that the budget of the University was not prepared nor controlled by the Comptroller's Office. The budget had been prepared by the Office of Institutional Planning, a function that reported directly to the Chancellor. In reviewing the budget for the years 1959–60, I discovered a serious weakness in the budgetary control, in that department heads were allowed to modify their original budgets for additional programs without approval or evaluation from the financial area. Many of the modifications were financially unsound, and there were no real cash funds available to support the expenditures. I also discovered that complete budgeting for plant funds—capital expenditures—had not been done, especially a realistic cash requirements forecast. This area of expenditure had many projects under way that were under-financed, and funds were being advanced from current operations to support the expenditures. . . .

I discovered that the budget was prepared without regard to the financial reporting format of the University, nor to sound accounting requirements and practice. It was impossible for the Comptroller's office to reconcile day-to-day operations to budget performance in major areas. I found that the so-called budget was unrealistic in income estimates and expenditure requirements.

One serious error in the budget, Hudson said, arose from the practice of the Office of Institutional Planning of estimating lapses in expenditures. For the 1959–1960 budget, it estimated the lapse would be more than $500,000—that is, it predicted that the departments would expend $500,000 *less* than was called for in the budget that had been allocated to them. But this $500,000 figure was never made known to the department heads, and as a result they operated their departments within the approved budget without any knowledge of or consideration to lapses. "This immediately made the current operations budget out of balance with the projected deficit that, in fact, was never revealed to the Trustees.

"These factors resulted in a $1,909,322 deficit for the 1959–60 fiscal year. In addition, the ineptness and lack of disclosure of plant funds budgeting contributed further to serious cash deficits."

Hudson had several private conferences with Vieh and told him his findings and his estimate of where the University was heading. Vieh agreed, "but stated that the Chancellor was a very difficult person to control in his ambitions for the University and had little regard for the details of financial requirements." Hudson asked if the trustees were aware of the situation and was told that this was the responsibility of the chancellor.

Vieh had announced in early March of 1960 that he was retiring and that Lawrence L. Monnett, Jr., would be joining the University to replace him as assistant chancellor for business affairs and finance. Monnett, a graduate of St. John's College in Annapolis, was executive vice president and a director of an insurance company in Mt. Vernon, New York. Vieh hoped that Mr. Monnett would have more influence with the chancellor in bringing about a balanced financial program for expansion and growth.

The day before Monnett arrived, the former comptroller was released and Hudson was appointed to the position for which he had been recruited almost a year earlier. Because of the uncertainty and vagueness of his position, he had not moved his family from Richmond; now he made plans to relocate in Pittsburgh. "It was obvious," he said six years later, "that the University needed sound financial management, and I felt that I could make a contribution to the goals it had set for itself. I was happy to be a part of this in spite of the obvious difficulties that were ahead."

When plans were being made late in 1960 to negotiate the first long-term loan in conjunction with the ten-year forecast, Hudson told Monnett that the University would need $20 million to become financially sound and to carry forth programs that had already been adopted. This was determined to be too high, and the ten-year forecast was tailored to a $10 million requirement. Hudson wrote in his report to the chairman of the board, "The forecasts of tuition income, current fund expenditure, gifts, and appropriations from the Commonwealth prepared by the Office of Institutional Planning were as unsound and unrealistic as the previous budgets. This was disclosed by the Comptroller's office, but at that time the loan had been consummated and an air of unconcern developed."

Hudson's report to the board chairman continues:

In the meantime, the University vigorously pursued the program of expansion. Plant fund expenditures mounted, most of which were under-financed. . . . Research contracts that required additional faculty and space were accepted with few exceptions without an analysis of the financial impact. The Comptroller's office objected to this procedure but was told that we were to keep the required records and nothing more. . . .

During this period, quarterly financial reports were prepared by the Comptroller's office for distribution to the Trustees. I strongly suggested that these reports be reviewed in detail with the Executive Committee and that forecasts of actual operations be disclosed. It was my opinion that this review should be made with the Comptroller present in order that a clear understanding of the University's financial statement be made. I was again told that this was the Chancellor's responsibility, and that he would handle the matter. Up to this time I had never had a conference with the Chancellor and discussed all items with Mr. Monnett. I felt that this was strange, in that I was an officer of the Board of Trustees but had no access to the Trustees, nor was I ever invited to a meeting.

Hudson also "strongly suggested" that the budget responsibilities be transferred to the comptroller's office and that the budget be prepared to follow the financial format of the University on a basis of sound accounting practice. He discussed this with Monnett and with Herbert L. Koerner, the Price Waterhouse partner who was responsible for the University account. Both were in complete agreement with him. But after pursuing the matter for a time, he was told that the chancellor desired that the budget and budget research be administered by the vice chancellor. There was one change, however: in a realignment of duties, the budget responsibilities were transferred from the Office of Institutional Planning to Monnett's Office of Business and Finance. Despite the change, Hudson was still not included in the preparation or control of the 1962–1963 budget. "We were again told that these plans were none of our concern and that our function was to maintain the records."

The ten-year forecast was completely out of reach. The full financial impact of the past two years was a reality, and a curtailment of some of the programs that could have averted the impending crisis was not developed. When the need for the additional $5,000,000 was planned and the ten-year forecast revised, the estimates of income and expenditure did not reflect the actual situation. . . . In spite of the objections by the Comptroller's Office, the forecast made by this office was never seriously discussed. Many new programs and developments . . . occupied the

Chancellor's administrative staff, and little time could be devoted to day-to-day requirements.

Gwilym Price had been aware as early as 1961 that he had a problem on his hands and that, as chairman of the board, he would have to take some action. He was alerted when he realized that Monnett was giving him an unusually large number of notes to sign—notes to Mellon Bank that were in addition to the substantial loans outstanding. He was further alerted at a meeting with Litchfield and H. L. Koerner, the outside auditor. Koerner made his report and concluded with the usual statement: "The books are in order and fully reflect the condition of the University." Price said, "Mr. Koerner, is there anything else you would like to add?" Litchfield interrupted, "I do not believe it is the function of the auditor to comment on the fiscal management of the University." Koerner was silent. Price said years later:

I should have challenged Litchfield right there and then, but I did not. You didn't challenge Ed very often. He was so damned positive.

There were several other occasions when I thought seriously of calling him to account, perhaps with a threat to resign, but decided not to do so. He had a coterie of people in the University. He had some friends on the Board and was popular with his associates in administration and with most of the faculty. Besides, I liked Ed personally. I had accepted the chairmanship in order to help him, and I wanted to do so. I knew that if I was too damn precipitous I could split the Board wide open, with almost irreparable harm to the University. If I rushed things I could tear the University inside out. I had to wait.

When he recalled these events almost twenty years later, at the age of eighty-six, there was a look of remembered distress on his face.

A special committee of the board several years later drew up a report, never used or released, in which it attempted to explain why it had not recognized trouble earlier and acted sooner. "The trustees had faith in Dr. Litchfield as an educator," it said in the spring of 1966. "We respected his reputation as an administrator, both in government and in business, and the record of accomplishment in his first four years at the University. We wanted very much to see the University succeed in what it had set out to achieve."

The report continued with a shrewd evaluation of Edward Litchfield: "As chancellor [he] was energetic, optimistic, and persuasive. He was also a man of dominating personality who was determined to have his own way and was disinclined to look kindly on anyone who opposed him, either from the Board or from the Administrative staff."

Price began to meet privately every week or so with Koerner "just to keep track of how things were going. Koerner kept telling me that things were not improving. We were going deeper into our resources, and sooner or later we would run out of money." In 1962 Price took Koerner with him to see Frank Denton, who was still a relatively new trustee, told Denton what they knew, and said: "Frank, you're the principal bank for this outfit, and they need money, and they usually owe you something. You better take a look at this."

Denton recalled his problems with the University's accounting system:

I became interested in the thing and tried to intelligently understand [it, but] I had trouble. It's quite different from corporate bookkeeping. It's just a foreign language compared to ordinary corporate bookkeeping, because it's fund accounting as against just a profit-and-loss statement. The complexity of the accounting makes the analysis of cash flow and the evaluation of financial position quite difficult. There were a great number of major accounts at Pitt, including tuition, income from sports events, research grants, federal aid, state appropriations, and various kinds of private, corporate and foundation gifts. There were thousands of transactions within these accounts.

So I became involved in it, and I went to Litchfield and asked him how he was going to cover this mounting deficit year by year. He said, "Just in accordance with our ten-year plan. You sat in on the development of the ten-year plan." So I said to him and used the phrase, "You better get some partners in crime, because you have trouble as I see it." He said, "Oh, it will work out." He was always optimistic. I told him he was really in trouble because he didn't even have a budget committee. He had an Audit Committee who were good men but who were not specialists in audit work. They just really accepted the audit from the outside auditing firm and reported it to the

board and that was the extent of their activity. This was insufficient.

Litchfield said, "You've got a point there." At the next meeting of the board he proposed that there be designated a combination budget and audit committee with new members. Price immediately made me chairman of it. Having complained, I got the job of being chairman of the committee.

Price gave Denton three qualified trustees to serve on the Budget and Audit Committee. They were Frank L. Magee, president of Alcoa, Malcolm E. Lambing, president of Pittsburgh National Bank, and Alfred W. Beattie, head of Allegheny County schools. These were busy, hardworking men who had nothing to gain personally in accepting their new assignment: no pay, no increase in power or prestige. They had not been asked to serve by someone to whom they were indebted and whom they could not refuse. They must have realized that they were undertaking a time-consuming and thankless job that promised trouble. For want of any other explanation, one may assume that they accepted the assignment because of a sense of duty, or because of a moral commitment to the University, or perhaps because of a simple desire to return a bad situation to good working order.

Stanton Crawford, called by some the wisest man on the campus, told the chancellor, "Ed, Mr. Denton can help you, in the long run."

The Budget and Audit Committee began its work by having Price Waterhouse make a complete appraisal of the University's financial situation. Price Waterhouse reexamined the budgets and budget forecasts in an effort to determine what the true figures were, and it interviewed Litchfield. It did not get all the data it wanted, but it learned enough to become increasingly concerned. Gwilym Price attested: "Frank and I could clearly see that a financial crisis was fast approaching unless the Chancellor controlled his expenses and balanced the budget, which we were constantly urging him to do. We did our damnedest to set him straight, to get him to a place where he had things under control. It was to our interest to do that. We had three or four meetings with Litchfield: 'Ed, you've just *got* to stop spending more money than you're taking in.' Each time he said, 'You'll see an improvement—you'll see it in the next quarter.'"

Edison Montgomery, a keen observer through three decades of work on the campus, believes that Charles Peake, vice chancellor for the academic disciplines, was the key architect of the academic success achieved by the University during the Litchfield years. Peake, he says, "had a capacity to recruit people and to recognize targets of opportunity that was unexcelled. And although Edward Litchfield could conceptualize, it is Peake that brought the people here, and it is people that make a great university, not the man at the helm. The entire philosophy department explosion, the chemistry department, are all attributable to Charles Peake. Litchfield might have found another Charles Peake, and obviously Peake couldn't have operated without Litchfield's backing. But if Peake hadn't been in that position at that time, much of Litchfield's accomplishment, I think, just wouldn't have occurred."

Yet if one viewed Charles Peake from the perspective of fiscal soundness and balanced budgets, as Price and Denton found they must, he became a part, a cause, of the problem. "He was a brilliant person," Price recalled, "but he was the worst offender. He could get anything from Ed by just saying, 'We need to do this to make it the kind of university you want it to be.' I remember once I was so mad at Litchfield and Peake—one of the times Ed had promised Frank and me that things would be better, but Peake came to him on something and he just went right ahead on it, even though he didn't have the money."*

When the auditor's appraisal of University finances was completed and hard information became available, Price, Denton, and their working associates on the Executive and the Budget and Audit committees began to comprehend the extent of the damage and the causes behind it. The Price Water-

house report revealed that the chancellor had concentrated power and decision making solely in his own hands, that he was relying on staff members not associated with the University's financial operations, and that the budgets he personally presented at formal trustees meetings once each year had been prepared without the knowledge or participation of the University's comptroller and its treasurer. Price Waterhouse revealed that at two meetings of the now-superseded Audit Committee held on October 1, 1961, and October 8, 1962, both attended by the chancellor and University staff members, its representative had warned the chancellor that he was spending beyond his means. The representative told him that he was borrowing excessively from funds earmarked for specific purposes, and that while such borrowing was a normal and accepted practice among universities where ability to repay was obvious, the chancellor was doing it to a degree that could lead to trouble.

The birth of the Litchfield fiscal disaster occurred in a routine but critically important process for any organization: the preparation of an annual budget. "The mistake that was constantly being made," recalls Edison Montgomery, Litchfield's first budget director,

was over-estimation of income. Each year I would present the budget to Litchfield to present to the board. I'd give it to him in a draft form showing him a massive deficit, and he would say, "Well, let's up this item here in gift income," and he would raise it by a million dollars. So the paper that was handed to the Board showed a balanced budget, but the income figures were totally unrealistic. In 1961 I began to develop a five-year plan for the University. I made my income projections, I made my expenditure projections based upon programs that I felt had been validated as far as the Chancellor was concerned, and I made a report to him and his cabinet that the University would go bankrupt in 1966. I predicted that the annual deficit in that year was going to be about $5 million, and the cumulative deficit would have grown to something like $18 million.

Litchfield would not discuss my paper. He wouldn't even look at the paper. So I went to him and said, "If this is the financial course, although I'm sure you know what you are doing, I cannot continue as budget officer. I will leave the University if you want me to. I don't want to

---

*On September 12, 1963, Peake wrote a "Dear Bill" letter to Price to impart some "happy news." He had just signed up ten mathematicians and had made arrangements for signing up four more the following year.

leave, but I just don't want to have any responsibility for the budget." So Litchfield kept me in a kind of miscellaneous administrative role.

In what is probably the best analysis of how Litchfield worked his way with the Board of Trustees, Montgomery recalls:

What he did was to carry on years of sleight of hand. Everything was in full view, but he would distract the Board to the point that they would not see the bad things. I've seen a financial statement which, knowing what was behind it, I thought was horrible. And he would . . . speak about how we were on the move, and the excellence, and here, look at this, how our income has gone up here. . . . Technically, all the figures were there. The only thing—I never really understood this—maybe he believed what he was saying. . . .

Edward was a brilliant debater. His forensic ability was just superb, and I suppose there was a certain fear by the trustees that if they asked a question he would present the answer in such a way that it would make the question sound as if it were a silly thing to ask. And this would embarrass them. So they didn't ask the question. That's a possibility. They certainly didn't ask the right questions.

Some surviving participants in this drama later agreed that 1963 was the crucial year in the history of the University and in the career of Edward Litchfield. With mounting deficits and alarming revelations of the circumstances under which they were incurred, the University found itself in an exigency that was close to being out of control. One thing might have retrieved the situation: an effective working alliance between the key trustees and the chancellor. It didn't happen. The chairman of the board and the four Budget and Audit Committee members tried "to straighten out the University's finances, and to help Dr. Litchfield survive his problems, in the interest of carrying on the academic program he had started." But in discussions they had with the chancellor, the trustees thought they saw little chance of developing a working alliance. Frank Denton personally came to two not very reassuring conclusions. He decided that the chancellor had been using his budgets solely to pacify the trustees and, once they were approved, simply ignored them. He decided further that the chancellor had resorted to deficit operations as a

considered policy. This conclusion resulted from an observation Litchfield made to him as they were leaving a meeting together, walking down the corridor of the chancellor's suite in Bruce Hall. Litchfield said pleasantly, "You know, Frank, there is more than one way to reap the advantage of a large endowment, even if you don't have one. If you have a deficit and it's made good, the effect is the same." Denton concluded from the remark that Litchfield had been carrying out the mandate given him, regardless of the cost, in the belief that the trustees and the Pittsburgh business community, when presented with the bills, would bail him out to save face. "If this was his assumption," Denton said in 1966, "he was wrong. Too many trustees and donors recognized that if they bailed Dr. Litchfield out by writing checks, they would have to bail him out again and again, with larger and larger checks."

When the budget for 1963–1964 was prepared, the situation was well out of hand. Jesse Hudson wrote in his report to the chairman:

The budget that was presented to the Trustees was completely out of balance in relation to expenditures and income. The impact of the past had developed, but the complete facts were not disclosed, in that income projections were predicated upon substantial gift income. . . . Early in 1964 the Comptroller's office made a detailed forecast of the crisis we would face in the spring. This forecast was never taken to the Trustees, and it was related to me that it could not be disclosed to them, since plans were being developed to meet the crisis. These plans, as I found out, were not sound, and it was quite improbable that they would develop. I was of the definite opinion that this should be discussed with the Budget and Audit Committee, but did not have the authority to go direct to its members. In view of the above, the situation seemed hopeless, and I decided to seek employment elsewhere. . . .

I must say that my decision to leave the University was a painful and regrettable one. I had hoped that I could have made a real contribution in my stay there. Beyond question, the University excelled and progressed in many areas during this period. Unfortunately, progress is sometimes very expensive, and this was certainly the case here. It was a pleasure to serve with the distinguished persons associated with the University.

In the ten-year plan unveiled in 1961 at Rolling Rock, Litchfield had forecast for the fiscal year 1963–1964 a surplus of $730,000. On January 21, 1963, he revised that figure to forecast a deficit of almost $1.4 million. On May 14, 1963, he made another revision and forecast a deficit of nearly $2.1 million.

At a number of meetings with Litchfield and Monnett, the Budget and Audit Committee had ordered that the budgets henceforth be balanced and the University's expenses brought within available income. Its members were pleased to hear on May 6, 1964, three-fourths of the way through the same fiscal year, a detailed statement from Litchfield in which, thanks to economies and improved effi-ciency, he was able to predict a surplus of $187,000. They congratulated the chancellor on the improvement. Five months later, in October 1964, in the annual audit, they learned the actual result. It was a deficit of $4,503,311.

Litchfield had quietly brought Walter Vieh back to the campus for a few days to study and report to him on the University's financial situation. Vieh told him, "The figures seem to justify the belief that the operating results for 1964–1965 will show a very encouraging improvement over 1963–1964, just as the budget had led us to hope they would." In fact, he was so encouraged that he predicted an operating surplus for the next year of $1.2 million.

25
Panther Hollow

What OakCorp proposes to do, in summary, is to take an ugly, useless ravine located in an immensely valuable area and transform it into a research complex which will serve as a focal point of a great cultural-educational-scientific center, and by so doing lift Pittsburgh into first rank among world cities.

Prospectus for "Panther Hollow: The 21st Century City," 1963

PANTHER HOLLOW, so called, is a stretch of vacant land that carried a railroad freight track through Oakland to steel mills on the Monongahela River. It is a ravine 650 to 900 feet wide at the top and 150 to 200 feet deep, with a broad floor extending southward about a mile. To the west of the ravine at its northern end stand the buildings of the University of Pittsburgh, its five hospitals, Mellon Institute, Carnegie Institute and Library, and other buildings of the Oakland Civic Center. To the east are Phipps Conservatory, the buildings of what was then Carnegie Tech, and Schenley Park. The wasteland of this ravine was the object of Chancellor Litchfield's most ambitious, most daring plan for the University, estimated to cost $250 million, give or take a few million.

Civic planners, architects, real estate developers, and University of Pittsburgh administrators had been looking speculatively for decades at that idle land set down near one of the busiest parts of the city. Early in the century a spur of the ravine at the near edge of the park had been filled in, burying a stone bridge, to form a plaza in front of Carnegie Library. A venerable city father, James C. Rea, once proposed that the Jones and Laughlin Steel Company be asked to dump its blast furnace slag in the ravine, "which in the course of thirty or forty years would probably fill the hollow . . . a long way down toward the river." In September 1953 Philip S. Broughton (with the A. W. Mellon Educational and Charitable Trust) took Theodore L. Hazlett, Jr. (called the legal architect of Pittsburgh's renaissance), and M. Graham Netting (director of Carnegie Museum) with him to walk the length of the hollows.* He then wrote a six-page letter to Chancellor Fitzgerald on the theme "Why not accept the Hollows as civic opportunities, put them to constructive use either as the site of dormitories, faculty housing, an art museum, an auditorium, science laboratories or an inter-university library? . . . There is no reason why beautiful buildings could not be constructed on the floor of Junction Hollow." Entrance to such buildings would be at both top and bottom.

*The ravine begins at Junction Hollow and becomes Panther Hollow on the way to the river.

"Storage facilities, auditoria, kitchens, spare bedrooms, etc. could be back against the cliff; rooms requiring outdoor exposure could face the central plaza at the bottom of the Hollow. . . . Frank Lloyd Wright has said that auditoria might just as well be underground, yet we ignore a God-given excavation."

Fitzgerald had earlier made a rendering of such a building for the University, going down five stories from the level of Carnegie Museum, and he had proposed to Robert E. Doherty of Carnegie Tech that they consider building a joint library against one of the slopes. But Dr. Doherty died, and Fitzgerald concentrated his attention on expanding toward the upper campus, and the idea withered away.

In 1961 the Pittsburgh Regional Planning Association produced a long-range master plan for the redevelopment of Oakland. The plan included a development body, called OakCorp, to produce leadership and financial support for the program. The corporation was to acquire, own, sell, lease, mortgage, manage, construct, maintain, and operate real and related personal property in Oakland. It was to sell stock, make a profit if possible, and pay taxes. The planning association turned over both the plan and the corporation to the University of Pittsburgh because it was the dominant institution in Oakland. OakCorp had seven owners: Pitt, Carnegie Tech, Carnegie Institute, Mellon Institute, the United Jewish Federation, the Catholic Institute of Pittsburgh, and Mount Mercy College. Pitt owned 50 percent of the voting stock. Litchfield was chairman. He hired as president an advertising executive, Fred Smith, who was a specialist in urban development and who, as a vice president of Prudential Insurance Company, had played a role in developing the $150 million Prudential Center in Boston.

One of the goals of OakCorp was to build a large research park in a bid to win a share of the $20 billion U.S. research industry, which was expected to double in size by 1970, and to build a new local economy on industries that would be spun off from its research and development accomplishments. In the search for a site, Litchfield's eye fell on Panther

The reality of Panther Hollow. Photo from the Charles Anderson Memorial Bridge, Boulevard of the Allies.

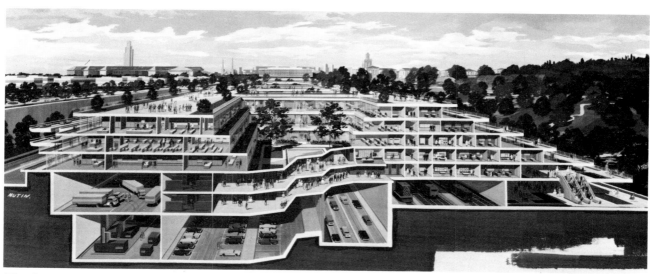

University Archives

The dream of Panther Hollow. Max Abramovitz designed this "building-on-its-side" to fill the hollow. Estimated cost was $250 million.

Hollow. There, he decided, was the ideal place. It had room not only for the research park but also for a new stadium (thus freeing the site of the old stadium for other University uses) and for a symphony hall, which the downtown interests, over his protests, were trying to move from Oakland to the Golden Triangle. He presented Max Abramovitz with the challenging site and the commission to design the most beautiful research park in America. Abramovitz went to work on the project with enthusiasm.

On the evening of June 5, 1963, in Carnegie Music Hall, Litchfield, Smith, and Abramovitz gave a select audience of 300 civic and industrial leaders a dramatic preview of what they called "Panther Hollow: The 21st Century City" and "the world's greatest research park." To show what they proposed to do in Panther Hollow, they had a magnificent scale model, thirteen feet long, with removable parts.

Instead of designing the usual high, monolithic structures, Abramovitz laid the equivalent of a 150-story building on its side in the ravine, its "roof" or upper side forming a seventy-five-acre mall that enlarged Schenley Park and tied together the Pitt and Carnegie Tech campuses. The buildings would

stand on thirty-foot stilts over the bottom of the gully, with the existing railroad tracks and a new cross-Oakland expressway beneath them. Structures would rise as many stories as necessary to reach ground level. Between the lowest level and the roof level, a series of horizontal layers would house the center's offices and laboratories, as well as roads, parking areas, utility substations, service facilities, and restaurants. A series of courtyards at intervals would bring fresh air and sunlight to the layers of the building.

At the near or north end of the development, two cantilevered buildings would rise several floors above grade; they would hold an instrumentation center and 150,000 square feet of exhibition space for Carnegie Museum, or perhaps the Pittsburgh Playhouse. (The stadium and the symphony hall had been dropped by the wayside.) At the far or south end, seven levels of terraced and cantilevered hanging gardens would descend to Panther Hollow Lake. Appropriate shops and other facilities would serve the expected 10,000 daytime residents. Eventually there would be apartments and town houses for those who preferred to live in the Twenty-first-Century City. The first building, about fifteen hundred feet long, would extend from the bridge at Forbes Avenue to the Schenley Drive Bridge that runs from Carnegie Museum to Phipps Conservatory. Two later buildings would extend to the Boulevard of the Allies bridge. In all, they would provide 18 million square feet of usable, income-producing space.

OakCorp officers announced that they believed they had tenants lined up for half the space in the first building. They would borrow the initial $60 or $70 million, and they hoped to break ground in the spring of 1964 and complete construction in 1966.

Richard K. Mellon made a rare public appearance on the platform and gave an even rarer talk in which he supported the project. But the next day Joseph D. Hughes (vice president and general counsel of T. Mellon & Sons and administrative trustee of the Richard King Mellon Foundation) sought out Litchfield to warn him that there was just not that much money available. Gwilym Price asked him, "Edward, don't you have enough balls up in the air now?" Litchfield parried with a reply that was much quoted: "Maybe I do. But don't call me down on it until I drop one."

The publicity on Panther Hollow, local and national, was all that the most ardent advocate could ask. *Business Week* ran a long and admiring article, *Time* gave it 2½ pages with two pictures, and *Paris-Match* ran a spectacular center-fold spread. The *Pittsburgh Press* printed two pages, and the technical and architectural journals gave the story extensive coverage. Then less and less was heard of Panther Hollow. The model was set up in the Babcock Room, where it attracted attention for a while at board meetings, but there were no more successes to report. There was some resentment on the Carnegie Tech campus that President Warner had not been consulted on the Panther Hollow development until it was delivered to him in an almost finished form and because the design would force road changes that were detrimental to Carnegie Tech's plans. Mayor David Lawrence had been told about the project belatedly and casually, and he gave it no support. Alcoa was not interested; IBM was lukewarm; there were many turndowns. Ground was not broken in the spring of 1964.

November 1964 was an important but confusing month in the OakCorp and Panther Hollow story. The corporation was still recruiting tenants in that month, but it had firm commitments for only 202,600 square feet, of which 100,000 was from the University itself. The corporation, which had started out with a capitalization of $536,000, now had $59,215 left, after spending $195,676 on promotion and development. President Smith resigned on November 2; Litchfield made Monnett president and asked Smith to serve as a consultant at $1,000 a month. On November 3 Monnett declared: "Unit One of phase one of the Panther Hollow project is close to becoming a reality. A public announcement will be made within the next three weeks. A major portion of the land in this site has been obtained, and cost estimates have been received that are within the budget."

On January 18, 1965, when the Greek Orthodox diocese offered to buy OakCorp stock, Litchfield told Monnett to decline their offer "in view of the uncertainty of OakCorp's future." On March 5 Monnett telephoned Abramovitz with instructions to terminate his work on Panther Hollow. OakCorp had $7,563 in the bank and the project was dead.

Litchfield, in a candid moment three months later, confessed: "We were unrealistic in thinking we could attract large Pittsburgh companies. They have their own research facilities. . . . I think we've been too free in our predictions."

Two other men left a testament that might lead one to think that the Panther Hollow project is not dead but dormant. Max Abramovitz declared, "Architects, city planners and others need to take a long look at the 'useless' and marginal land in our urban areas. To the extent that we can break precedent and design not only for the topography but also to meet the needs of the community, we will help materially to solve a major problem—the decay of our cities."

And Frank Denton said vehemently in 1981, "All that land wasted in the heart of the city! It's still a good idea. It should be done."

26
The Crisis

Much of the Pitt experience is not unique. It was the first institution to make the break for instant excellence, and it was the first to stumble. But many others can be seen laboring along the same path.

D. S. Greenberg, "Pittsburgh: The Rocky Road to Academic Excellence," *Science*, February 18, 1966

I N the meantime, the University's financial problems were becoming more serious. Frank Denton and his Budget and Audit Committee were deeply involved in a desperate effort, with the help of the administration, to find money to meet expenses and develop remedies for what was now a full-scale financial crisis. The committee held four long meetings between November 17 and December 18, 1964, with all its members present, as well as Price, Litchfield, Monnett, Crawford, Koerner, and Jesse Hudson. Because of the "confidential nature" of the problems discussed at these meetings, Secretary Crawford distributed only the barest outline of his Notations to the Board of Trustees as a whole. His Notations reveal disheartening scenes in which ten troubled men are struggling to save the University from financial collapse.

At the first meeting Denton said that the budget forecasts had been so inaccurate as to be useless, and it was now apparent that there had been no controls to limit budget expenditures. There was a large accumulated deficit in the current account, and the University had invested in fixed assets substantially more money than it had available. The result was a drastic cash shortage. The chancellor and his staff, he said, had done a remarkable job of using each available dollar several times over, but they were now at the end of that road. They had taken $10.578 million from research and restricted funds, and they had an accumulated loss in current funds of $12.553 million. Thus the University needed a total of $23 million to bring itself back to current balance, without paying any of its debt. In addition, if in the current fiscal year 1964–1965 the University did not at least break even, the situation would be still worse.

Litchfield said that when he accepted his appointment in 1955 he should have insisted on receiving a firm commitment on the financial support the community would give, and he should have insisted again in 1961–1962, when the deficits began to mount. He regretted, he said, that he had not asked the trustees to make their own commitment clear at the start. He lamented that most of the gifts received since 1955 had been earmarked for medicine and public health and that, with only one major exception, little of the money was for University endow-

ment. He complained that a succession of Health Center fund drives had excluded him from seeking gifts for nonmedical purposes. Donors, in fact, were still paying off installments on pledges they had made in 1959. He agreed that budget controls had not been adequate, but this was because the institution was changing so rapidly that each year brought a new budget situation. "There is little that can be done about all of that now," he said, "except to make desperate efforts to reduce the indebtedness. Management will do anything that this group agrees upon as a plan for action."

Price asked Litchfield, Denton, and four others to work with him as a task force to develop by mid-December a workable plan of action.

At the first task force meeting, Denton declared that it would be fruitless to approach industry for gifts until the University had become solvent. Nobody liked to pay for a deficit. Foundations, corporations, alumni, and other persons, he said, had given the University $80 million since 1955, and it was clear to him that they would not increase their giving until the institution had put its financial house in order. For that reason, he had declined Price's request that he lead a fund drive.

The Budget and Audit Committee decided to recommend two other steps. First, to ask Governor Scranton to give the University a large special legislative appropriation. Second, to put the question to the Executive Committee of the board. Would it recommend and support a drive for massive endowment funds in order to keep moving forward? Or, alternatively, would it recommend that the University fall back to a greatly reduced academic program, knowing that it would be very difficult to recover and regain stature after such a retreat? Denton stated the proposition simply: "We have been building a greatly improved University with increased merit in teaching and research staffs, physical plant, and general reputation, but this improvement has moved faster than income. . . . Do the community and the state like what we have developed here, and do they wish it to continue?" Litchfield agreed to carry out a stern cost-cutting program he had begun in October following a meeting with his Administrative Committee.

Litchfield's program "to cut costs wherever possible in order that the most essential programs may continue to grow" was put in a letter to his deans, directors, department heads, and vice chancellors. He listed thirty areas where economies should be made in the fiscal year ending July 31, 1965.

He ordered student aid to be cut back to save at least $50,000 and perhaps $100,000.

He told Edison Montgomery "to drag out the acquisition of new books" to reduce the library budget at least $100,000.

He declared that receptions and entertainment in his own office, which cost about $60,000 a year, were to be reduced down to the absolute bare bone. Commencement and honors convocation luncheons, normally held for 200 to 250 people, henceforth were to be limited to not more than 50 people. He would cut back sharply on his domestic and foreign travel, except when he did it on his own corporation accounts. Whenever possible, the staff was to save fares by riding with him in his plane. The motor pool was discontinued.

Heinz Chapel musical programs were to be cut drastically, including the distribution of free souvenirs and the hiring of guest organists. The women's swimming pool was closed.

A list was to be compiled of people from whom the University consistently bought materials, finished products, and services. The names were to be used for systematic canvassing, starting at once. A small trustees committee was to visit these people and ask for regular annual contributions.

He ordered a reduction in the number and cost of telephone calls, eliminated three positions in the top administrative offices by forming a secretarial pool, and accepted Gwilym Price's offer to have one secretary transferred to Price's personal payroll.

There would be no June or July meeting at Tumble Run, his farm near Coudersport in Potter County, and the August meeting would be attended by fewer people. An effort was to be made to persuade "our friends in the downtown corporations" to use the dormitories vacant in the spring term for holding special institutes and other programs.

While academic programs were to remain uncut as such, no faculty vacancies were to be filled before August 1 without his personal and written approval, and no salary increases were to be given "unless it is imperative to do so to retain a key employee. Exceptions are to be made by me only."

Litchfield, Monnett, and Montgomery, having had ten days of "searching conversations" with the deans and vice chancellors, were able to take $1.8 million out of the 1964–1965 budget and about $2.6 million out of the budget for the following year, just shy of the goal of $3 million. Unfortunately, despite these economies, the 1964–1965 budget was out of control and was going through a series of gyrations that exceeded anything that had gone before.

The budget, when Litchfield submitted it on May 12, 1964, had forecast an estimated operating surplus of $1.2 million. The trustees approved that figure. On November 17, 1964, at a joint meeting of the Executive and the Budget and Audit committees, Litchfield raised the predicted surplus to $2.6 million. Denton declared that the figure was patently absurd. Litchfield defended the figure. He asked Monnett: "Larry, is this figure correct?" Monnett said it was correct. He asked Hudson, "Jesse, do you agree with this?" Hudson said, "No." "You *don't?*" "No. It will not be that way."

On December 14 Litchfield submitted still another interim forecast, this one a reversal to predict a deficit of almost $2.4 million. When the final figure was in some months later, it showed a deficit of $1.1 million—$3.7 million off the chancellor's November 17 estimate.

The crisis came to a climax in seven anxious months in 1965.

January 20. The chancellor told his Administrative Committee of plans he had made for a very extensive program of solicitation by a volunteer staff. The drive would be headed by Edgar Cale, his vice chancellor for development (who had built up a large, expensive, and not very productive staff). The campaign, the chancellor said, would require the investment of little new money, except for the printing of pledge cards and other such materials.

January 21. Dr. Litchfield announced that the University would phase out the programs of its Allegheny Observatory and possibly close its building in

Riverside Park. The University, he said, could no longer justify the $50,000 it cost annually to maintain the operation. It had no graduate program and no undergraduate major; it had conferred its last Ph.D. degree in 1937.

If the chancellor felt that the observatory was an operation with few constituents and was therefore a safe place to make a deep cut, he was wrong. The announcement created a furor in local circles, in state politics, and among national scientists, with a heavy protest received by mail, telegram, and telephone. Charles A. Federer, Jr., editor-in-chief of Harvard Observatory Publications, declared, "We are appalled to hear of the possible closing and destruction of Allegheny Observatory, one of the world's great observatories both past and present. Its continuing program of measuring distances in space is of the greatest fundamental importance to all—and we emphasize *all*—branches of modern astronomy, including space travel.

"As there is no substitute for this program at other observatories, irreparable damage will be done by stopping this work now. Such false economy would badly degrade the University of Pittsburgh's reputation throughout the entire scientific world."

The decision to phase out programs at the observatory was reversed eight months later.

January 27. The chancellor, who was now beginning to show overt signs of the stress he was under, told his administrators that he had been reviewing the letters he had exchanged with Alan Scaife in 1955. He had found much evidence, he said, that the leaders among the trustees had intended to build up a massive endowment to strengthen the University. In fact, some large sums of money were mentioned in newspaper reports of that time. He said he would circulate copies of the correspondence to the top administrators.

February 4. A *Post-Gazette* editorial declared that the trustees should consider converting Pitt from a private institution to a semipublic, state-related university. It pointed out that Pennsylvania was near the bottom of all fifty states in the amount it contributed to higher education, but at the same time it was the only state that permitted use of public funds for

private institutions of higher learning. The state was under increasingly heavy fire to contribute much more than it did, for which it would get lower tuition rates in return. There was a bill in the legislature to convert Indiana State College, forty-five miles northeast of Pittsburgh, into Pennsylvania's second state university, to serve the southwestern counties. The University of Pittsburgh, the editorial said, would be a better, less costly choice.

February 9. At a historic meeting of the Board of Trustees, with Litchfield and his administrative staff present, Denton for the first time presented to the whole board, in full detail, the sad story of the University's financial condition. Litchfield responded that he would personally assume responsibility for what had happened. But he noted that the main cause of the trouble was the failure of the trustees to raise "a projected increase of $125 million in unrestricted endowment. . . . It is true that no specific commitment was made by any person or group at that time, but Board members had seemed to recognize the necessity of finding this kind of major endowment support."

That evening the trustees read in the *Press* an interview in which the chancellor said he was frankly disappointed with financial support of the University by its friends and alumni. Only one Pitt graduate in nine was giving anything to the University— "a pitiful percentage for a school with Ivy League aspirations."

February 11. Price and Litchfield together made a formal report on the board meeting to the Faculty Senate, in which for the first time they revealed the $4.5 million deficit in the last fiscal year.

February 14. The *New York Times,* using a press release issued after the Senate meeting, gave twelve paragraphs to the University of Pittsburgh and its problems.

March 6. Jesse Hudson agreed to return to the University for five months on a part-time basis with the title of vice chancellor for finance. He had departed in December to take a position as treasurer and financial vice president of Colonial Stores, Inc., a 438-store supermarket chain headquartered in Atlanta. Now he would work two full weeks of each month in Pittsburgh and parts of other weeks to help formulate plans to solve some of the University's financial problems. He set his own modest fee: $500 a month and out-of-pocket expenses.

March 15. Pitt trustee Deane W. Malott, president emeritus of Cornell University, wrote Litchfield a letter of encouragement and advice. "Your great forte," he said, "is as an imaginative builder, probably impatient of the minutiae of budgets and detailed cost control. Those qualities seldom abide together in the same carcass. But somewhere under you, you should have the ablest of budget directors—controllers who ask hard facts as every new idea emerges; who can stop 'Mr. President' in his tracks if his inspirational leadership gets too far out of hand."

March 16 (Tuesday). Some 135 college students and two ministers from Pittsburgh participated in a giant civil rights demonstration in Selma, Alabama, organized by the Student Nonviolent Coordinating Committee. Two days earlier, late on Sunday night, the leader of 100 Pitt students had called the chancellor at home and asked for help: the students wished to take chartered buses that would soon leave for Montgomery, Alabama, but on such short notice that they had no way, on Sunday midnight, to get the money they needed. The chancellor was able to help; he arranged to open a safe and make money immediately available for those students who wished to cash checks, which he personally guaranteed. But this was a time when civil rights protests were not commonplace, and his generous, well-meaning act had unfortunate repercussions.

The Monday morning *Post-Gazette* ran a front-page picture of the students boarding the bus. It featured the "Pitt student president," who bore a striking resemblance in dress and physiognomy to Fidel Castro. Protests came barreling in to the chancellor's office, one of them from a wealthy young heiress who had attended the University and was a benefactor, one from an engineering alumnus who had just headed a successful drive to raise money for petroleum engineering scholarships. Litchfield answered these with personal letters, but to counter the public outcry he issued a statement.

The University, he said,

does not, as an institution, take action on political issues . . . and, in my judgment, it never should. . . . These are moving moments in the life of our generations generally and in the lives of students particularly. Our students, more than their elders, are acutely aware of the wounds our society inflicts upon itself. For them the opposite sides of every issue stand forth in stark outline and vivid perspective. Students are not in agreement with one another, and in these circumstances it is hardly to be expected that there will be agreement between every student and his parent, between every student and his academic advisor, or between the total student body and its university.

This University takes for granted the right of every student to speak of what is on his mind and encourages him to do what he considers appropriate to pursue his convictions and that he seek his objectives through our democratic processes. For him to do less is to ignore his responsibilities. We insist only that he speak and act with regard to the law of the land, the regulations of the University, and the rights of his fellow men.

April 28. What was called the most extensive fund drive in the University's history began with a rally for Pitt alumni held at Mt. Lebanon's junior high school. The drive, which was to run through July, was organized by Vice Chancellor Cale, with more than 1,000 volunteer workers and 10,000 letters mailed to graduates in twenty-five regions of the nation. Seventy-five of the University's alumni and friends showed up in the junior high school auditorium, which had seats for 356. In what he later apologized for as an unfortunate eruption of disappointment, Litchfield in his talk criticized the alumni for lack of interest in the University, the general community for failing to fully support the University, the trustees for not producing the large endowment they had promised him, and the press for not embracing the ideals the trustees had established a decade earlier.

May 11. At the annual meeting of trustees, the board named a twenty-member committee to study the future of the University and to outline goals for the next decade. Price was named chairman. He was, in effect, given authority by the trustees to work out the school's salvation in whatever manner he thought best.

Trustee Emil E. Narick, a star halfback on the

powerful Pitt teams of 1937–1939, then a member of the legal staff of the United Steel Workers (and in 1986 a judge of the Allegheny County Court of Common Pleas), read a four-page letter aloud. In a stinging rebuke to the Litchfield administration, he charged that "incredible mismanagement" by the administration leadership had permitted a crisis to develop and then prevented the trustees from learning of it early enough to take preventive action. He gave the secretary the letter to be attached to the minute of the meeting and sent a copy to each of the trustees.

May 18. The Council of Deans and Campus Presidents, with thirty-three persons attending, met from 9:00 A.M. to 9:00 P.M. at the Litchfield residence on Warwick Terrace. Edgar Cale reported that the fund drive had received $156,000 in pledges and cash. One of the deans reported that some persons had been offended at receiving unsigned form letters from the University asking for money and that others who were not alumni were displeased at receiving unsigned form letters that addressed them as "Dear Alumnus." Cale explained that he did not have the equipment or personnel to sign 10,000 letters and that everyone who ever had any connection with the University was considered an alumnus for campaign purposes. He promised to correct all this in the future. Several months later he asked the Administrative Committee what he should do with 4,000 leftover copies of a pamphlet, "Renaissance and the Role of the Patron at the University of Pittsburgh."

May 21–23. The Administrative Committee, numbering twelve persons, gathered for a three-day meeting at Tumble Run, beginning with dinner on Friday evening. The chancellor talked about a return trip he planned to make that summer with Peake and Van Dusen to Ecuador, Guatemala, and possibly Costa Rica. He reported on four new areas of teaching and research the University was entering, which he had named the TOPS Programs (*T*ropical Rain Forests, *O*ceanography, *P*olar Studies, and *S*pace Program). He talked optimistically of the new Center for Latin American Studies, which was being set up by Cole Blasier. (This was the young State Department officer who in 1958 had

Stanton Chapman Crawford, chancellor from June 1965 to January 1966.

accompanied the Litchfield group visiting the Soviet Union; Litchfield had persuaded him, after a long courtship, to join the faculty.) There was a long discussion of possible accommodations the University might make in a new relationship with the Commonwealth.

That last session on Friday was followed by dinner. During the meal Litchfield rose, took a few steps, said he was ill, and collapsed. Van Dusen, Peake, and Montgomery placed him on a mattress, put it in a Land Rover, and carried him and Mary Litchfield to the hospital in Coudersport. Montgomery drove, because he was the only one who could manage a stick shift. Litchfield was unconscious during the drive; his illness was diagnosed as a heart attack. Mary Litchfield spent the night on the floor of her husband's hospital room, sleeping on the mattress. The others spent the night at Tumble Run and departed early Saturday morning "with feelings of deep concern for their leader's health."

Litchfield was flown to Pittsburgh three days later and taken to Presbyterian-University Hospital. There his physician, Dr. Jack D. Myers, chairman of Pitt's Department of Medicine, said the attack was a mild one, the occlusion would heal, and the patient probably would be able to return to work by Labor Day. He was discharged on June 2 and thereafter took telephone calls, held small meetings, and dictated letters at Warwick Terrace. After consulting Litchfield, Price appointed Stanton Crawford as acting chancellor.

He could not have made a more popular choice. Dr. Stanton Chapman Crawford, then sixty-eight years old, an ordained minister as a young man, had served the University since 1924 as an instructor and professor of biology; for six years as head of the Johnstown Center while still carrying a teaching load in zoology; as dean of the College of Arts and Sciences; and since 1956 as secretary of the University and dean of the faculties. An amiable man, he wrote beautiful minutes of the meetings he attended and graceful articles (several of them in collaboration with a talented daughter) for zoological, historical, and educational journals.

June 2. The trustees passed a resolution asking the state legislature for an immediate emergency appropriation of $5 million to meet operating deficits. Although the University's assets exceeded $190 million, they said, "the University today contemplates a shortage of cash receipts needed to meet its current obligations during the next fourteen months." Five days later six Pitt trustees—Price, Denton, Frank Magee, former governor David Lawrence, Mayor Joseph Barr, and state senator Albert Pechan—called on Governor William Scranton to explain the crisis they faced and to justify their unprecedented

request. Price told the press, "There is little possibility for the present of making up the current and anticipated deficit through large scale giving or borrowing. Frankly, we are at a loss at this time for any other solution to our problem except to turn to the Commonwealth for special aid."

Scranton made no commitment, but he promised to give the request thoughtful consideration and to discuss it with the State Board of Education, its subsidiary Council of Higher Education, and leaders of the legislature from both parties. Members of the council shortly thereafter, in the course of drawing up a recommended procedure for the governor to follow, visited the campus and met privately for several hours with Price, Denton, and three of their supporting trustees.

June 18. Litchfield wrote a confidential letter to Acting Chancellor Crawford in which he listed nine sources where $4.270 million might be borrowed, anticipated, transferred, or juggled. That would be $1.470 million more, he said, than the cash needs for June and July. "I recognize," he wrote, "that not all of these things are realizable, but among them, they accumulate a figure that suggests that the largest part of our cash needs between now and the end of the fiscal year are *quite possibly* available to us, despite comments that have been made elsewhere."

It was Litchfield's refusal to believe that there really was a financial crisis, as indicated in this letter and in other later correspondence, that by now had convinced Price and the other members of the Budget and Audit Committee that the chancellor was unable to produce or manage a program for saving the University, and that if such a program was to be developed, it would have to be developed without Dr. Litchfield. One contributing cause of the lack of such a program was the failure of Cale's badly managed fund drive.* Another was the chancellor's hostility to a closer relation with the state, which he felt

---

*On June 24 Litchfield wrote to Edgar Cale: "Your development people simply don't know Pittsburgh and I don't think they are going to get to know it. I think it is imperative that we get at least one person in who knows the community thoroughly, who is socially acceptable in the most 'social' circles, and who can do all the things that we simply can't do with a hired staff brought in from the outside."

was not necessary and which he said would result not only in control and censorship of the University but also in an end to contributions from private sources. It was during these days that Gwilym Price acted on his conviction that the chancellor must go. He discussed the matter with various trustees, and "when Litchfield was well on his way to recovery, I called on him at his home and informed him that when he returned to his office I intended to call a meeting of the Executive Committee and urge them to request his resignation." Litchfield was then on the eve of departing for a vacation of some weeks at Virgin Gorda in the British West Indies.

June 25. Price appeared for several hours before a subcommittee of the State House of Representatives meeting in Pittsburgh to study Pitt's request for a special appropriation. He was flanked by David Lawrence and Mayor Joseph Barr and backed by Stanton Crawford and Herbert L. Koerner. His testimony, according to one news report, was unusually candid and detailed. He said that both the trustees and the administration had exercised bad judgment. With benefit of hindsight, the trustees would not have taken some of the actions they had taken five years earlier.

June 28. The trustees, aware of the concern of the faculty and students, passed a resolution expressing its unanimous determination to do everything in its power to maintain academic standards and the current high level of quality in the years ahead. The next day, giving the forthcoming emergency appropriation as security, they borrowed $1.25 million from two Pittsburgh banks at 4½ percent. Almost 1,100 people on faculty and staff had feared, with good reason, that they would not be paid at the end of June. They were paid; the bank loans were used to meet the June 30 payroll.

Crawford sent a cable:

Litchfield
Dixbay
Virgin Gorda   BWI

Bank loans against special appropriation meet payroll regards from all to each

Crawford

July 2. The state legislature passed and Governor Scranton signed emergency appropriation legislation granting the University of Pittsburgh $5 million for the 1964–1965 and 1965–1966 fiscal years.

The trustees announced the appointment of David H. Kurtzman as vice chancellor for finance, succeeding Jesse Hudson. Kurtzman had left the Pennsylvania Economy League to serve as secretary of administration in the cabinet of Governor Lawrence; in 1965 he was senior research and educational associate for Fels Institute of Local and State Government at the University of Pennsylvania when David Lawrence, backed by Denton and Price, called and offered him the post.

One of his first duties was to pass judgment on a proposed new way to raise money. Vice Chancellor Monnett, in studying *Fortune* magazine's list of the 500 largest industrial corporations, observed that twenty-two of them were headquartered in Pittsburgh. They had total net profits after taxes in 1964 of $1,138,031,000. Now, if each of those twenty-two Pittsburgh corporations would contribute only 1 percent of their net profits to the University of Pittsburgh for this and the next four years, they would give $11,380,310! But since such gifts would be tax deductible, they could give two times $11,380,310 and still have the same net effect on taxes! Thus they could give approximately $100 million to the University in five years! That would wipe out the University's total cumulative deficit in the first year, would pay off the total debt in about 2½ years, and would add $50 million to the University's endowment funds! Monnett conveyed this discovery to Crawford with questions: "Would this be an unreasonable request to make of our home-based industrial corporations? Is this too much to ask?" On the filed copy of Monnett's letter, Crawford wrote, "Dr. Kurtzman thinks this is unrealistic."

Time magazine for that week, reporting the Pitt story, began by retelling the 1963 exchange between Price and Litchfield referring to Litchfield's outside activities. ("Edward, don't you have enough balls up in the air now?" "Maybe I do. But don't call me down on it until I drop one.") *Time* said, "It was clear that Litchfield had finally fumbled a big one: Pitt."

July 7–8. The House Appropriations Committee

The strain of the fiscal crisis showing, Gwilym Price, board chairman, and Frank Denton, head of the board's Budget and Audit Committee, testify before the State House Appropriations Committee, July 7, 1965.

conducted a two-day hearing on the Pitt crisis at 10:00 A.M. in Room 106—the chancellor's office—where a long table had been set up. Ten of its nineteen members were there to see if Pitt actually needed the additional $5 million it was seeking from the state. Price revealed that in addition to the emergency grant recently voted, the University in the foreseeable future would have operating costs totaling $2.5 million more per year than expected income. He emphasized Litchfield's understanding

that Kurtzman was to be in charge of fiscal matters and would report directly to the trustees. Denton testified, "Litchfield has built a machine here . . . that . . . just takes more gas to run than we have." David Lawrence said the University was too important to the state to be allowed to lapse into bankruptcy: "I submit that the growth and expansion of Pitt has not been in some fanciful, aimless ivory tower approach, but rather has been of direct and measurable relevance to the economic, intellectual and cultural needs of the citizens of the Commonwealth."

July 13–14. "Students for Litchfield" obtained some nine hundred signatures on a petition defending the chancellor against his attackers; ran a full-page advertisement in the *Pitt News* in the form of an open letter to the trustees; and held a well-mannered rally of some six hundred students in the Schenley Quadrangle. There were placards: "Do you want a bookkeeper for a Chancellor?" "We must not let Dr. Litchfield be crucified on a cross of debits and credits." "We must not now become a sacrificial lamb on the altar of State aid."

July 16. Emil E. Narick, in the last days of his non-renewable term as alumni trustee, delivered his second letter to the board:

In my view, the administration knew or should have known of the developing symptoms of the University's financial crisis long before the trustees were compelled to uncover it themselves. Further, if the administration was aware of the unfavorable financial condition, it had the responsibility of bluntly and forthrightly presenting the information to the trustees. . . . I am convinced and respectfully submit to the trustees, with all due respect to Chancellor Litchfield, that this is the time for a change in the management and leadership of the University.

July 19. The Ford Foundation, which from time to time used its resources to commission and direct studies-in-depth of the problems of education, was receptive to a request from the trustees that it make such a study of the plight of the University of Pittsburgh. The study group, five educators headed by Herman B. Wells, chancellor of Indiana University, met for the first time in Pittsburgh on this date. They were charged by the foundation to analyze the University's progress, study its role in the region, make recommendations for its future, and investigate its relationship with the state. Their study, it was estimated, would take six months.

July 21. Jesse Hudson wrote to Denton and Price, "I have had a few sessions with Dr. Kurtzman and I am very favorably impressed. You . . . have made an excellent choice and I am certain that he will make a material contribution to the future of the University."

Hungerford portrays Litchfield as a fallen Superman, July 14, 1965.

July 23. Acting Chancellor Crawford presided over a meeting of the Administrative Committee. He asked Kurtzman to review with the group the proper way of handling his new budget sheets. The minute of the meeting reads: "Dr. Kurtzman explained that a new control system has been established which he hopes will be effective in maintaining budget controls in the future. He stressed that he did not want his office to become a substitute for appropriate administrators, but to be regarded as a help in maintaining a meaningful fiscal soundness. Dr. Kurtzman said that he was willing to do anything he could to understand individual problems which he knew would arise. He also said that he thought it vital that his office keep all concerned informed of fiscal matters in which they would have interest. But to perform well he would need the cooperation of the administrative staff in such matters as commitment control which had not had a reliable system of control in the past."

July 27. Joseph G. Colangelo, Jr., Pitt's public relations director, called a press conference to be held in the chancellor's office. Speaking for the University, with no trustees or other officers present, he read aloud and distributed copies of two letters and a statement.

Letter from Dr. Edward H. Litchfield
to Gwilym A. Price
Chairman of the Board of Trustees

Coudersport, Pa.
July 20, 1965

Dear Bill:

While I was in the Virgin Islands, I had time to think about our general situation at some length. I concluded then that in the light of many considerations it would be best if I asked the Board of Trustees to accept my resignation. I did not write to you then, for I felt that further reflection would be prudent.

I have been back for a time now, and further reflection and review of our circumstances only deepens my conviction that this is the proper course of action. Will you therefore be good enough to convey this to the Board at your convenience.

I am enclosing a statement to the press which was sketched in various forms both in the Virgin Islands and here. You may also care to send it to the trustees.

Sincerely,
Edward H. Litchfield

Letter to Dr. Edward H. Litchfield
from Gwilym A. Price
Chairman of the Board of Trustees

July 26, 1965

Dear Edward:

It is with a sense of deep appreciation for the decade you have given us that I accept your resignation for the Board of Trustees.

I can say no more to you personally than I already have said of you publicly: You have done more for the University of Pittsburgh in one decade than most men could have accomplished in a half century. I believe this feeling on my part is shared by the trustees. As I also have stated, I am confident that the difficulties of the last few months are on the way toward a solution and that it will be possible to recapture the momentum toward quality and excellence which you have so brilliantly defined for us.

In a very real sense, you can never leave Pitt, for the community of scholars which is Pitt today is inextricably bound up with your vision. My hope is that those who guide its future will be able to carry this vision forward.

Sincerely,
Gwilym A. Price

Price did not attend the press conference, Colangelo said, because he felt his views were expressed in his letter. Dr. Litchfield had not said anything publicly about his embattled position until now, Colangelo added, because he felt he should not seek the limelight unless it would be for the good of Pitt.

The trustees had not actually met to accept the resignation, he said; Mr. Price had canvassed them in person and by telephone.

Acting Chancellor Crawford made the announcement that afternoon at the start of a meeting of the Council of Deans and Campus Presidents. He asked Deans Frank Wadsworth, Sargent Cheever, and Paul Masoner to draft an appropriate resolution expressing the tributes voiced, and he asked Peake to telephone Litchfield and convey to him the spirit of the meeting.

Book V
1966-1985

The [Vietnam] war became the organizing principle around which all the doubts and disillusionments . . . all the deeper discontents hidden under the glossy surface of the confident years coalesced into one great rebellion.

Godfrey Hodgson
America in Our Time

Many accepted it as a given. Millwork would pay the bills—buy the cars, pay the mortgage, put food on the table and clothes on their backs, even send the kids to college. . . . And it was never supposed to end. Now Western Pennsylvania has 58,700 fewer steel jobs than it did six years ago. Another 54,500 manufacturing jobs have also vanished. And precious little has taken their place—the area has lost a total of 89,200 jobs since 1979.

Jane Blotzer
Pittsburgh Post-Gazette
December 30, 1985

The recent precipitous decline of heavy manufacturing in the Pittsburgh region has increasingly shifted the mantle of civic leadership from the corporate chief to the community's university and college presidents. Today, our institutions of higher education and health care are as potentially important to a productive economic future as steel and coal were in the not too distant past.

David Bergholz, Assistant Executive Director, Allegheny Conference on Community Development, 1986

27
Toward Recovery

It was a great personal tragedy, but in the long sweep of the history of this institution, the Litchfield chancellorship was not a tragedy, not a failure. It was an enormous success.

John H. Funari, November 2, 1982

THE five educators and the staff members who worked on the Ford Foundation independent study ("The Wells Report") spent six months on the assignment. They interviewed forty-five faculty members, administrators, and trustees, talked with eighty-five state and community leaders, and produced a fifty-two-page document that is a model of its kind: frank, discerning, a work addressed solely to the circumstances of this one institution.* They saw their assignment as "a search for the particular steps the Pittsburgh administration had taken which had made advance toward its aspirations too costly. The striving for improvement is characteristic of college and university administrations. . . . Why, then, had the University of Pittsburgh experienced difficulties in pursuing a natural course? It seemed crucial to discover whether improvement can be forced too rapidly and if particular kinds of change are contraindicated"—or if a special financial vulnerability underlay some of the choices made. They were "keenly aware that Pitt is not just another University, that it has a distinctive personality, matched by the exciting city in which it is located," whose "'Renaissance' has been an inspiration to civic groups throughout the nation."

Some findings:

● Costs had been reduced in various ways in 1965 without impairing the quality of well-established academic programs or lowering the University's sights "except to the extent that they were unrealistic when set a decade ago."

● Dormitories were financed through revenue bonds and by a surcharge on student tuition. The recent building program did not constitute a drain on University resources, but the tuition increase may have been part of the cause of the slowdown in enrollment.†

● The committee suspected that there was a seepage of regular University funds into payment for overhead and other indirect costs of contract research.

● The University's administrative structure in July 1965 consisted of a chancellor and eight vice chancellors. Many universities of greater size and complexity were operating efficiently with fewer top executives. The ratio of administrative expenditures, moreover, appeared high in comparison with the ratio at other universities.

● Enrollment of postbaccalaureate students increased sharply from 1,701 in 1960–1961 to 2,938 in 1964–1965. Graduate instructional cost per student credit hour ranged from double to triple the undergraduate costs in the academic and nonhealth professions. The policy of encouraging such enrollment without taking measures to assure steady undergraduate growth had resulted in a material weakening of the University's cost structure.

● The University doubled the size of the faculty and doubled faculty salaries during the 1957–1965 period of wavering enrollment. One result was that each faculty member's teaching load was considerably below the old norm of fifteen credit hours. This reduced the ratio of students per faculty member, which probably meant that a high proportion of the faculty was working full-time on research or other duties.

● Because of the trimester program adopted in 1959–1960, approximately 70 percent of the total faculty held appointments on a twelve-month time and salary basis, while the academic year was eight months long. Other comparable universities limited this percentage, with reason, to 33.3.

The assumptions and hypothetical economies of

*The educators were: Chairman Herman B. Wells, chancellor of Indiana University; T. Keith Glennan, president of Case Institute of Technology; Roger Heyns, former vice president for academic affairs of the University of Michigan, later chancellor of the University of California at Berkeley; Edward Levi, provost of the University of Chicago, later U.S. attorney general; and Clarence Hilberry, former president of Wayne State University, later with the Ford Foundation. Dr. Hilberry died in January 1966 in the week the report was released.

†Full-time equivalent enrollment declined from 12,962 in 1957–1958 to 9,350 in 1961–1962, a drop of 28 percent while other private universities were experiencing a net increase. A major cause was the heavy loss of students from New York when that state instituted a vigorous program of support for a state system of public higher education, creating new units on fifty-eight campuses.

the trimester system were persuasive, but they had not been realized in the Pittsburgh experiment. The spring (third) trimester had not proved any more attractive to regular students than the summer session of the conventional school year. Three-fourths of the full-time undergraduates chose to forego the opportunity to speed up their studies. This disappointing student response "has made the experiment extraordinarily expensive. . . . The committee has therefore come to the conclusion that the trimester calendar is probably responsible for a major share of the increased operating expenses per student credit hour at the University of Pittsburgh. University officers disagree with this deduction, however, without a comprehensive cost study of the trimester—a singular lack in view of the strong University backing of this system. . . . Caution should have dictated that such a far-reaching and financially hazardous experiment be attempted only with specific underwriting of the risk by a foundation or a similarly enterprising source.*

"The consequences of proposed changes or new directions should be explored as fully as possible before implementation, and priorities should be set so that the University can concentrate its scarce resources on a select number of endeavors which have high promise and limited financial risk. . . . It takes time, judgment, dedication, money and good luck to build a great university."

The committee's strongest recommendation was that the University develop financial support to carry on its optimal future mission: that of assuring opportunities for high-quality, four-year undergraduate education in Western Pennsylvania and of meeting selected national and regional goals for graduate and professional education extending to the doctoral level where strength and resources warranted. Pennsylvania had unfulfilled demands for

collegiate opportunities and a need for expanded low-tuition undergraduate education. The needs were so pressing that no private college or university in the region could ignore them. In 1963 the national average for high school graduates enrolling in college was 51 percent. Pennsylvania's average was 38 percent, with only seven of the fifty states ranking lower. Its total full-time college enrollment of 208,000 was projected to reach 377,000 by 1975, a growth of 80 percent.

The committee saw no way that Pitt could meet such needs without a substantial increase in state aid. It should make an accommodation with the state under which it would receive such aid. It should do so with such a posture that private support would not be discouraged. (The trustees and administrative officers had come to a similar conclusion somewhat earlier; their efforts over much of the next year would be directed to that end.)

The committee made a special effort in attempting to judge the University's progress. It obtained confidential statements "from educators of note" about the qualifications of the faculty, adequacy of resources, and quality of the academic programs. It reviewed published rankings of institutions based on such measures as the numbers of Woodrow Wilson Fellows, National Defense Education Act Fellows, and National Science Foundation awardees. It obtained ratings of Pitt departments and programs by juries of deans and chairmen of comparable programs throughout the country. It analyzed library holdings, ratio of students to faculty, highest earned degrees of faculty members, sources of faculty doctorates, and distribution of expenditures to academic programs. It compared scores of interviews with members of the University community. This mass of material "demonstrated conclusively" that the University had made definite progress and was "distinctly superior to the institution it was a decade ago. . . . The University is certainly to be commended for improving the quality of education available to the upper Ohio River region. . . .

"The past decade has been a time of rapid progress for American higher education. . . . To the question whether Pitt has held its own or bettered its

---

*At a joint meeting of trustees and faculty members, Adolf Grunbaum reported that generally the faculty regarded the Wells Report as superficial and illogical in reasoning, questioned the statement that 70 percent of the faculty were on twelve-month appointments, and were disappointed that it gave no indication of what the Ford Foundation might do by way of financial support of the University.

place in this advance, it would be fair to answer that the University has made more progress than its detractors will admit, but less than its most ardent admirers assert."

The committee was open-handed in its praise for the faculty: "Ex-Chancellor Litchfield accomplished the remarkable feat of building a graduate and research faculty while strengthening and restructuring the entire faculty in less than ten years. . . . For most academic architects not one decade but several are needed to build a fine and seasoned faculty. The constituents of the University can be justifiably proud of the galaxy of scholars attracted to the city of Pittsburgh."

In their comments on the faculty, the committee members touched on a matter of particular interest and of critical importance: "It would be an irreparable loss if so fine a faculty were dispersed as a result of the present crisis. Keenly aware of this danger, the Pittsburgh officers and Board of Trustees have taken numerous constructive steps to avoid faculty losses during these difficult times. To their great credit countless faculty members have remained loyal to the University during the past six months, displaying an admirable sense of unity and responsibility. The Committee believes that its findings justify the faculty's confidence in the durability, promise, and destiny of the University of Pittsburgh."

The retention of the faculty almost intact in the years 1963–1966 is indeed one of the remarkable developments in the 200-year history of the University. That was a time when good teachers were in high demand, opportunities were open, and headhunters from other universities were on the prowl. It was a time when costs at Pitt were being cut, salaries and new appointments were frozen, and several monthly payrolls were met only by last-moment stratagems. There was, moreover, a feeling among the faculty members that they were not being consulted about the University's problems and were not being fully informed about measures that were being taken to remedy them; and they forthrightly so informed the top administrators. And yet, with only a few exceptions, they stayed. (The top administrators felt they had to be reserved in what they revealed, for fear they might cause a general exodus of good people from the campus.)

The records show that this was a considered decision on the part of key faculty members, reached independently or in group discussions with their deans and department heads. Gwilym Price recalled: "I made one speech to the University Senate acquainting them with the stark details of our financial situation and promising nothing but 'blood, sweat and tears,' a real austerity program, for an indefinite time. Stanton Crawford, a mild, elderly man, devoted to Pitt, had the affection and loyalty of the faculty, and he, with Vice Chancellors Peake and Van Dusen, kept them from panicking."

Stanton Crawford agreed to carry on as acting chancellor following Litchfield's departure, though he had accepted the position unwillingly in May and was reluctant to continue in August. He would be sixty-eight in October and he had suffered a serious heart attack. He routinely left his office with a briefcase full of papers to study and letters to answer. His wife objected as vociferously as her mild nature allowed. Now she felt that her husband would not survive the stress of his new responsibilities. There were others who agreed with her, but they knew that no one else at that time could do what he was called upon to do. He was an indispensable man.

During Crawford's eight months in office, the University enrolled 1,586 students on the Cathedral campus in one of its largest and best-qualified freshman classes. Governor Scranton signed an appropriation bill that gave the University $5 million in emergency aid and $5.8 million for regular maintenance, thus resolving the immediate financial crisis. The trustees formally announced their decision to seek closer ties with the state under a plan, still to be developed, that would provide low-tuition mass education for Western Pennsylvania students while maintaining the essential private character of the institution. Crawford spoke on their plans at the annual fund-raising dinner of the Century Club, explaining that the trustees' decision placed Pitt on the verge of a unique three-way partnership among private donors, the state, and the University. The state House of Representatives on January 7, 1966, created a subcommittee to work with University trustees and administrators in developing such a plan for a new relationship with the state.

Stanton Crawford died of a heart attack in his home on January 26. Four months later he was posthumously named the University's thirteenth chancellor. Five months after that, ground was broken for a new science building that was to be named for him to honor his memory.

Litchfield was fully recovered by September 1965 and resumed his active life. He had declined to stand for re-election to the Studebaker board because his ideas were not being followed, but he was now able to give more time to Avco (of which he and his wife owned 6,000 shares worth about $150,000), to Smith-Corona-Marchant (of which they controlled shares worth about $2,045,600), and to the Governmental Affairs Institute. He started a new enterprise, a subsidiary of the GAI, and put Edgar Cale in charge of it. It was a service that provided guidance to colleges and universities in their search for federal grants, loans, and contracts. In 1967 he announced the formation in New York of the Capital for Technology Corporation, which would specialize in new products and techniques in such fields as electronics, plastics, and spatial navigation. He was board chairman. He considered running for governor of the state until Kurtzman, whom he consulted, advised him that his candidacy would be a mistake. A Pittsburgher who saw him on a street in Washington in 1967 thought that he seemed much older and without his usual vigor and élan.

Questions have lingered in the minds of those who have studied the events of 1956–1965, or lived through them as participants. Why did they turn out the way they did? What can be learned from them? Was there some course Edward Litchfield could have followed that would have carried him to honored and triumphant retirement as chancellor emeritus in 1979, or launched him on the larger career in national affairs he contemplated? Or were

the sequelae implicit, inevitable, as in a Greek tragedy, predestined by the character, perhaps the hubris, of the protagonist?

John Funari, who was Litchfield's administrative assistant from 1958 to 1962, believes that one motif ran through the tragedy, the most human part of the drama. This was the personality of Edward Litchfield himself when brought face to face with the Pittsburgh community. As Funari sees it:

"If someone were to ask me what are the fundamental characteristics of a Western Pennsylvanian, I would say, chip on the shoulder, chin out, hands on our hips, telling the rest of the world to bug off. There is an element of resentment in that, of the power of the east, its bankers and sophisticates—a motif that appears over and over in our Western Pennsylvania, Whiskey-Rebellion, Scotch-Presbyterian history. One way absolutely to insult us and to gain our undying enmity is to patronize us. We put great pride in hard work and attention to detail. We distrust fops and dandies, dislike glibness, maybe even articulateness.

"Against that background, put in Edward Litchfield. Vain, sophisticated, moves with ease and grace, with confidence and aplomb, in high business circles. Part of the eastern establishment—his patron was General Lucius Clay. Has his own airplane and flies from place to place. His exterior personality is everything that Pittsburghers instinctively dislike. Here was a man who was contrary to every other chancellor the University had ever had. The clothes he wore, his whole manner and bearing and presence. He had a stage presence, with an orator's resonant voice, and it was as much in evidence in the board room as it was on an academic podium.

"He had his own niche carved out in American business. He was in a certain sense as much of a businessman as some of the business leaders he dealt with. Business leaders simply weren't used to that kind of relationship with a university chancellor. The university chancellor comes, sometimes hat in hand but always somewhat deferential. But Litchfield would come and talk with them about business organization and management as an equal—at least he thought he could. I believe that maybe down deep they resented that and saw it as patronizing."

There is ample testimony that Litchfield did indeed antagonize a considerable part of the Pittsburgh "power structure." William Rea, trustee, later board chairman, declared, "He did not get the full confidence of the community. He was very much of a one-man team, he was not a great leader of the community. I think he was a great academic leader within the University, but he antagonized a good many outside people." Gwilym Price said: "He could be very friendly if he wanted to. At other times he was as arrogant as hell. Who was the nice old man they got rid of to bring in Litchfield? Fitzgerald. I liked him. I liked him very much. I don't blame them for wanting to get rid of him and get somebody else in. My recollection is that even after I got there [in 1959] I felt sorry for him. Litchfield never mentioned him, never mentioned anything he had done. Ed treated my good friend Jake Warner as if he were dirt under his feet. Certainly as a junior in everything they did together. Polite as hell. Ed was very seldom impolite."

Some of the alienation certainly arose because of Litchfield's scale of living. D. S. Greenberg, a skillful reporter on educational matters, wrote to this theme in an article in *Science:* "Whether Litchfield enjoyed generous entertaining, or felt it was part of his duties, or both, the fact is that the stately halls of the Heinz Mansion became the center of a conspicuous social whirl. Prospective faculty recruits were given what was referred to as 'the treatment,' leading some of them to conclude that Pitt must indeed be an affluent institution. . . . Those so disposed could find ample data to arrange in a hostile pattern. If the University had financial problems, why did Litchfield live in the Heinz Mansion? Litchfield had a chauffeured Cadillac; the president of nearby Carnegie Tech got along with a chauffeured Oldsmobile. Litchfield, still holding on to his corporate interests, regularly was flown about the country in his own plane, charging the costs to the university when on university business. At least a dozen university presidents in this country are provided with planes from the university budget, but those who wished to look askance could find grounds for doing so."

Ben Spiegel

Litchfield in an unguarded moment.

Price said further of Litchfield: "Ed was a very persuasive man. There were times that I really thought he was a genius. In many ways he was. But with it all he lacked some common sense." As evidence of this failing, he cited the events following the untimely death of Alan Magee Scaife: "One of his great mistakes was that after Alan died, instead of recognizing that the situation had changed and he had a new ball game, he didn't recognize that. I don't think he wanted to."

Most people holding an opinion on the matter believe that Litchfield's troubles began with Scaife's death, and that if he had lived, the troubles of 1962–1965 would not have occurred. Frank Denton refused to speculate on the point. "I cannot conjecture," he said, "about what would have happened. If Alan Scaife had lived, Litchfield might not have

Ben Spiegel

Litchfield walks to his car in the Schenley quadrangle, accompanied by an assistant, Bernard Adams. His chauffeur is to the left.

acted the same. He might not have run wild." Price dissented from the common viewpoint: "I always had a feeling, after I got a little better acqainted with Pitt and Litchfield, that if Alan Scaife had lived, Litchfield would have been out long before he was. I think if he had lived and had felt the pulse of the business community, Alan would have found that Litchfield was not very popular. Whether he would have dug into the financial affairs very much or not I don't know, but I think he might have lost faith in Litchfield long before the rest of us did."

A main cause of Litchfield's downfall was unquestionably a series of misjudgments he made begin-

ning in 1958. Edison Montgomery recalls that he was gambling on two things. "He banked on being able to fill our undergraduate slots at greatly increased tuition. He sincerely believed . . . that enrollment pressure would enable us to raise tuition, and the increasing quality of the school would attract people even though tuition was high. What happened . . . was that we priced ourselves out of the market.

"The other thing he banked on . . . was that the rich people of Pittsburgh would not begin to give until we showed them that we had a truly distinguished university. So in effect we were investing in deficit financing in the expectation of having distinction that would make them give."

From this considered decision, Litchfield progressed still further to a dangerous conclusion: If he created the great new university the trustees had asked for in 1955, at whatever cost, with whatever deficits, the power structure would back him up and pay his debts. If they did not do so out of pride in what they saw, they would do it because they were backed into a corner and would have to bail him out to save face. In acting on that belief, he incurred the distrust and dislike of the one man in the community he could not afford to offend: Richard Mellon.

Mellon was certainly not offended by the chancellor's style of living, nor by his confidence and aplomb, nor by his air of a successful businessman. He was very much offended when he learned of the chancellor's financial strategy. Denton declared in an interview in 1981: "Litchfield decided on his own to go on building without the funds to do it. No one ever gave him a mandate to spend money he didn't have. [In] his desire for a great university, he figured that if he went ahead and did it and produced the good result, the trustees would have to back him and pay for it.

"I never advised Dick Mellon as to his charities, nor on Pitt, but I never believed for a moment that he was going to bail out Litchfield.

"Litchfield was not willing to grow slowly. If he had been willing to build in stages he could have weathered the storm and stayed in office."

Price asked Denton early in 1965 to go with him to R. K. Mellon's office to discuss the University and its problems. Denton described the meeting: "So we went to see Dick and he made the pitch to him about the problems and asked if Dick would be willing to help out on this deficit that had been created. At no surprise to me, Dick said no. He said he was an admirer of Pitt, he had given Pitt substantial funds and would give more money in the future from time to time, but he was not going to be put in the position of having somebody spend money and then be called upon to pick up and pay for whatever they decided to spend." He said privately to Denton after this meeting, "I do not give money by blackmail."

Edison Montgomery, in a published statement in 1972, set the record straight on the claim that Mellon should have given the University $125 million because Alan Scaife may have hoped he would do so. "When you're talking about $125 million," he said, "that just doesn't happen. There is a difference between an expression of support and a firm promise. At staff meetings, Litchfield stressed that he had been promised nothing, though he expected to receive the money he needed. . . . [One should not] fall into the trap of referring to 'the Mellons' as if there exists such an entity. The fact of the matter is that Alan Scaife and Richard King Mellon were two distinct individuals. Litchfield had every right to hope that Mellon's commitment to Pitt would prove as strong as Scaife's, but he had no right to expect that Mellon's preferences would coincide with those of his deceased brother-in-law. Moreover, if Scaife made a de facto commitment to Litchfield, Mellon was not obliged to keep it."

Edward Litchfield made no public defense of his record through the first six months after his retirement in July 1965. John Funari, who had left the University to join the State Department and saw him from time to time in Washington, says, "His demeanor was obviously that he felt he had been wronged, but I never detected a single note of bitterness. There was regret, as there must be when a man's career has just been completely blasted out of the water, but I saw no sense of retribution. He turned his attention to other things."

That restraint ended in the spring of 1966, when Litchfield decided to strike back at those who had driven him out of the University. Mary Litchfield gave Funari a box of documents and asked him to report Edward and his cause aright, which he found he was unable to do. ("I could not find the smoking gun—a firm promise of $125 million in endowment.") Litchfield, instead of writing an account himself of his ten years at Pitt, then paid a local journeyman writer a fee of almost $5,000 to tell his story. He told it badly. Two incredible documents the writer produced for Litchfield charged that there was actually no financial crisis in 1965; that the fund drive the chancellor had launched was "jeopardized by the distorted financial reports" the trustees gave the community; that Frank Denton refused to allow Litchfield to present a proposal to the trustees that would have made state aid unnecessary; that Denton had conspired to manufacture a crisis to relieve Mr. Mellon of his "responsibility" to pay off the University's operating deficit; that by accepting state aid, the trustees were jeopardizing academic freedom; that the image of Pittsburgh as a renaissance city was now tarnished; and that the University had been diverted from greatness and would no longer "play a major fruitful role in community development." Pittsburgh had deserted the goals it had set for itself; the future was in jeopardy, as was the confidence in a people's capacity for constructive social action.

Edward and Mary Morrill Litchfield spent some weeks early in 1968 vacationing in Central America. They returned to New York by commercial flight and there, at La Guardia on Friday afternoon, March 8, they boarded their own plane. This was a blue and white all-metal construction De Havilland Dove Reilly, Model DH–104–6A, with a capacity for eight passengers and two crew. Its twin British De Havilland engines had been replaced in March 1967 by American Lycoming Engines made by Avco, the "conversion" performed by Riley Aeronautics Corporation, Fort Lauderdale. The Litchfields had bought the plane on October 3, 1967.

Their pilot, James Edmund Looker, had flown the aircraft from Wellsville, New York, to La Guardia on the afternoon of March 6. Fifty years old, he was a resident of Wellsville and had been certified a commercial pilot in 1937, rated for airplane single and multiengine, land and instrument. He had been a revenue-carrying pilot, a test pilot with Piper Aircraft, and an air taxi-charter pilot with the Wellsville Flying Service. He resigned the last position to become a pilot for Smith-Corona-Marchant, which assigned him to perform pilot duties exclusively for its chairman of the board. He had earlier piloted Litchfield's Beech 65, Queen Air. As of February 1, 1966, he had logged 8,600 hours as pilot-in-command, 470 hours actual instrument flight time, 205 hours hooded flight time, and 75 hours synthetic trainer time. His last letter of competency was issued February 7, 1966, and his cur-

rent Second Class Medical Certificate was issued February 2, 1968, with no limitations.

James Looker did not like the converted De Havilland Dove. He told M. J. Tarantine, manager and operator of the Wellsville Flying Service, that the plane had mechanical problems—more than came with most aircraft. It had gear trouble and the turbos would not always engage—one would work, but one, generally the right one, gave him trouble. He also had trouble with the magneto ignition. An instrument shop had come to Wellsville to do a static check to assure the instrument system was working properly, but Tarantine thought this had never been completed.

Looker had his inboard tanks topped at La Guardia and a broken cover on a beacon light replaced. He received a weather briefing from the meteorologist on duty. The dispatcher checked him out at approximately 2:00 P.M. EST, Friday, March 8. The intended destination was Topeka, Kansas, with stops at Wellsville and Chicago. The aircraft departed La Guardia at 4:12 with three persons aboard: the Litchfields and the pilot. It landed at the Wellsville Municipal Airport at 5:30, taxied across the field to its hangar, and had the inboard tanks topped with 74.4 gallons of 100 octane gasoline. Tarantine told Looker that he appeared to be tired. Looker replied that he still had to go to Kansas with a stop at Chicago and that he was not looking forward to it, particularly with the marginal weather at Chicago.

John L. Palmer, whose Palmer Air Motive Company hangared and cleaned the aircraft, placed the luggage of three additional passengers in the rear baggage compartment. He saw there two tan attaché cases, a shopping bag filled with gift-wrapped packages, and a plastic garment bag that contained a suit or topcoat and a dress. He placed a twenty-four-inch suitcase on the rack and another plastic bag containing children's clothes. On an earlier occasion, before a flight to South America, Palmer had seen six life jackets stowed under the forward two-seat couch, each sealed in a plastic bag that could be ripped open by pulling a cord, but he did not look to see if the jackets were there on this occasion. Before a South American trip made in 1964, Litchfield had borrowed a life raft from Lawrence Litchfield, Jr. (president of Alcoa, no relation), but there was no raft aboard the Dove, though it would cross some sixty miles of open Lake Michigan water. Everyone, Palmer observed, was in a hurry to depart. There was no indication then or later that the pilot was being pressured to make a flight he did not wish to make.

The additional passengers were Litchfield's mother, eighty, and his two youngest children, Edward Harold (Ted), ten, and De Forest Dexter, five. They were all headed for a Morrill family reunion in Hiawatha, Kansas, and a birthday celebration for Mary Litchfield's mother. During the stop at Wellsville, Litchfield had telephoned Meigs Airport in Chicago and talked with Ralph T. O'Neil of Munster, Indiana, husband of Mary's sister. The Litchfields would pick them up at Meigs and continue on to Topeka. The plane would still be two persons under its rated load capacity.

The aircraft departed Wellsville at 6:00 P.M. EST. It now had six persons aboard: four adults and the two Litchfield children. At 5:33 CST Looker asked for and received the weather forecast for Chicago: ceiling 400 feet obscuration, visibility one-half mile, moderate rain, fog with a surface wind from 080° at 4 knots, temperature 41°, dew point 33°. He reported his altitude to the Chicago Center as 4,500 feet and his altimeter setting as 29.72. He said, "I haven't been able to figure out from my charts. I'm totally unfamiliar with your area. I can't find my charts for Meigs."

At 8:03:45 CST Looker advised the center, "We're still VFR [visual flight rules] at four point five. I'll descend to three point five if it's O.K. with you." The center replied, "Altitude's at your discretion." At 8:06:45 the pilot reported, "Thirty-two from Benton Harbor" (on the shore of Lake Michi-

gan). At 8:20 the tower operator issued a special VFR clearance for the aircraft to enter the Meigs control zone. The aircraft did not acknowledge the clearance instructions, and there was no further communication. Radar contact had been lost.

A missing aircraft alarm was issued. The U.S. Coast Guard and two private agencies conducted visual surface and sonar searches at the last reported position but with negative results. It was estimated that a person might live three hours in water the temperature of Lake Michigan.

Edward Litchfield's body, clad in a business suit and supported by a life preserver, was found at midmorning Saturday, floating five miles off Meigs Field. James Looker's body was found a few days later. The bodies of Litchfield's mother, wife, and son Edward were not recovered until early in May. They were identified at the Cook County Morgue by Ralph O'Neil. The body of De Forest Litchfield was never found.

The University of Pittsburgh campus was stunned by the morning news on March 9. The new chancellor ordered flags to be lowered to half staff. He asked for a memorial service to be held in Heinz Chapel on Sunday afternoon, March 17. He began proceedings to have the three new circular dormitory buildings named Litchfield Towers. And he issued a statement:

While we mourn his loss, we know that he has earned a secure place as one of the outstanding American educators of this generation, as well as one of the most productive leaders in the 181-year history of the University. We benefit from and will build upon the academic values that he created here. . . . I, personally, have the obligation not only to preserve them, but to advance them. For the basic character of this University, so capably enhanced by Edward Litchfield, is forward momentum.

28

"Our House Is in Order"

In view of your continued interest in the University of Pittsburgh's affairs, I am taking this opportunity of sending you a copy of our Financial Report for 1966. You will note that for the first time since 1958 we have shown an operating surplus. . . .

More importantly, the point that I know you were concerned about, based on our previous verbal discussion, is that we did not achieve this balance at the expense of our academic status. . . . Our educational expenditures show . . . that we have been able to make our economies in the areas which did not hurt our academic standing. . . . During this period we were able to grant salary increases on an average of about 10% to our faculty. . . .

We are hoping to be able to begin now to aim for continued growth in excellence.

David H. Kurtzman to Richard K. Mellon, November 9, 1966

THE day after Stanton Crawford's death, the trustees Search Committee and the faculty Advisory Committee met jointly in the chancellor's office. Gwilym Price, presiding, observed that the two committees now had an additional task to perform; to chose a chancellor and to name an acting chancellor to serve until the choice was made and the new man inducted.

Four names, he said, had been brought up in a meeting of the trustees held an hour earlier: Vice Chancellors Edison Montgomery, Charles Peake, Albert Van Dusen, and David Kurtzman, the new vice chancellor for finance. Trustee William Booth had proposed the name of J. Steele Gow, but Price said that while Mr. Gow would have been able to fill the office of acting chancellor admirably, the present state of his health, at age seventy-one, ruled him out of consideration. Dr. Grunbaum suggested the name of Professor Jack D. Myers of the School of Medicine.

Price had earlier suggested to Montgomery that he should take the office, but Montgomery declined and suggested that Kurtzman was the logical choice for the times, since he had worked more closely than anyone else with Crawford and the trustees in the University's attempt to work out a relationship with the Commonwealth. The minute of the January 27 meeting reads: "The qualifications of each individual were discussed, for it was recognized that each one has special merit. This discussion led to the unanimous decision that Dr. Kurtzman would make an excellent choice as Acting Chancellor. . . . He could represent the University well in Harrisburg because of his political knowledge and his acquaintance with the legislators themselves.

"It was agreed . . . Dr. Kurtzman should assure the faculty of his desire to maintain the integrity of the University, its forward progress, and the excellence of its faculty. Such assurance will help us to keep those faculty members who may be contemplating positions elsewhere."

Price was asked to talk with Kurtzman. He first telephoned the other trustees, obtained their concurrence, and then asked Kurtzman to accept the post, with the understanding that an intensified effort would now be made to find a permanent chancellor. He announced the appointment of David Harold Kurtzman as acting chancellor on January 30, 1966.

It was not a unanimously popular choice with the faculty. Kurtzman had been on the campus only seven months. He was not a physically impressive man, standing only five feet three inches. He was a financial man, an accountant type, with limited experience in university administration. He was thought to be "a Mellon man," one who for twenty-two years had been the brains of the Mellon-dominated Pennsylvania Economy League. He was also a Denton man—the person Frank Denton had brought in to cut back on expenditures, balance the budget, and (in some minds) to find a way to turn the University over to state control.

He could not have been more unlike those who had occupied the chancellor's office before him. Born in a village near Odessa, Russia, in 1904, the son of a successful wholesale grocer, he could not attend his local *gymnasium* (high school) because its 10 percent quota of Jewish students had been filled. His parents sent him at age eleven to live away from home, in Odessa, where the quota had not been filled. He saw and lived through pogroms. In 1920–1921, traveling by way of Romania, Belgium, and London, the family was able to assemble in Philadelphia. Young Kurtzman entered high school there as a nineteen-year-old sophomore, graduated in eighteen months, second in his class, and was given a scholarship to Temple, where he majored in accounting with a senior minor in political science. Now married, supported by a working wife and two jobs of his own, he took a doctorate at the University of Pennsylvania; his dissertation was entitled *Methods of Controlling Votes in Philadelphia*. In 1933, after two years of teaching political science at Temple, he became an assistant research director at the Pennsylvania Economy League in Philadelphia. In 1938 he moved to Pittsburgh to become director of research at the league's western division. At this end of the state, the league was an early "think tank" for city, school, and regional municipal governments. His fondest wish—never realized—was to put Pittsburgh and Allegheny County on a pay-as-you-go basis, retiring their debt, eliminating bond issues, and thereby saving millions of dollars in interest payments.

Kurtzman was one of the key aides to Mayor Law-rence and Richard Mellon in their joint effort to build a Pittsburgh renaissance. When Lawrence became governor in 1959, he took Kurtzman with him as his secretary of administration. Lawrence left office in 1963, not permitted to succeed himself, and Kurtzman became a senior research and educational associate of the Fels Institute of Local and State Gov-ernment. The University of Pennsylvania built him an air-conditioned office adjoining the old Fels man-sion and made no demands other than that he be there and talk occasionally with special students. Celia Kurtzman, his widow, says, "He was bored. It was a dull life." In the spring of 1965 came the tele-phone call from David Lawrence asking him to become vice chancellor for finance at Pitt.

Acting Chancellor Kurtzman called a joint meet-ing of deans and Senate councils in the Babcock Room at 4:00 P.M. on Tuesday, February 1, 1966. The address he delivered there was surely the most important of his life.

I have received many messages of encouragement and I will rely heavily on all of you for aid in fulfilling my new duties.

I realize many of you may have misgivings about a man from the finance area moving into the chief administrative spot even temporarily. You might feel that the most im-portant thing in my mind is to balance the budget without regard to maintaining our academic achievements. Let me assure you that such is not the case. I can do nothing here today to convince you of that, except to give you my word. I do give you my word. . . .

If we really want to save money, the best way to do it would be to close the University.

If we do not capitalize on the gains we have made—if we do not continue to go forward—if we attempt to merely stand still with the academic status we have achieved—then we will slip back. If we slip back in any way, money spent will go down the drain.

I hope to see us build up our financial backing to enable us to maintain that status, to maintain our gains and to move forward. For a while, we will do so with our belts a little tighter.

The talk was a sensational success; it received the rare accolade of a standing, applauding audience. It

David Harold Kurtzman, acting chancellor in 1966 and chancellor from January to May of 1967.

Pittsburgh Press

marked the beginning of admiration and affection for David Kurtzman that was sustained throughout the next decade. Professor Walter Evert said it best: "He was everybody's favorite uncle."

The Board of Trustees, Kurtzman said some months later, "gave me its confidence and the freedom to act. That, in itself, was a tremendous advantage, and a particularly brave thing to do when they themselves were, in some respects, under the gun, and I was untried, especially as a chief university administrator." He had no intention of performing a holding operation; it was not his inclination, nor did he think that was what the trustees, faculty, or students expected. He had already, as vice chancellor for finance, restored some of the excessively deep cuts in services and personnel made in the 1964–1965 economy drive, and he had set up monthly projections of income and expenditures, in contrast with the yearly projections of the previous administration. Acting on a report prepared by Price Waterhouse and Company, "A Program for Improving the Effectiveness of the Financial Function—March 1966," he began a series of other changes in financial procedures, including computerization of general ledger accounting and reporting. Acting on the Ford Foundation–Wells Report, he reorganized the top administration, reducing the number of vice chancellors from eight to three: Peake, academic disciplines; Van Dusen, professions; and Kurtzman, finance. The Budget and Audit Committee, with a $1.426 million operating surplus for 1966–1967, began to return the funds borrowed from endowment accounts, with back interest so that they could be reported as income-producing. The Panther Hollow project was officially dropped as not economically feasible. The four-person domestic staff at Warwick Terrace was dismissed and the house sold to the Catholic Diocese of Pittsburgh. Three of the chancellor's secretaries were reassigned. The handsome and historic Croghan-Schenley Room was cleared of files, desks, clothes racks, and excess furniture (it was later restored to its original appearance). Gwilym Price wrote to his friend Deane Malott the happy news that the University had now put its house in order.

Price was being somewhat more optimistic than the facts would seem to warrant in the spring of 1966. The University had emerged almost intact from a crisis, but it still faced serious and puzzling problems—problems that were linked in such a way as to make their solution extraordinarily difficult. The University needed A to get B, but it could not get A until it had B. It needed a permanent chancellor, but a good man would not be interested in the chancellorship until he knew the kind of university he was being asked to head. The University needed greatly increased support from the state, but it was not clear what arrangement could be worked out that would be acceptable to the governor, legislators, trustees, administrators, alumni, faculty, taxpayers, and a new chancellor. The current session of the legislature, moreover, was confined by law solely to fiscal legislation, and so Governor Scranton would have to be persuaded to call a special session in 1966 that would run concurrently with the regular session. The University also would need increased support from private sources, but it was not at all certain that the community, alumni, friends, foundations, and corporations would contribute to what would be an institution supported by the state. Nor would a prospective chancellor consider taking the office until he knew for sure that private support would be forthcoming. A *Post-Gazette* columnist wrote in July 1965, "It will require a search committee uncommonly gifted with the poker face to confront a candidate with an uncertain budget and an unclarified structure, particularly if the candidate has not been around Pitt during its recently tumultuous past."

Some of the faculty members were unsure and nervous about the possibility of political types, patronage hacks, and ultraconservative snoopers determining curricula, salaries, and academic standards. Word spread of an ominous conversation George Murdock had in February 1966 with Detlev Bronk, president of Rockefeller University and formerly president of Johns Hopkins and of the National Academy of Sciences. Murdock asked Bronk for suggestions on the choice of a new chancellor. Bronk criticized Pitt for attempting to become state related, said he foresaw increased state control and decreased private aid, and refused to recommend any candidates.

The situation was worsened by the appearance of a three-part article in *Science* magazine: "Pittsburgh: The Rocky Road to Academic Excellence." The piece was well researched and honest, but it threw an unmerciful light on the University's problems, and some top faculty people shared the view that it would make it more difficult to obtain a first-class chancellor.

The faculty, on the other hand, had stood firm, and the rate of attrition in 1965–1966 actually had dropped from a normal 11 percent to 8 percent. James A. Kehl, newly appointed dean of the School of Liberal Arts, wrote to Kurtzman on July 6, 1966, on returning from a deans conference at the University of Rochester:

Eighteen major universities . . . were represented. On numerous informal occasions discussions turned to the problem faced by the University of Pittsburgh over the last year and a half. . . .

One dean told me that when he heard of the financial situation in Pittsburgh a year ago, he made offers to two members of our Department of Philosophy and was impressed by the fact that neither was tempted by his Ivy League invitation. In addition, the representatives from Stanford and Michigan indicated that they had observed our ability to retain crucial members in spite of the financial picture and competition in the "academic market.". . . If this idea is widespread (and it appears to be), it will do much for the image of the University and its faculty.

Kurtzman sent copies of the letter to the trustees with a note: "I hope that you will agree with me that we on the Board have a responsibility to our faculty to make sure that we continue to warrant such loyalty."

Nevertheless, the ties were being strained. There had been a slippage in the past two or three years to the point where Pitt's academic salaries in many cases were now $2,000 to $4,000 below the going rate. Charles Peake addressed himself to that problem in an alarmed letter to Kurtzman handwritten during a plane trip. "Time is critical. We have

reached, I think, the point of maximum danger in our effort to stave off raids and thus retain our outstanding faculty. The situation calls . . . for dramatic action, if possible, to prevent imminent disintegration." He cited a conversation with one of his top younger sociologists. "After I explained the favorable characteristics of the bill you [Kurtzman] are negotiating and said that we had been assured that private support would be forthcoming, he retained serious reservations. What assurances do we have, he asked, that private support will be forthcoming, or that it will come in time and in sufficient amounts to save the situation? Something positive, he said, must be done right now." Peake begged for a dramatic act by the private sector that would immediately provide a fund for faculty salary improvement. Kurtzman looked at the existing salaries of his eighteen academic deans, compared them with the salaries paid by the twenty-six principal competitors, found that Peake's figures were correct, and promised to take up the subject with the trustees.

Two weeks later Peake had to acknowledge the resignation of the dean of the School of Social Sciences, who had accepted a position at Ann Arbor: "The thought of your not being with us next year fills me with dismay. . . . You have done an outstanding job. . . . I regret keenly the sudden turn of events which shortly after your arrival destroyed your high hopes for a creative task of building the Division and instead plunged you into a painful routine of retrenchment. . . . I know you understand that I would not have persuaded you to come here had I known the University was on the brink." (The top young sociologist, however, was still a member of the faculty in the 1980s.)

The University received surprisingly strong support from community spokesmen in its bid to create what one educator called a joint venture in public-private support for higher education. Some headlines of those months read: "Civic Chiefs Back Pitt on State Tie." "Scranton Backs Aid to Pitt as Helpful—Can't Be Ignored." "City Appeals to State to Pull Pitt Out of Hole." "State Ponders Way to Bail Out Pitt." "Pitt Needs a Transfusion." "Bishop

Office of Governmental Relations

On August 23, 1966, House Bill Number 2 of the General Assembly of Pennsylvania was signed, and the University of Pittsburgh became state related. Seated, left to right: Rep. K. Leroy Irvis (D), Governor William Scranton, and Sen. Robert D. Fleming (R). Standing, left to right: Robert H. Bailie, Pitt's Director of Commonwealth Relations, Rep. Thomas F. Lamb (D), Rep. Earl Sidney Walker (R), Rep. James J. A. Gallagher (D), Sen. James S. Berger (R), Rep. Donald O. Bair (R), Rep. H. Beryl Klein (D), Sen. Albert R. Pechan (R), and Martha B. Michalik, Assistant Director of Commonwealth Relations.

Wright Asks Pitt Aid." "Church Backs Aid to Pitt." "Pitt Key to Area Progress." "Let's Rally to Pitt's Aid." A *Press* editorial read: "This is an institution which repeatedly has shown its ability to weather rough going and advance its academic plans and programs. This is true chiefly because many civic leaders have recognized that the existence here of a big quality university is necessary to the welfare of the area and to our hopes for industrial develop-

ment, no less than for the educational opportunity it offers to students."

Even the humiliating articles that were reporting the financial crisis itself were producing a peculiar benefit in that almost all stressed the outstanding progress the University had made academically. A typical piece appeared in the *Philadelphia Sunday Bulletin:* "Pitt Ends Decade of Fantastic Gains—In Trouble for Over $25 Million."

The bill making Pitt a state-related institution was signed on August 23, 1966. About one hundred persons, most of them from Pittsburgh, crowded into Governor Scranton's office in Harrisburg to observe or participate in the ceremony. Three of them were Pitt undergraduates selected for the occasion. The governor used several dozen pens in signing his name; some of them still hang on home or office walls, boxed and under glass, with brass plates recording the momentous event.

The trustees had amended the bylaws to accept the designation "state-related" and to change the name to that of a private corporation called "University of Pittsburgh—Of the Commonwealth System of Higher Education." Under the terms of the agreement:

1. The state increased its contribution to the University's annual budget. Much of the increase was a direct subsidy to enable the University to lower its tuition for Pennsylvania residents. Pitt lowered its tuition for two trimester terms on the main campus from $1,450 to $450 for Pennsylvanians. Out-of-state students would continue to pay $1,600 a year. Pitt's four branch campuses—Johnstown, Greensburg, Bradford, and Titusville—reduced their tuition to $390. Night school tuition was cut from $38 to $14 per credit.

2. Part of the increase was to go for general overhead and for support of specific programs that the state wished to encourage in the public interest—for example, the School of Medicine and the Computer Center.

3. Pitt became eligible to receive General State Authority (GSA) construction grants to expand campus facilities. Some building projects, such as dormitories and student unions, did not qualify for GSA support; academic buildings did qualify.

4. Pitt was empowered to issue tax-exempt bonds to finance new construction not eligible for GSA support.

5. The board was increased from thirty-six to thirty-nine trustees. Twenty-four of these were University trustees, privately elected in the usual manner. Twelve were Commonwealth trustees—four of them appointed by the governor, four by the president pro tempore of the State Senate, four by the speaker of the State House of Representatives. Thus the state was given a voice, though a minority one, in the management of the University's affairs.

The University remained legally a private entity and, in practice, retained the freedom and individuality of a private institution, both administratively and academically. It set its own standards for student admission and retention, faculty, and teaching. Its assets remained in the hands of the corporation, its employees were employed by the corporation, and its affairs continued to be governed by an independent Board of Trustees. In return, the Commonwealth obtained the services of a state university in educating its young people, and did so without the huge capital investment that would have been required to build such an institution, as had once been contemplated.

The effort to find a chancellor up to this time had been unproductive and discouraging. William Rea said in a joint meeting of the committees on July 11, "We are now at the end of our list of active prospects. If we do not agree on [name not recorded], we will probably not have a new chancellor before the fall of 1967." Two weeks later Rea reported that the trustees felt that three choices should be considered: to select one of the two available prospects now and have a new chancellor by fall; or to continue on as before and intensify the search for the right kind of man, but with the realization that there would be no chancellor for possibly another year; or to appoint Dr. Kurtzman as chancellor for his three remaining years at the University, when he would reach sixty-five, and then select someone to succeed him.

To encourage and inform the search teams, a book was distributed, one sponsored by the American Council on Education: Frederick D. Bolman's *How College Presidents Are Chosen*. Bolman told the sad story of a selection panel that, having gone through a list of candidates, found one man who had all the qualifications except one: he was no longer alive. What the universities really hope to find, he wrote, "is a paragon of human virtues."

Gwilym Price observed at one of the committee meetings, "There is only one man in world history who had all those virtues," whereupon someone else added, "And He did not have a doctor's degree."

With the signing of the bill establishing the University's relationship with the state in August, the search committees were stimulated to renew their efforts. They were further encouraged by a series of happy developments:

• Richard King Mellon made a new series of gifts to the University in 1966. His foundations gave $70,000 for the purchase of land adjoining the Johnstown campus; $250,000 for development of the Greensburg campus; $250,000 for faculty salaries in the basic sciences; $100,000 for the Child Guidance Center; $50,000 for recruiting students to the School of Medicine; $3.3 million to develop a neurology department in the School of Medicine; and $1,075,475 to enable the University to refinance and retain possession of the Ruskin Apartments so they could be used for members of the house staffs of the University-affiliated hospitals and their families.

The A. W. Mellon Educational and Charitable Trust, of which Paul Mellon was chairman, gave $250,000 to increase the library collections for the Andrew Mellon Professorship and Fellowship programs. Mrs. Alan Magee (Sarah Mellon) Scaife, who died in 1966, left $5 million to the University "for endowment alone." These gifts had a special value, a special significance in that, with other gifts received in 1966, they expressed a restoration of confidence in the University's fiscal integrity and gave evidence that private donors, including "the Mellons," would indeed continue to support the University.

• The flood of freshman applicants when the University hung out its $450 tuition sign was overwhelming. There were 2,000 openings, and the number of applications would have reached 10,000 if the window had not been shut at 6,500. With such numbers to choose from, the University was able to make a more careful selection, with better than 90 percent of those accepted coming from the upper two-fifths of their high school classes. More applicants, moreover, came from lower-income working class families. So many students registered that the trimester system was rescued, with larger numbers enrolled in the spring term.

• The caliber of the new Commonwealth trustees was a pleasant surprise to anyone who had felt misgivings about them. Two were businessmen who had just ended terms as trustees. The other ten were two presidents of steel companies; a young vice president of Gulf Oil; the legislator who had done more than anyone else to negotiate Pitt's state-related bill through the State Senate; a distinguished lawyer who had been a track star at Pitt (the first black trustee); two other distinguished lawyers; a judge; the superintendent of Pittsburgh's public school system; and a top labor leader. Seven were Pitt alumni. The Pitt board now had the unique distinction of having as members the president of United States Steel Corporation and the president of the United Steelworkers of America.

• The new relationship developed in Pennsylvania was not only working well, it was also seen as a new development in higher education. The combination of public funds and private giving was recognized as a plan, a system, that could improve the institution and ease the financial pressure that was plaguing virtually all colleges and universities other than those with endowments in the hundreds of millions of dollars. It could result in what one writer called "a third kind of university."

The search for a chancellor was on dead center at the end of 1966. The trustees Search Committee was well into its second year with nothing to show but a long list of prospects, much correspondence, and the records of many inquiries, many visits to and from, and a score of interviews there and here. The committee had approved one candidate, but the faculty advisors voted against him and the man withdrew. The trustees thereupon retained Henry T. Heald to recommend new candidates and speed up the selection process. Dr. Heald was a good choice. As chancellor of New York University (1952–1956) and as president of the Ford Foundation (1956–1965), he knew everyone; and he had recently established a consulting firm to put that knowledge at the service of colleges in need of it. But he had produced no chancellor for the University of Pittsburgh.

Chairman Price would be seventy-two on June 10, 1967, when he would face mandatory retirement. For personal reasons he had moved the date up five months, to January 10. After eight grueling years on the Board of Trustees, seven of them as chairman, he wanted to move on "with a good conscience to the life of a retired country gentleman, to hunt, fish, read, play bridge, travel—something I had looked forward to doing when I was sixteen years of age." As an administrator, he disapproved of unfinished business, and he had a burning desire to complete two duties before he left. One was to have a trained, competent, willing member of the board to succeed him as chairman, and this he had in William Rea. The other was to have a permanent chancellor in office at the University, and this he apparently was not going to get.

The break came unexpectedly and quite by chance during the Christmas weekend when Clifford Nelson was lying in bed thinking about things before falling asleep. He was president of the American Assembly at Columbia University, and he knew that Pitt was still searching for a chancellor.* He had heard that morning that a certain man had been considered for the post. The drowsy thought occurred to him that the man had a physical resemblance to another person, a friend of his, Wesley W. Posvar, an air force colonel, chairman of the Division of Social Sciences at the Air Force Academy in Colorado Springs. A further thought occurred: "My God! Why not Wes Posvar for Pitt?"

Christmas fell on a Sunday in 1966, and Monday was a holiday. On Tuesday morning in his office at Columbia, Nelson telephoned Gwilym Price, whom he had met at one of the assembly's gatherings in Pittsburgh. He was told that Mr. Price would not be in his office until the next morning. Rather than wait, Nelson called another Pittsburgh friend, Joseph D. Hughes, officer of T. Mellon & Sons. He asked Hughes to convey his idea to Price and gave him some background information on Posvar. He had first met Posvar, he said, when Posvar came to the American Assembly in 1957 and persuaded him to hold one of his meetings at the Air Force Academy. It was the first time the program had been tried with college students, and it had become an annual affair, with Wesley Posvar in charge of it at the Air Force Academy. As later recalled by Nelson and Hughes, Nelson's recommendation went something like this: "He is a bright, keen man with a very wide knowledge. I have observed him in action at the assemblies with people from forty or fifty colleges, and he handles himself very well. I know that he has been in government service for twenty years and that he is considering a change. He wants a career as an academic administrator."

Joseph Hughes called Price on Wednesday morning and relayed Nelson's message, adding some information of his own. Price immediately called Henry Heald and asked him to investigate and advise. Heald did some checking, made some calls, and reported back the same day: "From all I can learn, Mr. Price, he might be a very interesting prospect. I suggest you get in touch with him." Price then called Falk and Rea. On the slim basis of the information they had been given, they made tentative plane reservations for three from Pittsburgh to Colorado Springs on Thursday, January 5.

Pitt's Joseph G. Colangelo, Jr., described the procedures that custom demands in searching for the head of a university. No one ever applies for the job—an application, if received, will be dropped into the wastebasket. Kibitzers and their suggestions are always welcome. At a certain stage the art of chancellor making takes a delicate turn. The process is like a slow tarantella, in which the wooer and the wooed circle each other, exchanging sly initiatives.

"The introduction often is arranged through an intermediary, and always with great discretion. The intermediary must be carefully chosen; he must represent the institution, without committing it too deeply, yet be able to put the question with sufficient

---

*The American Assembly had been founded in 1950 by Columbia president Dwight D. Eisenhower as an instrument for staging meetings around the country where leaders from many fields could discuss major issues of public policy.

authority so that a good man will not dismiss it out of hand. Also, the desire for information on the candidate has to be tempered against the knowledge that premature disclosure of interest could embarrass the man with his present associates or, as sometimes happens, arouse the interest of the institution's competitors."

According to custom, then, Price, Falk, and Rea decided to ask Heald to make the first contact with Colonel Posvar. If he was receptive to a visit, they would like to see him alone, possibly on January 5, before bringing in their colleagues on the search committees. Heald tried to reach Colonel Posvar in Colorado Springs but learned that he was with his family in New York, where they were spending Christmas week seeing plays and exhibits, with a trip to the Metropolitan Opera on December 23 for a performance of *Die Meistersinger von Nürnberg*. Heald reached him at his hotel, said what he had to say, listened, and then called Price. Colonel Posvar, he said, was not *un*interested.

At this point Price, a man in a hurry, called Colonel Posvar in New York and told him that he, Mr. Falk, and Mr. Rea would like very much to visit him at the Air Force Academy on January 5. Posvar said, "Well, unless you three gentlemen have a great desire to do some skiing, I can send my wife and the children back home and stop by Pittsburgh on Tuesday." Price agreed to that.

Colonel Posvar appeared early Tuesday morning at the Duquesne Club, where he had breakfast with Price, Falk, and Rea. He was wearing civilian clothes—in fact, an unmilitary gray topcoat with a Chesterfieldian velvet collar and a green Tyrolean hat bedecked with a multicolored brush and four ski resort insignia. He was forty-one years old, of medium height, and had reddish hair. He had a Ph.D. degree and was commonly addressed as Dr. Posvar rather than Colonel.

The four men spent the morning in Price's office in the Cathedral, discussing Dr. Posvar's academic background, the University's recent history and long-range goals, and the ways to achieve academic excellence. During the afternoon Price introduced Dr. Posvar to Frank Denton, gave him a tour of the campus, and showed him what would be the new chancellor's residence on Devonshire Street, recently given to the University by Leon Falk and now being refurbished. Posvar agreed to return to the campus on Saturday, January 7, bringing his wife with him, and to stay through Tuesday, the tenth. By this time everyone was aware that Mrs. Posvar was also Mildred Miller and that the family had been at the performance of *Die Meistersinger* at the Met because she was singing one of the lead roles, that of Magdalene.* She had been, in fact, a principal artist at the Metropolitan Opera since her debut in 1951, a recitalist and recording artist of international stature, and a familiar personality from her regular appearances on two popular radio and television programs, "The Bell Telephone Hour" and "The Voice of Firestone."

Price telephoned each of the six members of the Faculty Advisory Committee and asked them to attend a dinner at Bruce Hall on Sunday evening, January 8. He then managed to reach twenty-three of the thirty-six trustees and invited them to dinner with their wives the following evening at the Duquesne Club. He told the members of each group that they would meet a very promising candidate for the chancellorship but did not reveal his name or background. In the meantime, Heald was telephoning a dozen people or more who knew Posvar—at the U.S. Military Academy, at Oxford University, at the Pentagon, at Colorado Springs. His evaluation for the trustees reads: "In summary, I can say that . . . all the reports have been uniformly favorable. I have been unable to turn up any negatives. . . . Everyone seems to believe that he has the feeling for education and the dedication to quality which faculty members expect and hope a president might have."

Now, for the first time, Price began to think that he might have a chancellor before his retirement on January 10. Vice Chairman Rea was worried. The faculty advisors, he said, had not met the candidate. Although the power to appoint was reserved to the board, their approval was essential. Some of them, and possibly some of the trustees, were likely to feel

---

*The critic Harold C. Schonberg praised her performance in a *New York Times* review.

concern at the idea of a chancellor with a military background. They would want to question him on his concept of academic freedom and his scholarly values. There were, on the other hand, factors very much in his favor, and there was no doubt that he would survive such questioning handily. He had a record dating some years back as a thoroughly academic person; he was a permanent professor and a department head who was widely and favorably known among political scientists; he moved in the inner circles of foreign policy studies at Harvard and MIT; he was being recruited by other universities when he was approached by Pitt.

The rapport between the trustees Search Committee and the faculty advisors up to that time had been admirable. Dr. Grunbaum said, "The trustees made it a matter of policy that the board would not appoint a man the faculty would not accept." The meetings of the two committees produced "extremely valuable faculty-trustee communication. It gave the trustees an understanding of our views and, during the crisis, when the scavengers came around and people wanted to raid the place, it gave the advisors a basis for telling our colleagues not to abandon the ship. We were consulted on every important decision."

Against the background of trustee-faculty cooperation, the faculty advisors were somewhat disturbed that the identity and background of the man they were asked to meet were now, suddenly, withheld from them. Price was aware that he was forcing the issue. "I wanted a new chancellor before I left office, and there wasn't much time. If I gave the faculty as long as they were used to, we wouldn't have a chancellor for a long time. So I called for an end run."

The faculty advisors appeared at 1201 Bruce Hall at 6:30 P.M. on Sunday, January 8: Adolf Grunbaum, philosophy; George Murdock, anthropology; Daniel Cheever, School of Public and International Affairs; Jack D. Myers, medicine; George Fahey, psychology; Holbert N. Carroll, political science. Price and Heald met each man at the door, led him into a side room, and there handed him a biography of the candidate. When they were all assembled, Price gave them a short briefing on what he had done, emphasizing that only four trustees—Falk,

Rea, Denton, and Price—had met Dr. Posvar before they would meet him. He reported their approbation. He also explained why he had withheld information about the candidate in his telephone calls; because of Dr. Posvar's military background, he wanted them to meet the man in person at the same time that they studied his written record.

The candidate's biography spoke for itself:

§ Wesley Wentz Posvar, the son of a newspaperman, was born in Kansas in 1925 of Czech antecedents and reared in Cleveland. (In 1966 his father was an editorial writer for the *Indianapolis Star*.)

§ He graduated first in his class from the U.S. Military Academy at West Point in 1946, achieving one of the highest averages in the academy's history in the largest class (875 men) ever graduated from that institution. His B.S. degree in engineering was the first of five academic degrees he was to earn.

§ He was an aircraft project officer and fighter aircraft test pilot at the Air Force Proving Grounds in Florida from 1946 to 1948. He became a command pilot and was licensed to fly twenty-seven different types of aircraft.

§ He was the first air force officer to win a Rhodes Scholarship, earning a B.A. and an M.A. at Oxford University (1948–1951) in philosophy, politics, and economics. He spent a midterm two-week vacation as co-pilot of a C–54 in the Berlin Airlift.*

§ His first teaching post was as an assistant professor of social sciences at the U.S. Military Academy at West Point from 1951 to 1954.

§ He served from 1954 to 1957 as a member of the Long-Range Objectives and Program Group for the Directorate of Plans at air force headquarters in Washington.

§ He became professor of political science at the Air Force Academy in 1957 at age thirty-two—the youngest full professor at any of the service academies—and was later appointed chairman of the Division of Social Sciences—the youngest division head in the history of the academy. He still held these positions in December 1966.

§ The Junior Chamber of Commerce named him

*Sixty aircrew men were killed during the airlift—thirty-one Americans, eighteen British, eleven civilians.

one of the country's Ten Outstanding Young Men in 1959.

§ He was a research associate at the Center for International Study at MIT in 1963–1964, specializing in arms control and disarmament.

§ He was a Littauer Fellow in the Graduate School of Public Administration at Harvard from 1962 to 1964, earning an M.P.A. and a Ph.D. in political science. His doctoral dissertation was on the effect of military expertise on national defense policy in the United States.

§ He served a tour of duty in the Southeast Asian Theater in 1965 as a consultant to various government planning agencies in the areas of political-military relations and economic development.

§ He was editor of the book *American Defense Policy* (1964) and contributor of articles to *Orbis*, *Worldview*, *Western Political Quarterly*, *Public Policy*, and *Air Force/ Space Digest*, among other journals.

§ His wife, Mildred Miller, mother of the couple's son and two daughters, was an internationally renowned opera and concert artist, a mezzo-soprano who had performed leading roles at the Metropolitan, Vienna State, Berlin, Stuttgart, and San Francisco opera houses.

After their briefing in the side room, Price, Heald, and the six faculty advisors joined the other guests at Bruce Hall. These were Leon Falk, Jr., William Rea, Joseph Barr, their wives, and Mrs. Price. Mayor Barr, a University trustee, was there because he could not attend the Monday night dinner. Dr. Posvar had not yet arrived, but Mildred Posvar had come with the Reas. George Murdock was "very favorably impressed" with Mrs. Posvar. "She was a very personable woman indeed, and we liked her immediately. . . . She would be a great asset to a chancellor."

Posvar arrived a short time later. Price, Falk, Rea, Barr, their wives, and Mildred Posvar were driven the one mile to the Pittsburgh Golf Club, where they had a leisurely and relaxed dinner. Heald, Posvar, and the six faculty members retired to a room at the University Club for a working meal, with no wives and no trustees present. Their meeting lasted four hours. Posvar said, "It was like two oral doctoral examinations put end to end." Heald said, "I had never seen anything like it." George Murdock: "We questioned him very, very rigorously on all points. We didn't pull any punches. We didn't pussyfoot. After all, if *we* weren't persuaded, how could we persuade our colleagues in the Senate?" Adolf Grunbaum: "He had studied philosophy at Oxford and he made some very interesting remarks on the philosophy of science." Holbert Carroll: "We didn't need much selling, Dan Cheever and I. [Both were political scientists.] I knew that there are, among military men, people with very high standards, and clearly he was one of them." Grunbaum on the University's goal of national excellence: "He had a basic understanding that this would be exactly his mandate—naturally, in a fiscally responsible manner." Murdock: "He did not make a single mistake. His qualities, personality, and attitude gradually made a dent on us. We liked his forcefulness, his frankness. He was tough-fibered, but had original ideas, and he's near genius in intelligence. He was somebody who would see a challenge in Pittsburgh. This was precisely the kind of man we had hoped for but didn't think we could find."

The dinner meeting ended around eleven o'clock. Heald and Posvar left together. The faculty people talked among themselves for another half-hour. Price had asked Heald to telephone him at home before he took his midnight plane to New York. Heald called from the airport: "The meeting was a success. Posvar conducted himself very well. He answered questions fully and with dignity and sincerity. I think you're going to have a visit in the morning and it won't be too tough."

The visit came from the faculty advisors, who appeared at Price's office at 9:30 the next morning, Monday, the ninth. Adolf Grunbaum was spokesman. He said, as Price remembers it, "We agree that Dr. Posvar will be a good chancellor for the University. We agree with what you have done. But we do not approve of the way you did it. You didn't give us much time to consider such an important matter." Price apologized. "I understand exactly how you feel. I did rush it, but I was very anxious to get this job done before the annual organization meeting of the board tomorrow afternoon. I know you would have liked more time, but I did arrange for you to see Dr. Posvar, for you to voice your objection if you thought I was making a mistake."

"What finally decided us," Grunbaum said later, "was that Dr. Posvar had all the essential characteristics which are inherent and can't be acquired— brains, warmth, and so forth. Those that were acquireable—such as experience in certain areas— he could acquire because he had the intellectual power to do so, and he would know how to get good advice."

The dinner that night for trustees and their wives was held in the Duquesne Club. Posvar made a short talk before the dinner and answered a few questions afterward. William Rea then took Posvar and the women to another part of the club, while Price gave the trustees a full report on what had been done up to that point. "I told them all I knew about Dr. Posvar, which was a great deal by this time. I told them I thought he would make a very interesting and fine chancellor. The questions they asked me were numerous but friendly." A trustee suggested that a resolution electing Dr. Posvar chancellor should be voted on at once. Price ruled that the vote must be cast at the regular board meeting the next afternoon.

The next few days were hectic but in a sense anti-climactic, for the issue had now been resolved. Mrs. Posvar went to inspect the chancellor's residence. Telephone calls were made to commanding officers at Colorado Springs and to undersecretaries in Washington to ensure that Colonel Posvar would be released from military service. The board had met at 4:00 P.M. on January 10, 1967, on the fortieth floor of the Cathedral, and voted unanimously to offer the chancellorship to Dr. Posvar. Exactly fif-

teen days had elapsed from the time Clifford Nelson called Joseph Hughes to suggest a candidate for chancellor.

The board elected Price chairman emeritus. As chairman it elected William H. Rea (Princeton 1934, president of Oliver Tyrone Corporation, the city's largest real estate management operation, a trustee since 1950). An elaborate scroll was presented to Gwilym Price at his retirement dinner that evening. In his farewell speech, Price said:

I am pleased that just eighteen months after one of the most serious crises in the University's history, I am able to relinquish this job with full confidence that my successor is taking over the chairmanship of an institution that is solvent, viable and strong. . . .

To me, the biggest single task facing this Board in the immediate future is to establish and help fulfill a new goal for the University. That goal should be to make Pitt a really fine regional University, serving southwestern Pennsylvania, Pennsylvania, and the Upper Ohio Valley. I think it should be a University of such stature that it will rate an excellent national reputation.

I, for one, do not see any contradiction between a desire for genuine excellence and a regional orientation.

A news release was given to the press on Friday, January 13, 1967: "The University of Pittsburgh's Trustees announced today that Dr. Wesley Posvar, 41, a political science professor and former Rhodes Scholar who is Chairman of the Social Sciences Division of the Air Force Academy, will become the University's 15th Chancellor on June 1 this year."

At the same time, the trustees, at Dr. Posvar's request, appointed David Kurtzman to the full rank of chancellor, to serve until the chancellor-elect arrived on the campus in June.

29

The Frick Fine Arts Building

We have tried to avoid a direct confrontation, but it is now clear that the University is paying too great a price in the vague hope of some future bequest. Our patience and our repeated concessions have become cowardice in the eyes of the faculty and we cannot continue to ignore the spreading faculty discontent which has its source in the Henry Clay Frick Fine Arts Building.

Charles H. Peake, Provost, to Acting Chancellor David H. Kurtzman, March 7, 1966

In a conversation during the interregnum in 1967, David Kurtzman briefed Chancellor-Elect Posvar on an unpleasant situation that had developed on the Oakland campus. It concerned a disagreement with Helen Clay Frick, who had given the University the new Henry Clay Frick Fine Arts Building on Schenley Plaza. Miss Frick had agreed to construct "a fine arts building for the University," but now it appeared that she expected to maintain a proprietary and semi-autonomous control over the operation of the building, the people who used it, and the courses that were taught there, in a manner the University was finding unacceptable. Dr. Kurtzman believed that the relationship with Miss Frick must have been mishandled, and he hoped that he could settle the matter before Dr. Posvar took office on June 1.

The matter was indeed settled before June 1, but in a way that produced national headlines and drew the fascinated attention of the whole academic community. The "misunderstanding" with Miss Frick caused resignations of newly recruited professors in the Department of Fine Arts, worked anguish in the hearts of administrators, and produced recriminatory charges that are painful to read today. It almost ruined the department, and it gave the University some of the most harmful local publicity it has ever received. At the best, Pitt appeared to have acted ungratefully to a generous benefactor—to have needlessly, foolishly, offended an elderly lady of wealth who had given the University a $3.5 million fine arts building. At the worst, Pitt appeared to have signed an agreement on how the donor's money should be spent in the fine arts project and then repudiated that agreement. In some measure the story was reported as a kind of neighborhood backyard quarrel whose causes were trivial and somewhat amusing—a quarrel that the University could and should have settled by a simple exercise of accommodation, good will, and understanding.

Far more was involved than that. The pervading, fundamental issue of the disagreement was critically important to the University, and would have been to any university. And yet Pitt was not without responsibility. In running its course, the affair gives a textbook demonstration of what may happen when a donor makes, and an institution accepts, a gift without either understanding the intentions of the other. It also shows what may happen when a gift is accepted that is heavily encumbered with conditions.

Helen Clay Frick was the daughter of Henry Clay Frick, an industrial genius of the nineteenth century, controversial because of his attitude toward labor. She had a life-long passion for art and for protecting her father's memory, and she had the means to indulge both. When she died in 1984 at the age of ninety-six, she was considered one of the wealthiest women in the United States. She was a generous giver, but her philanthropy was highly personalized and participatory—like that of her father and, indeed, of her generation. As John McCarten wrote of her in the *New Yorker* magazine in 1939, she "has a straightforward mind, and she defends hotly the right of the giver to choose the gift and to wrap it up exactly as he wants to." They were words of portent for the University of Pittsburgh more than two decades later.

Pitt owed a debt of gratitude to the Fricks, father and daughter. Henry Clay Frick had supported the University before his death in 1919, one of his more imaginative recurring gifts being $15,000 to the Allegheny Observatory in 1910 for a program of entertainment for the lay public, particularly children. Helen Frick had given money to found the Department of Fine Arts in 1927 and had supported it for some four decades. She had sent Frederick Mortimer Clapp, first director of the department, on a year-long book-buying expedition abroad in which he quietly and anonymously acquired the nucleus of one of the best libraries of fine arts in the country. With John Bowman she had a friendly relationship that was unbroken through three decades. She had worked with him in directing the production on the top floor of the Cathedral of Learning of a catalogue of the Frick Collection in New York: elephant-folio in size, printed by hand with hand-set type on English hand-made paper (175 copies, none for sale). She had paid the salaries of the small fine arts staff and passed time with them when she was in Pittsburgh. Unlike many rich Pittsburghers, she had never cut her ties with the city, spending some months of each year in Clayton, the Frick mansion in Pittsburgh's Point Breeze district.

The department was headed, after Frederick Clapp became director of the Frick art museum in New York, by Walter Read Hovey (B.A. Yale 1918 and M.A. Harvard 1926). Hovey felt that Pitt was among the early institutions of higher learning to recognize the study of works of art as an academic subject. He also believed that a course he developed, Art as a Language, was of some importance to the University and the art world. Working with a modest budget, he showed a remarkable series of exhibitions in the department's small gallery in the Cathedral of Learning—twenty exhibitions in the three years between 1939 and 1941 alone. Throughout his thirty-five years at Pitt, he enjoyed the high confidence of Helen Clay Frick.

Miss Frick had for some three decades been recognized as a prime prospect for giving the University a fine arts building, preferably one with a large endowment, and three chancellors had importuned her to that end. In 1959 she agreed to give the building as a living memorial to her father, if the University provided a site satisfactory to her. The University obtained permission to build on city-owned park land at the south edge of the campus, on Schenley Plaza.

All seemed to be well: a generous long-term donor had promised a major gift in memory of her beloved father. But the next seven years were to show that this joint venture was foredoomed because the two parties had vastly different conceptions of the building. From the first, Miss Frick saw the Frick Fine Arts Building as an art museum with a permanent collection of art objects she would supply. The University saw it as a primary resource for classroom instruction in the history and appreciation of fine arts and for the advancement of knowledge through research, perhaps with the aid of a small gallery for exhibitions. But the Litchfield administration apparently had never discussed with Miss Frick this basic difference in the perceptions of the building's function and purpose.

There was nothing in Miss Frick's past to suggest that she would defer to the wishes of the recipient of a major gift. She had frequently disagreed with the other members of the Board of Trustees of the Frick Collection in New York (founded by her father and one of the great art collections in the United States), ultimately resigning in 1961 when they wished to accept gifts from the Rockefeller family. The collision between this donor and a university that had standards of academic independence to maintain may have been inevitable, but a university official who raises money is in the role of a matchmaker between the needs of the institution and the interests and wishes of the donor. Certainly this match was poorly made, and the basic cause was the apparent failure of the University to understand Miss Frick's wishes before accepting her commitment to fund the building.

In March 1960, while the building was being designed, Miss Frick was surprised and distressed to learn that Hovey, on reaching age sixty-five in July, would have to retire and be replaced by a new chairman of the department. She wrote to Litchfield to express her wish that Hovey be retained as chairman so that he could execute some conceptions she valued highly. If he was forced to step down even before construction began on the fine arts building, she would not hold the same views about some of the art objects she had intended to donate. She was convinced, moreover, that the University had never properly valued Hovey's performance. Despite his long and faithful service and his brilliant work, she said, the University had never given him a doctorate, nor had it recognized his strong desire to become a Mellon Professor.

Rather than cause trouble, offend a wealthy donor and friend of the University, lose certain gifts of art objects, and perhaps scratch one fine arts building, Litchfield agreed to extend Hovey's service as chairman, at least "until the building is well along." Mellon Professors, he explained, were selected from a panel of names prepared by an outside, non-Pittsburgh group of experts, and neither he nor the Mellons themselves could depart from that procedure. Professor Hovey had never been on the lists of those recommended. Litchfield deleted from the first draft of his letter the information that no respectable institution gave honorary degrees to its own faculty.

The Department of Fine Arts was not in good condition in 1960. In February an Andrew Mellon Predoctoral Fellow, Sam C. Gholson, specializing in the history of oil painting techniques, described it in a letter of resignation. The department, he wrote, "is not adequately staffed to provide qualified supervision for a predoctoral program. Such important areas as Greek art, Baroque art, and French art are not covered in the courses offered there. Aesthetic and technical approaches to the history of art are equally neglected. Complicating this deficiency of curriculum is the fact that no one on the Fine Arts faculty there has any clear idea what a doctor's degree is or what the requirements for the degree should be." Accordingly, he had decided to accept a two-year Rinehart Fellowship in Baltimore. In September 1962, Jean Seznec, an Andrew Mellon Professor with a background in art history, on being asked to give an opinion of the department, advised that the fine arts library had an admirable foundation. It "is extremely well stocked with reference works and periodicals; or rather, it was: for the sound policy along the lines of which the Library was originally planned does not appear to have been kept up for the last thirty years or so. During that recent period the buying seems to have become somewhat scanty and haphazard; this is noticeable even in the collection of monographs on major artists which is now unbalanced, and presents some surprising gaps." The photographic collection, he said, was "pitifully inadequate," and the slide collection was "so poor as to be almost useless."

The remedy, of course, was to improve the administrative supervision of the department and to bring in first-rate faculty people. This Litchfield set out to do. In October 1962 he wrote Miss Frick that he had appointed a new dean of the humanities, Frank Whittmore Wadsworth, graduate of Princeton, former English professor there and at the University of California, former Woodrow Wilson Fellow, Folger Shakespeare Fellow, and Guggenheim Fellow. The Department of Fine Arts was one

of the eleven in his division for which he was responsible. Wadsworth took his fine arts responsibility seriously. He called on Miss Frick at her Pittsburgh home with his wife, Roxalene, and he wrote her long, frequent, and beautifully composed letters reporting all the developments in the department and his progress in pursuit of what he assumed was their common goal: to make the Department of Fine Arts the best teaching and research unit in the University and one of the best in the country.

In the meantime, Hovey had resigned as chairman of the department to become the first Henry Clay Frick Professor of Fine Arts, a new position Miss Frick created for him. Wadsworth, in his second letter, described his vigorous search for a departmental chairman of scholarly distinction and administrative ability to replace Hovey, a search, he said, that would be somewhat easier now that Hovey had resigned. Calling himself "a new and untried administrator," he said he looked forward to making Hovey a valued partner in all his plans; he intended to ask him to take an active part in the ongoing activities of the department and would count on having the full benefit of his great experience and professional ability. In his next letter he cited some of the deficiencies of the department that he hoped to correct.

In their first conversation, Miss Frick had let Wadsworth know that she did not like Germans and that she wanted none in the department.* Wadsworth therefore felt obliged to write her that one of the people he was considering as chairman of the department was of German origin: Professor Karl Birkmeyer, distinguished art historian of the Northern Renaissance. Birkmeyer, he explained, "has been strongly recommended to us both for his scholarship and for his personal qualities" and "has

---

*Miss Frick's feelings about Germans were well enough known to have been discussed in McCarten's *New Yorker* article: "To Miss Frick, Germans, whether scholarly or not, are distasteful." Yet her dislike did not include German Jews who had been persecuted by the Nazis. She had a strong sense of patriotism, having served in France with the Red Cross during World War I. During World War II she had cared for British refugee children in her home.

been an American citizen for many years." (He came to the United States in 1948 and was naturalized in 1955.) He had worked for the U.S. government and had taught at Stanford and the University of California. "I know Professor Birkmeyer well and consider him not only an excellent scholar and a first-rate teacher but a charming person, one of the most delightful people socially I have met."

Miss Frick replied within the week. She did not, she wrote, wish to have any scholars of German extraction in the department. She asked Wadsworth to give up any intention of hiring one, regardless of his qualifications. She could not countenance a German director. Since the building was a large and very costly venture, she felt that she was within her rights in asking Dr. Wadsworth to accede to her wish in this matter.

Wadsworth, more than a little perturbed, replied on May 2:

Although I do not agree with your position about German scholars I fully realize how important the matter is to you and I should not personally wish to do anything to cause you uneasiness. At the same time, I should be less than honest were I not to state that I too feel strongly about a great university's obligations to society. I believe these obligations include the duty to recognize and honor scholarly excellence regardless of peoples' origins. I have a deep conviction that no institution can achieve greatness unless it honors this principle. . . . As one who served as a pilot in the last war and lost many dear friends, I take great pride in my country's willingness to forgive and to extend citizenship to people who love and respect her even though their own countries may once have been her enemies. When a man is naturalized, I think of him as an American and nothing more. My feeling for Karl Birkmeyer is of this sort. . . . He is a wonderful human being, gentle and kind. I admire him very much.

Actually, he said, the question was academic, since Professor Birkmeyer was not interested in becoming an administrator. He hoped, however, that he could persuade him to come for a trimester as a visiting professor.

He wrote Miss Frick shortly thereafter about another candidate for chairman: William C. Loerke, a *magna cum laude* graduate of Oberlin, Phi Beta Kappa, a Harvard Fellow at Dumbarton Oaks, a Fulbright Fellow in Italy, holder of M.F.A. and Ph.D. degrees from Princeton, a medievalist who had won the Porter Prize for an article, now an associate professor at Bryn Mawr. Miss Frick asked her secretary to find out from Wadsworth whether Loerke was a German. Wadsworth replied that he was "as American as a man can be"—born in Toledo, Ohio, a navy pilot during the war (on our side). Wadsworth added that Loerke was highly thought of by his students and colleagues. He described Loerke to Litchfield as "a good man to revive a moribund department," but he felt some concern. "Loerke is a very masculine, aggressive person who not only quivers with energy but is unusually direct. These qualities give him his own peculiar strength; they might also be a handicap in this particular situation." Could Loerke be an effective chairman "in view of our relationship with Miss Frick?"

Loerke was offered the job. At the time he was considering the offer of a fine arts chair at a California university, and he devised a test to help him make a choice. He drew up a list of twenty rare but important books on the history of art and checked to see which of his prospective employers had more of them. Whatever else was wrong with the fine arts library in 1963, Pitt won by a considerable margin. On June 19 Wadsworth gave Miss Frick the good news that Loerke had accepted the chairmanship of the department. She acknowledged the letter two days later, repeated her objection to employing Birkmeyer as a visiting professor, and expressed surprise that, despite what she had written Wadsworth about her dislike of Germans, he had ignored her request. As the only benefactor of the new building, she expected him to respect her wishes. She added that a copy of her letter was being forwarded to Dr. Litchfield.

Wadsworth replied:

I am most unhappy that you feel I have been discourteous in connection with Professor Birkmeyer. . . . It was imperative that we be assured of having on campus next fall someone who could give vigor and direction to our graduate program. We were in no position to delay. Professor Birkmeyer was far and away the best person available; indeed, he was the only person with the requisite qualifications who could be persuaded to come for the Fall Trimester upon such short notice.

I am most anxious to respect your wishes as fully as my own obligations to the University will allow.

Three weeks earlier, Wadsworth had asked Charles Peake to warn Litchfield of trouble that could lie ahead, enclosing copies of Miss Frick's letters as evidence and shrewdly analyzing the conflict.

What disturbs me, Charlie, is this. I take it that my description of the role of the Art Department is substantially in accord with your ideas and Edward's. I am not at all sure that it squares with what Miss Frick has been led to believe or with what Walter Hovey has in mind. I don't believe that I can hire a good staff or create a productive department until certain things are understood clearly by Miss Frick and by Hovey. I do not believe that Miss Frick should be allowed to think that she can in any way dictate the choice of personnel. I think Edward should tell her this and that in the long run we will gain from his frankness.

Wadsworth understood what the University might lose by a break with Miss Frick over the building. A great fortune was involved, and there could be other gifts.

I am very sympathetic to what Edward described the other day at lunch as "a gamble worth taking." Nevertheless, I think it would be a great mistake to fail to achieve a breakthrough now because of the distant promises of this gamble. The Department has a bad reputation around the country and if Miss Frick's Germanic phobia is encouraged it will have a worse one. . . .

Therefore I strongly urge that you ask Edward in his meeting with Miss Frick to define clearly those areas in which the University must have autonomy. . . . I would then be free to get on with the job, bring some professionals on the scene, and start something which Miss Frick would be glad to acknowledge as worthy of her father's memory.

Litchfield had met with Miss Frick on June 10, 1963, having read Wadsworth's letter, and followed the meeting with a letter to her in which he defended Birkmeyer's appointment as a visiting professor and pointed out that funds other than her own were involved. "I hope you will understand if I remind you that we have a very substantial amount

of Mellon money going into the [Fine Arts] Department and we must be free to exercise our own best judgments in spending not only your funds but Mellon funds, as well. This, of course, only underscores the importance of an educational institution's exercising its best judgment about professional competence of people."

Miss Frick replied that she certainly had no intention of telling the chancellor how to run his University. The selection of a director, however, was a matter in which she had a strong personal interest. She did not wish to be dictatorial, and she never had been in the years the department had operated. The best possible talent should be engaged. But neither she nor her father had ever felt that they could trust Germans. She hoped that Dr. Birkmeyer would prove to be an exception and that his appointment would not be regretted, and she extended her best wishes for a pleasant summer.

A calamitous development occurred while Loerke was shuttling back and forth between Bryn Mawr and Pitt before taking over as full-time head of the department. Virginia Lewis, a protégée of Miss Frick, Hovey's assistant for several decades and thought to be his intended successor, had become the department's librarian in addition to her teaching and other administrative duties. In February 1964 she made a policy change that restricted the use of the fine arts library, issuing cards to departmental faculty members and graduate students that permitted them to go into the library stacks if they signed in and out. One of the professors who had not yet received his card was denied entrance to the stacks; he complained to Loerke, who, still at Bryn Mawr, had not been consulted on the change of policy. Loerke thereupon exploded with a burst of indignation that seems disproportionate to the heinousness of the crime committed. His letter to Miss Lewis began: "No policy decision in respect to the library is ever to be made or promulgated without my approval. . . . Your recent issuance of stack permits . . . is so brazen an arrogation of authority beyond your competence that I must spell out in detail what should have been clear to you long ago." It concluded: "A library is supposed to be an efficient, pleasant center for serious study; it is not to be turned into a malevolent, penal institution in which pettifogging martinets maintain a constant state of irritation." Miss Lewis, stung by this assault, showed the letter to Miss Frick.

The situation was now beyond retrieval. Miss Frick wrote a letter to Loerke that (perhaps for the best) is not in the University archives. Loerke replied that he had already apologized to Miss Lewis "for the tone of my letter to her to which you rightly take exception." Wadsworth added his apologies to Loerke's and informed Miss Frick, somewhat optimistically, that all the differences between Dr. Loerke and Miss Lewis "have been settled amicably." He was proud, he said, that the department was now offering eleven classes, including two graduate seminars, compared to only five regular classes and no seminars under Mr. Hovey the previous year.

Over the next year and a half Miss Frick wrote letters of record to six people of stature and influence asking them to put pressure on the University to carry out her wishes. Three were trustees, three were outsiders. She began with a letter to Richard King Mellon dated February 27, 1964.

She wrote that Loerke's letter to Miss Lewis, a copy of which she enclosed, would show General Mellon* why she was so concerned. Loerke had made an apology and Miss Lewis had accepted it, but she—Miss Frick—did not believe that anyone who would write such a rude letter was a suitable director of the department. In her opinion, Loerke should be removed at the end of the semester. Dean Wadsworth, moreover, had impressed her quite unfavorably. He was, she felt, too inexperienced to be in charge of engaging faculty members for the department. A few months earlier he had spoken unfairly to her about Mr. Hovey, who, rather than Dean Wadsworth, should make the selections, for he had better judgment and more experience than Wadsworth. She thanked General Mellon in advance for acting in this matter.

Mellon sent the letter to Litchfield with a request for information. Litchfield supplied it in a long letter in which he deplored Loerke's action but defended him as a first-rate person despite his youth

*Lieutenant General, United States Army Reserve (Retired).

and hot temper. The Loerke matter, Litchfield said, was only an example of a larger problem: "That problem is largely centered around Professor Hovey. . . . [He] has been a consistent troublemaker during my years here. . . . [He] has been uncooperative with the dean and a source of constant difficulty with Dr. Peake, the vice chancellor in his area. His normal method of operation is to take his problems to Miss Frick first and, having obtained her reaction, then return to force his colleagues within the University to accept his view. Thus decisions are made between Hovey and Miss Frick, which the rest of the University has little opportunity to participate in." Miss Frick, he said, "is a delightful lady with great competence in her field and with a dedication to Pittsburgh and the University which it is absolutely essential that we maintain. . . . On the other hand . . . she has what we might call 'unorthodox' views about the academic world. For example, she is strongly opposed to the appointment of anyone to the fine arts faculty who is of German extraction even of several generations removed. I am sure you can readily imagine what would happen to our position in the academic world were we to be known as precluding any particular nationality from our faculty."

Miss Frick wrote again to Mellon on April 14, 1964. Since she was making such a large gift to the University, she said, she felt obliged to demand that Professor Loerke be separated from the Department of Fine Arts and that Dean Wadsworth be denied the right to select a director to replace Professor Loerke.

Mellon, addressing Miss Frick as "Helen," replied that in his opinion the fine arts department would be harmed by removal of its faculty members in the manner she suggested. The University, he said, had tried that once before, and as a result suffered for almost twenty years by being blacklisted. (He referred to the discharge of Dr. Ralph Turner in 1934.) Such an action would be a defiance of academic tradition recognized around the world. It would, moreover, blemish the great record that Helen Frick and others had accomplished in the department.

On April 24 Miss Frick wrote William Rea, a

trustee and a distant cousin, about Loerke. Despite all other conditions, she would not be content if he was kept on as department chairman. Rea told her that John Walker, director of the National Gallery in Washington and a member of Wadsworth's Advisory Board for the Humanities, had spoken highly to him of Loerke and Wadsworth. To this she replied that if John Walker judged Loerke so highly, why did he not engage him for the National Gallery? As for Wadsworth, she wrote, he lacked experience, was not considerate, and did not have the manners of a gentleman; she intended to have no further communication with him.

To Peake she had said of Loerke, "I will not have that man in my building." She followed with a letter of warning on October 5 that Peake should make no more assignments to the fine arts building until she was thoroughly convinced that Loerke had been transferred elsewhere. The rudeness and thoughtlessness she had encountered from the time the building first started to go up, she said, were such that they could cause her not to give it to the University.

On May 26, 1965, Miss Frick, in a private ceremony for her friends, held a donor's dedication of the Henry Clay Frick Fine Arts Building. The University held its own dedication when the fall trimester classes began. Miss Frick was represented at this ceremony by her attorney.

In the spring of 1965, when it became apparent that the differences between the principals could not be settled amicably, the attorneys were called in to draw up a formal "Memorandum of Understanding Between Miss Helen C. Frick and the University of Pittsburgh." David B. Buerger, of the law firm Buchanan, Ingersoll, Rodewald, Kyle and Buerger, represented Miss Frick; Charles C. Arensberg, of Patterson, Crawford, Arensberg and Dunn, represented the University, with Peake sitting beside Arensberg at the meetings. An agreement was completed and signed on June 16, 1965, Buerger and Secretary Stanton Crawford signing as witnesses and Miss Frick and Litchfield (one month away from his unhappy resignation) signing as principals. The memorandum is a crucially important document in

any attempt to understand the right and wrong of Frick vs. the University of Pittsburgh. An angry fine arts professor called it "A Memorandum of Submission"; an in-house Pitt attorney later said, "Our problems arose from Miss Frick's insisting upon her rights under the agreement." The point should be recognized, of course, that the memorandum was not written on a clean slate at the beginning of friendly negotiations. It was, cobbled up, rather, in the middle of a situation that had already deteriorated badly. It contained, despite the legal experts, provisions that were in conflict with each other and so could be resolved only by major concessions or generous interpretation by one side or the other. The University administrators gave Miss Frick extraordinary power and control over the department, its buildings, and its people, apparently in the hope that she would eventually act in what they considered a reasonable and understanding manner. Certainly it is clear, with the benefit of hindsight, that they should never have conceded certain points and that they would have refused the gift if they had foreseen the results of her interpretation of the document. When the terms became public, Charles Peake was criticized by his colleagues for selling the University short without consulting the faculty. He protested that he had conferred on the terms with Wadsworth and Loerke during the negotiations, and he said in August 1966, "More than a year ago, when Miss Frick threatened to go to court to take back 'her' building, I was asked, under pressure from 'above' [Litchfield and Crawford] to do everything possible to pacify her, on the grounds that . . . she would leave a vast sum of money to the University for art."

The eleven legal-size pages of this ill-advised document set forth the following stipulations:

● The University recognized that Miss Frick had special competence in fine arts. Accordingly, on certain matters relating to the management of the Frick Fine Arts Building, she was to be consulted or her approval obtained.

● Miss Frick recognized that the University could not abrogate its responsibilities regarding such matters as program objectives, appointment of faculty and other personnel, tenure and academic freedom, and policies and regulations established under the sanctions of the Board of Trustees.

• The fine arts department was to be physically separated into two parts. The academic staff (including Loerke) charged with teaching and research was to remain, for the foreseeable future, in its offices in the Cathedral of Learning. Those having functions related to the fine arts building were to be housed in that building.

• The library was to be moved permanently to the new building. It was to be operated in accordance with University policy, as administered by the director of the University libraries.

• Classrooms in the new building were to be used only for instruction in the fine arts and other humanities.

• The direction of the building was to be supervised by a director and an assistant director. Both were to be persons satisfactory to Miss Frick. Their responsibilities were the supervision of all museum and exhibition areas, the scheduling and management of exhibits, the preparation and printing of catalogues, the care of the objects of art, the arrangements for special lectures, and the purchase of works of art.

• Hovey was to become Henry Clay Frick Professor of Art Emeritus, but he would continue his teaching until a qualified successor was obtained. His successor was to be satisfactory to Miss Frick as well as to the University.

• The chancellor was to appoint Hovey director of the fine arts building.

• Miss Virginia Lewis was to be appointed assistant director.

• Miss Frick was to be consulted on candidates for the position of librarian, and every reasonable effort was to be made to appoint a librarian satisfactory to her, but final decision would rest with the University.

• Both parties agreed that modern or contemporary art had its place but that such art would not be shown in the new building.

• So long as the University followed all the provisions of the memorandum and provided $65,000 a year for operation of the building, Miss Frick would provide $135,000 a year.

• The University was to furnish Miss Frick with annual statements on the disposition of funds.

• The vice chancellor of academic disciplines was to confer with Miss Frick regarding "various developments" so that she would be informed and the University would have the benefit of her counsel.

• The University was asked to be cognizant of and to respect Miss Frick's feeling that Professor Hovey and Miss Virginia Lewis had served well the cause of fine arts at the University for many years and deserved grateful treatment—particularly since it was primarily they who inspired Miss Frick to make the gift of the building.

During the preparation of this remarkable document, Buerger presented a further condition from Miss Frick that was not to be made public or placed on the record. He spoke of it in a telephone conversation with Peake and again in a letter, addressed to himself and headed "Personal and Confidential," which he asked Peake to sign and return to him. This letter to Buerger would have Peake attest that he recognized that Miss Frick did not wish to have Professor Loerke teach classes in the fine arts building and also that Miss Frick would not continue to contribute to its operations if he did teach there. The University (Peake was asked to affirm) could not, of course, agree that Loerke should not teach there, but it did understand that Miss Frick was free to make or not make donations to the University. Therefore, the University recognized that if Loerke did teach in the building, then the signed Memorandum of Understanding would be invalid. Buerger would hold the only signed copy of the letter in trust for Miss Frick.

Peake was outraged. In refusing to sign the letter, he wrote to Buerger: "The University is being asked to enter into a secret agreement to do something which Miss Frick admits is in violation of the ethical and professional code of the Administration as a member of the academic world, and to do so under the daily and continuous threat of having her promised financial support withdrawn. Should perchance Professor Loerke teach a lecture course in the new Frick Building, and should then Miss Frick cease her financial support for the building, presumably the University would either (1) remain silent and suffer the loss of the support; or (2) protest, and thereby betray the fact that the University had entered into a secret and unethical agreement regarding one of its faculty members, which when known to the faculty and academic world would bring disaster upon the Administration and the University."

He suggested that Miss Frick and the University sign the Memorandum of Understanding when it was completed and "get on with the business of achieving something important for Miss Frick, the University, and the Pittsburgh region."

The memorandum was signed and, in Peake's words, it satisfied nobody. The following developments took place from July 1965 to June 1967— during the two years in which Litchfield resigned, Crawford became acting chancellor, Kurtzman succeeded him, and Posvar became chancellor. During the last months, Miss Frick refused to communicate in any way with Peake.

On August 31, 1965, Miss Frick wrote to George D. Lockhart, trustee, to ask him to see that Peake's name was removed from any list of candidates being considered for the chancellorship. Peake, she said, was not to be trusted, and he would cause as much trouble as an administrator as Dr. Litchfield had. On the same day she sent trustee Edward Weidlein the identical request and added that if Peake was given more authority, there would be constant friction. She did not trust him, and if he did not reverse some of the steps he had taken, she would cancel the Memorandum of Understanding.

On September 17 a professor of sociology was refused permission, under the terms of the memorandum, to teach a class scheduled in the fine arts building's 200-seat lecture hall. The ruling produced indignant professors and incensed students.

Some time late in 1965, Miss Frick wrote two letters to Herman B. Wells, who was heading the Ford Foundation group reporting on the problems of the University. From the context of Wells's delayed reply, it appears that she described the fine arts situation and asked him to take some action or to render some judgment on the University. Wells regretted that he could be of no help, because the report had been completed, and he and his fellow members of the committee felt they should now dis-

associate themselves from the institution. He suggested that she tell her story to Gwilym Price, chairman of the board, "who is a man of great wisdom."

On December 6 Acting Chancellor Crawford sent a memo to Dean Helen Rush on the subject: "Opportunity for Miss Helen Frick to Meet University People." He suggested that Miss Rush hold a tea in the Heinz Room on the twelfth floor of the Cathedral, "where a large group of the ladies could be invited. (Certain misunderstandings have been built up involving men, and I think it would be better to omit them at this stage.)"

On January 17, 1966, Crawford, Price, Rea, Lockhart, and Weidlein met to consider whether it would please Miss Frick to have an honorary degree conferred upon her. They decided to send Crawford (with whom she was on good terms) to Bedford, New York, to ask if she would accept a doctorate of fine arts at the commencement convocation on June 6 with certain social events arranged, or at a dinner in the fine arts building, or, if she thought these were too ostentatious, at a ceremony in Crawford's office followed by a buffet dinner in the Bruce Hall suite. The degree either was not offered or was rejected.

On February 17 the Faculty Senate asked its Committee on Tenure and Academic Freedom to begin a quiet inquiry into what was going on in the Department of Fine Arts.

Peake advised Price on March 7 that the Memorandum of Understanding had failed and that the University now should take a firm stand against Miss Frick's "prejudices and personal interferences."

On May 11 Leonard Slatkes, a new assistant professor, resigned from the department to protest against provisions in the memorandum. About the same time Charles Minott, a new young assistant professor, resigned to join the faculty at the University of Pennsylvania. In a temperate four-page letter to Kurtzman, he asked leave to call attention to "a progressively worsening situation."

As it now stands the Department has shrunk in terms of physical space and has depleted in faculty to the point where our offerings are so slim that it has been difficult and will soon be impossible to offer a sufficient number of courses for our undergraduate majors. . . .

I feel that the Department still has a potential for recouping its losses and growing to one of the fine secondary departments in the country. . . . From the questions asked me at the last professional meeting of Art Historians, I would say that the problems of the Fine Arts Department are being carefully watched by all of those universities from which it can hope to draw good graduate students and faculty members.

Wadsworth sent a plea for help to Kurtzman on May 20, again asking that the University take a stand:

As a result of unwarranted interference in academic affairs . . . there has been created an atmosphere of such tension and ill will that it can only be described as a cancer which is slowly eating its way into the heart of the Division of the Humanities. . . . Professor Haskins was thinking seriously of leaving, and it was only with difficulty that he was persuaded to remain here. Professor Cantini has been threatening to resign. . . . Most significantly, we have been unable to replace those people who have resigned, and the reason is largely that the unhappiness here is known across the country. . . . The Fine Arts Department has now become known in this country and abroad as an unhealthy place to be, and we will face increasing difficulty in staffing it unless we can clarify the present unhealthy situation. . . .

I have tried to help Vice Chancellor Peake in his long and laborious efforts to effect some sort of helpful compromise. Now, however, I believe that the time has come to take a stand and to ask that the academic integrity of the University be respected in the future.

On December 12 Wadsworth informed Kurtzman that the University's fine arts department, because of its troubles, had been dropped from the National Defense Education Administration's Title IV Program and would no longer receive its support.

Early in January 1967, William Rea made calls on "Cousin Helen" and her attorney in an attempt to come to some workable understanding. Pertinent to the situation was the fact that Miss Frick had not paid her 1966 contribution to the fine arts department. Rea's visits failed. Rea and Kurtzman then met with the Executive Committee of the board and received authority to take such action as they considered necessary. They decided to begin by moving the fine arts department and its people into the Frick Fine Arts Building and taking over the entire fine arts program.

Kurtzman told Wadsworth of the decision. Wadsworth asked for "some concrete indication of our new posture" as soon as possible. He wished to show it to his faculty members before they left for a College Art Association meeting, where they "might start looking around for other jobs." Kurtzman asked him to consult Peake, to advise him on who should sign the necessary letters, and to show him drafts of the letters.

On February 1 Charles Arensberg wrote David Buerger of the University's intended course of action. The administrative duties of Hovey and Miss Lewis would be terminated on April 15, 1967. They would be duly notified of these decisions by the proper authorities. The University would take over the fine arts building on April 15 so that full use of it could be made for teaching and research. (The University's ownership of the building had never been in doubt.)

Kurtzman made the announcement to the University Senate at its Friday meeting. He was given an ovation.

Peake informed Hovey the following Monday that his services as director of the fine arts building would cease on April 15, since the Memorandum of Understanding had been abrogated by both parties. On the same day Wadsworth wrote Virginia Lewis that her positions as assistant director and librarian were terminated and that her sole appointment would be that of professor of fine arts on a two-term salary. She resigned that position two months later.

The story broke on the morning of February 8. The rare, perhaps unique, act of a university— especially one known to be in financial trouble— telling off one of its big donors was national news. *Time, Newsweek,* the *Philadelphia Evening Bulletin,* and the *Chicago Tribune* ran major stories. A wire service (UPI) sent out a sizable piece to its subscribers, and so Pitt was news in the *Punxsutawney Spirit,* the *Morgantown Dominion News,* the *Erie Daily Times,* the *Allentown Call,* the *Tulsa Sun,* the *Albuquerque Journal,* and a score of others. The *New York Times,* which gave the story a column, set the tone by stating that the defense of academic freedom was the basic issue in the rupture. A typical headline read, "'Skyscraper U' Rates Academic Freedom High." Surprisingly, a number of articles averred that the right to teach and exhibit contemporary art was the main or even the sole issue between Miss Frick and the University.

The Pittsburgh papers gave major space to the story over a five-day period. The coverage tended to lean in Miss Frick's direction, but the University's basic points were made. Most letters to the University came from academic people and hailed the administration for its courage to be independent. Most letters to the newspapers sharply criticized the University. A long letter from Hovey in the *Post-Gazette* closed with, "The whole affair now looks as though from the very first they had planned to use Miss Frick as a means of obtaining for their own glorification even to the extent of millions of dollars that they could not otherwise acquire." In a mimeographed letter he distributed to "Dear Friends" he declared, "I cannot believe that academic freedom means the freedom to break solemn promises and to obtain money under false pretenses. Yet that is exactly the result of the distorted ego of the administrative personnel." In a letter to the *Press*, Miss Frick lamented that her dream to add beauty for the enjoyment of the public had been shattered by the mistakes of the present faculty. Her most damaging charge, which shocked and influenced many Pittsburghers and is still remembered today, was that not one person at the University had ever spoken a word of thanks to her for her gift of the fine arts building.*

The *Pitt News* printed two strong editorials, one headed "A Brave and Wise Stand," and two major articles, including the only detailed interview with the acting chancellor on the subject. Kurtzman declared that the basic issue was simply "whether anyone outside the University should have control over the faculty." He charged publicly for the first time that Miss Frick had demanded that Dr. Loerke and Dean Wadsworth be discharged. "If we gave in to those demands," he said, "we might just as well sell professorships." He did not reveal Miss Frick's orders not to employ Germans, nor did anyone else at the University.

Arensberg had sent Buerger a bill for $29,000 for "expenditures made at the specific request of Miss Frick." Buerger chose to consider the bill a request for a contribution, and in so doing introduced a note of mordant humor into an otherwise humorless situation. Miss Frick, he said in a letter to the *Pitt News*, declined to make any further contributions, as they might interfere with the University's academic freedom. He denied in that letter that Miss Frick had ever tried to have anyone discharged.

Hovey requested a meeting with William Rea and a hearing before the board. Rea replied that the circumstance affecting his relationship with the University had to do with his retirement and was entirely an administrative matter. The Executive Committee, therefore, declined to intervene. If Hovey wished further conversations about his situation, he should contact Peake or Kurtzman.†

The art objects Miss Frick had placed in the building on loan were gathered up under the supervision of Theodore Bowman and returned. They included thirteen paintings and the antique furniture she had provided for the offices of Hovey, Miss Lewis, and Robert Lord, organist. She generously did not remove certain art objects or any other items that might interfere with the operation of the building or the library. These included office tables and chairs, stone benches, wrought-iron standards, ninety-six upholstered folding chairs, a museum case, a fifteenth-century refectory table, two fifteenth-century consoles, two frescoes, two marble statues of the Annunciation carved by Alceo Dossena in the 1920s, and slide projection equipment. She also left twenty-two Lochoff frescoes, copies of Renaissance masterpieces (which she had bought from Lochoff in Florence for $40,000); the Aeolian organ (brought from the Frick's summer home in Pride's

---

*The University archives contain many written and spoken expressions of thanks, beginning with Litchfield's speech at the groundbreaking ceremony in 1962.

†William Rea told an interviewer years later that he had seen two great tragedies at the University—those of Edward Litchfield and Helen Clay Frick. He said that he alone, as chairman of the board in 1967, was responsible for the decision to break with Miss Frick.

The Henry Clay Frick Fine Arts Building.

Crossing, Massachusetts); a $200,000 endowment for buying books; the fine arts library; a trust fund that was returning some $14,000 annually; and the Henry Clay Frick Fine Arts Building (two rooms unfinished). She asked for the return of her latest large gift, which was still in storage: twenty-two Chinese porcelains, thirty-three Renaissance bronzes bought from the J. P. Morgan collection, and seven early French chairs. These objects, she said, came from her parents' home and were full of personal association. The Executive Committee voted to return the gifts.

Life went on, and public attention shifted to other matters. Students and faculty moved into classrooms and offices in the fine arts building. Hovey's position as director of the building was abolished; the Henry

Clay Frick Professorship, not being endowed, was allowed to expire. Miss Frick erected another fine arts building, this one behind the family mansion in Point Breeze, several miles east of the University. Virginia Lewis was its director.

On July 9, 1969, Miss Frick wrote to the *University Times* to announce that the current exhibition in the fine arts building, "Art of the Fifties," was illicit because it violated the purpose for which the building was erected. In October 1972 she wrote Posvar to protest that an ugly modern work was hanging in the lobby of the building; she hoped he would remove it. She thanked him for having had removed the dark stain on the front doors of the building.

On March 8, 1977, Chancellor Posvar arranged for a series of lectures and a reception to be held in the fine arts building to honor Walter Read Hovey on the fiftieth anniversary of his appointment to the University. Still living in Pittsburgh most of each year, he agreed to be present.

In April 1981 the fine arts department's doctoral program in art history was surveyed by a committee of the Conference Board of Associated Research Councils. Among the forty-one departments surveyed, Pitt was tied with two others (Chicago, North Carolina) for fourteenth place in quality of faculty. It had now become a department with nine faculty members, eight of them tenured. It began a planned program to make itself more a part of community life. The department's University Art Gallery in the years 1967–1983 held eighty-three exhibitions of art, ranging from "The Cybernetic Sculpture Environment of Wen-Ying Tsai" to "Diaghilev and Russian Stage Designers" to "Art Nouveau" to "Contemporary Andean Art."

In May 1982 an external evaluation committee headed by directors of the Schools of Fine Arts of Indiana University and New York University reported: "We found a healthy and productive department. Its major problems are 'good' problems, in the sense of challenge to do even better in the future. . . . We met an engaged faculty, completely professional in outlook, and . . . unusually productive as publishers. . . . Odious as ranking is, we are agreed the Pitt department should be seen as solidly in the ranks of the top dozen or so graduate departments in the country."

In June 1982 the report of an internal review committee concluded: "As a whole, the Department is well regarded by its peers outside Pittsburgh. . . . The committee found a Department which appears to function in an unusually smooth fashion. The friendly atmosphere of faculty meetings was mentioned more than once. Some speak of mutual pleasure and 'really' warm feelings. . . . The collegiality and harmony displayed is one of the greatest assets of the Department—a treasure on whose preservation lasting success can be built."

30

"The Creative Eye"

Our foremost concern is with quality. We will become more concerned with our own unique character and purpose—to know our special strengths and to reinforce them.

Wesley W. Posvar, Inauguration Address, March 27, 1968

WESLEY WENTZ POSVAR, forty-two, was inaugurated as the fifteenth chancellor of the University of Pittsburgh on a Saturday, in bright, balmy, first-day-of-spring weather. The academic ceremony and festival began at noon with an inaugural procession from the Stephen Foster Memorial to Carnegie Music Hall. Two hundred and two delegates from colleges, universities, and learned societies marched in academic regalia; they came from five continents and represented institutions that spanned seven centuries, from Oxford University (1249) to the University of Indonesia (1950). An audience of some nineteen hundred students, faculty members, and guests filled the Music Hall. William Rea, chairman of the Board of Trustees, conducted the investiture. In his response the chancellor spoke on what he foresaw as the new role of the University in the discovery and preservation of knowledge through research and scholarship.

Now, I suggest, we are on the verge of a new era of public involvement of the university. . . . I refer to an unprecedented and qualitative change in the role of the university, a role that will relate to a fundamental transformation of the human condition in this country during the next thirty years.

The university, because it is more stable and more independent than governments and corporations, will become the creative eye for the new society—for its communications systems, its social patterns, and its political and economic structure.

This, I submit to you, is the keynote of the next major stage of advancement of the University of Pittsburgh.

He dwelt on the continuing need for private funds, promised that administrators would listen carefully to the voice of the students, and predicted that during the next dozen years Pitt would gain more in qualitative improvement than in physical growth.

At the conclusion of his address, the chancellor conferred honorary degrees on four educators who had been influential as advisors and friends during his career. A luncheon for 350 guests in the Commons Room followed. (Six faculty wives and two top administrators had met in 1201 Bruce Hall one week earlier to test the menu.) At 3:00 P.M., dedication of the $12 million Hillman Library. At 4:00, a conducted tour of the twenty-one Nationality Rooms.

At 6:30, cocktails and dinner (black tie) for 150 guests in the Schenley ballroom. From 9:00 to 1:00 A.M., an inaugural ball in the Commons Room, to which all full-time and part-time members of the faculty, of all ranks, and their spouses, were invited. The rooms of the Cathedral of Learning were lighted at dusk and the exterior of the building was illuminated by floodlights.

The University mailed printed copies of the inaugural address to all the delegates, the trustees, and the permanent professors of the Air Force Academy. The chancellor sent personal copies to several of his particular friends, among them Zbigniew Brzezinski and Henry Kissinger.

The Posvar family had arrived at the University early in June 1967 following a round of farewell parties at Colorado Springs: Wesley, Mildred, Wesley William, sixteen, Margot Marina, thirteen, Lisa Christina, seven, and a large, black poodle named Beau-Beau. They took up housekeeping on Devonshire Street, about a half-mile east of the campus, in the residence Leon Falk had recently given for the purpose. Some repair work on the house was not finished: there had been a painters' strike, lumber was piled in the hallway, the furniture was covered with throw-cloths, and Mrs. Posvar cooked for the family for several days on a two-burner hot plate, one burner of which soon stopped functioning.

His neighbors were shocked or amused on seeing the chancellor, in a Pitt track suit, accompanied by Beau-Beau, jogging around his back yard before breakfast. ("I intend to use Devonshire Street," he said, "when I think the neighbors are ready for it.") He created further interest on those days when he rode to the campus on a bicycle. The tone, the style, of Posvar's first year were colored by such small occurrences as these. He brought an element of casual humor to a campus that had known little of it in several decades.

He received a pleasant letter from Dean Putnam Jones: "The Graduate Faculty in the Department of Political Science has voted unanimously that you be recognized as a full member of the Graduate Faculty." He joined the Duquesne Club, Rolling Rock

Wesley W. Posvar

Wesley Wentz Posvar, forty-two, became chancellor on June 1, 1967. Portrait by Jean Spencer.

James Kriegsmann

Mrs. Wesley Wentz Posvar, more widely known as the singer Mildred Miller. In 1978 she founded and became artistic director of the Pittsburgh Opera Theater.

Club, West Point Society of Western Pennsylvania, and the Executive Committee of the Allegheny Conference on Community Development, and he became a director of the Pittsburgh Symphony Society, the Civic Light Opera, and Pittsburgh's educational television station, WQED. He paid his respects to one of the country's great military figures, General Matthew B. Ridgway, a Pittsburgher since 1955, and took the Ridgways to the Pitt-Army home game. He persuaded Dwight D. Eisenhower to speak at the dedication of the totally new $8 million campus at Johnstown, with its ten buildings of steel, glass, and native field stone in a rural setting. He persuaded Richard K. Mellon to become a trustee emeritus of the University. He and Mrs. Posvar attended a "community reception" given in their honor on the lawn in front of Heinz Chapel and a University reception for 3,000 people at the Cathedral of Learning. And he took up the unending duties of courtesy correspondence. Among others, he wrote congratulations to Miss Paula Molnick, a senior, for taking first prize in the *Atlantic* creative writing contest, against 206 competitors; to Paul Jerry Ritchey for winning the two-mile championship at the NCAA meet in Detroit; to the Pitt team that distinguished itself in three appearances on television's General Electric College Bowl, in which it won $7,000 in scholarships; to the members of the William Pitt Debating Union for winning the Pennsylvania State Debating Championship ("Resolved: That the Federal Government Should Guarantee a Minimum Income to All Citizens").

Mildred Miller came to Pittsburgh near the peak of her career, with a full booking in opera, recitals, and television appearances, but she soft-pedaled her professional identity until she became established as the chancellor's wife. A ripple of laughter stirred the campus over an incident at the chancellor's residence. Members of the Pitt glee club appeared there during Christmas week to serenade the Posvars. Mildred Posvar was so moved that she offered to sing "Silent Night" if they hummed the accompaniment. One student was heard to groan, "Oh, the chancellor's wife thinks she can sing!" At the end of the song he approached her with a compliment:

"Mrs. Posvar, have you ever considered a career in opera or something?" The few who knew it also cherished the story of the conference between the chancellor's wife and the administrator in charge of the affair at which she would first meet the faculty. Unsure of himself and of the situation, he asked her if she would like to sing on the occasion. "If my predecessor sang," she said sweetly, "I will be happy to sing."

Several years before Pitt approached Posvar, she had contracted to sing the role of the gypsy girl Carmen with the Pittsburgh Opera during the 1967 season. (She had sung the part with that company in the late 1950s.) Knowing that people tend to identify actresses, actors, and artists with their stage portrayals, she decided that the University community and the community at large should come to know her for herself before they identified her with a stage role; and so she canceled her 1967 Carmen. Pittsburghers smiled when they read a *New York Times* feature article on her, syndicated in Pittsburgh, in which she gave an added reason why she canceled. Her Carmen, she said, was not sultry but young, kittenish, and much too sexy for the wife of a newly appointed university chancellor. For the Pittsburgh Opera she later sang Rosina in *The Barber of Seville*, Dorabella in *Così fan tutte*, and, in 1969, Carmen in a Syria Mosque performance sold out to both Mildred Miller fans and Mildred Posvar admirers. In November 1968 she sang before an audience of 1,500 in a performance for the Mount Lebanon Community Concert Series as a last-minute substitution when Renata Scotto became ill. Of that performance of lieder, art songs, and arias in English, German, French, and Italian, critic Carl Apone wrote in the *Press:* "She is a thoughtful, probing, intelligent performer whose excellence becomes slowly more apparent with each song. . . . She's charming on stage, an extremely attractive brunet, lovely to look at in a pink satin gown, and was comfortable in her assignment." In 1973 she gave a benefit recital for the University's Women's Association in which her fee—normally $2,500—and the proceeds—more than $19,000—went to establish a scholarship in perpetuity for a music student.

Mildred Miller had favored the move to Pitts-

Mildred Miller, with rose in hand, as Octavian in the Metropolitan Opera production of Richard Strauss's Der Rosenkavalier.

burgh: it brought her closer to New York and the Metropolitan; it would ease the travel problems involved in crisscrossing the country to fill other engagements; it would give the children the advantage of city life; and after ten moves in seventeen years of marriage, it gave promise of a settled domicile in a place and among people she liked.

Before June 1, 1967, she had managed to carry out a heavy schedule as an artist while maintaining a household, rearing three children, practicing at least one hour every morning, and performing the duties expected of an air force officer's wife. Difficult as that was, it was as nothing compared to the demands the University was now to make on her time and energy.

In the 1967 season Mildred Miller was Meg Page in *Falstaff* at the Metropolitan, gave an all-lieder concert in New York's Town Hall, appeared on television on the Bell Telephone Hour, gave a series of performances with civic opera companies, and sang some thirty times in twenty states in recital and with orchestras. (Requests for her appearances had increased after 1965, when she won the Grand Prix du Disque for a Columbia recording of Brahms's *Alto Rhapsody* and Mahler's *Songs of a Wayfarer*.) In "The Chancellor's Lady Sings" (*Pitt,* Spring 1968),

Helen Knox listed some of the additional duties of the chancellor's wife. She attended at least one official gathering each day—a dinner given by women students, or an alumni luncheon, or a meeting somewhere in the community. She stood for hours in reception lines. She served as hostess to those invited to the chancellor's residence: faculty members, staff members, trustees, their spouses, donors, student leaders, special out-of-town guests, and those who came to the Saturday brunch before home football games. To accommodate those demands, she asked her agent, Columbia Artists Management, not to book her on any of those days when she had to be present at the University. Her appearances as an artist, of course, were curtailed. Young and with her star still in ascent, she gave up a good part of her professional career to fulfill her required official duties at the University. The Posvars always considered the Pitt job a partnership. Even so, in recognizing this, one is led to the general conclusion that wives of university chancellors and presidents (like wives of ministers) are badly exploited, in that they are not free to pursue careers apart from their husbands', they are required to perform long and hard duties competently and cheerfully, and for this they are not paid. No husband of a woman college president—an attorney, perhaps, or a physician, or a business executive—would be expected to fulfill such obligations under such conditions.

The University, when its new chancellor took office, in June, 1967, had come safely through a three-year crisis of management. The faculty and most of the top administrative staff were intact. The state had contracted to assist the institution financially in a promising new relationship. With the concomitant sharp drop in tuition cost, enrollment was at a record high. At the same time, the University faced grave problems—decisions to be made, directions to be determined, questions to be resolved, pieces to be picked up and put together again.

The University was still heavily in debt—$15 million to a life insurance company and about $12 million that had been borrowed from the school's endowment funds, research grants, and construction capital.

The University was receiving extremely bad local publicity in the quarrel with Miss Frick over who was to control the new Frick Fine Arts Building and the Department of Fine Arts.

The University was hurt by a development in which Carnegie Institute of Technology merged with the Mellon Institute of Industrial Research to become Carnegie-Mellon University. Mellon Institute had been a Pitt affiliate for almost half a century, and its handsome columned Oakland building had long been an ornament of the Pitt campus. The merger was interpreted in some quarters as an action taken by Richard Mellon to show his displeasure with Pitt and its administrative leadership before 1966. The truth is simpler, less interesting, and therefore less likely to be believed. Stoddard Stevens, a wealthy New York lawyer, introduced his friend Paul Mellon to William Oliver Baker, young research director of Bell Telephone Laboratories. Baker had important connections, influence, and responsibilities in industry, higher education, the government, and the military, and he wanted to talk to Paul Mellon about a burning conviction he had. He felt that the nation needed a technical university—one with a broad base in the arts and humanities, in engineering and research, and in scientific technology. He had decided that Carnegie Tech *cum* Mellon Institute was the perfect combination to bring this off—a merger of two great American names. The idea was helped along by an adverse tax ruling on the institute's work by the Internal Revenue Service, and it drew support from those who feared the institute would no longer play an important role in an industrial economy in which so many corporations now had their own research laboratories. Paul Mellon took Baker's proposal to Richard Mellon (fellow board member of the institute), who opposed it mildly. "Let Andy Carnegie," he said, "continue to have his glory." When Paul Mellon pressed the idea, however, Richard Mellon concurred, and the merger between Mellon Institute and Carnegie Institute of Technology took place in the autumn of 1967.

Johnstown Tribune-Democrat

Dwight D. Eisenhower with Posvar at the dedication of the new Johnstown campus, September 26, 1967.

University Archives

Of the University's four regional colleges—Bradford, Greensburg, Johnstown, and Titusville—Johnstown (above) is the largest.

There were, of course, the continuing issues that cause tension, and controversy on almost all campuses. As Posvar described them wryly in 1970: "competing needs for library budgets, computer budgets, and instructional budgets; the issue of centralization versus decentralization of libraries and computers; the question of improving teaching quality; the continuing task of improving community relations and portraying expansion plans so as to make them acceptable to neighboring citizens; the need to develop better and more explicit understanding of faculty rights and responsibilities; the difficulty of obtaining and sustaining financial support for programs for minority students; the problem of internal communication . . . the state of decrepitude of the business systems—the slowness of registration, the inaccuracy and delays in invoicing, the laborious processing of work orders, and the often incredibly high charges for maintenance."

In addition to these known problems, there were incertitudes that could develop into problems that were even more serious, depending on how they were resolved.

● With the drop in tuition from $1,450 to $450

and the doubling in enrollment that resulted, would the caliber of incoming students decline? Would it be necessary to lower the quality of undergraduate study and the standards of the University itself to accommodate the new state relationship?

• Would state legislators attempt to control the University, as ex-Chancellor Litchfield had predicted?

• Would the legislators and successive governors continue to make adequate appropriations for the four state-related universities and do so on schedule? Penn State had a new president who was expert and fiercely competitive in the fight for state monies. Would Pitt successfully meet that competition?

• Would private donors—alumni, friends, and foundations—contribute to an institution that was receiving state support? Could a case be made that would produce private gifts and grants in substantial amounts? Would the public understand and accept the subtle distinction between a state-*supported* university, which was generally not thought of as needing private money, and a private state-*related* university, which must have private gifts to survive?

• Could Wesley Posvar, graduate of the Military Academy at West Point and erstwhile colonel in the U.S. Air Force, win the confidence and cooperation of the faculty? His statements on academic quality, freedom of speech, tenure, racism, the draft, and the war in Vietnam were all that a faculty member could ask, and his career was solidly based on performance as an academic administrator and teacher; but suspicion lingered about this former career military officer. Would his emphasis on balanced budgets, his programs based on sound management and "efficient allocation and use of resources" harm academic activities?

• The stirring of student unrest that had surfaced at the University of California at Berkeley in 1964 and was now spreading to other campuses—would it reach the University of Pittsburgh? If so, when, where, in what degree? What could a chancellor and his administrators do to divert it, control it, or absorb it into constructive channels?

From his first days in office, Dr. Posvar bore down on the need to review the principal goals of the University and "to define more clearly what kind of university we want Pitt to be." A two-day off-campus meeting attended by the top twelve administrators produced a restatement of objectives. It began by examining and dismissing Litchfield's goal of placing Pitt among the top ten schools in the country in every field in ten years as imprecise and unrealistic.

Excellence has many faces, and we must not define the term too narrowly. . . . Clearly, the University cannot be among the top ten in the country in every field. Moreover, it is simply too difficult to define the basis for such relative numerical rankings. . . . Where does quality/excellence reside? In subject matter content? The communication process/learning process? Teaching? Research? Public service?

Emphasis on the national ranking of the University is in itself meaningless, for we are already among the top twenty universities in the country in most important respects. We should set our own style and our own standards, and aim to be the best institution possible according to our own terms. . . .

The University of Pittsburgh should aspire to be among the best in the nation in those programs that we decide to pursue. . . . We should develop our own programs on the basis of our unique resources, interests, and strengths, and the educational needs of society as we perceive them.

In the course of these deliberations and after months of study with his staff and outside consultants, Posvar effected a major administrative and academic reorganization. He replaced the School of Liberal Arts with the College of Arts and Sciences, which combined the social sciences, natural sciences, and humanities under a single dean. He established a directorship of communications programs that included libraries, academic computer systems, and related research and science centers. He combined the separate offices of dean of men and dean of women under a single assistant chancellor for student affairs, "in keeping with the most modern practices of student affairs organization" and "to better coordinate our living and learning programs for all students."* And he placed all academic pro-

---

* In a further giant step forward, McCormick Hall in February 1970 was made a coeducational residence for 165 students. The

grams, graduate and undergraduate, under the direction of a provost. Posvar retained and used the key people from his predecessor's staff in carrying out these changes (Alan Rankin had left in 1965 to become president of Indiana State University), but as provost he named Rhoten A. Smith, dean of the College of Liberal Arts at Temple University for six years and president since 1967 of Northern Illinois University.

To succeed Kurtzman as vice chancellor for finance, Posvar persuaded Edison Montgomery to return to the University and gave him the additional position of director of communications programs.* As his executive assistant in fiscal management, Posvar recruited Jack E. Freeman, thirty-six, Baylor graduate, air force major, assistant professor of political science at Colorado Springs, military affairs officer at air force headquarters, and, before resigning to go to Pitt, executive assistant to the deputy undersecretary of the air force in Washington.

Posvar gave top priority to fiscal management; he personally controlled the making of the budget and the allocation of funds. He and his aides found the basic operating systems and procedures of the University out of date and inefficient in such areas as payrolls, personnel and student records, and financial accounting. To remedy these deficiencies they set out to develop a planning-programing-budget system similar to recent advanced programs in government and industry. "Ours," Posvar told his trust-

ees, "is something of a pioneering undertaking in higher education. We have been working on a master plan for the entire University. . . . In addition to a long-range planning and programming-budgeting system, we want to develop a complete management information system that will store data and help to schedule classes and instructors, record registration payments, and so on." This turned out to be a far more difficult task than even the most pessimistic participant had expected. Seven years and several misfires would ensue before the pioneering master plan was perfected; and not until 1985 were the chancellor and his advisors convinced that they would finally have in 1986 "the complete management information system" they had hoped for.

In these early years of the Posvar administration, the University learned the answers to some of the questions that had been raised in 1967.

First, the academic quality of incoming freshmen did not decline with the vastly greater numbers that came with state-relatedness and low tuition costs. On the contrary, the quality rose. Total enrollment increased 62 percent in the first four years, reaching 20,018 full-time equivalent students in 1970. Among entering freshmen, the percentage coming from the top fifth of their high school classes rose from 59 to 68. Scholastic Aptitude Test scores rose from a mean of 549 to 556 (verbal) and 570 to 592 (math). Analysis confirmed that the state's tuition subsidy was enabling many bright students from working class backgrounds to attend Pitt and that more of them—51 percent—were sons and daughters of parents who had not gone to college. The parents of 57 percent of the entering classes were earning less than $10,000 a year.

Second, except on two specific, manageable issues, the state legislators made no attempt to interfere in the running of the University. The twelve Commonwealth trustees continued to be useful board members of high quality. Three legislators in Harrisburg who had introduced bills that were considered regressive and were opposed by the University became its warm friends and stout supporters.

On the other hand, there were unfortunate delays for four successive years in passing and paying the state appropriation, and this cost the University a

announcement distributed by the Joint Coeducational Housing Subcommittee of the Women's Housing Board and the Men's Dormitory Council reads: "We hope that this will provide a more relaxed and natural environment where students will get a more complete understanding of the opposite sex. We hope that proximity of men and women in a residence hall will stimulate more sincere and meaningful relationships, while still encouraging academic excellence."

*Montgomery had left the University to become president of the Interuniversity Communications Council, an organization of some eighty major colleges and universities in the United States and Canada. It dealt with problems of communications in higher education, particularly as they involved the use of computers and high technology. As director of communications programs, a new post, Montgomery was in charge of the University's libraries, Computer Center, Knowledge Availability Systems Center, and the Health-Law Center.

considerable amount of money paid out in interest on loans from banks.

A third question hung for a time in a trembling balance: would private donors contribute to Pitt as a state-related institution?

In the matter of fund raising, the University was operating under a special restraint. It had been made clear to Posvar when he took office that the foundations, large corporate givers, and major private philanthropists expected Pitt to stand in the wings until a campaign mounted by the new Carnegie-Mellon University was near its end. It was not until 1972, therefore, that Pitt was able to undertake its own large campaign, a drive to obtain $35 million in the remaining eight years of the 1970s. In the meantime, Pitt developed a "low-horizon" campaign that was tailor-made to explain why it deserved to get private funds when it was already getting state support. This campaign strategy was used with the Annual Giving Fund, addressed primarily to alumni, and with the University's faithful, steady donors. Private gifts, Posvar explained, were the funds that provided the margin of excellence for special purposes for which state and federal funding would not be forthcoming. "We get a secure financial base from the state," the chancellor said. "Our private support gives us the quality of increment—the essential extra amount we need to support superior programs and special professorships and facilities. The private gifts make the difference between an adequate educational enterprise and a university of which the state and the nation may be proud."

Posvar emphasized a second point: that private universities actually receive much more public support than is generally recognized. "If you consider the whole spectrum of American universities today, from Harvard to Berkeley, you will see that the public or private nature of each is really a matter of degree. Harvard, which is supposed to be the epitome of private education, receives as much each year in federal academic support as Pitt receives from the federal government and the state. By the same token, the 'public' University of California system collects more private gifts than Pitt. So, most universities today receive large amounts of both public and private support."

Morris Berman/Pittsburgh Post-Gazette

William H. Rea, elected chairman of trustees on the same day that Posvar was named chancellor, shared with him the turmoil of the next five years.

At least partly because of this persuasive rationale, one of the University's basic questions was in time answered affirmatively: private donors would indeed contribute generously to Pitt as a state-related institution. In the two school years 1967–1969, private gifts and grants to the University from sources in Pittsburgh alone totaled about $11 million. The largest single benefactor was Richard K. Mellon, who in the five years before his death in 1970 gave $9 million—all this after it was feared that he had abandoned the University in 1965. Grants in 1967–1968, other than those from the state, included $200,000 from the National Aeronautics and Space Administration; $5.6 million from the U.S. Office of Education for the construction of facilities for the new Learning Research and Development Center (LRDC); $1.2 million from the National Science Foundation for LRDC program expansion; and $3.6 million from the National Science Foundation to develop national centers of quality in the departments of physics, crystallography, and chemistry.

Paul Solyan, who had worked on the account while with Price Waterhouse, joined the University as comptroller in December 1964, and he and his office developed for the chancellor a programed schedule for liquidating the University's internal and external debt. In his first two years, through economies and more stringent controls, Posvar was able to repay $8 million. His target date for discharging the debt entirely was April 1976. Comptroller Solyan says today, "State-relatedness, of course, helped us. But there was some indication that it may not have been necessary. The University, under the new management and with proper fiscal controls, could have survived and paid its way, but it would have taken longer. Also, the University would not be as large as it is now, and it would not have been able to continue to provide a quality education to Pennsylvania resident students to the extent that it has done since becoming state-related."

Seth Lubove, a *Pitt News* reporter who wrote a two-part profile of the chancellor, described Posvar's method of operation at a budget meeting with his top administrative officers:

"Posvar removes his jacket and sits at the head of the table. . . . [He] remains quiet, tapping his fingers on the table and keeping slightly distant from the discussion. Occasionally [he] asks a question concerning the long-term effects of a certain proposal or a question [Jack] Freeman has neglected. . . .

"As he is wont to do at lengthy meetings, Posvar has laid out before him a series of color-coded index cards and a blue pocket datebook. The index cards—prepared by his secretary—are his schedule for the day down to each quarter hour, and the datebook is 'booked six months in advance.'

"Since he must balance his time between academia, business, countless trusteeships and directorships, and thousands of other detailed obligations, Posvar is extremely conscious of his time—how it is used, how it is managed, and how productive it is. Unlike people who take 'each day as it comes,' Posvar thinks in terms of how most effectively to use the minutes of his upcoming days and months. He often gets up in the middle of a meeting to make a call to his secretary to confirm an appointment, change a date, or make final plans on an upcoming business trip. . . .

"He maintains a slight air of detachment about him, communicated by his restlessness, an impression that he would much prefer to get on with some more pressing concern. . . . But as removed as he may appear to be, Wesley Posvar is fiercely attentive to the scene before him. Like a hawk, he hovers above the participants, sighting and carefully measuring the entire situation from all angles of the discussion, then he swoops down aggressively and asks a precise question deserving a specific answer. He is annoyed with facetiousness and impatient with indecisiveness, qualities Posvar has always rejected."

Posvar is not proud of the impression he conveys and does not defend the pace he maintains. He has called his style more "frenetic" than it needs to be. "If we were vacationing at Martha's Vineyard," he says, "I would be organizing a trip to Nantucket." In answer to an inquiry on lessons he has learned in running a university, he laments that a college president is so busy that he has too little time to meditate on what he is doing and what he should be doing. "I think I could be praised," he says, "but probably criticized even more, for maintaining an excessively fast pace and in keeping a wide span of attention to various problems at the same time."

On another occasion he said, "I would be disappointed if my observers did not perceive in me a management style that includes my cultivation and appreciation of criticism of my own ideas and performance, and also my determination to have around me the ablest and most competitive intellects that I can find."

He has not hesitated on occasion to criticize his own performance. He blames himself for not having seen earlier that unification of the Health Center—his attempt to bring together the faculty of the School of Medicine through the six hospitals—

would not work. (See page 432.) He regrets the delay, year after year for more than a decade, in developing a truly advanced management-information system. "The magnitude of the task," he says ruefully, "had until now out-run the capacity to meet the need."

The Posvar administration, now nearing the second longest tenure in the history of the University, has received remarkably little adverse criticism from the state and local press and from interests in "the city," but it has never lacked censure from its own faculty members. For the most part, this seems to have been carried on in the professional, traditional, academic manner that sometimes puzzles those who are responsible for the governance of other U.S. institutions. A professor who in 1970 notified the chancellor formally in writing that he had found it necessary to present a motion of "no confidence" in him at the next meeting of the local chapter of the AAUP was seen enjoying himself not long afterward at a reception and buffet dinner at the chancellor's residence.

The new chancellor's qualities, performance, and style were inevitably compared to those of Edward Litchfield, his predecessor twice removed, for whom there was a persistent residual loyalty. The comparison tended to conclude that the status of faculty members was higher and the authority greater under Litchfield than it is in the Posvar administration. One faculty member who had known both men addressed himself to this conclusion in an interview in November 1982. John Funari, then dean of the Graduate School of Public and International Affairs, said, "I have two perspectives on the matter. I served under Litchfield from 1958 to 1962 as his executive assistant for administration, when I left to take a post with the Department of State. When I returned to the University in 1974 I talked with some of those who had been old friends and old hands here in the Litchfield years, and I heard them singing his praises and how good it had been in the old days. But it was those very same people who were most critical of Litchfield and felt threatened by him when he was actually on the job. They saw him then as something of an authoritarian, even bordering on a tyrannical figure who was not partic-

ularly sympathetic to their pace of academic life. In those days the chancellor had far more power and authority to act than does the present chancellor, in the sense that the concept of faculty participation in management just simply wasn't there. The power is far more dispersed in this University now than it was then."

In the course of months, semesters, and seasons that followed, the chancellor's views became known on the campus—his guiding principles, cast of thought, strongest convictions, and fixed ideas; his philosophy as an educator; the way he saw the relationship of the University to the city, region, and state; his opinions on academic freedom, student unrest, the draft, the arms race, the campaign to drive ROTC off the campus, the war in Vietnam; his response when confronted by stubborn opposition or a confessed serious blunder; how far he would go to protect a faculty member whose radical views had the community howling for his dismissal. Posvar's opinions became known from speeches made to University groups (freshmen, new faculty members, the University Senate, the Women's Association); from a hundred addresses delivered to audiences ranging from the Oakland Kiwanis Club to the Army War College at Carlisle; from interviews with the press and formal public statements released on controversial issues; from memoranda and letters; from the words recorded in the minutes of a thousand meetings on the campus.

On academic freedom

"I consider it to be my primary obligation to defend academic freedom at this University, no less against external demands that the professorial or student expression of unpopular views be stilled, than against internal campus movements that seek to roll over everything that stands in their way. If academic freedom submits to either of these onslaughts, the system of higher education based on open inquiry will come to an end, perhaps to be replaced by a system of great vocational academies. I have no intention of presiding over such an institution." (Chancellor's Annual Report, December 1, 1970)

"I have read your thoughtful letter of May 5 concerning the article in the Pittsburgh *Press* in which Dr. James G. Holland was mentioned.

"Let me say that I personally disagree with the views expressed by Dr. Holland as reported in the article. Nevertheless, he has the constitutional right to hold those opinions and to express them. . . .

"As you may know, once a faculty member is given tenure, he may be terminated only for cause upon the recommendation of the faculty, with the right to a full and impartial hearing by a committee composed of members of the faculty and the Board of Trustees. Dr. Holland is a tenured member of the faculty. To my knowledge, there has been no question concerning his professional qualifications, nor has he been found guilty of any illegal act." (Letter to an alumna of the University, May 21, 1968)

On minority students

"Because of their greater resources and their capacity for varied programs, the large universities can and should move faster than smaller institutions in recruiting minority students. Further, they must make strong efforts to expand minority enrollment in schools of nearly all-white professions, including engineering, medicine, and law. Looking beyond this phase, once higher enrollments are obtained the university will also have a key role in the adjustment of our whole society to a new set of forces: one sixth of our people having been denied economic and social mobility finally gaining it." ("The University as an American Institution," June 22, 1974)

On the draft

"To use the draft as a punitive instrument against those who engage in student protest activities is, in my opinion, not only improper and unfair, but also clearly contrary to the most important substantive and procedural guarantees of the Constitution. As a former military officer, I must register strong disagreement with the use of the draft as 'punishment' for illegal activity of any kind. . . . If a person is guilty of an illegal act, he should be punished as provided by law, not drafted into the armed forces where the lives of others may depend upon his actions. If he is not guilty of an illegal act, he should

be treated in regard to the draft on the same basis as anyone else." (Pitt news release, January 11, 1968)

On the war in Vietnam

"There are times to be silent and times to speak. This is a time to speak. . . . More and more we see the war in Vietnam deflecting energies and resources from urgent business on our own doorstep. An end to the war will not solve the problems on or off the campus. It will, however, permit us to work more effectively in support of more peaceful priorities. . . . We urge upon the President of the United States and upon Congress a stepped-up timetable for withdrawal from Vietnam. We believe this to be in our country's highest interest, at home and abroad." (A public statement signed jointly by seventy-seven college presidents, including Wesley W. Posvar, October 12, 1969)

On the University and the city

"As much as, and perhaps more than, any urban institution in the country, the University has been linked to the destinies of its host city. The relationship goes back to the earliest history of both, while today a thousand and one concerns unite Pitt and Pittsburgh in an intricate web of mutual associations. . . . One set of strands in this relationship has been woven by the University in fulfilling its 'public service' function. . . . Properly directed, public service activities can enrich many facets of the teaching and research functions of the University." (Chancellor's Annual Report, December 1, 1970)

"I think the University of Pittsburgh is most fortunate to be in the City of Pittsburgh. There are not more than a handful of the nation's large universities that exist in the heart of the city. There is none in a city with the civic pride, industrial leadership, and impulse for self-improvement of Pittsburgh. We are glad we can say that this city provides our clientele, . . . our support, . . . our habitat, . . . and our urban research laboratory. If it chose, Pittsburgh could become one of the most important centers for urban studies—and for higher education—in the nation." (Remarks at the annual dinner of the Negro Educational Emergency Drive, June 12, 1967)

On the University and the state

"We are finding in the State Legislature considerable support for our contention that an investment in higher education is one of the most productive appropriations a government can make for the future of its own people." (Remarks at a Women's Association meeting, May 6, 1969)

"The state received a considerable bargain when the University became state-related, since the state acquired the use of the very extensive physical plant that had been constructed primarily with private funds. . . . In Pennsylvania the necessity to build whole new campuses at a cost of many hundreds of millions of dollars, as both California and New York have done, was obviated—and the resources of three great private universities [Penn State, Temple, Pitt] were placed at the disposal of the state, along with their private endowments, their high-quality faculties and long-established programs." (Minute of a meeting of the Council of Deans and Campus Presidents, October 15, 1968)

On the role of the academic disciplines

"A new concept of the role of the academic disciplines has been advanced. The disciplines are seen as pursuing a three-fold function based on providing undergraduate liberal arts instruction, conducting graduate and postdoctoral study and research, and giving major support to the professional schools. Closer relationships among related fields have been sought. . . . There are no longer sharp distinctions between the academic disciplines and the professional schools." (Chancellor's Report to the Trustees, 1973–1974)

On the role of the university in the United States

"The American university is a unique and valuable American institution. . . . Two of our most important guiding principles, academic freedom and recognition of an obligation to serve the public interest, were not inherent but evolved qualities of the university, and . . . they have a more powerful effect in the American setting than they do elsewhere. . . . The public service mission on

a large scale was almost entirely an American development. . . .

"The American university bears resemblance to its counterparts in other continents, and it fosters the traditions of scholarship common to all places of higher learning. Yet it differs in its larger scale, its resources, and the degree of its commitment to research and service. It is a major and quite visible part of the whole social landscape.

"In America the university not only trains the members of the leading professions, but through them and its sponsored programs it helps generate the ideas and the motivations that govern the establishments of the schools, the health care system, the welfare system, the legal system, agencies of government, and industrial corporations. It democratizes the populace through expanding educational opportunity, and its responsibility to do this . . . stems from the political philosophy of our national founders and is, in effect, part of the unwritten political constitution of the United States. It is a center for investigation, discovery, and invention. It is all these since its one commodity is knowledge, and its one organizing principle is to make knowledge useful." ("The University as an American Institution," June 22, 1974)

"Most of us tend to think of the future in terms of the technological forecast—and such a forecast is not too difficult to provide. . . . I would like to make a special plea for realism. These forecasts represent what I would call the Sunday supplement syndrome. . . . They add up to a simplistic view of the future—a world's fair setting equipped with astonishing and handsome hardware, but a world without reference to people and their problems.

"It is the people, of course, who will really make the future. They must be taught to master the hardware, to understand the social consequences of new technology, and to use their intelligence and their wealth to create the kind of world in which they would like to live.

"This adds up to a massive task of education that must be done now, today—even before we have a clear idea of what the future will bring. And it is, today, a task affecting every aspect of University life." ("Education and the 21st Century," remarks to the Pittsburgh Personnel Association, October 11, 1967)

On the use of armed force

"Those who make decisions about the employment of military force are *ipso facto* in the domain of ethics. The commodity in which they deal is human security or human suffering. This point is more than a platitude; it means that decision makers must *not* restrict themselves to questions of what they *can* do in response to physical circumstances—things they can see and hear. They must also consider what they *ought* to do in the pursuit of ethical values." ("Justice in the Use of Armed Force," an address delivered at the U.S. Air Force Academy, November 1966)

"We must keep alert to the fact that a policy of nations relying upon nuclear deterrence as the principal basis of their security has an ultimately fatal flaw. For deterrence to be effective, the threat of inevitable retaliation must be credible. This means that deterrence rests on the continuing finite possibility that nuclear war will, in fact, occur—that deterrence *could* fail. Hence the gradual movement toward greater international cooperation has a vital urgency. We must invent a new system for preserving peace before the nuclear clock runs out." (Lecture to the Army War College, Carlisle, Pennsylvania, May 7, 1971)

On U.S. foreign policy

"It is obvious that Communism is not or is no longer a monolithic opponent of the Free World— witness some of the vehement conflicts that have taken place among communist states themselves. . . . The old simplistic view of Communism as a world monolith has a strong hold on American strategic thought, and U.S. diplomacy does not show great sophistication as yet in differentiating among socialist states that are more or less malevolent and more or less threatening to peace and to U.S. interests. In much of the Third World, and particularly in Latin America, we often seem blind to the pos-

sibilities of cooperation with forces of revolutionary change that are still amenable to nonviolent solutions. . . . It is hard to see how the establishment of normal relations with Red China could do anything but advance the cause of international communication and, in net effect, improve U.S. security." (Address to the seventy-fifth annual meeting of the American Academy of Political and Social Science, Philadelphia, April 3, 1971. President Nixon visited Red China in February 1972, the first president of the United States ever to do so.)

On the international dimension

"Given the postwar changes in the international arena, a comprehensive university cannot exist . . . without a powerful set of international studies, international programs, and international relationships. . . . There are some great universities without law schools or medical schools, or even football teams. But there are no great universities without a strong international dimension." ("Expanding International Dimensions," *Change*, May–June, 1980)*

On Wednesday, January 15, 1969, Posvar was spending an evening at home with friends. He took a telephone call at about ten o'clock. He was told by a security guard at the Cathedral of Learning that twenty-five to thirty black students had seized and barricaded themselves in the computer center on the eighth floor. They were wearing leather jackets and black berets and called themselves members of the Black Action Society. They intended to stay there until certain demands they had made some months earlier were met. They wanted to see the chancellor at once. The violent stage of the campus revolts of the 1960s had arrived on the campus of the University of Pittsburgh.

*In 1968 Posvar had established the University Center for International Studies, a comprehensive organization housing international academic programs and coordinating all international activities within the University. Its first director was Carl Beck. In 1969 the Western European Studies Program, directed by John Neubauer, joined the other major UCIS units: Latin America, East Asia, and Russia and East Europe.

31

Confrontation I

Various forms of public expression, protest, debate, demonstration and peaceful picketing are a normal part of the scene in a free and open society. At the same time, we must realize that physical obstruction of university activities or interference with the right of others to meet with persons of their choice or to study is not consistent with the political values of western society. To many, the "rule of law" may sound like a trite phrase, but it happens to be the cornerstone of all the civil liberties, minority rights, and democratic institutions that have been carefully nurtured and developed through 3,000 years of human progress. The man who places his own beliefs above the rule of law . . . clears the way for the advent of totalitarians who make precisely the same argument as he does to justify their actions: "What I do is right because it is what I believe."

Wesley W. Posvar in the *Owl*, 1968

THE country had never known anything like it. During an eight-year period beginning in 1965, students on several hundred U.S. campuses erupted in protest demonstrations. They denounced the power structure, the establishment, a corrupt society, the character of an entire culture. Their demands ranged from the ridiculous to the long-overdue reform of educational and social practices. They wanted an end to economic injustice, racism, political oppression, the draft, and the war in Vietnam. They variously demanded a restructuring of the university system: open admissions; ungraded courses; communal control of courses; an end to the ROTC; access to professors' papers; open trustees' meetings; a voice in the hiring, firing, and promotion of professors and the granting or denying of tenure; departments or schools of black studies, taught by black professors approved by black students; all-black dormitories; the expulsion from the campus of recruiters from the Dow Chemical Company, the Central Intelligence Agency, and the armed services; large contributions to the legal defense fund for imprisoned Black Panthers; the right to rule on what university research and what university investments were permissible; and at the State University of New York in Oneonta, a thirty-five dollar weekly allowance to each of the members of the protest committee.

The student protests of the period were a manifestation of the country's anguish over an increasing military involvement in what Wesley Posvar called "a miserable war" in Vietnam. The protests were further sparked by racial injustice and the riots it was causing in the inner cities. The 1960s had been an uneasy decade for Americans of any age, even when students were still being faulted for their lack of assertiveness as "the silent generation" and before the campuses erupted in violence. President John F. Kennedy had dealt with what have been called "the most massive demonstrations by civil rights groups since reconstruction." Other nonviolent protests headed by the Reverend Martin Luther King, Jr., were punctuated by riots that ignited the black communities of Los Angeles, Chicago, Newark, Detroit, and other American cities. Substantial progress was being achieved in a drive to end social injustice and economic deprivation, but the beneficial changes brought with them the seemingly inevitable unrest that accompanies promises and rising expectations. In the five years between 1963 and 1968, the country was stunned by four assassinations: those of President Kennedy, Robert Kennedy, while campaigning for the presidency, Dr. King, and Malcolm X, a black leader. Nor was violent death limited to the leadership. On May 4, 1970, Ohio National Guardsmen on the campus of Kent State University shot and killed four students who were protesting the U.S. incursion into and bombing of Cambodia; and eleven days later two black students at Jackson State College in Mississippi were killed by police gunfire.

Americans of draft age, and their friends and families, watched the number of American troops in Vietnam rise from the 16,700 sent by President Kennedy by 1963 to the 536,000 sent by President Johnson by 1968. If their attitude was an uncertain mixture of principle and self-interest, that war had strong critics who had little else in common with young campus protesters. Matthew B. Ridgway, a hero of World War II and the field commander who rescued South Korea from the Communists of North Korea, opposed the Vietnam war from the first as a mistaken political decision. He declared in 1971, "No truly vital U.S. interest was present to threaten our national security; [our] commitment to a major effort there was a major blunder."

An editorial in the *Washington Post* called Vietnam "a generation-wide catastrophe," and so it was. But as the student protest movement exploded on their campuses, college and university administrators had difficulty in equating the violence with the reality that the war was being fought by those young men who were not in college: by the undereducated, the poor, the minorities. At the same time, some faculty members were placed in an insufferable position in grading their students, for to fail a male student in his courses made him subject to the draft.

And so black students and white, generally in separate organizations, rose up in protest and struck at the institution nearest at hand: the college. Thus the years of the 1960s and early 1970s lent an intensity to student concerns that had never before existed in this country.

Most protest demonstrations were conducted peaceably, and few protesters were violent; but some of their leaders, a minority of politically extreme students and dedicated agitators, caused enormous damage and disruption on campuses in the years of the troubles. In the first six months of 1968, about 39,000 students were involved in 221 major demonstrations on 101 campuses. In the two school years between 1968 and 1970, some 11,200 students were arrested. Legislators were under fierce pressure, particularly from their middle class and blue collar constituents, to bring the student rebellion under control. The Congress and more than half the states enacted laws to fine, imprison, and withhold financial aid from any student found guilty of instigating or taking part in campus violence. *The Chronicle of Higher Education* surveyed twenty-eight of the campuses that suffered disruptions in 1968 and found that they had suspended or expelled more than 900 students. They had placed another 850 on warning or probation that could result in harsher penalties on a second offense.

The scenes of violence and destruction at Berkeley, where it all began in 1964 as a free-speech movement, the riots at Columbia and the armed students at Cornell, the deaths at Kent State and Jackson State—these have been imprinted on the national consciousness and are not forgotten. But a hundred other episodes on the campuses have been allowed to fade away from memory like a bad dream. To understand what university people experienced in the troubled years, one must recall some of the other unremembered academic happenings of that time.

At the University of Wisconsin, a bomb ripped through the Army Mathematical Research Center. It injured four people and killed Robert E. Fassnacht, a thirty-three-year-old professor, a postdoctoral researcher in low-temperature physics. The six-story $3.5 million building and its $1.5 million computer were destroyed. A revolutionary group warned that it would set off more bombs if its demands were not met.

At Pomona College in Claremont, California, Mary N. Keating, twenty, a secretary, was injured when a bomb wrapped as a package exploded while she was removing it from a mailbox in one of the college halls. She lost two fingers of her right hand, was blinded in one eye, and required plastic surgery to repair facial damage.

At San Francisco State College, Tim Peebles, a nineteen-year-old freshman, was blinded, his hands were torn, and his chest was crushed when he placed a dynamite pipe bomb in the office of a faculty member. A second bomb was discovered before it exploded.

At Fresno State College in California, fire bombs thrown through a window completely destroyed a new $1 million computer center.

At the State University of New York in Buffalo, 400 city police were dispatched to the campus at the request of the acting president to restore order after fourteen days of violence and disruption. A band of some two hundred students destroyed property, blocked access to buildings, terrorized secretaries, disrupted classes, and closed several buildings. Fire bombings and other forms of campus vandalism destroyed thousands of dollars of university property, including irreplaceable books.

During the years 1967–1971, "trashing," or window breaking, cost Stanford University about a quarter of a million dollars. Five sit-ins were conducted by Students for a Democratic Society (SDS). They torched the naval ROTC building and started a fire in the president's office that caused about $200,000 in damage. The house of a staff member was fire-bombed; another staff member was shot at through a window of his living room.

At the University of California in Santa Barbara, a custodian, Dover Sharp, was killed when he picked up a packaged bomb leaning against an outside door of the Faculty Club.

At Washington University in St. Louis, a student, an SDS member, was seized by authorities as he placed a fire bomb at the campus headquarters of the university ROTC. He was convicted in federal court and sentenced to five years' imprisonment.

At Lane College in Jackson, Tennessee, the science building was destroyed by arson. Damage was estimated at $400,000.

In Cambridge, Massachusetts, Harvard Yard was trashed in a night of rioting led by the November

Action Committee, an offshoot of the SDS. Thirty-five persons were arrested and 214, including 35 policemen, were treated for injuries. Damage to shops, banks, and Harvard buildings caused by rock throwing and arson was estimated at $100,000. In a separate incident, students imprisoned the dean of the college in his office for an hour and a half while, in the words of a *New York Times* reporter, they "chanted, shouted and screamed at him." Sixteen of the students were told to withdraw from Harvard, two of them permanently.

Jacques Barzun of Columbia told a House Education Subcommittee, "American universities will not recover for decades from the damage they have suffered as teaching institutions at the hands of student militants." Colleges, he said, would have to take strong means to overthrow student despotism if they were to recover at all.

The person who absorbed the impact of these assaults was the president of the college. It was he who had to make the decisions and develop the course of action. He was under increased pressures in these days from a dozen interests, each with its own opinions and advice, each with its claim on the president's time, and some with conflicting demands. He and his aides had to spend endless hours in discussion with the faculty, in answering letters from incensed citizens, in a nonstop "dialogue" with protesting students, and in developing reforms to accommodate some of the protests. Some students, however—often the leaders—had no real interest in dialogue, or reform, or accommodation through "open channels of communication." Their goal, expressed frequently in public statements, was to tear the university apart or to make it an instrument of political action. They worked to provoke the president into calling in the police, whom they then hoped to goad into conduct they could equate with overreaction and police brutality. This would demonstrate that the university was as reactionary and repressive as they wanted others to believe it was. Benjamin DeMott, Mellon Professor of Humanities at Amherst, wrote that the basic premise of the militants was absurd. "The fantasy," he said, "lies in the notion that if you're upset about Vietnam, racism,

poverty, or the general quality of life, the bridge to blow is college."

Under such pressures, some presidents found themselves unable to function effectively, or were unwilling to take the obscenity and abuse directed at them, or could not in good conscience avoid trouble temporarily by seeking peace through capitulation masquerading as reform. Some thirty presidents left their posts prematurely in 1967–1969. Successors were hard to find; some three hundred colleges were without presidents in 1969. James Perkins, who had been assaulted by his students, resigned from Cornell after concluding that the modern-day university was "anarchic at heart." Douglas Knight left Duke because he felt that he was "standing at the crossroads and there were five herds of buffalo coming down and you're in the middle." John Cafferty of the American Council on Education advised that a new breed of president was needed—"one who gets along with the police, has a thick skin, and lives in a fort." Wesley Posvar observed wryly: "University administrators find that by a single act they can at once alienate students, faculty, alumni, and the general public. As a consequence, the university seems trapped in the middle of the generation gap, drawing fire from both sides."

Student protest at the University of Pittsburgh was less radical than it was on many other campuses. It was directed first, of course, at U.S. participation in the civil war in Vietnam and at Pitt's apparent sufferance of that war in permitting the training of ROTC units, in permitting the CIA to recruit on the campus, and perhaps in conducting secret research for the military. Protest was also directed at social injustice in an attempt to extend the rights of black students, specifically through programs and reforms called for by the Black Action Society (BAS). On an independent but parallel course, women faculty members, staff, and students demanded equal opportunity and pay and an end to institutionalized discrimination against women. Finally, protest was aimed at increasing the extent of student representation in University governance and participation in decision making. The four areas of protest overlapped and merged: the protesters did not always distinguish among them as separate, unrelated issues.

From its first weeks in office in 1967, the Posvar administration took steps to anticipate, head off, absorb, or make constructive use of the protest movements arising on its own campus. Posvar began with precautionary measures: he had two documents revised to accord with changed circumstances. One was the handbook titled *Student Code of Conduct and Judicial Procedures;* the other was "Campus Disturbances," which gave guidelines for the security people to follow during student disorders. He developed contingency plans and instructions his administrators were to follow during confrontations with protesters. ("Minimal force may be employed in situations requiring self-protection. A responsible secretary should remain near a telephone to summon assistance if necessary.") He had some forms printed with blank spaces for names to be filled in and a place for the chancellor's signature and a date. The form read: "In case I am incapacitated or unable for any reason to run the University, I appoint the following people to take charge." At commencement exercises, a signed document on the lectern stated that if the ceremony was disrupted, those persons whose names appeared on the attached printed list were to be considered as having received their degrees. Posvar made known to the University community again and again "the limits of acceptable dissent and our firm intention to insure the observation of those limits."

To the Executive Committee of the Board of Trustees he said, "The University has no choice but to insist upon freedom of speech if it is to remain a university."

To the faculty: "We shall respond to the urban and racial crisis with immediate programs of community service and with educational and administrative reforms."

To administrators: "It is the duty of every university officer to maintain an orderly academic environment and to insure the personal safety of university members. We are prepared to take whatever steps are necessary to make certain that such an environment is maintained."

To a general audience: "We are today in a politics of confrontation that is quite serious in its implications. . . . Americans have the constitutional right peaceably to assemble and to petition their government for a redress of grievances. But protest at a university goes too far—and has to be stopped—when it tries to block orderly proceedings and infringes upon the rights of those who want to work and study there."

To the students: "I find much that is admirable in student demands for social justice and international peace, and if our democratic institutions are to survive, we must not only tolerate, but encourage their efforts at constructive change. Failure to eliminate injustice and war or to find easy solutions to the complex social problems that plague our nation, however, is no justification for bedlam, violence or hateful incivility. If we value our freedoms, we must value equally the exercise of those freedoms by others with whose views we may disagree. . . . Free inquiry, open discussion of issues and continuing search for truth are the heart of academic freedom, and academic freedom lies at the heart of the university."

Posvar accepted the faculty's resolution not to enter into contracts for secret research with the government, the military, or private corporations. He revealed that in one of his first administrative acts he had canceled the University's program for rewriting military manuals in readable, understandable prose. He accepted without protest the decision of the Faculty of Arts and Sciences to discontinue ROTC as a credit course, since that action was within their jurisdiction. He publicly called for an end to the incursion into Vietnam (see page 377).

Concerning the status of women at the University, Posvar affirmed that "the University of Pittsburgh is opposed to all forms of discrimination. . . . The University favors equal opportunities for women in respect to both education and employment." He defended the University's record but acknowledged that "much improvement is still needed" and initiated a comprehensive study of programs, policies, and procedures as they related to women.

In the matter of governance, the administration's considered course was to attempt to weave the rising demands for student power into the administrative fabric of the University. "I strongly believe in student participation in the decision-making and formulating policy," Posvar said in 1968. "Students are underrepresented. Many questions facing us could be better answered with a continuing input of student opinion and advice. . . . In almost every instance in which we consulted students—on dormitory design, registration procedure, library regulations, rules for student conduct, academic options, and degree requirements—we found their advice useful and original."

In September 1968 Posvar announced a means for developing such student participation in policy making. He asked each dean to expand the use of an undergraduate and a graduate student cabinet in his school. These cabinets were henceforth to give the dean advice on curriculum and instructional matters. Department chairmen as well as deans were urged to seek more student opinion in academic policy issues.

The provost, chief academic officer of the University, was asked to establish an academic council in each of the undergraduate schools. This would be composed of representatives chosen by the Student Cabinets, and it would meet regularly under the chairmanship of an assistant provost. It would be matched with a similar council at the graduate level.

In all this, a basic principle was upheld: that final authority in all scholarly affairs was still vested in the faculties of the schools and departments. "I am proposing," Posvar said, "what many people would consider to be drastic innovations in university governance. It is my hope that you, as students, will take most seriously my desire for the University to benefit from your views on matters that go beyond the social life of the campus, matters that embrace the fundamental values of the educational process."

Pitt students now had a major voice in major decisions—if they cared to use and work at it. Their cabinets could help write the rules on their own behavior and on breaches of those rules. They controlled the student organizations, including the funds that they paid to operate them. They were represented in policy meetings of the University academic community at a time when the councils were considering important revisions of curriculum, degree requirements, grading requirements, and admissions policies.

Some students believed that the councils were a delaying tactic, an attempt to pacify militant students without actually permitting any change. One of the campus leaders, Richard Bernstein, an industrial engineering senior from Cleveland, did not agree. In a letter to the *Pitt News,* with four cosigners, he challenged the attitude "that meaningful change is impossible within the present power structure." Creation of the administrative councils, he said, "will give students as much a voice in decision-making as I feel is feasibly possible. Dr. Posvar is intent on making it a reality. . . . As a student, I can't pursue a full load of courses and decide what I am going to take next term and decide how it's to be taught." Posvar, he said, "is a man concerned with the wishes of faculty and students. He said he would act on recommendations and not ignore them. He has shown he is with the students. Last spring, when about thirty students were arrested, he left a formal party in his tux and went down to the police and bailed them out."*

Bernstein had left the ranks of the student power advocates on two main issues. They based their demands, he said, on a democratic University structure, but they represented less than 1 percent of the student body. And they demanded that if their recommendations were not acted on within two weeks they would automatically go into effect, which was totally unrealistic. "You can't enact changes in two weeks; you have to consider the trustees and the legislators. And what if ten or twenty demands were turned in at one time?"

In October 1968 Posvar held the first of several Speak Your Peace conferences in the Student Union ballroom. "Administrators," he said to some fifty students and thirty faculty and administrative people, "are concerned with what their position should be. The administration should not have interests of its own, but should serve the welfare of the institution as a whole. The essence of the University

---

*On this occasion one of the students being released looked at the chancellor's black tie and dinner jacket and said, "Oh, Dr. Posvar! You didn't need to dress for us."

is the relation between faculty and students. When this relationship is faulty, the institution breaks down. This is what happened at Columbia." He joined a coffee hour that followed his talk and sat in on some of the ten group sessions that met to discuss social regulations, the commuter problem, off-campus housing, language requirements, admissions and counseling, the decision-making process, athletics, social rules of fraternities and sororities, grades and teaching, the role of student government, and academics. These meetings were typical of the administration's approach to the student rebellion that was fermenting in the 1960s.

Other steps were taken that went beyond dialogue, discussion, and the promised benefits of "open lines of communication."

• The University began a program in which Pitt students volunteered a tutorial service to disadvantaged children.

• Pitt faculty and graduate students began a voluntary operation to offer their expertise in response to community requests for technical assistance.

• The University opened Trees Hall to the neighboring community. This program, paid for by the University and outside donors, brought some fifty-five thousand people a year to the University's swimming pools and gymnasium at no charge during free periods in the afternoons and evenings. A committee that included persons from the community, largely black, planned and supervised the activities.

• The University supported a coalition of minority leaders in Pittsburgh who were working to bring more minority members into the building-trades unions. To that end the chancellor announced a suspension of new construction on the campus pending satisfactory progress. At the same time the University asked state and federal agencies to investigate construction jobs on its campus for possible discriminatory hiring practices by contractors and craft unions. If there were violations of the 1964 Civil Rights Act, Posvar said, and if unlawful discrimination could not be eliminated by negotiation, he would consider halting projects already under way in the University's $200 million building program.

• "Sensitivity training" sessions, organized by a professor of psychiatric medicine, were held for forty key University people, including the deans. Once a week for six to eight weeks they met in groups of eight with two black discussion leaders. The purpose: to help people to recognize and discuss racial biases and attitudes and to create a good climate for the social justice programs the University was undertaking.

• The University held a day-long seminar on black-white relations for 300 student leaders.

• The University began a training program to make the campus police more fully aware of the causes of racial unrest and friction.

• The University entered into a consortium with Temple and Penn State to encourage recruitment of black students and to set up a plan for fellowship support.

• The University began a special graduate fellowship program to increase the numbers of women's and minority groups among the faculty and administrators. It did this through the Provost's Development Fund, which awarded grants or loans to support those "who have evidenced both a desire to teach or administer at the college level and . . . a capacity for such undertakings." The financial support enabled candidates to acquire the advanced training and credentials that would lead to Ph.D. degrees and to positions of substantial responsibility with the University.

A saying among educators in the 1960s was "You can't understand it unless you are on the campus." Blacks in the 1960s told whites, "I can't explain it to you. You have to be black."

In the spring of 1968 Posvar held a number of meetings with representatives of the BAS. In reporting to the Council of Deans and Campus Presidents, he said that he had initiated steps "to meet the more reasonable demands of the group." The demands were:

To establish a black studies program with black professors to teach such subjects as black history and culture, sociology, music, English, fine arts, and anthropology, which would portray the true role of

HARD TO SERVE TWO MASTERS

CHANCELLOR POSVAR

HARD BOILED TREATMENT OF DEFIANT STUDENTS

SOFT TREATMENT OF STUDENT TROUBLE MAKERS

DEMAND OF STATE SENATE

DEMAND OF PITT REBELS

$ STATE AID?

PITT

CATHEDRAL OF LEARNING

The multiple dilemmas of the chancellorship, seen by Hungerford as a determined balancing act by Wesley Posvar.

black people in history;

To establish a black history research center in the library;

To recruit more black faculty and staff;

To recruit more black students. (The BAS originally demanded that at least 51 percent of the next freshman class be black, but it dropped that point.)

Posvar's goal in 1969 was to double the number of black freshmen and to do so without damage to academic standards. It was important, he told his deans, "that lines of communication be kept open and that we strive for sincerity, for the young black leaders want to believe us but they are skeptical and suspicious." He told of one member of the black community who said, "For 300 years, blacks and whites have been playing a ball game in America, and they've completed 4½ innings. Now our white brothers say to us, 'For the past 4½ innings we've been cheating you, but we're not going to do that any more. From now on we're going to play fair.' The only trouble with this is that the score is 100 to nothing."

Posvar and his staff faced two major problems in attempting to make academic reforms and to fulfill their commitments to students, black and white. For one thing, there was by no means a unanimity of opinion on the campus that such an effort should be made, let alone how it was to be carried out if made. Trustees, administrators, teaching and research faculty, staff people, and students were far from united on changes in academic policy and the introduction of affirmative action programs calculated to rectify past and present injustices. The divisions in society, in fact, with their doubts and prejudices, were reflected to a degree on the campus. Some faculty members who supported protesting students on the Vietnam issue did not welcome their drive to throw open to scrutiny professors' records on student performance. Some were uncomfortable discussing departmental policy before an audience of students. Some were offended at those students who not only opposed U.S. actions in Vietnam but also cheered the successes of the Communist army invading from the north. There was some indifference and some foot dragging in these months. BAS leaders knew it, and they decided to take what they considered appropriate action. One of them said later, "We had to do something that would attract their attention."

The second problem in meeting black demands was the wide gap between commitment and capacity to perform. It was one thing to promise sincerely to enroll some hundreds of black students and another to find students with the ability and educational background to succeed in courses at the university level. It was one thing to promise a black studies program and quite another to produce the professors qualified to teach it. There were at that time, for example, only a few more than 100 blacks in the

United States with Ph.D. degrees in political science. Most black militants refused to recognize shortage as a problem; to them, failure to sign on twenty black professors and enroll 500 black undergraduates was simply a willful refusal by white administrators to act. Some black leaders, however, saw the problem whole. They warned of the damage that would be done to black students by a double standard on admissions and grades and by a degree that was suspect to those concerned with academic standards. Bayard Rustin, civil rights activist who organized the famous 1963 March on Washington, called on college officials to stop capitulating to extreme demands of black students and instead to "see that they get the remedial training they need."

The irony of the situation was not missed by educators. The universities desperately needed qualified black teachers and administrators. They could not find them. The reason they could not find them was that the universities had made no effort in the past three or four decades to search out qualified young black people, train them, and employ them. Now when they were needed, too few of them existed.

The first confrontation at Pitt began on Wednesday, January 15, 1969, shortly before one in the afternoon, when some seventy black students crowded into the chancellor's outer office and the hallway on the first floor of the Cathedral of Learning and demanded a meeting with Dr. Posvar. When the secretary-receptionist told them he was not in, they said they would wait. The students placed guards at the outer door. In one of the truly remarkable scenes in the history of the University, one of the trustees—a jurist, a recent Republican candidate for mayor of the city, and a man of some dignity—appeared at the chancellor's office at this moment to fulfill an appointment. He was greeted at the door by two towering students dressed in dashikis and carrying spears who told him he could not enter. The judge was outraged and expected the police to be called instantly. Thereafter, the guards allowed people to enter and leave on the request of the secretary.

Posvar returned to his office from a meeting downtown at 3:00 P.M. and talked with the students for a half-hour behind closed doors. They were orderly but tense; their manner was hostile and their language intemperate. Their main complaint was that agreements made with the BAS in May, eight months earlier, had not been carried out; nothing was happening and they would wait no longer. When they presented a list of grievances and demands, Posvar, surrounded by milling students, refused to read or discuss it under such conditions of intimidation. Even if he did, he said, no commitment he made under coercion would be valid. In that case, he was told, something terrible was going to happen. The students then demanded that he declare that day, the birthdate of Martin Luther King, Jr., a permanent University holiday. He said he did not have the authority unilaterally to declare any University holiday, but he would refer their request to the faculty, deans, and department chairmen. He would suggest to them that blacks be allowed to miss classes on that date without penalty and that no exams be scheduled. He gave them official permission to be absent from classes for the rest of the day and agreed to meet with them at a later date under calmer circumstances. The students marched off to make the rounds of the campus in groups of ten or twelve to demand that classes be dismissed to honor King.

When reporters asked him if the students had made any threats, Posvar replied, "There was some angry rhetoric that probably included tacit threats." He added, "I am dissatisfied myself with the lack of progress on last summer's demands. We have made commitments. We are going to continue our efforts to fulfill them." He recalled privately a decade later, "It was a dreadful experience. All the meetings had a tinge, a threat, of extreme violence."

Posvar had taken steps as the new chancellor to recruit black undergraduates and so "to bring to the campus for the first time a freshman class that is racially composed in a way that is reasonably reflective of the general American population." He hired several black recruiters, directed a recruitment program at black veterans returning from the war in Vietnam, encouraged black students at the local two-year community college to apply to the University, and developed transitional-tutorial programs for those who arrived at the campus insufficiently prepared for university-level work. He endorsed a program in the School of Arts and Sciences called Project A, which brought fifty young blacks to the campus in the summer of 1968 for precollege preparatory work and an early start on the college curriculum. Project A students were "high risk" cases, but they were considered to be academically worth the gamble. They were given scholarships based on financial need in a program called "compensatory" and were provided with tutoring, after which they would be required to meet the same academic standards as all other University students.

The opposition to Project A that arose from unexpected sources demonstrated the appalling complexity of attempting to overcome the effects of generations of poverty and racial prejudice. Blacks who were not Project A students, having qualified for admission on their own merits, in the same manner as white students, were disturbed when they were looked upon as high-risk cases. The BAS complained that they had not been consulted on the selection of Project A students. Some national black leaders charged that in such programs the colleges were skipping over competent blacks to admit "authentic ghetto types."

In the drive to increase the number of black faculty members and staff, Pitt followed the dubious course of all other colleges at that time and raided the black colleges in the south. These new recruits were in turn subject to enticements from other colleges and from the corporate head-hunters with their big checkbooks. In order to win and hold his own in a fierce and growing competition, Posvar informed his staff that he would "be willing to pay higher salaries than we would pay to white persons of similar qualifications"—preferably within approved budgets. "If, however, the lack of a few hundred dollars will mean the loss of a black candidate, I want you to seek the additional funds from your dean, campus president, vice chancellor, provost, or, if necessary, from me." The action became known publicly, and fifteen letters of protest were received from people who lacked a clear understanding of the mandate worked by the law of supply and demand in a seller's market, even in academia.

Pitt began to establish a department of black studies in May 1968. More than a year later Posvar was "so far, not impressed by the quality of the program being developed . . . but it is too early to judge finally the outcome." The School of Engineering, with alumni help, enrolled twelve well-qualified black students in the freshman engineering class. An Afro-American collection had been set up in Hillman Library, aided by a sizable grant for books from the Hillman Foundation. But in 1969 the University had only 230 black students in a freshman class of 2,100, only 20 black faculty members in a full-time faculty of 1,400, and only 10 black students among 404 in the School of Medicine. On January 15, 1969, the day the students from the BAS crowded into his office, Dr. Posvar had reason to talk to his staff of the difficulty, as well as the importance, of the task they had undertaken and to express dissatisfaction publicly at the lack of progress they had made.

32
Confrontation II

Whatever women do they must do twice as well as men to be thought half as good. Luckily, this is not difficult.

Charlotte E. Whitton, former mayor of Ottawa, May 1979

THE "terrible thing" promised by the seventy members of the BAS took place on the same day as their visit to the chancellor's office. At eight-thirty that evening, thirty students wearing black berets went quietly to the eighth floor of the Cathedral of Learning and there burst into the machine room of the University's Computer Center. They ordered everyone to leave but permitted the operators to shut down the machines properly, thereby avoiding erasure of computer data. They then blockaded the elevator doors, barricaded the glass door of the center, and settled down for a "lock-in."

Campus police were given authority to dismiss all classes and to tell everyone—students, reporters, and curious onlookers—to leave the building. Shortly before ten o'clock, the time the doors of the center were normally locked, other black students appeared with blankets and provisions for their friends on the eighth floor. The campus police barred their entrance. Fifteen minutes later twenty city police officers arrived and took up strategic positions around the building.

Posvar arrived at his office about 10:00 P.M. He assembled a small task force: Jack Freeman, secretary of the University and his executive assistant; Jack Critchfield, assistant chancellor for student affairs; James Wolf, the University counsel; Jack Matthews, president of the Senate Council; and Jack Daniels and Norman Johnson, black faculty members. Posvar talked with the students by telephone, several of his aides taking part on extension phones. If they refused to leave, he told them, the matter would be turned over to the city police, who would eject them by force and place them under arrest. He did not want to do that. The students charged that promises made to them had not been kept. They read a list of new demands. They would not leave until the demands were met.

The task force members proceeded to analyze the situation and weigh the responses available to them. An assault by the police would almost certainly cause physical injury to some of the students, would possibly result in damage to an $8 million computer facility, and would leave a wound that could poison future relationships with black students and the black community. On the other hand, this was not a terrorist attack and so far there had been no real violence. There was no reason to believe that hardcore nonstudent agitators committed to destruction were part of the group. Under these circumstances, every effort should be made to keep the response internal and under control of the University. There was still time to choose a course between firmness and flexibility. Educators who had been through this ordeal had advised in their reports that it was best to "wait it out" as long as the conduct was not violent. One of them spoke of the need to listen for the message behind the shrillness of the rhetoric.

Everyone agreed that the new demands could not be accepted, since they could not be fulfilled, even with the best intent and the strongest effort. The new demand that "the true role of the black man" be incorporated in various University courses was clearly unreasonable, and the demand that there be a halt to University construction on land needed by the black community for residential purposes would open up a whole new area beyond academic matters. Capitulation, moreover, would set a dangerous precedent for even more extreme demands; it would leave the University vulnerable to further disorder; it would narrow the options available in responding to later disruption. The terms of the capitulation would have to be acceptable to the governing body of the University, the trustees, who could overturn it. Capitulation would anger alumni, state legislators, and much of the public.

Posvar's black advisors, after talking privately with the students, had a feeling that they would accept, perhaps welcome, a face-saving settlement if it preserved their dignity and pride. Posvar suggested, "Suppose we ignore the new demands and offer to agree on other reforms—the same reforms we discussed and agreed on last May. We can do better on those reforms than we have."

The task force drew up six points of agreement with the students:

• "The University will appoint a team to recruit additional black students. Appointments will be made as soon as BAS has screened and endorsed candidates for the recruiting team.

• "The University will recruit additional black faculty members, administrators, and other personnel. The BAS will recommend to the University where black faculty members, administrators and other personnel should be placed.

• "Material that could be used in writing a doctoral thesis relevant to Afro-Americans will be made available in sufficient quantity at Hillman Library.

• "Dr. Posvar will urge the faculty to establish an institute for black studies, with a director and assistant to be appointed by June. The two officials will be provided with necessary working capital upon their arrival at the University.

• "Dr. Posvar will recommend to the University Senate that black students and employees be excused from their duties on February 21, the assassination date of Malcolm X, without penalty. The Chancellor will also recommend that the Senate declare January 15, birthday of the late Reverend Dr. Martin Luther King, Jr., a University holiday.

• "Dr. Posvar will address himself to the other demands made by the BAS last May 20 without unnecessary delay."

The students said they would not agree to these points unless there was a written commitment that no punitive action would be taken against them. Posvar was willing to run the risks of adding amnesty to the terms of the agreement, but only if the students vacated the machine room without committing any damage.

The students left the Computer Center peaceably at three o'clock in the morning, after 6½ hours of occupation and 5 of negotiation. They had done no damage to property, and they had, in a Western Pennsylvania colloquialism, "redd up the room."

Joseph Colangelo called the news media and read them the seven-part agreement. He did not convey the point, or the media ignored it, that the issues were almost identical with those that had been agreed on in May and were slowly being introduced on the campus. The *Press* headline read, "Black Rebels Get 7-Point Program—Pitt Sit-in Ends: Posvar Grants Demands." The *Pitt News* had a page-one banner: "'Pressured' Chancellor Complies 'Positively' with Black Demands." There was public outcry and dissatisfaction that the perpetrators of the lock-in had escaped punishment. A brave call to battle, expressed in letters to the editors and to the chancellor, seemed to be built on the message "Let's you and him fight. I'll hold your coat."

In reporting to alumni and friends of the University, Posvar wrote: "There was no violence, no injury to persons, and no damage to property. The University did not agree to any demands to which it was not already committed or that were considered unreasonable.

"While I do not condone the students' actions, I believe our response to this incident was in the best interest of the University, and that the majority of the faculty, students and trustees agree. Those who say that we should have reacted to this situation by immediately calling the police and expelling the students, before any attempt to communicate with them, do not, in my opinion, understand the facts of this incident. . . . It must be understood that the actual situations we face do not always present us with simple and unambiguous choices."

A second and milder confrontation began on February 7, 1969, when some eight hundred students and spectators staged a demonstration in the Commons Room to rally support for six demands that were being presented to the administration:

• remove the ROTC from the campus.

• take a public stand against a state bill that would punish students engaged in campus disturbances.

• "unequivocally expose and oppose" students who, the demonstrators believed, were informers for the FBI. (One student recommended that a suspected informer should be publicly exposed and his picture printed in the school newspaper.)

• allow faculty and teaching fellows to discard the grading system if they wished.

• stop the practice of the Office of the Dean of Students of keeping secret and unauthorized personal files on nearly all undergraduate female students.

• pay for and print a student magazine called *Alternatives*, which the University printer had refused to touch because it had what he felt was obscene language. The students considered this a violation of free speech and later demanded that the printer be fired.

Posvar spoke for forty-five minutes, commenting on each of the demands and fielding questions from the floor.

On March 11 an all-white group that called itself Concerned Students and Faculty announced that it would conduct a round-the-clock fast in Lawrence Hall for three days but that its action would be peaceful and nondisruptive. Some 200 members of the group met in the Commons Room at noon to discuss their plans, and about 180 of these marched to Lawrence Hall and occupied the lobby of the building. Two faculty members canceled their evening classes in the building, which displeased the night students. The group demanded that henceforth all University policy meetings should be thrown open to everyone for hearing and discussion. No files should be kept on a student that he or she could not see at any time. Student failures and withdrawals from classes should not be recorded. Scholastic grade averages should be abolished. All physical education facilities should be open to the public. The University should publish a list of all its defense contracts. All employees working for the contractor that supplied the food service should be paid at least the federal minimum of $1.60 an hour. And the University should give the organization a hall, furniture, money, and maintenance for an "open university," which would give courses without structure, running twenty-four hours a day, in which "meaningful discussions" could be held continuously.

The Concerned Students and Faculty, now 350 strong, had brought in sleeping bags and were holding meaningful discussions, playing cards, listening to rock music, and studying. Three official attempts were made to persuade them to leave Lawrence Hall, which had a ten o'clock closing time, and move to the Student Union, which had no classes and no deadline for closing. That proposal was rejected.

At 9:00 P.M. Jack Critchfield announced that the building would be closed in one hour. At 10:00 P.M. the University police began to lock the doors, per-

mitting students to leave but no one to enter. About 170 students left. At 10:45 Jack Freeman made an announcement: "It is expected that this building will be vacated by 11 o'clock." At 11:15 the acting chief of the University police declared, "This building is officially closed."

Posvar, in the meantime, had decided "with deep regret" to ask for a court injunction requiring the students to vacate the building, since they were obstructing the orderly administration of University business and were threatening the rights of other students. Ronald Pease, dean of student affairs, announced this decision in a "last warning" at 11:30. Anyone who did not leave, he said, would face suspension or dismissal. The Concerned Students and Faculty pondered this development and voted to depart peacefully, but only after the court order had actually been served. In this way, they said, they would maintain their position by not capitulating and yet would not resort to violence, which they all opposed.

A constable appeared in Lawrence Hall about 3:30 A.M. A frail, elderly gentleman, he introduced himself as "your new professor" and, standing in the middle of the lobby, began to read the court order. He had forgotten his glasses, however, and had to borrow a pair from one of the students. When he finished the students cheered and applauded his performance. They packed their gear, cleaned up the lobby, and at 4:30 A.M. left the building. About seventy went to the Student Union ballroom to continue the sit-in and fast. The next day they moved again, to a large, unfinished room in the Social Sciences Building (now Thackeray Hall).

On March 14 at 12:32 P.M. the three-day sit-in and fast ended. About one hundred students were present to applaud the survivors, whose leaders immediately called a press conference. A statement released by the University said: "The original principle on which the University had insisted has been preserved: that unilateral action on the part of students in the occupation and use of campus facilities is never an acceptable procedure for academic discourse. But it also recognizes that throughout this period the students conducted themselves in an

A press conference in the chancellor's office at the time of the March 1969 sit-in of Concerned Students and Faculty.

orderly, non-disruptive, non-violent and otherwise reasonable manner, which must be commended."

A *Pittsburgh Press* editorial complimented the University for handling the situation with restraint; a news story carried the lead "Posvar Keeps His Cool in Strife."

About the same time the Concerned Students and Faculty began their Open University in space provided in the Social Sciences Building. The seminars in this program were titled The Importance of the Working Class, Student Movements in Spain, Counter Culture, An Alternative to the Lecture System, and The New Right. Students were not interested; they failed to attend; the Open University folded.

Another national movement that was to affect the University profoundly in the late sixties and early seventies derived from women's growing awareness that they, like blacks and other minorities, suffered from institutionalized discrimination. Spurred on by Betty Friedan's *The Feminine Mystique* (1963), by the report of President Kennedy's Commission on the Status of Women (1963), and by inclusion in the Civil Rights Act of 1964 of a ban on job discrimination based on sex, women's groups all over the country were calling attention to the inequities they suffered and demanding redress.

In the fall of 1969, the issue of discrimination against women at the University was raised by a newly formed organization of students, staff, and faculty headed by Ina Braden, assistant professor of dental behavioral science. The University Committee for Women's Rights (UCWR) charged that in every area of its operation the University worked to the disadvantage of women. Not only were the decision makers in the administration and faculty almost exclusively male (there were two female deans, one at the School of Nursing and one at the School of Health Related Professions), but their attitudes and actions, intentionally or not, kept University women from realizing their full potential. Admissions policies resulted in undergraduate classes where males outnumbered females but had somewhat lower qualifications, and a medical school with only 7 percent women. Financial aid was awarded more frequently and in larger amounts to men than to women. The job placement service, run by men, steered women graduates into traditionally low-paying, dead-end jobs. Among both staff and faculty, women were clustered in low-status jobs, with low pay and little chance for promotion. Only 3 percent of the full professors were women (nationwide the figure was 9 percent, and within the twenty leading universities, 5 percent). Only 9 percent of the associate professors and 17 percent of the assistant professors were women. Of the instructors, the lowest academic rank, 31 percent were women. The UCWR also attacked the University's staff grievance procedure, its antinepotism policy, and the use of sex-segregated want ads even when sex was not a bona fide occupational qualification.

Throughout the fall and winter of 1969–1970, the UCWR continued to air women's grievances against the University. With support from other Pittsburgh feminists—among them Eleanor Smeal, who later became national president of the National Organization for Women (NOW); Jo Ann Gardner, founder of KNOW, Inc., a feminist press; and Wilma Scott Heide—the UCWR held a series of meetings with departmental chairmen, deans, and administrators. Its goal was "to foster the welfare of women associated with the University of Pittsburgh . . . by promoting change in all University practices which work to the economic, social, or psychological detri-

ment of women." Women also made presentations before the University Senate and the Senate Council demanding equal treatment for women, child care services, and a program of women's studies.

In response to this broad-ranging attack, Posvar acknowledged that discrimination against women was prevalent in society at large but asserted that University policy prohibited it. He addressed a memo to deans, directors, department chairmen, and regional campus presidents: "The University of Pittsburgh has a policy on non-discrimination in employment and in educational opportunities, consistent with federal, state, and local laws. . . . This policy means that the sex of a student shall not be a factor in determining who will be admitted, given financial support, and recommended for placement after the student has completed his academic work. Women employees must be recruited, hired, paid, and promoted on the same basis with men. It is the responsibility of each of you in carrying out the regular duties of your office, to insure that discrimination does not exist in the areas for which you are responsible and that any discrimination now existing is removed as soon as possible."

As a public protest organization, the UCWR reached its peak when it staged a "teach-in" in the chancellor's office on May 18, 1970. Arriving at 9 A.M., only to find that Posvar had a dental appointment, the women settled down to wait. He arrived at 11:15 and immediately held a meeting with them that lasted until shortly after noon. The women presented a series of demands that included the appointment of women to top administrative positions, the establishment of an interdisciplinary school for women's studies, immediate changes "to insure equality between the sexes" in the policies and practices of all schools and departments, and a public report every six months on the progress made toward full equality for women. Appended to these demands were suggestions for implementation: free child care; flexible work schedules; realistic job classifications; unemployment benefits; equal pay for equal work; full status and proportional pay for part-time faculty and staff; nondiscriminatory retirement benefits accessible to both staff and faculty;

Pittsburgh Press

Posvar attends a student meeting in 1970.

appointment of women to search committees, tenure review committees, and other decision-making bodies; nondiscriminatory criteria for financial aid to students; active recruitment of women faculty and graduate students; equal housing for men and women students; and legal enforcement of fair admissions practices. They were demanding, in short, a "curriculum and atmosphere designed to give women a sense of self-esteem and to maximize their leadership abilities."

Posvar told the women: "I admit this problem of injustice exists and something will be done. I will respond as quickly and as reasonably as possible." At 5 P.M., when the women returned, he had an answer. Although rejecting a quota system for hiring, he supported "a policy of rectifying injustice by making efforts to recruit for appointment members of groups that are discriminated against, based upon criteria of full qualification for the positions involved." Regarding committee assignments he said, "I am requesting the President of the University Senate to take the interests of women into account when he makes committee appointments. . . . I shall do the same." The proposals for women's studies and child care he put off for further study. In a supplementary memo of May 25 he said: "First, let me reiterate that the University of Pittsburgh is vitally interested in the advancement of women in our society and within the University itself. . . . After careful consideration of the concerns that you and others have expressed, and after reviewing generally the status of women at the University, I have decided to ask the various elements of the University to undertake a thorough examination of their programs and procedures to determine what additional steps the University can take to improve the educational and vocational opportunities of women."

After months of protest activity, the women were discouraged by what they perceived as stonewalling—assertions of good intentions and referrals to committees for further study. Unlike the other protest movements that had shaken the University in the sixties, the women at Pitt turned to legal action to support their charges and demands. A letter from Braden to George Schultz, then secretary of labor, in March 1970, initiated a formal complaint against the University under Executive Orders 11246 and 11375, which prohibit sex discrimination by federal contractors. In this letter she wrote: "At the University of Pittsburgh women observe that the Blacks have achieved at least a beginning toward most of the goals of full and equal participation in University life which are now being denied women. The method which was effective in producing these accomplishments for Blacks was violence at both the local and national level. If this is not to become the only method of achieving equality in this country then peaceful methods *must* be afforded immediate attention and action." The complaint was referred to the Department of Health, Education, and Welfare, which scheduled a compliance review for later

that summer. One result of the visit by federal officers to the Pitt campus was the withholding of $15 million in new federal funding until the University developed an affirmative action plan.

Other lawsuits followed. Ina Braden filed a class action suit in July 1971 accusing the University of a variety of discriminatory acts against herself and all other professional women employed at Pitt since January 1968. This case was still in the courts when Braden died in early 1979. Other women filed with the U.S. Equal Employment Opportunities Commission. Prominent among them was Sharon L. Johnson, an assistant professor in the School of Medicine's biochemistry department, a member of the American Society of Biological Chemists and the American Chemical Society, who had received over $300,000 in research grants between 1963 and 1972 from the National Institutes of Health and the National Science Foundation. She charged that the medical school had denied her tenure because of her sex. The case was finally decided in August 1977 when U.S. District Court Judge William W. Knox ruled that statistics showed that sex discrimination did exist in the School of Medicine in 1972, but that there was no discrimination evident in the denial of tenure to Dr. Johnson.

In response to the feminist activity of 1969–1970, Chancellor Posvar in June 1970 called on the University administration to institute a "comprehensive study of University programs, policies, and procedures relating to the education, employment, and career development of women in the University." He concurrently established the Advisory Committee (later Council) on Women's Opportunities (ACWO), composed of representatives of faculty, students, administrators, and one member of the UCWR, with task forces to study various areas of concern to women. The ACWO, along with other groups and individuals, developed two programs of lasting benefit to women at Pitt. One task force succeeded in obtaining approval for a women's studies program to begin in the fall of 1972. Three new faculty were hired: Mary Briscoe, a joint appointment with the Department of English; Irene Frieze (Psychology); and Maurine Greenwald (History). The second outgrowth of the ACWO's deliberations was the establishment, with the approval of the Faculty Senate, of the Women's Center, whose purpose was to provide walk-in support services for women and to address such nonacademic problems relating to women as child care, maternity and paternity leave, salary scales, and fringe benefits. The center opened in the autumn of 1973 and was funded by the University until 1982, when it became the Oakland Women's Center.

Protests and demonstrations continued on the Pitt campus through 1971 and 1972. Students marched from the campus to Mellon Square downtown in the nationwide student-coordinated all-day moratorium to protest the war in Vietnam. They demonstrated when the United States bombed Cambodia and when National Guardsmen killed four students at Kent State. Posvar sent a telegram to London: "I regret very much that I must cancel attendance at the Institute for Strategic Studies meeting this week. The possibility of civil disorders in this city requires my presence near my university." The Concerned Students and Faculty announced that they would attend a full meeting of the Board of Trustees, where they intended to discuss ways by which the University could "disengage itself from the clutches of corporate power." When denied permission, some forty members of the group on the day of the meeting blocked the elevator to the Babcock Room on the fortieth floor of the Cathedral. Posvar was held by force for a time in the elevator; he kicked himself free. Fire bombs were found early one morning taped to the windows of the chancellor's and Jack Freeman's offices; the fuses had burned out. Vice Chancellor Van Dusen's office was fire-bombed. Posvar, inspecting the charred interior, suggested that it be left unchanged and named "The Twentieth Century Room." Four members of SDS, visitors from another city, seized an area in Hillman Library and threatened to fire bomb it. They were persuaded to depart by a team headed by history professor Samuel P. Hays.

The protests continued, but now they began to take on a milder tone and even, on occasion, a touch of humor. Miss Rebecca Gittings, Class of 1973, sent the chancellor a stern letter: "I will expect a refund of $6.93 for each class that is cancelled." Bernard Kobosky, director of admissions, lamented that a federal agency required him to report how many black students were enrolled at Pitt, and another federal agency forbade him to ask the racial origin of any student. One of the ephemeral student papers charged Posvar with a most horrendous offense: he was "a representative *of the administration!*" Heavy plexiglass was installed on the windows of the first-floor Cathedral of Learning offices. The chancellor's reception room was remodeled so that it could be cut off from the rest of the suite. The campus community laughed at the story, told in a commencement address, of the student who filled in a government application form that asked, "Do you believe in force, subversion, or civil disorder?" Thinking it was a multiple-choice question, he put a circle around civil disorder. In January 1970 the birthday of Martin Luther King, Jr., was declared a University holiday. The Black Studies Program, chaired by Jack Daniels, now had sixteen courses, a faculty of ten instructors, and 270 students; it gave promise of becoming an academically viable department in the College of Arts and Sciences. The Women's Studies Program opened with some four hundred students enrolled in courses in anthropology, English, history, psychology, and sociology. By 1976–1977 it had 1,800 students, with more than fifty certificate candidates. The personal records on female students in the Office of the Dean of Students were burned under the watchful eyes of a student committee. The hourly wage of the food service workers was raised from the minimum allowed for nonprofit institutions to the full $1.60 required of commercial establishments, which the administration said it had intended to do all along. The University Computer Center was moved to a suburb on the northern edge of the city.

By 1973 it was clear that the University had survived the years of violent protest without loss of life, without physical harm to any person, and with minimal damage to property. Various explanations are given for that escape from serious trouble or disaster, but the dominant reason has to be the course of action followed by the University administration.

The chancellor, despite fire from all sides, held fast to a moderate strategy aimed at solving the problem, determined not to fan the flames, not to be provoked into unwise action, not to oblige those who advised an unrestrained response. He and his staff managed to endure the long negotiations that called for much tolerance and infinite patience. (Time after time Posvar emerged from conferences at which agreements for reforms had been made only to find the student representatives brandishing papers before television cameras with bellicose assertions that these were the demands the administration was going to be forced to meet.) There were the contingency plans; the flexible responses; the sensitivity-training classes; the sharing of decision-making powers and administrative responsibility with students; the serious efforts to carry out needed reforms—preferably before they were demanded, though that displeased the students. The goal was to preserve a relationship in which—when the unrest subsided—the work of the administration, the faculty, and the students could continue without tension or disruption.

On October 5, 1970, appeared *The Scranton Report—Text of the President's Commission on Campus Unrest,* a well-researched and intelligently written document produced under the direction of William W. Scranton, former governor of Pennsylvania. In a carefully thought-out analysis of a national problem, the causes and conditions of student unrest were examined, and advice was given on the best course to follow during the different forms and phases of campus violence. The advice bears a striking, almost chapter-and-verse resemblance to those responses developed earlier by the Posvar administration.*

The University was also fortunate in the character and background of its students. Many were the children or grandchildren of immigrants who still lived in or had ties to ethnic neighborhoods where the church, the social hall, and the family next door influenced customs, manners, and morality. Many were children of blue collar wage earners, factory or mill workers, who, though well paid in the 1960s, were making sacrifices to send their sons and daughters to the University—the first of some families to try that giant step. Such children, it is believed, did not readily take to campus riots or to the risks of rebellion against academic authority over issues that were not terribly important to them, or on which they did not agree with the dissenting students.

Other reasons were also given. The University fortunately seems to have had few New Left professional agitators among its students and faculty—that is, destructive-minded representatives of SDS, the Student Nonviolent Coordinating Committee, the Weathermen, the December 4th Movement (D4M), and the Maoist Progressive Labor Party, some of them not students, who provided leadership and monitored classes for political content on campuses in California, New York City, and New England in 1966–1972.† A top administrator believes further that Quaker leadership, with its total devotion to nonviolence, had a beneficent influence on the students at critical moments, notably in ending the SDS threat to Hillman Library. He believes that the substantially increased participation of students in University governance and the trend of students to seek their goals through political action were also factors. He sees the killing of students at Kent State and Jackson State in May 1970 as a turning point: it had a sobering effect on those student leaders who realized that they had brought to a tragic point a movement they could no longer control; and it shocked society with the realization that it was shooting its own children.

In any event, by March 1973 American troops were out of Vietnam. Students now became concerned about finding jobs on graduation, and moderates were wielding influence in student power

---

*Wesley Posvar and Vice Chancellor Bernard Kobosky testified before the Scranton Commission. The University gave it free secretarial and legal services.

†The Pitt chapter of SDS on October 5, 1969, changed its name to the Revolutionary Socialist Union. It did so, officers explained to the Oakland Rotary Club, because it differed sharply with two other SDS factions. Both of those factions were "Maoist oriented" and both were "closer to anarchistic tendencies," while the Pitt wing was "oriented toward socialist goals." The national SDS headquarters, the officers complained, was controlled by anarchists.

groups. Some students had decided to "work within the system" and were doing so creatively and productively. Some others had become bored with the tedious work of restructuring the University—a task Wesley Posvar once described as trying to kick a mastodon into action.

Whatever the lasting effects of the protest movement nationwide—good, or bad, or both—brutal and dangerous in its excesses, constructive in some of the issues it raised, there can be no doubt of the importance of goals now generally agreed upon. A university must make its students partners in the educational adventure and representatives in university governance. A university has special obligations to its racial minorities and to the less-privileged segments of society. As educator and employer, the university has both a moral and legal obligation to treat men and women equally.

33

1976: The Turning Point

Liberal education is concerned with what is worth knowing about people and their world, not for the sake of something else but in its own right. Such an education deals with perennial questions about human nature, the meaning of life, good and evil, the physical universe. The educated person is one who has become accustomed to asking such questions with some degree of skill, partly as a consequence of familiarity with how others have asked and answered these questions.

Among the ways in which the perennial questions have been addressed, three are particularly appropriate to liberal education. These three ways may be labeled reason, art, and history.

Committee on Curriculum Reform, "Report to the Faculty," September 24, 1981

On August 23, 1976, the University marked its tenth anniversary as a member of the Commonwealth System of Higher Education. The record of those ten years, despite their coincidence with the dislocations of the Vietnam War era, is impressive. The figures and the facts are good—that is, the numbers commonly used to measure physical growth and, if possible, to dazzle university watchers, as well as the honors, awards, and commissions commonly cited to prove enhancement of quality. There were problems, too, and misfires, but Pitt did indeed have sustained growth and demonstrable achievement in the ten-year period that Wesley Posvar has described as "unreal" and "a time of great budgets and euphoria."

• The University doubled its enrollment on the five campuses, growing from approximately 17,800 students in 1966 to 35,374 in 1976.

• It delivered 55,811 trained and educated young men and women into the world, most of them to live and work in Western Pennsylvania: 30,166 with undergraduate degrees; 25,645 with postbaccalaureate degrees.

• It increased its full-time faculty from approximately 1,580 to 2,200.

• It increased its library holdings by more than 1.6 million entries, to a total of 3.5 million volumes, including microtext, in twenty departmental and associated libraries. The Law School library and the Falk medical library became the University's prime reference sources within their areas of specialization.

• In these ten years the faculty competed for and won grants and contracts for externally sponsored programs and research worth more than $325 million.

• The University in 1975 became by invitation a member of the Association of American Universities, a select group of fifty institutions strong in graduate work, professional schools, and research. According to the perceptions of the other forty-nine members, Pitt was thus recognized as one of the top publicly supported research universities in the United States.

Some of the most important developments took place in 1976—the year that Wesley Posvar called "a turning point between our efforts of the past ten years and of the next ten"—the year in which the University "entered an era of reality, a new stage in its evolution."

• The University became a founding member of Urban Public Universities (UPU), an organization established in April 1976. UPU called for a program somewhat similar to the land-grant concept of a century earlier that had produced legislation to support colleges in the rural community. Federal urban grants, the founders of UPU said, "would enable us to better serve the cities and metropolitan areas in which we live and to address urban problems." Among the twenty founding members were Temple, UCLA, Indiana, City University of New York, and the University of Illinois at Chicago.

• In April 1976 the University paid certain debts, including $6.375 million to Equitable Life, and in so doing discharged its back obligations, internal and external, incurred during the Litchfield administration. In a small, happy ceremony in the chancellor's office, Posvar put a match to the mortgage on the University's buildings.

• The administration in 1976 developed the University's first full-fledged formal program to honor academic achievement—an Honors Program that was to reward outstanding scholarly performance among the students as well as superior skills and demonstrated excellence among the teachers.

• The annual giving fund in 1976 for the first time passed the $1 million mark—a sum contributed by 20,011 donors, also a record.

• In 1976 three unions sought to represent faculty, nonteaching professionals, and clerical staff as their collective bargaining agents. After many months of hearings, the Pennsylvania Labor Relations Board ordered five universitywide elections. Although the vote was close in a runoff election, all attempts to win bargaining rights failed.

• On January 13, 1976, the trustees in full session approved a massive document loosely called the University Plan. In preparation for several years under the direction of the Office of Planning and Budget, the plan was created as part of a comprehensive program to guide the orderly development and management of the University. The plan was an attempt to overlay the complexities of academe with corporate-style cost accounting, taking measure where measurement is almost impossible. At the core was the Planning and Resources Management System (PRMS), which was designed to provide an objective and equitable system for setting priorities and allocating resources.

● In the first ten years of Posvar's administration, the University added almost 2 million gross square feet of usable space, bringing the total of available space to more than 8 million square feet. Some 600,000 more were under construction or committed. Within the next year, one-third of the University on the Pittsburgh campus would be relocated.

Posvar in 1970 had begun a series of discussions with residents and citizens' groups in the adjacent communities, as well as with representatives of city and state governments. His purpose was to explore ways of keeping the local community informed about campus development plans and of basing those plans on mutual understanding and consent. Accommodations were made and a pact was signed. To mastermind the architecture and siting of the new buildings, Posvar arranged for Max Abramovitz to resume his advisory and architectural services to the University.

University expansion between 1967 and 1976 included the construction of four especially notable buildings and plans for the construction of the massive Forbes Quadrangle complex, completed in 1978. The four buildings are large. They are distinctive in architectural design. They were erected for four burgeoning departments or centers desperately in need of more space. In each instance, faculty, staff, and students moved happily from offices and classrooms widely scattered about the campus into a relatively spacious home in a building bearing the name of the school or center.

The first branch of the University to occupy one of the new buildings was the School of Engineering. In 1846 that school had become the second or third in the United States to award engineering degrees. In 1868 it announced a formal four-year course of study leading to the B.S. degree in civil and mechanical engineering. It was the first school in the world to establish a petroleum engineering department and the first in the United States (in 1927) to introduce a part-time graduate program for

engineers in industry. Between the Civil War and 1907, engineering students at Pitt were more numerous than all other students combined. In 1951 an engineering research division was formed to undertake applied and theoretical research.

By the fall of 1970 the school had awarded B.S. degrees to 10,932 engineers and had in that year 1,757 full-time and 676 part-time students, both undergraduate and graduate. The cost of its high enrollment was a serious space problem. Its facilities were scattered in nine different locations.

Early in 1971 the school took over its own new building—the $15 million Michael L. Benedum Hall of Engineering, built with a gift from the Claude Worthington Benedum Foundation and funds from the General State Authority. It stands on the west end of the campus on the 1.8-acre site formerly occupied by the National Guard's Logan Armory. With its fourteen stories (two below ground) and its 419,000 square feet of space, it has a floor area equal to 80 percent of that of the Cathedral of Learning. It has 199 offices, 200 laboratories, 44 classrooms, 13 conference and seminar rooms, and a 528-seat auditorium divisible into 3 lecture halls. Its George M. Brevier Engineering Library contains 38,000 volumes.

Concurrently with its move to Benedum Hall, the School of Engineering introduced a new program structure. Among other changes it developed interdisciplinary graduate programs in energy resources and environmental engineering, and introduced a new curriculum aimed at sensitizing engineers to the economic, political, and cultural impact of technology on society.

At the end of the 1970s, the school had 409 female engineering students, or 19 percent of its enrollment. This was, according to a study made by the Georgia Institute of Technology, the highest percentage in the nation.

In 1969 the Learning Research and Development Center received a $5.6 million grant from the U.S. Office of Education, to be used to erect a $7 million eight-story building. Founded five years earlier, LRDC was one of the fastest-growing of the University's academic units and was already among the

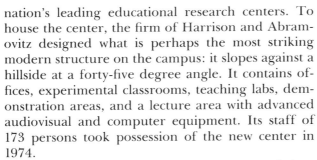

The Michael L. Benedum Hall of Engineering.

Michael L. Benedum.

nation's leading educational research centers. To house the center, the firm of Harrison and Abramovitz designed what is perhaps the most striking modern structure on the campus: it slopes against a hillside at a forty-five degree angle. It contains offices, experimental classrooms, teaching labs, demonstration areas, and a lecture area with advanced audiovisual and computer equipment. Its staff of 173 persons took possession of the new center in 1974.

LRDC conducts basic and applied research into the learning process; tests prototype materials stemming from that research; and constructs educational environments that are adaptive to the differences that each learner brings into the classroom. It carries out research in the field, working with policymakers in school districts in the Pittsburgh area. It works with children from Falk School, the University's laboratory school, situated nearby. Fifty to sixty pupils in an ungraded class ranging from kindergarten through third grade attend school in the LRDC building. LRDC researchers were celebrated in the 1960s for their work in individualized instruction. Recent efforts have stressed the linkage of cognitive science research and contemporary educational needs. Major work in the 1980s emphasizes learning processes in mathematics, science, and social studies.

The Department of Chemistry, having grown

UCIR

Learning Research & Development Center.

Herb Ferguson/News & Publications

Chemistry Building.

steadily since World War II, was by 1962 the largest department in the University. Still expanding in 1970, it was occupying space in many scattered locations, including three house trailers above Alumni Hall. The end of this logistical nightmare came with the decision to construct a new chemistry building at University Drive and Parkman Avenue. State Hall, the first building erected on the Oakland campus, had occupied that site since its completion in 1910. It was demolished. An impressive fifteen-story building, costing an even more impressive $14.7 million, was dedicated in 1974, and the department at last found itself in unified quarters. At the same time,

the National Science Foundation awarded a grant of more than $2 million to the Science Development Program for the expansion of the chemistry department.

Chemistry had about forty faculty members in 1974; it taught 3,500 undergraduate students and 150 graduate students, many of whom planned to enter careers in biomedical and other technical fields. In that year the department ranked third in the nation in the number of bachelors' degrees awarded, sixth in masters' degrees, and about twenty-fifth in the number of doctorates.

A major achievement in recent years has been the

establishment of the $3 million Surface Science Center, for which the first floor of Alumni Hall was remodeled. The center contains an advanced measurement facility for both analytical and physical chemical research in surface science—a new interdisciplinary field concerned with pheonomena that occur exclusively on the surfaces of solids and liquids. The detailed understanding of surface layers is crucial to the control of a number of industrial technologies; thus the center represents a link between the academic and industrial resources of the Pittsburgh area.

By 1985 the Department of Chemistry had increased its annual research grant and contract support to $5 million, making it one of the country's leaders in external research support per faculty member. Of that amount, more than $500,000 is for buying state-of-the-art instrumentation.

The Law School, founded in 1895, a charter member of the Association of American Law Schools, spent its first eighty-one years in cramped quarters. In January 1976 it moved into a handsome new structure on Forbes Avenue beside Lawrence Hall. The $8.5 million six-story building contains tiered classrooms, seminar rooms, an expandable courtroom seating 475 observers, offices for the faculty, and a library containing 160,000 volumes.

The school's seventy-one faculty members are learned in, among other fields, the law as it applies to health, energy policy, corporations and banking, taxation, divorce, and the penal code. Most of the students (nearly seven hundred of them in 1985) follow the basic course of study leading to a law degree. Some students apply for internships in various legal clinics in the Pittsburgh area or for positions as clerks in local appellate courts and in the U.S. Attorney's office. Some earn dual degrees (through the Graduate School of Public and International Affairs) by combining legal training with courses in law and public administration, in law and international affairs, and in law and public planning. Some take courses in law and industrial management through the Graduate School of Business or Carnegie-Mellon's Graduate School of Industrial Administration. Some take courses in law and public

Law Building.

management jointly offered with CMU's School of Urban and Public Affairs.

The faculties of 176 schools of law were recently evaluated on the number and quality of their publications in the country's best law reviews. Pitt ranked twentieth.

After the dedication of the Law School in 1976, Posvar announced that the twenty-year expansion program would come to a close after the construction of one more major building. This was to be the Forbes Quadrangle complex, a concrete and limestone building erected on the site of Forbes Field, home of the Pirates from 1909 to 1970. (Home plate

Ray Cristina/News & Publications

Forbes Quadrangle.

occupied a position now marked by a plaque embedded in the floor fifty paces east from the Bouquet Street entrance.) Consulting architect Abramovitz decided to limit the building's height to five stories so that it would not exceed that of the Carnegie Institute and Library across Schenley Plaza; but Forbes Quad is otherwise colossal in all its statistics. It cost $38.26 million. It has 744,695 square feet of floor space, roughly equivalent to the Cathedral of Learning's. It has 574 academic offices, 30 seminar rooms, 3 lecture halls, and working space for about 3,000 faculty and staff. It has one mile of corridors, five miles of partitions, and 435 underground parking spaces. A control center in the basement maintains the temperature in the Quad and in seven other buildings, including Engineering, five blocks away. An enclosed overhead passageway spanning Forbes Avenue connects Lawrence Hall, the Law School, and Forbes Quad to the Litchfield Towers dormitories, the Schenley Quadrangle, and the student union.

The logistics of moving into the new building was so complex that an occupancy schedule went through twenty drafts before being approved. The move took place in February 1978, involving the Graduate School of Public and International Affairs, the University Center for International Studies, the School of Education, the Departments of Anthropology, Black Studies, Geography, History, Political Science, Sociology, and Urban Studies.

The Cultural Resource Management Program (CRMP), a new University research activity established in 1976, also joined the move into Forbes Quad. One of the three top university operations in its field, the largest in the East if not in the country, CRMP is the archeological contract branch of the

Department of Anthropology. It contracts with private and government agencies to carry out studies in cultural resource management—that is, in "contract archeology." The program has superb equipment, laboratories, and several floors of space for the processing, analysis, and storage of archeological data. Facilities for geological, sedimentological, and invertebrate paleontological studies are shared with the Department of Geology and Planetary Sciences.

CRMP contracts have taken their collaborators to Ohio, Texas, West Virginia, Mississippi, Kentucky, Delaware, and, of course, to several areas of Pennsylvania, where they often work with oil and gas exploration companies, with municipalities, and with various federal agencies, including the U.S. Army Corps of Engineers, the Forest Service, and the National Park Service. CRMP was also the archeological consultant during the construction of the Pittsburgh subway, where some 35,000 artifacts were recovered and are being analyzed under the direction of Ronald C. Carlisle, the program's historical archeologist and editor of reports and publications. The program publishes the results of its larger research projects in the Department of Anthropology's *Ethnology Monographs* series.

The most widely celebrated undertaking of the department is the Meadowcroft–Cross Creek Archeological Project, led by James M. Adovasio, professor, department chairman, and director of CRMP. When he joined the faculty in 1972, Adovasio set out to find a local site where students could learn field excavation techniques and where he could pursue one of his specialities, rockshelter excavation. Rockshelter and cave excavations are common in the American West, where Adovasio received his training, but at the time such archeological sites were underexplored in much of the East.

Just such a site was pointed out to Adovasio by Phil Jack, a social scientist at California University of Pennsylvania. It was thirty miles southwest of Pittsburgh, on Albert Miller's 800-acre Meadowcroft Farm, which had been in the Miller family since 1795. A remarkable feature of the farm was a rock overhang, sixty-five feet high, on the steep north bank of Cross Creek in Washington County. This broad, deep site had a protected southern exposure, ample water, plentiful game, and lush vegetation. It had not been disturbed by looters and was well cared for by Miller, a man devoted to the archeology and history of Western Pennsylvania.

At Miller's invitation, Adovasio and summer field school students over the next six years worked 446 days at Meadowcroft, supported by the National Science Foundation, the National Geographic Society, several Pittsburgh foundations, and the University. The field work consisted of removing by hand and screening 230 cubic meters of sediment in eleven strata more than five meters deep. The entire excavation was recorded in field notes and thousands of photographs. The National Geographic Society made a film of the early years of the excavation.

Eventually, 100 charcoal samples from firepits and other archeological "features" at the site were sent to the Radiation Biology Laboratory at the Smithsonian Institution. Adovasio and his collaborators were expecting reasonably old dates to come back, but even they were startled by the very early age of many of the samples from strata near the bottom of the site. Meadowcroft now has seventy radiocarbon dates on its features and artifacts, more than any other single site in the eastern United States.

The Meadowcroft Rockshelter excavations have resulted in the most and earliest well-dated prehistoric flaked stone tools in North America. Later occupations, extending with no major gaps from prehistoric time nearly to the middle of the eighteenth century, left behind a human record that can be read in thousands of findings as diverse as animal bones, plant remains, ceramic potsherds, and flaked stone projectile points of many different types. Squash and corn remains from Meadowcroft indicate that horticulture was practiced by Indians in the Upper Ohio River Valley some five hundred years earlier than previously thought. The earliest Indian ceramics in the Upper Ohio region also come from the site and date from about 1,000 B.C.

Meadowcroft, moreover, has established the basal time line for the presence of humans in the New World. It has caused archeologists to rethink old ideas about when the earliest Americans reached

The east face of Meadowcroft Rockshelter near the end of the excavations. The small white tags mark significant archaeological features.

J. M. Adovasio/Anthropology

North America across the Bering land bridge, an area now marked by the Bering Strait. Until recently, that event was dated at no more than 10,000 to 12,000 years ago. But prehistoric men and women may have been at Meadowcroft and in the surrounding area as early as 19,000 years ago, and they were certainly there by 15,000 years ago. They were there, too, in 8,500 B.C., when the southern edge of the great Wisconsin-age glacier, seventy miles north of the site, began its final recession, an event

that marked the beginning of the present climatic regimes.

Hunters and gatherers seem to have used the shelter throughout its long history, probably on seasonal migrations to and from the Ohio River. Thus Meadowcroft has proven to show, in the words of Robert Stuckenrath, head of the Smithsonian's Radiation Biology Lab, "the earliest well-dated evidence of human occupation and the longest occupational sequence in a stratified site in the entire hemisphere." As Wesley Posvar put it, these findings "have, in effect, moved American archeology 2,000 miles eastward and will be discussed by anthropologists for years to come."

The work at Meadowcroft Rockshelter itself has been expanded to take in the entire Cross Creek watershed and now includes the study of the archeology of nearby drainages. Hundreds of other sites have been recorded, tested, or completely excavated in this vast outdoor "laboratory." Many articles and interim reports on the Meadowcroft–Cross Creek Archeological Project have appeared over the years, and a comprehensive book on the project is being prepared.

These successes, of course—the good figures of the past decade; the growth and advances; the new schools, centers, and programs; the new buildings—were accompanied by difficulties. Some problems had origins other than academic; they came with a changing economy, cutbacks in state and federal funding, and the revolution in social and moral attitudes. Some problems were quite unlike anything experienced before; most were common to all colleges and universities in the country. Posvar saw the 1970s as a decade during which higher education must begin to face reality. "Colleges and universities of the past thirty years," he had said in 1972, "were able to expand and add programs in response to external financial stimuli. [They] are now in a position that may be less aptly described as a depression than as the advent of economic reality—a state in which resources expand in modest, justifiable amounts, and in which our new programs can be adopted only by assigning them higher priority than some existing programs. Having gotten out of the habit of hard thinking in terms of priorities, we academicians may have some difficulty in doing so."

There were two specters in these years that haunted college administrators all over the country. One was inflation—10 to 12 percent a year in the middle seventies—which was dramatically increasing costs of materials, services, utilities, insurance, books, periodicals, paper products, payrolls. In Pitt's fiscal year 1975–1976, the cost of three utilities alone—electricity, gas, and steam—rose 76 percent,

adding more than $2 million to a budget that was already strained.

Beside inflation stood the specter of a problem frequently, almost incessantly, discussed: the demographic crisis of the next decades concerning the size, growth, and ages of the population after 1980 and its geographic distribution. The machines of the Census Bureau gave back a magic figure on September 23, 1972: the fertility level for the first time in U.S. history dropped on this day to replacement level—to zero population growth. The bureau reported that the number of persons fourteen to twenty-four years of age would peak in 1980 and decline by 3 million in 1985. Pitt's loss in the undergraduate pool could be worse: it could drop more than 30 percent by 1990 because of a decrease in the state's population, out-migration from Western Pennsylvania in hard times, and the larger numbers of those unable to pay the costs of a college education.

A more immediate problem at Pitt, however, was a fiscal system that was not working. Planning and budget control in the early 1970s were enmeshed in an elaborate, complex system involving three committee-task forces of thirty members each. This system was based on a model that simply could not be applied to the University. Much of the planning and budget was, in effect, removed from the chancellor's control.

Jack Freeman in 1974 returned from the Johnstown campus, where he had served for three years as president, to become Posvar's vice chancellor in charge of Planning and Budget—a post he had declined to accept in 1971. Freeman dismissed the task forces and set out to develop and install a new planning budget and control system.

Posvar and Freeman were both convinced that "the University must decide the extent to which it should attempt to determine and control its own future, as opposed to simply responding to external changes." They believed that only those colleges equipped to adjust to future changes in the academic environment were likely to remain strong and vital over the next several decades. They held that with a good faculty, a first-rate plant, a budget of $178 million, and the underrated advantages of

Gary Tweed/News & Publications

Litchfield Towers B and C, with Benedum Hall (right foreground) and Holland Hall and Brackenridge Hall (left), formerly two of the five Schenley Apartments. The Frick Middle School of the Pittsburgh School District is in the foreground. The towers were dedicated in 1963.

operating in a city, the University had exceptional opportunities—but only if it was prepared to face continued inflation, declining revenues, and sliding enrollments—only if it made the hard choices, cut costs, and set priorities.

For the most part, Provost Rhoten A. Smith and the deans and department heads felt a broader optimism about the future of their schools and departments. They generally held that by hard work, perseverance, and some modest adjustments in the system, it would be possible for them to continue over the next ten to fifteen years to do pretty much what they had been doing. Posvar and Freeman did

not agree; they predicted slow but sure decline if steps were not taken in time. The deans suggested that the need for such steps was being over-emphasized. A classic, continuing, high-level debate followed between the top administrators and the academic leadership.

Catastrophe did not befall the University when the 1980s arrived; its enrollment, in fact, reached an all-time high in 1983. Since it is difficult to measure non-events, one can never be certain whether catastrophe did not come because the assumption that it would come was wrong; or because the steps taken to head it off were effective; or because the catastro-

Herb Ferguson/News & Publications

Mervis Hall, Graduate School of Business, built on the site of Forbes Field and dedicated in 1983.

phe was still to come. It is significant, however, that Pittsburgh's record-high enrollment in 1983 ran counter to the national trend in higher education.

Neither Posvar nor Freeman was naive about what planning could accomplish, nor was either unaware of the limitations and pitfalls involved in forecasting future trends. "I have a humble view," Posvar declared, "of what planning can do." On the other hand, he continued, "some of my colleagues argue, with much anecdotal evidence, that long-range planning is fruitless, an exercise remotely connected to reality, if connected at all. However, the purpose of long-range planning is not to predict what is going to happen in the year 2000, nor is it to

make year-2000 decisions now. It is to enable us to make this year's decisions more enlightened—at least slightly better informed—by our current rough understandings."

Work on the planning system involved faculty, administrators, trustees, students, task forces, and ad hoc committees. Each dean, director, and department head was asked to submit a statement, not to exceed 1,000 words, on the goals of his or her operation. Some six hundred pages were submitted. Freeman made a national study of the planning of resource management systems in other large research universities. The planning and management document was based on the findings of these combined efforts. Three drafts were sent to the trustees before they approved it at a meeting in January 1976. Years later the chairman of the board who presided over that meeting, William H. Rea, commented with understandable pride, "I think the University of Pittsburgh has a better control of its budget than any other university in the country. They can give you a cost-accounting analysis of each department. It's a really beautiful operation."

Between 1967 and 1976, the College of Arts and Sciences (CAS), the largest degree-granting unit on the Pittsburgh campus, substantially increased its enrollment and the number of courses it offered. A college within the University, CAS represents the undergraduate component of the Faculty of Arts and Sciences (FAS), which provides the College with its 600 faculty members. CAS enrolled some eight thousand students in 1976, most of them full-time, most of them eighteen to twenty-two years of age. The College curriculum emphasizes the liberal arts, but many courses are also oriented toward careers in the professions.

Notwithstanding its accomplishments and generally good reputation, CAS encountered growing difficulties in the late 1960s and early 1970s. These were caused partly by the rising spirit of popular protest generated by the civil rights movement and by activism directed against the war in Vietnam. Other sources of problems were the growing debate among faculty and administrators over different philosophies of education; students' demands for greater control over their educational careers; the burgeoning enrollments that resulted when the baby-boom cohort reached the campuses; and Pitt's decision to become state-related, which meant admitting more students from a smaller geographical pool and across a wider social spectrum.

A shortage of faculty now began to be apparent. Many departments, having discontinued large lecture classes in response to vociferous protest, were at the same time faced with increasing numbers of students. Unable to staff enough courses with regular faculty and graduate student teachers, they began to hire additional temporary, term-by-term instructors. Inevitably, that practice was soon at-

tacked; critics called for increasing the number of regular, tenure-stream appointments instead of relying so heavily on temporary personnel. Administrators, however, having recently seen great fluctuations in enrollment, were wary of adding to the regular faculty because of the possibility of future declines. More tenure-stream faculty were indeed added, but students continued to crowd into the classrooms and the use of temporaries continued to grow.

The problem, although not limited to any one discipline, came to be most serious in the English department. There the great majority of composition and basic-level writing and literature courses were being taught by part-time instructors or by graduate students with assistantships. In 1974 only 12 percent of the undergraduate writing and composition courses offered by the English department were staffed by full-time faculty. The remaining 88 percent were taught by graduate students and temporary part-time instructors, labeled by one of them as "marginal, expendable, underprivileged, and underpaid." Of the total of 281 undergraduate English sections offered in 1974, no fewer than 71 percent were staffed by teachers outside the tenure stream. In 1975 such faculty taught 68 percent of all English sections.

Another factor encouraging the continued use of temporary faculty was the growing oversupply of Ph.D.s unable to find full-time employment: the baby boomers were going to graduate school. Temporary faculty protested their insecurity, their inadequate salaries, their low status—even the lack of mailboxes and other signs of membership in their departments and their profession.

Critics of the system did not oppose the employment of qualified teachers who could not or preferred not to devote themselves to full-time work. They did not attack the use of teachers whose primary commitment lay outside the University, such as musicians, real estate brokers, journalists, engineers, and lawyers, who were used to enrich the curriculum. Rather, they objected to a system that exploited all three constituencies: the students, who were often taught by instructors without full department status; the regular faculty, who had to assume

News & Publications

The William Pitt Union, originally the Schenley Hotel. The renovated building was dedicated in 1983.

proportionately larger shares of noninstructional work; and the temporaries themselves, who paid the price of being perceived as contingent.

The dependence on nonregular faculty was especially noticeable in the College of General Studies (CGS), which holds evening and weekend classes and classes at various off-campus locations. In 1975 CGS had 460 full-time and 5,790 part-time students, and it drew its faculty of about 260 from various University departments and faculties. In November 1980 an evaluation team from the Middle States Association reported, "Concern was expressed by some students and administrators of the College regarding the level of instructors assigned the College of General Studies sections. Many believed that too many TAs, TFs [teaching assistants, teaching fellows—two categories of graduate student teachers] and instructors are assigned to teach CGS sections.

Data provided by the Student Council and the Dean of the Faculty of Arts and Sciences indicate that in disciplines other than business, a high proportion of CGS sections are taught by these categories of instructors without professional rank. . . . Less than 40 percent of the CGS's courses are taught by instructors that hold faculty rank."

On January 11, 1976, acting on a request of the Senate Council, the trustees of the University in some measure righted a long-standing injustice. They amended the bylaws to read, "Tenure may be held by either full- or part-time faculty." Qualified part-time teachers "may, on request, be considered for appointment to the tenure stream faculty on a part-time basis. . . . Such persons should be under contract with the University for no less than half-time. . . . They should receive salary proportionate to the time contracted for, as well as other fringe benefits, perquisites of space, and facilities." Part-time teachers were only partly mollified; only a few such appointments were made, and part-timers continued to believe that they were not being properly considered when a full-time teaching post was being filled. But now, at least, the problem had been addressed, and whether or not they were in the tenure stream, part-time faculty received pay increases, were assigned office space, mailboxes, and campus telephone numbers, and were listed in the *Faculty and Staff Directory.*

A concurrent and not unrelated problem was the use of foreign-born teaching assistants and fellows—primarily for courses in math, science, engineering, and other technical fields—whose English could not be understood by the students or could be understood only with great difficulty. The nationwide shortage of faculty in these fields, in which private industry offers more lucrative careers, and the increase in students from abroad, most of whom require teaching assistantships, make this a thorny issue. As part of an attempt to address this problem, faculty resolutions have been introduced that would provide foreign-born graduate students with language instruction and screening before they are allowed to serve as teaching assistants.

With other institutions Pitt joined in the battles of this volatile period over what constitutes a liberal arts education and how to achieve it. Many questioned traditional student-faculty relationships and called for a rejuvenation in methods of teaching and learning that would foster creativity and intellectual responsibility among students. As was being demonstrated on campuses across the nation, the mood of the times was hostile to authority and advocated student self-determination.

On February 19, 1969, some thirty undergraduates, including the new president and vice president of the student government, called on James Kehl, dean of the College. In a ninety-minute meeting, the group demanded the abolition of the foreign language requirement. College students, they held, were old enough to select their own courses, and force-feeding was alien to a genuine educational experience. Such a visit to a dean by a student group would have been unthinkable ten years earlier, but by the late 1960s students were asserting themselves as never before. One hundred and twenty faculty members supported the students' stand, even providing some of the leadership in challenging existing standards.

That meeting was the beginning of the movement to liberalize the undergraduate liberal arts curriculum at Pitt. On January 11, 1970, the FAS faculty met in Clapp Hall and after 2½ hours of "strenuous discussion" voted 91 to 86 to abolish the foreign language requirement.* Other required courses also came under attack during the tenure of College dean Jerome Schneewind, including mandatory freshman composition. There were also strong objections, from students and faculty alike, to massive classes, old-fashioned lecture methods, and the passivity that traditional classroom practices inevitably encouraged. The reformers demanded new life in the curriculum. They insisted that required courses aroused hostility and were detrimental to learning.

Extensive changes were made in the College curriculum, especially for freshmen and sophomores. The faculty argued that if students were to be given

*Departmental qualifications were not affected by the abolition. Majors in such areas as fine arts and chemistry were still required to complete language courses according to departmental stipulations.

more freedom to direct their own educations, they needed more advice in the first years on what a liberal arts education meant. The College thereupon expanded its Advising Center and eventually created the position of advising director to provide individualized guidance to a course of study that would replace the across-the-board requirements that were being withdrawn. Freshman seminars were introduced—small classes taught by specially chosen faculty members. The Alternative Curriculum was set up—a thirty-credit program of totally unconventional, nonstructured education for the freshman year. Students and teachers together mapped out a program of learning, without grades, papers, or exams, tailored to the students' interests and capabilities. A course of study might stress investigation of current problems through mini-courses, lectures by invited speakers, private reading and research, or community service. At first, the Alternative Curriculum was much in demand. Then, gradually, it declined in popularity.

As further curricular changes followed, a student could earn a B.A. degree without a conventional major, choosing Liberal Studies instead. Requirements of the College's Distribution of Studies (DOS) were significantly reduced. Led by the English department, the FAS faculty readily agreed to abolish the freshman composition requirement, although, to everyone's surprise, composition came to be more in demand than before its removal as a requirement because students returned for additional courses. This was a tribute to the students' ability to assess their own weaknesses, to the quality of student advising, and to the more interesting variety of offerings in composition that came with the new and expanded curriculum. Eventually the pendulum was to swing in the other direction, but the sentiment of that period favored experimental approaches to college learning. Students and faculty alike endorsed these moves toward liberalization—and certainly there was need for a change in courses that were dull and unchallenging and in programs that permitted too few electives.

By 1975 some results of these curriculum changes were apparent and measurable. Many were disappointing. The hope that students would find their own motivation for taking a wide-ranging assortment of courses and that faculty would help them in making choices seemed to have been ill-founded. One dean later said, "It didn't happen. The faculty went about their business as usual, which means they went to class and the students were left unguided." There were complaints from various quarters, including local employers, regarding the uncertain literacy skills of graduating students, blaming the problem on the removal of the composition requirement (despite the continuing heavy enrollments in writing classes). As time passed, many questioned the extent of the liberalization of the curriculum, and were alarmed by the declining SAT scores for each freshman class. The causes of that decline were complex, and such declines were occurring in other colleges and universities across the nation, but some observers felt that curriculum reform was to blame. Others attributed the decline to the changed makeup of the Pitt student body that had come with state-related status. In any case, by 1976 the College reported that more than one-third of entering freshmen scored below the national average of 440 on their SAT verbal exams. Yet most had been in the upper fifth of their high school senior classes.

In 1976 the CAS Council debated the issue of changing the curriculum again to meet the current situation and new student needs. It took no action other than to reject unanimously a motion to raise admissions standards, explicitly recognizing the need to maintain enrollments. There continued to be complaints from various positions across the political spectrum. It was charged that those engaged in remedial work and in the teaching of skills were not adequately rewarded, that high-quality teaching and student achievement were not being recognized, that "grade inflation" had destroyed grading criteria, and that entrance standards were too lax.

Counterreform of the curriculum began to be discussed with the appointment of Irwin Schulman as dean of the College in 1978. A curriculum reform committee was appointed, made up of twenty-two faculty members and four students. They visited other liberal arts schools and conducted a survey of

700 graduates from the class of 1979. Three to one, the graduates favored a return to a mandatory writing requirement, and two to one they favored regularizing requirements in the humanities. There was more opposition to reinstating the foreign language requirement, but even so, just under half voted in favor of this change. By the fall of 1981 the committee had completed its work and the FAS Council had seen its proposal. In a standing-room-only gathering on December 1, almost twelve years after it abolished the foreign language requirement, the FAS faculty approved with minor changes the entire curriculum reform package.

The committee had intended from the first to go further than merely restoring the requirements of the 1960s. Without specifying what courses students had to take, it adopted a general set of core requirements that could be met in various ways. Students entering the College in 1983 would be required to take a total of thirty-six credits in courses in the humanities, natural sciences, and social sciences. They include:

Foreign language: Unless students are exempted by having studied three years of a language in high school, or can demonstrate proficiency on a placement test, they are required to take six credits in a language (all in the same language).

Writing: Entering freshmen are assigned to writing classes according to a placement test that determines their level of ability. (Only a handful have ever been exempted from this requirement.) Those needing remedial work take basic writing. Beyond this level, students must complete a course in composition by the end of the sophomore year, plus two more courses emphasizing writing. One of these can be an advanced composition course. At least one must be a course in another department—preferably in that of the student's major—in which a specific number of written assignments are made.

Mathematics: Students must demonstrate basic proficiency in algebra upon entrance or take an algebra course in the first year. Beyond this, students must take another math course or a course in some other quantitatively oriented field, such as statistics.

Foreign culture: Students are to take six credits in a single foreign culture area. These may be distributed among another term of a foreign language, study abroad, or related courses in such other disciplines as political science, history, or literature.

Although excellence in student scholarship and faculty teaching had been sought in various ways down through the years, after 1976 new ways of rewarding superior performance were developed and formalized. The University Honors Program (UHP) was introduced on the Pittsburgh campus in 1977. The chancellor, who had advocated such a program since his first year in office, appointed a task force of selected faculty, administrators, and students who were concerned that the University was not meeting the needs of its most able undergraduates. They realized that several hundred of each year's entering students, largely those enrolling in CAS and engineering, had SAT scores in the ninetieth percentile and that these students often spoke of a lack of academic stimulation at Pitt.

The Honors Program that evolved from the work of this task force—aided by a $100,000 grant from U.S. Steel—was aimed at providing demanding courses for talented and motivated students. These students would be offered instruction in small classes (of fifteen to twenty students) by outstanding teacher-scholars. Incoming freshmen could take as many honors courses as they wished if they had a combined SAT score of at least 1,200 and ranked in the top tenth of their high school class. Already enrolled students could register for courses if they had quality point averages of at least 3.25. Others who demonstrated genuine interest and promise could also apply. The program began with fifteen courses and stabilized at thirty-two courses after 1970. By its fifth term, 513 students were enrolled in courses in twenty-five departments.

In 1986 the administration and faculty established the Honors College, which made it possible to earn an academically distinctive undergraduate degree. G. Alec Stewart, director of the UHP, notes that when Pitt administrators went before the state legislature in 1982 with budget requests, the University was praised for three programs: organ transplants in the Medical Center, a new mining

Paul Liebhardt/Semester-at-Sea

The passenger liner SS Universe, *shown here docked at La Guaira, Venezuela, is home of the University's Semester-at-Sea program. Since 1981 it has allowd students to earn 12 to 15 liberal arts credits during a 100-day voyage around the world.*

engineering program, and the Honors Program.

The Honors Convocation was reinstated after some years' lapse as part of the general program to recognize superior achievement. In a ceremony held in March 1977, awards were once again given to eleven Chancellor's Scholars (in addition to the already existing awards given to Chancellor's Undergraduate Teaching Fellows). One hundred and nineteen juniors and seniors in the top 2 percent of their classes were honored, as were forty-seven Andrew Mellon Predoctoral Fellows. Twenty-five students were honored for leadership; and forty faculty members were recognized for scholarship,

research, teaching, and public service. The most prestigious awards given to entering freshmen pay full tuition, fees, room, and board for up to four years. Two hundred students from among those competing for the Chancellor's Scholarship are offered the Provost's Scholarship of $1,000 a year for up to four years. Others are eligible for one of the 400 merit scholarships valued at $500 a year for up to four years.

At the same time, with the strong advocacy of the College dean and a Senate committee, programs were being developed to evaluate and improve the quality of teaching. In 1974 the dean of FAS was given an extra $2.5 million for recruiting exceptionally accomplished faculty. In 1978 he established the Office of Faculty Development under the directorship of Robert Wolke. Wolke's office provides seminars and demonstrations in techniques of teaching as well as videotaped records of actual classroom performances ("See yourself teach—are you curious about how you appear to your students in the classroom?") and awards prizes for distinguished teaching. It was announced in 1983 that up to eight Chancellor's Distinguished Teaching Awards of $1,000 each would be presented annually, matched by another $1,000 to be given to the teacher's department.

Faculty and administrators in 1971 introduced a collateral program in the College of Arts and Sciences to achieve and recognize excellence in teaching. It created the Office for Evaluation of Teaching and charged it with administering a systematic, professionally directed evaluation by the students themselves of classroom teaching effort and effectiveness. The office has since become a center and has been raised to the campuswide provost's level. In 1984–1985 it administered 2,579 surveys in the classes of 1,306 instructors on the Oakland campus. (It surveyed 3,241 classes on all campuses in that year.) Some administrators and faculty members now support a proposed five-year program that would make student evaluation mandatory and would introduce evaluation of the instructor by his peers.

34

The Precisely Measurable Triumph

High achievement in the classroom and success on the playing fields, far from being contradictory, are mutually beneficial, and there is good reason to expect an institution with stellar academic programs to support similarly successful athletic programs.

Wesley W. Posvar, 1983

THE numbers commonly used to measure growth and progress may turn out to be deceptive. Planning programs, critical evaluations, and curriculum reforms are hard to measure. But in 1976, a turning point year for the University, Pitt mounted an athletic program that was a perfect and precisely measurable triumph. The whole nation watched, and, excepting only a small enclave in California, it was in total agreement that in this one endeavor, this one sport, the University of Pittsburgh was first, best, unsurpassed, and unequaled. There is some difference of opinion on exactly what the endeavor had to do with higher education, but the people of Western Pennsylvania, of Pittsburgh, and of the five University campuses rejoiced and applauded. They marveled, too, that the University had accomplished so much so soon. Starting from an apparently hopeless situation early in 1973, it climbed to the very top in only four years. That achievement has been called one of the most dramatic comebacks ever seen in college football.

The athletic situation could hardly have been worse when Wesley Posvar took office in June 1967. Compared to his more serious problems and new responsibilities, that was a small matter—but as athletics-minded alumni are wont to say, perhaps more than half seriously, few things make a chancellor look worse than a losing football team.

Litchfield had invited Coach Michelosen to resign early in 1966 after a mediocre season (3–7) in which Pitt had successive losses to Syracuse (51–13) and Notre Dame (69–13) and could recruit only sixteen freshman prospects. Dave Hart became head coach in 1966 and began with three 1–9 seasons, two of them witnessed by the new chancellor, who, it turned out, took his football seriously. In Hart's 1968 season, considered the most disastrous in the school's history, Pitt lost four games by forty-eight points or more, and it suffered the ultimate indignity at South Bend when both head coaches agreed to let the clock run in the second half to bring the game mercifully sooner to an end.

Carl De Pasqua, Pitt fullback in 1949, became Pitt's twelfth head coach in thirty-one years. Pitt had begun to appear rather frequently on a cruel list of the ten worst teams. Inevitably, Pitt varsity sports

other than football were enduring referred pains; even basketball was a deficit sport in the 1960s. W. Dean Billick, associate director of athletics, remembers the 1960s: "We had real problems. There simply wasn't any money."

In that year the new chancellor began to involve himself deeply and personally in the strategy and tactics of reorganizing the University's athletic department. He came on stage with a set of convictions. He believed that "an athletic experience imparts a discipline seldom found elsewhere in the learning process." Athletics, he said, "provide a large measure of the fun of attending a university." Beyond that, it "elevates community spirit and morale [and] offers to the spectator the opportunity for involvement and dedication to a cause." A good athletic program, moreover, "projects an image of institutional well-being and helps attract to the classroom intellectually alert young people from near and far." The University, he felt, should have winning programs in everything it did, certainly including athletic competition. Posvar also believed strongly that the University could put teams on the field whose players met or surpassed the required academic standards.

On a very practical level he once posed a rhetorical question to his staff: "What other University activity can manage to have the University of Pittsburgh's name listed in every Sunday paper across the nation?"

Before attempting to formulate a program to rescue Pitt athletics, Posvar characteristically set out to gather all available pertinent information and sought the best advice on what needed to be done. A main unanswered question was whether he was right in believing he could reconcile academic and athletic values.

He first assembled a blue-chip committee to advise him on changes in practice and policy. Tom Hamilton, former Pitt athletic director (1949–1959), now director of the Athletic Association of Western Universities, was on that committee, as was Lieutenant Colonel Casimir J. Myslinski, forty-seven, All-American center and captain of the 1943 West Point team, commander of an air force fighter squadron, and for the past five years assistant football coach and head of physical education at the Air Force Academy. Posvar also asked his athletic department people to prepare a white paper on the assets and liabilities of the University's membership in the so-called Big Four (Pitt, Penn State, Syracuse, and West Virginia), and he asked the presidents of those three other universities to meet with him as his guests to review the Big Four agreement. When Pitt was playing Florida State at Tallahassee in 1971, he invited a group of supporters from within and outside the University, including alumni, faculty members, and administrators, to meet with him. They spent an entire afternoon reviewing the steps that had led Pitt to its disastrous records of recent seasons. He extended the same invitation to a similar group at Tulane, and he met with Miami's athletic director and the former Penn State athletic director.

On the basis of his own findings and the advice he received, Posvar made a moral and money commitment to the athletic department and to the University. He would keep Pitt in big-time football. He would increase the investment in coaching, scholarships, and facilities. He would attempt to produce the kind of winning teams he felt a great university deserved and that his students and other constituencies wanted. He would do it without "spreading around red ink" and within NCAA regulations.

The following actions were taken during or after Posvar's search for a redemptive athletic program.

• Casimir Myslinski, having retired from military service, replaced Frank Carver as athletic director.

• Pitt withdrew from the Big Four. The agreement was supposed to maintain high academic standards and reduce athletic expenditures; but the research study revealed clearly that Pitt had involved itself in a kind of modified modern Code Bowman. Pitt was subject to restrictions that were not being followed elsewhere in college athletics nor, indeed, fully by the three other Big Four universities. The agreement permitted Pitt fewer athletic scholarships. Its athletes had to satisfy foreign language requirements stiffer than those at Penn State. It followed stricter rules on redshirting* The Big Four then collapsed.

*Holding back a player for a season, with continued eligibility, because of injury, immaturity, or other legitimate reasons.

Edward Bozik, athletic director in the 1980s, said in reviewing the canceled agreement, "For some reason, University of Pittsburgh athletic programs have had a tendency toward abnegation and self-flagellation—qualities which, I believe, are better left to saints than to athletic departments."

• John Terrill Majors was signed on as head coach early in 1973, replacing De Pasqua. An All-American tailback at Tennessee, first runner-up for the 1956 Heisman Trophy, Majors had just turned the Iowa State football team around with an 8–3 season and a trip to the Liberty Bowl. He was considered perhaps the hottest young (thirty-seven) coach in college football. When Pitt approached him, he sent his brother Joe, traveling under an assumed name, to negotiate a contract. It was clear that Majors would not have come if Pitt had remained a member of the Big Four.

• The Panther Foundation (formerly the Bellefield Trust), made a gift of $250,000, which the athletic department used to remodel and refurbish "that absolute dungeon," the dressing room area of Pitt Stadium. Installed were 147 spacious lockers, wall-to-wall carpeting, a sauna bath, new showers, a lounge for the players, color television, a stereo set, and a hospitality room for the parents of the players.

• Sharp new uniforms followed—bright gold pants, gold helmets, royal blue jerseys with names on the backs in block letters. New outfits were given to the cheerleaders and new uniforms to the 200-member Varsity Marching Band, which, founded in 1911, now for the first time barred outside players and admitted female students to its ranks.

• The administration persuaded an alumni group to establish another organization called the Golden Panthers to provide the primary outside financial support for Pitt's athletic programs. The Golden Panthers collected money from alumni and friends of the University and turned it over to the senior vice chancellor for administration, who disbursed it on the recommendation of the athletic director and with the approval of the chancellor. The donors had only one right in the allocation of their money: they could name the sport to which it should go. The Golden Panthers flourished; it turned over $3.3 million in its first ten years, of which about 85 percent went for athletic scholarships and the rest for facilities, equipment, travel expenses, and training costs.

- Posvar authorized Majors in his first year as head coach to grant seventy-eight football scholarships. (It was the last year that could be done under changed NCAA rules.)
- Posvar created the Office of Support Services for Athletes, assigning three full-time counselors to serve the members of the varsity teams. Football and basketball players—almost 75 percent of them in the College of Arts and Sciences or the College of General Studies—now had to maintain a minimum 2.0 Quality Point Average (QPA). If they did not attain that by the end of their sophomore year, they were subject to possible suspension or probation.

Majors understood and used two new developments in college athletics. One was the arrival of a new breed of athlete—tall, heavy, and muscular, but at the same time agile and incredibly fast. The other was a dramatic rise of the black athlete. Having been encouraged and sometimes aided under new liberalized policies to enter the universities, black students were of course eligible to compete in athletics, provided they met academic requirements. Their athletic abilities were such that they at once achieved full participation in, and sometimes domination of, teams in college sports. Majors was also a demon recruiter. In the most extensive off-season effort ever launched at Pitt, he spoke in early 1973 to 46 banquets, 23 alumni gatherings, and 19 coaching clinics, and he visited 100 high schools and countless homes.

One prime recruiting prospect in that year was a protégé of Dr. Michael Zernich, prominent orthopedic surgeon and former basketball star at the University. He was Tony Drew Dorsett, son of Wesley and Myrtle Dorsett of Aliquippa, on the Ohio River below Pittsburgh, where his father was a steelworker. Zernich introduced Dorsett to the chancellor, who introduced him to the athletic department. Majors or his assistants called on the Dorsetts several times and persuaded Tony to turn down sixty-seven other colleges and go to Pitt, which

was then the last university a potential star would be expected to choose.

The 1973 football season opened with a game against Georgia, in which Pittsburgh was a thirty-nine-point underdog. To general amazement, Georgia was outplayed and could barely manage to get a tie. Pitt had its first winning season in ten years: 6–5–1. Majors was named National Coach of the Year, season ticket sales rose from 7,000 to 10,000, and the team went to the Fiesta Bowl—the first invitation to a bowl in eighteen years. With higher ticket sales and a bowl game on national television, athletic department income and expenditures broke even. Dorsett was a season-long sensation. He was not a powerhouse, standing only 5 feet 10¼ inches tall and weighing 157 to 193 pounds during his four-year career, but he had, as a running back, a sixth sense of where the other twenty-one players were on the field, a remarkably fluid running style, and the ability to suddenly accelerate as though, it was said, he had turned on an afterburner. In his third game, a victory over Northwestern, he ran 265 yards on thirty-eight carries—still the University's third-highest single-game rushing performance and an all-time NCAA freshman record. He rushed 209 yards in a loss to Notre Dame, the most yards ever gained against a Notre Dame team. He ended the season second nationally in rushing with 144.2 yards per game and was a consensus All-American—the first freshman named in twenty-nine years and Pitt's first first-team All-American since 1963. He was called "the greatest freshman running back in college history."

One of the chancellor's duties from time to time was to travel to some distant city and there report to the Pitt Club in that community on the state of the University. Accordingly, on September 3, 1976, Wesley Posvar appeared at a reception and gave a half-hour address to the Greater Chicago Pitt Club. As an added attraction, the club gave a door prize—a pair of tickets to the Pitt–Notre Dame game at South Bend the following week. After relating the accomplishments of the University, Posvar closed with a phantasm: "Finally, our football team has

One of the new fraternity houses located on Trees Field, between the Veterans Administration Medical Center and Pitt Stadium.

injected a heavy dose of adrenalin into our institutional system. We have a chance this year to become one of the top ten teams. With a little luck in the first game . . . the last game . . . and the nine games in between, we may turn up our first undefeated season in years. We have a fair shot at the national championship, a major bowl bid, a Heisman Trophy winner, and if you want to dream, maybe all three."

There was indeed a sense of hope and expectation in the spring and summer of 1976. Pitt had had winning seasons in 1974 and 1975 (7–4 and 8–4). Dorsett has rushed an unbelievable 303 yards in defeating Notre Dame. Pitt beat Kansas decisively in the Sun Bowl at El Paso. Majors's large squads of freshman recruits were impressive. Sports writers agreed that Pittsburgh was a team to watch.

Pittsburgh won the first game, the opener at South Bend, 31–10. It beat Georgia Tech 42–14. It beat Temple 21–7 and was raised to a number 3 rank. It beat Duke, and Louisville, and Miami. On October 23, when Pitt played Navy at Annapolis in a nationally televised game, Dorsett was on the verge of surpassing 5,177 yards to become the leading rusher in the recorded history of college football. In the fourth quarter, with the ball on Navy's thirty-two-yard line, with Dr. Michael Zernich and his parents watching, he needed four yards to break the record. At 4:05 P.M. he took a pitchout from quar-

Pitt Sports Information

With dazzling speed and agility—and the blocking of Matt Carroll—Tony Dorsett carries the ball against Duke in 1976, the year he was awarded the Heisman Trophy. The score: Pitt 44, Duke 31.

terback Tom Yewcic and rambled for his third touchdown of the day. The crowd of 26,346, having witnessed a historic event, rose simultaneously for a standing ovation. The navy cadets fired their can- non in a one-gun salute. The entire Pitt team, including those on the bench, rushed to the end zone for a massive, prolonged, and joyous pile-up, for which they were penalized fifteen yards. The final score was 45–0.* Dorsett gave his game jersey to Dr. Zernich.

Pitt beat Syracuse on October 30 and Army on November 7. The Associated Press now rated it number 1 in the nation. Pitt beat West Virginia on November 14. All that now stood in the way of a perfect season and a possible national title was Penn State, that spoiler of dreams, the begetter of bitter memories. Penn State had beaten Pittsburgh in ten straight games, the last one, in 1975, in a 7–6 heartbreaker when Carson Long, probably the most accurate and dependable placement kicker in Pitt history, still the school record holder with 260 points, missed three field goals, two of them close-in attempts in the last ninety seconds of play.

The Penn State game was moved to Friday night and to Three Rivers Stadium, and the time was changed to 9:00 P.M. to accommodate national television. There was a slight drizzle. The score was 7–7 at the half, 24–7 at the final whistle. Penn State was out-matched, out-played, and out-coached. Dorsett rushed 224 yards and became the first college back in history to surpass 6,000 yards in rushing.

Four days later he was named winner of the Heisman Trophy as the outstanding college football player in the nation.

Pitt players now had a choice between the Orange Bowl in Miami and the Sugar Bowl in New Orleans. They elected to meet the higher-ranked team and went to the New Orleans Superdome on New Year's Day. There, in a game they played perfectly on both offense and defense, they defeated fourth-ranked (Associated Press) or fifth-ranked (United Press International) Georgia by a score of 27–3. Thus Posvar realized his dream of four months earlier: an undefeated and untied team, a national championship, a major bowl bid, and a Heisman Trophy winner. He also had just about every other football trophy awarded that year. (He displayed four of them in the Commons Room.) He also had $900,000 in Sugar Bowl receipts (before expenses), of which he allocated $100,000 to the University libraries.

---

*It should be remembered that the service academies face a competitive handicap in that they have no cadets who are on their way to careers as professional athletes.

In a short talk at the Heisman Award ceremony, Posvar said, in paraphrasing a famous remark attributed to Sophie Tucker: "We have been on the bottom, and we have been on the top, and believe me, top is better."

In the meantime, other startling events were taking place. Majors resigned to become head coach at the University of Tennessee, his alma mater. Jackie Sherrill, who had been Majors's assistant coach and defensive coordinator, returned from a year as head coach at Washington State to succeed Majors. He had five phenomenally successful seasons (1977–1981), with a record of 9–2–1, 8–4, 11–1, 11–1, 11–1, and he took teams to five bowl games, winning four. The national championship eluded him, twice because of losses to relatively weak opponents. The 1980 team, called by some the greatest of all Pitt teams, was rated number 2 in the nation, though the *New York Times* declared, on the basis of a sophisticated computer study, that it was really number 1. That claim was strengthened when eleven Pittsburgh players, a record number, were chosen in the first five rounds of the National Football League draft—three of them—Hugh Green, Randy McMillan, and Mark May—in the first round. May, when he signed with the Washington Redskins, sent back a gift of $10,000 to the Golden Panthers' fund.

Sherrill departed in 1961; he was succeeded by his assistant head coach, Serafino Dante (Foge) Fazio. Myslinski retired as athletic director, and Assistant Chancellor Edward E. Bozik moved from the Cathedral of Learning to the new stadium offices to take his place. In December 1985, following two unsuccessful seasons, Fazio was replaced by Mike Gottfried, head coach at the University of Kansas. At his first press conference after assuming his new position, Gottfried told the assembled media, "I've always had a goal to win a National Championship, and here at the University of Pittsburgh you have that opportunity."

Chancellor Posvar had set out in 1971 to accomplish three things in the University's athletic program. People who were close to him then, in the athletic department or elsewhere, are convinced

Time out.

Lynn Johnson

that if he had failed he would have decisively reduced Pitt athletics to a class B level or removed them altogether from intercollegiate competition. All but his severest critics are likely to agree that he accomplished all three of his objectives.

First, he carried out his financial commitment. In the past twelve years, the University has spent well over $10 million on—among other things—substantial improvements to the stadium and to the football coaching and administrative offices and on the complete renovation of Fitzgerald Field House. Most of the money has come from the football and basketball programs and from contributions made by the Golden Panthers and the Panther Foundation. Fund-raising organizations that are independent of university or institutional control have a potential for causing serious problems; but the rules under which the Golden Panthers and the Panther Foundation operate, and the discretion exercised by their officers, have created a rare working model for aid to athletics that is acceptable to association and conference authorities.

Second, Posvar made a commitment to produce winning teams and to do it within the regulations of the NCAA. This he did.

Third, he set out to improve the academic performance of varsity athletes. The athletes that the University was recruiting were of a better quality than they were before the middle and early 1970s. There were problems, however, in football. The graduation rate of football players differed very little from the rate of students in the College of Arts and Sciences, but grade averages "suddenly suffered a major drop" in the fall of 1984, after three terms of improving quality point averages. There were more serious problems in basketball, which has more grueling traveling schedules and practice sessions, combined with a long season. With the drop in basketball academic performance in the fall of 1984, a fourth counselor was added to the Office of Support Services to work full time with the team. In March 1985 the University Senate Athletic Committee, in its annual report to the Senate Council, declared that academic achievement among Pitt's student athletes was "certainly respectable, and in the case of some teams, outstanding."

The University Senate committee report pointed out that the measuring of academic performance was complicated by new and changing factors. For one thing, the College of Arts and Sciences in 1981 had adopted more rigid academic requirements for undergraduates, setting higher standards for performance in writing, mathematics, and general education and in foreign language and culture studies. Furthermore, athletes had traditionally coasted through their electives, but now the academic requirements for electives had tightened, in line with Pitt's tougher standards for undergraduate education in general, and the teaching staff was taking more seriously the administration's emphasis on "quality education."

There were cheers from those who were watching the program for support services to athletes when Jay C. Pelusi, middle guard, an economics major with a 3.38 QPA, and Rob Fada, offensive guard (3.26 QPA), were named to the Academic All-American National Team.

In the spring of 1985, Chancellor Posvar arranged to give a new name to the street that runs along the west side of the stadium. It was renamed Jock Sutherland Drive. The ceremony was modest, and little explanation was given for the change. But in the chancellor's mind, this was a symbol of his effort to resolve a quarrel a half-century old and of his drive to reconcile John Bowman's dream of academic purity, Jock Sutherland's dream of athletic prowess, and Wesley Posvar's conviction that the values of scholarship and the values of athletics need not be mutually exclusive.

35

The Future of
Academic Medicine

*The Medical Center is based on the premise
that you can have five or six independent
institutions and still have one educational unit.
It's always been an uneasy truce. You can't
always draw a sharp line between administration and service.*

Paul McLain, M.D. April 28, 1980

I N 1918, Ogden Edwards, Jr., acting dean of the University of Pittsburgh's School of Medicine, put forth his idea of a University health center, and it is not entirely unlike the center that exists today. It should include, he said, "the Medical School building, the Laboratory of Hygiene and Public Health, a research laboratory, the Medical Library building . . . a small general hospital, an eye and ear hospital, a children's hospital, a general dispensary, a psychopathic hospital and a dormitory for 200 students."

The School of Medicine's interest in an alliance with hospitals was based on its need to obtain access to clinical training for its students and interns. As early as the 1920s, the university had worked out informal agreements with a number of hospitals to gain teaching and staff privileges. A few of these early agreements gave the medical school a voice in the appointment of department chairmen at the teachers' hospitals and even, some said, in the naming of staff physicians.

Within the hospitals, the prerogatives of the School of Medicine were sometimes met with hostility or completely ignored. Each hospital had its own special history, its own traditions, its benefactors, and its particular public. Magee Hospital, for example, owed its existence to a bequest from a wealthy and powerful political figure, Christopher Lyman Magee, and members of the Magee family still exerted control over the hospital's administration. Presbyterian and Montefiore hospitals owed special allegiance to religious groups. Each hospital was reluctant to cede any authority that might endanger its relationship with its special allies. More important, all the hospitals had powerful governing bodies. Although these factors weighed heavily against a centralized health center, the hospitals, the School of Medicine, and the University have moved, with a certain perversity, toward an ever-tightening alliance. Only recently, after years of irresolvable clashes, was the effort at cohesion abandoned in the name of harmony and peaceful coexistence.

In 1965, the last year of the Litchfield administration, largely because of Litchfield's leadership, the hospitals and the University took an important step: they incorporated as the University Health Center of Pittsburgh (UHCP). The original hospitals were Presbyterian-University, Magee and Womens (which had merged in 1962), Eye and Ear, and Children's. Montefiore joined them in 1969. The Western Psychiatric Institute and Clinic, which was managed by the School of Medicine, was also included in the affiliation. UHCP was to be managed by a twelve-person board—two representatives from each of the hospitals and two from the University. The goal of this venture was to centralize the operations of the already existing Health Center and to improve its ability to carry out the three basic functions of teaching, research, and patient care.

Important changes in post-war medical education and in the delivery of health care had led to the creation of the Health Center. In the first place, an increasing emphasis on specialization in medicine and in basic research added new dimensions to the field of medicine. If the University (and by extension the Health Center) wished to take part in this emerging thrust toward basic research, it could no longer afford to concentrate single-mindedly on service but must attract medical researchers and research funds. The Medical School did recruit a small core of outstanding researchers in the basic sciences, men like Jonas Salk; Klaus Hofmann, who in 1961 achieved the first laboratory synthesis of the pituitary hormone ACTH; and Panayotis Katsoyannis, who in 1964 synthesized insulin in the laboratory. This cadre of scientists needed expanded research laboratories and other facilities. Their loyalties were to their research teams, which might include scientists from related disciplines and even from other institutions.

The Health Center hospitals also had begun to emerge as a regional medical resource. Physicians in outlying areas looked to them for the most advanced treatment and for specialized knowledge and assistance. A postgraduate program called Grand Rounds on Television linked the School of Medicine with more than sixty hospitals in the tri-state area. As part of a regional outreach program, the School of Medicine's continuing education program annually offered to health practitioners more than eighty short courses and seminars on patient treatment.

Finally, the University had been steadily moving to increase its control over the hospitals. Dr. Robert A. Moore, named vice chancellor for the health professions in 1954 (see pp. 207–08), was carrying out, as best he could, his development plan, his "detailed prospectus," for the Health Center. He was a powerful administrator, and he proceeded to do what was expected of him: to bring the medical center hospitals into closer cooperation with the School of Medicine. He met resistance from the independent hospital boards, who were united in a suspicion that the University was trying to usurp their power. By the time Moore resigned in 1957, after clashes with Litchfield, he had set a new course for the Medical School and the University that future vice chancellors and deans were to carry out.

The thrust behind these changes was the School of Medicine's determination, by whatever means, to move into the front rank of U.S. medical schools. If the school was to prosper, it must enroll a competent student body from all over the country, attract outstanding practitioners, and increase endowment. It must raise research monies and recruit first-rate researchers, and it must become known both for excellent hospital care and for superior research. The centralization of the Health Center hospitals was the cornerstone of the plan to achieve these ends, not only because modern medicine was now increasingly interdisciplinary but because centralization would help to standardize the level of teaching and patient care within the hospitals. By 1964 the plan was demonstrably successful. Thirty percent of the student body in the School of Medicine now came from outside Pennsylvania. Sponsored research funds had catapulted from $750,000 per year to about $5 million. The School of Medicine, which previously had consisted almost solely of part-time volunteer faculty, was now building a full-time faculty who were interested in furthering the success of the school.

Although the hospitals were suspicious of the University and uncomfortable with centralized control, they were persuaded to come together because on many levels it made sense to do so. They could plan together, they could share some of their facilities, and they would benefit from the cross-fertilization of so many medical professionals working in close proximity. This union, nevertheless, would have to overcome deeply divisive issues.

One major conflict centered on the appointment of hospital staffs. To the School of Medicine, it was imperative that each physician appointed to a hospital staff be worthy of appointment to the faculty of the School of Medicine; but to the hospitals this requirement seemed a usurpation of the right to choose their own staffs. F. Sargent Cheever, who served as the first president of the Health Center, later recalled the conflict:

> The requirements of members were not stringent but even these had to be sold to the wary institutional members of the UHCP with great care and tact. . . . A necessary requirement was that before a physician could join the staff of one of the affiliated hospitals, he or she must have an appointment on the faculty of medicine. This caused some difficulty with grandfather clauses, and two institutions in particular . . . were very suspicious of the whole business, feeling that the School of Medicine would want to freeze out certain worthy physicians simply because they were not acceptable to the "holier than thou" academically minded physicians on the fulltime faculty of the School of Medicine.

Valuable time was spent settling jurisdictional disputes. An ongoing complaint was that the University was exerting too strong an influence over the other members of the affiliation. The rule that there had to be unanimity among the six institutions—Pitt and the five hospitals—made it extremely difficult to reach a decision. Some decisions were reached, but only on trivial matters; important issues rarely got to a point of decision.

When Cheever retired in 1974, he spoke out publicly about the lack of true progress in the Health Center: "Our present rate of progress . . . is not rapid enough," he said, and, "Are we willing to sacrifice that degree of institutional autonomy necessary to permit the Health Center to plan and to govern itself as an organic whole for the good of the whole complex?"

In 1974 Nathan J. Stark, a Kansas City business executive and attorney, was brought in to succeed Cheever as president of UHCP, and for a time matters, from an administrative standpoint, looked more hopeful. The Health Center received a $1 million grant from the Richard King Mellon Foundation to hire a full-time planning director to coordinate finances and development. Stark predicted that within three years the Health Center would be self-supporting through grants, member contributions, and the cultivation of new sources of income. The conflicts between the University and the hospitals, nevertheless, continued to fester.

In March 1983 Chancellor Posvar made a stunning announcement. The University of Pittsburgh was withdrawing from membership in the Health Center, which henceforth would be limited to the hospitals themselves. The Health Center Board would continue as a confederation of medical service institutions. The University would make separate bilateral agreements with each hospital on any issue of shared interest.

"This action," Posvar said, "clarifies the mission of the University (through its Medical School) as a center for medical teaching and research, inasmuch as the University is no longer to be regarded as one among others in respect to its mission, but rather a strong partner with each member hospital." At the same time, he said the action "acknowledges as unrealistic the aspiration of years past that the University Health Center should be a vehicle for increasing centralization, combination, and expansion of operational activity."

An editorial in the *Pittsburgh Post-Gazette* titled "Pitt's Impossible Dream," published immediately after Posvar's announcement, characterized the relationships between the University, its medical school, its other health schools, and the six UHCP hospitals as "a spaghetti snarl of interrelationships and lines of command that only the most sophisticated fully understand." The editorial warned, "If the institutions in the University Health Center are not careful, they may find that hanging separately is the penalty for not having hung together."

Posvar spoke of the importance of basic biological research and called for a stronger voice from clinical department chairmen and medical scientists in making policy for the Health Center hospitals, implying that the University and the Health Center could not really be separate because the faculty in the Schools of the Health Professions and the clinical staff of the hospitals were actually one and the same. One successful transformation of the postwar era had been the increasing cooperation among researchers and practitioners, and a greater reliance on team efforts.

The vacancy on the Health Center board created by the resignation of the University was filled by the Western Psychiatric Institute and Clinic (WPIC). This institution, chartered by the Commonwealth of Pennsylvania in 1931, had been run since 1949, in a special arrangement with the state, by the School of Medicine. As a health care provider, WPIC seemed a more appropriate partner on the Health Center board than the University itself. The addition of WPIC indicated the growing influence of this institution under the leadership of Thomas Detre. Detre, of Hungarian birth, had received his medical education in Rome and his postgraduate psychiatry training at Yale. He came to Pittsburgh in March 1983 from the Yale–New Haven Hospital, where he was psychiatrist in chief. At the University he assumed the joint position of director of WPIC and chairman of the Department of Psychiatry in the School of Medicine.

One of Detre's early priorities at WPIC was the recruitment of faculty. His predecessor, Henry Brosin, had been deeply influenced by the work of Sigmund Freud, and he had built a faculty with a strong psychoanalytic orientation. The psychoanalytic approach to treating emotionally disturbed patients, so popular in the 1950s and 1960s, was now giving way to new pharmacological and neurological methods, and this approach was preferred by Detre. He sought distinguished academicians with multiple expertise ranging from the social and behavioral sciences to the neurobiological aspects of psychiatry.

Under his direction, WPIC attracted national attention, and its budget increased nearly tenfold. Additional federal and foundation grants enabled the institute to develop new programs, to expand those already established, and to carry out a major restructuring of the clinical services. Detre and his team turned WPIC into a center for creative research and new treatment modalities. The institute became known for its work on sleep disorders and affective disorders (particularly depression), biologic drug therapies, and innovative treatment programs for such specialized groups as children and geriatric patients.

Detre, who was soon to become associate senior vice chancellor for health sciences, began to refine his thinking between 1981 and 1983 about the principles on which the future of medicine would be based. Central to his philosophy was an emphasis on strengthening the university hospital. He drew a distinction between the "teaching hospital" and the "university hospital." In the teaching hospital, he said, the mission of the hospital predominates, with academic programs vying with other services for scarce funds, staff, and space. In the university hospital, by contrast, the primary mission is academic. Within the Health Center, all the hospitals except WPIC were technically teaching hospitals. They provided training to medical students and residents on the house staff, while ministering to patients from throughout the tri-state area, but were not actually controlled by the medical school. "Clearly," Detre wrote, "the mandate of the university hospital is to be in the forefront of health training, research, and service delivery. Looking beyond the borders of its local area, it strives to be a standard-setter nationwide."

In the summer of 1984, Nathan Stark, having held the top position in Health Sciences for ten years (interrupted by a year as under-secretary of health, education and welfare), left to join a Washington law firm. Detre succeeded him. Under his direction, the University's hold on academic medicine has been strengthened and a redefinition of the Health Center is in progress. Eye and Ear Hospital is now operated by the University, which also has taken over the management of Falk Clinic. While Magee and Montefiore seem to have drifted away from the University's orbit, Presbyterian-University Hospital may be moving closer to it. The UHCP board now handles only routine operating matters and exhibits little appetite for decision-making by consensus.

The School of Medicine was troubled in the early 1980s by accumulating problems. The state had not increased its $4 million annual appropriation between 1974 and 1981. School tuition skyrocketed from $710 a year for Pennsylvania residents in 1970 to almost $7,000 a decade later, but even these sharply increased tuitions did not enable the school to operate on a balanced budget. Each year the University had to add $2 to $3 million to its operating budget to prevent a deficit. Although the clinical departments were strong, the five departments of basic biological sciences (biochemistry, anatomy and cell biology, microbiology, physiology, and pharmacology) needed more faculty and a reorganization of programs and curricula. Several of these departments lacked heads. A $2 million grant for nutrition research had to be returned to the donor because of a lack of trained researchers. There was a publicly aired dispute on the issue of "practice income"—on whether the income generated by clinical faculty services should accrue to the department that earned it for departmental use, or be placed at the general disposal of the medical school.

Through all the problems and discord, the medical school made remarkable progress in medical research and teaching and slow but steady progress in rebuilding the departments. By 1985 a number of departments had achieved national stature, and seven of the vacant departmental chairs had been filled. The seed for the new Pittsburgh Cancer Institute (PCI) had been sown and its first director recruited, and the new building that housed the nation's largest nuclear magnetic resonance diagnostic scanning machine had been opened to the first patients.

Medical research at Pitt was conducted at both the basic and clinical levels. For example, at the same time that a group of clinical investigators began a study to determine the earliest signs and symptoms of Alzheimer's disease in human beings, researchers in basic pharmacology were developing an animal model of the illness using a neurotoxin to mimic the symptoms of dementia. Although scientists with major reputations headed many research projects, the team concept was emphasized. Once a research team had been assembled, its members were encouraged to follow their intuition in selecting the research direction they believed most promising.

There is no better example of this philosophy of creative collaboration than the work of Bernard Fisher and his colleagues. Fisher, a native of Pittsburgh and professor of surgery at Pitt's School of Medicine, is one of the world's leading cancer researchers. It was Fisher's intent to take a scientific look at current clinical practices, analyze the effectiveness of each practice, and systematically examine alternatives. His area of interest was a disease of major concern to women: breast cancer. When Fisher began his research, the current clinical treatment of breast cancer was radical mastectomy, a disfiguring and physically debilitating surgical procedure that calls for the removal of the entire breast, the lymph nodes under the arm, and the underlying chest muscles. The treatment was based on the belief that cancer cells spread from the tumor directly to the adjacent tissue and were then incorporated by the lymph nodes.

Early work at Pitt demonstrated that breast cancer is a systemic disease rather than a localized one; from its onset cancer cells get into the bloodstream rather than progress in an orderly fashion into surrounding tissues. This discovery suggested a marked change in treatment.

In 1963 the National Cancer Institute asked Fisher to head a major study of the various approaches to treating breast cancer. The National Surgical Adjuvant Breast Project (NSABP), a consortium of more than 100 medical centers, experimented with less extensive surgical procedures and with the use of chemotherapy rather than radiation after surgery. If breast cancer is a systemic disease, as Fisher believed, then chemotherapy, which is a systemic treatment, is a more appropriate follow-up to surgery. The results of the NSABP experiments, announced in 1979, changed the way breast cancer is treated. For 85 percent of all women in the United States who get breast cancer and discover it early, the radical mastectomy is rejected in favor of the less extensive simple mastectomy. And because of the use of chemotherapy, for the first time in fifty years mortality rates for the disease began to decrease.

The next step in the NSABP project was to determine whether even more limited surgery such as lumpectomy and segmental mastectomy could be as effective as removal of the entire breast for many women with early-stage breast cancer. Researchers from eighty-nine institutions cooperating in the study concluded that segmental mastectomy (removal of the cancerous lump and an adequate amount of normal tissue to ensure that the area is tumor-free), plus chemotherapy, is appropriate for treating breast cancer patients with tumors four centimeters or less in diameter. The NASBP-proven theories on the spread of breast tumors are now being applied to other solid tumors. Today the whole field of oncology is shifting toward understanding cancer as a bodywide disease and treating it as such.

The history of Pittsburgh's organ transplant program provides a second example of how medical science can be shaped for use in clinical practice. By 1985 surgeons of the School of Medicine had performed more than 1,400 operations in which they replaced failing or irreparably diseased organs with healthy organs. The story begins more than two decades earlier, however, with the arrival of Henry T. Bahnson in 1963 as chairman of the Department of Surgery at the medical school and chief of surgery at Presbyterian-University Hospital. In his courses in cardiovascular physiology at Harvard and Johns Hopkins, Bahnson had studied the great landmarks in heart surgery: the mechanical aortic valve developed by Charles A. Hufnagel at Georgetown University (1952); the invention of the heart-lung machine (1953); Michael DeBakey's development of a plastic heart pump in Houston and his replacement of damaged arteries with synthetic tubing (1953); the first coronary bypass operation, performed by René Favoloro at the Cleveland Clinic (1967); and, in 1967, Christiaan Barnard's transplantation of a human heart at Cape Town, South Africa (the patient lived eighteen days). In 1969 Bahnson performed the first successful heart transplant in Pennsylvania; the patient lived for eighteen months. Eight percent of heart transplant patients at this time, however, died within a year. As a result, enthusiasm for human heart transplant surgery waned, and all programs except the one at Stanford were terminated pending reevaluation.

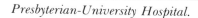

Presbyterian-University Hospital.

Stanford's Norman Shumway was experimenting with Cyclosporine-A, a Swiss-made product that seemed to suppress the white blood cell growth that causes rejection of the transplanted tissue.

Bahnson and his colleagues carried on animal research and experiments after 1969, at the same time planning to resume the human heart program when surgical techniques were improved and the means found to counteract tissue rejection. In 1980, with Robert Hardesty and Bartley Griffith, Bahnson performed another heart transplant. About the same time he persuaded Thomas E. Starzl, a pioneer transplant surgeon working in Denver and a long-time friend, to join the Pitt faculty.

Born in Iowa, Starzl did his first successful kidney transplant in 1961 at the University of Colorado. A little more than a year later he transplanted a human liver in an operation that, because of the extraordinarily high degree of surgical skill required, had never before been attempted. The patient lived twenty-two days. Starzl performed three more liver transplants in the next three months, all unsuccessful.

For the next four years, Starzl and his team performed kidney transplants only, at the same time studying and experimenting with various drugs designed to combat the body's natural tendency to reject grafted organs. In 1967 they resumed liver transplant surgery, and a transplant operation performed in that year enabled the patient to survive for more than twelve months. Success with liver transplants improved steadily, and with the development of Cyclosporine, the survival rate rose dramatically.

Starzl joined the Pitt faculty early in 1981 and soon began to impress the public and the national media not only with his surgical skills but also with the brilliant team he pulled together within the Health Center. In June 1984 Starzl and Bahnson, with the support of a large team of surgeons, nurses, and other medical specialists, performed the world's first double transplant operation. The patient was Stormie Jones, a six-year-old from Cumby, Texas. She was afflicted with a rare disease known as homozygous hypercholesterolemia and had recently undergone two unsuccessful heart operations. Stormie's damaged heart and liver were replaced during a sixteen-hour operation at Children's Hospital, and for several weeks thereafter she was the heroine of a nationally reported drama.

In 1984 the University of Pittsburgh was the only place in the country where transplant surgery on all six major organs (heart, liver, kidney, pancreas, lungs and corneas) including simultaneous replacement of the heart and lungs, was being done. As evidence of its success, within a one-year period it carried out the largest number of successful childhood liver transplants done anywhere in the world. The demand for such operations became heavier than the Pittsburgh team could handle. They were under pressure to accept more patients, but they could do "only two or three livers a week." And so Starzl began to train surgeons from other cities to perform liver transplants. In passing on his methods to other surgeons, Starzl hoped to establish liver transplant centers around the world. By the summer of 1984 there were about one dozen surgeons who were capable of heading liver transplant teams—all of them taught by Starzl—and about ten hospitals performing the operation.

Many of the breakthroughs in medicine at the University have come about as the result of interdisciplinary and cooperative efforts. In Posvar's words, "The University contains the collective intellectual power to attack such problems as disease, environment, and energy, but to do so effectively it must cross internal boundaries and break patterns. . . . Expertise is compartmentalized within traditional academic disciplines and departments. This system of organization has strong historic and current merit, but interdisciplinary and interschool efforts are mandated by new social imperatives. The bridging process has begun."

One of these interdisciplinary bridges has resulted in the development of Caduceus, a computer program designed to make medical diagnoses. It is the creation of two professors, Jack D. Myers and Harry E. Pople, Jr. Myers, who headed Pitt's Department of Medicine from 1965 to 1970, is one of the country's leading specialists in internal medicine. Pople, associate professor in the Graduate School of Business, is a computer scientist with far-ranging interests. Together Pople and Myers co-direct the University's Decision System Laboratory, where Caduceus, operating in a Digital Equipment Corporation VAX mainframe computer, lives.

Physicians need a computerized consultative system for two reasons. First, the base of medical knowledge in any broad specialty has grown to the point that no physician can hold such knowledge in his working memory. Second, the number of tenable diagnostic hypotheses is so great that the physician may not consider any given diagnosis adequately or at all. "The ablest clinician," Myers says, "can recall no more than about 20 percent of what he's read, seen, or heard about any particular ailment. The brightest human brain can juggle no more than six or seven hypotheses simultaneously. In contrast, today's computers can weigh dozens at once. The machines of the next decade will be even brainier."

With expert medical knowledge stored in the computer's memory, the physician can obtain a complete and up-to-date profile of a disease in minutes. He can command the computer to display the interconnections of that disease with all other diseases. He can obtain a listing of all diseases in which a given symptom, laboratory measurement, or radiological abnormality occurs. When confronted with a complex or obscure clinical problem, he can feed all the clinical information he has obtained about the patient—history, physical observations, and laboratory findings—into the system. If the evidence is adequate, Caduceus will supply all possible diagnoses and will then determine the actual disease through the process of elimination and the weighing of evidence. In a dialogue carried on with the physician, it may suggest additional tests or ask for more clinical information before arriving at a diagnosis.

In 1982 Caduceus passed parts of the National Board examination in internal medicine. It is used in the education of medical students, the continuing education of physicians, and the clinical testing and evaluation of both students and physicians. By the end of 1985 the system contained information about more than 4,000 symptoms of nearly six hundred diseases. Pople and Myers emphasize, however, that while the system has performed well, it is still some years away from routine use in the doctor's office or in the hospital.

Another example of emerging cooperative patterns in modern medicine is the Pittsburgh Nuclear Magnetic Resonance Institute, a nonprofit consortium formed by the University of Pittsburgh, Carnegie-Mellon University, the six UHCP hospitals, and other area hospitals. At the heart of the project is new technology: a magnetic resonance scanner that makes images of the body's tissues, not just the skeletal structure, and does so without using harmful ionizing radiation or contrast agents. NMR has been called "a clearer window into the brain and central nervous system."

Federal and state agencies approved the $8.6 million project in December 1983, and ground was broken in May 1984 for a new building to house the 14,000-pound donut-shaped body scanner. The machine surrounds the body with a strong static magnetic field and a small radio-frequency field. Signals are sent from the scanner to a computer, which analyzes the information and color-codes it to display soft tissue as well as bony structure in almost photographic detail.

Magnetic resonance spectroscopy can be harnessed to examine not only the cell's structure but also its chemical composition over time. The diagnostic and research potential of this technology is thus virtually doubled. Tissue biochemistry can be measured directly to yield a running picture of normal and abnormal processes occurring in the body. Because the clinician can examine the same tissue site again and again, he can detect physiological alterations before they are able to create the anatomical changes that would appear on an image. Likewise, the effects of treatment can be monitored to determine whether drug intervention has been of therapeutic value.

Magnetic resonance is not a new invention; its developers won a Nobel Prize in physics in 1952. It is new to medicine, however, and the potential of this technology for treatment and prevention is just beginning to be realized. Much of the promise that magnetic resonance imaging and spectroscopy holds is still in the phases of research and development. These activities are under way in Pittsburgh through the NMR Institute.

The National Cancer Act of 1971 established the concept of cancer centers as focal points for coordination and multidisciplinary cancer research in universities. It resulted in another major medical collaboration in Pittsburgh—the Pittsburgh Cancer Institute, which involves efforts by the University of Pittsburgh, Carnegie-Mellon University, and the six medical center hospitals. The Richard King Mellon Foundation launched the center with a grant of $3 million, and the university and hospital participants pledge yearly operating funds for diagnostic treatment services and cancer research.

As the first step in the collaboration, Falk Clinic, the ambulatory care clinic operated by the University, assesses adult cancer patients. Laboratory facilities are housed within various member institutions. Each institution draws on the personnel and resources of its affiliates and works closely with the Pittsburgh NMR Institute.

In 1985, Ronald Herberman left his position at the National Cancer Institute to become director of PCI. Also tied in with PCI is the establishment with CMU of a program to prepare research scientists. Graduates of this program will have earned an M.D. degree from Pitt and a Ph.D. from a biological science department at either Pitt or CMU.

A major chronic problem of our society is the care of the elderly. People sixty-five years old or older make up a steadily increasing proportion of the population; the fastest-growing segment is the group characterized as the "oldest old"—those eighty-five and older.

One of the many illnesses likely to strike older people, Alzheimer's disease, is a bewildering brain disorder that affects between 1 and 2 million people in the United States. At first manifesting itself in slight memory lapses, the disease continues its inexorable course toward complete mental confusion and dementia, a period that may take only a few months or as long as ten years. The disease strikes indiscriminately across all social groups. There is no known cure. Researchers in the Departments of Psychiatry, Neurology, and Medicine of the University of Pittsburgh's School of Medicine are involved in intensive efforts to solve the mystery of Alzheimer's disease, while clinicians attempt to care for and comfort its victims. One of these efforts is a five-year project funded by the National Institute on Aging to determine the earliest signs and symptoms of the disease.

However, Alzheimer's disease is by no means the only medical problem confronting the elderly. Because they often face both multiple health problems and the frailties that accompany the aging process, the elderly are best treated in a consolidated and comprehensive care system. For this reason Pitt has created the Benedum Center for Geriatric Medicine. Its history dates to 1977, when Posvar designated the development of academic programs in geriatrics and gerontology as one of the University's highest priorities. Money to recruit the first director of the University's gerontology program was provided by a $250,000 grant from the Richard King Mellon Foundation. In 1980 the Claude Worthington Benedum Foundation gave $1 million to the Departments of Medicine and Psychiatry to establish a program that would integrate these specialties for the benefit of elderly patients.

The Benedum geriatric program operates on the premise that the biological, psychological, and social aspects of aging cannot be separated. Therefore, the University has assembled a faculty of nationally recognized experts in a wide variety of fields—medicine, public health, pharmacology, epidemiology, social work, and other relevant disciplines. The Benedum Center has as its goal the development of a model service facility for the elderly. To this end it seeks to create innovative programs in geriatrics and to influence the curricula in which those who will one day provide health care for the elderly receive their training.

The Pittsburgh Cancer Institute and the University's programs in geriatrics and gerontology are built around a single critical issue. Like other programs at the University, they are multidisciplinary and multiinstitutional. As such, they break the bounds of traditional academia and point the way to the future. Research and development, and even teaching, often take place on a horizontal plane, cutting across disciplines and departments, cutting across even traditional university boundaries and rivalries. Collaborative efforts are the future of a society that must be concerned with efficient use of health care resources. Whether these new modes of research and health care delivery will require new management structures is still open to question. What is clear is that the area of Western Pennsylvania will continue to benefit from the vibrancy and innovation that characterize academic medicine today.

36

The Campus of the Future

We shall not cease from exploration
And the end of all our exploring
Will be to arrive where we started
And know the place for the first time.

T. S. Eliot,
"Little Gidding,"
Four Quartets

THERE were important developments on the campus in 1983–1985 that serve to illustrate major themes of the Posvar administration. They are typical of the style and represent the deepest convictions and aspirations of the chancellor/president* who throughout 1987 will celebrate his own private anniversary—the twentieth of his arrival on the University of Pittsburgh campus. They reflect his belief that the survival of a university depends on its capacity to set priorities and allocate resources by planning; that the university must expand its international dimension; that research universities are acquiring a new role in the American economy; that the state should use research universities to create new industrial growth through advanced technology; that research faculties and business entities will increasingly carry out research and development projects cooperatively.

Consider:

• A giant corporation gives its $100 million research center to the University—a community of fifty-four buildings on eighty-five acres in a Pittsburgh suburb. The gift includes laboratories, a computer telecommunications center, an executive office building—all completely furnished and equipped—and a $3 million fund to pay the costs of taking it over.

• The University begins a multi-million-dollar joint venture with the American Telephone and Telegraph Company to build, by early 1987, a telecommunications network that "will be the central nervous system of a fantastically new sophisticated communications environment—the underpinning of the whole forthcoming information revolution."

• The University embarks on a set of programs that involve radically new ideas and relationships. The programs are grounded on the concept of closer working ties between and among higher education, corporate industry, sources of venture capital, and local and state government.

• Large universities do not often engage in an overall comprehensive planning effort in which they revise their priorities and redeploy their resources.

Corporations commonly do. So, too, in 1985, did the University of Pittsburgh. It completed a year-long debate on its mission and its methods—what it has called "a strenuous year of institutional self-examination, collegial deliberation, creative thinking, and a good dose of mutual criticism." It examined the work and plans of every school, center, and department, every aspect of "the education business" at Pitt, including budgets, academic quality, and cost effectiveness, and it took appropriate action on its findings.

• President Posvar becomes the first U.S. university president to visit Cuba in twenty-five years. He returns with a preliminary agreement with the University of Havana involving an exchange program between the two universities.

The $100,000,000 Gift. In 1985 Western Pennsylvania lost a major corporation, Gulf Oil, which had contributed to the economic well-being of the region, the city, and the University for many years. Gulf was acquired by Chevron Oil, headquartered in California, which had its own research facilities at Richland and had no need for the Gulf research and development center in Harmarville, a few miles up the Allegheny River from downtown Pittsburgh. The center had a replacement value of $100 million. Pitt proposed that it be given the research center, pointing out, first, that the community would benefit if the center remained open and, second, that Pitt had the array of academic, research, managerial, and financial resources to undertake the responsibility of such an operation. Gulf and Chevron agreed to that proposal. Chevron added a $3 million start-up grant, and the Commonwealth offered a $3 million matching grant for economic development.

Posvar announced at a press conference in April 1985: "This unprecedented action . . . is really a gift to the people of Pennsylvania and the Pittsburgh region. It will enable us to maintain an operational resource of growing benefit to the public and the business and educational sectors. We expect it to be a significant factor in the economic revitalization of the region as well as becoming a national asset for the advancement of American science and technology." The University took over the facilities, renamed the University of Pittsburgh Applied Re-

---

*The University dropped the title *chancellor* and adopted the title *president* on October 18, 1984.

search Center (UPARC), in early 1986 and on March 17 signed a four-year, $13 million contract with its first major tenant, General Motors Corporation.

UPARC, Posvar says, represents "a unique initiative in American scientific research. It . . . is an operational complex of multipurpose laboratories and support services ranging from a sophisticated center to analytical labs and machine and instrumentation shops."

Research and development have always been a part of any corporate structure, but UPARC may represent a revised model of the research process known as technology transfer. "It is worth contemplating," Posvar says, "how the accelerated dynamics of this transfer often compress, bend and even reverse the old, standard sequence of basic research, applied research, technological development, and ultimate production. Now, instead, basic research in genetics becomes instantaneously applied research or technology. In surface science, for example, basic research can be quickly transformed into material results. This means that applied developers and technologists can intervene and even control the direction of basic research. . . . Clearly, society gains from any contraction of the time span between discovery and a finished product."

The Campus of the Future. In December 1983 the University of Pittsburgh and AT&T Information Systems announced their intention to equip Pitt with an innovative telecommunications network. On November 1, 1985, Pitt became the first university in the world to adopt the system: an optic fiber communication network that transports voice (telephone), data (computers), and video (television). This knowledge network, known as the Campus of the Future, represents a partnership that, Posvar says, "will revolutionize the way we analyze and share information here in Western Pennsylvania and around the world." AT&T describes the system as the basis for a global information society. It will give students, faculty members, and administrators anywhere on campus access to information, literally at the touch of a button, from libraries, host computers, and video sources. It will also serve as a testing ground for computer and electronic companies to evaluate experimental equipment and products.

The information capacity of this system is phenomenal, though barely tapped as yet. For instance, a pair of optic fibers can carry more than a thousand telephone conversations. By 1988, light-wave cables will transmit data fast enough to send the entire contents of the *Encyclopedia Britannica* in two seconds. A trans-Atlantic optic fiber will link North America and Europe by 1988. This is being called a postindustrial equivalent of Marconi's breakthrough in radio. Optic fiber networks may soon compete with or even supplant satellite transmission of information on a global scale.

The sophisticated system makes Pitt its own telephone company, linking all 11,000 phones on campus more efficiently and cheaply than the old system. In fact, the bond indebtedness for the first phase of the entire Campus of the Future project will cost no more than the annual bill of the old telephone system.

The data component of the project will link the University's mainframe computers, microcomputers, personal computers, and printers by means of an AT&T invention called the Information Systems network (ISN). The Pitt link-up is the largest in the world, with 1,400 ports in place, and—since ISN is compatible with all other computer brands and models—it has the capacity for unlimited growth.

The video component is controlled by a prototype video switch that sorts incoming signals, deciphers them, and routes them to classrooms, lecture halls, and seminar suites. Within a few years 120 classrooms will be linked by video. Teachers can call up by phone existing video resources or specially created video discs, each with a capacity of 15,000 images. They can tape a lecture and automatically store it at the University's video center for later playback. External-studies students and those at Pitt's regional campuses will "attend" the lectures by light wave.

AT&T, in conjunction with the Campus of the Future undertaking, is supporting a new master of science program in telecommunications that promises to be large, diversified, and innovative. The primary purpose of the Pitt-AT&T collaboration, however, is not to produce telecommunication experts or even computer specialists. "Our aim,"

Posvar says, "is to understand how students—how anyone—can use computers and other emerging technologies to acquire, analyze, and share an unprecedented scope of information. We seek new potentials for creative discovery in the arts, literature, sciences and engineering. Pitt will become an unprecedented testing ground to learn how pivotal changes in information technology affect our universities, our society."

New Ideas and Relationships. Early in the 1980s, aided by grants from industry, the University established the Foundation for Applied Science and Technology. FAST, a wholly owned nonprofit research organization, assists University researchers in patenting inventions and acquiring ownership in resulting products. University scientists, Posvar has pointed out, "have traditionally conducted most of the *basic*—far-sighted, open-ended— research in this country. . . . We believe the Foundation will add relevance to our educational mission by offering students exposure to applied research projects. We also believe it will be a factor in moving Western Pennsylvania towards a more secure technology-based economy." A board of directors is responsible for overseeing FAST's operations and policies.

In February 1983 the University's trustees established a new nonprofit corporation—the University of Pittsburgh Trust—to oversee designated corporate entities affiliated with the University but not strictly educational in nature. The corporation is a vehicle for organizing activities that would benefit the University but that should function as separate entities. FAST became its first subsidiary.

Pennsylvania Governor Dick Thornburgh, a graduate with high honors from Pitt Law School, is the moving force behind what may be the state's most ambitious development program: to organize and use universities of the Commonwealth to create new industrial growth and new jobs through advanced technology. This program, called the Ben Franklin Partnership, functions through four regional centers of advanced technology based at or near universities around the state. It got under way in February 1983 after the state legislature appropriated $1 million for its operation and the state's

Ben Franklin Partnership Board awarded $250,000 in matching grants to each of the four centers.

The Western Pennsylvania Advanced Technology Center, largest of the four, is administered jointly by the University of Pittsburgh and Carnegie-Mellon University through their wholly owned affiliate, the Mellon-Pitt-Carnegie Corporation (MPC). Twenty Pittsburgh corporations promptly pledged $600,000 for its first six months of operations. The Partnership Board then awarded MPC a second grant of $3.3 million in August 1983. To this was added $7 million from other sources, primarily industrial, to support a $10 million job creation effort. (The money is paid directly to the Technology Center, not to the universities.)* Forty-three research and development projects are now well under way. By early 1986 these regionally sponsored projects created 58 new companies.

The University of Pittsburgh, in partnership with CMU, began a major undertaking in January 1986 when the National Science Foundation awarded them $40 million to establish the fifth and most advanced supercomputing center in the United States. The center will be responsive to and serve the national community as well as local research efforts. The $22 million Cray X-MP/48 supercomputer installed at Pitt is the most powerful of its kind in the world. Total value of the project is more than $70 million. Posvar sees it "as a magnet for attracting new high-technology business and industries to the Pittsburgh area."

The Institutional Self-Examination. Roger Benjamin, provost and senior vice president of the University, was charged late in 1983 with conducting what came to be called "the most sweeping and detailed planning activity in the University's history." A political scientist and administrator from the University of Minnesota at Minneapolis, Benjamin did not foresee an easy future for higher education; he felt that all the indices pointed to a transformation in postindustrial societies and to hard times in the universities. He believed that the University of Pittsburgh "was going to have to make some choices, or

*The other advanced technology centers are at Penn State, the University of Pennsylvania, and Lehigh University.

somebody else is going to make the choice for us.

The planning program he developed with executive vice president Jack Freeman and with senior vice president for the health sciences Thomas Detre called for the scrutiny of every aspect of operations at Pitt. The entire academic program was examined in the light of projected declines in enrollment, reduction in tuition, and rising costs. Each academic unit was asked to make a self-study in which it evaluated its programs on the basis of quality, centrality, comparative advantage, student demand, and cost. A task force on planning then examined these studies and made its recommendations. Thus the University was willing to ask the most searching and painful questions of itself.

The provost's "preliminary recommendations," which contained dramatic, even revolutionary recommendations for change, were distributed on November 29, 1984. There followed intensive discussions between the schools and the provost's office aimed at devising mutually agreed-upon recommendations. In this process of free inquiry and review, a number of the original proposals were modified. The provost submitted his "final recommendations" to President Posvar on March 19.

Posvar on June 18 submitted to the trustees a revised document, sixty-four pages in length, titled "Report to Trustees, June 1985: The University Plan." The trustees ratified this document.

This process gripped the attention of a great many people in 1984–1985, and the documents are still good reading for anyone interested in an intimate look into the workings of a large urban research university; but the decisions and recommendations on scores of issues cannot possibly be covered in this history. One proposal (adopted in 1986) was for an undergraduate Honors College to provide an advanced curriculum for gifted students. The University Plan also calls for greatly increased interdisciplinary studies. According to Posvar, academic strengths and intellectual resources at the University can be intensified and even multiplied by cutting across administrative and professional boundaries. He cited specific areas where the University's competitive advantages can lead to major advances: in sophisticated materials science; neural sciences; molecular and cell biology; biotechnology; logic and linguistics; information sciences; corporate and public management; international studies; and philosophy of science.*

An American in Cuba. Accompanied by Cole Blasier, professor of political science and an expert on Latin America, Posvar visited Havana in May 1985. After several days of talks with University of Havana and government officials, they returned to Pittsburgh to announce preliminary plans for an exchange of scholars, students, and library materials. The "program is to be small and of high quality," the president said, "yet it has the potential to be the most comprehensive one involving the United States since the Cuban revolution, as it spans the social sciences and also the natural sciences and professions." This arrangement will give Pitt's experts on Cuba unparalleled opportunity for research and teaching. Acknowledging the political difficulties between the United States and Cuba, Posvar commented, "We believe that the intellectual dimension contains no threat to any government and may help foster ultimate ways to diminish dangerous tensions."

The University's Center for Latin American Studies (CLAS), is regarded as one of the University's truly distinguished units, which is somewhat surprising in a city with a Hispanic population of less than 1 percent. CLAS encompasses studies of countries throughout Latin America, but it has developed a particularly strong program in Cuban studies. The Center's library collection on Cuba is one of the most valuable anywhere; and together with the CLAS Monograph and Document Series, it forms an indispensable resource for anyone undertaking research on Cuba.

Wesley Posvar has enormously extended the International Dimension in his two decades in office. He has said in the strongest terms permitted a university president: "As we approach the twenty-first century, no educational institution in this country can claim to serve American students, American science, and American policy if it fails to incorporate

---

*For a statistical account of the state of the University at the beginning of Year 1986, see Appendix III.

internationalism at the core of its educational mission." Pitt now has academic exchange agreements with institutions in more than one hundred countries, including those in Western Europe and in China, the USSR, Poland, Yugoslovia, Bulgaria, and Hungary.

As of early 1986, some of Posvar's long-standing aspirations remain to be fulfilled. For example, he still aspires to make greater gains in recruiting black students and black faculty. There has been improvement, but not nearly enough, says Posvar, in appointments for women and blacks in the administration, faculty, and staff. And some internal issues are yet to be resolved. For instance, a segment of the faculty favors unionization; the president remains opposed, believing the concept of shared governance preferable to labor-management bargaining.

On a grander scale, the University approaches its bicentennial challenged and intrigued by an apparent duality of mission: to be a regional institution serving the communities and people of the immediate area, or to be a national/international university with a strong emphasis on research and teaching. Posvar argues that "we cannot be one or the other; that to serve the needs and be a leader within the context of our region—whether defined narrowly as Western Pennsylvania or as the Upper Ohio Valley or as the Middle Atlantic—we must be a national/international university ranked among the very best of the comprehensive, urban centers of research and teaching in the world."

Epilogue

One of the conclusions I have come to in writing this history is that this is essentially a success story—a happy chronicle of a sound and worthwhile accomplishment. For almost two hundred years there has been an output of a good product: an annual harvest of young people admirably trained to earn a living, to make a contribution to their community, their profession, and their country.

The author, in an address at a University planning conference on the Johnstown campus, May 31, 1984

A MAJOR ACADEMIC ANNIVERSARY is customarily an occasion when amiable platitudes are permissible. A university stands at the Threshold of a New Era. It faces heightened responsibilities and even more insistent demands. It must fill a role of vigorous leadership as it moves into the coming (decade) (half-century) (century), which will be marked by even broader capabilities, challenges, and expectations. If it does so, it will serve the community through future generations as it has in the past. It will be a cutting edge of progress. It will fulfill its promise and be true to its heritage.

There are times, of course, when platitudes convey an honest sentiment and describe an actual situation. The marking of a University's two hundredth anniversary is perhaps such an occasion. The University of Pittsburgh, two centuries old in February 1987, is moving into a period of accelerated change. And yet, some things will not change—they will be constant and recognizable on the Campus of the Future.

- There will certainly be a continuing debate on the roles and relative importance of teaching and research, of teachers and researchers. The debate will not be resolved.

- Young men and young women in college will not always act as their parents and teachers think they should act. From time to time they will opt to see how far they can push.

- Athletics will continue to be the one area of endeavor where, in the words of Jacques Barzun, all parties are serious about what they do.

- The University will never have as much money as it needs. It will also never have as much time. Nor as much space.

- The University will be the locus of divergent interests and activities, of conflicting aims and personalities, of heartaches, misfires, rivalries, human fallibilities, and angry disputes.

- The governance of an institution so large and so varied will continue to be fearfully complicated and difficult.

- The eternal questions will still be asked: What have we given our graduates to prepare them for life in this century and the next? What *should* we have given them?

- The happy chronicle, the sound and worthwhile accomplishment, will continue: the annual output of a good product—the harvest of young people admirably trained.

- There will be, God willing, a 250th anniversary at the University of Pittsburgh. Members of the Class of 1987, still in their early seventies, will return to the campus in Oakland, to the Student Union and the Quadrangles and the Cathedral of Learning, where they will attend a reunion in the twenty-first century, in the incredible year 2037.

"Universities," President Posvar said in the spring of 1985, "are lasting institutions, enduring for centuries, and no final horizon is in sight." He said:

We are reassured by their capacity to survive wars, political suppression, financial privation, public hostility, and student fickleness, and even from time to time self-inflicted wounds of intellectual smugness and academic apathy. There is, as well, a cycle in the life of a university; the needs of one generation or era differ from those of others. . . . Indeed, if there is one characteristic that marks not just the survivors, but the select and successful universities, it is the capacity to foresee change and move to meet new opportunities. . . .

While it certainly is a prime function of a university to preserve human civilization, what makes civilization vital is a ceaseless drive to discover and to reinterpret truths, and to nurture wisdom. The point-counterpoint of preservation and innovation becomes even more salient, even ironic, when one realizes that the radical notions of only several decades ago have become the weighted orthodoxy of today. The real danger for any university is the leaden hand of self-satisfaction and apathy. Recognizing that change and controversy are uncomfortable, the responsibility of all academic professionals is to the future, in awareness of the widening scope of public benefit offered by a great university.

Pitt at 200
Photographs by Lynn Johnson

Hillman Library

Henry Clay Frick Fine Arts Building

William Pitt Student Union

Mervis Hall, Graduate School of Business

The Greek Room

The Swedish Room

Litchfield Towers

Football

Health

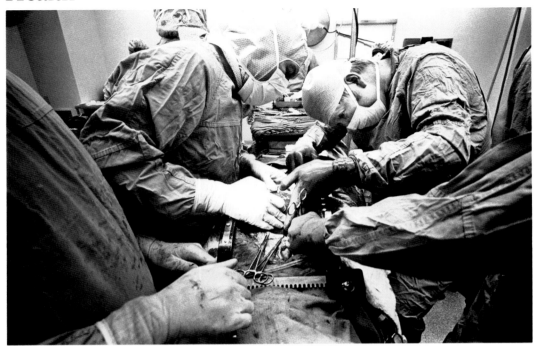

The Presbyterian University Hospital transplant team under the direction of
Thomas R. Hakala, M.D.

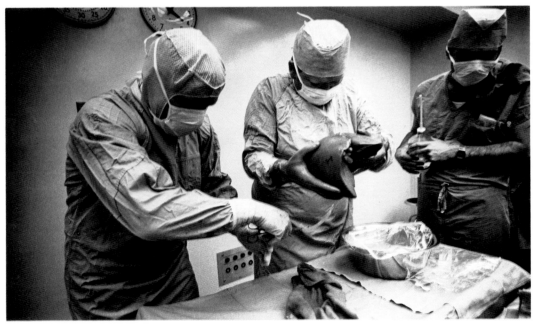

Dr. Hakala prepares a liver for transplant

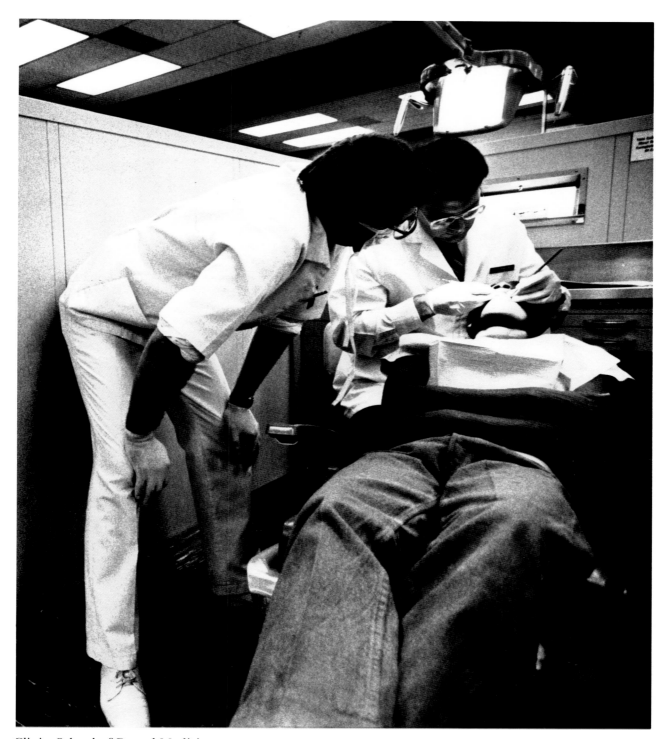

Clinic, School of Dental Medicine

Governance

Elizabeth Baranger, Dean of Graduate Studies, Faculty of Arts and Sciences

President Wesley W. Posvar and President of the Senate Barbara K. Shore

Jerome L. Rosenberg, Vice Provost and
Dean of the Faculty of Arts and Sciences,
confers with Thomas Detre,
Senior Vice President for the Health Sciences

A meeting of the Council of the University Senate

The Age of the Computer

The Chancellor's medallion, worn by the president on such occasions as commencement and the honors convocation.

Acknowledgments
Appendices
Notes and Sources
Bibliography
Index

Acknowledg-
ments

I wish first to thank, without implicating, those thirty-six persons (eleven of them now deceased) who kindly consented to tell me in extended conversations and correspondence what they knew about the University and its people. They are listed by name and position in the Bibliography. My notes on the interviews and the tapes of those that were recorded are now on file in the University archives, where, one hopes, they may be as useful to future historians as they were to me.

A number of University people other than those interviewed at length gave me information on University affairs. Needless to say, they are not responsible for the views expressed in the text, for errors or omissions. Among these were Charles E. Aston, Jr. (Special Collections, Hillman Library), W. Dean Billick (Department of Athletics), E. Maxine Bruhns (Nationality Rooms), Ronald C. Carlisle (Department of Anthropology), Lucille Crozier (University Trustee), Robert E. Dunkelman (Office of the Provost), Frances L. Drew (Department of Community Medicine, School of Medicine), Marcia Grodsky (Darlington Collection), Fletcher Hodges, Jr. (Stephen Foster Memorial, retired), Peter D. Karsten (Department of History), James Kelly (Department of Education), Bernard J. Kobosky (Office of Vice President for Public Affairs), Margaret C. McDonald (WPIC Office of the Associate Director), Robert D. Marshall (Department of English), Joseph A. Merante (Office of Admissions), James P. O'Brien (Department of Athletics), Jeffrey A. Romoff (Department of Psychiatry), Deane L. Root (Stephen Foster Memorial), Matthew J. Roper (Department of Fine Arts), Savina Skewis (Dean of Women, Emerita), Paul Solyan (Office of the Comptroller), Adelaide W. Sukiennik (Hillman Library), Neil H. Timm (Office of Vice President for Management and Budget), John R. Vrana (Office of Vice President for Business and Finance), Buell Whitehill (Emeritus, Department of Speech, Pitt-Johnstown), David G. Wilkins (Department of Fine Arts), Robb R. Wilson (Office of Institutional and Policy Studies), Julius S. Youngner (Department of Microbiology, School of Medicine), Frank A. Zabrosky (Archival Service Center), and Timothy F. Ziaukas (News andPublications).

I am also indebted to others not associated with the University who gave me information on certain events and people. Among these were Harriet Branton, Arthur Glaser, Mrs. Warren Dana, Robert E. Fulton, Joseph D. Hughes, Rita Judge of the *Pittsburgh Press*, Angelika Kane of the *Pittsburgh Post-Gazette*, Edward Lee, Jr., M. Graham Netting, William R. Oliver, Thomas C. Pears III, Herb Stein of WQED, the late Charles M. Stotz, Harry L. Wechsler, Lawrence C. Woods, Jr., and John D. Wright. The following individuals were also helpful: Philip Hallen, Paul Jenkins, Sandra Pyle, Clyde H. Slease III, and George Taber.

I also wish to express my gratitude to Barbara Tobias and Louise Bem, who aided me as researchers. They helped me to find information in any of a hundred places and then, months later, re-entered alone the trackless forest of historical bibliography in search of information I used but could not identify as to source. Louise Bem, who had talked with Arkady Shevchenko at Indiana University of Pennsylvania, called my attention to the fact that he had accompanied Khrushchev on his visit to the Pitt campus in 1959. Macy Levine and Linda Comis generously shared information from the forthcoming history of the Medical School. Jeffrey C. Cepull and his staff at the University Center for Instructional Resources provided essential photographic services. Glenora E. Rossell and Lelia W. Jamison, in command at the University archives, were both obliging and creative in their help. Frank J. Kurtik unearthed photographs of Forbes Avenue in the 1930s. Ruth Reid and Helen Wilson at the Western Pennsylvania Historical Society, and Maria Zini at the Pennsylvania Room, Carnegie Library of Pittsburgh, were also helpful.

Catherine Marshall, managing editor at the University of Pittsburgh Press, in addition to performing the usual editorial services involved in converting a manuscript into a finished book, also helped me with the copy on the women's movement in Chapter 32. Kathy McLaughlin, editorial assistant at the Press, Jill Neely, formerly of the Press, and June Belkin were very helpful in myriad ways. Jane Flanders, assistant editor at the Press, helped with the copy on curriculum reform in Chapter 33. Susan McCloskey was copy editor for the entire manuscript. Responsibility for design and production of this book was entrusted to Gary Gore and Richard Hendel. Barbara I. Paull helped to whip into shape a particularly difficult chapter that required specialized knowledge, that on the modern medical center, Chapter 33. Mary Ann Aug, director of News and Publications, and Thomas E. Ehrbar of her staff, rendered a similar service on Chapter 36, "The Campus of the Future," the last in the history. Walter Kidney of the Pittsburgh History and Landmarks Foundation was patient and helpful in checking details of architectural history. Frederick A. Hetzel, director of the University Press, researched and wrote Appendix A, "West of the Alleghenies."

It is a pleasure to express my indebtedness to Agnes Lynch Starrett, who inspired me to write my first biography in 1965 and who produced two books herself that were invaluable in the present history: *Through One Hundred and Fifty Years*, a history of the University to 1937, and *The University of Pittsburgh in World War II*.

I thank *Time* magazine for permission to use their cover portrait of Richard King Mellon, and the following for permission to reproduce photographs from their files: *Pittsburgh Post-Gazette, Pittsburgh Press*, the Historical Society of Western Pennsylvania, and the Pennsylvania Room, Carnegie Library of Pittsburgh. The lines from "Little Gidding" in *Four Quartets* (copyright 1943 by T. S. Eliot, renewed 1971 by Esme Valerie Eliot) are reprinted by permission of Harcourt Brace Jovanovich, Inc., and Faber and Faber, Ltd. Excerpts from the letters of Richard King Mellon in chapter 22 are quoted with the permission of the trustees of the Richard King Mellon Foundation.

Robert C. Alberts

Appendix A   West of the Alleghenies

Institutions in the shadow of the Allegheny Mountains tend to define their age in terms of this formidable geographical barrier. The "first-west-of-the-Alleghenies" is a beguiling and complex genealogical game. For example, in a speech in 1919 Chancellor William Holland claimed that Pitt was the oldest institution of higher learning west of the Alleghenies. In so doing, he held that the only other two contenders—an unknown academy in Nashville and another school in Lexington, Kentucky (obviously Transylvania College, now Transylvania University) had "more or less lost their identity."

In *Through 150 Years*, the sesquecentennial history of Pitt which was published in 1937, Agnes L. Starrett wrote that Pitt was "the first institution of higher learning, so chartered, west of the Alleghenies and north of the Ohio." This is correct, although the use of the Ohio River as a boundary to the south rules out Transylvania and another competitor that Holland failed to mention—Washington & Jefferson College, in Washington, Pennsylvania.

The claim of W & J to be the oldest institution of higher education west of the Alleghenies is based on letters from John McMillan, a Presbyterian minister who mentioned that students were attending his academy, known as McMillan's log school, in 1781. McMillan founded Washington Academy, which was chartered in 1787, and began classes in 1789—exactly the years that Pittsburgh Academy was founded and began classes. He also founded Canonsburg Academy in 1791. From Canonsburg Academy evolved Jefferson College, chartered in 1802, and Washington College, chartered in 1806. The two merged in 1865.

Pittsburgh Academy was chartered on February 28 and Washington Academy on September 24. McMillan was a founding trustee of both academies.

Transylvania was chartered in 1780, combined with Kentucky University in 1865, and under a modified charter existed as Kentucky University until 1908, when it resumed its original name. Through its two ancestors—Pittsburgh Academy and the Western University of Pennsylvania—Pitt has been continuously chartered since 1787, although its charter was also modified to allow for changes in name. For several years after the fire of 1845 the University did not operate. When one considers that many schools went out of business periodically, with or without charter (modified or unmodified), the impossibility of establishing ground rules for the oldest-west-of-the-Alleghenies contest becomes apparent. Does the existence of a charter count, even when the school is not functioning? If it does, how many years should be allowed the school with a continuous charter which was founded later than its competing institution without a continuous charter? Ultimately, this race for years is like counting the number of angels on the head of a pin: engaging but not useful.

Of the three leading contenders for the oldest-west-of-the-Alleghenies appelation, the University of Pittsburgh is today the largest and strongest research institution. And yet perhaps the only sensible resolution to this competition is to be found in *Alice in Wonderland.* The Dodo has organized a race (the participants "began running when they liked, and left off when they liked, so that it was not easy to know when the race was over"), and after a time he declares that it has ended. He is asked, "But who has won?" After a great deal of thought he responds, "*Everybody* has won and all must have prizes."

Appendix B

Principals, Chancellors, and Presidents

PITTSBURGH ACADEMY
1787	Hugh Henry Brackenridge (founder)
1789	George Welch
1796	Robert Andrews
1800	Robert Steele
1801	John Taylor
1803	James Mountain
1807	Robert Patterson
1810	Joseph Stockton

WESTERN UNIVERSITY OF PENNSYLVANIA
1819–1835	Robert Bruce
1835–1836	Gilbert Morgan (first president)
1836–1843	Robert Bruce
1843–1849	Heman Dyer
1849–1855	David Riddle (acting)

(Operations were suspended in 1849 after the second major fire; the University reopened in 1854.)

1855–1858	John F. McLaren
1858–1880	George Woods (first chancellor)
1880–1881	Milton Goff (acting)
1881–1884	Henry MacCracken
1884–1890	Milton Goff
1891–1901	William Jacob Holland
1901–1904	John A. Brashear (acting)

UNIVERSITY OF PITTSBURGH
1904–1920	Samuel B. McCormick
1921–1945	John G. Bowman
1945–1955	Rufus H. Fitzgerald
1955–1956	Charles B. Nutting (acting)
1956–1965	Edward H. Litchfield
1965–1966	Stanton C. Crawford
1966–1967	David H. Kurtzman
1967–	Wesley W. Posvar

(Title changed from chancellor to president in 1984.)

Appendix C

Pitt Statistics

This is the way it is at the University of Pittsburgh in the week of February 24, 1986, when the last proofs of this book are being initialed for release to the printer, and no more changes—no additions, no deletions, no corrections—can be made in text or pictures.

There are, in what is known as the "head count," 34,453 registered students. These represent a "full-time equivalent" (FTE) of 27,000 enrolled students—a figure that is obtained by adding the number of full-time students (22,033) to 40 percent of 12,420 part-time students.

University enrollment for fall 1984 accounted for 6.6 percent of all students enrolled in colleges and universities in Pennsylvania. This was also 13.6 percent of the state's graduate students.

89 percent of the students are from families resident in Pennsylvania. 59 percent of the students at the Pittsburgh campus are from Allegheny County.

17,958 of the students are male. 16,495 are female.

20,173 are FTE undergraduates. 6,827 (FTE) are in graduate work.

1,249 are non-Hispanic black males. 1,448 are non-Hispanic black females.

There are 1,349 students from foreign countries at the Pittsburgh campus. The largest number, 159, are from the People's Republic of China (up from 1 student in 1982). From India, 133. From Taiwan, 115. Saudi Arabia, 114. South Korea, 112. Nigeria, 67. Malaysia, 61. Egypt, 35. Indonesia and Iran, 28 each. Lebanon, 26. Thailand, 25. Turkey, 24. Japan, 23. Greece, 21. Canada, 19. Venezuela, 18. Pakistan, 14. Libya, 13. Hong Kong, 12. Bangladesh, Jordan, Sri Lanka, and Sudan, 11 each. Argentina, Iraq, United Arab Emirates, and West Germany, 10 each. Students also come from sixty-nine other countries, including France, Ireland, Kuwait, Mexico, Peru, and the Philippines.

Most of the foreign students are male, and most are graduate students.

The College of Arts and Sciences has the largest enrollment, with 8,633 students. The College of General Studies is next with 5,748. Engineering is third with 2,116 undergraduate and 831 graduate students.

There are 2,519 full-time freshman students enrolled in all schools at the Pittsburgh campus (excluding the College of General Studies). 5,438 were accepted from 7,238 applicants.

98 percent of these freshmen ranked in the upper two-thirds of their high school classes, and a majority ranked in the top fifth.

The average high school Quality Point Average for Pitt freshmen is 3.34.

At the Pittsburgh campus, Scholastic Aptitude Test scores for Pitt freshmen average 479 verbal. (The national average for college-bound students is 431.) Pitt freshmen averaged 533 math. (The national average is 475.)

83 percent of the freshmen at the Pittsburgh campus are eighteen years old. 51 percent are male.

48.5 percent of the freshmen are in the first generation of their family to go to college. The fathers of 30.0 percent are blue collar workers. The median family income is $34,839.

Two-thirds of the freshmen receive some form of financial aid.

A majority of the students are Roman Catholic. 25 percent are Protestant. 10 percent are Jewish.

Degrees were conferred on 6,355 students in 1985. Of these, 398 were Ph.D.s and 450 were other professional degrees.

There are 2,450 full-time faculty members at Pitt—626 professors, 776 associate professors, 755 assistant professors, 149 instructors, 36 lecturers, and 108 "others," which means faculty in libraries and several other special offices.

Virtually all the full-time faculty members have advanced degrees. 1,888 have doctorates. 1,133 are tenured faculty; 426 others are in the tenure stream. There are 660 regular part-time faculty members.

There are 103 non-Hispanic black full-time faculty members, of whom 39 are women.

There are 145 full-time faculty whose ethnic background is Pacific Island or Asian.

There are 24 endowed chairs for distinguished scholars.

The library collections total 4,741,201 entries, including volumes on microtext, and 23,755 subscriptions. The Hillman, the largest of the library facilities, can seat 2,500 users at one time.

The main campus has 131 acres of land, 56 buildings, 16 schools (of which 13 grant both M.A.s and Ph.D.s), 139 academic departments, and 7 research centers.

The University of Pittsburgh at Titusville has a 5-acre campus and a head count of 289 students.

The University of Pittsburgh at Bradford, situated near the New York state border, has a 125-acre campus and 845 students.

The University of Pittsburgh at Greensburg has a 160-acre campus and 1,395 students.

The University of Pittsburgh at Johnstown has 635 acres, 29 buildings, all completed since 1967, and 3,214 students.

The University ranks 43rd in the nation in the size of its endowment: $130 million at the current market value.

Its budget for 1985–1986 is $383,808,000.

Its sponsored research and other sponsored programs total approximately $84.3 million.

It pays about $13.1 million annually in payroll taxes.

Collectively, the University, its students, faculty and staff on five campuses, its affiliated hospitals, and its visitors infuse over a half-billion dollars annually into the regional economy.

With 3,110 full-time and part-time faculty, research associates, and a support staff of 5,277, the University on the main campus is the largest employer in the city and is among the six largest in Allegheny County. Its payroll in 1985 was $226.3 million.

Notes and Sources

Each backnote is keyed to the main text by a page number and an identifying phrase and by a short title of the book, article, or document cited. The full title is given in the bibliography.

The following abbreviations are used:

HSWP   Historical Society of Western Pennsylvania
JAMA   Journal of the American Medical Association
MSA   Middle States Association
PROHP   Pittsburgh Renaissance Oral History Project
WPHM   Western Pennsylvania Historical Magazine

Unless otherwise stated, "Starrett" refers to Agnes L. Starrett's history of the University, *Through One Hundred and Fifty Years,* 1937.

Chapter One. The Articulate Audible Voice of the Past

3 The title is from Thomas Carlyle's *Heroes and Hero Worship, the Hero as a Man of Letters.*

5 Could have served with distinction. Rossiter, 149.

5 "I saw no chance." Newlin, 57.

5 None distinguishable by house. Ibid., 59.

5 1,500 in the area. Anderson, 11.

5 "Bulk of the inhabitants." Marder, *Reader,* 113.

5 Brackenridge biography. Newlin; Marder, *Reader;* Marder, *Brackenridge; Dictionary of American Biography;* Anderson, 298–300.

5 177 boats. *Pittsburgh Gazette,* June 2, 1787.

5 H. H. B. and Sabina Wolfe. Newlin, 108–09; Marder, *Brackenridge,* 48–49. Her name also appears as Sabrina and Sophia. H. H. B. was admitted to the bar in Western Pennsylvania in 1781. His son by his first wife was born on May 11, 1786. He married Sabina Wolfe in 1790.

8 Plant the values of Enlightenment. Marder, *Brackenridge,* 38, *Reader,* 4, 29, 113, 115–17.

8 H. H. B. and John Scull. Andrews, *Post-Gazette,* 2–6; Marder, *Brackenridge, 37–38, Reader,* 12; Rosensweet, "The Post-Gazette—175 Years." The first number of the *Gazette* appeared on July 29, 1786, sixpence per copy, published weekly except when the supply of paper ran out.

8 Zadok Cramer. Baldwin, 161–62; Anderson, 101–02, 105–07; Elizabeth Hawthorne Buck, 6, 7.

Cramer sold sermons, journals of travel, song books, law books, spelling books, dictionaries, catechisms, stationer's supplies, playing cards, wallpaper, patent medicines, and his own best-selling books, the *Pittsburgh Almanack* and the *Navigator*, a guidebook produced annually for travelers on the rivers.

8 Sale of lands. Newlin, 76; Albo, 36.

8 New western county. Marder, *Reader*, 12.

8 Made Pittsburgh a borough. Ibid.

8 Road to Bedford. Andrews, *Post-Gazette*, 30; Newlin, 78.

8 Nonsectarian church. Andrews, *Post-Gazette*, 13; Newlin, 85; Marder, *Reader*, 29–30, 120–25.

8 Bill and article to charter academy. Starrett, 7–10, 546–48; Marder, *Reader*, 12, *Brackenridge*, 41–42; Newlin, 76–77.

9 Gift of land from Penn family. Starrett, 549–50; *Pittsburgh Gazette*, January 6, 1787.

9 5,000 acres. Starrett, 24; Newlin, 85.

9 Did not begin for two years. *Pittsburgh Gazette*, April 11, 1789. The first term began April 13, 1789. Sack, 79.

9 Mostly log houses. *Niles Weekly Register*, Baltimore, vol. 30, p. 436; Anderson, 10–11; Andrews, *Post-Gazette*, 12.

9 Faculty, catalogue, night school. Starrett, 26–35; *Pittsburgh Gazette*, May 28, 1796.

10 H. H. B. sent son to Canonsburg. Baldwin, 169.

10n H. H. B. supported Constitution. Marder, *Brackenridge*, 43, *Reader*, 13–14. He gave more than support; he aided the Pennsylvania Federalists when they used steam-roller methods to get approval from the assembly in September 1787. See Alberts, "Business of the Highest Magnitude."

10 Erected brick academy. Starrett, 28–29.

10 1804 examination. Ibid., 37.

10 7,000 inhabitants. Ibid., 58.

10 Passenger traffic. Ritenour, 80–82; Baldwin, 186–87; Wade, 43, 46–48.

10 Glass-making industry. See Innes.

11 "'Pittsburgh' is the answer." Baldwin, 218.

12 1818 charter. Starrett, 60–69, 551–59.

12 Gift of $12,000. Ibid., 68.

12 Installation of Robert Bruce. Ibid., 73–74; Young, 19.

12 Five different religions. Young, 20.

13 Thomas A. Mellon at W.U.P. Thomas Mellon, 56–63.

14 Had 43 students. Young, 19.

16 Statutes of 1822. Starrett, 81.

16 Tuition, "boarding." Ibid., 72.

16 Classes of 1823–35. Starrett, 91; Young, 21.

16 Curriculum. Young, 23–25; Phillips, *The Western University*, 2–7.

17 Tocqueville on faith in education. George Pierson, *Tocqueville and Beaumont and America*, 452.

17 Why classical languages were taught. Young, 26.

17 Trustees asked for new curriculum. Ibid., 30; Starrett, 106, 118–20, 124–27, 129–31.

17 Modified course, younger trustees. Young, 30.

17 Morgan appointed. Ibid., 30; Starrett, 92.

17 Recommended by Union College. Young, 31.

17 Pledge of support. Ibid., 30–31; Starrett, 96.

18 Statement of fund raisers. Young, 30–31.

18 Morgan's inaugural address. Ibid.; Starrett, 96–97.

18 Shortage of money. Young, 32–33.

18 "Destitute of means." Sack, 82.

18 Morgan advised institution to close. Young, 33.

18 Morgan's regret at age 82. Ibid.; Starrett, 98.

18 Bruce had faculty of three. Young, 33.

18 Recrimination in 1838. Ibid., 34; Starrett, 106.

18 Bruce left University. Young, 36–37; Starrett, 107.

18 Degrees to Duquesne students. Young, 37.

18 Great fire of 1845. Baldwin, 228–30; Starrett, 109–11; "When the University Burned," *University Record*, May 1927, pp. 210–14; WPHM, April 1979, pp. 190–91.

19 City councils "remonstrated." Minutes of trustees' meetings, May 8, June 17, 1845.

19 Architectural monstrosity. Young, 37.

19 Heman Dyer. Starrett, 111–15. But see Johnston, 155–56.

20 $26,000 in assets. Linhart, 43.

Chapter Two. "Great Diversity of Talent and Attention"

21 Epigraph. Minute of trustees' meeting, June 1, 1875.

23 Bought mineral collection. Ibid., April 29, 1853; Phillips, *The Old Western University*, 2.

23 Committee to select site, 1854. Minute of trustees' meeting, February 14, 1854.

23 Chose Ross Street and Diamond. Ibid.; Phillips, *The Old Western University*, 1–2.

23 Ross estate sold for $8,200. Baynham, 53; Minute of trustees' meeting, February 15, 1854.

23 "God save the Union." Starrett, 137, 146; Phillips, *The Western University in 1822*, p. 1.

23 Ross Street Building cost $18,300. Baynham, 45.

23 16 large rooms. Ibid., 48.

23 Interrogated the principal. Minutes of trustees' meetings, June 18, July 19, August 12, 1858.

23 G. Woods background. Starrett, 141; author's conversation with Lawrence C. Woods, Jr., his grandson; Lawrence C. Woods, Jr., letter to Prudence Trimble, HSWP, May 28, 1969, in Woods Papers, University Archives, File Folder (FF) 1.

23 Woods accepted post. Minute of trustees' meeting, February 11, 1859; Sack, 677.

24 "When I assumed charge." Holland Papers, University Archives, Woods to Holland, Box 1, FF 3.

24 Suggestion on increased enrollment. By Starrett, 142.

24n "The devil seemed interested." Young, 35.

24 *Gazette* editorial. Starrett, 142.

25 Students drilled. Baynham, 55.

25 Colonel Black. Starrett, 146.

25 Brunot. Ibid., 147; Baldwin, 321–22; Andrews, "The Civil War," 141 (in Lorant's *Story of an American City*).

25 Fort Pitt Foundry. Baldwin, 238, 317; Lorant, 132, 137, 139.

25 Privates paid $13. Faulkner, 386.

25 Soldiers very young. Ibid.

25 Margaret Wade Deland. *If This Be I*, 26–28; Starrett, 147.

25 College students digging entrenchments. Baldwin, 319.

25 Trustees seeking endowment. Minute of trustees' meeting, July 13, 1863.

25 William Scaife diary. Schoyer, 79.

25 Pittsburgh industry. Baldwin, 317–18; Andrews, "The Civil War," 132; Starrett, 147; Penna, 49–52.

26 Fahnestock and Carnegie. Lecture at HSWP on Carnegie by Joseph Frazier Wall, October 5, 1983. As every Western Pennsylvanian knows, the name is properly pronounced Car-NEG-ie.

26 Woods's 1864 report. Minute of trustees' meeting, June 20, 1864.

27 Sale of 780,000 acres. Ibid., April 13, 1863, February 6, 1864; Starrett, 149.

27 Endowed chair. Minute of trustees' meeting, June 16, 1871.

27 Chair of Military Science and Civil Engineering. Baynham, 55.

27 Allegheny Observatory and Langley. *University Times*, March 6, June 8, May 22, 1980; *Pittsburgh Post-Gazette*, March 8, 1981, August 13, 1983; *Pittsburgh Press*, November 18, 1983; *Pitt*, May 1980; Beardsley, "The Allegheny Observatory"; Beardsley, "Early Conflict"; Beardsley, "Samuel Pierpont Langley"; *Pittsburgh Dispatch*, February 23, 1919; Frank Schlesinger, dedication booklet, August 28, p. 19.

28 Diplomas in English, Minutes of trustees' meetings, Vol. 1–9, in University History Series: Starrett, Historical File 0/311, Box 19, FF 157.

28 Attempt to start law course. Minute of trustees' meeting, September 28, 1870.

28 Committee to investigate conditions. Ibid., January 10, June 16, June 19, 1871.

30 Thaw's $100,000 gift. Ibid., June 16, 1871, June 17, 1872, June 1, 1875.

30 Special arrangement for Langley. Wallace Beardsley, when astronomer of the Allegheny Observatory and instructor of astronomy at the University, disclosed the Thaw stipulation and the Woods-Langley quarrel. Using the William Thaw papers deposited in the Historical Society and the records at the observatory, he saw the situation in terms of the rivalry in academic circles between the teaching and the research missions. Beardsley

believes that Langley may have been the first professor in American higher education to work solely in research. He also believes that a peculiar, hushed-up episode of July 8, 1871, in which the observatory was vandalized and the lens of the equatorial telescope stolen, may have had its cause in the Woods-Langley quarrel.

31 Legislature approved changes. Baynham, 52.

32 $25,000 Avery bequest. Minute of trustees' meeting, November 29, 1875. He had founded Avery College for black students in Pittsburgh in 1849.

32 Preparatory department needed as a "nursery." "The Nucleus of This Institution," *Pittsburgh Post-Gazette,* January 18, 1920.

32 Preparatory department in new building. Starrett, 153.

32 Citizens broke in doors. Minute of trustees' meeting, October, 25, 1877.

32 $100 paid to canvassers. Ibid., August 30, 1877.

32 Asked permission to drill. Ibid., June 11, 1878.

32 Scientific course extended. Ibid.

32 Pharmacy school. Ibid., September 30, 1878.

32 Woods's 1879 report. Ibid., June 1879.

32 Actions by investigating committee. Ibid., June 26, 1879, April 1880, April 14, June 16, 1882. The trustees' minutes of this period frequently give the month only, omitting the day.

33 Woods's resignation. Ibid., April 30, 1880.

33 Committee comment on Woods. Ibid., June 26, 1879.

33 Woods to Holland. Holland Papers, University Archives, Box 1, FF 3.

33 $20,000 deficit. Minute of trustees' meeting, June 16, 1862.

33 Sale of Ross Street building. Ibid., May 31, 1882.

33 Liquor License Fund. Ibid., June 5, 1882.

33 Move to North Avenue. Ibid., June 16, 1882; Starrett, 166–71.

34 MacCracken: "thrice as much work." Minutes of trustees' meetings, June 21, 1881, June 5, 1882, June 2, 1884.

34 Langley's departure. Beardsley, "Early Conflict," 370.

35 William Thaw eulogy. Minute of trustees' meeting, October 24, 1889; Starrett, 154.

35 Darlingtons. Minute of trustees' meeting, June 19, 1890; *Pittsburgh Press,* July 2, 1892; Starrett, 179–80.

35 Record enrollment of 95. Minute of trustees' meeting, June 2, 1890.

35 Francis C. Phillips. Starrett, 140. See his two works cited in the bibliography.

35 Daniel E. Carhart. Ibid., 170–71, 174; minute of trustees' meeting, June 4, 1883.

35 Desired qualities of a chancellor. Minute of trustees' meeting, July 7, 1884.

35 Resolutions Governing Faculty. Ibid.

35 Absent from chapel. Ibid., July 7, 1884, June 1885.

36 Professor Barber. Ibid., June 17, 1886.

36 Librarian needed space. Ibid., June 6, 1887.

36 Columbian Exposition. Ibid., May 9, 1892.

36 Classification of the instructors. Ibid., July 2, 1889.

36 Department of Interior pamphlet. Ibid., June 2, 1884.

36 Must move from badly ventilated buildings. Ibid., June 4, 1888.

36 Committee advice on site location. Ibid.

36 Alumni committee on site. Ibid., January 3, 1889.

36 James Steen's plan. Ibid., April 16, 1889; Baynham, 65–66.

37 Goff's last report. Minute of trustees' meeting, June 2, 1890.

37 Park Institute. Ibid., July 2, 1889.

Chapter Three: "The Greatest Work I Have Ever Undertaken"

38 Epigraph. Holland Papers, HSWP, Series XVIII, Box 22, FF 61.

39 Holland background. *Dictionary of American Biography; Who's Who in America* (1916–17); Starrett, 187–88; *Pittsburgh Post-Gazette* obituary, December 14, 1932; *Pittsburgh Sun-Telegraph,* November 1, 1953.

39 Holland to parents. Holland papers, HSWP, Series XVIII, Box 21, FF 61.

40 First Annual report. Minute of trustees' meeting, June 6, 1892.

40n "Lectures extraordinary." Ibid.

40 Professor 45 years later. Scribner, 4.

40 Holland in *Courant*. December 1895, p. 9.

40 Admonition to trustees. Minute of trustees' meeting, June 17, 1895.

40 Asked alumni to raise $40,000. Ibid., June 3, 1895.

40 Had granted 453 degrees. *First Alumni Year Book*, June 1983, pp. 8–13.

41 Nothing from state since 1822. Ibid.

41 Asked for $300,000. Holland Papers, HSWP, Series XVIII, Box 21, FF 59, Holland to parents, February 23, 1895.

41 Got a promise of $50,000. Minute of trustees' meeting, June 1, 1896.

41 Began postgraduate degree program. Starrett, 213.

41 The Misses Stein. Scribner, 12; Starrett, 203; Holland Papers, Archives, undated speech by Holland to faculty and students on history of the University, FF 7.

41 "A momentous decision." Scribner, 12.

41 Medical College. Minutes of trustees' meetings, June 25, 1891, June 6, 1892, March 10, October 4, 1894, June 1, 1896, January 27, June 1902; Holland Papers, HSWP, Series XVIII, Box 21, FF 64, Holland to trustees, December 21, 1897.

41 College of Pharmacy. Minutes of trustees' meetings, October 3, 1895, March 12, June 1, 1896, June 1902.

41 Dental School. Ibid., June 1, 1896, June 1902; Holland Papers, HSWP, Series XVIII, Box 21, FF 64, Holland to trustees, December 21, 1897; Sissman, 13.

41 School of law. Minutes of trustees' meetings, October 3, 1895, June 1, 1896; Starrett, 341; *University Times*, November 26, 1975; Holland Papers, HSWP, Series XVIII, Box 21, FF 64, Holland to trustees, December 21, 1897.

41 "Work is prospering." Holland Papers, HSWP, Series XVIII, Box 21, FF 57, Holland to parents, October 30, 1893.

41 "Men with financial power." *The Western University Courant*, December 1895, p. 10.

41 Mrs. Thaw was angry. Holland Papers, University Archives, FF 4, Mrs. Thaw to Holland, April 10, 1895.

41 Benjamin Thaw gave $2,500. Minute of trustees' meeting, June 3, 1895.

42 $10,000 pension fund. Ibid.

42 $10,000 from Isaac Kaufmann. Ibid.

42 "The most prosperous of all communities." So described, critically, in *The Pittsburgh Survey*, 6 vols., 1908–14. See Alberts, *The Good Provider*, 190–91, and Penna, 53–54.

42 Sanitary Fair. Baldwin, 323.

42 "Large gifts are being made." Minute of trustees' meeting, June 1, 1896.

43 Holland on Andrew Carnegie. Holland Papers, HSWP, Series XVIII, Box 20, FF 56, Holland to parents, February 10, 1890.

44n Junta. Holland Papers, HSWP, Series XXII, FF 6, "The Beginning of the Junta," a paper by Holland delivered in 1919.

44 Holland and Hornaday. Ibid., Box 21, FF 57.

44 "Pittsburgh is a queer place." Ibid., Holland to parents, October 15, 1892, Box 21, FF 61.

45 "I feel discouragement." Minute of trustees' meeting, October 8, 1896.

45 Linhart on Pittsburgh. *Pittsburgh Record*, June–July, 1933, p. 46.

46 Fessenden background. Fessenden; *Dictionary of American Biography; Who's Who in America* (1930–31); Starrett, 193–94; Scribner, 5; Holland Papers, HSWP, Series XXIII, Box 49, FF 3, speech by Holland, June 12, 1919, on the history of the University; Lauffer, 339; *University Times*, December 14, 1978, "Why Isn't Fessenden a Household Word?" (Alta Rusman, the author, interviewed G. R. Fitterer, former Pitt metallurgy professor and dean of engineering, an authority on Fessenden.)

46 "Spent seven happy years." *University Times*, December 14, 1978.

46 Holland promised $60,000. Minute of trustees' meeting, Fessenden to Holland, June 14, 1895.

47 Inscription on grave. Fessenden, frontispiece.

47 A. W. Mellon elected. Minute of trustees' meeting, June 4, 1894.

47 D. E. Park gave 200 acres. Minute of trustees' meeting, June 3, 1895.

47 Carnegie agreed, Westinghouse refused. Ibid., June 17, 1895.

47 Keeler and Saturn rings. Ibid., report of Observatory Committee, June 3, 1895.

47 Holland gave his office to first female students. *Pitt*, Autumn 1945, p. 35.

47 Law department, 35 students. Holland Papers, HSWP, Series XVIII, Box 21, FF 64.

47 $5,000 for new observatory. Minute of trustees' meeting, June 7, 1897.

47 Holland on "athletic students." Ibid.

47 110th anniversary celebration. Ibid., January 19, March 8, 1897; Holland Papers, Archives, FF 13, "Report of Committee"; Scribner, 12. (Scribner was on the anniversary planning committee.)

48 Thanks to A. W. Mellon. Minute of trustees' meeting, June 6, 1898.

48 Stein sisters graduated. Scribner, *Old Days*, 12; Sack, 566.

49 Athletic committee. Minute of trustees' meeting, June 6, 1898.

49 Brashear on Keeler. Ibid., March 16, April 25, December 28, 1898.

49 Holland on engineers. Ibid., June 4, 1900.

49 Holland on need to change site. Ibid., June 15, 1896, June 7, 1897; Scribner, 12; Linhart, 46.

49 Carnegie students expected to go to W.U.P. Minute of trustees' meeting, Brashear to trustees, October 7, 1903; Starrett, 211.

49 Negotiations with Mrs. Schenley. Minutes of trustees' meetings, June 7, December 21, 1897, June 9, 1898; Holland Papers, HSWP, Series XXVIII, Box 59, FF 1, trustees' resolution, June 15, 1896, and Holland's report to trustees, December 18, 1897.

50 Became director of Museum. Holland Papers, Archives, FF 13, minute of March 16, 1898 meeting. For Holland's negotiations with Carnegie, see Ibid., FF 7, an undated speech by Holland on the history of the University, pp. 19, 20.

50 Trustees accepted resignation. Minute of trustees' meeting, June 14, 1900.

50 Holland gave away much of his salary. Ibid.

50 Holland's farewell. Ibid., June 4, 1900; Starrett, 207.

52 Two regrets. Holland Papers, Archives, FF 5, correspondence with J. B. Lippincott Company, Philadelphia; HSWP, FF 17.

52 Addressed soldiers in French. Holland Papers, HSWP, Series XXIII, FF 3, June 7, 1918.

52 Stories told about him. Author's interview with M. Graham Netting, 1982, who was a long-time director of Carnegie Museum of Natural History and is now director emeritus.

52 "Brought distinction." *Pittsburgh Post-Gazette*, December 14, 1932.

Chapter Four. . . . And on into a Bright New Century

53 Epigraph. McCormick Papers, University Archives, FF 23.

54 Brashear. *Dictionary of American Biography; Who's Who in America* (1916–17); O'Brien, "John A. Brashear"; Brashear, *Autobiography*.

54 Served with reluctance. Minute of trustees' meeting, Brashear's letter of resignation, October 7, 1903.

54 Contemporary on Brashear. Author's interviews with Carlton G. Ketchum. Brashear was from 1909 to his death in 1920 director of the Frick Education Commission, endowed by Henry Clay Frick with an initial grant of $250,000 to provide scholarships, training, and summer school sessions for the self-improvement of Pittsburgh's public school teachers.

55 Background on McCormick. *Dictionary of American Biography; Who's Who in America* (1916–17); *New York Times*, May 27, 1904; *University Bulletin*, Vol. 1, p. 39; McCormick; *Pitt Owl*, 1907, p. 17; minute of trustees' meeting, December 11, 1928, resolution on his death; *Pittsburgh Post-Gazette*, obituary, April 19, 1928.

56 $6,000 salary. McCormick Papers, FF 2, McCormick to trustees, June 4, 1904. The salary was $5,000 plus $1,000 as the equivalent of a house.

56 McCormick's conditions. Minute of trustees' meeting, June 4, 1904.

56 Inauguration. *Pittsburgh Post*, February 22, 1905; Starrett, 216–17.

56 Purchased Dental College. Minute of trustees' meeting, October 5, 1905; Sissman, 42–43.

56 Purchased medical department. Minute of trustees' meeting, July 23, 1908.

56 Change in name. Ibid., June 1, 1903, March 1908.

56 Observatory property sold. Ibid., June 9, 1909; Starrett, 218. The sale was handled by A. J. Kelly, Jr., a trustee and head of Commonwealth Real Estate Company.

56 Five sites considered. Minute of trustees' meeting, November 29, 1907.

56 Mary Schenley preferred leases. *Pittsburgh Sun,* October 5, 1906.

57 She sold land to city. *Pitt,* November, 1977, p. 21.

57 Nicola, Bellefield Company, and Schenley Farms. *Pittsburgh Press,* April 18, May 23, 1982, April 4, 1983; *Pitt,* Summer 1948, p. 31; Starrett, 218.

57 Nicola residences. *Pittsburgh Press,* May 23, 1982. An architect living in one of the Nicola houses in 1982 estimated that some of them would cost more than $1 million to duplicate today.

57 Nicola planned a town hall. *Pittsburgh Press,* May 23, 1982.

57 University paid $537,000 for hillside. Ketchum, "Pitt: The Adolescent Years," 182. For the record, the exact boundaries were Bayard, Bouquet, Oakland Cemetery, Vera, Breckenridge, Aliquippa, Centre Avenue, and Parkman.

57 McCormick to Rockefeller. McCormick Papers, FF 6, August 28, 1905.

57 Frick gave $32,000 to Observatory. Minute of trustees' meeting, October 5, 1905.

57 Frick declined to see him. Ibid., April 4, 1906.

57 Westinghouse to McCormick. Ibid., April 6, 1905.

57 Lauder declined. Ibid., Lauder to McCormick, April 22, McCormick to Lauder, May 21, 1908.

58 Carnegie's secretary replied. Ibid., McCormick to Carnegie, March 29, James Bertram to McCormick, March 30, 1905.

58 Carnegie thanked McCormick. Ibid., April 24, 1905.

58 Carnegie donated $16.15 million. *Who's Who in America,* 1916–17.

58 Carnegie would give 19 names. *Pittsburgh Post,* November 19, 1904.

59 Got only $250,000. McCormick, 32.

59 $50,000 less than raised for San Francisco. Minute of trustees' meeting, June 4, 1906.

59 Two grants from legislature. Linhart, 48; McCormick, 32.

59 Gave state 50 free scholarships. Minute of trustees' meeting, May 21, 1909.

59 $7,700 from Nicola and state. Ibid., May 21, 1908.

59 Architectural contest. *Pittsburgh Post,* April 14, 1908; *Pittsburgh Leader,* February 12, April 14,

October 18, 1908; minute of trustees' meeting, June 1908; *Jewish Criterion,* August 1908; *Pitt Owl,* 1907.

60 *Leader* on design. October 18, 1908.

61 *Post* on design. April 14, 1908.

61 Designs exhibited. Minute of trustees' meeting, June 1908.

61 McCormick ordered sketches for donors. Starrett Files, University Archives, Board of Trustees' minutes, 0/3/11, FF 158, Chancellor's Report, November 1909; McCormick Papers, FF 6, 12.

61 Cornerstone laying. Minutes of trustees' meetings, July 1908, October 3, 1908; *Pittsburgh Post,* June 9, 1908, Starrett, 220–21.

62 Trees Gymnasium. Minute of trustees' meeting, December 12, 1910; *Pittsburgh Dispatch,* April 13, 1911.

62 Character of deans and department heads. Author's interviews with Carlton Ketchum; Ketchum, "Pitt: The Adolescent Years," 189–90.

63 Academic tenure. Minute of trustees' meeting, June 1916.

63 Brashear on enrollment, Ibid., June 1902, June 1, 1903, June 6, 1904.

63 Move to drop liberal arts. Starrett, 215, 504.

63 McCormick supported college. Minute of trustees' meeting, June 1905.

63 Three trustees agreed. Starrett, 504.

63 Students signed petition. Ibid.

63 Enrollment from 108 to 649 in College. Chancellor's Report for 1914–15, October 11, 1915.

64 First team organized in 1889. Vogan and Seckinger, Archives, Memorabilia, Case 3, Dwr. 2; Chester L. Smith, "As Far as Football Went . . . ," in O'Brien, *Hail to Pitt,* 60; Starrett, 526; Pitt interview and news release on Bert Smyers, August, 1930, Archives, Memorabilia, Case 3, Dwr. 2.

64 Early Pitt athletics. *1983 Pitt Football Media Guide,* 82; Hockensmith; minute of trustees' meeting, June 2, 1905; Guy D. Wallace to Starrett, February 12, 1936, Starrett Papers, University Archives, Memorabilia, Football I.

64 Two games a week. W.U.P. played Susquehanna on October 24, 1904, and California Normal on October 27. *Pittsburgh Leader,* October 24, 1904.

64 Got permission for head coach to play. Starrett

Files, "Important Dates Concerning University— J. C. Fetterman," 1903, p. 18.

64 Officials wore bowler hats. See early photographs.

64 Team disbanded, left $500 debt. Minute of trustees' meeting, May 9, 1904; Wallace to Starrett.

64 Clapp to trustees. Minute of trustees' meeting, May 9, 1904.

64 Alumni spoke up. "Informal Conference . . . July 19, 1904 . . . on the Importance of Athletics in an Institution of Learning," Archives, Memorabilia, Case 3, Dwr. 2.

64 McCormick agreed. Minute of trustees' meeting, McCormick to James D. Moffat, president of Washington and Jefferson College, September 13, 1904.

64 Mosse brought Kansas players. Wallace to Starrett; Ketchum letter to author, May 5, 1983.

64 Imported Geneva players. Wallace to Starrett; *Pittsburgh Times*, November 12, 1904; author's interview with Ketchum, April 27, 1984.

65 Drive for $2,000. Wallace to Starrett; Minute of trustees' meeting, Clapp to trustees, May 9, 1904.

65 Agreement with Dreyfuss. Wallace to Starrett.

65n Height and weight of 1904 team. "How WUP and State Compare"—an undated, unidentifiable newspaper article among the University Archives' mounted clippings.

65n Later career of 1904 team. Joseph H. Thompson, "University Athletics," an address at the dedication of Trees Gymnasium, October 3, 1912, Archives, Memorabilia, Football, Case 3, Dwr. 2.

65 Press coverage. *Pittsburgh Dispatch*, November 25, 1904, November 25, 1905; *Pittsburgh Post*, November 12, 1905.

65 Small group of alumni. Author's interviews and correspondence with Carlton Ketchum, 1981–84.

66 "Firm stand for purer athletics." *Pittsburgh Press*, April 15, 1908.

67 Alumni hired Glenn Warner. Harry Keck, *Pittsburgh Sun-Telegraph*, February 28, 1948. In 1915 Warner introduced numbers on jerseys to identify the players and sell more programs. It is said that his was the first team to wear numbers. Riesman and Denny, 321.

67 Walter Camp on 1916 team. O'Brien, *Hail to Pitt*, 70.

67 Chamber of Commerce banquet. *Pittsburgh Leader*, January 18, 1914.

67 A victim of his own success. Ketchum interviews.

67 Fetterman on congestion. McCormick Papers, FF 26, Fetterman to the College Committee, October 10, 1913.

67 State had been giving grants. Correspondence with Paul Solyan, comptroller, 1985, in author's files.

67 Campus improvements. Ibid., FF 26, undated 5-page paper, "Matters Meriting Mention in Report of Chancellor for 1913–14."

68 High School of Medicine rating. Ibid.

68 Seven Chinese students. *Pittsburgh Sun*, October 3, 1913.

68 Gift of an automobile. McCormick Papers, FF 169, Babcock to the University, June 13, 1911.

68 Mellon Institute. Minute of trustees' meeting, "Special meeting called to act upon establishment of Institute of Industrial Chemical Research, 1913," Starrett Files, FF 63; *Pittsburgh Chronicle-Telegraph*, *Pittsburgh Sun*, March 26, 1913.

68 McCormick, Church, Carnegie exchange. McCormick to Carnegie, March 29, 1906, in minutes of trustees' meeting, FF 111; Starrett Files, FF 16A, Church to Carnegie, January 20, 1908; unsigned letter to Carnegie, January 9, 1911; Church to Carnegie, January 16, 1912; Carnegie to Church, January 30, 1912; Church to McCormick, February 2, 1912; McCormick to Church, February 8, 1912; Church to McCormick, January 13, 1914; Ketchum interview, April 27, 1984.

69 $3 million campaign. *Pittsburgh Leader*, December 1, 1913; January 12, 1914; *Pittsburgh Index*, January 17, 1914; *Pittsburgh Press*, January 6, 1914; *Pittsburgh Gazette-Times*, January 10, 1914; *Pittsburgh Sun*, January 13, 1914; *Pitt Owl*, 1915; author's interviews and correspondence with Carlton G. Ketchum.

69 Charles S. Ward, $60 million, *Who's Who in America* (1916–17).

69 Heinz gift of $100,000. Minute of trustees' meeting, July 1919; University clipping books, vol. 79, August 12, 1918.

69 McCormick trip to Europe. Starrett, 236.

69 George Ketchum, 155 words per minute. Author's conversation with George Ketchum in 1960.

69 George Ketchum to McCormick. Summer of 1914, otherwise undated, in McCormick's correspondence file for that year.

69 Germans held a victory parade in Pittsburgh in 1870. Author's conversation in 1940 with Smith Shannon, Pittsburgh lawyer, one-time city councilman and founding trustee of Carnegie Institute, who saw the parade as a teen-age boy.

70 Base Hospital 27. Crozier, chapter 3, pp. 2–5; Starrett, 369, 371.

70 The campus in World War I. Minute of trustees' meeting, June 1917, March 1918; Charles Arnold; Chancellor's Report, June 30, 1919, FF 19; Starrett, 235–41; author's interview with Helen Pool Rush, March 29, 1981.

70 DeHart visited Camp Hamilton. Archives, vol. 74 of early newspaper stories: a clipping dated September 24, 1917, name of paper indecipherable.

72 Effort to compress school year. McCormick Papers, Chancellor's Report, June 30, 1919.

72 915 students returned. Starrett, 241.

72 Alumni Hall campaign, B. D. Daubert, "Alumni Hall," *Pitt*, Spring 1951, p. 13; 1920 letterhead of the organization in correspondence; Starrett, 255; *Pittsburgh Post*, January 26, 1920; *Pittsburgh Gazette*, January 17, 1920; *Pittsburgh Dispatch*, January 1920; Ketchum, "The Adolescent Years," 183; Ketchum interviews.

72 Cut across the axis. Van Trump, "A Heritage of Dreams."

72 Floyd Rose to Hornbostel. Ketchum interviews.

72 Coal mine fires. Ibid.

72 Success of program helped by athletic prowess. Ibid.

73 W. C. White challenged McCormick. Minutes of Executive Committee meetings, October 29, 1915, January 15 and 30, 1917; Ketchum interviews.

73 McCormick note to his successor. McCormick Papers, FF 49, McCormick to Bowman, October 30, 1920.

73 McCormick and Holland discussing policies. Author's interview with Walter Rome, May 12, 1981.

73 McCormick and $2 million fund. Minute of trustees' meeting, January 24, 1921.

Chapter Five. "A New Kind of Schoolmaster"

The main sources for this chapter are:

1. Bowman, *Unofficial Notes.*

2. Bowman, "Notes about A. W. Mellon." University Archives, Bowman Papers, FF 50.

3. Bowman, "Affidavit," November 10, 1939. This peculiar, inexplicable document is a statement on 17 legal-size pages, signed, sworn to, witnessed, and notarized in Pittsburgh. It describes in 16 numbered paragraphs Bowman's association with A. W. Mellon. It covers some of the same events described in 1 and 2 above but with variations and valuable added material. The tone is not aggressive, but I suspect that someone may have doubted Bowman's story, perhaps that part on his half-time work in Washington over an 18-month period.

4. Bowman, Report to Trustees. July 1, 1922. This first Bowman report covered his first 18 months in office.

5. Bowman, "Speech Delivered at Dedication Dinner Following Dedication of Cathedral of Learning, March 8, 1955." An imperfect and incomplete but valuable tape recording. University Archives, Phonotape 3.

6. Author's interviews and correspondence with Carlton G. Ketchum beginning March 10, 1981, and continuing almost until his death on July 25, 1984.

7. Author's interviews with Walter Rome, Lawrence Irwin, Helen Rush, and Ruth Mitchell.

77 Chapter title. The phrase appears in Agnes L. Starrett's "John Gabbert Bowman," an essay in *Famous Men and Women of Pittsburgh*, 201.

79 Trustees wanted a modern university. Ketchum interviews.

79 Two trustees attended meeting. They are mentioned but not identified in *Unofficial Notes.* Carlton Ketchum provided their identity.

79 Bowman at hospital meeting and trustees' dinner. *Unofficial Notes*, 4–5; "Notes About A. W. Mellon," 1–2.

79 Dr. Mayo's advice. *Unofficial Notes*, 6.

81 Bowman's first days at Pitt. *Unofficial Notes*, 7.

81 University debt. Widely differing figures appear on the size of the debt when Chancellor Bowman took over. In his affidavit of 1939 he set the debt at $1,326,015. In his *Unofficial Notes*, written in his old

age, he set it at $2 million—the figure that is now uncritically accepted (pp. 8, 23, 58). Paul Solyan, comptroller, says the 1921 debt was $1.24 million. Letter to author, January 30, 1986.

Bowman also charged in *Unofficial Notes* (p. 8) that the trustees in 1920 had "put on a campaign to lift the debt. They spent $30,000 and raised $28,000." Carlton Ketchum, who with Karl Davis was in charge of the University's fund raising at that time, told me in the most positive terms that no such campaign was ever held.

81 Carnegie Library wished to end arrangement. University Archives, Fitzgerald Papers, FF 110, comment by Ralph Munn, May 16, August 28, 1947.

81 Classes in furnace room and on steps. Ketchum interviews. This happened only during the worst overcrowding of World War I.

81 School of Dentistry statistics. Starrett, 391.

81 Bowman on Alumni Hall. Report to Trustees, 1921–22, p. 8. But see Starrett, 255.

81 First call on A. W. Mellon. *Unofficial Notes*, 9; "Notes About A. W. Mellon," 3; Affidavit, 1. The three accounts differ somewhat; I have selected from and consolidated the three versions.

81 Calls on McEldowney, foundry president, Williams, Babcock, and McCune. *Unofficial Notes*, 10–12, 23–25, 33–36; "Notes About A. W. Mellon," 3–4.

83 Trustees' dinner for Bowman. *Unofficial Notes*, 20–22. The two leading attorneys present were probably George B. Gordon and Thomas Patterson. The steel company presidents were James Henry Lockhart and Homer D. Williams. The Presbyterian minister was Dr. William J. Holland. The glass company president was probably Pittsburgh Plate Glass Company's William L. Clause.

85 Bowman and Weber. *Unofficial Notes*, 27–29; Ketchum interviews.

85 Almost daily calls on R. B. Mellon. Ibid., 39.

85 Bowman and the plan. Ibid., 30, 38, 40.

85 Bowman's manner of walking. Ketchum interviews.

85 Frick Acres. *Unofficial Notes*, 40–42, 51–52; "Notes About A. W. Mellon," 7–8; Affidavit, 3; *University Record*, October 1926, p. 4.

86 Wrote to 7 schools of architecture. *Unofficial Notes*, 48.

86 Bowman and Klauder. Ibid., 49–50.

86 Described his plan to R. B. Mellon. Ibid., 53–56; "Notes About A. W. Mellon," 9.

87 Told Homer Williams about plan. *Unofficial Notes*, 59–60; "Notes About A. W. Mellon," 10.

88 "Mr. Harding has asked me." "Notes About A. W. Mellon," 4, 5.

88 Reform. Reports to Trustees, 1921–22, 1922–24; Affidavit, 5; Starrett, 255.

88 Dismissed 53 faculty members AAUP *Report*, 1935, p. 250.

88 Mellon: "It is unbusinesslike." Affidavit, 2.

88 Mellon Institute. Ibid., 4.

89 Bought Porter estate. Bowman, *Annual Report*, 1921–22, p. 9. Children's Hospital now stands on the site.

89 Bowman's work in Washington. "Notes About A. W. Mellon," 5–7; Affidavit, 1–2. He did not mention this work in his *Unofficial Notes*.

89 Bowman's failed marriage. Five of Bowman's associates have independently told me details of this situation.

89 Bowman and Mellon in Washington. *Unofficial Notes*, 57–58, 60–62, 63–69; "Notes About A. W. Mellon," 7, 10–20; Affidavit, 3–6.

90 A. W. Mellon to Nora Mellon. Hersh, 264–65.

92 A. W. Mellon paid University debts. Affidavit, 4.

Chapter Six. The Campaign

93 Epigraph. Bowman Papers, FF 131.

95 Bowman alienated his alumni. Ketchum interviews; Don Saunders's testimony before the Gow Committee, March 31, 1939 (see chapter 11).

95 Bowman's three resolves. *Unofficial Notes*, 80.

95 The tall building "an inspiration." Bowman Papers, FF 128, "The Building Program of the University," 2.

95 "A great central symbol." Bowman, "A Cathedral of the Spirit of Achievement." Bowman Papers, FF 128.

95 Klauder to "concentrate his thought." *Unofficial Notes*, 70.

95 Klauder's first design. Ibid., 70–71; Bowman, speech at dedication dinner.

95 Klauder: "Most excellent architecture." *Unofficial Notes*, 71.

96 Bowman to Weber, "visit weekends." Bowman Papers, FF 103, January 26, 1927.

96 Klimcheck on satisfying Bowman. *Unofficial Notes*, 72–73.

96 Bowman, Klauder, and *Die Walküre*. Ibid., 73–74; speech at dedication dinner.

97 The Commons Room. *Unofficial Notes*, 75–78.

97 Citizens' Committee to "implement strength." Bowman, *The Building Program*, 8, which names the 18 members of the Executive Committee, organized March 29, 1924.

99 Announcement dinner. *Unofficial Notes*, 80–84; Rome interview. Bowman errs in giving the date as September 6 (p. 81). All the documents show the date was November 6.

99 First copy to Calvin Coolidge. Bowman Papers FF 126, June 24, 1924.

99 Described building. Bowman Papers, FF 128, manuscript for a pamphlet on the high building, 12; Klauder to Bowman, May 12, 1926.

100n "Learning Tower of Pisaburgh." *Charette*, February 1931.

100 *New York Times* article. November 30, 1924.

100 Opposition to Bowman's plan. *Unofficial Notes*, 85–87. The trustee who wrote R. B. Mellon was A. L. Humphrey, president of Westinghouse Air Brake. He later withdrew the letter; his company joined Westinghouse Electric in making a $360,101 gift to the building campaign. Ibid., 88.

101 Bowman's unusable pamphlets. Bowman Papers, FF 121, J. P. Jones to Bowman, September 18, 1924; Ketchum interviews.

101 Jones-Bowman exchange of letters. Bowman Papers, FF 126.

102 Bowman's call to Ketchum office. Ketchum interviews.

102 Letter from Calvin Coolidge. Bowman Papers, FF 126, June 24, 1924.

102 Bowman-Ketchum professional relationship. Ketchum interviews. There is one brief mention in *Unofficial Notes* (p. 95) of work done by "a local firm or company of campaign managers," unnamed. Bowman was angry when the brothers mentioned their work on the Cathedral campaign in their later solicitation letters to potential clients.

102 "An insurance against radicalism." Bowman Papers, FF 93, 126, Bowman to Williams, March 3, 1925.

102 The campaign. Ketchum, "Pitt: The Adolescent Years," 196–97; *Unofficial Notes*, 93–100; running daily news and feature articles in all Pittsburgh print media and in the press of some other cities; Ketchum interviews.

103 Kickoff dinner with Judge Gary. *Unofficial Notes*, 88–92; Ketchum interviews. Gary had received an honorary Sc.D. degree from Pitt in 1915.

104 Large plaster model. Bowman Papers, FF 132, Klauder to Bowman, March 24, 1925.

104 U.S. Steel gift of $250,000. Later gifts, including a $50,000 bequest in Gary's will, brought the total to $500,000. *Unofficial Notes*, 92.

104 Rockefeller gift to University of Chicago. Nevins, II, 259–65.

105 Gillespie-Woods meeting. Ketchum, "Some Interesting Pittsburghers, 1911–1941," WPHM, January 1982.

106 Campaign workers' luncheon, May 5, 1925. Ketchum interviews; *Pittsburgh Gazette-Times*, May 6, 1925; Bowman Papers, FF 114.

107 Amount collected. Bowman Papers, Bowman to A. W. Mellon, February 25, 1926; *Unofficial Notes*, 97; Ketchum interviews; Ketchum, "Pitt: The Adolescent Years," 195–97; Bowman, Report to Trustees, 1924–26.

Chapter Seven. The Tall Building, and Some Others

108 Epigraph. Bowman Papers, FF 93, 128, "The Building Program of the University." Includes sets of undated galley proofs Bowman sent to each trustee.

109 "The summer of confusion." *Unofficial Notes*, 101. For additional information on the trustees' indecision, see Mark M. Brown, University Archives.

109 A. J. Kelly visit. *Unofficial Notes*, 101–03.

109 Howard Heinz's offer to pay. Bowman Papers, FF 93, June 30, 1925.

109 Joseph B. Shea letter. Ibid., FF 129, April 28, 1926.

109 Minutes of Building Committee. Ibid., FF 93, Digest; minute of trustees' meeting, June 8, 1925.

109 Stone and Webster contract. This firm had performed earlier services on the Cathedral of Learning on a fee and hourly cost basis. It drilled the four test borings "at a cost of not more than $900." In 1924–25 it built the Pitt Stadium.

110 Trustees approved, then postponed. Minute of trustees' meeting, September 29, 1925.

110 Gordon opposition. *Unofficial Notes*, 103–07; Ketchum interviews.

111 Building Committee reports, October 30, 1925. Bowman Papers, FF 93, 103, 128.

111 No building more than 100 feet high. *Unofficial Notes*, 112.

111 Bowman call on R. B. Mellon. Ibid., 112.

111 Bowman call on Charles Stone. Ibid., 113; Bowman, speech at dedication dinner.

111 Mellon silence. Ketchum interviews. Bowman says the Mellons twice ordered him to abandon the tall building and that he refused, offering once to tender his resignation. Bowman, *Unofficial Notes*, 116–17.

112 Plan for faculty houses on roof dropped. Bowman Papers, FF 132, memo of May 3, 1926.

112 400 feet, 29 stories. *University Records*, October 1926, p. 4.

112 Groundbreaking. Ibid.; Bowman *Unofficial Notes*, 121–22; Ketchum interviews.

112 Trustees accepted Bowman's refusal. Bowman, *Unofficial Notes*, 122–23.

112 "Most momentous step in architecture." Harvey Wiley Corbett, "Architecture," *Encyclopaedia Britannica*, 14th edition, II, 274.

112 Building the foundation. Bowman Papers, an unsigned, untitled, 8-page typescript datelined Boston, probably by A. L. Hartridge, Stone and Webster engineer on the project; Frederick H. Crabtree, supervising engineer for Stone and Webster, "Underneath the Cathedral," *Pittsburgh Record*, December 1928; unsigned article, "Notes Relative to High Type of Buildings, University of Pittsburgh, December 31, 1924," in *American Contractor*, September 15, 1928.

114 People were impatient. Bowman Papers, FF 93, Building Committee reports.

114 Bowman canceled board meetings. Bowman, speech at dedication dinner.

114 Bowman: "good reason for starting." Bowman Papers, FF 103, "Building Construction Program."

114 Many Klauder studies. Ibid.

114 Bowman's explanation for delay in construction. Ibid.

115 "Most important event." Ketchum, "Pitt: The Adolescent Years," 195–96.

115 Stadium. Ketchum interviews; author's interviews with Frank Carver; *Pitt Football Season Handbook*, 1925.

115 "Football-crazy alumni." Ketchum, "Pitt: The Adolescent Years," 194.

115 Why upper deck was not added. Ketchum and Carver interviews.

118 Dr. Huggins's opposition to stadium. Author's conversation with James S. Tipping, M.D.

118 School of Medicine. Crozier; Starrett, 354–407; Bowman, Reports to Trustees; R. R. Huggins; *The Relationship of the Pittsburgh School of Medicine to the Medical Profession of the Community*, 1920; *Peering Ahead in Medicine*, 1927; *On Sentry Duty*, 1927; *Address to the Class of 1930*, 1930; "The Advance of Medicine in Pittsburgh," *University Record*, October–November, 1931, pp. 64–67; "Pittsburgh Medical Center," ibid., January, 1927.

118 State board warning. Huggins, "Advance of Medicine," 66.

119 "Medicine advances most rapidly." Huggins, *Peering Ahead*, n.p.

119 Carnegie Foundation survey. Huggins, "Advance of Medicine," 66.

119 Bowman: "practical success." Report to Trustees, 1921–22, pp. 35–36.

119 Children's Hospital agreement, 1922. Bowman Papers, FF 50, agreement recorded April 18, 1924.

120 Falk Clinic. Dedication Program, September 28, 1931; Bowman Papers, FF 50, 2-page undated memorandum, "The Medical Center."

121 School of Dentistry. Sissman, 56–70; Starrett, 391–94.

122 Last rivet and first stone. *Pitt News,* October 25, 1929.

122 Contractor's dinner. *Pittsburgh Record,* February 1930, p. 66.

Chapter Eight. The 1930s: Fulfillment and Good Fortune

123 Epigraph: They shall find wisdom. . . . Much-quoted, it is engraved on the sesquicentennial gold medal.

124 Bowman, Gow, and the Falks. *Pittsburgh Bulletin Index,* September 8, 1932; *University Record,* February 1930, p. 65, April 1930, p. 69, June 1930, p. 63. According to Raymond F. Howes (*Low Point at Pitt*), Bowman in 1929 applied for the presidency of the University of Chicago, a post taken in that year by Robert Maynard Hutchins. *The Rebel Yell,* a short-lived off-beat campus newspaper, repeated the story on May 28, 1930, and added that Bowman's resignation was expected.

124 Walter Rome expense account. Rome interview.

126 Cathedral lawn. *Pitt,* October 1939, Spring 1941; *Unofficial Notes,* 124.

126 Historical Survey. Author's interviews with Lawrence Irwin, Agnes Starrett, and C. V. Starrett.

126 Society unable to pay. Fitzgerald Notes, Conference between Fitzgerald and John W. Oliver, December 5, 1939.

126 $30,000 for University Press. Litchfield Papers, "Mellon E. and C. Trust," Litchfield to Adolph Schmidt, May 6, 1960.

127 Admirably illustrated. Among the artists were Harvy Cushman, Clarence McWilliams, Ward Hunter, and Alex Ross.

127 Buhl Foundation bought and gave 1,250 copies. Agnes Starrett and Irwin interviews.

127 Bowman little interested in scholarly writing. Irwin interview, April 16, 1981.

127 Bowman against rushing into print. Fitzgerald Notes, March 21, 1938, November 28, 1939. Fitzgerald's Notes (FF 224 to FF 231) are a running record he made of daily operations.

127 George Carver's advice. Fitzgerald Notes, May 9, 1938.

127 Falk School. Fitzgerald Papers, FF 187, "Memorandum Concerning Establishment of the Falk Elementary School," G. S. Rupp, January 16, 1950. See also *Pittsburgh Record,* October–November, 1931, "The Falk Elementary School Opens"; ibid., June 1930, "The Fanny Edel Falk Elementary School"; *Pittsburgh Press,* September 13, 1981, Caren Marcus, "Falk School: 50 Years Old and Learning"; Starrett, 279, 429, 441.

128 Falk Clinic. *Pittsburgh Record,* October–November, 1931, p. 70; ibid., Joseph H. Barach, "The Story of the Falk Clinic," 71–72.

128 C. Glenn King background. *New York Times,* May 24, 1942; *Pittsburgh Press,* November 21, 1937, November 15, 1942; *Who's Who in America,* 1984–85; *University Record,* April–May, 1932.

128 Transcontinental and Western Air flight to West Coast. *Pittsburgh Press,* December 11, 1932.

128 Gave city a strip of Fifth Avenue. Bowman, Report to Trustees, 1932–34, "Progress of the Cathedral of Learning."

128 Fierce editorial outcry. *Pittsburgh Press,* December 5, 12, 15, 1933.

129 CWA figures. Bowman, Report to Trustees, 1932–34, FF 85; *Pittsburgh Sun-Telegraph,* December 23, 1933; *Pittsburgh Post-Gazette,* January 10, March 1, 1934.

129 Chalk marks weathered away. Information from Ruth C. Mitchell as supplied by Maxine Bruhns.

129 Scandal over union dues. *Pittsburgh Post-Gazette,* December 23, 1933; *Pittsburgh Press,* January 23, 1934.

129 1934 fund-raising campaign. Ketchum interviews; *Pittsburgh Sun-Telegraph,* April 22, 1934; Bowman Papers, Box 135, papers beginning July 30, 1934.

129 Bowman cut his salary. *Pittsburgh Bulletin Index,* November 7, 1935, p. 8.

129 Lowell Thomas. *Pittsburgh Sun-Telegraph,* April 25, 1934.

129 Editorials in favor. *Pittsburgh Sun-Telegraph,* March 2, April 18, May 17, 1934.

129 Bowman, A. W. Mellon, and Commons Room. Bowman Papers, FF 51, Bowman to Holgar

Johnson, March 31, 1936; Johnson to A. W. Mellon, April 21, 1936.

130 Separate reading rooms in library. Bowman, Report to Trustees, 1934–36, p. 96.

130 Woodruff: "Pitt in the 1936 Olympics." *Alumni Review*, August–September 1936; ibid., James H. Pott, "Impressions of the Olympics," October 1936; *Alumni Times*, March 1973, "John Woodruff Recalls 1936 Olympics."

130 Progress on Commons Room. *Pitt News*, November 6, 1936.

130 Bowman called for an end to mediocre teaching. *Alumni Review*, March 1937, contains his address, as well as those of Colmery, Sutherland, and Mayor Scully.

131 Sutherland ovation. *Pittsburgh Post-Gazette*, February 26, 1937; *Pitt News*, February 26, 1937.

131 A. W. Mellon: "You were right." *Unofficial Notes*, 126; "Notes About A. W. Mellon," 20.

131 Silver trowel. Preserved in a drawer at the University Archives.

132 Cornerstone statement. University History Starrett Files, 031, FF 133.

132 Open house statistics. "Finish the Cathedral," 1934, a 4-page pamphlet.

132 W. A. Jessup: "Most beautiful thing ever attempted." Spoken at the June 9, 1937, commencement exercises; *Alumni Review*, June 1937; *Pitt News*, August 13, 1937.

132 "Charm teas." Harry Kodinsky, "Dr. Bowman Bids for Support," *Pittsburgh Post-Gazette*, November 6, 1939.

132 Foster Memorial. Robert X. Graham, "Stephen Collins Foster Dedication," *Greater Pittsburgh*, May, 1937, pp. 19–20; Bowman, "A Singer to Pioneers," 83–88; *Unofficial Notes*, 140–48; Fitzgerald Papers, FF 190, Memorandum, December 31, 1948, "Gifts to the University from the Lilly Family"; *The Stephen Collins Foster Memorial . . . a Tribute to the Composer . . .*, Stephen Foster Memorial Committee, June 2, 1937; Tim Ziaukas, "Fletcher Hodges, 50 Years with Stephen Foster," *Pitt*, August 1982, p. 21; Rich Gigler, "Keeper of the Memories," *Pittsburgh Press*, June 27, 1982; Kurtzman Papers, University Archives, FF 104, Mrs. William B. Millard to Kurtzman, April 4, 1967.

134 Nationality Rooms. Author's interviews with Ruth C. Mitchell; interview of Ruth Mitchell in *Carnegie Magazine*, Summer 1975, pp. 247–56; Bruhns, "Pitt's Nationality Rooms," 45–48; Bruhns, *The Nationality Rooms*; Bowman, *Report of the Chancellor*, 1930–32, pp. 62–63; ibid., 1934–36, pp. 93–95; Starrett, 261–64; *Pittsburgh Press*, November 20, 1966, "Founder of Nationality Rooms Will Be Honored Today by Pitt"; *Christian Science Monitor*, October 4, 1930; Helen P. Rush, "The Story of the Nationality Rooms," Student Host Institute Address, June 24, 1957; *University Times*, December 13, 1979; *Pitt News*, April 7, 1982.

135 Population figures. Bowman Papers, FF 93, table by R. C. Mitchell.

140 Heinz Memorial Chapel. "$1,000,000 Memorial," *Pittsburgh Bulletin Index*, November 24, 1938, p. 8; Howard Heinz Dedication Address, *Alumni Review*, December 1938, pp. 3–8; "Heinz Memorial Chapel Dedicated as a Gift to Pitt," *Pittsburgh Post-Gazette*, November 21, 1938; *The Heinz Memorial Chapel at the University of Pittsburgh*, 40 pp., no date; *The Heinz Memorial Chapel—A Descriptive Guide*; "The Heinz Memorial Chapel," *Pitt*, October 1961, pp. 12–15; *University Times*, June 5, 1980.

140 Bowman to Weber. Bowman Papers, FF 103, September 25, 1928.

141 Adams on windows. *New York Times Sunday Magazine*, August 13, 1939, p. 2.

142 Bowman on Chapel. *The Heinz Memorial Chapel—A Descriptive Guide*, 7.

Chapter Nine. The 1930s: Dissension in the House

144 Liberal Club affair. Sabine and Wittke, 582; "Academic Freedom in Pittsburgh," *New Republic*, May 22, 1929; running accounts in the Pittsburgh newspapers; "Much Ado," Bowman Papers, FF 27, an unsigned, undated, unfinished, and never released 43-page manuscript defending the administration's actions; Legislative Committee Report, 1935.

144 Mooney-Billings case. See Frost, *The Mooney Case*.

144 *Pittsburgh Press*: "miscarriages of justice." April 25, 1929.

144 Albertson did not tell Barnes. AAUP *Bulletin*, 1929, p. 579; "Much Ado," 17–18.

145 Editorial attacks. *Pittsburgh Press*, April 24, 25, 27, 1929. The *Press*, part of the Scripps-Howard chain, had at this time and for some years thereafter a liberal, populist editorial policy.

145 "Some greater power." *Pittsburgh Press*, April 24, 1929.

145 Governor Fisher "mad as a hornet." *Pittsburgh Post-Gazette*, April 25, 1929; *Pittsburgh Sun-Telegraph*, April 27, 1929.

145 Woltman gave out notes of meetings. AAUP *Bulletin*, 1929, p. 584.

145 "Free Speech Gag." *Pittsburgh Press*, April 26, 1929.

145 Condemned the *Pitt Weekly*. *Pittsburgh Sun-Telegraph*, April 26, 1929.

146 Bowman interviewed in Erie. *Pittsburgh Press*, April 25, 1929. The reporter was William G. Lytle, Jr., who had been editor of the *Pitt Weekly*.

146 Bowman statement in *Post-Gazette*. May 3, 1929.

146 Barnes episode misreported. For example, in a *Press* editorial, April 24, 1929, which said that Barnes was "the announced speaker," and in a *Press* news story, March 31, 1935, which wrote of "the sensational episode when Dr. Harry Elmer Barnes was ejected from the campus by a policeman when he attempted to hold a meeting."

146 Albertson at trustees' hearing. Charles F. C. Arensberg, "From My Time at the Bar," 13, 14.

147 Woltman at the *World-Telegram. Current Biography*, July 1947, pp. 59–60.

147 W. Don Harrison and picketers. House Investigating Committee Report, 1935, p. 17; "Much Ado," 19–21; running newspaper accounts.

147 Three picketers. They were Leonard J. Grumet, 23, Alonzo D. Brewer, 21, and Lewis M. Teitlebaum, 23, the law student.

147 Appeals judge. He was Michael Musmanno. *Pittsburgh Press* editorial, September 17, 1932.

148 ROTC handbills. *Pittsburgh Sun-Telegraph*, September 20, 1933.

148 Loyalty oath. *Pittsburgh Post-Gazette*, September 24, 1932; *Pittsburgh Press*, October 10, 1933.

148 Weber statement. *Pittsburgh Post-Gazette*, September 24, 1932.

148 *Press* on loyalty oath. September 25, 1932.

148 Ralph Turner affair. AAUP, "*Academic Freedom and Tenure at the University of Pittsburgh*," 1935; *Brief Submitted by the University of Pittsburgh to the Committee of the House of Representatives*, May 18, 1935; C. F. C. Arensberg, "From My Time at the Bar"; Rose M. Stein, "Academic Cossacks in Pittsburgh," *Nation*, July 24, 1935; *Time*, March 4, 1935; C. Hartley Grattan, *Survey Graphic*, March 1936; "Much Ado," *Pitt*, Spring 1971 Legislative Committee Report, 1935.

148 Turner biography. AAUP *Bulletin*, 1935, pp. 224–26; *Who's Who in America*, (1944–45).

149 "Most popular professor." *Pittsburgh Press*, July 11, 1934.

149 *Campus Index*, 1934. The University Archives has a copy.

149 Meeting of Friends of the Soviet Union. Turner had agreed to preside but had to be with his publisher in New York on that day. *Pittsburgh Press*, February 7, 1933.

149 Turner to Presbyterian Church. It was the Hiland (sic) Presbyterian Church in the Perrysville section of the city.

149 Historical Society speech. *Pittsburgh Bulletin Index*, April 18, 1935. WPHS has a manuscript copy in its archives.

149 2,900 Turner students. AAUP *Bulletin*, 1935, p. 226.

149 Warnings to Turner by Gow, Sieg, and Oliver. Ibid., 227; Legislative Committee Report, 11, 16.

150 Turner promised Gow. Legislative Committee Report, 1935, p. 13.

150 Oliver: "Bowman not hostile." Bowman Papers, FF 137, Oliver to Bowman, July 8, 1934.

150 Bowman-Turner meeting. AAUP *Bulletin*, 1935, pp. 231–32.

150 Turner's letter to Bowman. Bowman Papers, FF 137.

150 Bowman to Ellenbogen. Ibid., FF 135, July 10, 1934; AAUP *Bulletin*, 1935, p. 237.

150 Turner denied attacks on religion. *Pittsburgh Sun-Telegraph*, July 9, 1934.

150 Pinchot to Bowman. *Pittsburgh Press*, July 11, 1934.

150 Lawrence to Bowman. *Pittsburgh Press*, July 6, 1934.

151 Students at Michigan. Author's interview with M. Graham Netting, who was at Michigan at the time.

151 A. W. Mellon disclaimer. Bowman Papers, FF 135. This is a 2-page typed document, undated and without a handwritten signature. It was never released, perhaps because Mellon's well-known reticence caused him to change his mind or because he decided, or someone persuaded him, that the letter seemed to undermine Bowman's position— which indeed it did.

151 Groups congratulated Bowman. *Pittsburgh Post-Gazette*, July 16, 1934; *Pittsburgh Sun-Telegraph*, July 9, 1934; AAUP *Bulletin*, 1935, p. 234.

151 Call for Bowman's resignation. *Pittsburgh Press*, July 8, 1934, editorial.

151 Farewell dinner for Turner. *Pittsburgh Post-Gazette*, *Pittsburgh Press*, August 15, 1934.

151 AAUP men with Himstead. They were Albert Benedict Wolfe, professor of economics at Ohio State, and James B. Bullett, professor of pathology at the University of North Carolina.

152 Bowman to AAUP. Bowman Papers, FF 137, February 20, 1935.

152 Avinoff to Bowman. Bowman Papers, FF 136, February 25, 1935.

152 AAUP secretary was shocked. *Pittsburgh Press*, March 24, 1935; W. W. Cook to George H. Clapp, February 26, 1935. The story, with the insult quoted in full, appeared in the *New York Times* on February 21, 1935.

152 AAUP *Report*. In the AAUP *Bulletin*, March 1935. There is a typescript of the version Bowman read as a draft in the University Archives.

152 Ignored Sieg and Oliver testimony. Bowman Papers, FF 137, Sieg Affidavit; Archives, "Much Ado," 27.

153 Legislative investigating committee. *Pittsburgh Press*, May 12, 1935; *Brief Submitted . . . to the Committee*, May 18, 1935; "Much Ado," 10–16. There are 8 volumes of typed transcript of the hearing in the University Archives.

153 Pitt publication comment. *Alumni Review*, May–June, 1935, pp. 3–11.

153 Turner and the 26 dismissed petitioners. "Much Ado," 37; House Investigating Committee Report, 12; C. F. C. Arensberg, "From My Time at the Bar," 15; *Brief Submitted . . . to the Committee*, 22.

156 Fitzgerald advice. Fitzgerald Notes, June 3, 1941. Fitzgerald's Notes, a daily record he kept of his activities comprising some hundreds of typed pages, are in the University Archives, Fitzgerald Papers, Boxes 27–34, FF 224–31.

Chapter Ten. Code Bowman and "The Most Discussed Controversy"

157 Epigraph. Bowman Papers, FF 89, March 11, 13, 1940.

158 All-Americans. *1984 Pitt Football Media Guide*, 86. See also *Greater Pittsburgh*, December 1937; *Alumni Review*, January 1938; *Pittsburgh Press*, March 6, 1939; *Pittsburgh Sun-Telegraph*, April 12, 1948.

158 Sutherland "a national hero." *Saturday Evening Post*, October 28, 1939, p. 14.

158 "The most discussed controversy." *Pittsburgh Post-Gazette*, February 26, 1937.

158 "Intelligent, honorable men." Carver interviews and correspondence.

159 Problems of recruiting, married players, Sutherland episodes. Ibid.

162 Pasadena quarrel. Ibid.; *Pittsburgh Post-Gazette*, February 22, 24, 26, 1937, March 6, 7, 1939; *Pittsburgh Press*, March 8, 1939; "Report of Special Committee of University . . . Trustees" (hereafter Gow Report), Sutherland testimony, April 24, 1939, pp. 1–2; Hagan testimony, May 9, 1939, pp. 24–25.

162 Pitt got $95,000. *Alumni Review*, January, 1937, p. 3.

162 Sutherland to Gow Committee. Gow Report, 1–16.

162 Bowman: "for the benefit of the students." Bowman Papers, FF 89, Bowman to Athletic Council, March 29, 1937.

162 "In accord with the best traditions." Gow Report, Sutherland testimony, John Weber letter to Sutherland, April 12, 1937.

162 Exceptional record on graduate athletes. See Norman MacLeod, "They Still Score Touchdowns," *Alumni Review*, November 1937, p. 19; Frank Carver, ibid., February–March 1935, p. 9; E. H. Litchfield and Myron Cope, "Saturday's Hero Is Doing Fine," *Sports Illustrated*, October 8, 1962, p. 66; James Michener, *Sports in America*, 237.

162 Writers chose Pitt to expose. For example, Francis

Wallace gave a detailed analysis of Pitt's aid to its athletes in two issues of the *Saturday Evening Post*, "Test Case at Pitt—The Facts About College Football for Pay," October 28, and "The Football Laboratory," November 4, 1939.

163 "We developed a bad name." Carver interviews.

163 Notre Dame dropped Pitt. Ibid. Trustee Herbert Riley maintained that Notre Dame dropped Pitt because Pitt had dropped Duquesne University when Elmer Layden (new coach at Notre Dame) was coach at Duquesne. Gow Report, Riley testimony, 33.

163 Notice by Middle States Association. Ibid., Weber testimony, May 3, 1939, p. 6.

163 Big Ten decided to eliminate Pitt. Manuscript in University Archives prepared by Department of Athletics for the chancellor's 1938–40 report to trustees, not used; report of James Hagan to Bowman in "Department of Athletics" file.

163 "Special equipment." Gow Report, Weber testimony, 2–4.

164 Big Ten opening. Carver interviews.

164 Athletic Council mediated. Bowman Papers, FF 89, Athletic Council to Bowman, March 19, Bowman to Council, March 20, 1937.

164 Harrison resignation letter. *Alumni Review*, March 1937, p. 1.

164 Sutherland very sorry. Gow Report, Weber testimony, 20.

164 Hagan refused to accept correspondence. Ibid., Sutherland testimony, 5; Wallace, "Test Case," 51.

164 The Hagan Plan. University Archives, Board of Trustees' Committee to Study . . . , Box 1; Gow Report, Sutherland testimony, 14; ibid., Saunders testimony, March 31, 1939, p. 23; ibid., Weber testimony, 2–3; Wallace, "Test Case," 51; *Pittsburgh Post-Gazette*, October 26, 1937; *Pittsburgh Press*, March 7, 1939.

164 Hagan Plan: "a greater sense of loyalty." Bowman Papers, FF 81, extract from the minutes of the meetings of the Athletic Council, July 21, 1937.

164 Weber: no need to recruit. Gow Report, Weber testimony, 26.

164 For a bizarre episode in which the football team voted not to accept an invitation to the 1938 Rose Bowl game, see *Pittsburgh Post-Gazette*, November 30, 1937; *Pittsburgh Press*, March 9, 1939; Gow Report, testimony by Sutherland, Weber, and Hagan.

164 Code Bowman. Gow Report, Sutherland testimony, 8–11; Wallace, "Test Case," 51, 52; *Pittsburgh Post-Gazette*, December 6, 1938; *Pittsburgh Press*, March 7, 11, September 28, 1939.

165 "A thorn in the side." Fitzgerald Notes, March 22, 1939.

165 Norman MacLeod protested. Chester Smith, *Pittsburgh Press*, March 7, 1939.

165 Trustee would need six months. Ibid. Late in 1938, newly recruited football and basketball freshmen rebelled against Code Bowman. See *Pittsburgh Post-Gazette*, November 24, December 2, 1938; *Pittsburgh Press*, March 8, December 2, 1939; Wallace, "Football Laboratory," 21, 85; Gow Report, Smyers testimony, 21; *Pitt News*, March 11, 1940.

165 Varsity Lettermen called on Bowman. *Pittsburgh Press*, November 22, 1938; Wallace, "Football Laboratory," 21; Gow Report, Ochsenhirt testimony, 2–6, Thompson testimony, 18.

165 Chamber of Commerce delegation. Gow Report, Thompson testimony, 18; Wallace, "Football Laboratory," 21.

165 As Thompson saw it. Gow Report, Thompson testimony, 18–27.

165 Bowman to student body. *Pittsburgh Press*, November 22, 1938; Wallace, "Football Laboratory," 21.

166 Fitzgerald to T. E. French. Fitzgerald Notes, November 11, 1938.

166 Alumni Association Report. *Pittsburgh Press*, March 10, 11, 12, 1939; *Pittsburgh Post-Gazette*, January 24, 1939; Gow Report, summary, 37.

166 Sutherland's resignation. Bowman Papers, FF 89, Sutherland to Bowman, March 4, 1939; Bowman to Sutherland, March 6, 1939; *Pittsburgh Press*, March 6, 7, 1939; *Pittsburgh Post-Gazette*, March 7, 1939; Wallace, "Football Laboratory," 20, 21, 85; Gow Report, Weber testimony, 12, 13; Fitzgerald Notes, March 22, 1939.

167 Difficult decision. *Pittsburgh Press*, March 6, October 26, 1939, April 13, 1948.

167 Bowman's response. Wallace, "Football Laboratory," 85.

167 Protest of students. *Pittsburgh Post-Gazette*, March 9; *Pittsburgh Press*, March 11, 1939.

167 2,000 students. *Pittsburgh Press*, April 19, 1939.

168 Farewell dinner. April 20, 1939; Wallace, "Test Case," 47.

168 Hagan's praise of Bowser. Fitzgerald Notes, March 13, 1939.

168 Saunders's resignation. Fitzgerald Notes, March 22, 1939. He became a top executive and served many years with George Gallup's marketing and attitude research company.

Chapter Eleven. The Ordeal of a Chancellor

169 Epigraph. Gow Report, Tippetts testimony, March 24, 1939.

170 Conversation between Bowman and Fitzgerald. Fitzgerald Notes, March 20, 1939, 4 entries.

170 Bowman's son paid by his father. Revealed in cross-examination of Bowman at House Committee hearings. Arensberg, "From My Time at the Bar," 16.

170 Fitzgerald and the Bowman crisis. Fitzgerald Notes, March 20, 1939.

171 Gow called on Bowman. Ibid., March 20, 22, 1939.

171 Gow Report (more properly the Braun Report). "Report of Special Committee of University of Pittsburgh Trustees. Final Revision," 49 pp., stapled folder, University Archives, Box 1 of 1.

172 Fitzgerald's advice to his colleagues. Fitzgerald Notes, March 22, 27, 28, 29, 1939, talks with Tippetts, Shockley, and Crawford.

172 Lanfear: "discontent and confusion." Testimony, Gow Report, March 31, 1939.

172 Graper: "riot act." Testimony, ibid., April 5, 1939.

172 Saunders: "Poesy." Testimony, ibid., March 31, 1939.

172 Bowman on an ideal teacher. Bowman Papers, Report to Trustees, 1921–22, pp. 18–19.

173 Bowman on "Red," the master workman. Bowman, Report to Trustees, 1922–24, pp. 14–16.

173 "Dad" buying trousers. Bowman, Report to Trustees, 1930–32, p. 19.

173 "If you have sent your child . . ." Bowman Papers, FF 148, *Pittsburgh Sun-Telegraph*, "Bowman Talks on Manners," November 25, 1933.

173 "Wanted an administrator, got a poet." Howes, *Low Point at Pitt*.

173 Only eight years' training in education. Five years (1902–07) as an English instructor at the State University of Iowa and Columbia; three years (1911–14) as president of the State University of Iowa.

173 Bowman had been a liberal. Howes, 21.

173 Handed back a large check. Ketchum interviews.

173 Would not use a bell. Starrett, "John Gabbert Bowman," in *Famous Men and Women of Pittsburgh*," 202.

173 Dressed people down in public. Three persons the author interviewed were witnesses to three such incidents: Walter Rome, Carlton Ketchum, and Lawrence Irwin.

173 Rumor a high official would be asked to resign. *Pittsburgh Press*, September 15, 1939.

173 Rumor about wealthy alumnus. Ibid.

173 Holbrook: interested in Turner case. Fitzgerald Notes, April 3, 1939.

173 Kerr: rumor on tenure. Ibid., April 22, 1939.

173 Friendly or critical? Ibid., September 7, 1939.

173 Clapp told Bowman. Ibid., September 5, 1939.

174 Bowman: "go into it hard." Ibid.

174 Kerr: some of committee were hurt. Ibid., September 16, 1939.

174 The Gow Report. The report is backed by Steele Gow's transcriptions of the interviews with 43 persons. These contain extraordinarily rich and readable material. The whole Gow Report, in my opinion, should be published.

177 Bowman intended to resign. Fitzgerald Notes, September 16, 1939.

178 Bowman: "loose statements." Bowman's reply to trustees' investigating committee, October 17, 1939.

178 American Historical Association. *Pittsburgh Post-Gazette*, March 11, 1939.

178 Alumni letter to Gow Committee, April 3, 1939. Bowman Papers, Special Investigating Committee, Box 1.

178 Bowman felt he could handle opposition. Fitzgerald Notes, October 4, 1939.

178 Bowman: "going after very strenuously." Ibid., October 10, 1939.

178 Fitzgerald: "Salvage the best things." Ibid., September 20, 1939.

178 Fitzgerald: "Build a picture of the next step." Ibid., September 25, 1939.

179 Tippetts to Fitzgerald. Ibid., September 18, October 5, 1939.

179 Crawford felt very deeply. Ibid., October 6, 1939.

179 Kerr: should swallow pride. Ibid., September 16, 1939.

179 Jessup: "Forget it." Ibid., September 25, 1939.

179 Bowman's reading. Ibid., October 15, 1939.

179 Weber on sharp questions to trustees. Ibid., October 14, 1939.

179 Bowman on monastic orders. Ibid., September 19, 1939.

179 Bowman's rebuttal. The Gow Report and Bowman's reply, besides appearing in full in the daily press, were presented in the *Alumni Review* (October 1939), which was distributed to 27,000 alumni. The *Pitt News* ingeniously broke both papers down and printed them in parallel columns according to subject: library, tenure, academic standards, etc.

180 "Chancellor Bowman Is Resentful." *Pittsburgh Press*, October 19, 1939.

180 *Post-Gazette* editorial. October 19, 1939.

181 David L. Lawrence. *Pittsburgh Press*, July 6, 1934.

181 *Time* magazine. "Tower of Trouble," March 4, 1935.

181 Raymond F. Howes. See *Low Point at Pitt*. Howes reprinted two earlier articles in 1972 as a warning to Californians as to what would happen to them if they elected Ronald Reagan governor. The articles were "Sweetness and Light in Pittsburgh," *Outlook*, December 4, 1929, and "A Poet in a Cathedral," *American Mercury*, September 1930.

181 Grattan. *Survey Graphic*, March 1936, p. 145.

182 Front-page apology in *Pitt News*. September 29, 1937.

182 Scaife opposed censorship. Bowman Papers, FF 72. Scaife had been an editor of the *Yale Daily News*,

where he was a colleague and friend of Briton Hadden and Henry R. Luce, founders of *Time*.

183 Paul Mellon to Bowman. Ibid., October 4, 1937. Mr. Mellon did not become a trustee.

183 Censorship modified. Fitzgerald Notes, May 17, 1938; *Pitt News*, October 1, 6, 1937.

Chapter Twelve. The University at War

185 Training of cadets. Fitzgerald, 2; Fitzgerald Papers, FF 363, Colonel E. L. Kelley to Fitzgerald, August 3, 1943; ibid., FF 341, "Preliminary Announcement of the Army Specialized Training Program," December 29, 1942; Bowman Papers, FF 98, "Memo for Mr. Fitzgerald," July 28, 1943; ibid., "Minutes of a Meeting with ASTP Negotiating Committee," July 29, 1943; ibid., FF 99, "Speech Delivered by Major General T. J. Hanley to the Commanding Officers and College Presidents of College Training Detachments," November 3, 1943; *Training to Win*, 15, 24–25; University Archives, *At Ease*, April 30, June 25, 1943; Starrett, *World War*.

186 Cadet routine. *At Ease*, various issues; Fitzgerald Papers, FF 333, "Directive on Guard Duty," June 19, 1943; ibid., Fitzgerald address to an alumni group in Roy McKenna's home, May 6, 1943.

186 Specialists for Military Government. Fitzgerald Papers, FF 360, John Geise to Bowman; Geise to S. C. Crawford, January 18, 1944; Bowman Papers, FF 96, "Division Memorandum Training Circular No. 4," April 30, 1943; ibid., Lieutenant Arnold L. Fein to University, "Letter of Intent," July 21, 1943; Starrett, *World War*, 16, 29. An interesting hypothetical occupation problem is given in Fitzgerald Papers, FF 360.

186 Psychological technicians. Starrett, *World War*, 15.

187 Area and Language Training. Bowman Papers, FF 96, unsigned and undated 2-page memorandum; Starrett, *World War*, 16, 30; University Archives, Helen Knox interview with John Geise, 1972.

187 General Hospital 27. Starrett, *World War*, 33.

187 Classroom conduct. Author's interviews with Agnes Starrett and Buell Whitehill; *At Ease*, various issues.

187 YM and YWHA canteen. *Pittsburgh Post-Gazette*, August 30, 1943; *At Ease*, June 25, July 30, August 13, September 3, 1943, January 7, 1944.

188 No more assignments, 150 deferments. Bowman Papers, FF 102, February 2, 1944.

188 Numbers trained. Starrett, *World War*, 17.

188 9,508 university people served. Ibid., 42.

188 Bowman on veterans. Biennial Report, 1944–46.

Chapter Thirteen. The Peacemaker

191 Epigraph. Fitzgerald Papers, FF 54.

192 Bowman's resignation. *Pitt,* Spring–Summer 1945, pp. 2–3.

192 Bowman's cerebral hemorrhage. Mrs. Gebhard Stegeman (Bowman's secretary) to Mrs. Elmer S. Blakeslee, September 1, 1948. Fitzgerald Papers, FF 4; Fitzgerald Notes, July 13, 1945.

192 Bowman promised chancellorship to Fitzgerald. He did so on his own in 1941 to persuade Fitzgerald not to accept the presidency of the University of Vermont. The board legitimated the promise by a vote of approval in a sparsely attended meeting not called for that purpose. Some absent trustees objected strongly in letters to Bowman, among them Floyd Rose (October 14, 1941), J. B. Nicklas (October 17), and William Archie Weldin (October 15). *Pittsburgh Post-Gazette,* October 24, 1941; Bowman Papers, FF 93, Bowman to trustees, October 9, 1941.

193 No one knew what a provost was. Bowman Papers, FF 142, May 20, 1942.

193 Fitzgerald had been managing affairs. This is amply evidenced in the Fitzgerald Notes—his office log from 1939 to 1945. For Fitzgerald's background, see *Who's Who in America* (1960–61); *Alumni Review,* Autumn 1945.

193 Called him peacemaker. Author's interview with Leon Falk, Jr., October 20, 1981; Carver interviews.

193 Heard a sigh of relief. Ketchum interviews.

193 Comparison with Eisenhower. Rome interview.

193 Caused code of tenure to be written. This is made clear by numerous entries in Fitzgerald's Notes, FF 4 and FF 30.

193 Fitzgerald-Himstead meeting. Fitzgerald Notes, April 18, November 15, 1946.

194 Phi Beta Kappa. Fitzgerald Papers, FF 172, memorandum of February 9, 1938; *Pittsburgh Post-Gazette,* January 20, 1953.

194 "Every possible veteran." Fitzgerald, Report to Trustees, FF 66, July 24, 1946.

194 Policy on accepting veterans. Fitzgerald Papers, FF 1, FF 32, Fitzgerald speech, untitled and undated, ca. 1945; Fitzgerald speech to University Senate, February 25, 1944.

194 Biddle's interviews. Fitzgerald Notes, March 5, December 27, 1946.

194 "Scholastic tramps." Ibid., Biddle to Fitzgerald, September 25, 1945.

194 Veterans' work excellent. Fitzgerald, Report to Trustees, July 24, 1946.

194 On quality of teaching. Fitzgerald Papers, FF 31, Fitzgerald to trustees, December 9, 1947.

194 Improved quality of students. Ibid., FF 54, address to community leaders, June 3, 1948; Fitzgerald, Biennial Report, 1946–48.

194 Teaching standards raised. Ibid., address to community leaders, Biennial Report.

195 Faculty morale good. Fitzgerald, to board, July 24, 1946.

195 Competition for teachers terrific. Fitzgerald Papers, FF 31, Fitzgerald to board, December 9, 1947.

195 Retained professors past 70. Fitzgerald Notes, September 18, 1945.

195 Employing members of same family. Fitzgerald Papers, FF 21, Memorandum, October 9, 1952.

195 Physicists would not budge. Ibid., FF 31, Fitzgerald to board, December 9, 1947.

195 Pitt better off in city. Ibid., FF 31, December 7, 1947; Fitzgerald, Biennial Report, 1946–48.

195 Only 18 classrooms plastered. Fitzgerald Notes, June 13, 1947.

195 Ellsworth Center. Ibid., September 7, 11, 13, 1948; Biennial Report, 1946–48; Fitzgerald Papers, FF 181, "Activities at the Ellsworth Center," no date, ca. 1948; Pitt news release, April 16, 1951.

195 "The impossible job." *Alumni Times,* Spring 1976, p. 5.

196 Two lace tablecloths; Santa Claus party; meeting in Harrisburg; luncheon for civic committee; $10 a month raise; Heinz Chapel curtains; Athletic

Department profanity; Foster program too long. Fitzgerald Notes, January 27, 1946; November 28, 1945; October 10, 1945; September 15, 1945; September 27, 1945; January 3, 1946; March 13, 1946; January 14, 1949.

196 Thirty-five areas reported to Fitzgerald. Edison Montgomery interview by Lawrence Howard, PROHP, May 21, 1975; Ray Steele, 6.

196 Prepared annual budget himself. Montgomery, PROHP, 5.

196 "Assume I may proceed." Author's conversation with Fletcher Hodges.

196 Six years without a vacation. *Pittsburgh Post-Gazette*, September 25, 1948.

196 Narrow margin physically. Fitzgerald Notes, October 28, 1948.

196 Democracy is time-consuming. Ibid., April 8, 1947.

196 "My interest is perennial." Fitzgerald Papers, FF 170, October 9, 1945.

196 Patterson call; student leader and Hall of Fame; mother quite hysterical; sculptor Frank Vittor; Fitzgerald to custodian; Mrs. Ream's call; sophomore asked for help; William Block and low salaries; Fitzgerald and corporation treasurer; president of Student Congress (his name is Howard Greenberger); "This little world"; Pitt Marching Band; Fitzgerald and fishing contest. Fitzgerald Notes, September 14, 1948; May 7, 1945; June 27, 1945; December 14, 1948; April 20, 1949; March 9, 1951; July 22, 1946; January 24, 1949; September 4, 1945; Fitzgerald Papers, FF 322, Biddle Memorandum, April 4, 1951; Fitzgerald Notes, October 3, 1952; July 26, 1946; August 28, 1951.

197 Fitzgerald asked Scaife to serve. Fitzgerald Notes, April 8, 1947.

198 "Energy, organizing ability." Fitzgerald Papers, FF 54. Speech to community leaders, June 3, 1948.

198 Hoped for drop in enrollment. Ibid.

198 R. K. Mellon interested. Ibid., April 8, 1947.

198 Scaife speech. Ibid., FF 30; *Pittsburgh Sun-Telegraph*, June 4, 1948.

198 Fitzgerald speech. Fitzgerald Papers, FF 54.

199 Refinancing stadium bonds. Ibid., FF 54, Fitzgerald speech to community leaders, June 3, 1948; *Wall Street Journal*, June 9, 1948.

199 Clapp career. *Alumni News Review*, April, 1949, p. 5; *Pitt*, Spring 1949, p. 4.

199 Clapp's attempts to resign. See, for example, Fitzgerald Notes, July 13, 1945.

199 MacLeod persuaded Clapp. Author's interview with MacLeod's business partner, Carlton G. Ketchum.

199 Clapp admonition on Yellin's gate. Fitzgerald Papers, FF 32, Clapp to Fitzgerald, December 2, 1948.

200 Ellsworth Center. Ibid., FF 181; Fitzgerald Notes, September 17, 1948; Fitzgerald, Biennial Report, 1946–48.

200 William Block and green lawn. Fitzgerald Notes, January 13, 1950.

200 Robertson and green lawn. Fitzgerald Papers, FF 31, Robertson to Fitzgerald, June 19, 1950.

200 Stotz and AIA resolution. Author's conversation with Charles Stotz, September 9, 1981.

200 Oliver to R. K. Mellon. Author's conversation with Oliver, April 22, 1983.

200 Legal papers on Cathedral open space. Litchfield Papers, Planning and Development A/C, Francis Pray to Charles Peake, June 13, 1957, enclosing "agreement abstracted from trustee book, legal agreement no more buildings until 1978 unless the Board of Trustees of the Mellon Institute agrees." See also minute of the special meeting of the Board of Trustees, December 28, 1953.

201 $11 million available for construction. Fitzgerald Papers, FF 87, Fitzgerald to Frederick Bigger, February 23, 1953.

201 Overture to YMHA. Ibid., June 27, 1950.

201 Masonic Temple and Duquesne Gardens. Ibid., September 12, 1951; Fitzgerald Papers, FF 36, W. F. Trimble, Jr., to Scaife, October 5, 1951, Scaife to Fitzgerald, October 9, 1951.

202 Talk of Panther Hollow. Fitzgerald Notes, May 10, 1949, October 5, 1953; author's conversation with M. Graham Netting, April 12, 1983.

202 Pitt and Allegheny Conference. Fitzgerald Notes, May 18, 22, 1950.

202 Bowman and Clapp Hall. Fitzgerald Notes, September 29, December 3, 5, 1949, January 6, February 21, 1950, February 1, May 10, 14, 1951.

202 R. K. Mellon and 3-acre plot. Ibid., June 27, 1950;

Pitt News, December 11, 1953, January 6, 1954; *Report of the A. W. Mellon Educational and Charitable Trust,* 105. It was sometimes called the town hall site because of a proposal early in the century to build a town hall there.

202 Scaife: no more buildings on lawn. *Pitt News,* April 29, 1953. Scaife said "never," but the agreement with the Mellon Trust said "the next twenty-five years," with permission to undertake buildings "if conditions warrant it" and there was common agreement of the Pitt trustees and the Mellon Institute.

Chapter Fourteen. The Letters of Gift

204 Founding of the school of Public Health. The main sources for this chapter are Zaga Blockstein, *Graduate School of Public Health,* 1977, pp. 1–69; *Report of the A. W. Mellon Educational and Charitable Trust,* 8–97; and the author's interview on June 15, 1984, with Adolph W. Schmidt, trustee, treasurer, executive vice president, and later president of the trust.

205 Pennsylvania ranked 42. *Report of the A. W. Mellon Educational and Charitable Trust,* 80.

205 Professional acceptance all-important. Author's interview with Adolph Schmidt, June 15, 1984.

205 None of 9 schools had developed industrial hygiene. Kurtzman Papers, FF 296, "Goals and Objectives of the Graduate School of Public Health," November 30, 1966, p. 2.

205 Schmidt, Broughton, and Reed called on Fitzgerald. Fitzgerald Notes, January 29, 1948.

205 Broughton to Parran. Blockstein, 40–41.

205 Fitzgerald to Parran. Ibid., 42.

205 Fitzgerald to Paul Mellon on meeting. Fitzgerald Notes, September 21, 1948; Blockstein, 47–48.

206 Parran to news media. *Pittsburgh Press, Pittsburgh Post-Gazette,* September 25, 1948.

206 Accredited before teaching. *Annual Report, Graduate School of Public Health,* 1949–50, p. 12.

206 Reed to Schmidt: must improve medical school. Blockstein, 33.

206 Parran report: need a great medical center. Ibid., 93.

207 $1 million endowment. Fitzgerald Notes, August 5, 1953.

207 Salk on faculty. Carter, 52.

207 Parran report to Mellon Trust. Blockstein, 61.

207 Schmidt on opposition to full-time faculty. Ibid., 61–62; Schmidt interview.

207 GSPH helped to produce a change. Schmidt interview.

207 Mellon Trust report: "essential place." p. 96.

207 Schmidt ultimatum to hospital administrators. Ibid.

207 Scaife proposed Parran. Blockstein, 67.

207 Parran and "socialized medicine." Ibid., 63–64; *Reader's Digest,* January 1951, p. 63; JAMA, January 12, 1946, p. 84.

207 Parran requested clarification. Blockstein, 67.

207 Fiedler's warning. Ibid.

207 Vice Chancellor Robert A. Moore. *Pittsburgh Post-Gazette,* September 19, 21, 1953; *Pittsburgh Press,* September 17, 1963.

208 Moore's conditions and plans. Fitzgerald Papers, FF 328, Moore to Fitzgerald, March 12, 1953; Fitzgerald Notes, December 6, 1952, June 11, July 3, August 4–5, November 19, 1954.

208 $15 million gift announced. *Pittsburgh Sun-Telegraph,* January 19, 1954; *Pitt,* Spring 1954.

209 Paul Mellon's speech at dedication. University Archives, Thomas Parran files, under "Paul Mellon," 1, 3–4, 10–11.

Chapter Fifteen. The Pitt Vaccine

210 Epigraph. Selvaggio, 44.

211 McEllroy not reconciled. *Pittsburgh Press,* October 6, 1957.

211 $15,000 Scaife grant. *Pitt,* Winter 1949–50, p. 40.

211 Salk biography. Carter, 28–53; Williams, 270–72; *Time,* March 28, 1954; Pitt news release, "Biographical Material on Dr. Salk," no date.

211 McEllroy: "I didn't have much to offer." *Pittsburgh Press,* October 6, 1957.

211 To gain some experience. *Pittsburgh Press,* April 5, 1952.

212 Weaver's call on Salk. Carter, 60–62.

212 Salk said he was ready. Ibid., 95–97, 99.

212 Weaver description of Salk at work. Ibid., 68–69.

214 Elsie Ward: "so much excitement." Ibid., 106.

214 William Hammon. *Time*, November 3, 1952, 73–75; Carter, 101–02.

214 Salk announced he would vaccinate. *Pittsburgh Press*, May 13, 1952; *Pittsburgh Sun-Telegraph*, May 13, 1953.

214 Jesse Wright. *Pitt*, Autumn 1952; author's conversations in the 1940s with Drs. Raymond Frodey and Richard Simon, who helped to send Wright through medical school.

215 Salk at Watson Home. Salk, JAMA, 1066; Carter, 137–78.

215 Salk's inoculations at Watson and Polk. Williams, 288–90; Carter, 138–39.

215 Salk: "You don't sleep well." Williams, 289.

215 Salk: "It was the thrill of my life." Carter, 140.

215 Salk, "Studies in Human Subjects. . . . " JAMA, March 28, 1953, 1081–98; *Pittsburgh Press*, March 29, 1953; Selvaggio, 44–45. The full text of the broadcast appeared in the *Pitt News*, March 27, 1953.

215 Hoped to have a moderating effect. Carter, 156.

216 Salk: keep his name out of news. Williams, 352; Carter, 166, 214–15.

216 Inoculation of 1,000 children. Carter, 217–18; *Time*, March 29, 1954, pp. 56–57.

216 Inoculated himself, wife, children. Williams, 292.

216 Second program of 6,500 children. Carter, 217–18.

216 The main field study. Ibid., 202, 206, 238; Williams, 297, 305, 317.

217 The meeting at Ann Arbor. Williams, 312–15; Carter, 256, 266–74, 286; *Harpers*, August 1955. See also *New York Times*, April 13, 1955; Cathy Covert, *Editor and Publisher*, April 16, 1955.

217 Salk at afternoon meeting. Carter, 277–82.

217 Associate: "The world is listening." Ibid., 279.

217 "Self-effacement is a luxury." Ibid., 280.

217 Ordeal after Ann Arbor. Williams, 315–22; Carter, 285–300.

218 Extra telephone for PR director. *Omnibus*, May 1955.

219 Tenth anniversary report. A 12-page pamphlet distributed by the NFIP; *Pittsburgh Press*, November 19, 1984.

Chapter Sixteen. "The Athletic Situation," or, Days of Rage and Anguish

220 Title: "Rage and Anguish." Paxton, 132.

221 Sports editor: "the annual dissatisfaction." Al Abrams, *Pittsburgh Post-Gazette*, October 22, 1947.

221 Carnegie Tech losses. Paxton, 134; *Pittsburgh Sun-Telegraph*, November 25, 1947; *Pittsburgh Press*, November 29, 1947.

221 Shaughnessy: "one of the finest." Jack Sell, *Pittsburgh Post-Gazette*, January 26, 1943.

221 Shaughnessy's resignation. Fitzgerald Notes, November 26, 1945; Fitzgerald Papers, FF 24, Shaughnessy to R. E. Sherrill, January 17, 1946; *Pittsburgh Sun-Telegraph*, February 5, 1946.

221 Training camp at Kiski. Carver interviews.

221 Bellefield Trust. Author's interview with Charles R. Wilson and Dr. George Fetterman, November 16, 1981.

221 Fitzgerald really cared. Myron Cope, *Pittsburgh Post-Gazette*, November 26, 1954. To Elaine Kahn of the Associated Press he said, "I love football. A weak football team doesn't make me happy." Fitzgerald Papers, FF 19.

222 Told Hagan to rebuild. *Pittsburgh Press*, June 3, 1948.

222 Chancellor's electrifying speech. Jack Henry, *Pittsburgh Sun-Telegraph*, October 22, 1947; Fitzgerald Papers, FF 23.

222 Fesler's salary raised. Fitzgerald Notes, January 28, 1947. Hagan knew he would lose Fesler but hoped to keep him at least three years. Carver interviews.

222 Bad condition of athletic facilities. Fitzgerald Notes, December 12, 26, 1945; *Pittsburgh Sun-Telegraph*, October 22, 1947.

222 Costs rising. Fitzgerald Notes, December 26, 1945; Jack Henry, *Pittsburgh Sun-Telegraph*, October 21, 1947; Fitzgerald Notes, Fitzgerald-Hagan conference, December 26, 1945.

222 "Strange flirtation." Arthur Daley, *New York Times*, February 1, 1949.

222 Pitt almost chosen by Big Nine. Carver interviews.

222 Will they win one game? Fitzgerald Notes, September 12, 1947.

222 $70,000 surplus. *Pittsburgh Press,* June 9, 1948; *Pittsburgh Post-Gazette,* June 9, 1948.

222n Fewer stadium seats. Information supplied by W. Dean Billick, athletic department.

223 Mayor Lawrence protest. *Pittsburgh Press,* December 23, 1947.

223 Fitzgerald calls for reexamination. *Pittsburgh Post-Gazette,* October 25, 1947; Fitzgerald Papers, rough manuscript of his speech, FF 23.

223 Babcock's meeting with Sutherland. Fitzgerald Papers, FF 30, May 19, 1947.

223 Sutherland's death. The young doctor who heard him in the hospital corridor was Harry L. Wechsler. Sutherland left his estate to his sister and other relatives. Carlton Ketchum, who was close to him from the time he enrolled him as a student in 1914, said that Sutherland had named Pitt in his will but changed it when Dr. Bowman made a slurring reference to him in the 1940s. *Pittsburgh Press,* April 15, 1948; author's conversation with Dr. Wechsler.

223 Investigating committee reports. *Pittsburgh Post-Gazette,* February 25, 1948; *Pittsburgh Sun-Telegraph,* February 24, 25, 26, 1948; *Pittsburgh Press,* February 25, 1948.

224 McClelland comment. *Pittsburgh Press,* February 26, 1948. Harry Keck, *Pittsburgh Sun-Telegraph* sports editor, called the faculty report "silly twaddle" (February 26, 1948).

224 Board's administrative committee. Fitzgerald Papers, FF 20, February 23, 1948; minute of trustees' meeting, FF 23, February 27, 1948. Floyd Rose was chairman of the Trustees' Committee.

224 Ochsenhirt Committee. Paxton, 132.

224 Fitzgerald: "Draw up a liberal code." Ibid.

224 Carver highly regarded. *Pittsburgh Sun-Telegraph,* February 26, 1948; *Pittsburgh Press,* June 14, 1948.

224 Best freshman squad. *New York Times,* November 27, 1948; Carver interviews.

224 Fitzgerald on Hamilton. Fitzgerald Notes, August 25, 1948, *et seriam.*

224 Paxton article. *Saturday Evening Post,* November 19, 1949, pp. 29, 131–34; Fitzgerald Notes, October 11, 12, 1949.

225 Comments on *Post* title. *Pittsburgh Press,* November 16, 1949.

225 Hamilton program. Fitzgerald Notes, September 22, 1949; Paxton, 133; *Pittsburgh Press,* December 12, 1951; *Pittsburgh Post-Gazette,* December 12, 1951; Carver interviews.

225 Hamilton, GSA, and field house. Carver interviews; author's interview with Edison Montgomery.

225 Fitzgerald on field house. *Pittsburgh Press,* December 12, 1951.

225 Scaife and Hamilton. Carver interviews.

225 Trips to inspect athletic plants. Ibid.; Fitzgerald Papers, FF 22, Scaife invitation to Fitzgerald, August 18, 1954.

226 Hamilton to Jensen. Fitzgerald Papers, FF 21, March 5, 1952.

226 Fitzgerald-Hamilton letters. Ibid.

226 Hamilton's clash with Milligan. Carver interviews.

Chapter Seventeen. Farewell, a Long Farewell

228 Epigraph. *Pittsburgh Press,* July 12, 1954; *Pitt,* Summer 1954, p. 3.

229 Geise met Fitzgerald on plane. University Archives, taped interview of John Geise by Helen L. Knox, 1972.

229 Letter of retirement. *Pitt,* Summer 1954, p. 3.

229 Weidlein on Fitzgerald. *Pitt,* Summer 1954.

229 "Gallant chancellor." *Pittsburgh Sun-Telegraph,* July 13, 1954.

229 Man of the Year. *Pittsburgh Post-Gazette,* January 22, 1955.

229 President, American Association of Colleges. *Pitt News,* January 14, 1954.

229 Chairman, student interchange. Ibid., April 12, 1966.

229 Stooped appearance. Author's interview with William Tacey, July 16, 1981.

230 Management study. Survey of Administrative Management: University of Pittsburgh, in seven parts, by Cresap, McCormick and Paget, Management Engineers, 1954; Fitzgerald Notes, June 26, 1953.

230 Fitzgerald handled mechanics. Fitzgerald Notes, May 28, July 15, 18, 1953.

230 Abrasive grilling. Ibid., October 21, 1953.

230 Montgomery statement. Taped interview with Montgomery, February 8, 1971, by Lawrence Howard, as part of the University's PROHP.

230 Assessment of Fitzgerald. Cresap Report, 3, 13, I–3, I–4, I–13.

231 Moratorium on contruction. Ibid., XXVIII–4.

231 Increased endowment. *Pitt News*, November 21, 1955, "University Ten-Year Report."

231 Increased enrollment. Ibid.

231 Enlarged faculty. Ibid.

231 Signed more than 42 percent of all diplomas. *Pittsburgh Press*, January 12, 1965.

231 New relationship with city planning. Fitzgerald Notes, May 18, 1950; Fitzgerald Papers, FF 87, Fitzgerald to Frederick Bigger, February 2, 1953.

231 Considered Panther Hollow. Fitzgerald Notes, May 10, 1949; Fitzgerald Papers, FF 219, Fitzgerald to Broughton, October 5, 1953.

231 One-third of all medical alumni. *Pitt News*, November 21, 1955, "University Ten-Year Report."

232 Storm Jameson. *Journey from the North*, II, 221–29, 238, 240; letter to Ruth C. Mitchell, March 22, 1982. She was accompanied by her husband, Guy Chapman, professor of history, a hero of World War I, and author of several works on William Beckford and on his war experiences, *A Passionate Prodigality*, 1966.

233 Change in Nationality Rooms. *The Nationality Rooms*, no date, introduction by E. Maxine Bruhns; "The University and World Affairs," typescript, by Ruth C. Mitchell, 22–23.

233 Pitt Press. "University Ten-Year Report," *Pitt News*, November 21, 1955.

233 "Most comprehensive study." He was Merritt Lyndon Fernald, director of Gray Herbarium, Harvard University. Ibid., II, xi.

233 Jennings: 6,000 miles. Ibid., II, xi.

233 Artist worked 1,600 hours. *Wildflowers*, II, ix, x, xii.

233 Andrei Avinoff. See Alex Shoumatoff, "Personal History: The Shoumatoff Family," *The New Yorker*, May 3, 1982, part of the book *Russian Blood: A Family Chronicle*, 1982.

234 Peterson on Percival Hunt class. *Pitt*, January 1962, "Professor Peterson's Magic Lantern," 15.

234 One of the best teaching schools. Helen Knox interview with John Geise.

234 "One of the founding writing programs." Author's interview with Walter H. Evert, July 10, 1981.

234 *Monitor* on Peterson. February 1, 1964.

234 *Herald-Tribune* on Peterson. April 27, 1961.

234 Weeks: "audacious discovery." *Atlantic*, January 1965, p. 124.

234 *Pittsburgh Post-Gazette*, on Peterson. November 22, 1946.

234 List of writing awards. Bowman Papers, FF 64; *Pittsburgh Post-Gazette*, November 25, 1972.

235 Peterson on his teaching method. *Pittsburgh Post-Gazette*, November 21, 1963; *Pitt*, January 1962, pp. 13–16; *New York Herald-Tribune*, April 27, 1961; *Atlantic*, January 1965, pp. 124–25.

235 Coined the phrase *word processing*. Author's conversations with Peterson in the 1960s.

235 Grant of $22,839. *Pittsburgh Post-Gazette*, November 25, 1972.

236 English professor wondered. In a conversation with the author, July 10, 1981.

236 Four presidents met in Stassen's home. Fitzgerald Notes, September 6, 1950.

236 Faculty approved compromise on loyalty oath. Fitzgerald Papers, FF 211, Tabulation of Vote, April 28, 1951; minute of special meeting of the faculty of GSPH, April 14, 1951, Dr. Parran presiding—one of a number of such meetings recorded in FF 211.

236 Fitzgerald's testimony. Fitzgerald Papers, FF 211, April 27, 1951; *Pittsburgh Post-Gazette*, May 1, 1951; *Pittsburgh Sun-Telegraph*, April 30, 1951.

237 "Our frenzied times." *Pittsburgh Post-Gazette*, May 1, 1951.

237 *Pitt News* editor wrote to *Press*. *Pittsburgh Press*, April 17, 1951. The *Press* editorial appeared on April 7, 1951.

237 Louis Budenz. *Pittsburgh Press*, December 10, 1951.

237 Penn State employee. He was Wendell Scott McRae, *Pittsburgh Post-Gazette*, September 3, 4, 1952; *Pittsburgh Press*, September 12, 1952.

237 Pechan: opponents are Communists. *Pittsburgh Press*, April 22, 1951.

237 Woodside did not wish. *Pittsburgh Sun-Telegraph*, April 30, 1951.

237 Dean addressing Phi Beta Kappa. *Chicago Sunday Tribune*, April 29, 1951. He was Dr. Carl F. Wittke, dean at Western Reserve University, who in 1929 had investigated the Pitt Liberal Club affair and coauthored an adverse report printed in the AAUP *Bulletin*.

237 Bill altered. *Pittsburgh Post-Gazette*, May 22, 1951; *Pitt News*, March 5, 1952.

239 Pechan regretted. Author's interview with Edgar Cale, September 14, 1981.

239 Loyalty oath declared unconstitutional. *Pittsburgh Press*, January 11, 1975.

239 Farewell dinner. *Pittsburgh Post-Gazette*, June 24, 1955; Program, Trustees' Dinner, June 24, 1955.

239 Qualifications of a chancellor. Fitzgerald Papers, FF 34.

239 Questions on University's future. Cresap Report, I–12.

239 Optimism for the future. Ibid., XVI–1.

Chapter Eighteen. The Twelfth Chancellor

243 Epigraph. Litchfield Papers, FF 96, "Scaife 1955."

244 Gow afraid he was being mesmerized. Shefler.

244 Gow to Litchfield, two letters. Litchfield Papers, October 19, 1954, FF 345, "Gow."

244 Litchfield to Gow: thanks. Ibid., October 26, 1954.

244 Falk: "He had everything." Greenberg, 551.

244 Peter Gray: "We were enchanted." Ibid.

244 Litchfield to Falk: "Do not consider me." Litchfield Papers, April 19, 1955, FF 90, "Falk."

244 Anne Litchfield's illness. Ibid., Litchfield to Francis Pray, July 9, 1955, FF 717.

244 Litchfield: "a great honor." Ibid., FF 345, Litchfield to Gow, April 19, 1955.

245 Litchfield to Scaife: my understanding. Ibid., FF 96, "Scaife 1955."

246 Scaife to Litchfield: favorable impression. Ibid., June 7, 1955.

246 Litchfield to Scaife: "not my proposal." Ibid., FF 673, June 7, 1955.

246 Outline of policy issues. Ibid.

246 Scaife to trustees: ready to nominate. Ibid., June 10, 1955, FF 96.

246 Falk reported to trustees. Minute of trustees' meeting, June 14, 1955.

246 Scaife to Litchfield: "splendid presentation." Litchfield Papers, FF 96, June 14, 1955.

247 "Electrified." Dorothy Kantner, *Pittsburgh Sun-Telegraph*, June 17, 1955.

247 Scaife, formal terms of pay. Litchfield Papers, Scaife to Litchfield, June 29, 1955, FF 96, "Scaife."

247 Litchfield announcement. *Pittsburgh Press*, July 18, 1955, *Alumni News Review*, October 1955.

247 Litchfield curriculum vitae. Litchfield Papers, FF 324, 913; Pitt news release, July 20, 1955; Litchfield to Francis Pray, July 9, 1955; Pitt news release, undated, "Edward H. Litchfield Narrative Biography"; "Dr. Edward Litchfield," 1-page manuscript, February 25, 1947; Litchfield letters to his wife from Germany; La Cossitt, 42; Solow, 122; *Who's Who in America*, *Who's Who in American Education*.

249 Foreign service in Germany. Litchfield Papers, FF 997; FF 1, Miscellaneous; personal correspondence with the Civilian Administration Division, December 13, 1945; FF 20, 90, 1945–46. Litchfield arrived in Germany in November 1945 as a State Department civilian looking for a post. In the telling and retelling in later years, the story was "improved" by the statement that General Clay sent a requisition back to Michigan to have Dr. Litchfield join him and set up a civil government in West Germany. See La Cossitt, 134; *Pittsburgh Sunday Press Magazine*, March 24, 1957.

249 Political Science Association. Solow, 124; La Cossitt, 134.

249 Governmental Affairs Institute. Solow, 123; La Cossitt, 132, 134; Pitt news release, July 20, 1955; Litchfield Papers, FF 717, Litchfield to Francis Pray, July 9, 1955.

249 Record at Cornell. Solow, 123–24; La Cossitt, 132; Pitt press release, July 20, 1955; Litchfield Papers, FF 717, Litchfield to Francis Pray, July 9, 1955. For an analysis of the school and its teaching methods, see *Newsweek*, April 4, 1955.

249 Principles of administration. Litchfield, "Notes on a General Theory of Administration," *Administrative Science Quarterly*, June 1956; Solow, 124. Herbert Simon, Carnegie-Mellon professor and Nobel Prize laureate, had also developed the theory that principles of administration common to all enterprises might be identified scientifically.

250 High elective or appointive office. Solow, 123; author's interview with John Funari, who believes that Litchfield would have been given a high federal post if Nixon had defeated Kennedy in 1960.

250 Clay: "You have no choice." La Cossitt, 132.

250 Mrs. Litchfield said to accept. Ibid., 134.

250 Salk on Pittsburgh. La Cossitt, 132.

250 Nobody had such an opportunity. Ibid.

250 Pitt the most underadministered. The professor was Peter Gray, and Litchfield answered that when he was finished, Pitt would be the most overadministered. Greenberg, 551.

250 Speech to Allegheny Conference. *Pittsburgh Press*, September 13, 1955; *Pitt*, Autumn 1955, p. 3.

251 Trustees didn't even blink. La Cossitt, 43.

251 Audience was stunned. Greenberg, 658.

251 Address to trustees. Minute of Winter Meeting, December 13, 1955; Litchfield Papers, FF 85; Litchfield to Schmidt, December 15, 1955.

251 Scaife to Litchfield. Litchfield Papers, December 14, 19, 1955, FF 96.

251 Asked Helen Pool Rush. Litchfield Papers, Litchfield to Dean (later vice chancellor) Rush, January 19, 1956; Rush to Litchfield, January 26, 1956, FF 237, "Dean of Women."

252 Address to Century Club. *Alumni News Review*, February 1956.

252 Hazard and Litchfield. Litchfield Papers, Hazard to Litchfield, March 1, 1956; Litchfield to Hazard, March 8, 1956, FF 42, "Hazard."

252 Address to faculty. Litchfield Papers, FF 717, 29-page transcript; *Alumni News Review*, May 1956; Francis Pray to Litchfield, March 28, 1956; Pitt news release, March 26, 1956.

252 Putnam Jones comment on speech. Dorothy Kantner, *Pittsburgh Sun-Telegraph*, March 27, 1956.

252 Litchfield to Van Dusen. Litchfield Papers, FF 665, March 31, 1956, "Van Dusen."

Chapter Nineteen. Toward Higher Ground

254 Pattern of time divided. Solow, 123.

254 $90,000 income. Ibid.

254 Trip to Iran. Litchfield Papers, FF 918, "General," X and Y, September 6, 1956; FF 854, Litchfield to President of Trustees, August 22, 1956.

254 Litchfield: "something troubling us." Ibid., FF 96, Board of Trustees, A. M. Scaife, October 3, 1956.

255 Litchfield Associates. Greenberg, 551; Litchfield Papers, FF 714, "Public Relations," Litchfield, answers to questions posed to him by Myron Cope, November 27, 1962.

255 Crawford on Litchfield's absences. Funari interview, November 2, 1982.

255 Rankin background. Litchfield Papers, FF 729, Litchfield to Crawford, November 21, 1955; FF 330, "General Affairs, Assistant Chancellor" (A. C. Rankin).

255 Brought back presents. Author's interview with Robert Bailie, May 13, 1981.

255 Unsolicited letter offering help. Litchfield Papers, FF 225, to A. Bailey Case, Westfield, N.J., January 17, 1959. Litchfield addressed him as "Dear Bailey"; Case wrote in reply, "Dear Dr. Litchfield."

255 To boyhood friend. Ibid., FF 523, Litchfield to Goddard Light, August 4, 1959.

255 Bought his first plane. *Pittsburgh Press*, October 26, 1956; *Newsweek*, November 12, 1956; Litchfield Papers, Personal File, October 31, 1956.

255 $150,000 insurance. Ibid., FF 240, "Development, Assistant Chancellor," memorandum on Edgar Cale.

255 Bought a Beechcraft. Ibid., FF 96, Litchfield to Scaife, October 26, 1956, "Chancellor's Staff"; Solow, 123.

255 "Central piloting system." Phrase used in an undated 8-page Pitt Information Services release, "Pitt: A Search for Excellence," by Helen L. Knox, second of three articles.

255 Assistant chancellors. *Pitt News*, July 18, 1956; *Alumni News Review*, February 1957.

255 Montgomery positions. Minute of Council of Deans meeting, December 17, 1956.

255 Vice Chancellors. *Pitt,* Autumn 1956, pp. 5, 17, 28–29.

255 Substantial injustices. Minute of Executive Committee meeting of Board of Trustees, January 8, 1957; minute of trustees' meeting, March 12, 1957; minute of Administrative Committee meeting, January 3, 1958; Litchfield Papers, FF 745, Litchfield to trustees, March 7, 1957.

255 Linhart persuaded not to join TIAA. Litchfield Papers, FF 345, J. Steele Gow to Litchfield, November 19, 1956; Litchfield to Gow, November 20, 1956.

256 Pensions paid. Ibid., FF 299, correspondence and reports in "Retirement Pension Material, July 1, 1955"; Table of Retired Faculty Members Still Living on December 31, 1956; FF 745, Leon Falk to Litchfield, April 3, 1956.

256 Crawford made list of retired. Minute of Administrative Committee meeting, August 22–25, 1957, "Summary of Major Studies in Progress."

256 Got $20,000 for retirees. Minute of Executive Committee meeting of Board of Trustees, January 8, 1957.

256 "Miracles are not past." Minute of trustees' meeting, Litchfield to Board of Trustees, March 7, 1957.

256 Professors emeritus. Litchfield Papers, FF 297, "Faculty Committee on Merit Recommendation," Crawford to Woodruff, July 6, 1957; FF 745, Litchfield to Demas Barnes, June 4, 1958.

256 Health and retirement. Minute of Administrative Committee meeting, March 13, 1957; *This Week at the University,* March 21, 1957, p. 4.

256 Teaching loads reduced. Litchfield Papers, FF 674, "Outline of Significant Programs and Developments," February 16, 1959.

257 New tenure plan. Litchfield, "Toward Higher Ground," September 17, 1962 (page 23, under Chronology).

257 Office of Cultural and Educational Exchange. Ibid.

257 All professional schools to graduate level. Solow, 190.

257 Faculty research carrels. "Toward Higher Ground" [23].

257 Tuition exchange program. Litchfield Papers, FF 674, "Montgomery," February 16, 1959, "Outline of Significant Programs."

257 Inexpensive second mortgaging. Undated 8-page pamphlet, "Faculty Home Purchase Plan," Litchfield Papers, FF 1.

257 Sabbatical leaves. Litchfield Papers, FF 572, Crawford to Litchfield, June 18, 1958, "Revised Statement on Policy on Sabbatical Leaves"; Pitt news release, January 7, 1957; minute of trustees' meeting, March 12, 1957; minute of Administrative Committee meeting, August 22, 1956.

257 "Unprecedented step." Helen L. Knox, "Pitt: A Search for Excellence."

257 Merit increase committee. Litchfield Papers, FF 297, Woodruff to Wood-Smith, February 13, 1958; Budget Committee on Merit Increases to Litchfield, February 13, 1958; Woodruff to Crawford, April 9, 1957; Crawford (as committee secretary) to Litchfield, April 22, 1957; Crawford, "Faculty Development."

257 Wriston's suggestions. Litchfield Papers, FF 917, Budget Committee on Merit Increases to Litchfield, February 4, 1957.

257 Litchfield's letters of merit. Ibid., letters by category, April 22, 1957; Stankard to Wood-Smith, April 22, 1957.

258 Not what Litchfield expected. Litchfield Papers, FF 777, Litchfield to Administrative Committee, Woodruff, et al., January 31, 1958 (in several drafts).

258 Renamed it Committee on Faculty Evaluation. Litchfield Papers, FF 640–42, minute of special meeting on faculty personnel, November 18, 1957.

258 Corrected grave injustices. Ibid., FF 297, Faculty Evaluation Committee to Litchfield, August 12, 1957.

258 Amended its judgment on teachers. Litchfield Papers, FF 297, Woodruff to Wood-Smith, February 13, 1958.

258 660 faculty members evaluated. Ibid.

258 Only 4 percent Pitt graduates. Ibid., FF 297, Report on Faculty Development, 1963, Summary, 2.

258 Had met Miss Morrill in 1954. Author's interviews with Alan Rankin, week of January 23, 1984.

258 Mary Morrill background. *Alumni News Review,* May 1957; University of Kansas *Alumni Magazine,* March 1956; *Pittsburgh Press,* April 16, October 30, 1957.

259 Gave Litchfield article on Morrill. Rankin interviews.

259 Litchfield to Mary Morrill. Litchfield Papers, FF 571, July 23, 1956.

259 Morrill to Pittsburgh. *Pittsburgh Press*, February 20, 1957.

259 Wedding. *Pittsburgh Post-Gazette*, April 1, 1959; *Pittsburgh Press*, March 30, 1959.

259 Minimum publicity. Litchfield Papers, FF 716, Jane Shaw to Francis Pray, March 11, 1957.

259 One afternoon at Mellon home. *Pittsburgh Press*, April 16, 1957; Rankin interviews.

259 Mrs. Litchfield as hostess. Author's conversation with Mrs. Warren Dana, October 6, 1982.

259 Feared would run University like a business. *Pitt*, Spring 1968, p. 28.

259 Complaint on merit increase committee. Litchfield Papers, FF 297, "Faculty Committee on Merit Increase," minute of special meeting of Advisory Committee on Faculty Personnel, November 18, 1957, comment by Elvis Stahr, 3.

259 Complaints on "bibliography-making." Ibid., memorandum to Wood-Smith from Woodruff, February 13, 1958.

260 Gow-Litchfield exchange on *Time* article. Ibid., January 24, 25, 1957.

260 "One of the phenomena." Minute of Council of Deans meeting, October 22, 1958.

Chapter Twenty. "New Dimensions of Learning in a Free Society"

262 Wished to be accompanied. Tacey interview, July 16, 1981.

262 Everyone should rise. Litchfield Papers, FF 769, Litchfield to Crawford and Rankin, October 28, 1960.

262 Medallion. Ibid., FF 14, "Academic Regalia," Crawford to R. K. Mellon; *Pitt*, May 1957, p. 4.

262 Gown. Ibid., "Academic Gowns," Rankin to Contrel and Leonard Co., April 4, 1957; *Pittsburgh Post-Gazette*, May 7, 1956.

262 Educator on civil war in education. Richard G. Browne, executive officer, Teachers College Board, Springfield, Illinois, delivered at the Founders Day Banquet, State Normal University, printed in *Vital Speeches of the Day*, April 15, 1958.

263 Schenley Apartments and Hotel. Fitzgerald Papers, FF 95, Minute of Conference of Chancellor Litchfield with Messrs. Fisher and Crawford, December 30, 1955; Litchfield Papers, Vieh to faculty members, March 25, 1957, "Schenley Apartments"; Report to Subscribers to the . . . Building Fund, March 19, 1956; Pitt news releases, February 14, 15, 1956; *Pittsburgh Post-Gazette*, December 23, 1955, February 15, 18, 1956, October 2, 1957; *Pittsburgh Press*, December 23, 1955, February 15, 1956, October 9, 1957; *Alumni News Review*, February 1956.

263 Dormitory regulations. Student Affairs Papers, Box 7, FF 61, Breckenridge House: Standards of University Residence.

263 ". . . enrich educational process." *Pittsburgh Post-Gazette*, December 23, 1955.

263 Salk Hall. *Pittsburgh Press*, October 23, 1957.

264 Ruskin Apartments. Minute of Council of Deans meeting, March 17, 1958; Report to the . . . Middle States Association (hereafter MSA), November 1960, p. 6; *Pittsburgh Press*, February 28, 1958.

264 Babcock Memorial Room. Report to the MSA, November 1960, p. 7.

264 Trees Hall. *University of Pittsburgh Building Program*, January 20, 1960; author's interviews with Alan Rankin, who was the administrator in charge of overseeing the design and construction of Hillman Library.

264 Hillman Library. Ibid.; *Pitt*, July 1960, "The Hillman Library—A New Concept in Library Design"; Van Trump, "The Book and the Land."

265 Langley Hall. *University of Pittsburgh Building Program*, 11.

265 Henry Clay Frick Fine Arts Building. *University of Pittsburgh Building Program*, 27; *Pittsburgh Post-Gazette*, November 5, 1956.

266 Total investment. Report to the MSA, November 1960, p. 93.

266 Replacement cost, $200 million. Litchfield Papers, FF 530, "Park Martin, Forbes Avenue Relocation," draft, November 19, 1958, of "Statement in Regard to That Part of the University of Pittsburgh Expansion Program. . . ."

266 Trustees' permission to retain Abramovitz. Minute of Joint Meeting of Executive Committee and the Committee on Physical Plant, November 13, 1958. Abramovitz had a $10,000 retaining fee per year; he did not charge it when he was paid for a commission.

266 Wriston recommended. Litchfield Papers, FF 648, December 28, 1955.

266 Litchfield's directives. Litchfield Papers, FF 648, "Planning and Development, Overall Architectural Planning," April 17, May 8, 1956.

266 Confidential conferences. Ibid. Litchfield's preference for *development*, not *expansion*, is shown in his editing of these papers.

266 Litchfield on noise. *Pittsburgh Press*, March 24, 1957; Litchfield Papers, FF 717, Litchfield to faculty, March 26, 1956.

266 Abramovitz ideas. Litchfield Papers, FF 648.

266 Cost per lineal foot. Ibid., Litchfield to Abramovitz, March 5, 1956.

266 Litchfield: "exciting." Ibid., Litchfield to Abramovitz, August 22, 1956.

266 Litchfield asked Van Dusen. Litchfield Papers, FF 666, "Planning and Development," Van Dusen to Litchfield, March 24, 1958.

266 Abramovitz on Cathedral. Litchfield Papers, FF 648, "Confidential Memorandum, Planning and Development, Overall Architectural Planning," April 17, 1956; ibid., "Notes on Conversations," S. C. Crawford, August 21, 1956.

266 Forbes Field. Minutes of Joint Meetings of Executive Committee and the Committee on Physical Plant, November 13, 19, 1958; *Pittsburgh Post-Gazette*, November 29, 1958; *Pittsburgh Press*, September 9, 10, 1958; Pitt news release, September 9, 1958. Thomas P. Johnson, vice president of the Pittsburgh Baseball Club, assured the chamber of commerce that the Pirates would stay in Pittsburgh, but said that if new and better facilities were not found, that attitude could change. *Pittsburgh Press*, October 20, 1960.

267 Long-range development plan. Litchfield Papers, FF 648, Litchfield to Abramovitz, July 26, 1956; ibid., "Memorandum for Committee on Site Planning"; comment on same by Litchfield, no dates; ibid., Litchfield to Abramovitz, August 22, 1956; *Pittsburgh Press*, September 10, December 14,

1958; *Oakland News*, September 11, 1958; *Pitt News*, November 10, 1958; Pitt news release, September 9, 1958.

268 Explosion of protest. *Oakland News*, May 21, 1959; *Pittsburgh Press*, January 23, 1963; *Pitt News*, July 21, 1971; many other continuing stories in the press.

268 *Press* editorial. October 24, 1938.

268 Previously prepared answers. Litchfield Papers, FF 530, Litchfield to Park Martin, November 3, 1958; ibid., several drafts of letters to W. Forrester, editor of the *Press;* ibid., "Park Martin, Forbes Avenue Relocation," November 1958; ibid., "Statement in Regard to . . . Expansion Program," November 19, 1958.

268 Trip to Soviet Union. Cole Blasier, "The Curious Origins of Latin American Studies at Pitt," *Pitt*, May 1975, pp. 2–8; *Report on Higher Education in the Soviet Union*, E. H. Litchfield, 1958; *New York Times*, July 14, 1958, December 29, 1964; *Pittsburgh Press*, July 18, 1958, October 12, 1960; *Pittsburgh Post-Gazette*, July 28, October 30, 1958; *Pitt News*, October 31, 1958; Litchfield Papers, FF 673, "Planning and Development, A/C," Litchfield to Van Dusen, August 20, 1958.

269 Death of Alan Scaife. *Pittsburgh Post-Gazette*, July 24, August 2, 1958; *Pittsburgh Press*, July 24, 1958; *New York Times*, July 25, 1958.

Chapter Twenty-one. An Episode in the Life of a Chancellor

272 Such a horde. Zora Unkovich, *Pittsburgh Sun-Telegraph*, September 25, 1959.

272 Warned not to appear at windows. Author's conversation with Mrs. Richard C. (Barbara) Tobias, October 18, 1982.

272 Khrushchev's visit, general. *Pittsburgh Post-Gazette*, September 24, 25, 1959; *Pittsburgh Press*, September 24, 25, 1959; *Pittsburgh Sun-Telegraph*, September 24, 25, 1959; *Pitt News*, September 28, 1959.

272 Khrushchev: "Wonderful! Wonderful!" *Pittsburgh Post-Gazette*, September 25, 1959.

272 Had seen Mesta products. *Pittsburgh Press*, September 20, 1959.

272 Waved cowboy hat. *Pitt News*, April 17, 1961.

272 Mrs. Khrushchev apologized. *Pitt News*, September 28, 1959.

272 She had been a teacher. *New York Times*, September 28, 1959.

272 Reminded her of Kiev. *Pitt News*, September 28, 1959.

272 State Department opposed invocation. Rankin interview.

273 Most unusual arrangement. Ibid.

273 Salads were switched around. Ibid.

273 Security people in grillwork. Ibid.

273 32 at head table. The number has been incorrectly given as 37. The best source on this point is Litchfield's program, in which he pasted names, pronunciations, and notes for his introduction.

273 Twelve students. Duquesne University had no students there, because the school term had not opened. *Pittsburgh Press*, September 24, 1959; *Pitt News*, September 28, 1959.

273 R. B. Finn's questions. Litchfield Papers, FF 475. Louise Bem, a researcher on this book, talked with Arkady Shevencho on February 20, 1985, when he lectured at Indiana University of Pennsylvania. He told her at that time that he was with the Khrushchev party in this country in 1959. He became a U.S. citizen in February 1986.

273 Refused to divulge his name. *Pittsburgh Sun-Telegraph*, September 25, 1959.

273 First time a prayer. *Alumni News Review*, October 1959, p. 1; *Pittsburgh Press*, September 23, 1959; Rankin interview.

273 Mary Litchfield-Khrushchev dialogue. Funari interview; *Pitt News*, September 28, 1959. The *News* coverage of the Khrushchev visit, with the writing and editorship of Murray Chass, was excellent.

273 One observer watched. Litchfield Papers, FF 475, "Khrushchev," H. Philip Mettgar, executive director of the Governmental Affairs Institute, Litchfield's house guest, to Litchfield, September 25, 1959.

274 Young woman from Cleveland. *Pitt News*, September 28, 1959.

274 "That's discrimination!" Ibid.

274 D. L. Lawrence speech. It and Khrushchev's speech were printed in full in the *New York Times*, September 25, 1959.

274 Audience rose and applauded. It did so four times: when Khrushchev entered, when he rose to speak, when he finished speaking, and when he departed. *Pitt News*, September 28, 1959.

274 Khrushchev's speech. *New York Times*, September 25, 1959.

275 Audience became restless. Ibid.; *Pittsburgh Sun-Telegraph*, September 25, 1959.

275 Khrushchev's extemporaneous talk. *New York Times*, September 25, 1959; *Pitt News*, September 28, 1959.

275 Litchfield's closing remarks. The quotations are taken from a tape recording of the events. (University Archives, Phonotape 18, Khrushchev luncheon, 2 reels, 1 hr. 45 min.) Litchfield had a prepared typescript of his remarks, anticipating what Khrushchev would say, and made revisions as Khrushchev spoke. He later edited the transcript, eliminating some minor solecisms but causing it to lose a bit of its emotional intensity. His agitation at the close of the meeting is evident in the recording.

276 Editorials praised city's conduct, Litchfield's reply. *Pittsburgh Press*, September 25, 30, 1959.

276 Pittsburgh gave warmest welcome. *New York Times*, September 25, 1959. This was unexpected, because of the large number of Hungarian refugees from the 1956 uprising who were in the city.

276 "What did she see in him?" Ann Zurosky, *Pittsburgh Press*, September 25, 1959.

276 Pushing a cart. Ibid.

276 Mrs. Khrushchev asked for copy of prayer. Litchfield Papers, FF 475, "Khrushchev," Rankin to Litchfield, September 25, 1959. Mayor Gallagher was later presented with a gold medal showing Lunik I in orbit, a lacquered wooden cigar box, 12 small jars of caviar, a color picture book on Moscow, an album of 20 phonograph records, and 3 pint bottles of vodka.

Chapter Twenty-two. The Golden Glow

277 Epigraph. Herbert G. Stein, *Pittsburgh Post-Gazette*, September 13, 1962; his letter to author, January 30, 1986.

278 Faculty salaries at median level. Pitt Report to the MSA, 28–29, 87–88, November 1960; Herbert G. Stein, *Pittsburgh Post-Gazette*, September 12, 1962.

278 More Ph.D. degrees. The percentage increased from 56 percent of the full-time faculty in 1954–55 to 62 percent in 1958–59. Pitt Report to MSA, November 1960, p. 28.

278 Sixty courses dropped. Herbert G. Stein, *Pittsburgh Post-Gazette*, September 12, 1962.

278 Higher median scores. Pitt Report to the MSA, 42.

278 Sixfold increase in sponsored research. Ibid., 38–39.

278 Change at graduate level. Litchfield Papers, Litchfield to Stahr, April 16, 1958; MSA, Preliminary Appraisal, November 1960, p. 48; The University of Pittsburgh, 1955–65, A Report to the Community, 1965, p. 11.

278 Has closed the gap. MSA Preliminary Appraisal, 3.

278 1958–60 financial figures. Ibid., 90–93; A Report by a Special Committee of the Ford Foundation (Wells Report), January 1966, p. 3.

278 Trustees acted with courage. Litchfield to faculty and administrators, no date [1958]. The first of a series of "informal reports."

278 Scaife disturbed. Litchfield Papers, FF 96, Scaife to Litchfield, February 12, 1958.

279 Pitt first in foundation grants. *Pittsburgh Press*, February 24, 1960, third biennial survey of the Council for Financial Aid to Education.

279 Eighth in gift income from business concerns. Ibid.

279 Peake: most grants to health. Author's interview with Charles Peake; Litchfield statement at the first meeting, November 17, 1964, of the Budget and Audit Committee.

279 Competing with Carnegie Tech. Wright, 229.

279 Weak in alumni support. Greenberg, 660.

279 Bowman had to "psych" himself. Irwin and Rome interviews.

279 Litchfield not a good fund raiser. Peake interview.

279 Litchfield to R. K. Mellon on endowment. Litchfield Papers, FF 93, "R. K. Mellon," August 19, 1958.

280 Decision of A. W. Mellon Trust not to liquidate. *Report of A. W. Mellon Trust, 1930–1980*, p. 16.

280 R. K. Mellon persuaded not to liquidate. Schmidt interview, June 15, 1984.

280 Broughton asked for a memorandum. Litchfield Papers, FF 673, "Planning and Development, A/C."

280 Litchfield's written record. Ibid.

280 Litchfield's secretary surmised. Ibid., Jane Wood-Smith to Litchfield, memorandum attached to correspondence.

280 Mellon Trust raised a question. *Report of A. W. Mellon Trust*, 99–100.

280 Litchfield's announcement of grant "magnificent." Litchfield Papers, FF 770, "Secretary," Crawford to Litchfield, December 17, 1958.

281 Litchfield on the Mellon Grant. *Report of A. W. Mellon Trust*, 99–103; *New York Times*, December 16, 1958; Pitt news release, December 16, 1958; Litchfield Papers, FF 553, "Mellon Fellowships, General," P. F. Jones to Peake, January 14, 1959; ibid., "Andrew Mellon Professorships," statements by Litchfield to faculty, September 30, 1959 and May 5, 1960; *Pittsburgh Press* editorial, December 17, 1958.

281 Crawford's record of comments. Litchfield Papers, FF 770, "Secretary," Crawford to Litchfield; ibid., "Comments from Mr. Brewer," December 17, 1958.

281 "Everyone talking about Pittsburgh." Ibid., Litchfield Papers, "Academic Disciplines, V/C," Peake to Litchfield, February 6, 1959.

281 Peake: Why not go to Pittsburgh? Herbert G. Stein, *Pittsburgh Post-Gazette*, September 13, 1962.

281 Eurich: "Pitt pioneering." *Atlantic*, June 1963, p. 52.

281 Wiggins on stipends. Litchfield Papers, FF 913. "Wiggins," Wiggins to Litchfield, April 27, 1959.

281 Peake ran the program. Peake interview, May 27, 1981.

281 94 applicants. Litchfield Papers, FF 553, "Mellon Professorships."

281 "Bend rules a bit." Ibid., Putnam F. Jones to Peake, January 14, 1959, FF 553, "Mellon Fellows, General."

281 Sir Anthony Blunt. Peake interview.

282 Mellon assessment of results. *Report of A. W. Mellon Trust*, 102.

282 George P. Murdock. *Who's Who in America* (1972–73).

282 John P. Gillin. University of Pittsburgh obituary release, August 5, 1973.

282 Alexander Spoehr. *Who's Who in America* (1972–73).

282 Only one other anthropology department with three presidents. Litchfield Papers, FF 10, "Academic Disciplines, V/C," Peake to Litchfield, November 21, 1964; ibid., Peake to Spoehr, Gillin, and Murdock, November 23, 1964; Wells Report, 38.

282 Description, philosopher of science. From *The Philosophy of Science*, a 17-page booklet, undated, produced by the Science Center.

282 Adolf Grunbaum. *Who's Who in America*, (1984–85); *Pittsburgh Post-Gazette*, September 13, 1962; Pitt news release, March 7, 1968; *University Times*, January 11, 1979.

282 Nicholas Rescher. *Who's Who in America* (1972–73); Litchfield Papers, FF 7, "Academic Disciplines, V/C," Rescher to Peake, February 4, 1963.

282 Wilfred S. Sellars. *Who's Who in America* (1972–73).

282 Grunbaum, Sellars, and Yale. Litchfield Papers, 645, "Academic Disciplines, V/C," Charles W. Hendel of Yale to Grunbaum, December 27, 1962; Grunbaum to Peake, January 29, 1963; Baier to Peake, January 20, 1963; Litchfield to Sellars, January 28, 1963.

283 N. R. Hanson: "something invaluable." Kurtzman Papers, FF 6, Hanson to Peake, June 10, 1965. See also *University Times*, January 27, 1983.

283 Litchfield's promises on salaries. Litchfield Papers, FF 7, "Academic Disciplines, V/C," Sellars to Litchfield, January 29, 1963.

283 Brzezinski. Ibid., FF 478, "KA–KZ General," V. O. Key, Jr., Professor of Government, Harvard, to Litchfield, March 17, 1957.

283 Litchfield wanted Price on board. Ibid., FF 665, "Planning and Development," Litchfield to Van Dusen, January 21, 1957.

283 Higgins asked Price. Author's interview with Gwilym Price, August 4, 1981.

284 Price background. Ibid.; author's previous association with Price, 1950–64; Nancy Mason's interview, September 8, 1972, PROHP, revised and edited by Price in May 1975.

284 Price called on Warner. Price interviews.

284 Price called on Denton. Author's interview with Frank Denton, September 7, 1981.

284 Denton and Litchfield. Ibid.

284 Price: 39th floor. Greenberg, 660.

284 Mellon's 7 letters. Litchfield Papers, "R. K. Mellon," FF 329, R. K. Mellon to Litchfield, August 14, November 18, 25, December 15, 1958, January 12, February 24, September 28, 1959; Litchfield to Mellon, August 14, 19, November 20, 1958, February 26, September 10, 28, 1959.

284 Mellon and Litchfield on *Fortune* article. Ibid., "Fortune Magazine," Litchfield to Mellon, et al., November 14–20, 1958.

286 Crawford on *Fortune* article. Ibid., Crawford to Litchfield, October 24, 1958.

286 Trouble identifying vice chancellors. Herbert G. Stein, *Pittsburgh Post-Gazette*, September 12, 1962.

286 Space center. *Pittsburgh Post-Gazette*, August 9, December 7, 1962, January 11, 1963; *Pittsburgh Press*, December 21, 1962; *Pitt*, January 1963; Wells Report, 38.

286 Met with J. F. Kennedy. Litchfield Papers, FF 186; *Washington Evening Star*, May 10, 1962.

286 Van de Graaf accelerator. Pitt news release, December 7, 1961.

286 GSPIA. *Pitt*, Winter, 1957–58, pp. 4–6, Fall 1964, p. 3; MSA Preliminary Appraisal, 64–69; Report to the Community, 17, 27; Wells Report, 34.

287 Library School. *Pittsburgh Post-Gazette*, September 28, 1961; Report to the Community, 18; Wells Report, 33; Austin Wright, *The Warner Administration at Carnegie Institute of Technology, 1950–65*, pp. 154–55.

287 Department of Languages. Litchfield Papers, FF 2, "Academic Disciplines, V/C," Peake to members of the department, October 22, 1959; Herbert G. Stein, *Pittsburgh Post-Gazette*, September 13, 1962.

287 Asian Center. Report to the Community, 22; Pitt news releases, January 18, December 3, 1962, February 13, October 6, 1970, March 2, 1977; James T. C. Liu to the author, September 12, 1981; T. C. Liu to Thomas Kuo, September 15, 1981; Lelia Jamison to Richard Reiker, January 21, 1982; Richard Chu to Thomas Kuo, September 15, 1981; East Asian Libraries Newsletter, September 1973, pp. 11–15; *Pitt*, Winter 1968; *University Times*, October 21, 1971, January 12, 1978, September 21, 1978.

287 Regional campuses. *Pitt,* "Pitt Regional Campuses," four issues, January–April 1982, one on each campus.

287 Ecuador. *Pittsburgh Post-Gazette,* August 3, 1962; Report to the Community, 26.

287 Book Center. Litchfield papers, FF 110, Monnett to Litchfield, October 7, 1960; *Pittsburgh Press,* March 15, 1960; Guide to Undergraduate Education, 9 (a pamphlet for high schools, no date).

288 Golden Glow. The phrase appears in "What Happened at Pitt?" *Fortune,* September 1965, p. 48.

288 "It was an exciting atmosphere." Peake interview.

288 "It's nice to have a problem." Litchfield to Walter Evert, 1965, as told in the author's interview with Evert.

288 Litchfield's financial plan. Wells Report, 3; Greenberg, 661; Budget and Audit Committee letter to the chairman of the board, October 25, 1966 (see chapter 24).

289 New comptroller's report laid aside. Jesse T. Hudson, "Statement of Events and Circumstances . . . ," September 1966, p. 3 (see chapter 24).

289 "Forward looking and constructive." Budget and Audit Committee letter to chairman of the board, October 25, 1966.

289 "General note of appreciation." Minute of Council of Deans meeting, April 14, 1961.

289 Warning of MSA team. MSA, Preliminary Appraisal, November 8–11, 1960, pp. 19–21, 24.

289 Mrs. Bowman killed in accident. *Pitt News,* October 24, 1950.

289 Bowman sold farm. George Swetnam, "Adventures in Retirement," *Pittsburgh Press,* October 31, 1954.

289 Cathedral of Learning dedication. *Alumni News Review,* May 1956.

289 Bowman to Litchfield. Litchfield Papers, FF 146, May 1, 1957.

Chapter Twenty-three. The Colodny Case

292 Colodny career. Pitt news release, March 7, 1959; *Who's Who in America* (1984–85); *Pittsburgh Post-Gazette,* January 19, 20, 1961, April 9, 1973, November 4, 1982; *University Times,* November 4, 1982; Litchfield statement, January 19, 1961.

292 Kansas recommended. Litchfield Papers, FF 188, Chancellor Franklin D. Murphy to Litchfield, March 18, 1959. Murphy in 1985 succeeded Paul Mellon as chairman of the board of the National Gallery in Washington.

292 "Let's congratulate ourselves." Ibid., FF 572, Litchfield to Murphy, March 24, 1959.

292 Castro's foreign minister. *New York Times,* January 11, 1961.

292 Sane Nuclear Policy. *Pittsburgh Press,* January 23, 1961.

292 Walsh on Colodny. *Pittsburgh Press,* January 17, 1961.

293 Said other teachers were suspect. Litchfield Papers, FF 188, Powers to Litchfield, January 25, 1961, February 2, 1961; *Post-Gazette* editorial, April 27, 1961; Pitt news release, Joseph G. Colangelo, "The Colodny Case."

293 Colodny said was misquoted. *Pittsburgh Post-Gazette,* January 18, 19, 1961; Colangelo, "The Colodny Case," 4.

293 "Fair Play for Professor." *Pittsburgh Post-Gazette,* January 19, 1961.

293 Called the last national case. Ibid., April 9, 1973.

293 Walters quoted. *Pittsburgh Press,* January 19, 1961. The six other listed organizations were American Peace Crusade, American Student Union, American-Russian Institute, Joint Anti-Fascist Refugee Committee, American Veterans for Peace, Spanish Refugee Committee.

293 *Pitt News* editorials. January 18, 23, 1961.

293 68 students signed. *Pittsburgh Press,* letter to the editor, June 22, 1961.

293 Walsh: did not get medal. *Pittsburgh Press,* April 26, 1961.

293 Did get medal. Litchfield Papers, FF 188, Samuel Hays to Charles Peake, August 25, 1964, with copy of letter from Adjutant General J. E. Hagood, August 17, 1964.

293 ACLU, *Pittsburgh Press,* and *Pittsburgh Post-Gazette. Pittsburgh Press,* January 23, 1961.

293 "Publicity stunt." *Pittsburgh Post-Gazette,* January 26, 1961.

293 Support by AAUP chapters. *Pittsburgh Press,* January 20, 24, 1961; Colangelo, "The Colodny Case," 4.

293 Earl Browder. *Pittsburgh Press*, June 19, 1961.

293 Charles Owen Rice. *The Pittsburgh Catholic*, January 26, 1961; Litchfield Papers, Litchfield to Rice, FF 749, February 9, 1961.

294 AAUP: Will defend any professor. *Pitt News*, January 23, 1961.

294 Litchfield appointed committee. Litchfield Papers, FF 188, Litchfield to Members of the House of Representatives, January 26, 1961; *Pittsburgh Press*, January 19, 1961.

294 Rules of hearings. Litchfield Papers, FF 188, W. George Crouch to All Members of the Faculty, January 20, 1961; *Faculty News*, January 1961.

294 K. Leroy Irvis. *Pittsburgh Press*, April 26, 1961; Colangelo, "The Colodny Case," 5.

294 Appearance before HCUA. *Pittsburgh Press*, June 1, 1961; *Pittsburgh Post-Gazette*, June 2, 1961.

295 Litchfield's three advisors. Litchfield Papers, FF 188, exchange of correspondence between Litchfield and Perkins, Moore, and Malott, May–June, 1961 (stapled together).

295 Litchfield's report. "A Matter of Principle," *Pitt*, July 1961, pp. 7–9.

295 Editorials on report. *Pittsburgh Post-Gazette*, June 25, 1961; *Pittsburgh Press*, June 15, 1961.

296 Cost in money and time. Herbert G. Stein, *Pittsburgh Post-Gazette*, September 13, 1962; Litchfield Papers, FF 188, Litchfield to Lowell J. Reed, July 6, 1961.

296 Phi Beta Kappa. *The Key Reporter*, Winter 1961–62, Autumn 1961; Litchfield Papers, FF 395–99, "Addendum: The Colodny Case," February 22, 1962, 22 pp.

296 "Cannot be intimidated." Herbert G. Stein, *Pittsburgh Post-Gazette*, September 13, 1962.

296 "Stated case elegantly." Funari interview.

296 "We were lucky it happened." Herbert G. Stein, *Pittsburgh Post-Gazette*, September 13, 1962.

Chapter Twenty-four. Trouble

298 GAI impropriety. U.S. House Committee on Appropriations. Mutual Security Appropriations for 1961 . . . Hearings . . . 86–2 Congress, Part 1; *Pittsburgh Post-Gazette*, May 26, 1960; *Pittsburgh Press*, May 26, June 14, 1960.

298 "I have abandoned Persia." Litchfield Papers, FF 888, "T-General," Litchfield to Lewis Thomas, October 12, 1962.

298 Salk's departure. *Pittsburgh Post-Gazette*, March 12, 1960; *Pittsburgh Press*, March 11, 12, 16, 1960; *Pittsburgh Sun-Telegraph*, March 16, 18, 1960; Litchfield Papers, FF 843, "Salk," December 14, 1962; Salk to Litchfield, December 19, 1962; Jalbert to Litchfield, no date, filed "P.R., Director of."

298 Hamilton's departure. Minutes of meetings of Executive Committee, June 22, 24, 1959; author's correspondence with Frank Carver; Litchfield Papers, FF 35, Walter Vieh to Hamilton, November 28, 1958, note appended by Carver, "Tom should have been in on this [Forbes Field] discussion from the very first."

298 Litchfield memorandum on Hamilton. Litchfield Papers, FF 23, "Director of Athletics," June 25, 1959; minutes of Executive Committee meetings, June 22, 24, 25, 1959.

298 McCluskey might have mastered rivalries. Author's interview with William Rea, November 23, 1981; Lawrence Howard's interview with Edison Montgomery, PROHP, May 21, 1975.

299 Litchfield's Arden House plan. Litchfield Papers, FF 563, "Warwick Terrace," Litchfield to Cale, Crawford, and Monnett, January 8, 1963.

299 Heinz mansions. *Pittsburgh Press*, August 3, 1961, November 18, 1964, April 20, 1965; *Pittsburgh Press*, August 3, 1961, November 18, 1964, April 20, 1965; *Pitt News*, January 6, 1965; minutes of Executive Committee meetings, September 11, 1962, June 19, 27, 1963; Litchfield Papers, FF 563, 900.

300 Entertained more than 3,300 people. *Pitt News*, January 6, 1965.

300 His fact book on the house. Litchfield Papers, FF 8, "Fact Book, Q and A," 3–5.

300 First black athlete to Sugar Bowl. Carver interviews; *Pittsburgh Post-Gazette*, December 3, 1955; O'Brien, *Hail to Pitt*, 143.

300 Litchfield's order to Michelosen. *Pittsburgh Post-Gazette*, February 21, September 18, 1963; *Pittsburgh Press*, October 2, 1963; *Pitt News*, January 23, 1963.

300 Good record of 1963 team. Conversation with Jim O'Brien; O'Brien, "Twentieth Reunion: '63 Football Squad Was Something Special," October 29, 1983, Pitt Football Program, 85.

300 Loss of bowl bid. Carver interviews; Cale interview, September 14, 1981.

300 Abrams: "And they criticize the pros!" *Pittsburgh Post-Gazette*, November 29, 1963.

300 The pages on the 1963–65 financial crisis in this chapter and chapter 26 are based on the following documents:

    1. "A Statement by the Trustees' Budget-Audit Committee Relative to Financial Matters at the University of Pittsburgh in the Years 1955–56," October 5, 1966, 14 pp. (hereafter Budget-Audit Statement), signed by Frank R. Denton, Alfred W. Beattie, Malcolm E. Lambing, and Frank L. Magee. Special file, University Archives.

    2. "A Financial Survey and Analysis—University of Pittsburgh—1955–65," July 19, 1965, 23 pp. Prepared by Joseph G. Colangelo, Jr., "under the supervision and direction of Stanton Crawford, Paul Solyan, Harry E. Daer, Edison Montgomery, Gwilym Price, and Frank Denton."

    3. Jesse T. Hudson, "Statement of Events and Circumstances at the University of Pittsburgh from October 1959 to July 30, 1965," September 1966, 6 pp.

    4. Rough draft of an untitled, undated document, 21 pp., on the financial crisis, prepared in 1964 by Walter Vieh "in resp(onse) to ques(tions) from EHL." (Vieh had left the University when Monnett came in 1960, but he returned briefly at Litchfield's request to prepare this document.)

    5. Author's interviews with Frank Denton, Edison Montgomery, and Gwilym Price in 1981.

    6. Interviews with the same persons in the 1970–75, PROHP.

    7. Minutes of meetings of the Board of Trustees.

301 Trustees felt they were asked unfairly. Budget-Audit Statement, 5.

303 Price aware in 1961. Price interview, August 4, 1981.

304 "We wanted the University to succeed." Budget-Audit Statement, 9.

304 The chancellor was energetic. Ibid., 8.

304 Price met with Koerner. Price interview, August 4, 1981.

304 Denton met Koerner. Denton interview, September 7, 1981.

304 Denton went to Litchfield. Ibid.

304 Budget-Audit Committee was formed. Ibid.

304 Crawford to Litchfield on Denton. Litchfield Papers, FF 44, Crawford to Litchfield, April 1, 1964.

304 Pleas to Litchfield to stop spending. Price and Denton interviews; Budget-Audit Statement, 6, 10.

305 Montgomery on Peake. Montgomery interview.

305 Peake could get anything from Litchfield. Price and Denton interviews.

305 Fourteen mathematicians. Litchfield Papers, FF 8, "Academic Discipline, V/C," FF 3, September 11, 1963.

305 Warnings by Price Waterhouse. Budget-Audit Statement, 8–9.

305 Montgomery on presentation of budget. Interviews by Lawrence Howard, February 8, 1971, for the PROHP series, and by the author, April 23, 1981. See also Litchfield Papers, FF 672, Montgomery to Litchfield.

306 1963 a crucial year. Price and Denton interviews.

306 Denton's two conclusions. Denton interview.

307 $4.5 million deficit. Budget-Audit Statement, 7.

307 Vieh predicted a $1.2 million surplus. Litchfield Papers, FF 161, Litchfield to his staff, June 14, 1965; FF 767, Litchfield to Crawford, June 14, 1965; Budget-Audit Committee Statement, Box 1, FF 1, letter to Gwilym Price, October 25, 1966.

Chapter Twenty-five. Panther Hollow

309 Panther Hollow. Litchfield Papers, Minutes of Council of Deans meetings, March 30, 1962, November 3, 1964, January 20, May 18, 1965; *Pitt*, July 1963; *This Is an Urban Area*, 24 pp., no date, University of Pittsburgh pamphlet; Burson-Marsteller news release, June 5, 1963; Pitt news release, November 28, 1962; minute of Executive Committee meeting, March 13, 1962.

309 James C. Rea suggestion. Litchfield Papers, FF 749, "Rea," J. C. Rea to Litchfield, April 25, 1963, Litchfield to Rea, May 15, 1963.

309 Broughton on Panther Hollow. Fitzgerald Papers, FF 219, Broughton to Fitzgerald, "Notes on Junction and Panther Hollows," September 17,

1953, with photographs and a blueprint; Fitzgerald to Broughton, October 5, 1953.

309 Fitzgerald proposed a library. Fitzgerald Papers, FF 219, Fitzgerald to Philip S. Broughton, October 5, 1953.

309 PRPA master plan, OakCorp. Minute of Council of Deans meeting, March 30, 1962; *Charette*, February 1962, pp. 6–15; "Preliminary Prospectus of Oakland Corporation," December 11, 1961.

311 Litchfield planned a new stadium. Minute of Council of Deans meeting, September 15, 1964; Howard interview with Edison Montgomery, PROHP, February 8, 1971, with supplementary comments, May 21, 1975.

311 Litchfield and Symphony Hall. Montgomery, PROHP interview, supplement.

311 Music Hall presentation. Ibid.; *Pitt*, July 1963, pp. 14–16.

312 Had tenants for half the space. *Business Week*, June 8, 1953.

312 Hughes to Litchfield. Author's interview with Joseph D. Hughes, December 25, 1982.

312 Price to Litchfield; balls in air. Cope, 22–23.

312 Publicity on Panther Hollow. *Business Week*, April 7, 1962, June 8, 1963; *Time*, June 21, 1963; *Pitt News*, June 12, July 3, 1963; *Pittsburgh Press*, January 21, 1964; *Wall Street Journal*, January 6, 1963.

312 Panther Hollow problems. Minute of Administrative Committee meeting, January 20, 1965.

312 Warner not consulted. Cope, 22–23.

312 Design would force road changes. Peake interview, May 27, 1981; Litchfield Papers, telegram to Litchfield, October 27, 1964 from Price and Denton, Sanantonio Abad, Ibiza, Balearic Islands.

312 Many turndowns. Litchfield Papers, Panther Hollow correspondence.

312 Only 202,600 square feet. Ibid., Oakland Corporation meeting, April 30, 1965; "Panther Hollow," Monnett to Frank Novak, February 15, 1965.

312 Capitalization. Litchfield Papers, "Oakland Corporation," minute of directors' meeting, November 30, 1964.

312 Smith at $1,000 a month. Ibid.

312 Monnett to Council of Deans. Minute of meeting of November 3, 1964.

312 Declined diocese offer. Litchfield Papers, "Oakland Corporation," January 18, 1965.

312 Abramovitz canceled. Litchfield Papers, FF 36, "A–General, Abramovitz," Monnett to Abramovitz, March 5, 1965.

312 $7,563 in bank. Ibid., Oakland Corporation meeting, April 30, 1965.

312 Litchfield: "We were unrealistic." *Pittsburgh Press*, May 2, 1965, Kenneth Eskey, "Chancellor Speaks His Mind."

312 Abramovitz: importance of marginal land. Burson-Marsteller news release, June 5, 1963.

312 Denton, still a good idea. Denton interview. On March 15, 1986, in announcing a ten-year expansion project, Carnegie-Mellon University said that it will erect a three-story electronic materials technology building against the Panther Hollow hillside.

Chapter Twenty-six. The Crisis

314 Crawford and Notations. Litchfield Papers, FF 41, Crawford to Litchfield, December 10, 1964, "B/T Budget Audit."

314 Denton's analysis. Ibid., FF 44, "Notations of Meeting of the Budget and Audit Committee," November 17, 1964.

314 Litchfield: should have got commitment. Ibid.

314 Task force meeting. Ibid.

314 Denton: fruitless to approach industry. Litchfield Papers, FF 41, "Notations on Special Task Force Meeting," December 10, 1964.

314 Ask for a special state appropriation. Ibid.

314 Question put to Executive Committee. Ibid.

315 Cost cutting program. *Pittsburgh Press*, December 2, 1964, February 7, 9, 1965; Litchfield Papers, FF 109, "Budget Cutting" and "Economies," Litchfield to staff, December 14, 1964; Litchfield to Hudson, December 14, 1964; to all vice chancellors, December 29, 1964 and January 21, 1965; to Montgomery, January 13, 1965; to Peake, January 15, 1965; Memorandum for the Record, November 12, 1964, February 22, 1965; to Monnett, Deck,

etc., April 12, 1965; minutes of Administrative Committee meetings, October 20–30, November 7, 1964; Memorandum for the Board, November 2, 1964; *Pittsburgh Post-Gazette*, January 28, 1965; *Pitt News*, January 29, 1965; *New York Times*, February 13, 1965.

315 1964–65 budget. Budget-Audit Committee Statement, 7–8.

315 Litchfield-Hudson exchange. Denton interview.

315 Cale's fund drive. Author's interview with Edgar Cale, September 4, 1981; Ketchum interviews; minutes of Administrative Committee meetings, January 20, September 24, 1965.

315 Allegheny Observatory. *Pittsburgh Press*, January 24, 1965; *Pitt News*, January 25, March 15, September 15, 1965; Pitt news release, December 2, 1965.

316 Litchfield reviewing letters. Minute of Administrative Committee meeting, January 27, 1965; Litchfield Papers, FF 165, "Bailie," Litchfield to Crawford, June 13, 15, 1965.

316 *Pittsburgh Post-Gazette* editorial advised state-related status. February 4, 19, 1965.

316 Historic board meeting. Minute of trustees' meeting, February 9, 1965.

316 Chancellor disappointed. *Pittsburgh Press*, February 9, 1965.

316 Price-Litchfield report to Faculty Senate. Pitt news release, February 11, 1965.

316 Hudson returns part-time. Litchfield Papers, FF 109, "Budget Cutting," Hudson to Litchfield, March 14, 15, 1965; "Finance," FF 305, "acting V/C for," Litchfield to Administrative Committee, March 10, 1965; draft of a canceled news release on the appointment.

317 Malott's advice. Litchfield Papers, FF 567, "Malott," Malott to Litchfield, March 15, 1965; Litchfield to Malott, March 22, 1965.

317 Selma. Pitt news release, March 26, 1965; *Pittsburgh Press*, March 15, 1965; *Pittsburgh Post-Gazette*, March 15, 1965; Litchfield Papers, FF 36, "Alabama," June, secretary to Litchfield, March 6, 1965; Colangelo to Litchfield, March 16, 23, 1965; Frank J. Lydick to Litchfield, March 17, 1965; Litchfield to Lydick, April 26, 1965; *Pitt News*, March 26, 1965. Litchfield ended a conference in his office when he received a telephone call from John Seidman, a liberal arts faculty member, who

reported from Montgomery that Pitt students had been beaten, trampled by horses, clubbed by Montgomery police and badly hurt; that students from other colleges had been clubbed and were dying; that the Pitt student leader had been injured and taken to an aid station; and that ABC and NBC cameramen had turned their cameras away when the violence started. The reports were not true.

317 Mt. Lebanon rally. *Pittsburgh Post-Gazette*, April 29, 1965; *Pittsburgh Press*, April 29, 1965.

317 Price given authority. Minute of trustees' meeting, May 11, 1965; *Pittsburgh Press*, May 11, 24, 1965

317 Narick letter. Minute of trustees' meeting, May 11, 1965; Litchfield Papers, FF 94, "B/T Narick," Narick to board, May 11, Narick to Crawford, May 12, 1965.

318 Meeting at Warwick Terrace. Minute of extended session of Council of Deans, May 18, 1965.

318 Meeting at Tumble Run. Minute of Administrative Committee meeting, May 21–23, 1965; Montgomery interview, March 20, 1985.

319 Asked state for $5 million. Minute of trustees' meeting, June 2, 1965.

319 Call on Governor Scranton. *Pittsburgh Post-Gazette*, June 8, 1965; *Pittsburgh Press*, June 8, 1965.

319 Council of Higher Education visited campus. *Pittsburgh Post-Gazette*, June 19, 1965; *Pittsburgh Press*, June 17, 1965.

319 Litchfield to Crawford on $4.27 million. Kurtzman Papers, FF 354.

319 Litchfield's refusal to believe. Budget-Audit Statement, 10; Denton and Price interviews.

319 Criticism of Cale's people. Litchfield Papers, FF 109, "Budget Cutting, 1964–65," Litchfield to Cale, June 24, 1965.

319 Litchfield opposed state-relatedness. *Pittsburgh Post-Gazette*, May 13, 14, 1965; *Pittsburgh Press*, March 17, April 30, May 13, 1965; draft of an article by Litchfield written February 15, 1965, for the *Post-Gazette* editorial page but not sent (Kurtzman Papers, FF 358). See also an article by William Rodd printed in the *Pittsburgh Forum*, February 4, 1972, and also in the *Pitt News*, February 21, 1972.

320 Asked Litchfield to resign. Price interviews and correspondence.

320 Meeting of House subcommittee. *Pittsburgh Post-Gazette*, June 26, 1965; *Pittsburgh Press*, June 26, 1965.

320 Trustees' resolution on excellence. Litchfield Papers, FF 63, "Board of Trustees," June 28, 1965.

320 Borrowed $1.25 million. *Pittsburgh Post-Gazette*, June 29, 1965; *Pittsburgh Press*, June 29, 1965.

320 Cable to Litchfield. Litchfield Papers, FF 767, "Secretary," June 29, 1965.

320 Kurtzman becomes vice chancellor for finance. Author's interviews with Denton, Price, and Celia Kurtzman; *Pittsburgh Press*, July 2, 1965; *Pittsburgh Post-Gazette*, July 3, 1965.

320 Monnett to Crawford on 1 percent. Kurtzman Papers, FF 354.

320 "Pitt's Juggler Fumbles." *Time*, July 2, 1965.

321 Two-day House hearing. *Pittsburgh Post-Gazette*, July 7, 8, 1965; *Pittsburgh Press*, July 7, 1965.

322 Student rally. *Pittsburgh Post-Gazette*, July 14, 1965; *Pittsburgh Press*, July 13, 14, 1965.

322 Second Narick letter. Litchfield Papers, FF 94, "B/T Narick," July 16, 1965; *Pittsburgh Press*, July 16, 1965; *Pittsburgh Post-Gazette*, July 17, 1965.

322 Ford Foundation study group. Pitt news releases, June 7, 14, 1965; Kurtzman Papers, FF 355, Minute of Study Group, Minute of Joint Meeting, July 19, 1965; *Pittsburgh Post-Gazette*, July 20, 1965.

322 Hudson on Kurtzman. Litchfield Papers, FF 94, "B/T, Price," July 21, 23, 1965.

322 Kurtzman talk to Administrative Committee. Minute of the meeting, July 23, 1965.

322 Colangelo press conference. *Pittsburgh Post-Gazette*, July 28, 1965; *Pittsburgh Press*, July 28, 1965. He had spent a weekend at Tumble Run working with Litchfield on the statement and resignation letter.

323 Crawford made the announcement. Minute of Council of Deans meeting, July 27, 1965.

Chapter Twenty-seven. Toward Recovery

327 Epigraph. Funari interview, November 11, 1982.

328 Drop in enrollment. Wells Report, 7.

328 Loss of students to New York. Montgomery interview.

329 Trimester, adverse. Wells Report, 10–12.

329 Grunbaum criticism of Wells Report. Joint meeting of the trustees' Search Committee with the Faculty Committee, January 17, 1966.

329 University's progress. Wells Report, 8–13.

330 Praise of faculty. Ibid., 7, 9.

330 Decision by key faculty members. Greenberg, 800.

330 Price on faculty. Nancy Mason interview, PROHP, 1975, p. 30.

330 Mrs. Crawford objected. Bailie interview, May 13, 1981.

330 Caliber of freshman class. *Pittsburgh Press*, September 5, 1965; *Wall Street Journal*, September 18, 1965.

330 Decision to seek state relationship. Pitt news release, December 10, 1965.

330 Crawford to Century Club. Pitt news release, December 11, 1965.

331 Litchfield left Studebaker. Litchfield Papers, FF 293, Litchfield to Sherwood H. Egbert, April 1, 1965.

331 Litchfield's stock ownership. Greenberg, 551.

331 Cale in charge of new service. Cale interview.

331 Capital for Technology. *Pittsburgh Press*, September 14, 1967.

331 Pittsburgher who saw him in Washington. Author's conversation with Mrs. Robert E. Fulton.

331 Funari on personality. Funari interview.

332 William Rea: "antagonized." Rea interview, November 23, 1981.

332 Price: "He was arrogant." Price interviews.

332 Scale of living. Greenberg, 660–61.

332 Price: "lacked some common sense." Price interviews.

332 Denton: if Scaife had lived. Denton interview.

333 Price: if Scaife had lived. Price interviews.

333 Montgomery: gambling on two things. Lawrence Howard interview with Montgomery, PROHP, 1971.

334 Denton: Was not willing to build slowly. Denton interview.

334 Price's call on R. K. Mellon. Price interviews.

334 Denton, blackmail. Denton interview.

334 Montgomery on promise of $125 million. This

appeared in the *Pitt News* on February 4, 1972. It was a rebuttal of some of the inaccuracies and aspersions in an attack on the University that appeared in the same issue, written by William H. Rodd, II.

334 Funari on Litchfield after retirement. Funari interview.

334 Two incredible documents. Both were written by William Rodd. The first is a nine-page manuscript on the financial crisis, distributed privately by Litchfield but never published. It is in the University Archives in the Special Budget and Audit Committee file. The second is a longer work written by Rodd in 1966 but not then published. It appeared on February 4, 1972, in a weekly tabloid called the *Pittsburgh Forum*, despite efforts of Litchfield's surviving children to stop publication. The *Pitt News* reprinted this five days later, adding a commentary on the text by Montgomery and Joseph G. Colangelo.

335 Events of March 8–9. *Pittsburgh Post-Gazette*, March 11, 12, 1968; *Pittsburgh Press*, March 9, 10, 1968; *Pitt News*, March 11, 15, 1968; *Chicago Tribune*, May 6, *Chicago Sun-Times*, May 5, 1968; National Transportation Safety Board, aircraft accident report; Federal Aviation report; Rand-McNally, "World Aircraft—Commercial, 1935–1960"; Litchfield Papers, FF 224, Litchfield to Lawrence Litchfield, July 31, 1964.

Chapter Twenty-eight. "Our House Is in Order"

337 Epigraph. Kurtzman Papers, FF 245, Kurtzman to R. K. Mellon.

338 Price to Search Committee and faculty. Minute of Search Committee meeting, January 27, 1966; Price interview.

338 Price offered chancellorship to Montgomery. Price interview; Kurtzman Papers, Personal, FF 121, Price remarks on awarding an honorary degree to Kurtzman, October 23, 1967.

338 Kurtzman named. Helen Knox, "From Odessa to Emeritus with Love"; Pitt news release, January 30, 1966; minute of Administrative Committee meeting, February 4, 1966.

338 Kurtzman at first not a popular choice. Rea interview; Rea address at dedication of Kurtzman

Room; Knox, "From Odessa to Emeritus with Love."

338 Kurtzman biography. Knox, "From Odessa to Emeritus with Love," 2–6; Price, Rea, and Celia Kurtzman interviews.

338 Pay as you go. This was the subject of several Pennsylvania Economy League news letters in the early 1940s, written by the author from material supplied by Kurtzman.

339 Kurtzman speech to Senate. Kurtzman Papers, transcription of tape of speech made by Helen Knox; Herbert G. Stein, *Pittsburgh Post-Gazette*, February 28, 1966; Carver interviews.

340 "He was everybody's favorite uncle." Evert interview, July 10, 1981.

340 "Board gave me its confidence." Kurtzman Papers, Personal, FF 121, Kurtzman address on receiving an honorary degree, October 23, 1967.

340 No holding operation. Herbert G. Stein, *Pittsburgh Post-Gazette*, February 28, 1966; Knox, "From Odessa to Emeritus with Love," 1.

340 Kurtzman restored cuts. Knox, "From Odessa to Emeritus with Love," 6.

340 Reorganized top administration. Kurtzman Papers, FF 51, Kurtzman to vice chancellors, deans, and directors, March 30, 1966; ibid., S. C. Crawford to Price, December 7, 1965; minute of Executive Committee meeting, August 10, 1965; *Pittsburgh Post-Gazette*, April 1, 1966; *Wall Street Journal*, September 15, 1965.

340 Dropped Panther Hollow. Minute of Administrative Committee meeting, October 1, 1965.

340 *Pittsburgh Post-Gazette* columnist. Herbert G. Stein, July 30, 1965.

340 Murdock and Bronk. Minute of Executive (Search) Committee meeting, February 8, 1966.

341 Articles in *Science*. February 4, 11, 18, 1966.

341 Faculty attrition dropped to 8 percent. *Pittsburgh Post-Gazette*, February 28, 1966.

341 James Kehl to Kurtzman. Kurtzman Papers, FF 30, July 6, 1966.

341 Peake to Kurtzman. Ibid., FF 6, February 2, 22, 1966, Kurtzman to Peake, February 16, 1966.

341 Peake to resigning dean. Ibid., FF 318, Peake to Richard Park, March 28, 1966.

341 "A joint venture in higher education." Colangelo, *Pitt*, Fall 1966, p. 2.

341 Headlines. Civic Chiefs Back Pitt, *Pittsburgh Press,* January 23, 1966; Scranton Backs Aid, *Pittsburgh Press,* December 19, 1965; City Appeals to State, *Pittsburgh Post-Gazette,* June 22, 1965; State Ponders Way, *Pittsburgh Press,* June 24, 1965; Pitt Needs Transfusion, *Pittsburgh Post-Gazette,* June 24, 1965; Bishop Wright Asks, *Pittsburgh Post-Gazette,* June 29, 1965; Pitt Key to Progress, *Pittsburgh Press,* June 5, 1965; Let's Rally, *Pittsburgh Post-Gazette,* June 9, 1965; Chamber of Commerce, *Pittsburgh Press,* June 16, 1965.

342 *Pittsburgh Press* editorial. April 17, 1966.

342 *Philadelphia Sunday Bulletin.* June 20, 1965.

343 State-related status. *Pittsburgh Press,* August 23, 1966; Colangelo, "A Third Kind of University"; Colangelo, draft of a manuscript for a brochure on state-relatedness, Kurtzman Papers, FF 358.

343 Rea: "We are at end of list." Minute of Executive (Search) Committee meeting, July 11, 1966.

343 Rea: three choices. Ibid., July 21, 1966.

343 Bolman's book. See review in *New York Times,* January 10, 1965.

344 Price: "only one man." Colangelo, "The Making of a Chancellor," 2.

344 Saved Ruskin. Minute of trustees' Executive Committee meeting, August 10, 1965; memorandum from G. S. Rupp, treasurer, to Kurtzman, ibid., May 26, 1965, agenda of the meeting; *Pittsburgh Post-Gazette,* May 6, 1966.

344 Gifts restored confidence. *Pittsburgh Post-Gazette,* December 3, 1966, "Pitt Back on Track."

344 Would have had 10,000 freshmen. Pitt news release, October 26, 1967; Helen Knox, "The 2000 Best," *Pitt,* Winter 1967, p. 7.

344 "A third kind of university." Colangelo, *Pitt,* Fall 1966.

344 One candidate withdrew. Nancy Mason interview with Price, PROHP, 1975, pp. 34–35.

345 Price and retirement. Ibid.; Price interview; *Pittsburgh Press,* January 16, 1967; Pitt news release, January 10, 1967.

345 Discovery of and negotiations with W. W. Posvar. Colangelo, "The Making of a Chancellor"; minute of Administrative Committee meeting, January 13, 1967; Nelson; Price, Rea, Posvar, and Joseph D. Hughes interviews.

346 Schonberg on Mildred Miller. *New York Times,* December 24, 1966.

347 Concern at military background. Nelson, 542; Price and Rea interviews.

347 Price and faculty advisors: "an end run." Price interviews.

347 W. W. Posvar's biography. *Who's Who in America* (1984–85); Pitt news release, January 13, 1967; Colangelo, "The Making of a Chancellor"; Nelson; Posvar interview.

348 Mildred Miller's biography. *Who's Who in America* (1984–85); Knox, "The Chancellor's Lady Sings."

348 Faculty advisors called on Price next morning. Price interviews.

349 Retirement dinner. Pitt news release, January 10, 1967; dinner program, "In Honor of Gwilym A. Price."

349 Kurtzman appointed to full rank. Posvar interview.

Chapter Twenty-nine. The Frick Fine Arts Building

350 Epigraph: Peake to Kurtzman. Unless otherwise noted, the cited letters and other documents are filed in the University Archives, Litchfield Papers, Box 51, FF 306–16, labeled "Helen C. Frick" and "Henry Clay Frick Fine Arts Department," or in 13/15 Buildings—Henry Clay Frick Fine Arts Building, FF 1–14.

351 $3.5 million gift. Kurtzman Papers, FF 274, William G. Fisher to Kurtzman, April 25, 1966, "Construction Projects Since 1957."

351 "A straightforward mind." McCarten.

351 Catalogue, Frick Collection in New York. *Alumni News Review,* April 1950; *Pitt,* Winter 1949–50; extensive correspondence on this undertaking among Miss Frick, John Bowman, Andrei Avinoff, Frederick Mortimer Clapp, and others in the University Archives and in office files of the Department of Fine Arts.

351 F. M. Clapp. *Who's Who in America* (1936–37).

352 Hovey felt his course influenced art. Hovey interview, April 7, 1981; Hovey letter to the author, April 9, 1981.

352 Twenty exhibitions. The author reviewed these in the weekly *Pittsburgh Bulletin Index,* 1939–41.

352 Resignation. *New York Times*, January 19, 1961.

352 Miss Frick on retaining Hovey. Frick to Litchfield, March 9, 1960; Litchfield to Frick, March 14, 1960.

353 Department in bad condition. Gholson to Putnam Jones, February 14, 1960; Seznec to Peake, September 1, 1962.

353 New dean of humanities. Litchfield to Frick, October 23, 1962.

353 Wadsworth called on Miss Frick. Wadsworth to Frick, April 4, 1963.

353 Described search for chairman. Ibid.

353 Called self "a new administrator." Ibid., January 25, 1963.

353 Hovey a valued partner. Ibid., April 4, 1963.

353 Deficiencies of the department. Ibid., April 8, 1963.

353 She did not like Germans. Ibid., April 4, 1963; McCarten.

354 In defense of Birkmeyer. Wadsworth to Frick, May 2, June 26, 1963.

354 Miss Frick on Birkmeyer. Frick to Wadsworth, April 10, June 21, 1963.

354 Wadsworth did not agree. Wadsworth to Frick, May 2, 1963.

354 Wadsworth on Loerke. Wadsworth to Frick, May 29, June 5, June 26, 1963.

354 Miss Frick asked her secretary. Wadsworth to Frick, June 5, 1963.

354 "A very masculine, aggressive person." Wadsworth to Litchfield, May 14, 1963.

354 Loerke listed twenty books as a test. John Walker to Helen C. Frick, August 25, 1964.

354 Miss Frick repeated her objection. Frick to Wadsworth, June 21, 1963.

354 "I am most unhappy." Wadsworth to Frick, June 26, 1963.

355 Asked Peake to warn Litchfield. Wadsworth to Peake, June 5, 1963.

355 Litchfield defended Birkmeyer. Litchfield to Frick, June 26, 1963.

355 Miss Frick would not presume to dictate. Frick to Litchfield, July 6, 1963.

355 Loerke to Virginia Lewis. An office memorandum, February 7, 1964.

356 Loerke apology to Lewis. Loerke to Frick, February 28, 1964.

356 Wadsworth also apologized. Wadsworth to Frick, February 27, 1964.

356 Letter to R. K. Mellon. Frick to Mellon, February 27, 1964.

356 Mellon asked for information. Mellon to Litchfield, March 30, 1964.

356 A long letter. Litchfield to Mellon, April 6, 1964.

356 She felt obliged to demand. Frick to Mellon, April 14, 1964.

356 Cannot remove faculty people. Mellon to Frick, April 24, 1964.

357 Would not be content. Frick to Rea, April 24, 1964; Walker to Frick, August 25; Walker to Wadsworth, August 11, 1964.

357 Walker spoke highly. Rea to Frick, May 14; Walker to Wadsworth, May 1, 1964.

357 Walker should engage him. Frick to Rea, May 16, 1964.

357 "I will not have that man." Peake interview.

357 Loerke must be transferred. Walker to Wadsworth, August 31, 1964.

357 Miss Frick dedicates building. Minute of trustees' meeting, May 11, 1965; *Pitt News*, May 26, 1965.

357 Memorandum of Understanding. June 16, 1965.

357 "A Memorandum of Submission." Loerke to Kurtzman, June 24, 1966.

357 "Our problems arose." Initialed, undated short memorandum, probably March 1968, by James R. Wolfe.

357 Peake protested. Peake to Minott, May 20, 1966; Peake to Kurtzman, August 3, 1966.

358 Buerger's undated letter to Buerger. May 1965; Peake interview; letter from Peake to Edison Montgomery, September 6, 1981, forwarded to author.

358 Peake refused to sign. Peake to Buerger, May 17, 1965.

359 Memorandum satisfied nobody. Peake to Kurtzman, August 3, 1966. Much effort was expended in 1966 on a proposal to set up a semi-independent art center controlled by a separate board. Buerger turned it down, saying frankly that Miss Frick

wanted "autonomy." Arensberg said it was illegal under state law and the University charter.

359 Miss Frick would not communicate with Peake. Peake to Crawford, November 30, 1965.

359 Peake's name should be removed. Frick to Lockhart, August 31, 1965.

359 Miss Frick to Weidlein on Peake. August 31, 1965.

359 Sociology professor denied access. *Pitt News*, September 17, 1965.

359 Miss Frick's request to Wells. Wells to Frick, March 29, 1966.

359 Miss Frick to meet University people. Crawford to Rush, December 6, 1965.

359 Honorary degree for Miss Frick. Memorandum, January 6, 1966.

359 Faculty Senate inquiry. Peake to John Walker, February 7, 1966. In this letter Peake wrote, "I wish so much that Miss Frick could get some insight into the nature of the academic world and understand how powerful are the sanctions of the faculty."

359 "Prejudices and personal interference." Peake to Price, March 7, 1966.

359 Slatkes resignation. Slatkes to Kurtzman, May 11, 1966.

359 Minott resignation. Minott to Kurtzman, April 7, 1966.

360 Wadsworth's plea for help. Wadsworth to Kurtzman, May 20, 1966.

360 Department dropped by NDEA. Wadsworth to Kurtzman, December 12, 1966.

360 Rea called on Miss Frick and her attorney. Kurtzman to Wadsworth, January 24, 1967; Rea interview.

360 Request for "some concrete indication." Wadsworth to Kurtzman, January 19, 1967.

360 Arensberg told plans. Arensberg to Buerger, February 1, 1967.

360 Kurtzman informed Senate. *Pittsburgh Post-Gazette*, February 9, 1967.

360 Peake informed Hovey. Peake to Hovey, February 6, 1967.

360 Lewis resignation. Wadsworth to Lewis, February 9; Lewis to Kurtzman, April 3, 1967.

360 Story was national news. Among others, *New York Times*, February 8, 1967; *Philadelphia Evening Bulletin*, February 9, 1967; *Chicago Tribune*, February 8, 1967; *Newsweek*, February 20, 1967; *Time*, February 17, 1967.

361 Pitt's basic points made. *Pittsburgh Post-Gazette*, February 9, 10, 1967; *Pittsburgh Press*, February 8, 9, 11, 1967; *Pittsburgh Catholic*, February 16, 1967.

361 Hovey on "the whole affair." *Pittsburgh Post-Gazette*, February 24, 1967.

361 Hovey to Dear Friends. February 10, 1967.

361 Miss Frick's dream shattered. *Pittsburgh Press*, February 27, 1967.

361 No one thanked her. *Pittsburgh Post-Gazette*, February 9, 1967.

361 Four pieces in *Pitt News*. February 10, 13, 15, 1967.

361 Pitt's bill for $29,000. Kurtzman to Arensberg, January 20, 1967; Arensberg to Buerger, January 25, 1967; Buerger to Arensberg, January 26, February 10, 1967.

361 Denied Miss Frick wanted anyone discharged. Buerger to *Pitt News*, February 27, 1967.

361 Rea refused Hovey. Hovey to Rea, February 8, 1967; Rea to Hovey, February 24, 1967; Hovey interview, April 7, 1981.

361 Rea solely responsible. Rea interview.

361 Disposition of art objects. Theodore Bowman to Kurtzman, April 5, 1967; Bowman to Rea, April 5, 1967; Bowman to Wadsworth, April 17, 1967; Wadsworth to Kurtzman, February 15, 1967.

361 Alceo Dossena figures. See Donald Miller, *Pittsburgh Post-Gazette*, December 5, 1968, "Pitt Fakes Given New Importance."

361 Lochoff copies cost $40,000. Hovey to G. S. Rupp, May 22, 1959; Litchfield to Frick, May 22, 1959.

362 $200,000 endowment for books. "List of seven points that must be agreed upon prior to submission of any proposal" to make a new agreement with Miss Frick. No date or signature.

362 Trust fund returning $14,000. Theodore Bowman to Rea, April 5, 1967.

362 Current exhibition illicit. Frick to *Pitt News*, July 9, 1969.

362 Ugly modern work; thanks for removing stain. Frick to Posvar, October 19, 1972.

362 Reception for Hovey. Pitt news release, March 4, 1977; Donald Miller, *Pittsburgh Post-Gazette*, March 8, 1977.

363 More a part of community life. "Proper Utilization of the Frick Fine Arts Building," 5 pp., no date, no signature.

363 Evaluations of Department. File folder in Frick Fine Arts Department records, "Department of Fine Arts Self-Study and External and Internal Evaluations, 1981–82."

Chapter Thirty. "The Creative Eye"

365 Inauguration. *Pitt,* Spring 1968; *Pittsburgh Press, Pittsburgh Post-Gazette,* March 27, 1968; *Pitt News,* March 29, 1968.

365 Conferred honorary degrees. On Charles J. Hitch, president, University of California; Colonel George A. Lincoln, head of social sciences at the U.S. Military Academy; Don K. Price, Jr., dean of the John F. Kennedy School of Government, Harvard University; Herbert G. Nicholas, fellow of New College, Oxford.

365 The menu was tested. Posvar Papers, FF 3.1.7 (1968).

365 Chancellor sent personal copies. Ibid., "Notes from Mr. Freeman," May 31, 1968.

365 Work on house not finished. Knox, "The Chancellor's Lady Sings," 15. Falk had also made a gift of $10,000 for work on the house. Posvar Papers, FF 3.19 (1966), letters dated May 25 and June 14, 1966.

365 Posvar running and pedaling. *Pittsburgh Press,* June 18, 1967, February 6, 1972.

365 Was made a member of graduate faculty. Posvar Papers, FF 1.1.1 (1967), Putnam F. Jones to Posvar, July 25, 1967.

368 Eisenhower at Johnstown. Posvar Papers, FF 2.5.3 and 3.7.3 (1967), Posvar to John Eisenhower, September 13, 1967.

368 R. K. Mellon as trustee emeritus. Ibid., 3.7.2 (1968), R. K. Mellon to Posvar, May 13, 1968.

368 Courtesy correspondence. Ibid., 1.1.1 (1967–68), Posvar to Ritchey, April 24, 1970; *Pitt News,* January 22, 29, February 5, 1968; 15.31 (1968), March 20, 1968.

368 "Thinks she can sing." Knox, "The Chancellor's Lady Sings," 13; author's interview with Mrs. Posvar, August 8, 1983.

368 Conference before meeting faculty. Mrs. Posvar interview.

368 Would not sing Carmen. *New York Times,* April 13, 1970; Knox, "The Chancellor's Lady Sings," 15.

368 Audience of 1,500 at Mt. Lebanon. *Pittsburgh Press, Pittsburgh Post-Gazette,* November 13, 1968.

368 Donated fee. Posvar papers, FF 6.2.1 (1973), Mrs. Posvar to Bernard Koperek, January 11, 1973; *Pittsburgh Post-Gazette,* February 28, 1972.

368 She favored move to Pittsburgh. Author's interview.

369 Ten moves in 17 years. Ruth Heimbucher, *Pittsburgh Press,* January 18, 1967.

369 1967 schedule. Knox, "The Chancellor's Lady Sings," 12.

369 Grand Prix award. Ibid., 16.

369 Her University duties. Ibid., 13.

370 Asked her agent not to book her. *New York Times,* April 13, 1970.

370 Merger of Mellon Institute with Carnegie Institute of Technology. Hughes and Schmidt interviews.

371 Posvar lists issues. Posvar papers, 5.101 (1970), Report to Trustees, December 7, 1970.

372 Review of goals. *Pittsburgh Press,* January 14, 1968; minute of the planning meeting at Seven Springs, December 1–2, 1967; minute of second meeting, February 5, 1968.

372 Administrative reorganization. *Pittsburgh Post-Gazette,* September 19, 1967; *Pitt News,* September 18, 1967; *Pitt,* Fall 1968, pp. 1–7; Posvar to trustees, August 18, 1968; to faculty and staff, September 15, 1967.

372 Deans combined in one office. *Pitt News,* April 8, 1968. Jack B. Critchfield, dean of student affairs, became assistant chancellor for student affairs.

372 McCormick Hall announcement. *Pitt News,* February 20, 1970.

372 Fiscal reform and planning. *Pitt,* Fall 1969, pp. 5–6; *Pitt Owl,* 1968, p. 5; Posvar Papers, FF 2.2.1 (1968), Posvar to William Graham, February 16, 1968; Report to Trustees, August 18, 1969; Freeman interview, June 6, 1985.

373 Enrollment, SAT scores. *Barron's Profiles,* 1968, p. 4; First Annual Report to Trustees, October 26, 1967; Fifth Annual Report, 1971; "Report on Student Socioeconomic Status, Fall, 1960," July 30, 1971.

373 Two legislative attempts to interfere. The 1969 Fleming Bill proposed to take punitive action against students who engaged in campus disturbances. The Snyder Bill required faculty members to report an hourly breakdown on their teaching, the courses they taught, the number of students in them, and the students' credit-hours germinated.

373 Three became stout supporters. Robert D. Fleming, Albert R. Pechan, and Richard A. Snyder.

374 Restraint on fund raising. Posvar Papers, FF 6.1.1 (1974), Posvar to David S. Ketchum, February 10, 1974.

374 Rationale for private gifts. *Pittsburgh Press*, January 2, 1972; Posvar to trustees, August 18, 1969; *Pitt Owl*, 1968, p. 6; Fifth Annual Report, June, 1972, p. 9.

374 Public support common for private colleges. Posvar papers, FF 4.5.2 (1968), Posvar to new faculty, September 4, 1968; Posvar address to trustees, 5.1.9B (1969), August 18, 1969.

374 Got $11 million. Posvar papers, FF 3.1 (1969), Posvar to trustees, August 18, 1969.

374 R. K. Mellon gave $9 million. Ibid., FF 5.1.9 (1972), Chancellor's Report to Deans, Directors, and Chairmen, February 29, 1972, including Pitt news release.

374 Public grants. Ibid., FF 3.1 (1969), Posvar to trustees, August 18, 1969.

375 Paid off $8 million. Interview with Paul Solyan, comptroller, January 31, 1986.

375 Solyan and state aid. Author's interviews.

375 Posvar at a budget meeting. Lubove, "Posvar: Pitt's Chancellor 'Thriving' Under Pressure."

375 Martha's Vineyard—Nantucket. Kennedy, 13.

375 "An excessively fast pace." Posvar to author.

375 "I would be disappointed." Ibid.

375 Criticizes own performance. Author's interview.

376 Funari comparison, Litchfield, Posvar. Funari interview, November 2, 1982.

376 On academic freedom. Posvar Papers, File of Writings, 5.1.10 (1970–71), Box 22, FF 88.

377 Letter defending Dr. Holland. Ibid., 11.11 (1968), Posvar to Mrs. L. B. Smith, May 21, 1968.

377 On recruiting minority students. Ibid., "The

University as an American Institution," June 22, 1974. An informal 22-page unprinted essay on Posvar's experiences in higher education.

377 The draft as a punitive instrument. Pitt news release, January 11, 1968.

377 The war in Vietnam. A position paper and news release distributed by Haverford College.

377 Pitt linked to Pittsburgh. Posvar Papers, FF 5.1.10 (1970–71), Posvar's file of writings.

377 Pitt fortunate to be in Pittsburgh. Chancellor's memorandum file, an address to a dinner meeting of the Negro Education Emergency Drive, June 12, 1967.

378 Investment in higher education. Posvar Papers, speech to women's association meeting, May 6, 1969.

378 State received bargain. Minute of meeting of Council of Deans and Campus Presidents, October 15, 1968.

378 The role of academic disciplines. Posvar Papers, FF 4.4 (1973–74), Report to Trustees.

378 "A unique and valuable institution." Ibid., FF 5.1.10 (1974), "The University as an American Institution."

378 Technological forecasts. Ibid., FF 5.1.101 (1967), remarks to Pittsburgh Personnel Association, October 11, 1967.

379 Military force is in the domain of ethics. Ibid., FF 5.1.10 I (1966), address to Air Force Academy, November 1966.

379 On nuclear deterrence. Ibid., FF 5.1.1 (1971), address to Army War College, May 7, 1971.

379 On U.S. foreign policy. Ibid., FF 5.1.10 (1971), address to American Academy of Political and Social Science, April 4, 1971.

Chapter Thirty-one. Confrontation I

381 Communal control of courses. Novak and Evans column, "The Strike at Berkeley and Academic Freedom," *New York Times*.

381 Access to professors' papers. *New York Times*, April 16, 1970.

381 Granting or denying tenure. Arnold H. Lubash, *New York Times*, April 14, 1970; Arnold Beichman, *New York Times Magazine*, December 7, 1969, p. 182.

381 All-black dormitories. *Pittsburgh Post-Gazette*, October 18, 1968.

381 Contributions to Black Panthers. *New York Times*, March 22, May 21, 1970; John Hersey, *Letter to the Alumni*, 1970, p. 112.

381 $35 weekly allowance. Sullivan, "Extremism," 4. Sullivan was assistant director of domestic intelligence, Federal Bureau of Investigation.

381 "A Miserable War." *Vital Speeches*, February 1, 1969, p. 235.

381 "The most massive demonstrations." *Encyclopedia of American History*, R. B. Morris, ed., 1982, p. 497.

381 Ridgway opposed. "Indochina Disengaging," *Foreign Affairs*, July 1971, pp. 591–92. See also Alberts, "Profile of a Soldier"; Hetzel and Hitchens, 279.

381 "A generation-wide catastrophe." Daskir and Strauss, xv.

382 39,000 students involved. Manchester, 1131–35.

382 11,200 arrested. Keniston and Lerner, 60.

382 More than half the states. *Scranton Report*, 1970, p. 6.

382 900 expelled or suspended. *Wall Street Journal*, September 30, 1969.

382 University of Wisconsin. *New York Times*, August 26, 1970; *Scranton Report*, 4. "Underground newspapers all over the country gleefully reported, after the bombing, that another blow had been struck against the 'pig nation.'" (*Scranton Report*, 6.)

382 Pomona. *Scranton Report*, 6; Sullivan, "Extremism," 3.

382 San Francisco State. *Scranton Report*, 6; Manchester, 1098.

382 Fresno State. *Scranton Report*, 6–7; *New York Times*, May 21, 1970.

382 SUNY at Buffalo. *Pittsburgh Post-Gazette*, March 8, 1970.

382 Stanford. *Scranton Report*, 6; Sullivan, "Civil Disorder," 9.

382 Santa Barbara. *Scranton Report*, 6; Sullivan, "Extremism," 3; author's correspondence with chancellor's office, Santa Barbara, February 13, 27, 1986.

382 Washington University. Sullivan, "Extremism," 3.

382 Lane College. Ibid.

382 Harvard. *Wall Street Journal*, May 27, 1969; *New York Times*, December 16, 1969, April 17, 1970; Hersey, 25; *Chronicle of Higher Education*, October 19, 1970, p. 5.

383 Barzun: "will not recover." *New York Times*, May 10, 1969. He was wrong.

383 Hoped to goad the police. *Scranton Report*, 6.

383 DeMott: "bridge to blow is college." Manchester, 1099.

383 Thirty presidents left posts. *New York Times*, March 15, 1970; *Wall Street Journal*, May 11, 1969.

383 300 vacancies. *New York Times*, May 18, 1969.

383 Perkins "anarchic." *New York Times*, March 10, 15, 1970.

383 Knight: "standing at the cross roads." Ibid., May 18, 1969.

383 Cafferty: "New breed." Ibid., May 18, 1969.

383 Posvar: "by a single act." Report to Trustees, December 1970.

384 Contingency plans. Posvar Papers, Box 22, FF 8.0, "Guidelines for Confrontations," no date, labeled "Oral Report—Not for Distribution."

384 "Insist on freedom of speech." Minute of trustees' Executive Committee meeting, November 10, 1970.

384 To faculty: programs of community service. Posvar Papers, Posvar to colleagues, June 17, 1968, "Memorabilia," 1968.

384 "An orderly academic environment." Posvar Papers, FF 5.1.10, Posvar to alumni and friends, February 28, 1969; *Pittsburgh Press*, March 14, 1969.

384 "Politics of confrontation." Posvar Papers, 1969/70, FF 5.1.10, speech to the Allegheny County Ministerial Union, November 11, 1969.

384 "Much that is admirable." Annual Report to Trustees, December 1970.

384 Status of women. Posvar memo to Provost, Vice Chancellors, Deans, . . . and Department Chairmen, May 29, 1970.

385 Student participation, cabinets. "Full Text of Student Power Statement," *University Times*, December 1968; *Pittsburgh Post-Gazette*, Alvin Rosensweet, October 11, 1968; Posvar Papers, FF 5.1.10 (1969), March 24, 1969.

385 Richard Bernstein. *Pittsburgh Post-Gazette*, October 11, 1968.

385 Posvar "bailed them out." *Pitt News*, March 20, 1968.

385 "Speak Your Peace" conference. Ibid., October 14, 1968.

385 Tutorial service for children. Posvar Papers, FF 3.1, Posvar to trustees, August 18, 1969.

386 Technical assistance. Ibid., 3.5, minute of meeting of University Senate, January 31, 1969; 1970 Report of the Chancellor, *Pitt*, Winter 1970, p. 11.

386 Trees Hall open. *Pitt News*, March 24, 1969; Posvar Papers, FF 5.1.10, Posvar to University community, March 24, 1968; minute of Council of Deans meeting, June 12, 1968.

386 Building-trades union. *Washington Post*, September 21, 1969; Posvar Papers, FF 6.7.2, Posvar to University community, September 22, 1969; *Pitt News*, September 25, 1969; *Pittsburgh Post-Gazette* (editorial), September 23, 1969.

386 Sensitivity training. Minute of Council of Deans meeting, October 15, 1968.

386 Seminar for 300 student leaders. Posvar Papers, FF 3.1.4, Chancellor's Report to Executive Committee, October 7, 1969.

386 Training for University police. Ibid., 4.7., James R. Wolfe to Donald Smith, September 13, 1968.

386 Provost's Development Fund. Ibid., 1.3A, no date: *University Times*, March 22, 1979.

386 Met BAS's reasonable demands. Minute of Council of Deans meeting, June 12, 1968.

386 BAS demanded 51 percent of freshmen. Minute of Senate Council meeting, February 24, 1969.

386 Goal was to double freshmen. Ibid.

387 "Black leaders want to believe us." Ibid.

387 Only 100 black Ph.D.s. *Wall Street Journal*, April 18, 1974.

388 Warned on double-standard. Thomas Sowell, *New York Times Magazine*, December 13, 1970, p. 49.

388 B. Rustin on remedial training. *New York Times*, April 28, 1969.

388 First confrontation with BAS. *Pittsburgh Press*, January 16, 1969; *Pitt News*, January 16, 1969; Posvar Papers, FF 7.3, statement by Posvar, February 21, 1969; FF 3.5, chancellor's remarks to University Senate, January 31, 1969; Posvar to trustees, August 18, 1969; author's interviews with Posvar, Bernard Kobosky, and Charles Arensberg.

388 Make freshman class reflective. Posvar Papers, FF 7.1, draft of an open letter to the students, no date.

388 Hired black recruiters. Minute of Council of Deans meeting, February 12, 1968.

388 Recruited black Vietnam veterans. Ibid.

388 Recruited community college. Ibid.

389 "Transitional tutorial program." Posvar Papers, FF 7.1, Kobosky to Posvar, May 7, 1970, "Student Affairs."

389 BAS complained not consulted. Ibid., "Student Aid and Admissions," FF 7.1.1, Kobosky to Critchfield, July 31, 1968.

389 "Authentic ghetto types." Thomas Sowell, *New York Times Magazine*, December 13, 1970, p. 37.

389 Raided black colleges. Minute of Council of Deans meeting, June 12, 1968, February 10, 1971.

389 Pay higher salaries. Posvar Papers, FF 1.18.1, Posvar to deans, March 31, 1969.

389 Fifteen protest letters. Posvar Papers, FF 5.1.12, letters of explanation to correspondents, May 1969.

389 Began Department of Black Studies. Ibid., FF 5.9, April 30, 1968; *University Times*, July 9, September 11, 1969, January 8, 1970.

389 Not impressed by quality. Posvar Papers, FF 3.1.4, Chancellor's Report to Executive Committee, September 10, 1969.

389 Twelve enrolled in Engineering School. Minute of Council of Deans meeting, May 7, 1969.

389 Hillman grant for Black History. Posvar Papers, FF 6.1.1, Henry L. Hillman to Posvar, December 22, 1969.

389 Only 230 black freshmen. Chancellor's Report to Executive Committee, September 10, 1969.

389 Ten blacks in medical school. *University Times*, September 25, 1969.

Chapter Thirty-two. Confrontation II

390 Epigraph: Charlotte E. Whitton. Nancy McPhee, *The Book of Insults Ancient and Modern*. New York; St. Martin's Press, 1978, p. 52.

391 Sit-in at Computer Center. *Pittsburgh Press*, January 16, 1969; *Pitt News*, January 16, 31, 1969; Posvar Papers, FF 7.3, statement by Posvar, February 21; FF 3.5, chancellor's remarks to Senate, January 31;

minute of Senate meeting, January 31; Report to Trustees, August 18, 1969; Posvar, Kobosky, Freeman, and Arensberg interviews.

391 Best to wait it out. *Scranton Report,* 15.

391 Listen for the message. *Scranton Report,* 15–16.

391 Incorporate "true role of black man." BAS to Posvar, no date, Posvar Papers, 1967/70 FF 5.1.6.8. *Pitt News,* June 25, 1968.

391 Halt University construction. Posvar Papers, FF 7.3.2, Posvar to University community, March 24, 1969.

391 Felt students would accept. Posvar interview.

392 *Pittsburgh Press* headline. January 16, 1969.

392 *Pitt News* headline. January 16, 1969.

392 "Perpetrators escaped." *Pittsburgh Press,* January 19, February 16, 1969.

392 Posvar to alumni and friends. Posvar Papers, FF 5.1.10, February 28, 1969.

392 Second confrontation, 800 students. *Pitt News,* February 10, 1969.

393 All-white group. *Pittsburgh Press,* March 16, 1969.

393 Proposals by Concerned Students. *Pittsburgh Post-Gazette,* March 15, 1969; Posvar Papers, FF 5.1.12, "To the Chancellor . . . ," no date.

393 Three-day sit-in by Concerned Students. *Pittsburgh Press,* March 12, 19, 1969; *Pittsburgh Post-Gazette,* March 14, 15, 1969; *Pitt News,* March 14, 1969; Posvar Papers, FF 7.3.3, typescript of Pitt statement read to the media over the telephone by Colangelo; FF 7.3.3, "Statement of the Chancellor," no date; minute of Council of Deans meeting, March 12, 1969.

394 *Pittsburgh Press* praised restraint. "Sit-In at Pitt," March 19, 1969.

394 "Keeps his cool." *Pittsburgh Press,* February 21, 1969.

394 Open University started but failed. *Pitt Owl,* 1969, "Posvar," no pagination [p. 113].

395 Admissions policies, financial aid, job placement. "Discrimination Against Women at the University of Pittsburgh: A Report Compiled by the University Committee for Women's Rights," November 1970 (hereafter UCWR Report).

395 Faculty statistics. Ruth Drescher, "Pitt Women Demand Their Rights," *The Point,* May 28, 1970, p. 2.

395 UCWR goal. UCWR Report, 1.

395 Presentations. Marcia Landy, "Academic Feminism: The History of Women's Studies at the University of Pittsburgh," 1973.

395 Posvar memo. *University Times,* February 5, 1970.

395 Teach-in. UCWR Report, 28; UCWR, "Statement presented to the Chancellor," May 18, 1970; *University Times,* May 28, 1970.

397 Memo of May 25. Drescher, "Pitt Women."

397 Letter to Schultz. UCWR Report, Appendix G–1.

397 $15 million withheld. *Pittsburgh Press,* April 8, 1979.

397 Braden class action suit. Ibid.

397 Johnson suit. *Pittsburgh Post-Gazette,* August 3, 1977.

397 ACWO established. *University Times,* June 25, 1970.

398 Moratorium March. *Pitt News,* October 17, 1969.

398 Telegram to London. Posvar Papers, FF 5.1.11, September 16, 1969.

398 "The clutches of corporate power." "Pitt Slates Beef Session of Dissent." *Pittsburgh Press,* October 25, 1969.

398 Blocked the elevator. Posvar and Freeman interviews.

398 Posvar restrained by force. Ibid.

398 Fire bombs. Ibid.

398 SDS seized Hillman. Freeman interview.

398 $6.93 refund. Posvar Papers, FF 5.1.11, September 16, 1969, Rebecca Gittings to chancellor, May 11, 1970.

398 Kobosky's problem. Minute of University Senate meeting, June 19, 1969.

398 Multiple choice question. Posvar Papers, FF 8.0. J. Harland Cleveland told this story in an address to the Pittsburgh World Affairs Council, May 28, 1968.

398 Black Studies Program, 270 students. Posvar Papers, FF 7.1, Kobosky to Posvar, May 7, 1970.

398 Burned female personnel records. *Pitt News,* February 10, 1969.

398 Food service workers. Posvar Papers, FF 7.3.2, Posvar to University community, March 24, 1969.

399 Students brandished lists of demands already agreed on. Posvar interviews; Chancellor's Report to Trustees, 1970, p. 3.

399 Pitt and the *Scranton Report.* Kobosky interview,

November 14, 1983; Posvar Papers, FF 8.4, Pitt news release, September 28, 1970.

399 Top administrator on Quaker leadership. Freeman interview.

399 Pitt SDS changed name. *Pittsburgh Press*, October 5, 1969.

400 Like trying to kick a mastodon. Minute meeting, October 12, 1972.

Chapter Thirty-three. 1976: The Turning Point

402 Posvar: "Great budgets and euphoria." Quoted in the *Wall Street Journal*, May 18, 1976.

402 Grants received. "The University of Pittsburgh 1976–1990," 2; Posvar Papers, FF 4.4 (1976), "The Quest for Quality"; Posvar to Chicago Pitt Club, September 3, 1976; Chancellor's Report to Trustees, November 19, 1976.

402 1976 "a turning point." *University Times*, September 9, 1976, June 16, 1977; *Pitt*, August 1977; Chancellor's Fifth Annual Report to Trustees, June 1972; chancellor Posvar to new faculty, September 15, 1976; minute of trustees' meeting, June 21, 1972.

403 Discussions with community residents. *Pitt*, Winter 1971–72, p. 31.

403 Abramovitz back. Posvar interview.

403 School of Engineering. Fitterer, *The School of Engineering*, pp. 3, 4; Kurtzman Papers, FF 86, H. E. Hoelscher, "The School of Engineering: An Overview," undated; *Pitt*, "The Engineer and Society," March 1985; Report to the MSA, November 1980, pp. 95–108.

407 Abramovitz limited height of Forbes Quadrangle. Rankin interview.

408 Meadowcroft. Adovasio and Carlisle, presentation to trustees, May 12, 1982; Adovasio and Carlisle, *Scientific American;* Adovasio lecture to HSWP, April 7, 1976; *University Times*, August 7, 1975, April 1, 1976, November 3, 1977, February 9, 1978, July 5, 1979; *We Chart the Future*, 43; Pitt news releases, July 25, 1975, May 19, 1977; *Pittsburgh Post-Gazette*, November 19, 1984; *Pitt*, August 1981.

410 Must face reality. Chancellor's Fifth Annual Report to Trustees, 1972; minute of trustees' planning meeting, June 21, 1972.

410 Demographic crisis. University Planning Policies for the 1980s, pp. 1–4, 12, 27, 29; *We Chart the Future*, 60.

410 The planning budget and control system. Posvar to new faculty, September 15, 1976; Posvar to State of the University Luncheon, May 18, 1977; *We Chart the Future*, 7; "The University of Pittsburgh, 1776–1990," September 1976; Pitt news releases, November 29, 1984, June 18, 1985.

411 Deans more optimistic. Posvar Papers, FF 4.4.2 (1977), Freeman to Posvar, March 29, 1977.

412 Humble views on planning. *We Chart the Future*, 8, 11, 12.

413 Rea on budget. Rea interview.

413 Concern over part-time faculty. Jane Flanders, *University Times*, November 14, 1974, November 13, 1975, February 17, 1977, October 2, 1980.

415 The battle over curriculum. Posvar Papers, FF 1.4.1 (1976), Robert Marshall to Posvar, July 27, 1976, "An Accounting of My Stewardship"; ibid., FF 1.4.1 (1977), Steele Gow and Robert Marshall, "Restructuring Undergraduate Education," March 17, 1977; *University Times*, February 5, 1970, January 6, 1977, December 15, 1977, January 12, 1978, September 7, 1978, April 9, 1981; *Pitt News*, December 3, 1969, February 7, 1970; *Pittsburgh Press*, February 2, 1970.

415 Students and Dean Kehl. *Pitt News*, February 19, 1969.

416 "It didn't happen." Irwin Schulman, quoted by Stein, *Pittsburgh* magazine, February 1982, p. 78.

417 Survey of 700 graduates. Ibid.

417 Honors Program. Posvar Papers, FF 2.10, minutes of trustees' meetings, with chancellor's remarks, April 17, 1975, May 18, 1976; FF 3.1.11 (1976), minute of Academic Affairs Council meeting, October 21, 1976; FF 5.1.10, October 21, 1976; FF 2.10 (1982), Posvar to College and University Personnel Association, October 11, 1982; C. Alec Stewart to Dear Colleague, Honors Program memorandum, September 9, 1977; *Where Do Bright, Concerned Students Go?*, an undated 24-page pamphlet; minute of Senate Council meeting, March 24, 1977; *We Chart the Future*, 19; Report to the MSA, November 1980, pp. 27–31, 219; *Pitt*, August 1980; *University Times*, February 17, March 17, November 3, 1977, July 6, 1978, May 20, 1982.

418 Wolke, faculty development. *University Times*, March 9, 1978, May 10, 1979, October 2, 1980, October 20, 1983, February 9, 1984; Report to the MSA, November 1980, p. 192; Posvar Papers, FF 7.17 (1980), "See Yourself Teach," November 1980.

419 Evaluation of teaching. Minutes of Senate Council meetings, October 13, December 13, 1976, February 14, 1977; "Report on the Evaluation of Teaching," Paul Beck, chairman, September 1976.

Chapter Thirty-four. The Precisely Measurable Triumph

420 Epigraph: Posvar. O'Brien, *Hail to Pitt*, 5.

421 Enclave in California. The University of Southern California, which was rated second and thought it should be first.

421 One of the most dramatic comebacks. O'Brien, *Hail to Pitt*, 163, quoting Russ Franke of the *Pittsburgh Press*.

421 Billick: "We had real problems." Conversation with the author.

421 Posvar on merits of athletic programs. O'Brien, *Hail to Pitt*, 5.

421 "What other university activity?" Letter to author from Edward Bozik, May 8, 1985.

421 Blue-chip committee. Author's interviews with Posvar and Edward Bozik. Letter to author from Dean Billick, May 3, 1985.

421 Posvar made a commitment. Ibid.

422 Withdrew from Big Four. Author's interview with Edward Bozik.

422 Majors sent brother Joe. *Time*, December 2, 1974.

422 Panther Foundation, $250,000 gift. Posvar Papers, FF 2.2 (1973), Posvar to directors of the Panther Foundation (Bellefield Trust), undated; C. R. Wilson, president, to Posvar, August 15, 1973; Posvar to Wilson, August 27, 1973.

422 Work on athletic facilities. *Pittsburgh Press*, April 9, August 21, 1973, April 20, 1983; *Time*, December 2, 1974; Department of Athletics, Board of Visitors, October 1, 1982.

422 Golden Panthers. *Pitt News*, March 19, 1982, January 1, 1983; Department of Athletics, Board of Visitors, October 1, 1982.

423 78 football scholarships. Letter to author from Edward Bozik, May 8, 1985.

423 Office of Support Services. *Pitt News*, April 3, 1985; *University Times*, April 4, 1985.

423 Majors' recruiting effort. *Pittsburgh Press*, August 21, 1973; *New York Times*, October 28, 1973.

423 Michael Zernich. Interview with Edward Bozik.

423 Season ticket sales rose. Author's conversation with Dean Billick.

423 Athletic Department broke even. Ibid.

423 "Greatest freshman." *New York Times*, January 2, 1977.

423 Posvar at Chicago Pitt Club. Posvar Papers, 5.1.10 (1976), September 3, 1976.

426 Gave jersey to Dr. Zernich. Bozik interview.

426 Displayed four trophies. Pitt news release, March 11, 1977.

426 $100,000 to libraries. *University Times*, January 20, 1977; *Pittsburgh Post-Gazette*, November 22, 1976.

426 *New York Times* said Pitt was number one. *Pittsburgh Press*, January 6, 1981.

426 Mark May gave $10,000. *Pittsburgh Press*, September 13, 1981; *Pittsburgh Post-Gazette*, September 23, 1981.

426 Spent more than $10 million. Letter to author from Edward Bozik, May 8, 1985.

427 Senate Athletic Committee Report. *University Times*, April 4, 1985.

Chapter Thirty-five. The Future of Academic Medicine

429 Epigraph. Interview with Barbara I. Paull, April 28, 1980.

430 Ogden Edwards in 1918. McCormick Papers, Edwards to McCormick, January 1918.

431 Cheever recalled conflict. Interview with Elaine Rudov, September 22, 1975. Archives, Falk Library.

432 Cheever on lack of progress. *Pitt*, Spring-Summer 1974.

432 Reorganization of the Health Center. Pitt news release, March 29, 1983; minute of Executive Committee meetings, March 16, April 12, 1983; Posvar, memorandum to his staff, March 8, 1983;

Pittsburgh Post-Gazette, March 31, April 6, 1983; *Pittsburgh Press,* March 31, 1983; *University Times,* April 7, 1983; *Pitt News,* July 11, 1984.

432 "Impossible dream." *Pittsburgh Post-Gazette,* April 6, 1983.

432 WPIC and Thomas Detre. Marcia Kramer Schachner, *Western Psychiatric Institute and Clinic of the University of Pittsburgh: Its Years of Research, Teaching, and Service,* 1984, pp. 305–06, 312, 319–20, 324, 354, 392, 433, 450–59; *Pittsburgh Post-Gazette,* October 7, 1982, November 6, 1984; *University Times,* November 8, 1984.

433 Had to add $2 to $3 million. *University Times,* January 12, 1984.

434 Bernard Fisher and NSABP. Reports by Gerhard Werner and Fisher to the Board of Trustees, January 13, 1976; *University Times,* March 8, May 3, June 14, July 12, 1984; *Pitt News,* March 9, July 11, 1984; *Newsweek,* July 13, 1981; *We Chart the Future,* 53; *Pittsburgh Post-Gazette,* March 14, 1985; *Pitt,* May 1984, pp. 1–2; *Time,* May 25, 1985.

434 Organ transplants. *Newsweek,* March 30, 1981, January 11, December 13, 1982; *Life,* September 1982; *Pittsburgh Post-Gazette,* March 11, September 24, 1982, December 20, 1983, February 16, April 23, April 25, 1984, May 30, 1985; *Pittsburgh Press,* January 3, June 30, 1982, March 11, 1984, May 5, May 30, July 14, 1985; *University Times,* October 20, 1983, June 28, 1984; *We Chart the Future,* 17–18.

436 Stormie Jones a heroine. See *Pittsburgh Post-Gazette,* February 16, 17, 1984.

436 Posvar: "Must cross internal boundaries." *We Chart the Future,* 8.

436 Caduceus. Pitt news release, November 30, 1982; minute of trustees' meeting, February 17, 1983, presentation by Myers and Pople; *We Chart the Future,* 8, 36; *Medical Economics,* November 22, 1982, p. 143; Henry W. Pierce, *Pittsburgh Post-Gazette,* December 30, 1985.

437 Nuclear Magnetic Resonance Institute. *University Times,* December 15, 1983, January 12, May 31, July 26, 1984; Henry W. Pierce, *Pittsburgh Post-Gazette,* May 23, 1984; *Pittsburgh Press,* June 26, 1983, March 11, 1984.

437 Pittsburgh Cancer Institute. *Pitt,* May 1984; *Pitt News,* March 9, 1984; *University Times,* March 8, May 3, 1984; *Pittsburgh Press,* June 25, 1985.

438 Geriatrics program. *University Times,* October 30, 1980; *Pittsburgh Press,* October 13, 1981; *Pitt News,* October 3, 1983; *Pittsburgh Post-Gazette,* October 3, October 8, 1985; Pitt news release, October 7, 1985.

Chapter Thirty-six. The Campus of the Future

440 *The $100,000,000 Gift.* University news release, March 29, 1985; *University Times,* April 4, 1985; *Pittsburgh Press,* April 1, 1985; *Pittsburgh Post-Gazette,* August 12, 1985; other continuing articles and news stories.

441 UPARC. University news release, April 1, 1985.

441 Posvar on technology transfer. *Pittsburgh Post-Gazette,* August 12, 1985.

441 *The Campus of the Future. Focus,* AT&T Information Systems magazine, March 1984; University news release, December 14, 1983; *Pittsburgh Press,* December 15, 1983; Posvar, "Campus of the Future Is Here Today," *Technotimes,* February 1985; Posvar speech at Hilton Head, S.C., November 18, 1984; *Pitt News,* January 20, 1984; *Pitt,* February 1984; *University Times,* December 15, 1983, February 9, March 8, June 14, 1984.

442 *New Ideas and Relationships. University Times,* October 2, 1982, February 24, June 2, 1983, April 19, 1984; University news releases, October 21, 1982, February 17, 1983; *Pitt News,* October 25, 1982; *We Chart the Future,* 25; minute of trustees' meeting, February 17, 1983; *Pitt,* August 1984.

442 Super computing center. University news release, January 17, 1986.

442 *The Institutional Self-Examination.* Posvar, *The University Plan,* June 18, 1985; Office of the Chancellor, University Long-Range Planning Policies (1985); Institutional Overview and Description of Process (1984); Benjamin, *Pitt,* November 1983; *University Times,* December 1, 1983, March 8, April 5, May 31, 1984.

443 *An American in Cuba.* University news release, June 4, 1985.

443 Posvar: "Incorporate internationalism." *Christian Science Monitor,* May 30, 1985.

445 "A national/international university." *The University Plan,* 37.

445 "Intellectuals cannot predict." *Report from the Chancellor,* Fall, 1983, p. 11.

Bibliography

The place to begin, of course, is the Hillman Library. Its University Archives and Special Collections contain an awesome store of bibliographic material on the Pittsburgh Academy (1787–1819), the Western University of Pennsylvania (1819–1907), and the University of Pittsburgh (1907– —). On their 2,498 linear feet of shelves there are, for example: seventy-nine volumes of press clippings on University people and affairs for 1904–1918; Board of Trustees minutes from 1845; chancellors' reports to the trustees; college, division, and department files; College bulletins and catalogues; directories, University pamphlets, brochures, and booklets; and files on students, faculty, administrators, and alumni—all admirably organized, catalogued, and retrievable.

There are 2 document boxes of Chancellor Holland's papers; 5 boxes of Chancellor McCormick's; 21 of John Bowman's; 61 of Rufus Fitzgerald's; 155 of Edward Litchfield's; 45 of David Kurtzman's; and 223 of Wesley Posvar's through the school years 1975–1976. All have been mined for this history. Working to master this material is, in the words of the U.S. Army recruiters, not a job but an adventure.

The other main source of information for this history has been the author's personal interviews with thirty-six persons who made University history, or attentively watched it being made, or both. These were in-depth interviews; most of them were recorded on tape; and they are all now part of the Archives. I started the interviews in March 1981, and for reasons that must be apparent I began with the oldest subjects. The names follow. The position given is the one for which the person was or is best known—not necessarily the position at the time of the interview.

Charles F. Arensberg, University counsel, interviewed on March 12, 1982.

*Robert Bailie, administrative assistant to four chancellors, May 13, 1971.

William W. Booth, trustee, April 28, 1981.

Edward E. Bozik, athletic director, May 13, 1985.

*Edgar Cale, administrative fund raiser, September 14, 1981.

*Frank Carver, athletic director, July 1, 1981, followed by continuing correspondence and conferences.

* Deceased.

Daniel Cheever, professor of international affairs, January 25, 1982.

*Frank Denton, trustee, September 7, 1981.

Walter Evert, professor of English, July 10, 1981.

Leon Falk, Jr., trustee, October 20, 1981.

George Fetterman, officer of the Panther Foundation, November 16, 1981.

Jack E. Freeman, senior vice chancellor, June 6, 1985.

John Funari, when dean of GSPIA, November 2, 1982.

*Walter Hovey, formerly director of the Department of Fine Arts, April 7, 1981.

Lawrence Irwin, founding director of the University of Pittsburgh Press, April 16, 1981.

*Putnam F. Jones, former dean of the faculty, October 29, 1982.

James Kehl, professor of history, February 29, 1984.

*Carlton G. Ketchum, director of the University's fund raising after 1923 and member of various athletic committees, March 10, 1981. Interviews, conferences, and correspondence continued until his death in July 1984.

James W. Knox, chairman of Nationality Room activities, December 9, 1981.

Celia Kurtzman, widow of Chancellor David Kurtzman, May 8, 1981.

*Abe Laufe, professor of English, October 20, 1982.

*Ruth Crawford Mitchell, founding director of the Nationality Room program, March 5 and 16, 1981.

Edison Montgomery, administrator in charge of many University departments, often as a trouble-shooter, April 23, 1981, followed by conferences and continuing correspondence.

Charles Peake, vice chancellor, May 27, 1981, followed by correspondence.

Wesley W. Posvar, chancellor, later president, August 8, 1983, and April 27, 1985.

*Gwilym Price, president of Board of Trustees, August 4, 1981, followed by correspondence.

Alan Rankin, vice chancellor, January 23, 24, 25, 1984.

William Rea, president of trustees, November 23, 1981.

*Walter Rome, trustee, May 12, 1981.

Helen Pool Rush, vice chancellor, March 19, 1981.

Adolph Schmidt, director of the A. W. Mellon Educational and Charitable Trust, June 15, 1984.

Agnes Starrett, director of the University of Pittsburgh Press, March 19, 1981.

C. V. Starrett, editor of the University Record, officer of the Buhl Foundation, March 19, 1981.

William Tacey, professor of speech and secretary of the Pittsburgh chapter of the AAUP, July 16, 1981.

Albert C. Van Dusen, vice chancellor, March 5, 1982.

Reginald Wilson, officer of the Panther Foundation, November 16, 1981.

Seven of these persons had been interviewed in the early 1970s by the Pittsburgh Renaissance project: The Stanton Belfour Oral History Program. They were Frank Denton, Edison Montgomery, Gwilym Price, Helen Pool Rush, Agnes Starrett, C. V. Starrett, and A. C. Van Dusen.

John Geise, professor of history, was interviewed by Helen Knox in 1972; a tape was made available to the author.

The William Holland Papers at the Historical Society of Western Pennsylvania are a valuable source of information not only about the University in the years 1890–1900 but also about the social history of Pittsburgh in that decade.

Printed Material

"Academic Freedom and Tenure at the University of Pittsburgh." American Association of University Professors *Bulletin*, December 18, 1935.

Adovasio, J. M., and Carlisle, R. C. "The Archeology of the Eastern United States: A View from the University of Pittsburgh." A presentation to the Board of Trustees, May 12, 1982.

———. "An Indian Hunters' Camp for 20,000 Years." *Scientific American*, May 1984.

Alberts, Robert C. *The Good Provider: H. J. Heinz and His 57 Varieties.* Boston: Houghton Mifflin, 1973.

———. "Business of the Highest Magnitude." *American Heritage*, February 1971.

———. "Profile of a Soldier: Matthew B. Ridgway." *American Heritage*, February 1976.

———. "Ten Years After." *Pitt*, Spring 1941.

Albo, Samuel V. "Sidelights on University History." *University Record*, October 1926.

Alumni Directory, University of Pittsburgh, 1787-1910. (Issued by the General Alumni Association.)

American Men and Women of Science. Multiple volumes in fifteen editions to 1982. New York: Bowker.

Anderson, Edward Park. "The Intellectual Life of Pittsburgh, 1786–1836." *Western Pennsylvania Historical Magazine,* January, April, July, October 1931.

Andrews, J. Cutler. *Pittsburgh's Post-Gazette.* Boston. Chapman and Grimes, 1936.

———. "The Civil War." In Stefan Lorant's *Pittsburgh: The Story of an American City.*

Apone, Carl. "Liberal Arts Under Fire." *Pittsburgh Press,* August 18, 19, 20, 1974.

Arensberg, C. F. C. "From My Time at the Bar." *Pittsburgh Legal Journal,* October 1, 1976.

Arensberg, Charles C. "Hugh Henry Brackenridge." In *Famous Men and Women of Pittsburgh.*

Arnold, Charles, ed. *The University and the War. University of Pittsburgh Bulletin,* vol. 14, July 1, 1918.

At Ease. A weekly newspaper produced by the Air Crew Cadets of the 60th College Training Detachment, University of Pittsburgh. Forty-six issues, April 30, 1943 through March 24, 1944. University Archives.

Auerbach, Stuart. "Ice Age Man Trod Pennsylvania Area." *Washington Post,* August 5, 1974, p. 1.

Avinoff, Andrey, and Jennings, Otto Emery. *Wildflowers of Western Pennsylvania and the Upper Ohio Basin.* vol. 1, text (Jennings), vol. 2, illustrations (Avinoff). Pittsburgh: University of Pittsburgh Press, 1953.

Baldwin, Leland D. *Pittsburgh: The Story of a City.* Pittsburgh: University of Pittsburgh Press, 1937.

Balta, George A. *The Cathedral of Learning: A Statement of Architectural, Educational and Social-Humanitarian Significance.* Unpublished manuscript submitted with an application for National Landmark Status, 1976. University Archives, Group No. 13/3/3, FF 1.

Barron's Profiles of American Colleges. Woodstock, N.Y.: Barron's Educational Series, 1964–.

Barzun, Jacques. *The American University: How It Runs, Where It Is Going.* New York: Harper & Row, 1968.

Barzun, Jacques, and Graff, Henry F. *The Modern Researcher.* 4th ed. San Diego: Harcourt, Brace, 1985.

Baynham, Edward Gladstone. "The Founding of the University of Pittsburgh." Master's thesis, University of Pittsburgh, 1935.

Beardsley, Wallace R. "The Allegheny Observatory During the Era of the Telescope Association,

1859–1867." *Western Pennsylvania Historical Magazine,* July 1981.

———. "Samuel Pierpont Langley." In *Famous Men and Women of Pittsburgh.*

———. "Samuel Pierpont Langley: 'Early Conflict' Between Teaching and Research at the Western University of Pennsylvania." *Western Pennsylvania Historical Magazine,* October 1981.

Bedingfield, Robert E. "Personality: He'd Make a Beaver Look Lazy." *New York Times,* July 21, 1957. (On Litchfield.)

Benedek, Susan. "Posvar Presents Broad View of University." *Pitt News,* April 10, 1985. (An interview with Chancellor Posvar on twenty years of state-relatedness.)

Biederman, Les. "Jock Sutherland: Pride in Perfection." *Pittsburgh Sunday Press,* October 27, 1974.

"Blacklist." *Newsweek,* January 11, 1936.

Blasier, Cole. "The Curious Origins of Latin America Studies at Pitt." *Pitt,* May 1975.

Blockstein, Zaga. *Graduate School of Public Health, University of Pittsburgh, 1948–1974.* Pittsburgh: Blockstein, 1977.

Board of Trustees, University of Pittsburgh. *By-Laws.* As adopted January 14, 1969, and amended through May 14, 1980.

Bowman, John Gabbert. *The Cathedral of Learning of the University of Pittsburgh.* Pittsburgh, February 1925.

———. *Inside the Cathedral.* Pittsburgh, October 1925.

———. *Notes Along the Way.* Illustrations by Theodore Bowman. Pittsburgh: Eddy Press, 1939. Privately printed, 150 copies.

———. *Unofficial Notes.* Pittsburgh: Davis and Warde, 1963. Privately printed, 450 copies.

———. *Within the Cathedral of Learning.* 1930. 23 pp. Foreword by Ruth Crawford Mitchell.

———. *The World That Was.* New York: Macmillan, 1926.

———. "A Cathedral of the Spirit of Achievement." Undated manuscript, University Archives.

———. "In Brief Review." Undated manuscript, University Archives.

———. "Notes About A. W. Mellon." Undated manuscript, University Archives, 32 pp.

———. "Pittsburgh's Contribution to Civilization." In

Pittsburgh and the Pittsburgh Spirit—Addresses at the Chamber of Commerce of Pittsburgh, 1927–1928. Pittsburgh, 1928.

———. "A Singer to Pioneers." *Atlantic Monthly,* July 1935.

———. Notarized affidavit containing sixteen statements. November 10, 1939. University Archives, 7 pp.

———. Speech delivered at dedication dinner, Cathedral of Learning, March 8, 1955. University Archives.

Brashear, John A. *The Autobiography of a Man Who Loved the Stars.* Edited by W. Lucien Scaife. New York: American Society of Mechanical Engineers, 1924.

Brief Submitted by the University of Pittsburgh to the Committee of the House of Representatives, May 18, 1935.

Brown, Mark McCullough. *The Cathedral of Learning 1921–1926: A History of an Architectural Design for the University of Pittsburgh.* Master's thesis, State University of New York at Binghamton, 1983. Copy in Hillman Library.

Brown, Nancy J. "Creating a Top-ranked Program: Many Consider Pitt the Place to Be for Philosophers." *University Times,* January 27, 1983.

Bruhns, E. Maxine. *The Nationality Rooms.* Undated manuscript with color illustrations, University Archives, 56 pp.

———. "Pitt's Nationality Rooms . . . That University Curriculum." *Pitt,* Summer 1973.

Buck, Elizabeth Hawthorne. "Early Literary Culture in Western Pennsylvania." *University Record,* Autumn, 1935.

Buck, Solon J. "Interpreting Pittsburgh Through Its Past." *University Record,* January–February, 1933.

Buck, Solon J. and Buck, Elizabeth Hawthorne. *The Planting of Civilization in Western Pennsylvania.* Illustrations by Clarence McWilliams. Pittsburgh: University of Pittsburgh Press, 1939.

Budget and Audit Committee, Frank Denton, chairman. "Report to the Chairman of the Board of Trustees." October 25, 1966.

Building Program [of the] *University of Pittsburgh.* January 12, 1960, 75 pp.

Burger, Mary Lou. "Reflections of a Scientist-Philosopher." *University Times,* January 11, 1979. (On Adolf Grunbaum.)

Carlin, Margie. "Life with the Litchfields . . . Down on the Farm." *Pittsburgh Post-Gazette Sunday Magazine,* December 4, 1960.

Carroll, Holbert. *A Study of the Governance of the University of Pittsburgh.* University of Pittsburgh, 1973.

Carter, Richard. *Breakthrough: The Saga of Jonas Salk.* New York: Trident Press, 1966.

Chute, Eleanor. "What Helps Child Learn to Learn? Scientists Ask." *Pittsburgh Press,* July 31, 1983.

"The City-Renaissance, Phase 2." *Time,* June 21, 1963. (On the Panther Hollow project.)

Clemmens, Daryl. "An Interview with Chancellor Posvar." University Archives. Undated draft of an interview, 3 pp.

"Closing in on Polio." *Time,* March 29, 1954. (Cover story on Jonas Salk.)

Colangelo, Joseph G., Jr. "The Colodny Case." A Pitt news release and policy statement, June 20, 1961.

———. "The Making of a Chancellor, 1967." *Pitt,* Winter 1967.

———. "The Precarious Angel." *Pitt,* Spring 1973. (On tenure and the Turner case.)

———. "A Third Kind of University." *Pitt,* Fall 1968.

———. "Who's in Charge Here?" *Pitt,* Fall, 1970.

"College of Arts and Sciences—Committee on Curriculum Reform—Report to Faculty." September 24, 1981, 8 pp.

Colodny, Robert Garland. *Spain: The Glory and the Tragedy.* New York: Humanities Press, 1970.

Cope, Myron. "King Edward of Pitt." *Saturday Evening Post,* April 6, 1963.

Covert, Cathy. "Reporters Sizzling over Polio Chaos." *Editor and Publisher,* April 16, 1955.

Crabtree, Frederick H. "Underneath the Cathedral." *University Record,* December 1928.

Cramer, Zadok. *Magazine Almanac.* Published annually under various titles from about 1801 to 1819.

———. *The Navigator; Containing Directions for Navigating the Monongahela, Allegheny, Ohio, and Mississippi Rivers, with an Ample Account of these Much-Admired Waters, from the Head of the Former to the Mouth of the Latter, and a Concise Description of Their Towns, Villages, Harbors, Settlements, etc., with Maps of the Ohio and Mississippi, to Which Is Added an Appendix, Containing an Account of Louisiana, and of the Missouri and Columbia Rivers Discovered by the Voyage Under Capts. Lewis and*

Clark. Eighth Edition—Improved and Enlarged. Pittsburgh: Cramer, Spear and Eichbaum, 1814.

Crawford, Stanton C. "A University-Wide Program of Faculty Development." *Educational Record,* January 1961.

Crawmer, Michael S. "Part-Time at Pitt: Teachers of Convenience for Departments in Need." *University Times,* October 2, 1980.

Cresap, McCormick and Paget. *Survey of Administrative Management, University of Pittsburgh.* 2 vols. 1954.

Crozier, Lucille B. "The Early History of the School of Medicine of the University of Pittsburgh." Unpublished manuscript, 1976, Historical Society of Western Pennsylvania Archives, 56 pp.

Current Biography, July 1947, "Woltman, Frederick."

Dahlinger, Charles W. *Pittsburgh: A Sketch of Its Early Social Life.* New York and London: G. P. Putnam, 1916

Daniel, Jack L., and Harris-Schenz, Beverly. "Black Student Access and Success at the University of Pittsburgh." Prepared for the 1984 Johnstown Conference.

Daskir, M., and Strauss, William A. *Chance and Circumstance: The Draft, the War, and the Vietnam Generation.* New York: Knopf, 1978.

Daubert, B. D. "Alumni Hall." *Pitt,* Spring 1951.

Davis, H. B. "Academic Freedom in Pittsburgh." *New Republic,* May 22, 1929.

Deland, Margaret Wade. *If This Be I, as I Suppose It Be.* New York: Appleton-Century, 1935.

Dictionary of American Biography. Edited by Allen Johnson and Dumas Malone. New York: Scribners, 1928. Hugh Henry Brackenridge, John Brashear, Robert Bruce, Reginald Fessenden, William Holland, Samuel Langley, Samuel McCormick, William Thaw, Andrew W. Mellon.

Dresher, Ruth. "Pitt Women Demand Their Rights." *The Point,* May 28, 1970, p. 2.

Dyer, Heman. *Records of an Active Life.* New York: Thomas Whittaker, 1886.

"Dynamo at Pitt." *Time,* January 7, 1957. (On Edward Litchfield.)

"The Engineer and Society." *Pitt,* March 1975, 38 pp.

"Ethnic Groups Invest Time, Money in Nationality Rooms." *University Times,* December 13, 1979.

Fact Book—University of Pittsburgh. Published annually in September by Management Information and Policy Analysis.

Famous Men and Women of Pittsburgh. Edited by Leonore R. Elkus. Pittsburgh History and Landmarks Foundation, 1981.

Faulkner, Harold U. *American Economic History.* New York: Harper and Brothers, 1924.

Ferguson, Russell J. *Early Western Pennsylvania Politics.* Pittsburgh: University of Pittsburgh Press, 1938.

Fessenden, Helen May. *Fessenden: Builder of Tomorrow.* New York: Coward-McCann, 1940.

"Fifty-two-Story Building Proposed for Pitt on Old Frick Estate." *Pittsburgh Post,* November 7, 1924.

Fitterer, G. Raymond. *Past: The School of Engineering.* Address given at the dedication of the Michael Benedum Hall of Engineering, 1971, 40 pp.

Fitzgerald, Rufus H. "The War Program of the University of Pittsburgh." *Alumni Review,* March 1943.

Flanders, Jane T. "The Problem That Won't Go Away in the English Department." *University Times,* November 14, 1974.

———. "The Part-Time Employment Situation in the English Department, Up-Date 1975." *University Times,* November 3, 1975.

———. "Caste System at Pitt." *University Times,* February 17, 1977.

Forbes, Karen A., and Konnelyn, Teig. *Kinder, Kirche, Küche—Women's Education and Employment in Higher Education: The Comprehensive Report of the Provost's Task Force of the Advisory Council on Women's Opportunities.* 1971, 49 pp.

Frost, Richard H. *The Mooney Case.* Stanford: Stanford University Press, 1968.

"G. G. Proves Itself." *Time,* November 3, 1952. (On the polio research work by Dr. William D. Hammon.)

Gigler, Rich. "Revisiting the Schenley." *Pittsburgh Press Roto,* April 18, 1982.

Giovengo, Annette. "The Hungerford Collection." *Western Pennsylvania Historical Magazine,* April 1983.

(Gow Report) "Report of Special Committee of University of Pittsburgh Trustees, Final Report." University Archives, 49 pp. (Transcriptions of confidential interviews with forty-three persons.)

Graham, Robert X. "Stephen Collins Foster Dedication." *Greater Pittsburgh,* May 1937.

Grattan, C. Hartley. "The Fight for Academic Freedom." *Survey Graphic*, March 1936.

A Greater Pittsburgh Needs a Greater University. Brochure by the Planning and Development Committee, 1947, 16 pp. (Shows buildings needed and intended for the Cathedral campus.)

Greenberg, D. S. "Pittsburgh: The Rocky Road to Academic Excellence." *Science*, February 4, 11, 18, 1966.

A Guide to the Heinz Memorial Chapel, University of Pittsburgh. Pittsburgh: University of Pittsburgh Press, 1938.

Gwinn, Sherman. "John Bowman's Fifty-Story Dream." *American Magazine*, May 1928.

Harpster, John W., ed. *Pen Pictures of Early Western Pennsylvania.* Pittsburgh: University of Pittsburgh Press, 1938.

Harris, Jonathan; Ogul, Morris S.; and Schulman, Irwin J. "Improving Our Student Body." *University Times*, January 6, 1977.

Hechinger, Fred M. "Pitt: A Case History in Cost of Excellence." *New York Times*, January 23, 1966.

Heimbucher, Ruth. "Founder of Nationality Rooms Will Be Honored Today by Pitt." *Christian Science Monitor*, October 4, 1930.

Heinz, Howard. "The Chapel's Purpose." *Alumni Review*, December 1938. (An address of presentation.)

"The Heinz Memorial Chapel." *Pitt*, July 1961.

"The Heinz Memorial Chapel." *University Record*, December 1929.

"Heinz Memorial Chapel Dedicated as Gift to Pitt." *Pittsburgh Post-Gazette*, November 21, 1938.

The Heinz Memorial Chapel—A Descriptive Guide. 1940, 44 pp.

The Heinz Memorial Chapel at the University of Pittsburgh. Pittsburgh, Herbick and Held. Undated guidebook, colored illustrations, 40 pp.

Hersey, John. *Letter to the Alumni.* New York: Knopf, 1970.

Hersh, Burton. *The Mellon Family.* New York: Morrow, 1978.

Herward, Maureen M. "Academy to University." Unpublished manuscript, 1981, University Archives, 200 pp.

Hetzel, Frederick A. "What Is a University Press?" *Pitt*, Spring 1966.

Hetzel, Frederick A., and Hitchens, Harold L. "An Interview with General Matthew B. Ridgway." *Western Pennsylvania Historical Magazine*, October 1982.

Hockensmith, Wilbur D. "The Good Old Days." *Alumni Review*, October 1935.

Hodges, Fletcher, Jr. "A Pittsburgh Composer and His Memorial." *Western Pennsylvania Historical Magazine*, June 1938.

———. "The Research Work of the Foster Hall Collection." *Pennsylvania History*, July 1948.

———. "Stephen Foster." In *Famous Men and Women of Pittsburgh.*

Holsopple, Barbara. "Women on Pitt's Faculty Contend: Our Colleges Are Fit to Be Tied." *Pittsburgh Press*, December 19, 1971.

Hornblower, Margot. "Pittsburgh's Past Competes with a New Image." *Washington Post*, December 17, 1984. (Interview with Wesley W. Posvar.)

Howes, Raymond F. *Low Point at Pitt: A Study of the Loss of Academic Integrity.* Riverside, Calif.: privately printed, 1972.

Hudson, Jesse T. "Statement of Events and Circumstances at the University of Pittsburgh from October 1959 to July 1965." September 1966, 6 pp.

Huggins, R. R. *Address to the Class of 1930.* Pittsburgh, 1930. Privately printed pamphlet.

———. *On Sentry Duty.* Pittsburgh, 1927. Privately printed pamphlet.

———. *Peculiar Problems Facing Industrial Medicine.* Pittsburgh, 1927. Privately printed pamphlet.

———. *Peering Ahead in Medicine.* Pittsburgh, 1927. Privately printed pamphlet.

———. *The Relationship of the Pittsburgh School of Medicine to the Medical Profession of the Community.* Pittsburgh, 1920. Privately printed pamphlet.

The Impact of the University of Pittsburgh on the Local Economy. Educational Systems Research Group, 1972.

"The Impossible Job: A Special Report on What It Takes to Run a College These Days." *Alumni Times*, Spring 1976.

Innes, Lowell. *Pittsburgh Glass, 1797–1891.* Boston: Houghton Mifflin, 1976.

Jameson, Storm. *Journey from the North. Autobiography of.* 2 vols. London: Collins, Harville, 1969.

Jennings, Otto Emery. See Avinoff, Andrey.

Johnston, William G. *Life and Reminiscences.* Pittsburgh, 1901. Privately printed.

Keffer, Karl. "The 125th Anniversary Celebration of the University of Pittsburgh." *Pittsburgh Dispatch,* February 4, 1912.

Kennedy, Matthew. "Chancellor Posvar." Posvar Papers, FF 5.1.6 (1976). A 30-page unpublished profile, January 1976.

Kenniston, Kenneth, and Lerner, Michael. "The Unholy Alliance Against the Campus." *New York Times Magazine,* November 8, 1970.

Ketchum, Carlton G. "Pitt: The Adolescent Years, 1908–1928." *Western Pennsylvania Historical Magazine,* April 1971.

————. "Some Interesting Pittsburghers, 1911–1941." *Western Pennsylvania Historical Magazine,* January, April 1982.

"Klauder, Charles Zeller." *Architectural Forum,* January 1939.

Knox, Helen. "The Chancellor's Lady Sings." *Pitt,* Spring 1968.

————. "From Odessa to Emeritus with Love." *Pitt,* Spring 1967.

————. "Pitt: A Search for Excellence." Pitt Information Services release, 1962.

————. "Profile: Stanton Chapman Crawford." *Pitt,* Fall 1965.

————. "The 2,000 Best." *Pitt,* Winter 1967.

Kodinsky, Harry. "Dr. Bowman Bids for Support— Chancellor Meets Students at Weekly Teas." *Pittsburgh Post-Gazette,* November 6, 1939.

La Cossitt, Henry. "$100,000,000 to Work With." *Saturday Evening Post,* June 9, 1956.

Lauffer, Max A. "Western Pennsylvania's Contributions to the Age of Science." *Western Pennsylvania Historical Magazine,* October 1977.

Linhart, Samuel B. "The Crucial Period in University History." *University Record,* June–July, 1933.

Litchfield, Edward H. *Report on Higher Education in the Soviet Union.* Pittsburgh: University of Pittsburgh Press, 1958.

————. "Colleges Can Operate All Year." *Saturday Review of Literature,* December 15, 1962.

————. "New Dimensions of Learning in a Free Society." Litchfield's inauguration address. It is a chapter in a volume of that title containing twenty other seminar addresses and public lectures delivered on that occasion. Pittsburgh: University of Pittsburgh Press, 1957.

————. "Notes on a General Theory of Administration." *Administrative Science Quarterly,* June 1956.

————. "Pitt Aims at Greatness." *Pittsburgh Press Roto Magazine,* March 24, 1957.

————. "Toward Higher Ground: A Five Year Progress Report, 1957–1962." An address, September 17, 1962.

————. Letter to chairman of Board of Trustees clearing Robert Colodny. *Pittsburgh Post-Gazette,* June 14, 1961.

Litchfield, Edward H., and Cope, Myron. "Saturday's Hero Is Doing Fine." *Sports Illustrated,* October 8, 1962.

Lorant, Stefan. *Pittsburgh: The Story of an American City.* New York: Doubleday, 1964.

Lowenstein, Arlene. "The Falk Clinic at the University of Pittsburgh." Ph.D. dissertation, University of Pittsburgh, 1985. Hillman Library.

Lubove, Seth. "Charting a Course for the University." *Pitt News,* September 5, 1980.

————. "Posvar: Pitt's Chancellor 'Thriving' Under Pressure." *Pitt News,* August 29, 1980.

McCarten, John. "Daughter of Her Father." *New Yorker,* July 15, 22, 1939. (On Helen Clay Frick.)

McCormick, Samuel Black. "Brief History of the University of Pittsburgh." *University of Pittsburgh Bulletin,* vol. 1, 1910.

McFadden, Daniel H. *The Commonwealth and the University: A Descriptive Study of the University of Pittsburgh as a State-Related University.* Ph.D. dissertation, University of Pittsburgh, 1972.

MacLeod, Norman. "They Still Score Touchdowns." *Alumni Review,* November 1937.

Manchester, William. *The Glory and the Dream: A Narrative History of America 1932–1972.* Boston: Little, Brown, 1973.

Marcus, Caren. "Falk School: 50 Years Old and Learning." *Pittsburgh Press,* September 13, 1981.

Marder, Daniel. *Hugh Henry Brackenridge.* New York: Twayne, 1967.

————. *A Hugh Henry Brackenridge Reader, 1770–1815.* Pittsburgh: University of Pittsburgh Press, 1970.

Markess, Valerie. "Archeology—Multi-million Dollar

Investment in Salvaging Human History." *Pitt,* August 1981.

Marshall, Robert D. "The Pitt and the Pendulum." *University Times,* September 7, 1978. (On curriculum reform.)

———. "An Account of My Stewardship: Report to the Chancellor." July 27, 1976.

———. "A Defender of Open Curriculum Looks at Proposals." *Pitt News,* October 9, 1981.

Mellon, Thomas. *Selections from Thomas Mellon and His Times.* Edited by Matthew T. Mellon. Belfast, Northern Ireland: Stanhope House, 1970, boxed.

"A. W. Mellon—An Extraordinary Alumnus." *Alumni Times,* Autumn 1980.

"Andrew William Mellon, Most Distinguished Citizen of His City and Loyal Alumnus of the University of Pittsburgh." *Alumni Review,* September 1937. (Obituary article.)

"Mellons Help School to Obtain 14-Acre Tract in Education Center." *Pitt Weekly,* November 23, 1921.

Meyer, Debra. "Oakland Plan: After Almost Five Years, the Plan Has Helped to Forge Better Relations Between Institutions and Neighbors." *University Times,* October 25, 1984.

———. "A Profile of Pitt's New Provost." *University Times,* December 1, 1983. (On Roger Benjamin.)

Michener, James. *Sports in America.* New York: Random House, 1976.

Miller, Linda, and Dennis, Joni. "The Inside Story: Women at Pitt." *Pitt News,* November 11, 1981.

"Much Ado." Unsigned, undated, and unpublished manuscript on the Ralph Turner case, University Archives, 43 pp.

Mulkearn, Lois. "'Pittsburgh in 1806' by George Beck." *Pitt,* Spring 1948.

"National Transportation Safety Board, Aircraft Accident Report." 125 pages of documents and 4 pages of photographs of the Edward H. Litchfield plane crash, March–June 1968.

Nelson, Bryce. "Pitt Picks Chancellor." *Science,* February 3, 1967.

Nevins, Allen. *John D. Rockefeller: The Heroic Age of American Enterprise.* 2 vols. New York: Scribner's, 1940.

Newlin, Claude Milton. *The Life and Writings of Hugh Henry Brackenridge.* Princeton: Princeton University Press, 1932.

"Notes Relative to High Type of Buildings, University of Pittsburgh, December 31, 1924." *American Contractor,* September 15, 1928.

"Oakland Corporation." Unsigned manuscript, March 1962, 64 pp. University Archives.

O'Brien, James E. "John A. Brashear." In *Famous Men and Women of Pittsburgh.*

O'Brien, Jim, ed. *Hail to Pitt—A Sports History of the University of Pittsburgh.* Pittsburgh: Wolfson Publishing Company, 1982.

The Owl. Published annually by the graduating class of the University from 1907 through 1980.

Patterson, Maggie. "Chancellor Posvar Marks 10th Year at Pitt." *Pitt,* August 1977.

Paxton, Harry T. "Purity Dies at Pitt." *Saturday Evening Post,* November 19, 1949.

Penna, Anthony N. "Changing Images of Twentieth Century Pittsburgh." *Pennsylvania History,* January 1976.

Phillips, Francis C. *The Old Western University at the Corner of Diamond and Ross Streets.* Pittsburgh, 1914. Privately printed.

———. *The Western University in 1822.* Pittsburgh, 1919. Privately printed.

Pierson, George. *Tocqueville and Beaumont in America.* Oxford: Oxford University Press, 1938.

Pitt Football Media Guide. Published annually by the Sports Information Office, University of Pittsburgh.

"Pitt Will Erect 52-Story Building." *Pittsburgh Chronicle Telegraph,* November 7, 1924.

"Pitt's Big Thinker." *Time,* September 7, 1962.

"The Pittsburgh Renaissance Project: The Stanton Belfour Oral History Collection." The University of Pittsburgh Graduate School of Public and International Affairs, September 1974.

"Planning and Resource Management System Procedures Manual." Office of Planning and Budget, 1976.

"Planning Directions for Academic Programs, 1980–1990." 1981, 24 pp.

Posvar, Wesley W. *Report of the Chancellor.* 1975, 32 pp.

———. *A Report to Trustees—The University Plan.* June 1985, 64 pp.

———. "Basic Research: The Federal Government and the Universities." *Pitt,* Supplement, August 1977.

———. "The Creative Eye of the New Society." *Pitt,*

Spring 1968. (The chancellor's 1968 inauguration address.)

———. "New Horizons for the University." *Science*, September 28, 1984.

———. "Posvar." *Pitt Owl*, 1968. (An interview on goals and plans.)

———. "The University in Pittsburgh. What Can Pitt Do for You?" *Pittsburgh Post-Gazette*, May 18, 1973.

———. "University Long-Range Planning Policies— Institutional Overview and Description of Process," 1985.

Pott, James H. "Impressions of the Olympics." *Alumni Review*, October 1936.

A Preliminary Appraisal of the 'Commitment to Excellence' of the University of Pittsburgh, November 1960.

"Professors' Group Taboos 'Cathedral of Learning,'" *Pittsburgh Bulletin Index*, January 11, 1936.

Regional Campuses, *University Times* Supplements. Bradford, January 28, 1982; Greensburg, February 25, 1982; Johnstown, March 25, 1982; Titusville, April 22, 1982.

"The Report: Findings and Conclusions of the Legislative Committee, Resolution No. 61, University of Pittsburgh." *Alumni Review*, May–June 1935.

Report of the A. W. Mellon Educational and Charitable Trust, 1930–1980. Pittsburgh [1981]. Privately printed.

Report of the Provost's Advisory Committee on Women's Concerns, June 1984.

"A Report to the Community—The University of Pittsburgh—1955–1965." April 29, 1965, 31 pp.

Resources for the Eighties: Toward Thresholds of Greatness in our Third Century. 1980, 39 pp.

The Response of an Urban University to Change. vol. 1: *Overview*. Middle States Association report, 1971.

Ridgway, Matthew B. "Indochina Disengaging." *Foreign Affairs*, July 1971.

Riesman, David, and Denny, Revel. "Football in America." *American Quarterly*, vol. 3, 1951.

Ritenour, John S. *Over the Old Roads to Pittsburgh*. *Western Pennsylvania Historical Magazine*, October 1921.

Rodd, William H. II. "The Litchfield Document." *Pittsburgh Forum*, February 18, 1972. (Contains a statement by Litchfield's heirs opposing publication.)

———. "The Litchfield Papers." *Pitt News*, February 21, 1972. (Contains corrections by Edison Montgomery

and Joseph Colangelo of errors, misstatements, and misrepresentations.)

Rooms with a View: Achievements of the Nationality Committees and the Office of Cultural and Educational Exchange. Illustrations in color by Andrey Avinoff and Richard Oden, text by B. Burtt Evans. Undated, no pagination.

Rosensweet, Alvin. "Pitt Finds Student 'Advice' Is Useful." *Pittsburgh Post-Gazette*, October 11, 1968.

———. "The Post-Gazette—175 Years." *Pittsburgh Post-Gazette*, July 30, 1961.

Rossiter, Clinton Lawrence. *1787: The Grand Convention*. New York: Macmillan, 1966.

Rusman, Alta. "Pitt Adopts More-Structured Liberal Arts Curriculum." *Pitt*, February 1982.

———. "Trustees Approve Five-Year Plan." *Pitt*, August 1985.

———. "Why Isn't Fessenden a Household Word?" *University Times*, December 14, 1978.

Sabine, George H., and Wittke, Carl. "Academic Freedom at the University of Pittsburgh." American Association of University Professors *Bulletin*, December 1929.

Sack, Saul. *History of Higher Education in Pennsylvania*. 2 vols. Harrisburg: Pennsylvania Historical and Museum Commission, 1963.

Salk, Jonas. "Studies in Human Subjects on Active Immunization Against Poliomyelitis: A Preliminary Report on Experiments in Progress, with the Collaboration of B. L. Bennett, L. J. Lewis, E. N. Ward, and J. S. Youngner." *Journal of the American Medical Association*, March 28, 1953.

Salmon-Cox, Leslie, and Holzner, Burkhart. "The Development of the Learning Research and Development Center, 1963–1973." LRDC, 1973, 68 pp.

Schachner, Marcia Kramer. "Western Psychiatric Institute and Clinic of the University of Pittsburgh: Its Years of Research, Teaching and Service." Ph.D. dissertation, School of Education, University of Pittsburgh, 1984.

[Schoyer, William, and Schoyer, Maxine.] *Scaife Company and the Scaife Family, 1802–1952*. Pittsburgh: Davis and Warde, 1952. Privately printed.

Schulman, Irwin J. "Reform: An Effort to Restate Purposes." *Pitt News*, October 9, 1981.

The Scranton Report—Text of the President's Commission on Campus Unrest. 1970.

Scribner, Henry S. "Old Days at W.U.P." *Alumni Review,* November 1934.

Selvaggio, Marc. "The Making of Jonas Salk." *Pittsburgh Magazine,* June 1984.

"Sesquicentennial: University of Pittsburgh Opens Four Months' Long Celebration of Its 150 Years." *Pittsburgh Bulletin Index,* February 25, 1937.

Sheehan, Robert. "The Rich, Risky Life of a University Trustee." *Fortune,* January 1967.

Shefler, Oscar. "Litchfield and the New Pitt." *Pittsburgh Quote,* vol. 8, no. 1, 1964.

Shoumatoff, Alex. "Personal History: The Shoumatoff Family," *New Yorker,* April 26, May 3, 1982. Part of the book *Russian Blood: A Family Chronicle.* Andrei Avinoff is the main figure.

Silverman, Alexander. *Research History of the Department of Chemistry. . . .* Pittsburgh, 1945. Privately printed.

Sissman, Isaac. *75 Years of Dentistry—University of Pittsburgh. A History of the School of Dental Medicine.* University of Pittsburgh, 1971.

Smith, Chester L. "The Truth Behind the Sutherland Case." *Pittsburgh Press,* March 7–13. Seven articles.

Solow, Herbert. "The All-Purpose Executive." *Fortune,* December 1958.

"Speed-up at Pittsburgh." *Time,* July 11, 1960.

Starrett, Agnes Lynch. *The Cathedral of Learning, 1921–1937.* University of Pittsburgh, 1937.

———. *The Maurice and Laura Falk Foundation.* Historical Society of Western Pennsylvania, 1966.

———. *Through One Hundred and Fifty Years: The University of Pittsburgh.* Pittsburgh: University of Pittsburgh Press, 1937.

———. *The University of Pittsburgh in World War II. University of Pittsburgh Bulletin,* 1947.

———. "John Gabbert Bowman." In *Famous Men and Women of Pittsburgh.*

Steele, Bruce. "Building a Winning Department." *University Times,* May 2, 1985. (On the Department of Chemistry.)

Steele, Ray. "The Ascending Fall: The University of Pittsburgh's Conversion from a Private to a State-related University." Undated, unpublished manuscript, 50 pp.

Stein, Herbert G. "Campus Counter-Revolution." *Pittsburgh* magazine, February 1982, p. 78.

———. "What's Going on at Pitt?" *Pittsburgh Post-Gazette,* September 12, 13, 14, 1962.

The Stephen Collins Foster Memorial—The Inspiration and Approaching Realization of a Memorial Building to Honor "America's Troubador." Stephen Foster Memorial Committee, 1936.

The Stephen Collins Foster Memorial of the University of Pittsburgh—A Tribute to the Composer. . . . Stephen Foster Dedication Committee, June 2, 1937.

Student Code of Conduct and Judicial Procedures. (Effective September 1981.)

Sullivan, William C. "Extremism and Businessmen." (An address at the Fifty-seventh Annual Meeting of the United States Chamber of Commerce, April 27, 1969.)

———. "Civil Disorder in Academic Communities." (An address at the Fifth National Conference of the Associated Student Governments of the United States, November 27, 1968.)

Swetnam, George. "Adventures in Retirement." *Pittsburgh Press,* October 3, 1954. (On John G. Bowman.)

"Taking Stock—Pitt Prepares for Middle States Evaluation." *Pitt,* August 1980, 18 pp.

Terte, Robert H. "Pittsburgh University Expansion Plans, Stalled by Financial Crisis, Under Study by Three Groups." *New York Times,* July 25, 1965.

This Is an Urban Area. Undated, illustrated brochure on the Panther Hollow Project, 24 pp.

Thompson, George Jarvis, comp. *Legislative Acts and Public Documents Relating to the University of Pittsburgh.* Board of Trustees, 1923.

"Tower of Trouble." *Time,* March 4, 1935.

Turner, Ralph E. "History in the Making in Western Pennsylvania." Unpublished typescript, 17 pp. Read at a meeting of the Historical Society of Western Pennsylvania, April 24, 1934.

"Undergraduates at the University—a Review for the Eighties." A report by the University to the Commission on Higher Education of the Middle States Association of Colleges and Schools, November 1980.

Underwood, John. "Pitt Wins (Boss's Orders)." *Sports Illustrated,* October 28, 1963.

"The University and the Regional Economy." *Pitt,* Supplement, August 1977.

University of Pittsburgh Building Program. Illustrated. January 20, 1960, 80 pp.

The University Plan, 1976. University of Pittsburgh, 110 pp.

"University Planning Policies for the 1980s." Introduction by Wesley W. Posvar. July 1979, 151 pp.

Van Trump, James D. *Life and Architecture in Pittsburgh.* Pittsburgh History and Landmarks Foundation, 1983.

———. "An Aerial View of Oakland in 1924." In his *Life and Architecture in Pittsburgh.*

———. "Bellefield from the Air." In *Life and Architecture in Pittsburgh.*

———. "The Book and the Land: The Hillman Library." *Charette,* July–August 1968.

———. "The Cathedral of Learning from the University Club Roof." In *Life and Architecture in Pittsburgh.*

———. "A Heritage of Dreams—Some Aspects of the History of the Architecture and Planning of the University of Pittsburgh, 1787–1969." *Western Pennsylvania Historical Magazine,* April 1969.

Van Trump, James D., and Ziegler, Arthur P., Jr. *Landmark Architecture of Allegheny County, Pennsylvania.* Pittsburgh History and Landmarks Foundation, 1967.

Vogan, Michael, and Seckinger, Richard. *A History of Pitt Football,* 1981. An unpublished manuscript in the University Archives.

Wall, Joseph Frazier. *Andrew Carnegie.* New York: Oxford, 1970.

———. "Andrew Carnegie." A lecture at the Historical Society of Western Pennsylvania, October 5, 1983.

Wallace, Francis. "The Football Laboratory Explodes." *Saturday Evening Post,* November 4, 1939.

———. "Test Case at Pitt—The Facts About College Football 'Play for Pay.'" *Saturday Evening Post,* October 28, 1937.

We Chart the Future: Report from the Chancellor. Fall 1983. (In the form of an illustrated news magazine.)

("Wells Report") *A Selective Review with Proposals for Future Paths—A Report by a Special Committee of the Ford Foundation.* January 1966, 47 pp.

"What Happened at Pitt?" *Fortune,* September 1965.

"When the University Burned." *University Record,* May 1927.

Who's Who in America—A Biographical Dictionary of Notable Living Men and Women of the United States. Produced biennially, first volume in 1899.

Who's Who in American Education—A Biographical Directory of Eminent Living Educators of the United States. Vol. 1, 1928.

Williams, Greer. *Virus Hunters.* New York: Knopf, 1959.

Wright, Austin. *The Warner Administration at Carnegie Institute of Technology, 1950–1965.* Pittsburgh: Carnegie Press, 1973.

Young, Arthur M. *The Voice That Speaketh Clear.* Pittsburgh: University of Pittsburgh Press, 1957.

Index

Books by
Robert C. Alberts

The Most Extraordinary Adventures of Major Robert Stobo. Houghton Mifflin, 1965.

The Golden Voyage: The Life and Times of William Bingham, 1752–1804. Houghton Mifflin, 1969.

The Good Provider: H. J. Heinz and His 57 Varieties. Houghton Mifflin, 1973.

Benjamin West: A Biography. Houghton Mifflin, 1978.

The Shaping of the Point: Pittsburgh's Renaissance Park. University of Pittsburgh Press, 1980.

FOR THE NATIONAL PARK SERVICE

A Charming Field for an Encounter: The Story of George Washington's Fort Necessity. 1975.

George Rogers Clark and the Winning of the Old Northwest. 1975.

Mount Washington Tavern: The Story of a Famous Inn, a Great Road, and the People Who Used Them. 1976.